DIFFERENT WORLDS PRESENTS

Gamers Guide
to
FEUDAL JAPAN

SHOGUN & DAIMYO
MILITARY DICTATORS OF SAMURAI JAPAN

By
TADASHI EHARA

DIFFERENT WORLDS PUBLICATIONS
SAN FRANCISCO
WWW.DIFFWORLDS.COM

DEDICATION

To my sons
George Atsushi Ehara & Anthony Hiroki Ehara
Gamers forever!

ISBN 978-0-9753999-5-8

Copyright © 2011 by Tadashi Ehara
All rights reserved.

Different Worlds Publications
San Francisco, CA • U.S.A.
www.diffworlds.com
info@diffworlds.com

MANUFACTURED IN THE UNITED STATES OF AMERICA

1st edition v1.0 September 2011
1st edition v1.1 October 2011

Contents

Map of Japan and its Provinces
    circa 1867 2

Introduction 3
Conventions 3
Calendar 3
Names 5
Pronunciation 5
Plurals 6

History 7
▸ Pre-Samurai History: to 1185 . . . 7
Ancient Period (to 710) 7
Nara Period (710-794 7
Heian "Aristocratic" Period
(794-1185) 8
Hogen Rebellion (1156) 8
Heiji Rebellion (1160) 8
Genpei "Minamoto-Taira" War (1180-1185) 9
▸ Kamakura Period: 1185-1333 . . . 10
Genko War (1331-1333) 10
Kenmu Restoration (1333-1336) 10
▸ Muromachi "Ashikaga" Period:
1333-1573 10
Nanboku-cho "Northern and Southern
Courts" Period (1336-1392) 11
Sengoku "Warring States" Period
(1467-1573) 11
▸ Azuchi-Momoyama Period:
1573-1603 11
▸ Edo "Tokugawa" Period:
1603-1868 12
Bakumatsu "Late Tokugawa" Period
(1853-1867) 12
Boshin War "War of the Year of the
Dragon" (1868-1869) 13

Government 14
▸ The Imperial Court 14
The Taiho Code 14
Provincial Government Organization . 15
▸ Kamakura Bakufu: 1185-1333 . . 16
Central Administration 16
Provincial Administration 17
▸ Muromachi Bakufu: 1336-1573 . . 17
Central Administration 18
Provincial Administration 18

▸ Tokugawa Bakufu: 1603-1868 . . . 18
Central Administration 18

Shogun 21
Kamakura Shogun 22
Kamakura Shikken 26
Muromachi Shogun 32
Edo Shogun 39

Daimyo 52
Heian Period 53
Abé 53
Fujiwara 54
Ministers, Statesmen, Warriors, Etc. 54
Men of Letters, Poets 74
Empresses 76
Kiyohara 77
Oba 78
Ono 78
Ono 79
Sakanoué 80
Sato 80
Taira 81

Kamakura Period 90
Adachi 90
Daibutsu 91
Hiki 91
Izumi 91
Kagami 91
Hojo 92
Jo 94
Kudo 94
Kumagai 95
Nawa 95
Minamoto 96
Saga-Genji 97
Daigo-Genji 98
Murakami-Genji 99
Uda-Genji 99
Seiwa-Genji 99
Miura 109
Nikaido 111
Oé 111

Contents

Shimokobé 112	Ashina 173
Wada 113	Aso 174

Muromachi Period 114

- Ashikaga. 114
  - Shogunal Branch 115
  - Kamakura Branch 117
- Akamatsu 120
- Hosokawa 122
- Isé 126
- Imagawa 127
- Ishibashi 130
- Ishido 130
- Itagaki 131
- Itami 131
- Jinbo 132
- Kikuchi 133
- Momonoi 136
- Oimi 136
- Kira 137
- Ko 138
- Kusunoki 139
- Nikki 141
- Oda 141
- Miyoshi 142
- Otaté 144
- Nitta 145
- Nagao 147
- Ogigayatsu 148
- Ouchi 149
- Oyama 151
- Rokkaku 152
- Shibukawa 153
- Saito 154
- Shoni 155
- Sasaki 156
- Suzuki 157
- Shiba 158
- Tawara 159
- Takeda (Aki) 160
- Togashi 161
- Wada 161
- Urakami 162
- Wakiya 162

Momoyama Period 163

- Akechi 163
- Akaza 164
- Amako 165
- Asai 168
- Asakura 170
- Anegakoji 172
- Chiba 175
- Chikusa 176
- Daidoji 176
- Hiratsuka 176
- Hasebé 177
- Ishikawa 177
- Hashiba 178
- Kagaé 178
- Hatakeyama 179
  - Kawachi-Hatakeyama 180
  - Noto-Hatakeyama 181
  - Mutsu-Hatakeyama 182
- Kakimi 182
- Hatano 183
- Kasai 183
- Ishida 184
- Isshiki 185
- Kasuya 185
- Katata 186
- Kimura 186
- Kodera 186
- Kitabataké 187
- Konishi 189
- Kobayakawa 190
- Maki 191
- Kono 192
- Marumo 193
- Miyabé 193
- Matsunaga 194
- Munakata 195
- Nanjo 195
- Ogawa 195
- Nishina 196
- Okamoto 196
- Onoki 196
- Onodera 197
- Otani 197
- Ryuzoji 198
- Sakazaki 199
- Sassa 200
- Shibata (Owari) 201
- Shibata (Echigo) 202
- Tagaya 203
- Takahashi 203
- Takayama 204
- Takigawa 205
- Takeda 206
- Tsukushi 212
- Ujiié 213
- Yamagata 213

Contents

Ukita 214	Yura 253
Wada 215	Tomita 254
Yamana 216	Yashiro 254
Utsunomiya 218	Yuki 255

Edo Period 219
- Chosokabé 219
- Bessho 221
- Fukushima 222
- Furuta 223
- Hineno 223
- Gamo 224
- Hiraiwa 225
- Ina 226
- Itami 226
- Kobori 226
- Kanamori 227
- Kimura 227
- Kato 228
- Horio 229
- Koriki 230
- Kuwayama 230
- Maeda 231
- Maita 231
- Masuda 232
- Matsushita 232
- Mizunoya 232
- Matsukura 233
- Minagawa 234
- Mori 234
- Nakamura 234
- Mogami 235
- Murakami 236
- Naito 237
- Nigao 237
- Nasu 238
- Okubo 238
- Otomo 239
- Saigo 242
- Sano 242
- Suganuma 242
- Sakuma 243
- Takenaka 244
- Satomi 245
- Sugihara 246
- Terazawa 246
- Tanaka 247
- Togawa 247
- Tokunaga 247
- Toyotomi 248
- Tsutsui 253

Samurai Cinema 257
- Characters in Chanbara 258
  - Samurai 258
  - Ninja 258
  - Peasants 258
  - Yakuza 258
  - Women 259
  - Townsfolk 259
  - Others 259
- Recommendations for Gamers 260
  - For Role-Playing 260
  - For Miniatures 260
- Notes 260
- Heian "Aristocratic" Period (794-1185) 261
- Sengoku "Warring States" Period (1467-1573) 262
- Azuchi-Momoyama Period (1573-1603) . 264
- Edo "Tokugawa" Period (1603-1868) 265
- Genroku "Golden Age of Edo" Period (1688-1704) 274
- Bakumatsu "Late Tokugawa" Period (1853-1867) 275
- Non-Specific 278

Kanji Primer 280

Campaign Setting 282
- Ahistorical Campaign 282
- The Tabi "Pilgrimage" 282
  - The Pilgrim Party 282
  - Party Protocol 283
  - The Route 283
  - For Adults Only 284

Roads 285
- Gokaido 285
- Other Routes 286
- Notes on Gazetteers 286

Tokaido Gazetteer 288

Osaka Kaido Gazetteer 296

Nakasendo Gazetteer 297

Minoji Gazetteer 303

Family Crests 304
- Random Mon Generator 305

Contents

PREFECTURES **309**
   PREFECTURE TO PROVINCE CONVERSION... 309
   OTHER REGIONAL NAMES 310

GLOSSARY **311**
   TITLES & OFFICES 311
   OTHER 318

BIBLIOGRAPHY **322**
   MAIN SOURCES 322
   HISTORY 322

BUSHIDO 322
CULTURE 322
MON "JAPANESE CRESTS" 322
SAMURAI CINEMA 322
TRANSLATIONS....................... 322
ILLUSTRATIONS 322
SPECIAL THANKS 323

INDICES **324**
   INDEX OF CLANS 324
   INDEX OF NOTABLE ANCESTORS 325

Gamers Guide
to
FEUDAL JAPAN

SHOGUN & DAIMYO

Map of JAPAN and its PROVINCES circa 1867

Introduction

Shogun & Daimyo

The samurai ruled the Land of the Rising Sun from the end of the 12th century to the middle of the 19th century. At the top were the Shogun, the military dictators who dominated Japan as regents to the Emperors. Below the Shogun were the daimyo, provincial warlords who governed their individual fiefs with virtual sovereignty.

It was the bushi "samurai class" that fought the wars, achieved the peace, and eventually kept the status quo for two-and-a-half centuries. From the beginning of the 17th century until the end of the samurai era, Japan enjoyed a period of relative peace and cultural development that is unmatched by any other civilized nation. During their rule, Japan was a virtual police state with ninja spies and informants everywhere, and was one of the most despotic, autocratic, and oppressive regimes in the history of mankind.

The world of the samurai no longer exists, but its influence lives on in the daily lives of the Japanese. *Go-rin-no-sho* "The Book of Five Rings," the treatise on military strategy by the legendary swordsman Miyamoto Musashi (1584-1645), much like *The Art of War by Sun Tzu*, has been translated into many languages, and has been read by generations of businessmen for its insights into business management and the principals of winning. Bushido "the way of the samurai," a code of conduct and ethics of the warrior class, explains a lot about the Japanese philosophies of life regarding duty, compassion, honesty, and their attitudes regarding death.

The samurai now exist only in history books, novels, comic books, cinema, and video games. This compendium is organized as an handbook for creating more realistic backgrounds for role-playing games, boardgames, miniatures games, and computer games. It is also useful for those writing historical novels, screenplays, graphic novels, comic books, animé, and other creative works.

Presenting an alien and exotic world from a bygone age, this tome is a companion to *Daimyo of 1876* (Different Worlds Publications) and covers all the daimyo clans that were defeated, dispossessed, or otherwise dissolved before the end of the samurai era, and not included in that book. The two books together cover all the major clans and prominent families of feudal Japan.

Like *Daimyo of 1876*, this guide is not a scholarly piece of work. Almost all of the information are from English-language sources. Many of the resources that I have used, however, were written by scholars who did use Japanese-language sources.

Comments are welcome, and encouraged; please send them to tadashi@diffworlds.com. I look forward to hearing from you.

Conventions

Calendar

Japan did not adopt the Gregorian calendar that is universally used today until 1873. Prior to that, the Chinese lunar calendar was used, and years

Introduction

were designated based on the nengo "era" name which was adopted in 645 from the Chinese system. Era names were decided by court officials and changed frequently. A new nengo was usually proclaimed within a year or two after the ascension of a new Emperor. Era names also changed due to other felicitous events or natural disasters. Custom changed over time and different reasons caused the change of nengo names. There are even some years that did not have a nengo designation. Traditionally, the first day of nengo started at the whim of the Emperor, and is considered its first year until the next lunar new year when the second year of the nengo begins.

Although lunar months have fanciful poetic names, they are numbered simply from 1 to 12 in regular usage. Since lunar months are 29 or 30 days, every two or three years, an extra intercalary month is added to keep in step with the sun. This month is numbered the same as the preceding month but with a special designation.

In Chinese calendars the rule is that the winter solstice occurs in the 11th month, so with rare exceptions the lunar new year begins in the 2nd new moon after this event. Lunar months begin on new moons when it is dark so the middle of the month is when the moon is full.

Days are numbered as in the Gregorian calendar, but Japan did not have weeks prior to its adoption. Instead the month was divided into periods of ten days. Shops that took a day off every ten days would, for example, close on the 4th, 14th, and 24th days of the month.

Since lunar months do not correspond at all with the Gregorian calendar, and the fact that lunar year starts anywhere from about three to seven weeks later than the Gregorian new year, there is frequently a mismatch of actual dates between the two calendars; the 15th day of the 2nd lunar month is never February 15. The last day of the 12th lunar month is in January or February of the next year in the Gregorian calendar. It is safe to say that not all historians bothered to convert lunar dates to the exact Gregorian equivalent. Even if the scholar had translate a date as being the 16th day of the 5th (lunar) month, the next researcher reading it may erroneously recast it as being May 16th.

If you ever see sources conflicting in dates, this may be why. Any date prior to the Imperial Restoration that you see is suspect in its accuracy, unless it specifically addresses this issue.

Age reckoning prior to the modern era is another point of possible inaccuracy. In east Asia, the practice that originated in China is that newborns are one year old at birth, and at the beginning of each successive new lunar year, a year is added. Ergo, a child born on the last day of the year is two years old the next day. This results in people being one or two years older than in western reckoning. Again, translations of age may or may not have accounted for this.

Note that birthdays were still celebrated as auspicious occasions, but the celebrant's age traditionally did not change on that day.

In 1902 Japan made the traditional system of age reckoning obsolete by law and adopted the western system. The traditional system, however, persisted and was still commonly used, so in 1950 they had to pass another law to encourage people to use the new system. I was born in 1954, and when I was young, I was confused as to my real age as my grandmother kept using the old method.

All this about problems with dates and ages, however, is academic. Does it really matter? Gamers need not be concerned. You are recreating history anyway. I am addressing these issues here just in case you may be confused

Introduction

by sources with conflicting information, and this happens often. How old was Ietsuna when he became the 4th Tokugawa Shogun?

For the sake of convenience, the Gregorian calendar is used herein. And, yes, dates and ages have not been thoroughly confirmed.

Names

Names of Shogun, daimyo, and their contemporaries are in the traditional Japanese order: family name first, followed by the given, or personal, name.

Modern Japanese names are in the western order with the family name last, as is customary in English text.

Pronunciation

The base of the Japanese language is syllables, and there are relatively only a small amount of them. It has five vowel sounds, and syllables that are equivalent of the vowel sound preceded by a consonant. It also has an 'n' sound, which sounds like the 'n' in 'sun,' and is never the first syllable in a word. Yo'uon are a slurring or contraction of two syllables, the second one being ya, yu, or yo.

The table below shows the main single-syllable sounds in the Japanese language. In each box, the top entry is the hiragana, the middle is the katakana version, and the bottom is its sound in Roman characters. The table is missing syllables that begin with g, z, d, b, p, and j, which are consid-

Vowels					Youon		
あ ア a	い イ i	う ウ u	え エ e	お オ o			
か カ Ka	き キ Ki	く ク Ku	け ケ Ke	こ コ Ko	きゃ キャ Kya	きゅ キュ Kyu	きょ キョ Kyo
さ サ Sa	し シ Shi(Si)	す ス Su	せ セ Se	そ ソ So	しゃ シャ Sha(Sya)	しゅ シュ Shu(Syu)	しょ ショ Sho(Syo)
た タ Ta	ち チ Chi(Ti)	つ ツ Tsu(Tu)	て テ Te	と ト To	ちゃ チャ Cha(Cya)	ちゅ チュ Chu(Cyu)	ちょ チョ Cho(Cyo)
な ナ Na	に ニ Ni	ぬ ヌ Nu	ね ネ Ne	の ノ No	にゃ ニャ Nya	にゅ ニュ Nyu	にょ ニョ Nyo
は ハ Ha	ひ ヒ Hi	ふ フ Fu(Hu)	へ ヘ He	ほ ホ Ho	ひゃ ヒャ Hya	ひゅ ヒュ Hyu	ひょ ヒョ Hyo
ま マ Ma	み ミ Mi	む ム Mu	め メ Me	も モ Mo	みゃ ミャ Mya	みゅ ミュ Myu	みょ ミョ Myo
や ヤ Ya		ゆ ユ Yu		よ ヨ Yo			
ら ラ Ra	り リ Ri	る ル Ru	れ レ Re	ろ ロ Ro	りゃ リャ Rya	りゅ リュ Ryu	りょ リョ Ryo
わ ワ Wa	ゐ ヰ Wi		ゑ エ We	を ヲ Wo			
				ん ン n/nn			

In each box, the top entry is the hiragana, the middle is the katakana, and the bottom is the romanization.

ered a variation of the syllables in the table, so there are actually a little over one hundred different syllabic sounds in the Japanese language.

The vowels a-i-u-e-o are pronounced in order: ah-ee-ooh-eh-oh. Therefore the second set of syllables are pronounced kah-kee-kooh-keh-koh, the third set sah-shee-sooh-seh-soh, and so on. As for youon, the pronunciation, as mentioned above, is a slurring of two syllables. In western media, the city of Kyoto is often verbalized as Kee-oh-toh, which is not at all the way it is pronounced in Japan. Just try slurring the two syllables 'kee' and 'yoh' together very quickly, practically eliminating the 'ee' sound, to come up with the 'kyo' sound.

Another type of contraction is in words like Nikko or teppan. Just pronounce these as they are spelled.

The spelling of Japanese words into the Roman alphabet used here is based on the Hepburn system that is widely used today.

Pronounce all vowels clearly. There are no silent letters. G is always hard as in 'good,' j is soft as in 'join,' and ch is soft as in 'chat.'

For the beginner, it will be easiest if you break up the Japanese word into syllables first. Ieyasu is i-e-ya-su, or ee-eh-yah-sooh.

Japanese words are generally pronounced without accents and each syllable is given equal stress. An example of an exception is a word like Omori, which could mean either small forest or large forest. To mean a large forest, the first o sound is stressed a little longer and given a slight emphasis. This is arguably a remnant of Chinese influence from pre-historical days.

To properly distinguish the correct syllables, an apostrophe is used: San'indo is sa-n-i-n-do, not sa-ni-n-do; San'yodo is sa-n-yo-do, not sa-nyo-do. Sometimes an apostrophe is used to make the reading easier in words like kon'nyaku, although this is not strictly necessary.

Since the vowel and consonant sounds are similar, it has been said that you can read Japanese like you were reading Italian or Spanish, but without the accenting.

EXAMPLES

- Abé is not as in Abe Lincoln, it is ah-beh. Daté is not pronounced like the fruit, it is dah-teh. In these cases, the letter e with an accent mark is used to help with the pronunciation.
- Ii is ee-ee, but say it fast.
- The last syllable of Shogun is not pronounced like the firearm, but rather shoh-goon, with the short oo sound as in book or foot.

PLURALS

Japanese words in this guide will not add the letter s to denote a plural form, which is the custom in the latest English texts, e.g., "many samurai" instead of "many samurais." Plural meaning should be deduced from its usage, e.g., "the samurai was" and "the samurai were."

History

Feudalism in Japan

Pre-Samurai History
to 1185

The first evidence of human life in Japan was around 35,000 B.C., from when the earliest stone tools have been found. Ground and polished stone tools from around 30,000 B.C., discovered in Japan, are the earliest known in the world, which in the rest of the world are not typically associated until about 10,000 B.C.

The first signs of civilization in Japan appeared about 14,000 B.C., with the advent of hunter-gatherers and the first evidence of rudimentary agriculture. The earliest pottery and other household items found in Japan date from around 11,000 B.C.

Ancient Period (to 710)

Traditional history of Japan begins with the enthronement of the mythological 1st Emperor of Japan Jimmu-tenno (711-585 B.C.) in 660 B.C., which is considered the foundation of the Empire, and the beginning of a dynasty of sovereigns which continues to this day.

From the 3rd to the 7th centuries, the political state of Japan centered in the Yamato and Kawachi provinces. Close relationships between Japan and the Three Kingdoms of Korea began during toward the end of the 4th century, and Japan started sending tributes to Imperial China in the 5th century.

In 538 Buddhism was introduced to Japan by King Seong (-554) of Baekje, one of the Three Kingdoms of Korea. The new religion was promoted by Prince Shotoku (574-622), who was inspired by Buddha's teaching to establish a centralized government.

Nara Period (710-794)

In 710, Empress Gemmei (660-721) established the capital of Heijo-kyo, commonly known by its present name of Nara, in Yamato province, patterned after the Tang China capital of Chang'an (present-day Xi'an). Prior

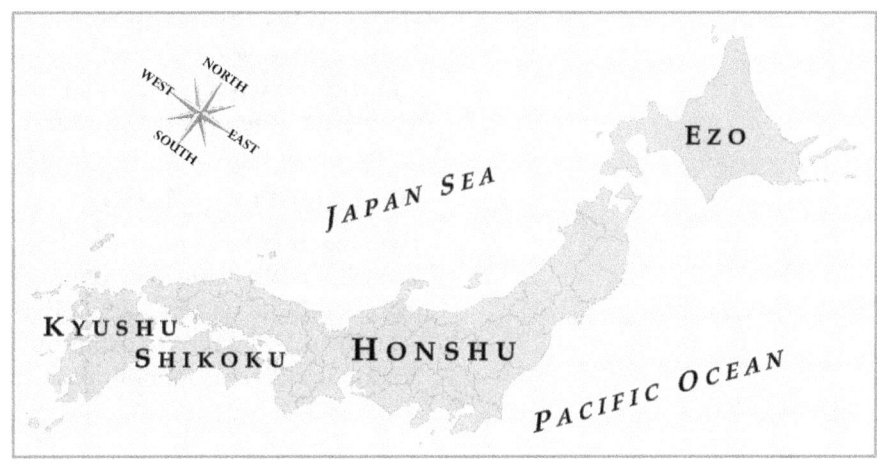

History – Heian Period

Emperor Kammu

to the establishment of Nara, the Imperial Court was customarily moved after the death of an Emperor due to the ancient belief that a place of death was tainted.

Nara became Japan's first truly urban center, and soon had a population of 200,000, or nearly 4% of the total Japanese population, with 10,000 of them working for the government.

Major cultural developments during this period included the *Koji-ki* and the *Nihon-ki*, the first national histories; the *Man'yoshu*, an anthology of poems; and the building in Nara of the Todai-ji, a temple which housed a 16-meter high gilt-bronze statue of Buddha called the Daibutsu.

HEIAN "ARISTOCRATIC" PERIOD (794-1185)

In 794, Emperor Kammu (737-806) estabished the capital of Heian-kyo (present-day Kyoto), 16 miles/26 km north of Nara.

The Heian Period is considered the apex of Japanese culture. Buddhism, literature, poetry, music, and art all flourished during this time.

Nominal sovereignty laid with the Emperors, but the Imperial Court was dominated by the Fujiwara clan, who married their daughters to the Imperial family, and thus became grandparents to the Emperors. The Fujiwara became Regents to the Emperors, and took absolute control of the Imperial Court, becoming hereditary dictators. Little authority was left for traditional officialdom, and all governmental affairs were handled through private administration by the Fujiwara.

It was during this period that the warrior class steadily gained in power and influence, threatening the authority of the central government. Decline in food production, growth of the population, and competition for resources among the great families all led to the gradual decline of Fujiwara power and gave rise to military disturbances in the mid-10th and 11th centuries. Members of the Fujiwara, the Taira, and the Minamoto families — all of whom had descended from the Imperial family — attacked one another, claimed control over vast tracts of conquered land, set up rival regimes, and generally broke the peace of Japan.

HOGEN REBELLION (1156)

The Hogen Rebellion is considered the beginning of the chain of events that would culminate in the establishment of the first military dictatorship in Japan.

Essentially a succession dispute over the next Emperor, it was fought between the supporters of the Emperor Go-Shirakawa (1127-1192), led by Fujiwara Tadamichi (1097-1164), Taira Kiyomori (1118-1181), and Minamoto Yoshitomo (1123-1160), and the supporters of the retired Emperor Sutoku (1119-1164), led by Fujiwara Yorinaga (1120-1156), Minamoto Tameyoshi (1096-1156), and Taira Tadamasa.

In the end Go-Shirakawa's forces prevailed, and Kiyomori and Yoshitomo established the two samurai clans of the Taira and the Minamoto as the new major political powers in Kyoto.

HEIJI REBELLION (1160)

The Hogen Rebellion set up a bitter rivalry between the ambitious Taira and Minamoto clans over political power. When in late 1159 Taira Kiyomori left Kyoto on a personal pilgrimage, in early 1160 Fujiwara Nobuyori (-1160) and Minamoto Yoshitomo abducted the now-retired Emperor Go-Shirakawa in a *coup* for political power.

History – Heian Period

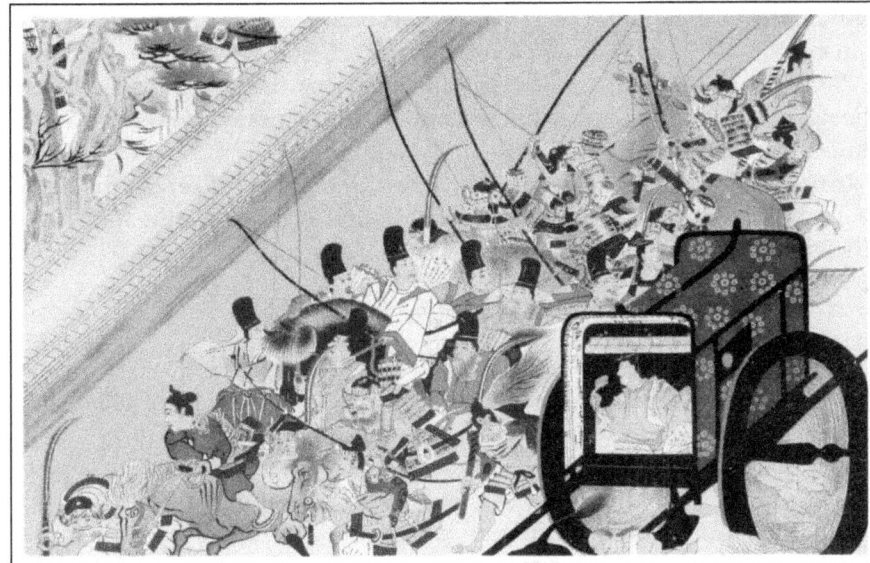

ABDUCTION OF THE EMPEROR GO-SHIRAKWA BY FUJIWARA NOBUYORI AND MINAMOTO YOSHITOMO IN 1159

– *Detail of an illustration by the painter-monk Sumiyoshi Keion (13th century) for the book* Heiji-monogatari *"Chronicles of Heiji" written by Hamuro Tokinaga (late 12th century).*

Ultimately, Kiyomori returned and killed Nobuyori and Yoshitomo. Yoshitomo's two eldest sons were likewise killed, but his other three sons, Yoritomo, Yoshitsuné, and Noriyori, were spared and exiled.

As head of the most powerful warrior clan, Kiyomori climbed the ranks of the Imperial Court, culminating in his 1167 appointment as Daijo-daijin "Chancellor of the Realm," the first from a military family to hold that title, and *de facto* head of government.

In 1179 Kiyomori imprisoned the cloistered Emperor Go-Shirakawa. In the following year, he forced his son-in-law, the Emperor Takakura (1161-1181) to abdicate, and placed his two-year-old grandson, the son of Takakura, as the new Emperor Antoku (1178-1185). This caused many of his allies, most of the provincial samurai, and even members of his own clan to turn against him.

Genpei "Minamoto-Taira" War (1180-1185)

In the middle of 1180 Prince Mochihito (-1180), brother of the Emperor Takakura, called on Kiyomori's old rivals of the Minamoto clan to rise against the Taira. Minamoto Yoritomo (1147-1199), the new head of the clan, raised an army and engaged the Taira with the help of his cousin

BATTLE SCENE FROM THE GENPEI WAR

Minamoto Yoshinaka (1154-1184), and his half-brothers Minamoto Yoshitsuné (1158-1189) and Minamoto Noriyori (1156-1193).

Although the Minamoto were initially unsuccessful, Kiyomori died early the next year from sickness, leaving his son Munemori (1147-1185) to continue the war.

In the final year of the war, the Minamoto defeated the Taira at the Battle of Yashima (Sanuki), and the conflict culminated at the Battle of Dan-no-ura (Nagato) where the Taira was completely destroyed.

KAMAKURA PERIOD
1185-1333

After the victory, Minamoto Yoritomo consolidated his power and established a new government at Kamakura (near present-day Tokyo). Yoritomo was officially appointed Shogun in 1192, dawning the feudal age of Japan, which lasted until the mid-19th century.

In 1199 Yoritomo died suddenly, and his son Minamoto Yoriié (1182-1204) succeeded as the 2nd Kamakura Shogun. Yoritomo's widow Masako (1156-1225) and her father Hojo Tokimasa (1138-1215) seized control of the Shogunate, and Tokimasa began rule as the 1st Hojo Shikken "Shogunal Regent" to his grandson Yoriié.

Henceforth, the Hojo installed puppet Shogun in Kamakura, and eventually brought the Imperial Court in Kyoto under Shogunate control. The Hojo established a council of military lords, and worked to bring the whole country under centralized military control.

GENKO WAR (1331-1333)

In 1331 a coalition against the Hojo emerged, and the Emperor Go-Daigo (1288-1339) tried to seize power and overthrow the Shogunate. He attacked the Hojo Shikken in Kamakura, but was defeated and exiled.

Two years later Go-Daigo escaped his exile, raised an army, and with the help of Nitta Yoshisada (1301-1338) and the head of the Hojo army, Ashikaga Takauji (1305-1358), who turned against the Shogunate, destroyed Kamakura and the Hojo.

KENMU RESTORATION (1333-1336)

After the Genko War, the Emperor Go-Daigo returned to Kyoto to commence the restoration of Imperial rule in Japan. Go-Daigo and his administration were inexperienced and inefficient, however, and did not pay proper tribute to their military supporters. They failed to properly reward the warlords, going so far as to levying extra taxes on them to restore the Imperial Palace. By the end of 1335 the Emperor and the nobility had lost all support of the warrior class.

In early 1336, Ashikaga Takauji rebelled against the Imperial Court, defeated Go-Daigo's forces, and took Kyoto, ending the Kenmu Restoration.

MUROMACHI "ASHIKAGA" PERIOD
1336-1573

After Ashikaga Takauji seized Kyoto, the Emperor Go-Daigo retreated to established a rival Court at Yoshino (southern Yamato), known as the Southern Court. In Kyoto, Takauji enthroned the Emperor Komyo (1322-1380), beginning the Northern Court. In 1338 Komyo officially appointed Takauji as Shogun. In 1378 Takauji's grandson, the 3rd Ashikaga Shogun

Emperor Go-Daigo

Yoshimitsu (1358-1408), set up the Bakufu headquarters in Kyoto's Muromachi district, on the northwest outskirts of the city.

NANBOKU-CHO "NORTHERN AND SOUTHERN COURTS" PERIOD (1336-1392)

Supporters of the two Courts fought a series of battles during this period. The Ashikaga Bakufu steadily gained power, and by 1392 Shogun Yoshimitsu was able to reconcile the two Courts and reinstate Imperial succession through the Northern Court line of the Emperor Go-Komatsu (1377-1433).

SENGOKU "WARRING STATES" PERIOD (1467-1573)

The Ashikaga Shogunate ultimately failed to maintain central control, and the power of the daimyo "provincial warlords" grew with little interference from the Bakufu. Opposition to the Shogunate initially grew in the region around Kyoto, with uprisings spreading to the Kanto region and elsewhere. The collapse of Ashikaga authority in 1467 unleashed internecine struggles for land control.

The Sengoku Period began with the Onin War (1467-1477) when a succession dispute within the Ashikaga sparked a civil war over military supremacy between Hosokawa Katsumoto (1430-1473) and his father-in-law Yamana Sozen (1404-1473). After some serious fighting in Kyoto, the conflict quickly evolved into a stalemate. When both Katsumoto and Sozen died, neither faction knew how to end the war. Eventually Kyoto was in ruins and both sides retreated. By then warfare had spread to the provinces, where it continued for the next century.

AZUCHI-MOMOYAMA PERIOD
1573-1603

By the 1560s, the period of anarchy was ending. The process of national unification began with three warriors of profound military and political skills: Oda Nobunaga (1534-1582), Toyotomi Hideyoshi (1536-1598), and Tokugawa Ieyasu (1542-1616). Beginning with Nobunaga, these three gradually defeated and annexed smaller daimyo.

In 1568 Nobunaga entered Kyoto to take control of the Imperial Court, and installed Ashikaga Yoshiaki (1537-1597) as the 15th, and ultimately final, Muromachi Shogun. By 1573 he had destroyed the Asakura-Azai alliance, suppressed the militant Buddhist monks, and consolidated his power around Kyoto. When Yoshiaki plotted against him, Nobunaga deposed him, marking the end of the Ashikaga Shogunate and the Sengoku Period. The Empire will have no Shogun until Tokugawa Ieyasu in 1603.

Nobunaga was now powerful enough to subjugate the outlying provinces. He destroyed the Takeda, the Uesugi were mired in succession disputes, and he was about to confront the Mori. In 1582, however, he was betrayed and assassinated by one of his generals, Akechi Mitsuhidé (1528-1582), at the Honno-ji, a temple in Kyoto.

When another of Nobunaga's generals, Toyotomi Hideyoshi, heard of the incident, he rushed to avenge his master, killing Mitsuhidé at the Battle of Yamazaki (between Kyoto and Osaka).

Hideyoshi then went on to consolidate his power. He conquered Shikoku, Kyushu, and finally the Hojo of Odawara in 1590, completing the unification of Japan.

Oda Nobunaga

History – Edo Period

Alas, Hideyoshi's ambition knew no bounds and he plotted the conquest of China by first taking Korea. The Korean Campaigns of 1592-1593 and 1597-1598 were both disasters, and the effort ended with his death in 1598.

After a Darwinian process of elimination, Tokugawa Ieyasu emerged as the new leader of Japan when he defeated his enemies at the decisive Battle of Seki-ga-hara (Mino) in 1600.

Edo "Tokugawa" Period
1603-1868

In 1603 the Emperor Go-Yozei (1572-1617) appointed Ieyasu as the 1st Tokugawa Shogun. The new Shogun set up his Bakufu at Edo, from where the Tokugawa Shogunate would rule Japan in relative peace for the next 250 years.

To keep the peace, the Shogunate installed the sankin-kotai "alternate attendance" system of residency which required that each daimyo set up a residence in Edo, and reside in alternate years between there and their fief. They also banned Christianity, and introduced seclusion laws allowing trade with only China, Korea, and the Netherlands.

Bakumatsu
"Late Tokugawa" Period (1853-1867)

At the beginning of the 19th century, foreign shipping increased in the area around Japan due to whaling and the China trade. Western traders wanted Japan as a base for supplies, and where shipwrecked sailors could receive assistance. The Tokugawa Shogunate rebuked all overtures.

In 1853, when Commodore Matthew C. Perry (1794-1858) entered Edo Bay with his four "Black Ships," the Bakufu was thrown into turmoil. The following year, the Shogunate was forced to sign a treaty with the U.S., opening ports in Japan for trade, effectively ending the country's isolation from the rest of the world. Treaties with the Dutch, Russia, United Kingdom, and France soon followed, and were signed in 1858.

In 1863, with the support of many key daimyo who opposed the treaties, the Emperor Komei (1831-1867), breaking with centuries of Imperial tradi-

Gasshukoku suishi teitoku kōjōgaki

"Oral statement by the American Navy admiral"

– Japanese print showing three men, believed to be Commander Anan, Commodore Matthew C. Perry, and Captain Henry Adams, who opened up Japan to the west.

The text being read may be President Fillmore's letter to the Emperor of Japan.

tion, began to take an active role in matters in state, and issue his "Order to expel the barbarians."

After a series of naval battles, it was clear that Japan was no match against the western powers, and that expelling of foreigners was not a realistic policy.

Boshin War
"War of the Year of the Dragon" (1868-1869)

Discontent over the Bakufu's handling of national and foreign affairs led to a movement to oust the Shogun and restore the Emperor at the head of a new government.

The 15th and final Tokugawa Shogun Yoshinobu (1837-1913) launched a campaign to seize the Imperial Court in Kyoto, but the military tide rapidly turned in favor of the more modernized Imperial faction. A series of battles culminated in the 1868 surrender of Edo, which was renamed Tokyo. The boy Emperor Meiji (1852-1912) moved the capital from Kyoto to Edo Castle, now the Imperial Palace.

In 1869 remnants of the Shogunal forces were finally defeated at the Battle of Hakodaté (Ezo), marking the close of the feudal era in Japan.

In 1877 Saigo Takamori (1828-1877) led a rebellion of samurai-class men from Satsuma to protest government corruption and to strengthen the military class. Heavily outnumbered by soldiers equipped with modern weapons, after a series of battles, the last of the samurai drew their swords, charged the Imperial forces, and were mowed down by Gatling guns. With these deaths, the samurai era came to an end.

Battle of Hakodaté, Ezo (1869)

Government

Imperial and Military Rule

The Imperial Court

The Imperial Court was the nominal ruling government during the feudal era of Japan. From 794 the Court was in Kyoto until the end of the Tokugawa Shogunate in 1868, when it was moved to Tokyo (previously Edo) and integrated into the new Meiji government.

Early civil power was primarily held by the ruling Emperors and their Regents, typically appointed from the ranks of the Imperial Court and the aristocratic clans. Military affairs were handled under the auspices of the civil government. By the 10th century, the Fujiwara Regents dominated, and official government offices had no power to speak of unless they were supported by the Fujiwara.

After Minamoto Yoritomo (1147-1199) launched the military rule of Japan, true power was held by the Shogun, who foreigners often mistook for the Emperor. Henceforth the Imperial Court was reduced to minor administrative duties. Court positions were no longer prestigious and not especially sought after. Office holders made their rounds as overseers, primarily as official record keepers.

Although powerless, and many offices often left vacant, the Imperial Court survived with relatively few changes in its organization, before it was completely abolished in 1885.

The Taiho Code

In 701, at the request of the Emperor Mommu (683-707), the Taiho Code was enacted to reorganize the government structure of Japan by adapting the system of Tang China. It was compiled at the direction of Imperial Prince Osakabé (-705), Fujiwara Fuhito (659-720), and Awata Mahito.

The Taiho Code was one of the first to include Confucianism as a significant factor in the Japanese code of ethics and government. However, it contained two major departures from the Tang model:

- Government positions and class status were based on birth, as had always been in the Japanese tradition, and not talent, as was the Chinese way.
- The Japanese rejected the "Mandate of Heaven" concept of China, and elsewhere, and asserted that the Emperor's authority came from his Imperial descent, not from his righteousness or fairness as a ruler.

The Code established two branches of government:

- **Jingi-kan** "Department of Shintoism" -- Handled all spiritual, religious, or ritualistic matters. It was responsible for annual festivals and official court ceremonies such as coronations, as well as the upkeep of shrines, the discipline of shrine wardens, and the recording and observation of oracles and divinations. Note that this branch governed all the Shinto shrines in the country, but had no jurisdiction over Buddhism.
- **Daijo-kan** "Council of State" -- Handled all secular and administrative matters. Originally, it was made up of ministers and counselors presided over by the Daijo-daijin "Chancellor of the Realm," and included the sadaijin "minister of the left," the udaijin "minister of the right," sadaiben "controller of the left," the udaiben "controller of the right," four dainagon "major counselors," and three shonagon "minor counselors."

The Daijo-kan proved to be flexible and useful, and eventually grew to include many members:

- **Daijo-daijin** "Chancellor of the Realm"
- **sadaijin** "minister of the left" -- Senior minister of state.
- **udaijin** "minister of the right" -- Junior minister of state. Deputy to the sadaijin.
- **naidaijin** "minister of the center"
- **dainagon** "major counselor" -- Commonly there were three, sometimes more.
- **chunagon** "middle counselor" -- Varied in number from two to ten.
- **shonagon** "minor counselor" -- Commonly there were three. Served as both chamberlain for the Emperor and secretary for cabinet members sangi and above. They also supervised the geki.
- **sangi** "Imperial advisor" -- The lowest-level cabinet member who discussed policies with the dainagon, the chunagon, and the ministers, but did not vote.
- **geki** "external secretariat" -- Appointees of the Emperor.

Government – The Imperial Court

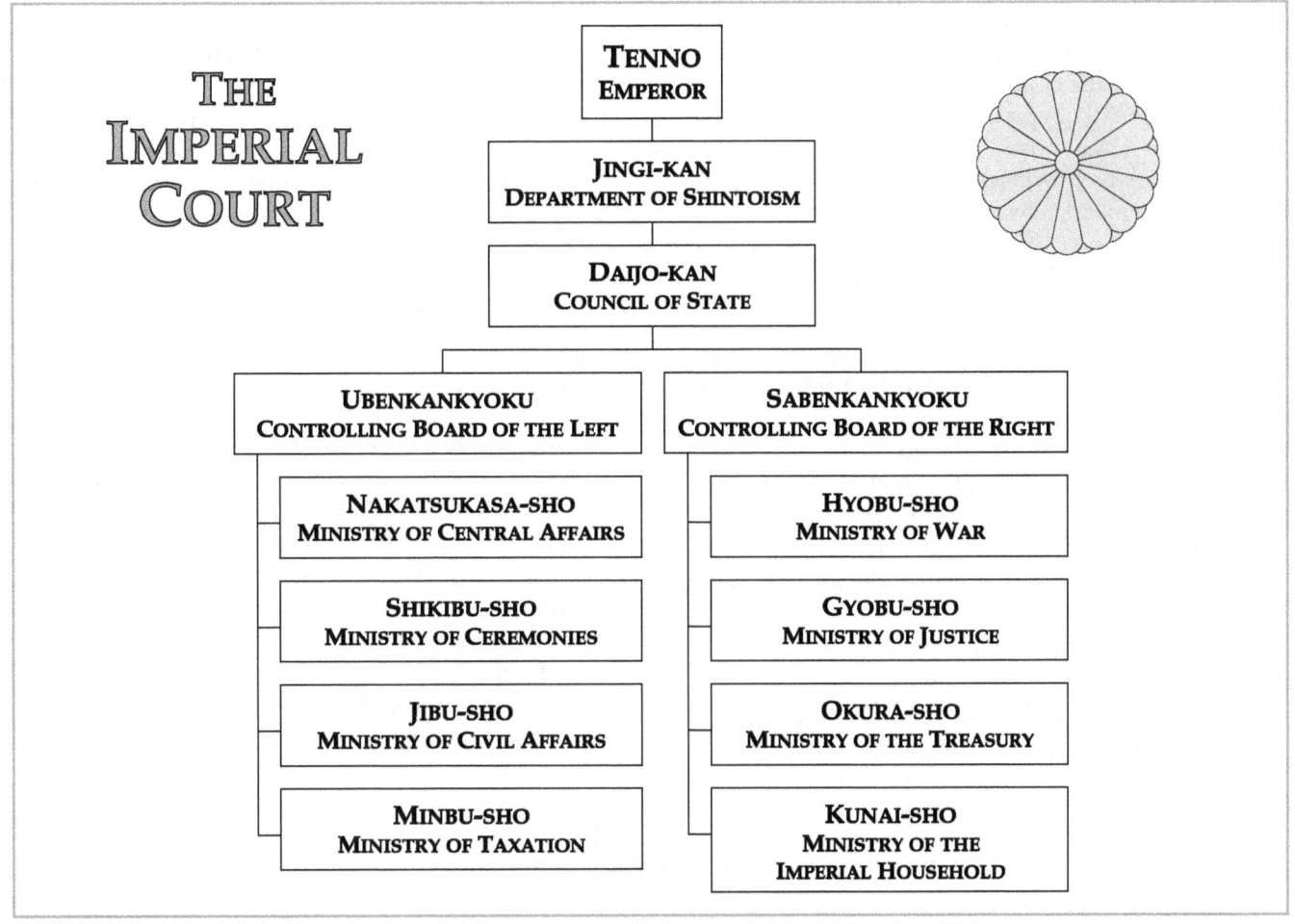

- **sadaiben** "controller of the left" -- Supervised the four ministries of the central affairs, civil services, ceremonies, and taxation.
- **udaiben** "controller of the right" -- Supervised the four ministries of the military, justice, treasury, and the Imperial Household.
- **sachuben** "1st assistant controller of the left"
- **uchuben** "1st assistant controller of the right"
- **sashoben** "2nd assistant controller of the left"
- **ushoben** "2nd assistant controller of the right"
- **sadaishi** "1st secretary of the left"
- **udaishi** "1st secretary of the right"
- **shisho** "assistant secretaries" -- Twenty officials held this position.

The eight ministries that were the responsibilities of the sadaiben and the udaiben were:

- **Ubenkankyoku** "Controlling Board of the Left"
  - **Nakatsukasa-sho** "Ministry of Central Affairs"
  - **Shikibu-sho** "Ministry of Ceremonies"
  - **Jibu-sho** "Ministry of Civil Affairs"
  - **Minbu-sho** "Ministry of Taxation"
- **Sabenkankyoku** "Controlling Board of the Right"
  - **Hyobu-sho** "Ministry of War"
  - **Gyobu-sho** "Ministry of Justice"
  - **Okura-sho** "Ministry of the Treasury"
  - **Kunai-sho** "Ministry of the Imperial Household"

Although the ministries existed primarily for keeping official records, during the time of the Shogun, the Bakufu had collateral officials who regulated, set policies, administered, and held actual control over their bureaucratic responsibilities.

Provincial Government Organization

At the time of the Taiho Code, Japan had 66 kuni "provinces." Each province had a group of kokushi "administrative governors," appointed by the Imperial Court, that were divided into four levels:

- **kami**
- **suké**
- **jo**
- **sakan**

Each kuni was further divided into gun "districts," which were administered by gun-ji "district officials," who were primarily responsible for keeping the peace,

Government – Kamakura Bakufu

collecting taxes, recruiting labor for the *corvée*, and for keeping registers of population and land allotment. Each gun was further subdivided, but local organizations varied greatly, typically into townships of around fifty homes led by a shoya "headman."

The number of provinces varied over time. As new land was developed, new provinces appeared.

Kamakura Bakufu
1185-1333

After defeating the Taira in the Genpei War (1180-1185), Minamoto Yoritomo (1147-1199) seized certain powers from the aristocracy and was given the title of Shogun in 1192. The system of government he established became formalized as the Bakufu "Shogunate," the first military dictatorship of Japan.

After the death of Yoritomo, the Hojo seized control of the Bakufu, and placed puppet Shogun as figureheads.

- **Shogun** "Commander-in-Chief"
- **Shikken** "Shogunal Regent"
- **rensho** "associate Regent" -- Established to share power and government administration with competing branches of the Hojo. Official documents required the signatures of both the Regent and the rensho.
- **Hyojo-shu** "Council of State" -- The highest decision-making body of the Kamakura Shogunate. Included statesmen, warriors, and scholars. Matters were decided with a simple majority vote. Initially there were 11 members, and the number steadily increased to 28.

Below the Hyojo-shu, administration was split into central and provincial administration.

Central Administration

- **Mandokoro** "Administrative Board" -- The main executive and general administrative office of the Kamakura Bakkufu. Formerly the Kumonjo "Office of Documents." The Hojo Regents used the office solely to oversee government finances.
- **Monchujo** "Board of Inquiry" -- Responsible for legal matters, especially dealing with lawsuits and appeals.
- **Samurai-dokoro** "Board of Retainers" -- Disciplinary board to regulate the activities of the war-

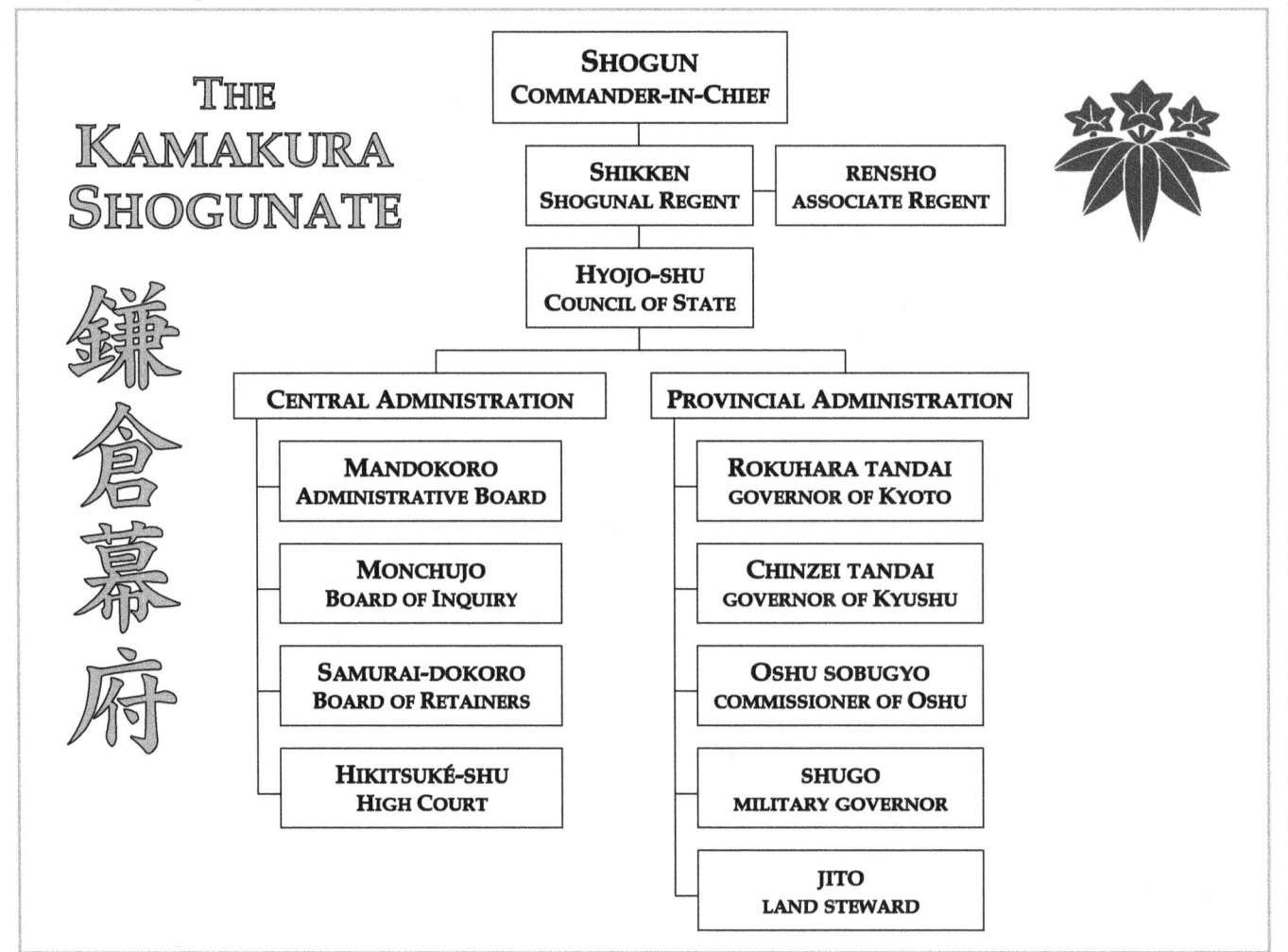

Government – Muromachi Bakufu

rior class. Its main responsibility was overseeing the police and the jito "land stewards."

- **Hikitsuké-shu** "High Court" -- Judicial court established to supplement the responsibilities of the Hyojo-shu. Among the legal issues it dealt with were land claims and taxation.

Provincial Administration

- **Rokuhara tandai** "Military governor of Kyoto" -- Responsible for overseeing Kyoto and the Imperial Court, as well affairs of southwestern Japan, for the Shogunate. Formerly the Kyoto-shugo. They were also a sort of secret police and widely feared. There were two positions: the higher-ranking kita-kata "northern governor," and the lower-ranking minami-kata "southern governor." Both posts were always taken by the Hojo.
- **Chinzei tandai** "military governor of Kyushu" -- Overseers of political, military, and legal matters in Kyushu for the Bakufu. It replaced the Chinzei-bugyo "commissioner of Kyushu" post which was originally created to oversee the defense of the island, acting as the first line of defense against Mongols.
- **Oshu sobugyo** "commissioner of Oshu" -- Managed Shogunal affairs in northern Honshu.
- **shugo** "military governor" -- Appointed by the Bakufu to maintain control over a province. Some shugo oversaw more than one province, in which case a shugo-dai "deputy governor" was appointed for each of the other provinces. Duties included policing, peacekeeping, administration, investigating crimes, and judging legal cases. They were the the forerunners of the daimyo.
- **jito** "land steward" -- Vassals appointed by the Shogunate to supervise estates. They were responsible for collecting taxes and ensuring their proper distribution. Appointments were considered as rewards for loyal service to the military government.

Muromachi Bakufu
1336-1573

The Ashikaga Bakufu inherited much of the administrative structure of the Kamakura government. Many key offices were retained. The Ashikaga ruled from the Muromachi district in Kyoto.

- **Shogun** "Commander-in-Chief"

Below the Shogun, administration was split into central and provincial administrations.

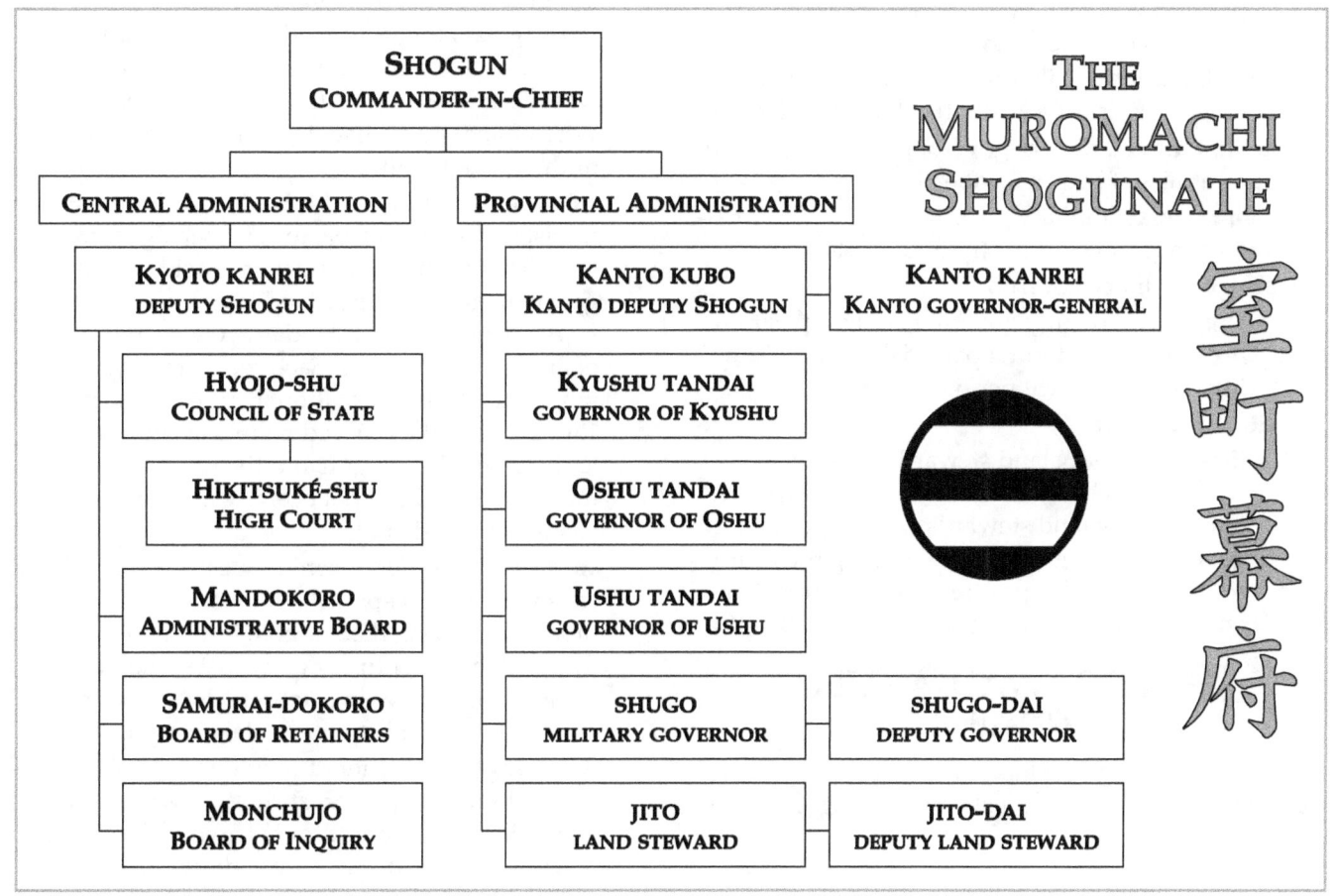

GOVERNMENT – TOKUGAWA BAKUFU

CENTRAL ADMINISTRATION

- **Kyoto kanrei** "deputy Shogun" -- Assisted the Shogun in administering the Bakufu. One important responsibility was to oversee the shugo "military governors." Three warrior families, the Shiba, the Hosokawa, and the Hatakeyama, shared this position on a rotating basis.
- **Hyojo-shu** "Council of State"
  - **Hikitsuké-shu** "High Court"
- **Mandokoro** "Administrative Board"
- **Samurai-dokoro** "Board of Retainers"
- **Monchujo** "Board of Inquiry" -- During the Muromachi period, many of the responsibilities of the Monchujo were reassigned to the Mandokoro, and the Board of Inquiry was reduced to recordkeeping.

PROVINCIAL ADMINISTRATION

- **Kanto kubo** "Kanto deputy Shogun" -- Kamakura-based representative of the Kyoto Ashikaga Bakufu. Responsible for governing eastern Japan. It was a hereditary position within the Ashikaga.
  - **Kanto kanrei** "Kanto governor-general" -- Kyoto-based overseer of the Kanto region. It provided assistance to the Kanto kubo. The position was held by members of various branches of the Uesugi.
- **Kyushu tandai** "military governor of Kyushu" -- Managed affairs of Kyushu for the Shogunate.
- **Oshu tandai** "military governor of Oshu" -- Managed affairs of Mutsu for the Shogunate.
- **Ushu tandai** "military governor of Ushu" -- Managed affairs of Dewa for the Shogunate.
- **shugo** "military governor"
  - **shugo-dai** "deputy governor" -- This position became a more formal part of the Bakufu during the Muromachi period.
- **jito** "land steward"
  - **jito-dai** "deputy land steward" -- When a jito received appointments to oversee multiple estates, deputy land stewards were appointed to govern the additional lands. During the Muromachi period, this position became important enough to become a formal part of the Bakufu.

TOKUGAWA BAKUFU
1603-1868

In 1603 the Tokugawa Bakufu was officially established in Edo by the 1st Tokugawa Shogun Ieyasu (1543-1616).

The Tokugawa Shogunate evolved into a political system where feudal power was split between the Bakufu in Edo, headed by the Shogun, and the provincial domains, ruled by the daimyo "feudal lords." For a fief holder to be considered for daimyohood, their land must be assessed at 10,000 koku of rice (50,000 bushels) or more.

The daimyo were categorized into three levels of relationship to the Tokugawa family:

- **Shinpan** -- Collateral families related to the Tokugawa and were deemed the most loyal.
- **Fudai daimyo** -- Vassals of the Tokugawa or allies in battle.
- **Tozama daimyo** -- Former non-allies who pledged their allegiance to the Tokugawa after the 1600 Battle of Sekigahara (Mino).

The daimyo had a degree of sovereignty and were allowed independent administration of their fiefs in exchange for loyalty to the Shogun, who was in turn responsible for national security and foreign relations. Each level of government administered its own system of taxation.

The Tokugawa bureaucracy grew in an *ad hoc* basis, with permanent and temporary offices added as needed. The following is a typical organizational structure of the Bakufu that existed during the Edo era.

- **Shogun** "Commander-in-Chief"
- **tairo** "great elder" -- Acted as interim leader in the absence of a Shogun, or when the Shogun was incapacitated. Position was often vacant. When filled, it was usually from the Sakai, the Ii, or the Hotta families.
- **roju** "senior counselor" -- Senior government administrators responsible for overseeing many offices. There were two under the first two Tokugawa Shogun, then five, and later four. They were selected from fudai daimyo with revenues of at least 25,000 koku. Each roju served one month at a time, in rotation. By the end of the 17th century, they served merely as intermediaries between the Shogun and the offices they administered, and did not exercise any power to change or decide policy.
- **sosha-ban** "master of ceremonies" -- Protocol officials who were responsible for conducting ceremonies involving the Shogun. Initially two held this post, but eventually grew to 24 who performed their duties in rotation. The title was restricted to the ranks of the fudai daimyo.
- **jisha-bugyo** "minister of religious affairs" -- Supervised temples and shrines, as well as their hierarchy and landholdings. Three or four held this post, and performed their duties one month

Government – Tokugawa Bakufu

at a time, in rotation. They were always fudai daimyo.

- **Kyoto shoshidai** "Kyoto governor-general" -- Official representative of the Shogun to the Emperor in Kyoto. Headquartered in the Nijo Palace. Oversaw the activities of the Imperial Court, Kyoto, and the surrounding eight provinces. Received an annual stipend of 10,000 koku. Had under him 50 yoriki "assistant administrators/guards" and 100 doshin "policemen." Reported to the Edo Bakufu every five years.
- **Osaka jodai** "keeper of Osaka Castle" -- Lord of Osaka Castle and senior military officer of central Japan.
- **sobayonin** "grand chamberlain" -- Responsible for relaying messages between the Shogun and the roju. The post holder received a stipend of 20,000 koku.
- **waka-doshiyori** "junior counselor" -- Assisted the roju and supervised the hatamoto and the gokenin. In addition, they also supervised artisans, artists, physicians, palace guards, and construction work. Officially there were six, but appointments were irregular, and there were between four and seven at a time.

The roju was responsible for responsible for many offices:

- **Edo machi-bugyo** "Edo city magistrate" -- Oversaw the Edo chonin "townsfolk" and had a full range of administrative and judicial responsibilities. There were usually two position holders

GOVERNMENT – TOKUGAWA BAKUFU

who alternately exercised control every other month. Usually selected from among the fudai daimyo, but were often hatamoto with 500 koku stipend. The position carried a 3,000 koku allowance.

- **yoriki** "assistant magistrates" -- Each magistrate had immediately under him 25 yoriki who were retainers with 200 koku stipend. The yoriki's office was not officially hereditary, but in practice the position was handed down from father to son, with the son entering service as a sort of apprentice around the age of 13. This family tradition meant that the yoriki knew their Edo well, and new magistrates depended on them for their experience and knowledge for the day-to-day running of their office.
- **doshin** "companions" -- Each magistrate had 120 doshin who worked under the yoriki and received a 30 koku stipend. Although they were samurai, they wore only one sword plus the jitté, a steel wand with a hook for catching the blade of the sword or knife of the attacker. They were the lowest-ranked peace officer, and they patrolled the streets of Edo with two or three deputies recruited from the townsfolk. The doshin acted as informers, and were the eyes and ears of the police.

▶ **kanjo-bugyo** "finance minister" -- Responsible for financial matters of the Bakufu. They numbered from four to six, selected from among the hatamoto, and had a large number of assistants.
- **daikan** "intendant" -- Local government officials who supervised and managed the Shogun's personal land holdings.

▶ **kanjo-ginmiyaku** "comptroller" -- Although structurally lower than the kanjo-bugyo, they were overseers of the activities of the higher office, investigating and auditing the commission as necessary.

▶ **ometsuké** "inspector general" -- Investigated internal affairs of government including the daimyo. There were four inspectors general.

▶ **ongoku-bugyo** "provincial magistrate" -- Essentially city magistrates, similar to the Edo machi-bugyo, who oversaw other localities such as Kyoto, Osaka, Sunpu, and Nagasaki. These appointees were hatamoto.

▶ **obangashira** "captain of the guard" -- Responsible for security at the three castles of Edo, Kyoto, and Osaka.

▶ **rusui** "keeper of Edo Castle" -- Supervisor of Edo Castle.

▶ **kinrizuki** "envoy to the Imperial Court" -- Inspectors of the Imperial Palace.

▶ **koké** "master of Court ceremonies" -- Hereditary officials responsible for carrying out official ceremonies and rituals. They also acted as Shogunal representatives for functions at the Imperial Court, temples, and shrines. The koké were made up of prominent families not of daimyo status. By the mid-19th century they numbered 26.

▶ **sobashu** "chamberlain" -- Officials in direct service to the Shogun, but bureaucratically reported to the roju.

▶ **hatamoto** "banner knight" -- High-ranking retainers who had the right to a personal audience with the Shogun. An early 18th century estimate had them numbering at about 5,000. Around 10% of the hatamoto were landholders, but not at a daimyo level.

▶ **gokenin** "household vassal" -- Lower-ranking samurai in service to the Shogun. They numbered around 12,000. Some in this group had higher incomes than some of the hatamoto, but the gokenin nevertheless were of lower rank and lesser status.

The waka-doshiyori supervised the following positions:

▶ **kosho-todori** "chief of the pages"
  konando-todori "chief of the attendants"

▶ **metsuké** "inspector" -- Played the role of an intelligence agency and internal spies. Investigated instances of maladministration, corruption, and unrest, focusing on those ranking below the daimyo. There were as many as 24 metsuké at any given time.

▶ **shoinban-gashira** "captain of the bodyguard"
  koshogumiban-gashira "captain of the inner guard"
  shinban-gashira "captain of the new guard"

▶ **magistrates**
  accountants
  tax collectors
  policemen

Although nepotism was a common practice, most higher-up positions in the Tokugawa Bakufu were not held hereditarily. Posts were stepping stones to higher offices, e.g., from jisha-bugyo to Osaka-jodai to Kyoto-shoshida to roju.

SHOGUN

MILITARY DICTATORS OF JAPAN

Dates are years of tenure.

KAMAKURA SHOGUN
1192-1338

Figurehead Shogun are listed below in italics.

1. **Minamoto Yoritomo** (1192-1199)
2. **Minamoto Yoriié** (1202-1203)
3. *Minamoto Sanetomo (1203-1219)*
4. *Kujo (Fujiwara) Yoritsuné (1226-1244)*
5. *Kujo (Fujiwara) Yoritsugu (1244-1252)*
6. *Prince Munetaka (1252-1266)*
7. *Prince Koreyasu (1266-1289)*
8. *Prince Hisa'aki (1289-1308)*
9. *Prince Morikuni (1308-1333)*
10. *Prince Moriyoshi/Morinaga (1333-1334)*
11. *Prince Narinaga (1334-1338)*

KAMAKURA "HOJO" SHIKKEN
1203-1333

Figurehead Shogunal Regents are listed below in italics.

1. **Hojo Tokimasa** (1203-1205)
2. **Hojo Yoshitoki** (1205-1224)
3. **Hojo Yasutoki** (1224-1242)
4. **Hojo Tsunetoki** (1242-1246)
5. **Hojo Tokiyori** (1246-1256)
6. *Hojo Nagatoki (1256-1264)*
7. *Hojo Masamura (1264-1268)*
8. **Hojo Tokimuné** (1268-1284)
9. **Hojo Sadatoki** (1284-1301)
10. **Hojo Morotoki** (1301-1311)
11. *Hojo Munenobu (1311-1312)*
12. *Hojo Hirotoki (1312-1315)*
13. *Hojo Mototoki (1315-1316)*
14. **Hojo Takatoki** (1316-1326)
15. *Hojo Sada'aki (1326)*
16. *Hojo Moritoki (1326-1333)*

MUROMACHI "ASHIKAGA" SHOGUN
1338-1573

1. **Ashikaga Takauji** (1338-1358)
2. **Ashikaga Yoshiakira** (1358-1367)
3. **Ashikaga Yoshimitsu** (1367-1395)
4. **Ashikaga Yoshimochi** (1395-1423)
5. **Ashikaga Yoshikazu** (1423-1425)
6. **Ashikaga Yoshinori** (1428-1441)
7. **Ashikaga Yoshikatsu** (1441-1443)
8. **Ashikaga Yoshimasa** (1449-1474)
9. **Ashikaga Yoshihisa** (1474-1489)
10. **Ashikaga Yoshitané** (1490-1493, 1508-1521)
11. **Ashikaga Yoshizumi** (1493-1508)
12. **Ashikaga Yoshiharu** (1521-1545)
13. **Ashikaga Yoshiteru** (1545-1565)
14. **Ashikaga Yoshihidé** (1568)
15. **Ashikaga Yoshiaki** (1568-1573)

EDO "TOKUGAWA" SHOGUN
1603-1868

1. **Tokugawa Ieyasu** (1603-1605)
2. **Tokugawa Hidetada** (1605-1623)
3. **Tokugawa Iemitsu** (1623-1651)
4. **Tokugawa Ietsuna** (1651-1680)
5. **Tokugawa Tsunayoshi** (1680-1709)
6. **Tokugawa Ienobu** (1709-1712)
7. **Tokugawa Ietsugu** (1712-1716)
8. **Tokugawa Yoshimuné** (1716-1745)
9. **Tokugawa Ieshigé** (1745-1760)
10. **Tokugawa Ieharu** (1760-1786)
11. **Tokugawa Ienari** (1786-1837)
12. **Tokugawa Ieyoshi** (1837-1853)
13. **Tokugawa Iesada** (1853-1858)
14. **Tokugawa Iemochi** (1858-1866)
15. **Tokugawa Keiki/Yoshinobu** (1866-1868)

Kamakura Shogun

1st Kamakura Shogun
Minamoto Yoritomo

- **Birth:** 1147 @ Heian-kyo (Kyoto)
- **Shogun:** 1192-1199
- **Death:** 1199 (aged 53)

3rd son of Yoshitomo and his official wife, a daughter of Fujiwara Suénori. His childhood name was Oni-musha.

Yoritomo made the genbuku at age of 13, a little before the beginning of the 1160 Heiji Rebellion (Kyoto). After the defeat of his father by the Taira, he fled with him, left him at Aohaka (Mino), and took refuge at the house of the ekicho "mayor" of the village of Oi. He was discovered by Taira Munekiyo and taken to Kyoto. Taira Kiyomori (1118-1181) intended to put him to death, but at the petition of his mother, he was contented with exiling him to Hiruga-oshima (Izu): Ito Sukechika and Hojo Tokimasa (1138-1215) had charge of him. He had a connection with Sukechika's daughter who bore him a son. In his fury Sukechika wanted to kill him, but Yoritomo managed to escape, and took shelter in the house of Tokimasa. There he acted in a similar manner with Tokimasa's daughter, the famous Masako (1156-1225), and it was in vain that her father sent her to the governor of the province, Taira Kanetaka. She eluded his watchfulness, and in 1179 returned to Yoritomo and married him.

In 1180, when Prince Mochihito (-1180) sent orders to levy troops to fight against the Taira, Yoritomo was the first to respond to the call, marking the start of the Genpei War (1180-1185). Yoritomo enrolled soldiers in Izu and in Sagami, but was defeated at Ishi-bashi-yama (Sagami) by Oba Kage-chika (-1180). He retreated then into the mountains of Hakoné, where he gathered his adherents, stopped at Kamakura and summoned the whole Minamoto clan from the different provinces. Kiyomori sent an army against him, but the soldiers, having heard of the superior numbers of Yoritomo's army, did not dare to attack him, and retired without fighting. Yoritomo then sent his troops towards Kyoto. At the Kiso-gawa (between Mino and

Owari), they joined the army brought up from Shinano by his cousin Minamoto (later Kiso) Yoshinaka (1154-1184) and his uncle Minamoto Yukiié (-1186), and defeated the soldiers of Taira Shigehira (1158-1185). Lastly, in 1183 they came to Kyoto, from whence the Taira fled to the west, taking with them the younger Emperor Antoku (1178-1185). Yoshinaka, once master of Kyoto, acted with such lawlessness that he provoked the anger of the ex-Emperor Go-Shirakawa (1127-1192) and the jealousy of Yoritomo, who sent an army commanded by his own brothers Minamoto Noriyori (1156-1193) and Minamoto Yoshitsuné (1159-1189) against him. In 1184 Yoshinaka was defeated and killed at the Battle of Awazu (Omi).

The victors then turned their efforts against the Taira, whom they repulsed at Ichi-no-tani (Settsu), at Yashima (Sanuki), and culminated in 1185 at Dan-no-ura (Nagato), where none of the Taira escaped alive, ending the Genpei War.

In 1186 Yoritomo charged his uncle Minamoto Yukiié with high treason, and had him beheaded.

Dissensions having arisen between Yoritomo and Yoshitsuné, the latter, to escape from his brother, who was watching for an opportunity to assassinate him, fled to Mutsu, where in 1189 he was defeated at the Battle of Koromo-gawa by Fujiwara Yasuhira (1155-1189), acting by Yoritomo's command, and committed seppuku.

Yoritomo then had undisputed sway. In 1190, he was named sotsui-hoshi "superintendent" of the 66 provinces. In 1192, he received the title of Sei-i-tai-shogun "Commander-in-Chief." A new era began for Japan that lasted for nearly seven centuries. The authority, no longer in the hands of the Emperor, was wielded by his powerful lieutenant-general, the Shogun. Yoritomo showed himself cruel to opponents and all those whose influence he feared: his uncle Yukiié and his brother Yoshitsuné had already been dispatched by his order; in 1193 he directed also that his other brother Noriyori be put to death. We have however to concede that he was an eminent administrator, and his organization of the Bakufu of Kamakura proved that he had real genius for government.

Yoritomo, often known under the title of Kamakura-udaisho or Kamakura-dono, died at the age of 53, from the effects of a fall from horseback.

2nd Kamakura Shogun
Minamoto Yoriié

- **Birth:** 1182 @ Kamakura
- **Shogun:** 1202-1203 (abdicated)
- **Death:** 1204 (aged 21)
  assassinated @ Shuzenji (Izu)

Eldest son of Yoritomo and Masako (1156-1225). Born at the residence of Hiki Yoshikazu (-1203) in Kamakura, and was first called Ichiman. He was 17 years old when his father died, and although he had then received the title of so-shugo-jito, his mother Masako formed a council, which was composed of her father Hojo Tokimasa (1138-1215), Oé Hiromoto (1148-1225), and eleven other members, who were entrusted with the government affairs. Yoriié showed great ardor in learning

the military arts of fencing, horse-riding, etc., but his morals were very low, and this estranged all men from him.

In 1199, after his father's death, Yoriié became head of the Minamoto, and in 1202 he was named Sei-i-tai-shogun, but fell ill the following year. His mother Masako then suggested that the 38 provinces of the Kansai should be given to his brother Senman (later Sanetomo), and the 28 provinces of the Kanto to his son Ichiman (1198-1203). Hiki Yoshikazu (-1203), Yoriié's father-in-law, thinking the partition unfair to his grandson, presented a complaint to his son-in-law, and formed with him the design of destroying the Hojo. Masako heard of this and informed her father Hojo Tokimasa, who sent Amano Tokagé to kill Yoshikazu. In 1203, when the news of this murder had spread, the whole family of the Hiki rose in arms, but Tokimasa ordered the palace of Ichiman at Hiki-ga-yatsu valley, where they had assembled, to be set on fire, and all perished in the flames. Yoriié was ordered to shave his head and was confined in Shuzenji (Izu), where Tokimasa had him assassinated the following year.

3rd Kamakura Shogun
Minamoto Sanetomo

- **Birth:** 1192
- **Shogun:** 1203-1219
- **Death:** 1219 (aged 26) assassinated @ Tsurugaoka Hachiman-gu (near Kamakura)

3rd and last Minamoto Shogun. 2nd son of Yoritomo and Masako (1156-1225), and younger brother to Yoriié. In 1203 he succeeded his father as head of the Minamoto and a figurehead Shogun, whilst the administration remained in the hands of his mother Masako, his uncle Hojo Yoshitoki (1163-1224), and his grandfather Hojo Tokimasa (1138-1215). At the age of 12 he changed the name Senman, which he had borne until then, to Sanetomo.

In 1205 Hojo Tokimasa planned to destroy his grandson Sanetomo, and to replace him by his son-in-law Hiraga Tomomasa, but the plot was revealed to Masako, who hastened with her son to the palace of Hojo Yoshitoki: Tokimasa was obliged to shave his head and retire to Hojo (Izu), whilst in 1205

he was put to death at his Kyoto mansion. Masako continued to govern with her brother Yoshitoki.

Sanetomo, understanding his own puppet status and ineffectiveness in comparison to the Hojo, feared for his life the rest of his days, and put all of his time and energy into writing poetry and gaining posts within the powerless but honorary Imperial Court. Sanetomo was a talented poet, writing over 700 poems between the ages of 17 and 22 while being tutored by Fujiwara Teika (1162-1241), even having one of his tanka "short poems" included in the anthology *Ogura Hyakunin Isshu* "*100 Poems by 100 Poets,*" a noted collection of poems of the Heian "Aristocratic" Period (794-1185) and the early Kamakura Period (1185-1333). Eventually he lapsed into inactivity and despair, plagued by fear of assassination, and tormented by chronic alcoholism, an addiction which the Zen Buddhist priest Eisai (1141-1215) once tried to break by replacing alcohol with tea.

At the beginning of the year 1219, Sanetomo, having received the title of udaijin "junior minister of state," the 3rd highest post of the Imperial Court, ordered a ceremony of thanksgiving to be held at the Senior Shrine at the Tsurugaoka Hachiman-gu near Kamakura. In the evening, under heavy snow, he was leaving the temple and standing on the steps when he was assassinated by his nephew Kugyo (1200-1219), son of Yoriié, who was for this act subsequently beheaded a few hours later. Sanetomo was then only 28 years old. He was the last of the Minamoto Shogun.

4th Kamakura Shogun
Kujo (Fujiwara) Yoritsuné

- **Birth:** 1218
- **Shogun:** 1226-1244 (abdicated)
- **Death:** 1256 (aged 38)

3rd son of Kujo (Fujiwara) Michiié. As he was born in the year of the tiger, in the month of the tiger, and on the day of the tiger, his given name at birth was Mi-tora "Three Tigers."

In 1219, when the 3rd Minamoto Shogun Sanetomo was assassinated, the 2nd Hojo Shikken Yoshitoki (1163-1224) sought a successor to the Minamoto family. Although the direct line of Minamoto Yoritomo (1147-1199) was extinct, his sister had been married to Fujiwara Yoshiyasu, and her daughter to Daijo-daijin "Chancellor of the Realm" Fujiwara Kintsuné (1171-1244). The daughter of the latter married Kujo Michiié, had a son Yoritsuné, then 2 years old, who was destined to succeed the Minamoto Shogun, while Masako (1156-1225), the widow of Yoritomo, was Regent. Masako was aided in her functions by her brother Hojo Yoshitoki (1163-1224), and in 1224, after the latter's death, by her nephew Hojo Yasutoki (1183-1242). In 1226 Yoritsuné, then 8 years old, was made Sei-i-tai-shogun, but the authority remained in the hands of the Hojo.

In 1230 Yoritsuné was married to the daughter of Minamoto Yoriié (1182-1204), 15 years his senior.

In 1244 Yoritsuné transferred the Shogunate to his son Yoritsugu, who was then 6 years old. In 1245 he shaved his head and became a Buddhist monk.

In 1252 Yoritsuné tried to create a revolt against the powerful Hojo Shikken, but the only result was the deposition of his son.

5th Kamakura Shogun
Kujo (Fujiwara) Yoritsugu

- **Birth:** 1239
- **Shogun:** 1244-1252 (deposed)
- **Death:** 1256 (aged 16)

Son of Yoritsuné. In 1244 he became Shogun when 5 years old at the abdication of his father, but the 4th Hojo Shikken Tsunetoki (1224-1246) and then the 5th Hojo Shikken Tokiyori (1227-1263) continued to govern. In 1246, when only 7 years old, he married the sister of Tsunetoki.

In 1252, Yoritsugu's father Yoritsuné having been implicated in a plot against the Hojo, the latter deposed the young Shogun and replaced him by Munetaka-shinno (1242-1274), eldest son of the Emperor Go-Saga (1220-1272).

6th Kamakura Shogun
Munetaka-shinno

- **Birth:** 1242
- **Shogun:** 1252-1266 (deposed)
- **Death:** 1274 (aged 31)

2nd son of the Emperor Go-Saga (1220-1272).

In 1252, at the age of 10, the Imperial Prince Munetaka was chosen by the 5th Hojo Shikken Tokiyori (1227-1263) to succeed the deposed Shogun Yoritsugu. As he was another puppet ruler controlled by the Hojo Shikken, he committed to waka "Japanese poetry" instead.

In 1266, pressed by the bonze Ryoki, the Imperial Prince took the resolution to free himself from the tutelage of the Hojo, but the plot having become known, he was deposed and confined in the Rokuhara (Kyoto). In 1272 he shaved his head and took the name Gyosho.

Munetaka had two sons: Koreyasu-shinno, who succeeded him in the charge of Shogun, and the bonze Shintaku, chief of Enma-in. His two daughters married the Emperor Go-Uda (1267-1324).

7th Kamakura Shogun
Koreyasu-shinno

- **Birth:** 1264
- **Shogun:** 1266-1289 (deposed)
- **Death:** 1326 (aged 62)

Son of Munetaka-shinno. He succeeded his father in the office of the Shogun at the age of 3, all the authority remaining in the hands of the 8th Hojo Shikken Tokimuné (1251-1284).

In 1289 the Imperial Prince Koreyasu was deposed by the 9th Hojo Shikken Sadatoki (1271-1311) at the age of 25 because he grew "too old" to be a puppet ruler. Whereupon he retired to Saga (west of Kyoto), where he shaved his head, and lived for 37 years more.

8th Kamakura Shogun
Hisa'aki-shinno

- **Birth:** 1276
- **Shogun:** 1289-1308 (deposed)
- **Death:** 1328 (aged 52)

7th son of the Emperor Go-Fukakusa (1243-1304). During the reign of his elder brother Fushimi-tenno (1265-1317), he was chosen by the 9th Hojo Shikken Sadatoki (1271-1311) to succeed the 7th Kamakura Shogun Koreyasu-shinno, who in 1289 was deprived of his dignity.

Having in his turn displeased the powerful Shikken, in 1308 the Imperial Prince Hisa'aki was deposed and replaced by his 7-year-old son Morikuni-shinno. He then retired to Kyoto, where he lived 20 years.

9th Kamakura Shogun
Morikuni-shinno

- **Birth:** 1301
- **Shogun:** 1308-1333
- **Death:** 1333 (aged 31 or 32)

Son of the 8th Kamakura Shogun Hisa'aki-shinno, and grandson of the Emperor Go-Fukakusa (1243-1304). In 1308, at the age of 7, he succeeded his father, who had been deposed by the 9th Hojo Shikken Sadatoki (1271-1311).

After the destruction of the Hojo, the Imperial Prince Morikuni became a bonze, and died the same year.

10th Kamakura Shogun
Moriyoshi-shinno

- **Birth:** 1308
- **Shogun:** 1333-1334 (deposed)
- **Death:** 1335 (aged 36 or 37) beheaded @ Kamakura

1st Shogun of the Kenmu Restoration. Eldest son of the Emperor Go-Daigo (1288-1339) and of Minamoto Chikako,

Fuchibé Yoshihiro comes to execute Prince Moriyoshi while he reads the Lotus Sutra in his cave.

– Woodblock print by Utagawa Kuniyoshi (1798-1861)

daughter of Kitabataké Morichika. Also known as Morinaga-shinno.

In 1326, at the death of the Crown Prince Kuninaga-shinno, Go-Daigo had resolved to replace him by Imperial Prince Moriyoshi, but the 14th Hojo Shikken Takatoki (1303-1333) opposed it, and brought the choice on Kazuhito-shinno (1313-1364), son of Go-Fushimi (1288-1336). Moriyoshi then became a bonze and took the name Son'un. In 1327 he was made zasu "chief" of the Tendai Sect in Hiei-zan (northeast of Kyoto). He established himself in the village of Oto (Yamato), hence the name of Oto-no-miya which was given to him.

In 1331, when Hojo Takatoki was marching against Kyoto to dethrone Go-Daigo, Son'un with his brother Munenaga-shinno (1311-1385) placed himself at the head of the troops levied by the bonzes, and tried to arrest the advance of the enemy, but he was defeated. He then concealed himself in the district of Kumano (Kii), put aside the garb of bonze, took his name of Moriyoshi again, and gathered together partisans to his father's cause.

In 1333, after the ruin of the Hojo, Moriyoshi was named Sei-i-tai-shogun, but the following year, having been calumniated before Go-Daigo by Ashikaga Takauji (1305-1358), he was deposed, imprisoned in the Nikai-do of Kamakura, and placed under guard of Ashikaga Tadayoshi (1306-1352). In 1335 Hojo Tokiyuki (1322-1353) came to attack Kamakura. Tadayoshi was defeated and fled. Before his flight he had his prisoner beheaded by the hands of Fuchibé Yoshihiro.

11TH KAMAKURA SHOGUN
NARINAGA-SHINNO

- **Birth:** 1325
- **Shogun:** 1334-1338 (deposed)
- **Death:** 1338 (aged 12) executed @ Kyoto

2nd Shogun during the Kenmu Restoration. 10th son of the Emperor Go-Daigo (1288-1339) and Fujiwara Renshi (1301-1359), daughter of Ano Kinkado. His brothers-uterine were the Crown Prince Tsunenaga (1324-1338) and the Emperor Go-Murakami (1328-1368).

In 1333 the Imperial Prince Narinaga was appointed Kozuké-taishu and Kanto-kanrei "eastern deputy Shogun," then sent to Kamakura and named Sei-i-tai-shogun after the deposition of his brother Moriyoshi-shinno. In 1338 the Emperor Komyo (1322-1380) of the Northern Dynasty, chose him kotaishi "heir." He then returned to Kyoto, was dismissed shortly after, confined at Kazan-in, and put to death by Ashikaga Tadayoshi (1306-1352), along with his brother Tsunenaga-shinno. He was 13 years old.

Kamakura Shikken

1st Kamakura Shikken
Hojo Tokimasa

- **Birth:** 1138 @ Izu
- **Shikken:** 1203-1205 (abdicated)
- **Death:** 1215 (aged 76) @ Izu

Son of Tokiié, descendant in the 6th degree of Taira Sadamori (-10th century). He was residing at Hojo (Izu) when Minamoto Yoritomo (1147-1199), exiled in 1160 by Taira Kiyomori (1118-1181), arrived there and received hospitality, first from Ito Sukechika, then from Tokimasa.

In 1180 Prince Mochihito (-1180) incited the samurai of Kanto to revolt against the Taira. Tokimasa set out with Yoritomo, killed Taira Kanetaka, but in 1181 was defeated at Ishibashi-yama (Sagami) by Oba Kagechika (-1180). He then entered Kai, applied to Takeda Nobuyoshi (1583-1603) for help, and came back with a large army of men. Yoritomo established himself at Kamakura, and married Tokimasa's daughter Masako (1156-1225). In 1185 Tokimasa was appointed Kyoto kanrei "Kyoto deputy Shogun," and by degrees became more influential.

After the death of Yoritomo in 1199, he was succeeded by his son and heir Yoriié (1182-1204), who was at the time 18 years old. Tokimasa, his grandfather, became his guardian, and took the title of Shikken "Regent." From that time, Tokimasa, together with his daughter Masako, governed without opposition.

In 1203, Yoriié having become ill, Tokimasa regulated the order of his succession, gave the 28 provinces of the east to Yoriié's son Ichiman (1198-1203), and the 38 provinces of the west to Yoriié's brother Sanetomo (1192-1219). Hiki Yoshikazu (-1203), Ichiman's grandfather, complained of the share given to his grandson. Tokimasa had him assassinated together with Ichiman. Yoriié, still Shogun, having manifested his dissatisfaction, abdicated, was exiled to Shuzen-ji (Izu), then in 1204 put to death, and replaced by his brother Sanetomo, who became the 3rd Minamoto Shogun.

After that, the 2nd wife of Tokimasa, Omaki-no-kata, intrigued to have her son-in-law Hiraga Tomomasa appointed Shogun. Tokimasa listen to her suggestions, and intended to have Sanetomo assassinated, but the plot was discovered, and in 1205 Masako and her son Hojo Yoshitoki (1163-1224) forced Tokimasa to return to Hojo (Izu) and exile there, where he became a Buddhist monk, and died 10 years later.

2nd Kamakura Shikken
Hojo Yoshitoki

- **Birth:** 1163
- **Shikken:** 1205-1224
- **Death:** 1224 (aged 60 or 61) assassinated @ Kamakura

Eldest son of Tokimasa and his wife Maki, and brother to Masako (1156-1225) and Tokifusa (1175-1240).

In 1184 Yoshitoki took part in the expedition of Minamoto Noriyori (1156-1193) against the Taira in Kyushu, and defeated Harada Tanenao in Bungo.

In 1205 Yoshitoki, with Masako, forced his father to abdicate, succeeded in the office of Shikken, and governed relatively uneventfully in concert with his sister.

In 1219, after the death of Sanetomo, Yoshitoki chose Kujo (Fujiwara) Yoritsuné (1218-1256) as Shogun, who was then only 2 years old, a son of Sessho "Regent to the Emperor" Kujo Michiié (1193-1252) and great-grandson of the eldest sister of Minamoto Yoritomo (1147-1199).

Soon afterwards the ex-Emperor Go-Toba (1180-1239) endeavored to overthrow the power of Yoshitoki, but his army was defeated during the 1221 Jokyu War at Uji, Seta, and Kyoto. The Emperor was exiled to Sanuki, as were also his sons the ex-Emperors Tsuchimikado (1196-1231) and Juntoku (1197-1242), the first to Tosa, the second to Sado, and his grandson the Emperor Chukyo (1218-1234) was deposed after a reign of 70 days.

To watch more closely the intrigues of the Court, Yoshitoki installed his son Yasutoki and his brother Tokifusa (1175-1240) in the Rokuhara (Kyoto). Thus all authority was in the hands of the Hojo: the Shogun and the Emperors were chosen and deposed according to the Hojo's will and pleasure.

Yoshitoki died at the age of 61, assassinated by a servant of the Imperial Court.

3rd Kamakura Shikken
Hojo Yasutoki

- **Birth:** 1183
- **Shikken:** 1224-1242
- **Death:** 1242 (aged 58 or 59)

Eldest son of Yoshitoki.

In 1218 Yasutoki became betto "chief" of the samurai-dokoro "board of retainers."

At the time of 1221 the Jokyu War (Kyoto), his father Yoshitoki sent Yasutoki to fight against the army of the ex-Emperor Go-Toba (1180-1239). It was

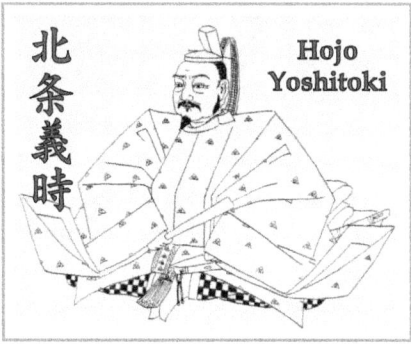

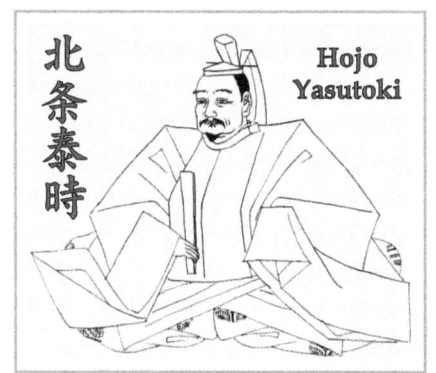

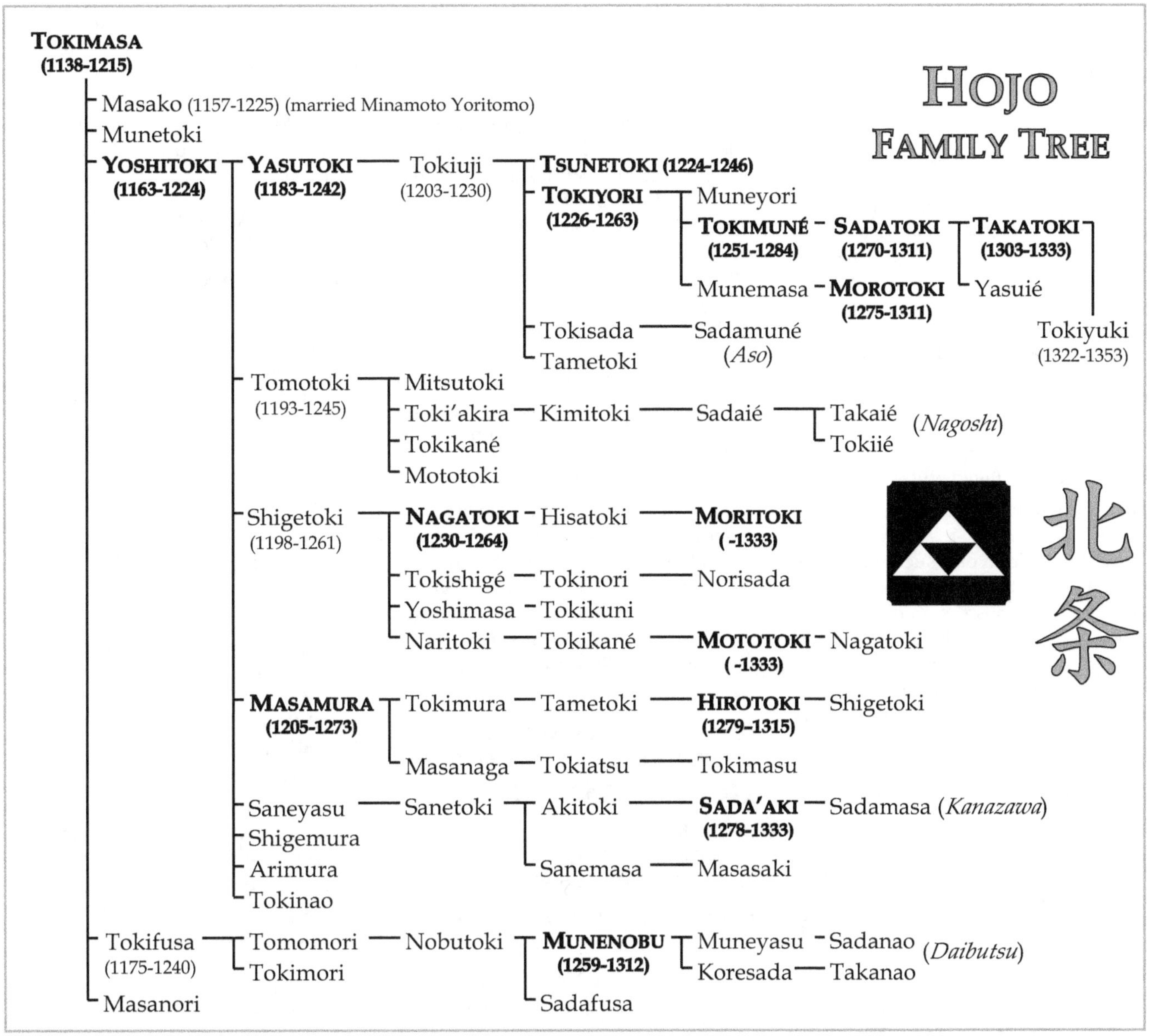

Kamakura Shikken

Hojo Family Tree

```
TOKIMASA
(1138-1215)
├─ Masako (1157-1225) (married Minamoto Yoritomo)
├─ Munetoki
├─ YOSHITOKI ─┬─ YASUTOKI ──┬─ Tokiuji ──┬─ TSUNETOKI (1224-1246)
│  (1163-1224)│  (1183-1242)│  (1203-1230)├─ TOKIYORI ─┬─ Muneyori
│             │             │             │  (1226-1263)├─ TOKIMUNÉ ─── SADATOKI ─┬─ TAKATOKI ─┐
│             │             │             │             │  (1251-1284)  (1270-1311)│  (1303-1333)
│             │             │             │             └─ Munemasa ─── MOROTOKI   └─ Yasuié
│             │             │             │                             (1275-1311)
│             │             │             ├─ Tokisada ── Sadamuné                    Tokiyuki
│             │             │             └─ Tametoki    (Aso)                       (1322-1353)
│             │             ├─ Tomotoki ─┬─ Mitsutoki
│             │             │ (1193-1245)├─ Toki'akira ── Kimitoki ── Sadaié ─┬─ Takaié (Nagoshi)
│             │             │            ├─ Tokikané                          └─ Tokiié
│             │             │            └─ Mototoki
│             │             ├─ Shigetoki ─┬─ NAGATOKI ── Hisatoki ── MORITOKI
│             │             │ (1198-1261) │  (1230-1264)             ( -1333)
│             │             │             ├─ Tokishigé ── Tokinori ── Norisada
│             │             │             ├─ Yoshimasa ── Tokikuni
│             │             │             └─ Naritoki ── Tokikané ── MOTOTOKI ── Nagatoki
│             │             │                                        ( -1333)
│             │             ├─ MASAMURA ─┬─ Tokimura ── Tametoki ── HIROTOKI ── Shigetoki
│             │             │ (1205-1273)│                          (1279-1315)
│             │             │            └─ Masanaga ── Tokiatsu ── Tokimasu
│             │             ├─ Saneyasu ── Sanetoki ─┬─ Akitoki ── SADA'AKI ── Sadamasa (Kanazawa)
│             │             ├─ Shigemura             │             (1278-1333)
│             │             ├─ Arimura               └─ Sanemasa ── Masasaki
│             │             └─ Tokinao
│             ├─ Tokifusa ─┬─ Tomomori ── Nobutoki ─┬─ MUNENOBU ─┬─ Muneyasu ─┬─ Sadanao (Daibutsu)
│             │ (1175-1240)└─ Tokimori              │  (1259-1312)└─ Koresada ─┴─ Takanao
│             │                                     └─ Sadafusa
└─ Masanori
```

北条

---

he that deposed the young Emperor Chukyo (1218-1234), replaced him by the Emperor Go-Horikawa (1212-1234), and exiled the three ex-Emperors to distant provinces, after which he installed himself in the Rokuhara Palace and governed the capital from 1221-1224 as the 1st Kita-kata Rokuhara tandai "northern governor of Kyoto," with his uncle Hojo Tokifusa (1175-1240) as the 1st Minami-kata Rokuhara tandai "southern governor of Kyoto."

In 1224 Yasutoki returned to Kamakura to succeed his father as Shikken, and sent his son Tokiuji (1203-1230) and his cousin Tokimori as governors to Kyoto.

At the death of the Emperor Shijo (1231-1242), Yasutoki sent Adachi Yoshikagé to Kyoto in order to prevent the election of the candidate of the Sessho Kujo (Fujiwara) Michiié (1193-1252), and to raise Go-Saga (1220-1272) to the throne. He died the same year.

During his 18 years administration, Yasutoki introduced numerous reforms and worked efficaciously at improving the state of the country, which had been impoverished by long civil wars. He was highly praised for his impartial justice. In 1232, he had Miyoshi Yasutsura draw up the *Goseibai-shikimoku* "Formulary of Adjudication," a legal code for the use by the samurai; it is also called *Joei-shiki-moku* from the era during which it was published. The Zen Buddhist monk Myoé (1173-1232) was his most loyal counselor.

4TH KAMAKURA SHIKKEN
HOJO TSUNETOKI

▸ **Birth:** 1224
▸ **Shikken:** 1242-1246 (abdicated)

Hojo Tsunetoki

> **Death:** 1246 (aged 21 or 22)

Son of Tokiuji (1203-1230), and grandson of Yasutoki. He was Musashi no kami.

In 1242 Tsunetoki succeeded his grandfather Yasutoki as Shikken. Having become ill, he abdicated in favor of his brother Tokiyori, and died soon afterwards. He is buried at the Komyoji in Zaimokuza (Kamakura), a temple he founded with the priest Nenna Ryochu (1199-1287).

5TH KAMAKURA SHIKKEN
HOJO TOKIYORI

> **Birth:** 1227
> **Shikken:** 1246-1256 (abdicated)
> **Death:** 1263 (aged 36)

Son of Tokiuji (1203-1230), and grandson of Yasutoki.

In 1246 Tokiyori succeeded his brother Tsunetoki as Shikken. He had scarcely taken possession of his office when his relative Nagoé Mitsutoki, Echigo no kami, supported by the ex-Shogun Kujo (Fujiwara) Yoritsuné (1218-1256), tried to have him assassinated in order to take his place, but the plot was discovered. Mitsutoki was exiled to Izu, and Yoritsuné sent back to Kyoto.

In 1247 Miura Yasumura, accused of endeavoring to re-establish Yoritsuné in his former office of Shogun, along with all his family, was destroyed by Adachi Kagemori (-1248) at the Battle of Hochi.

In 1252, Yoritsuné having continued to conspire against Tokiyori, the latter deposed the Shogun Kujo (Fujiwara) Yoritsugu (1239-1256), a son of Yoritsuné, whom he sent back to Kyoto, and replaced him by Prince Munetaka (1242-1274), a brother to the then-reigning Emperor Go-Fukakusa (1243-1304).

In 1256 his health failed. He shaved his head, assumed the name Doso, and retired to Saimyo-ji, hence the name of Saimyo-ji-nyudo, by which he is known, letting Hojo Nagatoki govern in the name of his son Tokimuné (1251-1284).

It is said that Tokiyori traveled *incognito* throughout the country in order to judge personally of the needs of the people, of the abuses of the administration, etc. He signalized his government by a wise economy, and a close and constant interest in agriculture. He had, as minister, Aoto Fujitsuna of legendary fame.

6TH KAMAKURA SHIKKEN
PUPPET REGENT OF TOKIMUNÉ
HOJO NAGATOKI

> **Birth:** 1230
> **Shikken:** 1256-1264
> **Death:** 1264 (aged 33 or 34)

Son of Shigetoki. From 1247-1256 he was the Kita-kata Rokuhara tandai "northern governor of Kyoto." In 1256 he returned to Kamakura to assist the young Shikken Tokimuné. He was made Musashi no kami and betto "chief" of the samurai-dokoro "board of retainers."

7TH KAMAKURA SHIKKEN
PUPPET REGENT OF TOKIMUNÉ
HOJO MASAMURA

> **Birth:** 1205
> **Shikken:** 1264-1268 (abdicated)
> **Death:** 1273 (aged 67)

Son of Yoshitoki, and brother to Shigetoki. He was on the Hyojo-shu "Council of State," and held the titles Mutsu no kami and Sagami no kami.

From 1256-1264 Masamura was rensho "assistant to the Regent" to Nagatoki. In 1264 he replaced Nagatoki as Shikken. From 1268-1273 he was again rensho to Tokimuné.

8TH KAMAKURA SHIKKEN
HOJO TOKIMUNÉ

> **Birth:** 1251
> **Shikken:** 1268-1284
> **Death:** 1284 (aged 32)

Eldest son of Tokiyori. He was only 6 years old when his father resigned the office of Shikken in his favor, but he was aided by the rensho "assistant to the Regent" Nagatoki. From an early age he evinced a resolute, energetic character. In 1266, having had some disputes with the 6th Kamakura Shogun Munetaka-shinno (1242-1274), he deposed and replaced him by the 3-year-old Koreyasu-shinno (1264-1326), son of Prince Munetaka.

From 1264-1268, prior to becoming Shikken, Tokimuné was rensho to Masamura.

In 1260 the celebrated Kublai Khan (1215-1294) had dethroned the Song Dynasty, and having established his capital at Khan-Baleck (now Beijing) he called upon all the former tributary states of China to acknowledge their fealty to the new Yuan Dynasty. In 1268 he sent an ambassador to Japan with a letter which Tokimuné considered offensive to the country, and was left unanswered. Kublai Khan sent more emissaries, twice in 1269, once each in 1271 and 1272, but they were driven away each time, without even permitted to land.

Hojo Nagatoki

Hojo Masamura

Hojo Tokiyori

In 1274 Kublai Khan sent a fleet of 150 war-vessels to Tsushima, to begin the 1st Mongol invasion of Japan. So Sukekuni, the governor of the island, tried to resist, but he died in a battle at Asaji-no-ura, and the island was laid waste. The invaders, after having devastated Iki-shima, tried to land at Imatsu (Chikuzen). The Kyushu clans, the Shoni, the Otomo, the Matsuura, the Kikuchi, etc., had intrenched themselves at Hakozaki, and at the 1st Battle of Hakata Bay (Chikuzen), offered vigorous resistance. The Mongols inflicted serious losses on the Japanese army, and would undoubtedly have gained the victory in the end had not Liu, their general, been killed in battle, and many of their vessels wrecked in a tempest, later dubbed the kamikazé "divine wind." The remainder of the fleet escaped, and returned to China.

Kublai Khan did not consider himself vanquished. In 1276 he sent another ambassador with the same proposal. Tokimuné had him beheaded at Tatsu-no-kuchi (Kamakura). In 1279 two others met with the same at Hakata (Chikuzen), and, by the orders of Tokimuné, Kyushu and the western provinces of Hondo "Honshu" made themselves ready to repel any invasion. In 1281 Kublai sent 100,000 Mongols and 10,000 Koreans to begin the 2nd Mongol invasion of Japan. After having devastated Iki-shima, and massacred all its inhabitants, the Mongols came to the coast of Dazaifu (Kyushu), where they encountered an energetic resistance. Having landed at Goryu-san (Hizen), they met with a large army upon which they inflicted great losses by their artillery without however being able to vanquished them. After a week of desperate fighting, known collectively as the 2nd Battle of Hakata Bay, the situation had not changed, when, for the second time, a kamikazé came to the succor of the Japanese. The Mongolian fleet was scattered, and thousands of soldiers perished in the sea. The survivors took refuge in the island of Takashima, where Shoni Kagesuké (-1285) pursued them, slew a great many, and brought back a thousand prisoners who were put to death. Only three escaped to carry the news of the disaster to China.

Meanwhile, expecting a new invasion, Tokimuné continued to fortify the coasts. In fact, Kublai Khan began to prepare a new expedition, but his plan could not be realized, and thus Japan was preserved from the only foreign invasion that threatened her in the course of her history. Tokimuné died soon after, and did not survive this triumph, which was greatly due to his energy.

Tokimuné is known for spreading Zen Buddhism in Japan, and, by extension, Bushido among the warrior class. He invited Chinese Zen monks, such as Sogen Mogaku (Wuxue), to Japan, and, with him, in 1282 had the Engaku-ji built at one of Kamakura's Five Mountains to honor those of both sides who perished in the two Mongolian invasions.

9TH KAMAKURA SHIKKEN
HOJO SADATOKI

- **Birth:** 1271
- **Shikken:** 1284-1301 (abdicated)
- **Death:** 1311 (aged 40)

Son of Tokimuné. He was only 13 years old, at the death of his father, when he became Shikken, and initially had his kinsman Hojo Naritoki (-1287) as rensho "associate Regent."

In 1285 Sadatoki's first act of authority, known as the Shimotsuki Incident, was to send Taira Yoritsuna to attack the Adachi clan, resulting in the death of Adachi Yasumori, his maternal grandfather, and the near extermination of the clan, killing 500. Yasumori's only crime had been to seek the honors of the Shogunate for his son Munekagé.

Soon afterwards, in 1289, displeased with the Shogun Koreyasu-shinno (1264-1326), Sadatoki sent him to Kyoto, and replaced him by Hisa'akira-shinno (1276-1326), brother to the reigning Emperor Fushimi (1265-1317).

In 1292 Sadatoki was advised by a Korean envoy to re-open relations with China in order to avoid another war. He had him imprisoned and scorned his advice.

In 1293 Sadatoki's soldiers killed Taira Yoritsuna and 90 of his followers in the Heizen Gate Incident.

Sadatoki was obliged to settle continual disputes between the two branches of the Imperial family, concerning the succession to the Chrysanthemum Throne. The Emperor Go-Saga (1220-1272) saw his two sons Go-Fukakusa (1247-1259) and Kameyama (1260-1274) crowned after him. The latter abdicated in favor of his son Go-Uda (1275-1287), whose successor was Fushimi (1288-1298), a son of Go-Fukakusa. When Fushimi abdicated in favor of Go-Fushimi (1288-1336), the ex-Emperor Go-Uda (1267-1324) requested Sadatoki to respect the will of Go-Saga, according to which the Emperor should be chosen alternately from the two branches of his descendants. Sadatoki deposed Go-Fushimi, replaced him by Go-Nijo (1285-1308), a son of Go-Uda, and decided that henceforth the Emperors should abdicate after a reign of ten years to surrender the throne to the rival branch.

Sadatoki also decided, in order to weaken the power of the Fujiwara, that the Sessho "Regent to the Child Em-

peror" and the Kanpaku "Regent to the Emperor" should alternately be chosen from among five of its many branches, called for this reason the Go-Sekké "Five Regent Houses." They were the Konoé, the Takatsukasa, the Kujo, the Ichijo, and the Nijo. These arrangements were evidently made with a view to fortifying the authority of the Hojo by dividing their adversaries. They were efficacious as long as energetic men like Tokimuné and Sadatoki were in power; but in weak hands they became a cause of troubles, which finally brought about the ruin of the powerful Shikken.

In 1301 Sadatoki had his head shaved, assumed the name Soen, and retired to Saishokoku-ji, which he had built. He continued to govern until his death.

10th Kamakura Shikken
Puppet Regent of Sadatoki
Hojo Morotoki

- **Birth:** 1275
- **Shikken:** 1301-1311
- **Death:** 1311 (aged 36)

Son-in-law of and successor to Sadatoki, who continued to govern in Morotoki's place.

11th Kamakura Shikken
Puppet Regent of Takatoki
Hojo Munenobu

- **Birth:** 1259
- **Shikken:** 1311-1312
- **Death:** 1312 (aged 52 or 53)

Also known as Osaragi Munenobu.

From 1297-1302 he was the Minami-kata Rokuhara tandai "southern governor of Kyoto," and from 1305-1311 was rensho "assistant to the Regent," prior to becoming Shikken.

12th Kamakura Shikken
Puppet Regent of Takatoki
Hojo Hirotoki

- **Birth:** 1279
- **Shikken:** 1312-1315
- **Death:** 1315 (aged 35 or 36)

From 1311-1312 was rensho "assistant to the Regent," prior to becoming Shikken.

13th Kamakura Shikken
Puppet Regent of Takatoki
Hojo Mototoki

- **Birth:** 1286
- **Shikken:** 1315-1316
- **Death:** 1333 (aged 46 or 47)

From 1301-1303 was Kita-kata Rokuhara tandai "northern governor of Kyoto," prior to becoming Shikken.

14th Kamakura Shikken
Hojo Takatoki

- **Birth:** 1303
- **Shikken:** 1316-1326 (abdicated)
- **Death:** 1333 (aged 29 or 30) @ Tosho-ji (Kamakura) by seppuku

Son of Sadatoki. He was the last ruling Kamakura Shikken, the latter ones being his puppets.

After Sadatoki had his head shaved, his son-in-law Morotoki became Regent. At the latter's death in 1311 Takatoki, then only 8 years old, received the title of Shikken, and was assisted by his kinsmen Terutoki and Mototoki. In 1316 he officially took the power, but being of weak intelligence and dissolute morals, he spent his time in assisting at dances and dogfights, leaving the government in the hands of his maternal grandfather Adachi Tokiaki (-1333) and his minister Nagasaki Takasuké (-1333). The latter, by his bad administration, excited general discontent, and in 1322 troubles arose in different provinces. The Emperor Go-Daigo (1288-1339) thought the time favorable for the overthrow of the powerful Shikken; emissaries sent by him found adherents even in Kamakura. But in 1325 Takatoki, having heard of it, obliged the Emperor, under pain of deposition, to disown his emissaries, and profess his good dispositions towards the Hojo.

Hojo Hirotoki

Hojo Takatoki

In 1326 Takatoki fell ill, retired, and became a Buddhist monk, though he still held some influence at the Shogunal court.

That same year Kuninaga-shinno, heir to the throne, having died, the Emperor Go-Daigo wished to have his own son Moriyoshi-shinno (1308-1335) nominated, but Takatoki opposed his nomination, and chose instead Kazuhito-shinno (1313-1364), 3rd son of Go-Fushimi (1288-1336). The Emperor, wishing to get support of the powerful Tendai sect, nominated Moriyoshi-shinno chief of the Hiei-zan temples (northeast of Kyoto), and a conspiracy was prepared in secret. In 1331 Takatoki sent Nikaido Sadafuji with a large number of men to arrest Go-Daigo, who fled to Mount Kasagi (south of Kyoto). Takatoki then pronounced his deposition, raised Kazuhito to the Chrysanthemum Throne as the Emperor Kogon, and sending troops to surround Kasagi-yama, he made Go-Daigo prisoner, confined him for some time in the Rokuhara (Kyoto), and at the beginning of the following year, exiled him to Chiburi (Oki). Defenders of the deposed Emperor now arose everywhere: the Kusunoki in Kawachi, the Nitta in Kozuké, the Akamatsu in Harima, etc. After one year's exile, Go-Daigo escaped from Chiburi island, landed in Hoki and asked Nawa Nagatoshi for protection. Takatoki sent an army to Kyoto under the command of Ashikaga Takauji (1305-1358). But when the latter had no sooner arrived at the capital, he declared himself in favor of Go-Daigo and besieged the Rokuhara, where Hojo Nakatoki and Hojo Tokimasu lost their lives.

Meanwhile, in 1333 Nitta Yoshisada (1301-1338), having brought an army from Kozuké, besieged and burned Kamakura, and Takatoki, after an attempt at resistance, committed suicide by seppuku with all his kinsmen and servants. Thus ended the power of the Hojo who, for over a century, had been the real rulers of Japan.

15th Kamakura Shikken
Puppet Regent of Takatoki
Hojo Sada'aki

- **Birth:** 1278
- **Shikken:** 1326 (abdicated)
- **Death:** 1333 (aged 54 or 55)

From 1302-1308 was Minami-kata

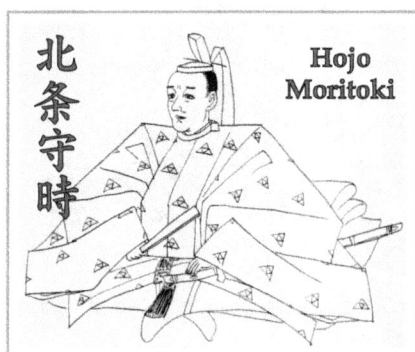

Rokuhara tandai "southern governor of Kyoto," from 1311-1314 was Kitakata Rokuhara tandai "northern governor of Kyoto," and from 1315-1326 was rensho "assistant to the Regent" to Mototoki and Takatoki, prior to becoming Shikken.

16th Kamakura Shikken
Puppet Regent of Takatoki
Hojo Moritoki

- **Birth:** 1295
- **Shikken:** 1327-1333
- **Death:** 1333 (aged 37 or 38)

Son of Hisatoki, and grandson of the 6th Hojo Shikken Nagatoki. He committed seppuku along with all his clansmen during the Siege of Kamakura by Nitta Yoshisada (1301-1338).

Muromachi Shogun

1st Muromachi Shogun
Ashikaga Takauji

- **Birth:** 1305
- **Shogun:** 1338-1358
- **Death:** June 7, 1358 (aged 52 or 53)

Son of Sadauji. His mother was of the Uesugi.

Ashikaga Takauji

At the beginning of the Genko War (1331-1333), Takauji was ordered by the 9th Hojo Regent Takatoki (1303-1333) to besiege Mount Kasagi (Yamashiro and Yamato), where the Emperor Go-Daigo (1288-1339) had taken refuge, and Akasaka (Kawachi), a castle of Kusunoki Masashigé (1294-1336). But in 1333, after becoming increasingly disillusioned with the Kamakura Shogunate, he declared for the Emperor and, aided by Akamatsu Norimura (1277-1350), conquered the Rokuhara (Kyoto), where Hojo Nakatoki and Hojo Tokimasu were killed. At the same time Nitta Yoshisada (1301-1338) of Kozuké completed the ruin of the Hojo by the taking of Kamakura, where Takatoki committed suicide, destroying the Shogunate. Go-Daigo thus became the *de facto* ruler of Japan.

After Go-Daigo's return to Kyoto to start the so-called Kenmu Restoration (1333-1336), the Emperor distributed rewards to those who had helped him to recover his throne, and Takauji received in fief Musashi, Shimosa, and Hitachi. He was not satisfied and wanted more: as a descendant of the Minamoto, he aspired to the dignity of Shogun, but the title was conferred on Morinaga-shinno (1308-1335), and later to Narinaga-shinno (1326-1338): Takauji was very much vexed. Sensing discontent among the samurai, he pleaded with the Emperor to do something before rebellion broke out, however his warnings were ignored.

In 1335 Hojo Tokiyuki (1322-1353), son of Takatoki, having levied troops in Shinano, attacked and conquered Kamakura, starting the Nakasendai Rebellion. Takauji, having been sent against him, drove him back, then, disclosing his ambitious designs, he took Kamakura for himself, distributed domains to his officers without permission from the Court, and claimed the title of Sei-i-tai-shogun "Commander-in-Chief."

Takauji announced his allegiance to the Imperial Court, but Go-Daigo declared him a rebel and sent Nitta Yoshisada to reclaim Kamakura. With the signature of retired Emperor Kogon (1313-1364), he prepared to resist the Imperial troops. Defeated by Nitta Yoshisada in Mikawa and in Suruga, he intrenched himself in the Hakoné mountains (Sagami), where he inflicted a bloody defeat on his adversary, who wanted to dislodge him. A great number of daimyo then took his side, and in 1336, with their assistance, Takauji marched against Kyoto, defeated the Imperial army, and entered the capital, while Go-Daigo took up with the warrior monks of the Enryaku-ji in Hieizan (northeast of Kyoto). Within days Kitabataké Akiié (1318-1338) arrived from Mutsu with fresh troops, united with Nitta Yoshisada, Kusunoki Masashigé, etc., and expelled Takauji from Kyoto. The latter, defeated again near Hyogo, went for help to Kyushu. There he defeated Kikuchi Taketoshi (-1341) at the Battle of Tatara-no-hama (Chikuzen), then hastened towards the capital with the support of the Kyushu warrior families: the Shimazu, the Matsuura, the Otomo, and the Shoni, along with those already in the Ashikaga camp: the Hosokawa, the Akamatsu, the Imagawa, the Isshiki, the Nikki, the Uesugi, the Ko, and the Ouchi. Yoshisada and Masashigé tried to check his advance at the decisive Battle of Minatogawa (Harima), but they were defeated; Masashigé committed suicide and Yoshisada retreated. A month or so later, Takauji entered Kyoto as conqueror, declared that Go-Daigo had forfeited his throne, and installed Yutahito, the 2nd son of the Emperor Go-Fushimi (1288-1336), as the new Emperor Komyo (1322-1380). From that day dates the schism in the Imperial descendance.

Takauji pursued Nitta Yoshisada to his stronghold at Kanagasaki (Echizen), and in 1337 it was brought down. Yoshisada escaped, but his son and Takanaga-shinno (1310-1337) were forced to commit seppuku. In 1338, at the Battle of Ishizu (Izumi), Kitabataké Akiié was killed. Two months later the Ashikaga forces engaged Nitta in the Battle of Fujishima (Echizen), and in the course of the fighting Yoshisada was killed.

For nearly sixty years, there were two Emperors at the same time: one, the legitimate Emperor, belong to the so-called Nan-cho "Southern Court," because Go-Daigo had retired to the south of Kyoto; the other belonging to the Hoku-cho "Northern Court," supported by the Takauji and his successors, who finally obtained the abdication of his competitor.

For twenty years, Takauji, aided by Ko Moronao (-1351), Shiba Takatsuné (1305-1367), etc., continued the war, with alternate successes and reverses, it is true. But he saw the supporters of the Southern Court fall one after another, the Nitta, the Kusunoki, the Kitabataké, etc. Then trouble came to his own family: his brother Tadayoshi (1306-1352) and his son Tadafuyu took side with the adverse party, and in 1350 he was obliged to wage war against them. This cast a deep gloom over his last years. In 1352 Tadayoshi was captured by Takauji's men in Izu and poisoned, presumably on Takauji's orders. While fighting Tadafuyu's army, Takauji learned that the new Emperor of the Southern Court, Go-Murakami (1328-1368), had recaptured Kyoto. Heavy fighting continued in the Kinai for the next three years with Tadafuyu on the side of the Southern Court. In 1355 Takauji rallied his forces in Omi and launched a counterattack that produced a string of fiercely contested

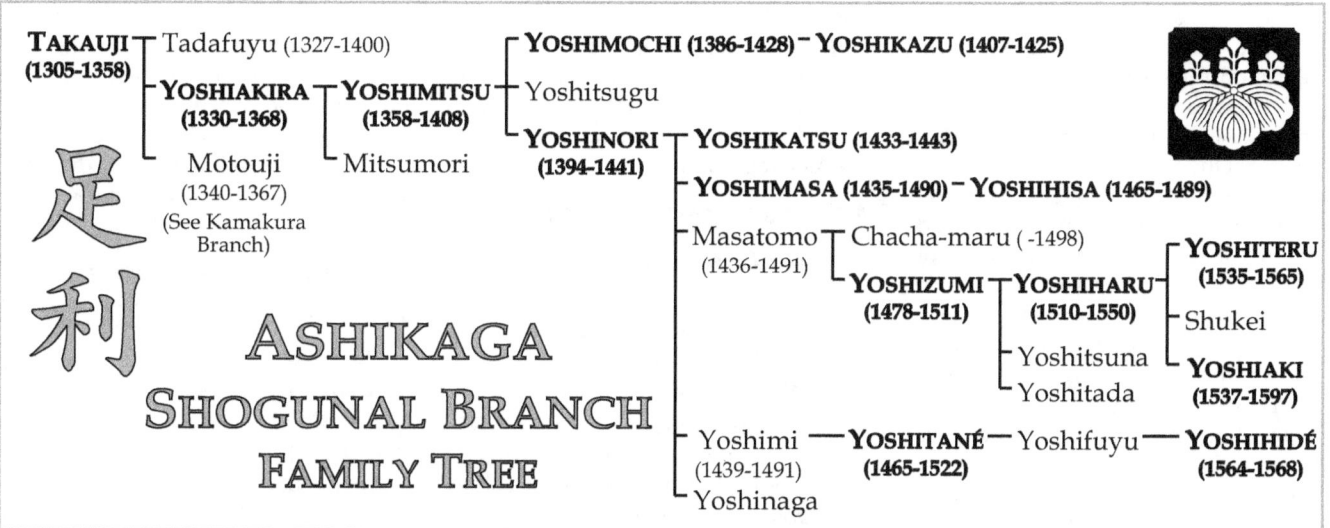

Ashikaga Shogunal Branch Family Tree

struggles that finally drove Tadafuyu and the Southern Court out of the capital.

Takauji spent the next three years reorganizing his administration, and in 1358 was considering the idea of personally leading a campaign to Kyoto against the Shibuya when he fell ill and died of a cancer, leaving his power to his son Yoshiakira (1330-1368).

According to famous Zen master and intellectual Muso Soseki (1275-1351), who enjoyed his favor and collaborated with him, Takauji had three qualities: he kept his cool in battle and was not afraid of death; he was merciful and tolerant; and he was very generous to those below him. Takauji was a devout Buddhist, an excellent poet of waka "Japanese poetry," a good painter, and a well-known musician of sho " "Japanese reed instrument."

2nd Muromachi Shogun
Ashikaga Yoshiakira

- **Birth:** 1330
- **Shogun:** 1358-1367 (abdicated)
- **Death:** 1367 (aged 37) of illness

Son of Takauji. He was brought up at Kamakura as a hostage of the Hojo, and then installed at Muromachi (Kyoto). He was dispatched back to Kamakura to maintain peace in the eastern provinces, but in 1349 an internal disturbance of the government caused him to be called back to Kyoto, where he found himself named as Takauji's heir.

In 1351, when the Southern army retook Kyoto, Yoshiakira went to Kyushu for reinforcements, returned, re-

entered the capital, deposed the Northern Emperor and replaced him by the Emperor Go-Kogon (1338-1374), although the three Imperial emblems were in possession of the Southern Emperor Go-Murakami (1328-1368).

In 1358, having become Shogun at the death of his father, Yoshiakira continued the war against the Southern Court, and by and by, obtained the submission of all the great daimyo, such as the Ouchi, the Yamana, the Nikki, etc. In 1362 Hosokawa Kiyo'uji and Kusunoki Masanori (-1390) attacked Kyoto.

Yoshiakira fled, but regained the capital 20 days later.

In 1367, overcome by illness, he abdicated in favor of his son Yoshimitsu then only 10 years old, and died some months afterwards. His tomb is in the Toji-in (Kyoto), where his father is also buried.

3rd Muromachi Shogun
Ashikaga Yoshimitsu

- **Birth:** 1358
- **Shogun:** 1368-1394 (abdicated)
- **Death:** 1408 (aged 49)
  @ Kyoto of illness

Son of Yoshiakira. Being only 10 years old when succeeding his father, he had as shitsuji "deputy Shogun" the celebrated Hosokawa Yoriyuki (1329-1392), to whom he greatly owed the success in his enterprises. Although the supporters of the Southern Court had been defeated nearly everywhere, Kyushu remained faithful to them owing to the son of the ex-Emperor Go-Daigo (1288-1339), Yasunaga-shinno, who being supported by the Kikuchi, the Ito, the Shimazu, etc., kept up the war in that part of the country. In 1374 Yoshimitsu, after having sent there Imagawa Sadayo (1326-1420) with the title of Tsukushi tandai, himself conducted an expedition. Resistance was short: Kyushu submitted, and Yasunaga was obliged to flee and hide himself.

Having returned to Kyoto, Yoshimitsu installed himself in the Muromachi Palace and soon raised the prestige of the Shogunal power to its zenith. By frequent embassies he kept up his relations with the Ming Dynasty, recently established in China, cultivated letters, and favored artists. Being a fervent adept of Zen Buddhism, he was liberal to the bonzes, and in 1382 built the Shokoku-ji (Kyoto), the most beautiful temple of the epoch.

Meanwhile the Yamana, availing themselves of the intestine wars, had become by and by the masters of 11 provinces. Yoshimitsu was uneasy at their increasing power, but in 1391, when Yamana Ujikiyo attacked Kyoto to open the Meitoku War, Yoshimitsu routed his army and distributed the immense domain of that family among his generals. This triumph definitively secured the power of the Ashikaga. In 1392 the Southern Emperor Go-Kameyama (1347-1424), himself submitted, and abdicated in favor of the Northern Emperor Go-Komatsu (1377-1433), to whom he transmitted the Imperial insignia under the condition that henceforth the Emperors should be chosen from the two Imperial branches alternately. It was the end of the Nanboku-cho "Northern and Southern Courts" Period, which for 56 years had divided the country into hostile camps.

In 1394 the Emperor Go-Komatsu gave Yoshimitsu the title of Daijo-daijin "Chancellor of the Realm."

In 1395 Yoshimitsu abdicated in favor of his son Yoshimochi, then 9 years old. He had his head shaved and became a bonze under the name Tenzan Dogi.

In 1397, on Kitayama (north of Kyoto), Yoshimitsu built a splendid palace, which the people called Kinkaku-ji "Temple of the Golden Pavilion" on account of the great richness in its ornamentation. From that place the powerful bonze continued to govern the land as adviser to his son.

In 1404 Yoshimitsu sent an embassy to China with rich presents. In return the Ming Dynasty Emperor sent him a message in which he recognized him as Nippon Koku-O "King of Japan" and authorized him to send a tribute only every 10th year. However strange this letter of the Chinese Emperor may seem, there is no doubt that he considered the presents sent to him from Japan as a tribute, and the embassies as a homage of vassalage.

Having become dangerously ill, Yoshimitsu was visited by the Emperor himself in the Kinkaku-ji. He soon afterwards died, requesting his son to stop the relations with China.

Yoshimitsu, who carried the glory of his family to such a high degree, was, after Takauji, the most remarkable of the Ashikaga Shogun.

4TH MUROMACHI SHOGUN
ASHIKAGA YOSHIMOCHI

- **Birth:** 1386
- **Shogun:** 1395-1423 (abdicated), 1425-1428 (2nd tenure)
- **Death:** 1428 (aged 41)

3rd son of Yoshimitsu. Having in 1395 named Shogun when only 9 years old by the abdication of his father, he let the latter govern until his death in 1408.

In 1398 King Taejong (1367-1422) of Joseon (Korea) sent a diplomatic mission to Japan, led by Pak Tong-chi. When it arrived in Kyoto, Shogun Yoshimochi presented the envoy with a formal diplomatic letter, and presents were given for the envoy to convey to the Joseon Court.

In 1412, when the Emperor Go-Komatsu (1377-1433) abdicated, Yoshimochi nominated Shoko (1401-1428), who also belonged to the Northern Court, contrary to the agreement made in 1392; hence several revolts of the supporters of the Southern Court in Yamato, Kii, and Mutsu. In 1418 he killed in the Shokoku-ji (Kyoto) his brother Yoshitsugu (1394-1418), accused of aspiring to the Shogunate.

In 1423 Yoshimochi abdicated in favor of his son Yoshikazu, and became a bonze in the Toji-in (northwest of Kyoto), but Yoshikazu having died two years later, he resumed the power and kept it until his death in 1428.

5TH MUROMACHI SHOGUN
ASHIKAGA YOSHIKAZU

- **Birth:** 1407
- **Shogun:** 1423-1425
- **Death:** 1425 (aged 17)

Son of Yoshimochi. In 1423 he became Shogun when 15 years old by the abdication of his father, but died two years afterwards. It is said his death was hastened by a life of drunken dissipation. Yoshimochi resumed the responsibilities of Shogunhood until his death in 1428.

6TH MUROMACHI SHOGUN
ASHIKAGA YOSHINORI

- **Birth:** 1394
- **Shogun:** 1429-1441
- **Death:** 1441 (aged 47) assassinated

3rd son of Yoshimitsu.

Yoshinori was a bonze at the Shoren-in (Kyoto) under the name Gi'en, when on the day of the death of his elder brother Yoshimochi, he was chosen as his successor. From amongst the handful of possible Ashikaga candidates, his name was selected by the kanrei "deputy Shogun" Hatakeyama Mitsuié (1372-1433), who drew lots in the sanctuary of Iwashimizu Hachiman Shrine (Kyoto), and it was believed that Hachiman's influence had affected this auspicious choice.

Ashikaga Yoshimochi

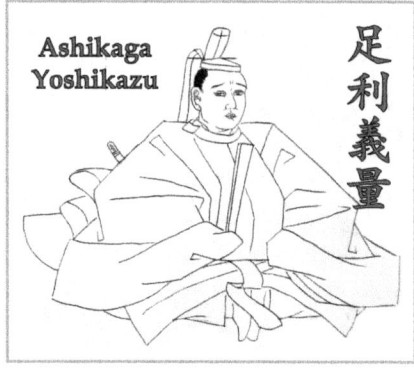

Ashikaga Yoshikazu

Ashikaga Yoshinori

The first act of Yoshinori's authority was to designate, as successor of Shoko-tenno (1401-1428), Go-Hanazono (1419-1471), a great grandson of Suko-tenno (1334-1398) of the Northern Court, whose choice caused a revolt in Isé.

Yoshinori had been elected Shogun contrary to the advice of the Kamakura-kanrei "deputy Shogun" Ashikaga Mochiuji (1398-1439), who himself aspired to the Shogunal dignity. On that account their relations were so strained that Yoshinori ordered Uesugi Norizané (1410-1466) to march with an army against Mochiuji. In 1438 the latter was defeated at Hakoné (Sagami) and invited to commit seppuku, ending what is known as the Eikyo Rebellion.

In 1440 Yoshinori reconstructed the Yasaka Pagoda at the Hokan-ji (Kyoto), which had been destroyed by fire in 1436.

Yoshinori was notorious for his oppressive measures and unpredictable dictatorial whims. When he wanted to take a part of the domain of Akamatsu Mitsusuké (1381-1441) in order to give them to Akamatsu Sadamura, Noriyasu, the son of Mitsusuké, having heard of that design, informed his father of it. In 1441 Mitsusuké, concealing his irritation, invited Yoshinori to a feast, and had him assassinated in the middle of the entertainment, in what is known as the Kakitsu Incident.

7TH MUROMACHI SHOGUN
ASHIKAGA YOSHIKATSU

- **Birth:** 1434
- **Shogun:** 1442-1443
- **Death:** 1443 (aged 9)

Son of Yoshinori. Succeeded his father when 8 years old. His advisor was the Kyoto-kanrei "deputy Shogun" Hatakeyama Mochikuni (1398-1455). Yoshi-

kazu died two years later after falling from a horse.

8TH MUROMACHI SHOGUN
ASHIKAGA YOSHIMASA

- **Birth:** 1435
- **Shogun:** 1449-1473 (abdicated)
- **Death:** 1490 (aged 55) @ Higashi-yama (Kyoto)

Son of 6th Ashikaga Shogun Yoshinori. Became Shogun when 8 years old at the death of his older brother Yoshikatsu. Originally named Yoshinari, several years after becoming Shogun, he changed his name to Yoshimasa, by which name he is better known.

In 1454 Yamana Mochitoyo/Sozen (1404-1473), who had stirred up troubles in Kyoto, was banished to Tajima, where he raised an army. Akamatsu Norinao was sent against him, but was defeated, and Mochitoyo marched against Kyoto, which he entered as conqueror, Yoshimasa being unable to check him. At the same time disturbances arose in the Kanto, and the Shogun sent his brother Masatomo to restore order in those provinces. Meanwhile the rivalries among the great families, the Hosokawa, the Hatakeyama, the Yamana, the Shiba, etc., caused continual wars, and the misery of the people was aggravated day after day. Instead of trying to remedy this sad state of affairs, the Shogun was thinking of nothing but pleasure in his palace of Muromachi (Kyoto).

It was in 1464 that Yoshimasa, having no children, adopted his brother, the bonze Gijin, who re-entered the world and took the name of Yoshimi. But the following year Yoshimasa's wife Hino Tomiko bore him a son, Yoshihisa. Yoshimasa immediately wanted to annul the promise made to his brother. The latter, to maintain his right, applied for help to Hosokawa Katsumoto (1430-1473), while the Shogun addressed himself to Yamana Sozen for the support of his son. All the great daimyo took one or other side: Hatakeyama Masanaga (1442-1493), Shiba Yoshitoshi (1430-1490), Akamatsu Masanori, Takeda Kuninobu, etc., sided with Katsumoto; while Hatakeyama Yoshinari (1437-1491), Isshiki Yoshinao, Ouchi Masahiro (1446-1495), Shiba Yoshikado (-1480), Toki Noriyori, etc., were seen on the side of Sozen; and in 1467 the Onin War commenced and lasted for ten long years, marking the beginning of Japan's Sengoku "Warring States" Period (1467-1573). Kyoto and the neighboring villages were reduced to ashes, and the artistic objects and documents which were then destroyed cannot be sufficiently regretted. In 1473 both Sozen and Katsumoto died: they had been fighting for seven years without any decided success.

Later that year, in the midst of ongoing hostilities, Yoshimasa abdicated in favor of his son Yoshihisa, then 9 years old, but continued to hold on to the reins of power.

In 1477 the hostile armies, tired of the war and unable to get provisions in the devastated districts, dispersed, each daimyo returning to his own province, ending the Onin War.

In 1482 Yoshimasa commenced building on Higashi-yama (east of Kyoto), a palace, which in opposition to the Kinkaku-ji "Temple of the Golden Pavilion" of his grandfather Yoshimitsu, was called Ginkaku-ji "Temple of the Silver Pavilion." He lived there for ten years, surrounded by bonzes, poets, actors, etc., continuing to exhaust the treasury by his prodigality.

His son Yoshihisa having died prematurely in 1489, Yoshimasa reconciled with his brother Yoshimi, adopted the latter's son Yoshitané, whom he nominated as Shogun. He died the following year, leaving the work built up by his predecessors in a very precarious state. On account of his palace at Higashi-yama, Yoshimasa is often named Higashi-yama-dono or Higashi-yama Shogun.

Muromachi Shogun

9th Muromachi Shogun
Ashikaga Yoshihisa

- **Birth:** 1465
- **Shogun:** 1473-1489
- **Death:** 1489 (aged 23) of illness

Son of Yoshimasa.

In 1473, in the middle of the Onin War (1467-1477), Yoshimasa retired. Yoshihisa's mother Hino Tomiko, with the support of the powerful daimyo Yamana Mochitoyo/Sozen (1404-1473), fought Ashikaga Yoshimi to ascend her son to the Shogunate. She prevailed, and Yoshihisa became Shogun at the age of 8 years, but his father continued to govern.

When the Onin War ended, Yoshimi retired to Mino, and Kyoto was left in peace, but the authority of the Shogun was shaken, and Yoshihisa applied himself to strengthen it.

Sasaki/Rokkaku Takayori (-1520), daimyo of southern Omi, began seizing land and manors owned by nobles of the Imperial Court, temples, and shrines. In 1487 Yoshihisa himself led an expedition against him, besieging Takayori in Magari-no-sato (Omi), but died of illness during the campaign.

Although Yoshihisa had given some hopes to the Shogunate by his energy, his untimely death did not permit him to realize them. He left no heir. Yoshimasa resumed administration, but died the following year, and Yoshitané became Shogun.

10th Muromachi Shogun
Ashikaga Yoshitané

- **Birth:** 1465
- **Shogun:** 1490-1493 (deposed), 1508-1521 (2nd tenure, deposed)
- **Death:** 1522 @ Awa (aged 56)

Son of Yoshimi. In his early life he was named Yoshiki (sometimes read as Yoshimura), and then Yoshitada. At the the death of Yoshihisa, he was adopted by his uncle Yoshimasa, and in 1490 became Shogun.

The following year, in 1491, Yoshitada marched against Sasaki Takayori (-1520), whom he put to flight. Then, supported by Hatakeyama Masanaga (1442-1493), he turned his arms against Hatakeyama Yoshitoyo, who hastened to ask Hosokawa Masamoto (1466-1507) for help. The battle was fought at Shogaku-ji (Kawachi): the army of the Shogun was completely defeated, Masanaga was killed, and Yoshitada had to flee into Etchu. In 1493 Masamoto then recalled from Izu, Yoshizumi, a son of Ashikaga Masamoto, and raised him to the Shogunate.

In 1498 Yoshitada left Etchu in order to seek an asylum with Ouchi Yoshioki (1477-1528) in Suo. He exiled there for ten years, preparing his revenge. In 1501 he changed his name to Yoshitané.

In 1508, Ouchi Yoshioki having furnished him with an army, Yoshitané marched against Kyoto, expelled Yoshizumi, whose supporter Hosokawa Masamoto had been assassinated, and resumed the title of Shogun. This unexpected success was afterwards crowned by a brilliant victory gained by Yoshioki over the Hosokawa, the Sasaki, and the Miyoshi, who had leagued against him.

In 1511, Yoshizumi having died, Hosokawa Sumimoto (1489-1520) wished to raise Yoshizumi's son Yoshiharu to the Shogunate, and started with an army to install him in Kyoto. Ouchi Yoshioki immediately went to Tanba to recruit an army. Having succeeded, he returned in great haste and completely defeated Sumimoto.

In 1520, after Sumimoto's death, Hosokawa Takakuni (1484-1531) replaced him as kanrei "deputy Shogun," but Yoshitané tried to thrust him aside. He did not succeed, and was obliged to take refuge in Awaji. Then Takakuni nominated Yoshiharu in his place. From Awaji, Yoshitané went to Awa (Shikoku), where he died. As he died in exile on an island, he is often called Shima-kubo.

11th Muromachi Shogun
Ashikaga Yoshizumi

- **Birth:** 1478
- **Shogun:** 1493-1508 (deposed)
- **Death:** 1510 (aged 32) @ Omi

Son of Masamoto, and grandson of the 6th Ashikaga Shogun Yoshinori, adopted by the 8th Ashikaga Shogun Yoshimasa. Yoshizumi was first called Yoshito (sometimes read as Yoshimichi), then Yoshitaka.

When his father died in 1491, Yoshizumi found an asylum in Suruga with Imagawa Ujichika (1473-1526), who took him to Kyoto and confided him to the kanryo "deputy Shogun" Hosokawa Masamoto (1466-1507). In 1493, when the 10th Ashikaga Shogun Yoshitané, defeated in Kawachi, left Kyoto and fled to Etchu, Masamoto replaced him by Yoshizumi, then 15 years old, as puppet Shogun.

Hosokawa Masamoto having been assassinated in 1507, and his successor Sumimoto (1489-1520) being only 17 years old, in 1508 Yoshitané raised an army in Suo, led by Ouchi Yoshioki (1477-1528), re-entered Kyoto, and reinstalled himself as Shogun. Yoshizumi fled to Omi, and died three years later.

Muromachi Shogun

12th Muromachi Shogun
Ashikaga Yoshiharu

- **Birth:** 1510
- **Shogun:** 1521-1546 (abdicated)
- **Death:** 1550 (aged 40) @ Sakamoto (Omi)

Son of Yoshizumi. In 1521 he was nominated Shogun, and entered Kyoto when 11 years old, after Hosokawa Takakuni (1484-1531) had expelled Yoshitané from the capital.

In 1526 Yoshiharu invited archers from neighboring provinces to come to the capital for an archery contest.

In 1528 Miyoshi Nagamoto having entered Kyoto with an army, Yoshiharu fled into Omi, to the residence of Kuchiki Tanetsuna. In 1531 Hosokawa Takakuni committed suicide, and his place was taken by Hosokawa Harumoto (1519-1563), who in the following year brought Yoshiharu back to Kyoto. At that time the power of the Shogun was at the mercy of the great daimyo, who, throughout the country, were at war with one another. It was the epoch of Sengoku "Warring States," which were brought to an end only when Oda Nobunaga (1534-1582) came into power.

In 1539 Yoshiharu, in order to escape from the Miyoshi, was again obliged to leave Kyoto, and retired to Hatsusé (Yamato), where he spent three years, and a second time, re-entered the capital.

At the end, in 1546, Yoshiharu abdicated the Shogunate over a political struggle between Miyoshi Nagayoshi (122-1564) and Hosokawa Harumoto, and appointed his son Yoshiteru as the 13th Ashikaga Shogun in exile. But in the following year Harumoto obliged him again to flee to Sakamoto (Omi), where he died after a few years.

13th Muromachi Shogun
Ashikaga Yoshiteru

- **Birth:** 1536
- **Shogun:** 1546-1565
- **Death:** 1565 (aged 29) by seppuku

Eldest son of the 12th Ashikaga Shogun Yoshiharu. His mother was a daughter of Konoé Taneié (1503-1566). In 1546 he became Shogun when only 11 years old, with his investiture ceremony being held at Sakamoto (Omi). At the time his name was still Yoshifushi, and did not change it to Yoshiteru until much later in 1554.

Scarcely had he been confirmed as Shogun when his father made a truce with Hosokawa Harumoto (1519-1563) in order to return to Kyoto. However, Harumoto's retainer Miyoshi Nagayoshi/Chokei (1522-1564) sided with Hosokawa Ujitsuna (1514-1564) and the two Hosokawa started a war that drove out Yoshiteru, his father, and Harumoto from Kyoto.

Afterwards in 1553, having reconciled with Miyoshi Nagayoshi, Yoshiteru was readmitted to Kyoto. But although invested with the title of Shogun, he had no authority: Nagayoshi and his vassal Matsunaga Hisahidé (1510-1577) were the real masters. To be rid of their domination, Yoshiteru recalled Harumoto, but Nagayoshi opposed his return, and the Shogun was obliged to banish Harumoto to Akutagawa (Settsu).

After that, Yoshiteru invited Uesugi Terutora/Kenshin (1530-1578) to pacify the Kanto, and Mori Motonari (1497-1571) the Kansai, but they refused to undertake such a difficult task.

Finally, in 1565, as Yoshiteru prepared to oppose the evil designs of Matsunaga Hisahidé, the latter in haste repaired to Kyoto with Miyoshi Yoshitsugu (1549-1573) and invested Nijo Palace. Yoshiteru, perceiving that any serious resistance was out of the question, killed himself by seppuku.

Yoshiteru was well respected for his actions and diplomatic skills, and many researchers credit him as being the last effective Ashikaga Shogun. Oda Nobunaga (1534-1582) and Uesugi Kenshin were among the many daimyo and samurai who traveled to Kyoto to pay their respects to the Shogun. Yoshiteru practiced kenjutsu "art of the sword" and had Kamiizumi Nobu-

tsuna (1508-) and Tsukahara Bokuden (1489-1571) teach him the art of using the katana, and became a master of it. He used over a dozen priceless katana "samurai swords" given to him by various daimyo to kill a large number of enemy troops before his death. He was closer to being a samurai and a warlord than any Shogun since Ashikaga Takauji.

14th Muromachi Shogun
Ashikaga Yoshihidé

- **Birth:** 1564
- **Shogun:** 1568
- **Death:** 1568 (aged 3 or 4)

Son of Yoshifuyu, and a grandson of Yoshitané. Three years after the death of the 13th Ashikaga Shogun, Miyoshi Yoshitsugu (1549-1573) and Matsunaga Hisahidé (1510-1577) chose him to succeed Yoshiteru, when Yoshihidé was only 3 years old. The Imperial investiture was however refused.

Soon Oda Nobunaga (1534-1582), who patronized Yoshiaki, a younger brother of Yoshiteru, marched against Kyoto. Unable to resist, Miyoshi Yoshi-

tsugu and Matsunaga Hisahidé retired to Awa (Shikoku), taking along with them Yoshihidé, who died soon afterwards, some say of illness, others that he was assassinated by Hisahidé.

15TH MUROMACHI SHOGUN
ASHIKAGA YOSHIAKI

- **Birth:** 1537
- **Shogun:** 1568-1573 (deposed)
- **Death:** 1597 (aged 59) @ Kyoto

15th and last Ashikaga Shogun. 3rd son of the 12th Ashikaga Shogun Yoshiharu, and brother to the 13th Ashikaga Shogun Yoshiteru. Was a bonze at the Ichijo-in in Nara (Yamato) under the name Gakkei.

After the death of Yoshiteru, his other brother Shuko, then a bonze at the Kokuon-ji (Kyoto) was killed by the order of Matsunaga Hisahidé (1510-1577). Yoshiaki likewise was going to be put to death, when, aided by Hosokawa Fujitaka (1534-1610), he managed to flee to Omi where he found asylum at the residence of Sasaki/Rokkaku Yoshikata (1521-1598). There in 1565 he took the name of Yoshiaki. Two years later he took refuge at the residence of Asakura Yoshikagé (1533-1573) in Echizen.

In 1568, as Asakura Yoshikagé found it too difficult to lead him victoriously to Kyoto, Yoshiaki sent Hosokawa Fujitaka as emissary to Oda Nobunaga (1534-1582), who enthusiastically accepted the mission. After accepting Matsunaga Hisahidé's surrender, Nobunaga entered the capital with his protégé. Yoshiaki received formal acknowledgement as the new Shogun from the Emperor Ogimachi (1517-1593). Nobunaga then rebuilt the Nijo Palace for him, and intrusted the guard of Kyoto to Kinoshita (later Hashiba, then Toyotomi) Hideyoshi (1536-1598). Then in concert with Tokugawa Ieyasu (1543-1616), Shibata Katsuié (1522-1583), etc., he attacked the Sasaki, the Asakura, and all the other adversaries of Yoshiaki, and defeated them one after another.

But soon the relations between the Shogun and his protector began to strain. Nobunaga dared to make representations to the Shogun, and presented a list of 17 articles containing the points in which the Shogunal administration ought to be reformed. His dignity wounded, Yoshiaki asked Takeda

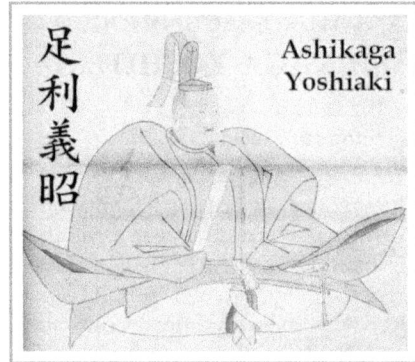

Shingen (1521-1573) to rid him of the one to whom he owed his fortune. Initially Shingen did not disappoint. He defeated allied Oda and Tokugawa troops at Mikata-ga-hara (Totomi), and in the spring of 1573 entered Mikawa. Perhaps emboldened by Shingen's success, Yoshiaki openly broke from Nobunaga, fortified Nijo Palace, and urged the Asai and the Asakura to renew their efforts. Unfortunately for Yoshiaki, the 'Tiger of Kai' was not destined to challenge Nobunaga directly.

Shingen died, and while the Takeda endeavored to keep his death a secret, Nobunaga moved quickly to surround Kyoto, and forced Yoshiaki to negotiate. The Emperor interceded, but a few months later Yoshiaki again defied Nobunaga: he left Nijo Palace in the hands of Mizubuchi Fujihidé, and set up camp near the Uji River, in the Maki-no-shima Stronghold, a formidable defensive location, but spirited attacks by Nobunaga forced Yoshiaki into submission. Yoshiaki pleaded for his life, which Nobunaga granted, but was never again to play a role in Kyoto politics. Nobunaga exiled the Shogun as a prisoner to Wakaé Castle (Kawachi). This ended the Shogunate of the Ashikaga, who had governed Japan from 1336.

In 1575 Yoshiaki became a bonze under the name Shozan, and applied to Mori Terumoto (1553-1625) for an asylum. He later returned to Kyoto, where he lived almost ignored, and died there.

Edo Shogun

1st Edo Shogun
Tokugawa Ieyasu

- **Birth:** 1543 @ Okazaki Castle (Mikawa)
- **Shogun:** 1603-1605
- **Death:** 1616 (age 73) @ Sunpu (Suruga)

Upon the hour of the tiger, in the year of the tiger, 1543, a child was born that would set the course of Japanese history for the next three hundred years. The future Shogun, who would establish a dynasty that would rule the Empire of the Rising Sun until the end of the samurai era, was born at Okazaki Castle (Mikawa) and received the name Takechiyo at birth. He was the son of Matsudaira Hirotada (1526-1549), the daimyo of Mikawa, and Odai-no-kata (1528-1602), the daughter of neighboring daimyo Mizuno Tadamasa (1493-1543). His mother and father were step-siblings, and they were just 17 and 15 years old, respectively, when Takechiyo was born. Two years later his mother was sent back to her family, and the couple never lived together again. As both husband and wife remarried, and both went on to have further children, Takechiyo (the future Ieyasu) in the end had 11 half-brothers and sisters.

In 1548 Oda Nobuhidé (1510-1551) attacked Mikawa, and Hirotada sought help from his more powerful neighbor Imagawa Yoshimoto (1519-1560), who was willing to do so, but on the condition, as was customary, that Takechiyo be sent to Sunpu Castle (Suruga) as a hostage. Hirotada reluctantly agreed, and sadly sent off his 6-year-old son on the road east with a staff of servants, a group of 27 other youngsters of his own age to serve as companions, and an escort of some fifty samurai bodyguards. During the journey, a certain Norimitsu, Hirotada's vassal, stopped the train and kidnapped Takechiyo into the hands of Nobuhidé, who confined him at Kowatari Castle, in custody of the Kato of Atsuta (Owari). Nobuhidé then offered peace to Hirotada but on such hard conditions that the latter preferred to continue the war, and Takechiyo was confined in the small temple

Tokugawa Ieyasu

Tenno-bo, where he had to undergo many hardships, notwithstanding the devotedness of O Cha no Tsuboné.

In 1549 both Hirotada and Nobuhidé died, leaving the Matsudaira leaderless, and the already splintered Oda weakened. Imagawa Yoshimoto wasted no time in capitalizing on this turn of events, and dispatched an army under the command of his uncle Imagawa Sessai (-1557) to attack the Oda's border castles. Sessai laid siege to Anjo, a former Matsudaira fort, which housed Oda Nobuhiro (-1574), Nobuhide's eldest son and the new head of the Oda. With the castle about to fall, Sessai offered a deal to Oda Nobunaga (1534-1582), Nobuhide's 2nd son: the siege would be lifted if Takechiyo was handed over to the Imagawa. Nobunaga had little choice but to agree, and so Sessai took Takechiyo, now 9 years old, to Sunpu (Suruga). Here he lived a fairly good life as hostage, and potentially useful future ally of the Imagawa. Sessai himself tutored the boy in military tactics and strategy.

In 1554, at the age of 12, Takechiyo for the first time put on a coat of arms. Two years later, at his genbuku "coming-of-age ceremony," he received the name of Matsudaira Jisaburo Motonobu, with the "moto" coming from Yoshimoto himself. In 1558 he married the daughter of Sekiguchi Chikanaga, a vassal of the Imagawa, and soon after received permission to return to his own province, where he again changed his name to that of Matsudaira Kurando-no-suké Motoyasu.

Motoyasu had scarcely returned to Okazaki, when he began to make preparations for war against Nobunaga, who was threatening to attack Mikawa. Having regained possession of his two castles of Terabé and Hirosé, as well as the western portion of Mikawa, he entered Suruga. At that very time in 1560, Imagawa Yoshimoto was attacking Nobunaga, but was defeated and killed at the Battle of Oké-ha-zama (Owari).

With Yoshimoto dead, Motoyasu decided to free himself of Imagawa influence. As a number of his close relatives, including his wife and infant son Nobuyasu (1559-1579), were held as hostages in Sunpu by Yoshimoto's successor Imagawa Ujizané (1538-1615), in secret he allied with Nobunaga. But in 1562, Motoyasu openly broke with the Imagawa, and laid the Siege of Kamino-jo, which he captured along with two sons of the slain castle commander Udono Nagamochi. As the Udono were an important Imagawa retainer clan, Ujizané unwisely agreed to release Motoyasu's family members in return for the children.

Later in 1561 Motoyasu, having forced his uncle Mizuno Nobumoto (-1576) to submit after defeating him at Ishigasé and at Kariya (Mikawa), returned to Okazaki to settle the terms of peace with Nobunaga.

In 1563 Motoyasu's eldest son Nobuyasu, at the age 5, was married to Nobunaga's daughter Toku-himé (1559-1636), also 5-years-old, to seal an alliance between the two clans.

In 1564 Motoyasu defeated the militant Mikawa Monto Buddhist sect in a sharp encounter that saw him actually struck by a bullet that had failed to penetrate his armor.

In the next few years Motoyasu applied himself to rebuilding a Matsudaira clan badly fragmented by years of strife, and a province weakened by war. To this end he carefully nurtured

Edo Shogun

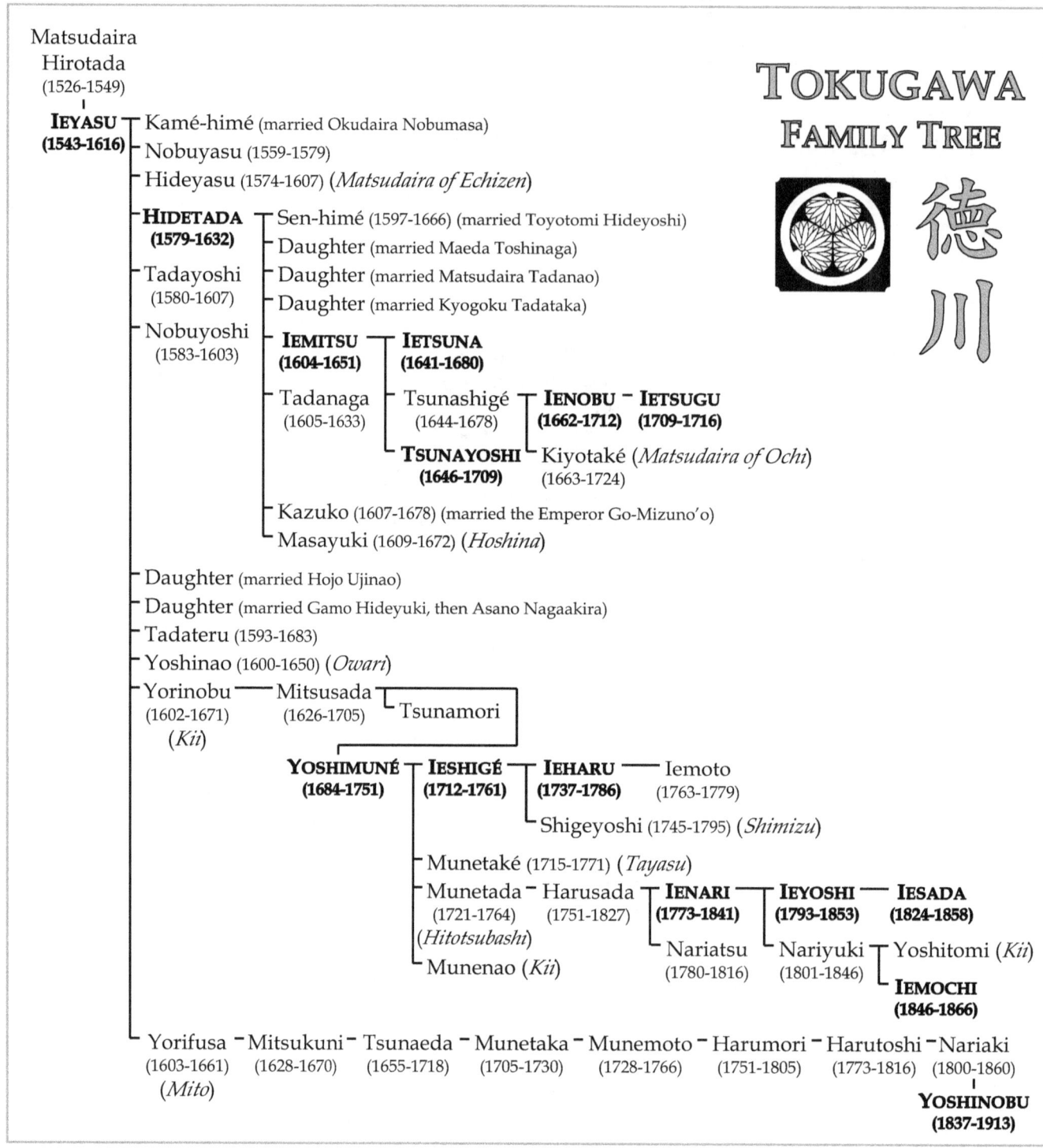

Tokugawa Family Tree

- Matsudaira Hirotada (1526-1549)
  - **Ieyasu** (1543-1616)
    - Kamé-himé (married Okudaira Nobumasa)
    - Nobuyasu (1559-1579)
    - Hideyasu (1574-1607) (*Matsudaira of Echizen*)
    - **Hidetada** (1579-1632)
      - Sen-himé (1597-1666) (married Toyotomi Hideyoshi)
      - Daughter (married Maeda Toshinaga)
      - Daughter (married Matsudaira Tadanao)
      - Daughter (married Kyogoku Tadataka)
      - **Iemitsu** (1604-1651)
        - **Ietsuna** (1641-1680)
        - Tsunashigé (1644-1678)
          - **Ienobu** (1662-1712) — **Ietsugu** (1709-1716)
        - **Tsunayoshi** (1646-1709)
        - Kiyotaké (*Matsudaira of Ochi*) (1663-1724)
      - Tadanaga (1605-1633)
      - Kazuko (1607-1678) (married the Emperor Go-Mizuno'o)
      - Masayuki (1609-1672) (*Hoshina*)
    - Tadayoshi (1580-1607)
    - Nobuyoshi (1583-1603)
    - Daughter (married Hojo Ujinao)
    - Daughter (married Gamo Hideyuki, then Asano Nagaakira)
    - Tadateru (1593-1683)
    - Yoshinao (1600-1650) (*Owari*)
    - Yorinobu (1602-1671) (*Kii*)
      - Mitsusada (1626-1705)
        - Tsunamori
        - **Yoshimuné** (1684-1751)
          - **Ieshigé** (1712-1761)
            - **Ieharu** (1737-1786)
              - Iemoto (1763-1779)
              - Shigeyoshi (1745-1795) (*Shimizu*)
          - Munetaké (1715-1771) (*Tayasu*)
          - Munetada (1721-1764) (*Hitotsubashi*)
            - Harusada (1751-1827)
              - **Ienari** (1773-1841)
                - **Ieyoshi** (1793-1853)
                  - **Iesada** (1824-1858)
                  - Nariyuki (1801-1846)
                    - Yoshitomi (*Kii*)
                    - **Iemochi** (1846-1866)
                - Nariatsu (1780-1816)
          - Munenao (*Kii*)
    - Yorifusa (1603-1661) (*Mito*)
      - Mitsukuni (1628-1670)
        - Tsunaeda (1655-1718)
          - Munetaka (1705-1730)
            - Munemoto (1728-1766)
              - Harumori (1751-1805)
                - Harutoshi (1773-1816)
                  - Nariaki (1800-1860)
                    - **Yoshinobu** (1837-1913)

---

and strengthened his retainer band by giving them lands and positions within his administration of Mikawa. Chief among his followers at this time were Ishikawa Kazumasa (1534-1609), Sakai Tadatsugu (1527-1596), Sakikabara Yasumasa (1548-1606), Koriki Kiyonaga (1530-1608), Honda Tadakatsu (1548-1610), and Hattori Hanzo (1542-1596).

In 1565, in order to free himself from all Imagawa influence, and to assert his independence, he put aside the name Motoyasu and took that of Ieyasu, by which he was to be henceforth known, and under which he has become so renowned.

In 1567 Ieyasu received the title of Mikawa no kami, then obtained permission from the Emperor to keep the name of Tokugawa for his own family, leaving that of Matsudaira to the lateral branch of the Nitta and the Serata families. In so doing, he claimed descent from the Minamoto, but, as little is known of the Matsudaira prior to the 15th century, no proof has actually been found.

Ieyasu remained an ally of the Oda. In 1568 his Mikawa soldiers were part of Nobunaga's army which captured Kyoto. At that time, he became acquainted with the famous Takeda Shingen (1521-1573) of Kai and made an alliance with him against Imagawa Ujizané. In 1570 the latter, attacked by his two foes, was routed and dispossessed of his domain, Shingen taking Suruga, Ieyasu receiving Totomi.

In 1570, leaving his son Nobuyasu at Okazaki, Ieyasu went to Hikuma, which name he changed to Hamamatsu (Totomi), and built a castle there. His fame spread by degrees and all the former vassals of the Imagawa offered him their services. At this time, he with 10,000 men aided Nobunaga to triumph over the Ashikaga and the Asai at the Battle of Anegawa (Omi), a victory owed largely to the efforts of the Tokugawa men.

Meanwhile, Takeda Shingen was fighting the Hojo of Odawara, who were trying to take the province of Suruga from him. He asked Ieyasu for help but was refused, and war between the former allies soon began. In 1571 Shingen entered Totomi and besieged the castles of Takatenjin, Yoshida, Niré, etc. Ieyasu, however, allied with Uesugi Kenshin (1530-1578), who attacked Shinano from the north, and Shingen had to turn his attention to this new enemy.

In the following year, however, war recommenced between the two rivals. Shingen's son and heir Takeda Katsuyori (1546-1582) took Futamata Castle (Totomi), and Ieyasu found himself besieged in Hamamatsu. He sent to Nobunaga for help, and the latter sent him a great body of men under the command of Sakuma Morinobu. In the beginning of 1572, Shingen with a large army camped at Mikata-ga-hara, north of Hamamatsu, and burned all the surroundings of the castle, but Ieyasu held his position. To induce him to accept battle, Shingen retired to Iidani, and Ieyasu left his castle and camped at Mikata-ga-hara. He was at once attacked and defeated. Morinobu fled, and Ieyasu was preparing for death, when one of his vassals, Natsumé Masayoshi, whom he had left at Hamamatsu, arrived in haste, and obliged his lord to return to the castle. With a small body of faithful samurai, Masayoshi boldly met death, a sacrifice to his master's welfare. Having returned to Hamamatsu Castle, Ieyasu, on the following night, made a sortie with his men, and attacked the enemy at daybreak. The vanquished of the preceding day came to his rescue, and defeat was soon changed into a decided victory.

In 1573 war with the Takeda resumed, but was interrupted for some time by Shingen's death. Katsuyori renewed the struggle, and in 1574 invaded Totomi and captured the important Tokugawa fort at Takatenjin. In 1575 Ieyasu, again with Nobunaga's help, defeated his enemy at the Battle of Nagashino (Mikawa). Katsuyori survived the battle and retreated back to Kai. A truce followed which lasted for several years, during which time both parties prepared for a final effort. In 1579 Ieyasu's wife and his eldest son Nobuyasu were accused of conspiring with Takeda Katsuyori to assassinate Nobunaga, whereupon Ieyasu summoned them to Hamamatsu. After an investigation, with pressure from Nobunaga, Ieyasu's wife was executed and Nobuyasu was ordered by his father to commit seppuku. It is said that Ieyasu deeply regretted the part he played in his son's death.

In 1581 war recommenced against the Takeda, and Ieyasu took the castle of Takatenjin from Katsuyori. The following year, an expedition conducted by Nobunaga and Ieyasu was directed against Katsuyori. It ended with the ruin of the Takeda at the Battle of Tenmoku-zan (Kai), and Ieyasu received Suruga, which bordered the Hojo of Odawara.

Ieyasu then paid a visit to Nobunaga in his castle of Azuchi (Omi), and Akechi Mitsuhidé (1528-1582) was chosen to receive so high a dignitary. From here, he went to Kyoto and thence to Osaka, where in 1582 he heard of the murder of Nobunaga by Mitsuhidé's treachery in the Incident at Honno-ji (Kyoto). Not having enough troops with him to oppose the traitor's forces, he narrowly escaped back to Mikawa, gathered a small army, and marched towards Kyoto, but at Atsuta (Owari), he heard of the defeat and death of Mitsuhidé by Hashiba (later Toyotomi) Hideyoshi (1536-1598).

Ieyasu then turned his attention to taking the Oda province of Kai, a move that prompted Hojo Ujimasa (1538-1590) to send his much larger army into Shinano, and then into Kai. No battles were fought between the two forces, and, after some negotiation, Ieyasu and the Hojo agreed to a settlement which left Ieyasu in control of both Kai and Shinano, while the Hojo took control of Kazusa (along with some parts of both Kai and Shinano).

Ieyasu returned to Okazaki, recruited surviving Takeda men into his army, and did not take part in the campaign of Shizu-ga-také (1583), where Hideyoshi defeated Shibata Katsuié (1522-1583) to become the single most powerful daimyo in the Empire.

The following year, Ieyasu accepted the advances made by Nobunaga's heir Oda Nobukatsu (1558-1630), and joined him to fight Hideyoshi in what is known as Komaki Campaign, in which Ieyasu won the only notable battle at Nagakuté (Owari). After months of fruitless marches and feints, Hideyoshi settled the war by making peace with Nobukatsu and offering a truce to Ieyasu, who confirmed it by his marriage with Hideyoshi's daughter Asahi-no-kata, and Ieyasu's 2nd son Hideyasu (1574-1607) becoming an adopted son of Hideyoshi.

In the following years Ieyasu busied himself with the administration of his domain, and as Hideyoshi was wary of him, he was left out of his invasions of Shikoku and Kyushu.

In 1590 Ieyasu resumed his military life in Hideyoshi's campaign against the last independent daimyo in Japan, Hojo Ujimasa of Odawara, who ruled the eight provinces of the Kanto region. After three months of the Siege of Odawara, bowing to the overwhelming power of the Toyotomi army, and an impending shortage of food supplies, the Hojo accepted defeat, and the top Hojo leaders killed themselves, ending the clan's reign of over 100 years. Ieyasu accepted Hideyoshi's offer of the eight Kanto provinces of the Hojo in return for the five provinces that he currently controlled: Mikawa, Totomi, Suruga, Shinano, and Kai. His revenues were now 2.5 million koku.

Ieyasu now moved all his soldiers and vassals to the eastern provinces. He set up his headquarters in the small port of Edo in Musashi, and from there began reforming the Kanto provinces: distributing domains among those who for 30 years had been fighting in his interest, controlling and pacifying the Hojo samurai, building an immense castle on the ruins of a fortress built there in the 15th century by Ota Dokan (1432-1486), and improving the underlying economic infrastructure of the lands. As the Kanto region was somewhat isolated from the rest of Japan, Ieyasu was able to maintain a unique level of autonomy from Hideyoshi's rule. Within a few years he had become the 2nd most powerful daimyo in Japan.

Although Ieyasu was not required to provide troops for the Korean Expeditions (1592-1593, 1597-1598), he was obliged to serve in Hideyoshi's headquarters in Kyushu as a military advisor, where he stayed off and on for the next five years. Despite his frequent absences, Ieyasu's sons, loyal retainers, and vassals were able to control and improve Edo and the new Tokugawa domain.

In 1598, Hideyoshi, with his health clearly failing, chose Ieyasu as one of the Go-Tairo "Five Regents" who be responsible for ruling on behalf of his young son, Hideyori, after his death. The others were Maeda Toshiié (1539-1599), Mori Terumoto (1553-1625), Ukita Hideié (1573-1655), and Uesugi Kagekatsu (1556-1623). When the Taiko died later that year, Ieyasu installed himself at Fushimi Castle (south of Kyoto) and began to rule as sole master. Troubles soon rose between him and the great daimyo who accused Ieyasu of usurping the power of his ward. The leaders of this faction were Maeda Toshiié and Ishida Mitsunari (1560-1600). Ieyasu however, through much cunning, was able to bring Toshiié to his side. But in 1599 Toshiié died, and many daimyo returned to their domain, plainly showing their dissatisfaction with Ieyasu's ambitious designs. Among them were the other three Go-Tairo, and Kagekatsu, in particular, so openly refused to recognize the authority of Ieyasu, who soon opened a campaign against him. Ieyasu had scarcely left Fushimi, going north, when his enemies issued a proclamation accusing him of 13 serious charges, and called to arms all the vassals that remained faithful to the Taiko. Ieyasu's adherents, however, were not idle, and prepared for battle. Thus, at very short notice, Japan was divided into two camps.

The war began in August 1600. Ieyasu's vassal Hosokawa Fujitaka (1534-1610) was attached in the castle of Tanabé (Tango), and resisted heroically. Torii Mototada (1539-1600) defended Fushimi well, but the assailants took the castle and Mototada died in battle. Meanwhile Tokugawa allies Fukushima Masanori (1561-1624) and Ikeda Terumasa (1565-1613) marched eastward and occupied the castles of Kiyosu (Owari) and Gifu (Mino). There, Nobunaga's grandson Oda Hidenobu (1580-1605) whom Ishida Mitsunari had won to his party, was taken prisoner and confined to Koyasan (Kii). Ieyasu however had come to Oyama (Shimotsuké), where he learned what had happened since his departure. He hastened to retrace his steps and gathering a large army of men, encountered Mitsunari's larger army in Mino. On October 21, 1600, at the Battle of Seki-ga-hara, Ieyasu gained a complete victory over his foes, and a huge number heads of the enemy were the trophy of the day.

This success gave Ieyasu undisputed authority, which he used most arbitrarily. Of his former adversaries, the principals, Ishida Mitsunari, Konishi Yukinaga (1555-1600), Ankokuji Ekei (1539-1600), etc., were beheaded at Kyoto; Ukita Hideié, Oda Hidenobu, Chosokabé Morichika (1575-1615), Maeda Toshimasa, Masuda Nagamori, Tachibana Muneshigé (1567-1643), Niwa Nagashigé (1571-1637), and others were deprived of their domains; others again, such as Mori Terumoto, Uesugi Kagekatsu, Satake Yoshinobu (1570-1633), Akita Sanesué (1576-1660), etc., who submitted to the victor, found their revenues considerably reduced. His adherents, the Kobayakawa, the Daté, the Kato, the Mogami, the Asano, the Fukushima, the Gamo, the Ikeda, the Kuroda, the Hosokawa, the Todo, the Tanaka, the Yamanouchi, the Okudaira, the Ii, etc., received very large domains, and the distribution of fiefs was made in such a manner that the last to submit to the new power (tozama daimyo) always found themselves near one or several of the ancient vassals (fudai daimyo), who watched them so as to prevent even the possibility of a rebellion.

Ieyasu, now securely established in power, showered greater honors on the person of the Emperor than had thus far been accorded to him, but reserved the executive power to himself. Installed in Fushimi, he summoned the learned Fujiwara Seika (1561-1619) and Hayashi Razan (1583-1657) to help him with their sagacity in the administration of affairs. He ordered the maps of the provinces and districts to be revised: brought the ancient books of the Ashikaga-gakko and Kanazawa-bunko to Fushimi or to Edo, and had the most important and rarest rewritten. It was he too who revived the edicts against Christianity and increased their severity. It was only in 1603 that he received from the Emperor Go-Yozei (1572-1617), the title of Sei-i-tai Shogun and those connected with it, such as the titles of Genji-no-choja, Jun'a-in, and Shogaku-in-no-betto.

Two years later, in 1605, Ieyasu abdicated in favor of his son Hidetada, then 26 years old, his principle motive being to secure the succession of his high dignity to his family. He took the title of Ogosho "Retired Shogun" at the age of 62, and relocated to Sunpu. Whilst taking an active part in the government, he devoted his leisure to hawking, swimming, literature, and poetry.

In 1611 Ieyasu went to Kyoto, and had an interview with Toyotomi Hideyori, to whom he betrothed his granddaughter, Sen-himé (1597-1666), daughter of the Shogun Hidetada. Notwithstanding all the precautions taken by Ieyasu and the surveillance exercised over him, Hideyori, having come of age, was taught by his surroundings, and in particular by his mother Yodogimi (1569-1615), to look upon Ieyasu as the usurper of his power. Thus the relations between him and the Tokugawa became steadily more strained, and the latter only waited for an opportune moment to get rid of him.

Ieyasu induced Hideyori to rebuild the Hoko-ji (Kyoto) at great expense. It had been previously built by Hideyoshi but was destroyed by an earthquake in 1596. Ieyasu well knew that the money used in this pious work would not be employed in recruiting soldiers. In 1614, when the temple was finished, Hideyori ordered a large bell to be cast, and invited Ieyasu to the opening ceremony. Now, it happened that in the inscription placed on the bell, the two characters of the name of

Ieyasu were employed, separated one from the other. The ex-Shogun affected to be insulted at this imprecation against him, bringing down the curse of heaven. He stopped the proceedings of the feast, asked an explanation and even wanted to force the Emperor to suppress the ill-omened inscription. Hideyori refused to submit to such unreasonableness.

Later that year Ieyasu and Oda Hidetaka (-1555) camped their formidable army under the walls of Osaka. The castle was well-fortified, and Hideyori's generals Ono Harunaga (-1615), Sanada Yukimura (1567-1615), Goto Mototsugu (1565-1615), etc., had assembled a large number of samurai, mostly ronin of ancient daimyo dispossessed by Ieyasu. Every man was determined to sell his life dearly. After some doubtful encounters, Ieyasu sent O Cha no Tsuboné to Yodo-gimi, and through her intermediary, peace was restored, Hideyori agreeing to dismiss his troops and to fill the moats of the castle of Osaka. Thus ended what is known in history as the Winter Campaign of Osaka, as it took place in the last months of the year 1614.

Ieyasu had scarcely returned to Sunpu when new difficulties arose. Hideyori consented to the demolition of the exterior defenses and to the filling up of the moats, which was supervised by Honda Masazumi (1566-1637), but he asked that his soldiers should be recognized as regular troops, which request met with a flat refusal. He then proposed to exchange his provinces of Settsu, Kawachi, and Izumi for those of Awa, Sanuki, and Iyo in Shikoku. Ieyasu offered him those of Shimosa, Kazusa, and Awa (Tokaido), but to accept this proposition would have been putting himself completely into the power of the former. Hideyori refused and the two parties again prepared for war. In May 1615 Ieyasu brought his army, and one month after, despite the bravery shown by the besieged garrison, Osaka fell. Hideyori and Yodo-gimi perished in the conflagration of the castle, and his infant son was executed, but his wife Sen-himé was sent back to the Tokugawa alive. This 2nd siege is called the Summer Campaign of Osaka. The power of the Tokugawa was now supreme and secure for a long period.

Before returning to Suruga, Ieyasu promulgated the Buké-hatto "Regulations for the samurai" in 13 chapters, taken from the Joei-shikimoku and the Kenbu-shikimoku Codes. He likewise established the Kugé-hatto "Kugé Code" in 17 chapters after having consulted the Kanpaku "Regent to the Emperor" Nijo Akizané (1556-1619) on the matter.

In the beginning of 1616, soon after his return to Sunpu, Ieyasu fell ill. He received the title of Daijo-daijin "Chancellor of the Realm" from the Emperor, but in the month of May, departed this life. Buried temporarily at Kuno-san, (Totomi), in the following year his body was carried with great solemnity to Nikko (Shimotsuké), where a magnificent temple of Tosho-gi was erected in his honor. He received the posthumous name of Tosho Daigongen.

Ieyasu had 19 wives and concubines, by whom he had 11 sons and five daughters, establishing three of them as the daimyo of Kii, Owari, and Mito, which were maintained for the sole purpose of providing an heir should the main branch fail to produce one.

Ieyasu was certainly a genius. He was a skillful warrior and a shrewd politician. Ieyasu claimed to have fought in 90 battles, either as a warrior or a general. He did not win all of his battles, but he won those that counted. Ieyasu finished the work of pacifying the country, a work begun by Oda Nobunaga and Toyotomi Hideyoshi, and endowed it with a powerful organization, securing the power to his own family for the next two-and-a-half centuries, until the end of the samurai era.

2ND EDO SHOGUN
TOKUGAWA HIDETADA

- **Birth:** 1579
  @ Hamamatsu Castle (Totomi)
- **Shogun:** 1605-1623 (abdicated)
- **Death:** 1632 (aged 53)

3rd son of Ieyasu and one of his many consorts. He was born Nagamaru at the castle of Hamamatsu (Totomi).

At the age of 10, Nagamaru was sent to Kyoto to stay with Hashiba (later Toyotomi) Hideyoshi (1536-1598) as hostage during the 1590 Odawara Campaign. In 1592 Hideyoshi presided over Nagamaru's coming-of-age ceremony, where he dropped his childhood name

and assumed the name Hidetada, the first kanji of his new name provided by Hideyoshi himself. He was named the heir of the Tokugawa, being the eldest surviving son of Ieyasu, and his favorite since Ieyasu's eldest son Hideyasu had been previously ordered killed, and his 2nd son was adopted by Hideyoshi while still an infant. In 1593 Hidetada returned to his father's side.

In 1600 Hidetada, with a large force of men, accompanied his father in the projected campaign against Uesugi Kagekatsu (1556-1623), and went as far as Utsu-no-miya (Shimotsuké), but hearing that Ishida Mitsunari (1560-1600) had risen in arms, he marched south through the Tosando (central mountains of northern Honshu), but allowed himself to be delayed by the Sanada at the Siege of Ueda (Shinano) for 15 days, and arrived in Mino after the Battle of Seki-ga-hara. Ieyasu, in his anger, refused to receive him, but at the intervention of Honda Masazumi (1566-1637) consented to give him audience.

In 1605 Ieyasu abdicated, and Hidetada was named Shogun, and married Oeyo (1573-1626), daughter of Asai Nagamasa (1545-1573) and Oichi (1547-1583), the sister to Oda Nobunaga (1534-1582). He aimed at maintaining and developing his father's policy, continuing to persecute the Christians, and under the most severe penalty forbade any Japanese to go out of the country. It is he who stopped commercial relations with all foreigners except the Dutch, the Chinese, and the Koreans.

In 1612 the Shogun Hidetada arranged a marriage between his daughter Sen-himé (1597-1666), Ieyasu's favorite granddaughter, and Toyotomi Hideyori (1593-1615), who was living as common citizen in Osaka Castle with his mother Yodo-gimi (1569-1615). This did not quell troubles between the two families, and Hidetada took part with his father in the two Sieges of Osaka (1614-1615), although the two argued more then once on the course the campaign should take.

In 1620 Hidetada married his daughter Kazuko-himé (1607-1678) to the Emperor Go-Mizuno'o (1596-1680). The product of that marriage, a girl, eventually succeeded to the throne of Japan to become the Empress Meisho (1624-1696).

In 1622 Hidetada abdicated the Shogunate in favor of his son Iemitsu, taking the title of Ogosho "Retired Shogun," but retained effective power.

Hidetada died ten years later, was buried in Zojo-ji at Shiba (Edo), and received the posthumous name Taitoku-in.

3RD EDO SHOGUN
TOKUGAWA IEMITSU

- **Birth:** 1604
- **Shogun:** 1622-1651
- **Death:** 1651 (aged 46)

Eldest son of Hidetada. Born Takechiyo. He was educated by Naito Tadashigé.

In 1617 he came of age, and dropped his childhood name in favor of Iemitsu, and was installed officially as the heir to the Tokugawa Shogunate. From an early age Iemitsu practiced the shudo "pederasty" tradition. In 1620, however, he had a falling out with his lover Sakabé Gozaémon, a childhood friend and retainer, aged 21, and murdered him as they shared a bathtub.

In 1623 Iemitsu became Shogun at the age 19, when his father abdicated, and devoted all his time to the study and perfecting of the government methods introduced by Ieyasu. He closed the country entirely to all foreign commercial transactions; in 1636 forbade the building of ships which would permit long voyages; in 1638, by a cruel massacre, suppressed the Shimabara Insurrection (Hizen); in 1640 put to death the Macao ambassadors who had come to ask for liberty of commerce; confined the Dutch, who were allowed to pursue commerce with the Japanese, to Deshima (Nagasaki); bore a blind and ferocious hatred to Christianity and destroyed it by a fierce persecution; made the law sankin-kotai "alternate attendance" which obliged the daimyo to reside alternately in Edo and in their domain, and leave their wives and children as hostages at Edo.

Iemitsu was a protector of Buddhism and Confucianism. For the former in 1626 he built the Kan-ei-ji (Edo), and in 1634 the Eisho-ji (Kamakura). He erected a temple in honor of Confucius, and protected the learned Hayashi Doshun (1583-1657), Nakaé Toju (1608-1648), etc.

Iemitsu's sister Kazuko-himé (1607-1678) had been married in 1620 to the Emperor Go-Mizuno'o (1596-1680), and from this union was born a daughter, Meisho-tenno (1624-1696), who was raised to the Chrysanthemum Throne at the age of 7. Thus Iemitsu's influence was great both at Kyoto and at Edo.

To prevent any attempt of insubordination on the part of the Imperial Court, Iemitsu required that a Prince of royal blood should be always at the head of the Ueno (Edo) and Nikko (Shimotsuké) temples, whom he was ready to oppose to the legitimate sovereign should he prove troublesome. By all these maneuvers Iemitsu brought the government of the Shogun to the highest degree of power.

When Iemitsu died, he was buried at Nikko where a magnificent temple was erected to his memory. His posthumous name is Taiyu-in. At his death, ten of his most faithful subjects killed themselves in junshi "suicide"; among these were: Hotta Masamori (1606-1651), daimyo of Sakura (Shimosa); Abé Shigetsugu, daimyo of Iwatsuki (Musashi); Uchida Masanobu; Saegusa Moriyoshi; Okuyama Yasushigé; etc. At the same time more than 3,700 maids of honor were dismissed from the Palace and, of this number, over 100 shaved their heads and embraced religious life as ama "Buddhist nuns."

4TH EDO SHOGUN
TOKUGAWA IETSUNA

- **Birth:** 1641
- **Shogun:** 1651-1680
- **Death:** 1680 (aged 38) of illness

Eldest son of Iemitsu and a concubine.

In 1651, although he was a frail child, Ietsuna succeeded his father as Shogun at the age of 10. His regents were Sakai Tadakatsu (1587-1662), Sakai Tadakiyo (1624-1681), Inaba Masanori (1623-1696), Matsudaira Nobutsuna (1596-1662), and Ii Naozumi. In addition, he handpicked his half-brother Hoshina Masayuki (1611-1673) as one of his advisors.

In the year of his accession to the Shogunate, Ietsuna repressed the rebellion of Yui Shosetsu (1605-1651) and Marubashi Chuya, who had planned an uprising, in which Edo would be burned to the ground, Edo Castle raided, and the Shogun executed, in what has come to be known as the Keian Uprising or the Tosa Conspiracy. The plan was discovered and Chuya was executed along with his family and Shosetsu's family. Shosetsu chose to commit seppuku rather than being captured.

In 1652 about 800 ronin led a small disturbance on Sado, which was similarly suppressed.

In 1657, when Ietsuna was almost 20 years old, a great fire erupted in Edo and burned the city to the ground. It took two years to rebuild the city.

In 1663, the regency of the Shogun ended, and Ietsuna's chief advisors were now Hoshina Masayuki, his uncle Itakura Shigenori (1617-1673), Tsuchiya Kazunao, Kuzé Hiroyuki, and Inaba Masanori.

During his reign, Ietsuna forbade junshi "suicide" at the death of a master, prohibited any translation of European works, and any writing concern-

ing the government, Edo morals, etc. We need not wonder therefore at the great number of authors who were imprisoned or banished during his reign.

In 1680 Ietsuna fell ill and died prematurely. As he had no children, his brother Tsunayoshi succeeded him. He was buried in the Kan'ei-ji (Ueno) and received the posthumous name Gen'-yu-in.

5TH EDO SHOGUN
TOKUGAWA TSUNAYOSHI

- **Birth:** 1646 @ Edo
- **Shogun:** 1680-1709
- **Death:** 1709 (aged 62) assassinated

4th son of Iemitsu by one of his concubines, Keisho-in (1627-1705), who was an adopted daughter of Honjo Munemasa. Born in Edo, he relied on his mother for advice until her death.

In 1661 Tsunayoshi received the fief of Tatebayashi (Kozuké -- 350,000 koku).

In 1680 Tsunayoshi was called to succeed his brother Ietsuna, who died without progeny. He was at that time 34 years old. Immediately after becoming Shogun, he gave Hotta Masatoshi (1634-1684), one of the most brilliant advisors of the Shogun's rule, the title of tairo "great elder" for his part in ensuring his succession. He then ordered a vassal of the Takata to commit suicide because of misgovernment, confiscating his fief of 250,000 koku. Showing his strict approach to the samurai code, during his reign he would confiscate a total of 1,400,000 koku. In 1684 Tsunayoshi decreased the power of the tairo after the assassination of Masatoshi by his cousin Inaba Masayasu (1640-1684).

Tsunayoshi was a patron of letters and sciences, encouraged military studies, worked at the reform of the calendar, founded schools, protected artists, etc. The finances being in a bad condition, he sought to improve affairs by altering the value of money and by awarding land to the hatamoto instead of giving them a pension in rice. These measures wrought a notable increase in the prices of all necessaries of life and occasioned general dissatisfaction. Tsunayoshi had acted on the advice of Yanagisawa Yoshiyasu (1658-1714), and on representations made by the kanjo-bugyo "finance minister" Ogi-

wara Shigehidé (1658-1713). At that time, 30 million koku composed the revenues of the whole Empire; of which 23 million belonged to the daimyo, 3 million to the temples and hatamoto, and the remaining 4 million to the Shogunate. This last sum, from which 150,000 koku were deducted, being the allowance made to the Court of Kyoto, could certainly not suffice because of the prodigality of Tsunayoshi, who had to find diverse expedients to increase his finances.

Owing to the influence of the bonzes, Tsunayoshi promulgated the Shorui Awaremi no Rei "Edicts of Compassion for Living Beings," which under the strictest penalty, forbade the killing of any living being, and had places of refuge erected for disabled or infirm horses and dogs. Owing to this, and the fact that he was born in the year of the dog, he earned the pejorative nickname of "Dog Shogun." Examples of the inhuman execution of this law are not wanting; thus, in 1686 a vassal of the daimyo Akita (Dewa), having killed a swallow was put to death and his children sent into exile.

Tsunayoshi presided during the Genroku Period (1688-1704), considered the golden age of the Edo Period (1603-1868). Major events during his reign include the 1701-1702 affair of the 47 ronin of Ako, the 1703 Genroku

earthquake, the 1706 typhoon that hit Edo, and the 1707 eruption of Mount Fuji.

In 1704 Tsunayoshi, having no children, adopted his nephew Tsunatoyo, son of Tsunashigé, who took the name of Ienobu.

Like most men of his position, he practiced shudo "pederasty," and was the nenja "older lover" of wakashu "young lover" Yanagisawa Yoshiyasu (1658-1714), who served the Shogun, and was 12 years Tsunayoshi's junior. The fief of Fuchu (Kai), which Tsunayoshi possessed up to that time, passed to Yoshiyasu, who then was continually rising in favor. In 1709, abusing the influence he had acquired over the mind of the weak and aged Shogun, Yoshiyasu asked that Suruga be added to the fief, which his son Yoshisato was to inherit. Tsunayoshi consented, but before placing his seal on the official document confirming the donation, his wife Mi-dai-dokoro, daughter of the ex-Kanpaku "Regent to the Emperor" Takatsukasa Fusasuké (1637-1700), exasperated that such an abnormal favor should be granted, stabbed the Shogun and killed herself. He was buried at the Kan'ei-ji (Ueno) and received the posthumous name Joken-in.

6TH EDO SHOGUN
TOKUGAWA IENOBU

- **Birth:** 1662
- **Shogun:** 1709-1712
- **Death:** 1712 (aged 50)

Eldest son of Tokugawa Tsunashigé and a concubine. Born Tsunatoyo.

In 1678, when his father died, Tsunatoyo succeeded as daimyo of Kofu (Kai).

In 1694 a ronin, Arai Hakuseki (1657-1725), was appointed as personal tutor and advisor to Tsunatoyo. Hakuseki used to be a teacher in Edo, but was recommended by the philosopher Kinoshita Junan (1621-1698) to become personal tutor to Tsunatoyo, and was summoned to his Edo residence. It is thought that Hakuseki gave him 2,000 lectures on the Chinese classics and Confucianism. Hakuseki became a great advisor to Ienobu until the end of his life.

In 1704 the Shogun Tsunayoshi chose as heir his nephew Tsunatoyo, who then changed his name to Ienobu.

In 1709 Ienobu received the title of Shogun at the age of 47. The first act of his reign was to abrogate the severe laws enacted by his predecessor against those who killed animals or caused them to suffer. Censorship was eventually discontinued; Ienobu told his subordinates that the thoughts and feelings of the populace should reach the high levels of the Bakufu. Cruel punishments and persecutions were discontinued, and the judicial system was also reformed. He recoined the altered pieces of money that Tsunayoshi had introduced, and gave them their former value, leading to economic reform and stabilization.

In 1711, on the petition of Arai Hakuseki, he suppressed the custom, which obliged the greater number of the Princes of the Imperial family to become bonzes, and the Princesses to become ama "Buddhist nuns," and he allowed them to marry. In fact, one of the younger daughters of the Emperor Naka-mikado (1702-1737) married one of Shogun Ienobu's younger sons.

When Ienobu died, he was buried in the Zojo-ji (Shiba), and received the posthumous name Bunsho-in.

7TH EDO SHOGUN
TOKUGAWA IETSUGU

- **Birth:** 1709 @ Edo
- **Shogun:** 1713-1716
- **Death:** 1716 (aged 6) of illness

Eldest son of Ienobu and his concubine Gekko-in. Born in Edo. His childhood name was Nobumatsu.

In 1713 he succeeded his father as Shogun at the age of 4, and took the name Ietsugu. As he was not mature or able enough to rule, he was put under the protection and counsel of his father's advisor, the Confucian scholar Arai Hakuseki (1657-1725).

It was in Ietsugu's name that a law was enacted, which obliged the daimyo of Kyushu to burn any European vessel that should land on their coasts and to kill the crew.

In 1716 Ietsugu died due to complications from a cold, was buried in the Zojo-ji (Shiba), and received the posthumous name Yusho-in.

8TH EDO SHOGUN
TOKUGAWA YOSHIMUNÉ

- **Birth:** 1684 @ Kii
- **Shogun:** 1716-1745 (abdicated)
- **Death:** 1751 (aged 66)

3rd son of Mitsusada (1627-1705) of the Kii branch, grandson of Yorinobu (1602-1671), and the great-grandson of Ieyasu. His childhood name was Genroku.

In 1697 he underwent the rites of passage, took the name Shin-no-suké, and received the fief of Niba (Echizen -- 30,000 koku).

In 1705, at the death of his father and two elder brothers, the ruling Shogun Ienobu appointed Shin-no-suké, at the age of 21, daimyo of Wakayama and chief of the Kii branch, taking the name Yorikata.

In 1707 a tsunami destroyed and killed may in the coastal of Kii. Yorikata did his best to try to stabilize things, but relied on leadership from Edo.

In 1716 the boy-Shogun Ietsugu died, and Yorikata was chosen as his successor. Though he refused the dignity of Shogun three times, he was obliged to submit to the decision of the family council, and took the name Yoshimuné, at the age of 32. The term of his Shogunate would last for almost thirty years.

When in power, Yoshimuné's first endeavor was to extirpate abuses and to bring about the happiness of his people. Now known as the Kyoho Reforms, he dismissed the conservative adviser Arai Hakuseki (1657-1725); entrusted the affairs of justice to the upright O'oka Tadasuké (1677-1752); made researches for the tombs of the ancient Emperors and had them repaired; ordered suggestion boxes to be placed in the cities of Edo, Kyoto, and Osaka to receive the petitions and complaints of the common people; repressed luxury and favored economy; distributed a book on popular medicine for the benefit of the poor; introduced the growing

of sweet potatoes and the making of sugar; established a trade system for the mutual benefit of the provinces; etc.

He was also a protector of the learned. In 1720 he started removing the prohibition since 1640 to read or translate European books, and personally supervised the printing of a great number of books, etc. In short, he became so popular by his wise administration, that the people called him Komé Shogun "Rice Shogun." Yoshimuné however did not revoke the laws closing the country to strangers; nay he redoubled the watchfulness and did much for the protection of the coasts.

In 1729 a certain Ten'ichi-bo, a native of Wakayama, pretending to be the son of Yoshimuné, came to Edo to assert his rights, but was arrested, convicted of falsehood, and put to death.

In 1745 Yoshimuné, at the age of 61, abdicated in favor of his eldest son Ieshigé, and took the title of Ogosho "Retired Shogun." He died six years later, was buried at the Kan'ei-ji (Ueno), and received the posthumous name Yutoku-in.

Yoshimuné is considered by many to have been the best of the Tokugawa Shogun.

9TH EDO SHOGUN
TOKUGAWA IESHIGÉ

- **Birth:** 1712
- **Shogun:** 1745-1760 (abdicated)
- **Death:** 1761 (aged 49)

Eldest son of Yoshimuné. His mother was Osuma-no-kata, the daughter of Okubo Tadanao. His childhood name was Nagatomi.

In 1725 Ieshigé underwent the genbuku "coming-of-age ceremony." His 1st wife was Nami-no-miya, the daughter of the Prince Fushimi-no-miya Kuninaga (1676-1726). His 2nd wife was Oko, the daughter of one of

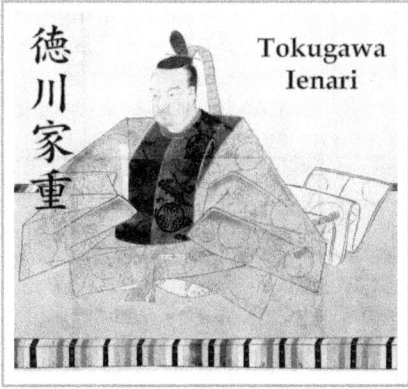

the Courtiers who had followed his high-born 1st wife from the Imperial Court to Edo. This famously good-natured 2nd wife was the mother of Ieharu, who would become Ieshigé's heir.

In 1745 Ieshigé succeeded his father as Shogun at the age of 33, but Yoshimuné continued to direct affairs after his official retirement. This attention was designed to ensure that Ieshigé was secure in his office and remained Shogun until 1760. After his father's death, uninterested in government affairs, Ieshigé left all decisions in the hands of his chamberlain, O'oka Tadamitsu (1709-1760).

In the 1758 Horeki Incident, the councilors of the Shogun began to fear the doctrines taught by the Shinto-Confucian scholar Takenouchi Shikibu (1712-1767) at Kyoto, wherefore he was imprisoned and 17 kugé were degraded or exiled.

Ieshigé's reign was beset by corruption, natural disasters, periods of famine, and the emergence of the mercantile class. His clumsiness in dealing with these issues greatly weakened the rule of the Tokugawa.

In 1760 Ieshigé abdicated at the age of 48 in favor of his eldest son Ieharu, and took the title of Ogosho "Retired Shogun." He died the following year, was buried at the Tokugawa family mausoleum at the Zojo-ji (Shiba), and received the posthumous name Junshin-in.

10TH EDO SHOGUN
TOKUGAWA IEHARU

- **Birth:** 1737
- **Shogun:** 1760-1786
- **Death:** 1786 (aged 49)

Eldest son of Ieshigé, whom he succeeded when 23 years old.

Ieharu ordered Dutch books to be translated and encouraged letters and science.

In 1767 Yamagata Daini and Fujii Umon were beheaded, and Takenouchi Shikibu exiled, for having proclaimed the authority of the Emperor to the prejudice of that of the Shogun.

When Ieharu died, since his son Iemoto died before him, a successor was chosen from the Hitotsubashi branch. He was buried in the Kan'ei-ji (Ueno) and received the posthumous name Shinmei-in.

11TH EDO SHOGUN
TOKUGAWA IENARI

- **Birth:** 1773
- **Shogun:** 1787-1837 (abdicated)
- **Death:** 1841 (aged 67)

Son of Hitotsubashi Harunari, his childhood name was Toyochiyo. In 1778, when only 4 years old, he was betrothed to Shigé-himé, the 4-year-old daughter of the tozama daimyo Shimazu Shigehidé (1745-1833) of Satsuma domain (Kyushu). The couple officially married in 1789.

In 1781 he was chosen by the childless Shogun Ieharu to be his heir. In 1787, upon the abdication of his adoptive father, Toyochiyo became Shogun Ienari at the age of 14.

In 1789 troubles occurred in the island of Ezo, but were repressed by Matsumaé Michihiro. This is the last revolt of the Ebisu mentioned in history.

During the rule of Ienari, the foreign powers again renewed their efforts to enter into communication with Japan: Russia in 1792, 1798, 1804, 1811, and 1814; England in 1797, 1801, 1803, 1808, 1810, 1813, 1818, and 1824; America in 1797, 1806, and 1837; but all advances were met with a refusal. The Shogun ordered the daimyo of the north to keep a good watch on the coasts, and to defend them. Forts were constructed in different parts of the country, communications with Annam (now Vietnam) and Luzon (now the main island of the Philippines) were interrupted, and the country was again secluded more than ever from the outside world.

The famous Matsudaira Sadanobu (1759-1829) reformed the regulations of the army and marines, obliged the hatamoto to pass examinations on military affairs, personally inspected the coasts, etc. In 1827 Ienari received the title of Daijo-daijin "Chancellor of the Realm"; he is the only one who bore that title whilst Shogun. In 1837 Oshio Heihachiro (1793-1837) revolted and attempted to occupy the castle of Osaka but was defeated by Doi Toshitsura (1789-1848) of Koga (Shimosa), and killed himself.

Soon after, Ienari resigned his position to his son Ieyoshi. He had ruled during 50 years, the longest serving of the Tokugawa Shogunate. He died four years later, received the posthumous name Bunkyo-in, and was buried in the Kan'ei-ji (Ueno).

Ienari was known as a degenerate who kept a harem of 900 women and fathered over 75 children, many of whom died in their youth, the others entering by adoption or by marriage into the noblest families.

12TH EDO SHOGUN
TOKUGAWA IEYOSHI

- **Birth:** 1793
- **Shogun:** 1837-1853
- **Death:** 1853 (aged 60)

2nd son of Ienari, he succeeded his father at the age of 44.

In 1842 Ieyoshi appointed Mizuno Tadakuni (1794-1851) to conduct the Tenpo Reforms, which were efforts to resolve perceived problems in the military, economic, agricultural, financial, and religious systems.

In 1842, as foreign vessels were more frequently sighted off Japan, orders were given to fire at those which came near the coasts. In the meantime the daimyo of Mito, Tokugawa Nariaki (1800-1860), ordered cannons to be cast, guns and weapons to be made, drilled his troops, and all this in view of a war with the Europeans, but the Edo government began to fear that he had some other purpose in view, and in 1844 confined Nariaki to his domains of Komagomé (Edo), together with his counselor Fujita Toko. The same year King William II of Holland wrote a letter to the Shogun requesting him to enter into commercial relations with the different powers of Europe. The Catholic missionaries, in spite of long-standing prohibitions, settled in the island of Okinawa, preparatory to their entry of Japan.

In 1846 the American vessel Columbus entered the haven of Suruga Bay (Sagami) and attempted in the name of her government to open commercial relations with Japan, similar to that carried on with China, but met with a polite refusal. However the French, English, and Russian flags frequently appeared in Japanese waters.

In 1852 the minister Ii Naosuké (1815-1860) set Nariaki free and entrusted him with the defense of the country. Nariaki constructed the forts of Shinagawa in order to protect Edo, presented the Bakufu with 72 cannons that had been cast in his domain, ordered guns to be made, etc. Meanwhile the Emperor had prayers offered in the Shintoist and Buddhist temples.

On July 8, 1853, an American fleet anchored in Suruga Bay, and the commander, Commodore Matthew C. Perry (1794-1858), asked to present a letter from President Millard Fillmore (1800-1874) to the Shogun. At this news, all that district was greatly excited. The bugyo "commissioner" of Uraga, in all haste, informed the Edo government, which at once sent an order to all the daimyo to prepare for war. In the meantime, a temporary building had been erected on the sea coast near Kurihama, and the bugyo of Uraga (Sagami) received the American envoy. On July 14, Perry landed with an escort of 300 armed sailors, handed over the President's letter, and announced that he would return the following year to get an answer from the Shogun Ieyoshi. After having made several soundings in Kanagawa Bay, he sailed away.

On Aug 20th, Poutiatine, a Russian, arrived at Nagasaki with a similar mission from his government, but Ieyoshi had just died five days before. He was buried in the Zojo-ji (Shiba) and received the posthumous name Shin-toku-in.

13TH EDO SHOGUN
TOKUGAWA IESADA

- **Birth:** 1824
- **Shogun:** 1853-1858
- **Death:** 1858 (aged 34)

Married to Atsu-himé, the adopted daughter of Shimazu Nariakira (1809-1858), daimyo of Satsuma. His reign marked the beginning of the Bakumatsu "Late Tokugawa" Period (1853-1867) of Japanese history.

Adopted by his brother the Shogun Ieyoshi, Iesada succeeded him at the age of 30 years, at a time when the arrival of foreigners and their petitions to enter into relations with Japan was about to place the government of the Shogun in a predicament. The council of the Shogun, together with the principal daimyo, deliberated upon the answer to be given to the United States of America, but could not agree as to how the letter should be worded. In the meantime, the Russian envoy demanded the opening of diplomatic and commercial relations and the settlement of the disputed boundaries in the island of Sakhalin. He was put off for another year.

On Feb 12, 1854, Commodore Matthew C. Perry (1794-1858) with seven

vessels arrived in the harbor of Uraga Bay (Sagami) and asked for the answer to his communication of the preceding year. Opinion differed. Nariaki urged a refusal and Hosokawa Narimori (1804-1860) of Kumamoto (Higo) asked permission to fire upon the American vessels. But the Shogun Iesada, after much vacillation, in March 31, 1854, signed a temporary treaty which opened the two ports of Shimoda (Izu) and Hakodaté (Ezo) to the American vessels with permission to traffic there and get provisions. Soon after, the port of Nagasaki (Hizen) was added to the two others.

The Bakufu, however, continued its preparations for war. In 1855 the Shogun Iesada sent Yatabori Ko and Katsu Rintaro to Nagasaki to obtain information from the Dutch about the construction and handling of European ships. The same year, in the month of November, a most violent earthquake was felt at Edo and occasion a big fire which destroyed several quarters of the city and killed 25,000 people.

In 1956 Townsend Harris (1804-1878) arrived at Shimoda as minister plenipotentiary of the United States, and the Bakufu sent Hotta Masaatsu, Bitchu no kami and daimyo of Sakura (Shimosa), to settle all questions in reference to foreigners. Notwithstanding the opposition of his daimyo, the Shogun gave audience to Mr. Harris and received a letter from him in which ten ports were asked to be opened to American commerce. Iesada dared not take such responsibility upon himself and sent Masaatsu to the Emperor to confer with him. The counselors of the Kyoto Court, through love for conservative traditions, and also in opposition to the authority of the Shogun, were of opinion that every petition of the strangers

should be refused, and that even those that had already been granted should be revoked. Masaatsu returned to Edo with this answer and the Shogun read it to the assembled daimyo in order to have their opinion on the subject.

In 1858 Ii Naosuké (1815-1860), Kamon no kami and daimyo of Hikoné (Omi), was named tairo "first minister" to the Shogun Iesada, and his energy was destined to hasten the solution of the pending difficulties. Hotta Masaatsu at first tried to evade the formal answer which the American envoy seemed to be expecting: Harris then spoke of addressing himself directly to Kyoto. The Bakufu, in order to gain time, sent a tardy answer to the Washington government. Harris however gave them to understand that France and England, who, after the capture of Canton, had just concluded a treaty with China (Treaty of Tientsin -- June 27, 1858), would send their combined fleets to Japan, and, if need be, take extreme measures to effect the opening of the country. In view of this threat, the Bakufu yielded, and on July 29th signed a treaty with the United States.

At this juncture Iesada fell dangerously ill, and having no children, the question of his succession brought about great difficulties. Tokugawa Nariaki (1800-1860) of Mito proposed his son Hitotsubashi Keiki (who would later become the 15th Tokugawa Shogun Yoshinobu), but the tairo Ii Naosuké was powerful enough to have this candidate set aside, and secured the majority of votes for Iemochi, a boy of 12 years and a member of the Kii branch. This secured the continuation of his influence, and he at once profited by it to confine Nariaki to his domain, and forbade Keiki to enter the Palace of the Shogun.

Iesada died at the age of 34. He was interred at Ueno (northeast of Edo), and received the posthumous name Onkyo-in.

14TH EDO SHOGUN
TOKUGAWA IEMOCHI

- **Birth:** 1846 @ Edo
- **Shogun:** 1858-1866
- **Death:** 1866 @ Osaka Castle (aged 20) of heart failure

Eldest son of Tokugawa Nariyuki (1801-1846), 11th generation Wakayama daimyo of the Kii branch. Cousin to the previous Shogun Iesada. He was known in his childhood as Kikuchiyo. In 1847, at the age of 1, he was adopted as the heir of the 12th generation daimyo Tokugawa Narikatsu (1820-1849), and succeeded him in 1849. In 1851, at his coming-of-age ceremony, he took the name Yoshitomi.

In 1858, through the influence of the tairo "chief minister" Ii Naosuké (1815-1860), he was chosen to succeed the heirless Iesada as Shogun, despite the opposition of Tokugawa Nariaki (1800-1860) of Mito, who proposed his own son Hitotsubashi Keiki (who would later become the 15th Tokugawa Shogun Yoshinobu). Upon assuming the office of Shogun, Yoshitomi changed his name to Iemochi. He was then only 12 years old, and the government remained in the hands of Naosuké.

It was the Shogun Iemochi who signed the treaties with Holland (Donker Curtius, Aug 19, 1858), with Russia (Poutiatine, Aug 20), with England (Lord Elgin, Aug 27), and with France (Baron Gros, Oct 9). This news caused great disturbances in Kyoto. The Emperor Komei (1831-1867) secretly wrote to Tokugawa Nariaki, and asked him to bring the Bakufu to change his line of conduct and to expel all foreigners. Ii Naosuké then sent the roju "elder" Manabé Norikatsu to Kyoto, who imprisoned 57 kugé and samurai who were hostile to the Shogunate, while 40 or 50 others received the same punishment at Edo. These measures calmed the people for some time.

The Emperor Komei had meanwhile entrusted the keeping of Kyoto to the daimyo of Tosa and of Satsuma, who were hostile to the Bakufu, and sent to Edo the kugé Ohara Shigenori with a large retinue commanded by Shimazu Hisamitsu (1817-1887). The Imperial envoy was to order the Shogun to repair to Kyoto with the principal daimyo in order to treat about the interior and exterior affairs of the country; to oblige him to name five tairo as in the days of Toyotomi Hideyoshi (1536-1598); and to receive Hitotsubashi Keiki (the future Shogun Yoshinobu) and Matsudaira Yoshinaga (1828-1890) of Fukui (Echizen) as counselors. Moreover, in 1858 amnesty was given to all con-

demned, and the revenues of the Ii and the Ando families were diminished.

At the beginning of 1859 Yokohama (Musashi) was opened to foreigners, but the Japanese were strictly forbidden to dress in European style. The following year the Shogun Iemochi sent an embassy to the United States. In the meantime Ii Naosuké was assassinated by the ronin of Mito, but his successor Ando Nobumasa (1819-1871), Tsushima no kami, followed the same policy. In 1861 plenipotentiary ministers were sent to all the countries that had signed treaties with Japan. Public opinion however did not abate in its resistance to the policy of opening the country, and foreigners were frequently murdered. The Bakufu then resolved to send an extraordinary embassy to the powers asking them to postpone the application of the treaties. The envoys to Europe left Japan on Jan 22, 1862, and were received in audience by Napoleon III (1808-1873) on Apr 13. But neither at Paris nor elsewhere did they find the government disposed to abandon the advantages promised in the treaties.

It was on his return to Kyoto that, on Sept 14, 1862, Ohara's retinue met some Englishmen at Namamugi (near Yokohama). Charles Lennox Richardson (1834-1862), one of the party, was killed and two others wounded by the Satsuma samurai, in what is now referred to as the Namamugi Incident.

At this time, the Bakufu abrogated the law sankin-kotai "alternate attendance," which obliged the daimyo to leave their wife and children in Edo, and on all sides troops were raised. Enomoto Kamajiro, Akamatsu Kosaburo, and Uchida Tsunejiro were sent to Holland to study the construction of warships.

On Feb 11, 1862, as part of the Kobugattai "Union of Court and Bakufu" movement, Iemochi was married in a magnificent ceremony to Imperial Princess Kazu-no-miya Chikako (1846-1877), daughter of the Emperor Ninko (1800-1846), and younger sister to the Emperor Komei (1831-1867). The couple apparently enjoyed the closest relationship of all the Tokugawa Shoguns, and Iemochi never took a concubine.

Meanwhile, the Shogun had sent Hitotsubashi Keiki and Matsudaira Yoshinaga to Kyoto, and on the 5th day of the 3rd month of the 3rd year of Bunkyu (April 22, 1863), he himself went. Iemochi traveled in a great procession to the capital, and had 3,000 retainers as escort, which included the Roshigumi (part of which became the future Shinsengumi). This was the first time since the visit of the 3rd Tokugawa Shogun Iemitsu 230 years before that a Shogun had visited Kyoto.

The samurai looked to the Shogun to be their leader, and proceed to expel the barbarians, but finding Iemochi loathe to comply with their requests, they went to the Toji-in (northwest of Kyoto), broke the statues of three Ashikaga Shogun, and exposed the heads at Shijo-ga-hara. Disorder soon reigned supreme in the capital.

The Emperor Komei went to the temple Hachiman of Otoko-yama (south of Kyoto), where he intended to present Iemochi with a sword, the emblem of authority to expel all foreigners. The Shogun, feigning sickness, requested Hitotsubashi Keiki to replace him at the ceremony, but Keiki likewise shunned this honor. This dissatisfied the samurai still more, and they asked the Emperor to place himself at their head. Soon after, however, Iemochi went to the Imperial Palace and promised to enter upon the campaign before the lapse of another month. He also manifested the desire to return to Edo, but was detained at Kyoto, and replaced at his castle by Tokugawa Yoshiatsu (1832-1868) of Mito.

At that time, England insisted on having the indemnity settled which she demanded for the murder of Charles Lennox Richardson. Hitotsubashi Keiki was sent to settle the affair, and at the same time, Ogasawara Nagayuki went to Yokohama to ask the representatives of the powers to desist from entering into relation with Japan. His request did not even receive consideration, whereupon Ikeda Chikugo no kami Nagaoki (1837-1879) was dispatched to Europe to treat directly with the governments, but he dared not attempt to accomplish his difficult mission, and on his return was degraded.

Meanwhile, on the day appointed by the Emperor Komei, the 10th day of the 5th month, 1863, Mori Takachika (1836-1871), the Choshu daimyo, gave order to fire on the American vessel, the *Pembroke*, which was passing the Shimo-no-seki Strait (Nagato), and in a few days, some French and Dutch ships experienced the same treatment. Takachika however received congratulations from Kyoto for this bold act. As England could obtain no redress for the Namamugi Incident, Admiral Sir Augustus Leopold Kuper (1809-1885) with seven ships was to bombard Kagoshima (Satsuma). The Bakufu now offered the Shimazu a loan of 70,000 ryo to pay the claimed indemnity.

In Sept 1863 the Shogun, despite the opposition of Mori Takachika, succeeded in having the custody of Kyoto taken from the Choshu troops and given to those of the Satsuma and the Aizu. Mori Motozumi, Sanjo Sanetomi (1837-1891), and six other kugé fled to Nagato and were at once degraded. The Bakufu thus recovered a little influence, a semblance of calm set in, and the hostility against the foreigners quieted down somewhat.

In the beginning of 1864, Iemochi, after only a few months' stay in Edo, returned to Kyoto, and to his great astonishment was ordered by the Emperor to punish the Mori and to postpone the campaign against the foreigners. The samurai of Choshu, unable to obtain the accomplishment of their wishes, openly rebelled and tried to overpower the guard of Kyoto. They were repulsed, but, in the fight, some stray balls found their way into the Imperial Palace. Mori apologized, but was not heeded, and Hitotsubashi Keiki named Tokugawa Yoshikatsu (1824-1883) of Owari commander-in-chief of the army that was to march against the Choshu troops. At the same time the Prince Arisugawa Taruhito (1835-1895), Ichijo Saneyoshi, and 70 other opponents of the Bakufu were imprisoned. In the month of November, the Shogun's army arrived at Hiroshima (Aki); the Mori, finding it impossible to resist, concluded peace, and the troops returned to Kyoto. Some time before, the powers made a call at Shimo-no-seki and their combined fleet bombarded and destroyed the forts (Sept 5-8).

The year 1865 was passed in preparing for an expedition against Choshu, which Iemochi intended to lead in person. Tokugawa Yoshikatsu and Katsu Yoshikuni tried in vain to make him desist from his design. The Mori did not remain inactive, and through the intervention of Saigo Takamori (1828-1877), he made peace with Satsuma. War began in July 1866, and the Shogun's troops were defeated by those of Choshu.

On Sept 19, 1866, Iemochi died at Osaka at the age of 20. The cause of death was reported as heart failure due to beriberi, a disease caused by a thiamine (vitamin B_1) deficiency. He received the posthumous name Shotoku-in, and his body, taken back to Edo, was buried in the Zojo-ji (Shiba).

15th Edo Shogun
Tokugawa Yoshinobu

- **Birth:** 1837 @ Mito (Hitachi)
- **Shogun:** 1866-1867
- **Death:** 1913 (aged 76)

15th and last Tokugawa Shogun. 7th son of Nariaki (1800-1860), head of the Tokugawa of Mito. He was born with the name Matsudaira Shichiroma. He was brought up under strict Spartan supervision and tutelage, and was taught in the literary and martial arts as well as in the principles of politics and government. At the instigation of his father, he was adopted as heir by the influential Hitotsubashi family in order to have a better chance of succeeding to the Shogunate. In 1847 he became family head, coming of age that year, receiving court rank and title, and taking the name Keiki.

In 1858, at the death of the Shogun Iesada, his father presented him as a candidate to the Shogunate, touting his skill and efficiency in managing family affairs, but the opposing faction, led by Ii Naosuké (1815-1860), won out, and Iemochi became the 14th Tokugawa Shogun. Soon after, during the Ansei Purge, Keiki and others who supported him were placed under house arrest, and Keiki himself was made to retire from Hitotsubashi headship.

In 1860 Ii Naosuké was assassinated, and Keiki was reinstated as Hitotsubashi family head. In 1862 he was made hosa "minister" to Iemochi, and from that time was an important factor in politics.

His two closest allies, Matsudaira Yoshinaga (1828-1890) and Matsudaira Katamori (1836-1893), were appointed to other high positions: Yoshinaga as seiji-sosai-shoku "chief of political affairs," Katamori as Kyoto shugo-shoku "guardian of Kyoto." The three men then took numerous steps to quell political unrest in the Kyoto area, and gathered allies to counter the activities of the rebellious Choshu domain. They were instrumental figures in the Kobugattai political party, which sought a reconciliation between the Shogunate and the Imperial Court. In 1864 Keiki, as commander of the Imperial Palace's defense, successfully defeated the Choshu forces in their attempt to capture the Hamaguri Gate, which was achieved with the use of the forces of the Aizu-Satsuma coalition.

In 1866, at Iemochi's death, Keiki was chosen to succeed him as Shogun, and took the name Yoshinobu. He was no sooner in office than he dispatched Katsu Yoshikuni (1823-1899) to Hiroshima (Aki) as negotiator to stop the war against Choshu.

Yoshinobu also quickly initiated a massive government overhaul to strengthen the Tokugawa Bakufu. In particular, the national army and navy under Tokugawa command were modernized and strengthened by the assistance of advisors from the 2nd French Empire and equipment purchased from the United States.

On Jan 30, 1867, the Emperor Komei (1831-1867) died. With his successor, who would be known as the Emperor Meiji (1852-1912), being only 15 years old, the influential kugé and daimyo, seeing they had nothing to fear from his personal initiative, openly expressed their intensions. The Prince Arisugawa Takehito (1862-1913) and the kugé, who had been imprisoned, were given freedom.

In the middle of 1867 the daimyo of Tosa, Yamanouchi Toyonobu, with his advisor Goto Shojiro (1838-1897), ad-

Tokugawa Yoshinobu

dressed a memoir to the Shogun, inviting him to resign his power into the hands of the Emperor, and preside over a new national governing council composed of various daimyo. Yoshinobu, frightened at the difficulties of his position, accepted the advice, and on Oct 14 he sent in his resignation.

He then withdrew from Kyoto to Osaka. However, Satsuma and Choshu, while supportive of a governing council of daimyo, were opposed to Yoshinobu leading it, and moved a massive number of their troops into Kyoto. On Dec 15 a great assembly of daimyo and kugé was called at the Imperial Court. In this meeting Mori Takachika (1836-1871) and his kugé followers were reinstated in their dignities and offices; the guard of the city of Kyoto was taken from the troops of Aizu and Kuwana and again confided to the troops of Satsuma, Choshu, Aki, Echizen, etc.; the titles of Sessho, Kanpaku, Sei-i-tai-shogun, giso, tenso, and shoshidai were suppressed; new offices of sosai, gitei, and san'yo were created, etc. These measures were promulgated on Jan 4, 1868.

Yoshinobu was stripped of all titles and land. He opposed this action, and composed a message of protest to be delivered to the Imperial Court. At the urging by the men of Aizu, Kuwana, and other domains, and in light of the immense number of Satsuma and Choshu troops in Kyoto, he dispatched a large body of troops to convey this message to the Court.

When the Tokugawa forces arrived outside Kyoto, they were refused entry. On Jan 27, 1868, they were attacked by Satsuma and Choshu troops, starting the Battle of Toba-Fushimi (be-

tween Kyoto and Osaka), the first clash of the Boshin War (1868-1869). Though the Tokugawa forces had a distinct advantage in numbers, Yoshinobu abandoned his army in the midst of the fight once he realized the Satsuma and Choshu forces had raised the Imperial banner, and escaped to Edo on the Shogunate warship *Kaiyo-maru*. He placed himself under voluntary confinement, and indicated his submission to the Imperial Court. However, a peace agreement was reached wherein Tayasu Kamenosuké (1863-1940), the young head of a branch of the Tokugawa, was adopted and made Tokugawa family head. Edo Castle was handed over to the Imperial army, and the city was spared from all-out war.

Together with Kamenosuké, who took the name Iesato, Yoshinobu moved to Shizuoka (Suruga), where centuries earlier Tokugawa Ieyasu (1543-1616), the founder of the Tokugawa Shogunate, had also retired. Iesato was made the daimyo of the new Shizuoka domain.

Many of the hatamoto also relocated to Shizuoka as a large proportion of them did not find adequate means to support themselves. As a result, many of them resented Yoshinobu, some of them to the point of wanting him dead. The ex-Shogun was aware of this, and was so afraid of assassination that he made special sleeping arrangements to confuse potential assailants.

Yoshinobu lived a life in quiet retirement, indulging in many hobbies, including oil-painting, archery, hunting, photography, and even cycling. It was the beginning of a new era for Japan.

Daimyo

Samurai Warlords of Feudal Japan

The following daimyo are those not included in the book *Daimyo of 1867*, and therefore represent the warlords that were defeated, dispossessed, or otherwise discontinued from the annals of history prior to the end of the samurai era. Together they comprise all the daimyo listed in Papinot's *Historical and Geographical Dictionary of Japan*, as well as those that were found while researching this compilation.

Although the title daimyo did not appear until the Muromachi Period (1336-1573), the following includes major warlords and powerful clans from the earlier Heian (794-1185) and Kamakura (1185-1333) eras.

The warlords are listed in order of period, and within each period, alphabetically by clan name. Please note that there are many families that lasted more than one historical time period, and these are listed in the era in which the last major clan leader lost his fiefdom.

Mon "family crests" were not universally adopted by the samurai until the Muromachi Period (1336-1573), and the mon of only a few prominent clans are available prior to this period. For families where the mon is unknown or otherwise missing, you can use the Random Mon Generator towards the end of this guide to roll up a family crest by chance for gaming purposes.

Fushimi-jo

Heian Period

ABÉ

Territory: Northern Honshu
Castles: Koromo-gawa (Mutsu)

Ancient family originating in Iga claiming descent from a legendary character named Abi, who in the 7th century B.C. opposed the conquest of Yamato by the 1st Emperor of Japan Jimmu (711 B.C.-585 B.C.), who drove the clan northward to take refuge in northern Honshu.

The *Nihon-shoki* "*Japan Chronicles*," completed in 720, records that the Abé descended from a son of the legendary 9th Emperor of Japan Kogen, who reigned around the 2nd century B.C.

The Abé became enormously wealthy by monopolizing the gold, iron, and horse trade in northern Honshu. They also designed a new type of stockade which could withstand a long siege.

By the 9th century the native northern Honshu Ainu were subjugated or displaced. The region, then split into Mutsu and Dewa, was settled by a mix of Japanese immigrants and former Emishi tribesmen, and the Abé were appointed "superintendent of the aborigines" to control the populace on behalf of the Kyoto government and the governor of Mutsu.

The Abé began to not pay taxes, be expansionistic, and generally be rebellious against the Imperial Court. In 1051 the Fujiwara, who held the office of governor of Mutsu, attacked the Abé, but were repulsed. Desperate to quell this affront to their authority, Heian-kyo (Kyoto) appointed Minamoto Yoriyoshi (998-1082) as Chinjufu-shogun "Defender of the North." In the ensuing Zen-kunen "Earlier Nine-Years" War (1051-1063), in 1057 Yoriyoshi and his son Yoshiié (1039-1106), with important aid from the Kiyohara of Dewa, killed Abé Yoritoki at the Battle of Koromo-gawa (Mutsu), and in 1062 defeated his son Sadato at the Kuriya-gawa Stockade (Mutsu), breaking the power of the Abé.

Throughout Japanese history there are many who have been called Abé, but it is difficult to say which are directly related to the old clan from Iga and Mutsu. A family in Musashi named Abé became prominent starting in the 18th century, but its relationship to the earlier Abé has not been definitively confirmed.

Notable Ancestors

Abé Hirafu (575-664)

Governor of Koshi (northwest Honshu). Also known as Abé no Hikita no Omi Hirafu.

In 658 the Empress Saimei (594-661) sent Hirafu to attack the Emishi in northeastern Japan with 180 ships. In 659 he attacked the Mishihasé, another racial group, possibly of Chinese origin, in northern Japan.

In 663 Hirafu, along with Oyaké no Omi Kamara, Kamitsukeno no Kimi Wakako, Iohara no Kimi, and Echi no Takutsu, was sent by the Emperor Tenji (626-672) to aid the Korean kingdom of Baekje (or Paekche), which was being attacked by both the Silla (or Shiragi) and the Tang China. In 663 the Japanese naval forces, believed to be from the Hokuriku region, were completely defeated at the Battle of Hakusuki-noé (Korea), which marked a long 900-year break of Japanese interaction in Korea.

Afterwards Hirafu was appointed military governor of Dazaifu (Kyushu).

His story is told in the Nihon-shoki. He is said to be the ancestor of the Abé, the Ando, and the Akita.

Abé Yoritoki (-1057)

Son of Tadayoshi. He ruled the six Emishi districts of Iwaté, Hienuki, Shiwa, Isawa, Esashi, and Waga. In the center of his domain he built the castle of Koromo-gawa (Mutsu), and established a sort of independent principality, keeping all the proceeds of the taxes, and refusing to contribute to the expenses of the province, etc.

In 1051 Yoritoki led an army of Emishi into northern Miyagi (Mutsu), and trounced at Onikiribé a government army, which was sent to stop the Abé raids that were fighting the Minamoto expansion into their territories. This triggered the Zen-kunen "Earlier Nine-Years" War (1051-1063). In 1053 the Emperor deputized Minamoto Yoriyoshi (998-1082) as Chinjufu-shogun "Defender of the North," and commissioned him to quell the revolt. Yoriyoshi took his son Yoshiié (1039-1106) with him. Yoritoki submitted, but rebelled a second time. In one of the first engagements, Yoritoki was killed by an arrow in battle south of the Koromo-gawa.

One of Yoritoki's daughters married Fujiwara Tsunekiyo (-1062), whose son Kiyohira (1056-1128) founded the Northern Fujiwara Dynasty.

Abé Sadato (1019-1062)

Eldest son of Yoritoki. He continued the Zen-kunen War (1051-1063) after his father's death in 1057.

In 1057, at the Battle of Kawasaki (Mutsu), fighting during a snowstorm, Sadato defeated Minamoto Yoriyoshi (998-1082), and obliged him to retreat.

In 1061 Yoriyoshi, reinforced by Kiyohara Takenori of Dewa, besieged Sadato at the Kuriya-gawa Stockade (Mutsu). After several days of fighting, with his water supply diverted, his defenses attacked, and his fortress set aflame, Sadato surrendered. The following year, the Minamoto returned to Kyoto with his head.

Abé Muneto (1032-1108)

2nd son of Yoritoki, and younger brother to Sadato. He was based at the Isawa Stockade (Mutsu).

Muneto at first rebelled against the Court during the Zen-kunen "Earlier Nine-Years" War (1051-1063), but when his elder brother Sadato was defeated and killed, he surrendered to Minamoto Yoshiié (1039-1106).

He was at first exiled to Iyo, then to Tsukushi (northern Kyushu), where he achieved bonzehood.

Muneto is considered one of the possible ancestors of the Matsuura of Hizen.

Abé Masato (11th century)

Son of Yoritoki. Occupied the Kurosawa Stockade (Mutsu).

Abé Norito (11th century)

Son of Yoritoki. Stayed at the Koromo-gawa Stockade (Mutsu) with his father.

 # FUJIWARA

Residence: Heian-kyo
"Capital of Peace and Tranquility"
(later Kyoto)

Family which descended from Amé no Koyané no Mikoto, one of the faithful followers of Amaterasu and of Ninigi no Mikoto.

Originally a clan of landowners called the Nakatomi, in the 7th century they took over the Yamato Court. From among their leaders came the Shinto ritualists, who were responsible for the prominence of the Kashima-jingu (Hitachi), with an Imperial grant overseen by them.

In their political and religious opposition to the Soga, in 645 they assassinated for the Throne the most influential members of that family, thus reinforcing their influence at Court.

In 669 the Emperor Tenji (626-672) permitted Nakatomi Kamatari (614-669) to take the family name Fujiwara as compensation for services rendered against the Soga. The first Fujiwara was thus Kamatari's son, Fujiwara Fuhito. One of his daughters married the Emperor Monmu (683-707), and another married the Emperor Shomu (701-756). Thus the custom of "marriage politics" was started for the Emperors to marry Fujiwara women. Thanks to these family ties, and careful political manipulation, by the late 9th to early 10th centuries the Fujiwara were all-powerful in the Court.

Throughout the Heian "Aristocratic" Period (794-1185) the Fujiwara politically dominated Japan through their monopoly of the Regency posts of Sessho and Kanpaku, in effect subject only to the Emperor. During this time the Fujiwara supplied Japan with its greatest statesmen and poets.

By the end of the 12th century, the abdicated Emperors exercised their power in Court, the provincial warrior class rose, and the Fujiwara gradually lost its control over mainstream politics.

Beyond the 12th century, the Fujiwara continued to monopolize the Imperial Regency for most of the time in the history until the 19th-century Imperial Restoration. If their influence was not anymore the same as what they had previously, they remained close advisors to the Emperors.

MINISTERS, STATESMEN, WARRIORS, ETC.

NOTABLE ANCESTORS

Fujiwara Kamatari (614-669)

Son of Nakatomi Mikeko. Born Nakatomi Kamatari, he is the founder the Fujiwara clan in Japan. He was a faithful servant of Imperial Prince Karu no Oji, later the Emperor Kotoku (596-654); and friend and supporter of Imperial Prince Naka no Oé, later the Emperor Tenji (626-672).

Kamatari was the head of the Jingi no Haku "Shinto Ritualists." As such he was one of the chief opponents of the increasing power and prevalence of Buddhism in the Court and in the nation. As a result, in 645 Prince Naka no Oé and Kamatari plotted the ruin of the Soga, whose ambition was unlimited, and made a *coup d'état* in the Court. Whilst the Empress Kogyoku (594-661) gave a public audience to the envoy of Korea, in her presence they assassinated Soga Iruka, who had a strong influence over the Empress. Thereafter Iruka's father Soga Emishi (587-645) was forced to commit suicide in his own house. The Empress was forced to abdicate in favor of her younger brother Karu no Oji, who ascended to the Chrysanthemum Throne under the name Kotoku-tenno.

Fujiwara Kamatari

Heian Period – Fujiwara

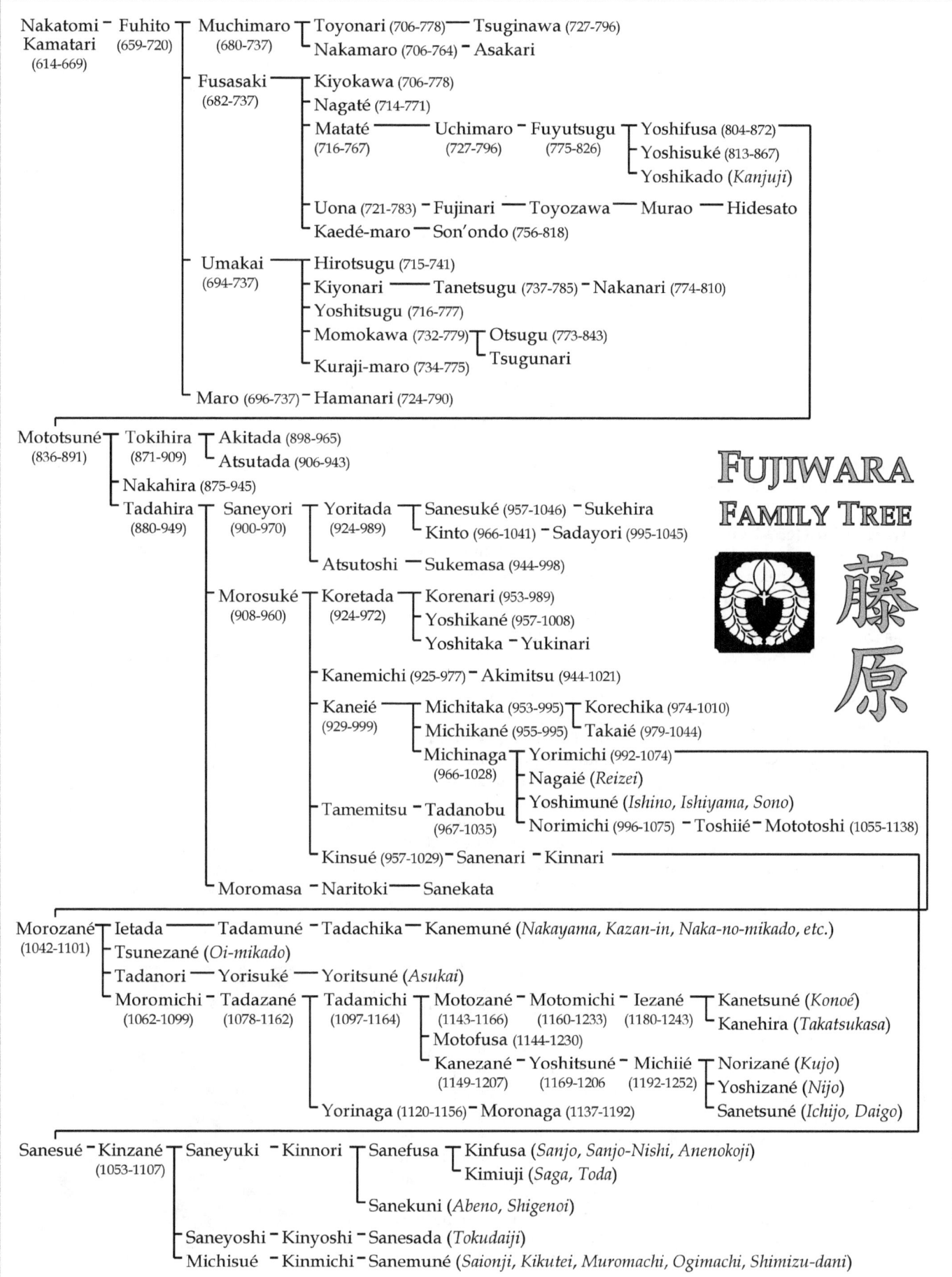

Fujiwara Family Tree

Heian Period – Fujiwara

The new Emperor inaugurated his reign by introducing great changes in the form of government. This system was called the Taika no Kaishin "Taika Reforms," which was based on Chinese institutions of the Tang Dynasty, and aimed at strengthening Imperial power.

In 669 Kamatari was appointed naidaijin "inner minister," and took an active part in public affairs during the reigns of the Emperor Kotoku, Empress Saimei (2nd reign of Kogyoku), and Emperor Tenji (626-672).

In 669 Kamatari fell dangerously ill. The Emperor Tenji then nominated him dai-shokukan, and granted him and his descendants the family name of Fujiwara. His temple is in Tamu-no-miné (Yamato).

His nephew Nakatomi Ominaro (-711) became the head of the national shrines of Isé, keeping the Nakatomi name.

Fujiwara Fuhito (659-720)

2nd son of Kamatari. His father died when he was only 10 years old. He was minister during the reigns of the Empress Jito (645-702), the Emperor Mommu (683-707), the Empress Gemmei (660-721), and the Empress Gensho (683-748).

In 672, when the Imperial succession dispute begat the Jinshin War, Fuhito was only 13 years old. As he was too young to hold government office, he was not involved in this conflict, and was taken in by a fuhito "scribe" named Tanabé Osumi in Yamashina. When the Imperial Prince Oama succeeded to the Chrysanthemum Throne as the Emperor Temmu (631-686), however, the chaos and troubles took a toll on the power of the Nakatomi and their kinsmen.

In 689 Fuhito was appointed a judge, and from there his fortunes took a turn for the better. He was chosen by the Empress Jito to aid her after the death of her husband Temmu, and as the guardian of her son Prince Kusakabé (662-689). Eight years later, he was granted 50 retainers.

In 697 the Prince Karu (683-707), the 2nd son of Kusakabé, and grandson of the Emperor Temmu and the Empress Jito, ascended as the Emperor Mommu. Fuhito supported this succession strongly, and received the favor of the ex-Empress Jito. Since then his promo-

Fujiwara Fuhito

tion in the Court began. In 699 the new Emperor conferred the Fujiwara surname to Fuhito.

In 701 the Taiho Code, an adaptation of the Tang China system of government, which Fuhito had helped to compile, was enacted.

Also that year, the Prince Obito, later the Emperor Shomu (701-756), son of the Emperor Mommu, was born by one of Fuhito's daughters Miyako. Fuhito succeeded in making Obito the Crown Prince, and had him marry one of his other daughters, Komyo-shi. Until then only a royal lady could be the Empress, and Komyo-shi was the first who did not derive from the Imperial household.

In 707 the Emperor Mommu, two months before his death, offered Fuhito a fief of 5,000 households. He declined, and the fief was decreased to only 2,000 households, with 1,000 being passed on to his desendants.

In 708 Fuhito was nominated udaijin "junior minister of state," along with Isonokami no Maro (640-717), who was made sadaijin "senior minister of state." Both were praised by the new Empress Gemmei (660-721) for their "equitable character." This gave Fuhito tremendous power over the administration.

In 709 Fuhito, in his capacity as udaijin, met with Kim Shin Fuku and the other members of the embassy from Silla (Korea). This was the first time a minister, rather than the Emperor, had officially met with envoys. In 710 he was also udaijin when the capital was moved to Nara.

In 718 Fujito refused the title of Daijo-daijin "Chancellor of the Realm," which title the Empress Gensho (683-748) however conferred on him after his death.

Fuhito moved Yamashina-dera, the main Buddhist temple his clan supported, to Nara, and renamed it Kofuku-ji. In 760 he received the posthuous name of Tankai. In 768 the Kasuga Shrine, the main temple of the Fujiwara clan was settled near the Kofuku-ji.

Fuhito had four sons by two women, and they became the ancestors of the four branches of the Fujiwara: Muchimaro (680-737), the Nan-ké "southern branch"; Fusasaki (681-737), the Hok-ké "northern branch," which became the Regent line of the clan; Umakai (694-737), the Shiki-ké "ceremonial branch"; and Maro (695-737), the Kyo-ké "Kyoto branch." He also had four daughters by two other women: three by Kamo-himé, and one by Tachibana no Michiyo. In 698 his eldest daughter by Kamo-himé, Miyako no Iratsumé, was chosen as consort for Mommu-tenno, and was the mother of Shomu-tenno. His 2nd daughter by Michiyo, Komyo-shi, married Shomu, and became the mother of the Empress Koken (718-770).

Fujiwara Muchimaro (680-737)

Eldest son of Fuhito, his mother was Shoshi, daughter of the udaijin "junior minister of state" Soga Murajiko (-664). He married a granddaughter of Abé Miushi, with whom he had two sons, Toyonari and Nakamaro. Among his daughters were consorts of the Emperor Shomu (701-756) and Fujiwara Fusasaki (681-737).

In 734 Muchimaro became udaijin, and on the eve of his death, sadaijin "senior minister of state."

He died during a smallpox epidemic.

Fujiwara Muchimaro

Heian Period – Fujiwara

As Muchimaro's domains were situated south of those of his brother Fusasaki, his family was called Nan-ké "Southern branch," and that of Fusasaki, Hoku-ké "Northern branch."

Fujiwara Fusasaki (681-737)

2nd son of Fuhito. In 702 he had charge of the inspection of the Tokaido and the Tosando. He was minbu-kyo "minister of police."

In 734 Fusasaki founded the Sugimoto-dera in Kamakura (Sagami) with the priest Gyoki (668-749). The temple's legend holds that the Empress Komyo (701-760) instructed Fusasaki, then the highest-ranking minister, to build the temple enshrining a statue of the eleven-headed Kannon (Ekadasamukha in Sanskrit) as the main object of worship. As he was a great sculptor, Gyoki himself fashioned the statue.

He died along with his brothers during a smallpox epidemic.

Fusasaki's son Uona was the founding ancestor of the Hoku-ké "Northern branch" of the Fujiwara.

Fujiwara Umakai (694-737)

3rd son of Fuhito. He was married to Kumé Wakamé (-780), with whom he had son Momokawa, whose daughter became the Empress (posthumously) of the Emperor Heizei (773-824).

In 717 Umakai was chosen as a kentoshi "ambassador" to China, and he returned the following year. In 719 he became Hitachi no kami, in which he was also in charge of inspecting the leadership of Kazusa, Awa, and Shimosa.

In 724 Umakai suppressed a rebellion of the Ebisu in Mutsu. As he was at the time shikibu-kyo "chief of protocol," he became the founder of the Shiki-ké "Ceremonial branch" of the Fujiwara.

In 726 Umakai was a construction supervisor of the new Naniwa Palace (Osaka).

In 731 Umakai was appointed sangi "Imperial counselor" when this title was created.

In 732 Umakai was the military governor of the Western Sea district.

Along with three of his brothers, Umakai died in 737 during a nationwide outbreak of smallpox that killed numerous aristocrats.

An accomplished poet, the *Man'yoshu* contains six of his works, with others in the collection *Yearnings for the Ancient Chinese Style*.

Fujiwara Maro (695-737)

4th son of Fuhito. His mother was Ioé Iratsumé, former wife of the Emperor Temmu (631-686), daughter of Fujiwara Kamatari (614-669), and half-sister of his father. Among his children was Hamanari.

Maro was hyobu-kyo "minister of war," sangi "Imperial advisor," sayu-kyo-tayu; hence the name of Kyo-ké "Kyoto branch" given to his family.

He and three of his brothers died of small pox the same year.

Fujiwara Toyonari (704-765)

Eldest son of Muchimaro, was minister during the reigns of the Empress Gensho (683-768) and the Emperor Shomu (701-756). He was also called Naniwa no Daijin.

In 757 Toyonari intended to have the Prince Shioyaki-o nominated Taishi "Crown Prince," but his brother Nakamaro, who enjoyed the full confidence of the Empress Koken (718-770), caused the Prince Oi-o, the future Emperor Junnin (733-765), to be elected instead, and Toyonari was exiled to Tsukushi (Kyushu).

In 764 Toyonari was recalled after the death of Nakamaro.

Fujiwara Nakamaro (706-764)

2nd son of Muchimaro.

In 757 Nakamaro succeeded in having Prince Oi-o nominated Taishi "Crown Prince." In 758, upon ascendance to the Chrysanthemum Throne as the Emperor Junnin (733-765), he loaded Nakamaro with favors, and bestowed on him the title of Emi no Oshikatsu.

In 764, jealous of the influence the bonze Dokyo (700-772) had over the ex-Empress Koken (718-770), Nakamaro plotted with the then Emperor Junnin, and raised troops in order to seize the monk, but pursued as far as Omi by his cousins Yoshitsugu and Kurajimaro, he was defeated and executed at Lake Biwa with his wife and two sons Materu and Kuzumaro.

Fujiwara Kiyokawa (706-778)

Son of Fusasaki. In 749 he became sangi "Imperial advisor."

In 750 Kiyokawa was sent to China as kentoshi "ambassador." He went as far as the then capital Chang'an (Xi'an since the 14th century) in Shaanxi province, where he was received by the 7th Tang Emperor Xuanzong (685-762), who told him, "I have heard that there is a virtuous ruler in your country. Now having observed your distinctive manner of walking and bowing, I would name Japan a country of ritual, righteousness, and gentlemen." Xuanzong later had portraits made of Kiyo-

kawa and his two deputies, and composed a poem upon their departure.

In 752 Kiyokawa embarked for a return trip to Japan with Abé Nakamaro (701-770), who had been in China since 717, but their vessel was driven by a storm to the coasts of Annam (Vietnam) where the natives massacred many of their servants. In 755 they were able to return to Chang'an, and later that year tried again to return to Japan, but this time the onset of the An Shi Rebellion (755-763) of general An Lushan (703-757) against the Tang Court made the trip unsafe.

Both Kiyokawa and Nakamaro decided to settle, at least for a while, in China. They took Chinese names, and obtained various offices and dignities from the Imperial Court. Neither ever made it back to Japan.

Fujiwara Nagaté (714-771)

Son of Fusasaki. He was sadaijin "senior minister of state" during the reigns of the Emperor Shomu (701-756), the Empress Koken (718-770), the Emperor Junnin (733-765), and the Empress Koken (718-770).

In 770, at Koken's death, Nagaté aided in the nomination of Shirakabé-shinno to the Chrysanthemum Throne as the Emperor Konin (709-782), who conferred on him sho-ichi-i "the 1st rank of the 1st class."

As he resided at Nagaoka, Nagaté is often known by the name of Nagaoka-daijin.

Fujiwara Mataté (716-767)

3rd son of Fusasaki. He was successively sangi "Imperial advisor," dainagon "counselor of the Imperial Court," and shikibu-kyo "minister of ceremonies."

Fujiwara Uona (721-783)

4th son of Fusasaki. He was in the service of the Emperor Shomu (701-756), the Empress Koken (718-770), the Emperor Junnin (733-765), and the Empress Koken (718-770).

In 782 Uona was sadaijin "senior minister of state" of the ancient Imperial Court of Japan when, at the accession of the Emperor Kammu (737-806) to the Chrysanthemum Throne, he was implicated in a conspiracy against the new Emperor, and exiled to Tsukushi (Kyushu). Having been pardoned soon afterwards, he returned to the capital where he died the following year.

Fujiwara Hirotsugu

Uona is the founder of the Oshu "northern Honshu" Fujiwara. He is the ancestor of the Daté, etc.

Fujiwara Hirotsugu (715-741)

Eldest son of Umakai. In his youth, he simultaneously studied Buddhism, military arts, astronomy, etc.

In 738 Hirotsugu was appointed to a minor position in Dazaifu (northern Kyushu). He took umbrage at the great influence of the bonze Genbo over the Court, raised an army, and in 740 rebelled. Ono Azumabito (-757) and Ki Iimaro were sent against him. At Itabitsu-gawa, Hirotsugu was defeated, arrested at Nagano (Hizen), and beheaded.

His death marked the end of the Shiki-ké "ceremonial branch" of the Fujiwara, and the rise of the Nan-ké "southern branch."

Some of his poems grace the *Man'yoshu*.

Fujiwara Momokawa

Fujiwara Yoshitsugu (716-777)

2nd son of Umakai. In 740, when his brother Hirotsugu revolted, he was exiled to Izu.

In 746, having been recalled at the death of the bonze Genbo, Yoshitsugu was appointed Kozuké no kami. Afterwards, hostile to his cousin Nakamaro, then all-powerful, he was degraded, and banished to Omi. In 764 he contributed to the defeat of Nakamaro, and was nominated Dazai-shi "governor of Kyushu," and afterwards naidaijin "minister of the center."

His daughter Otomuro became the consort of the Emperor Kammu (737-806), and the mother of the Emperors Heizei (773-824) and Saga (786-842).

Fujiwara Momokawa (732-779)

Son of Umakai. He was one of eight brothers. His mother was Kumé no Wakamé (-780). His childhood name was Oda-maro. He married Moroané, his niece and daughter of his brother Yoshitsugu.

Momokawa was minister during the reigns of the Empresses Koken (718-770) and Shotoku (718-770), two tenures of the same monarch. At her death, notwithstanding the opposition of the udaijin "junior minister of state" Kibi no Kabi, he succeeded with the help of Nagaté and Yoshitsugu in having Yamabé-shinno, who was then 62 years old, ascend to the Chrysanthemum Throne as the new Emperor Konin (709-782). When there was question of choosing the Taishi "Crown Prince," Momokawa proposed Yamabé-shinno, the eldest of one of Konin's concubines Takano no Niigasa (-790). Momokawa would not desist, and remained before the gate of the palace for forty days, without returning to his residence, when finally the Emperor yielded to his advice. So he gained his cause, and in 773 Yamabé-shinno, later the Emperor Kammu (737-806), was nominated.

Momokawa's children included sons Otsugu and Tsugunari, and daughters Tabiko and Tarashiko. Tabiko was the consort of Emperor Kammu, with whom she bore Prince Otomo, who later became Emperor Junna, during whose reign she was the Empress Dowager. Tarashiko was the wife of Emperor Heizei (773-824), and died in 794 during the moving of the Imperial capital to Heian-kyo (later Kyoto).

Heian Period – Fujiwara

Fujiwara Kuraji-maro (734-775)
Another son of Umakai. He was Izumo no suké and Bizen no kami.

In 764 Kuraji-maro took part in the campaign against his cousin Naka-maro.

In 767 Kuraji-maro had charge of inspecting Iyo and Tosa, and afterwards became successively hyobu-kyo "minister of war," Dazai-shi "military governor of Kyushu," and sangi "Imperial advisor."

Fujiwara Hamanari (724-790)
Son of Maro. His mother was an unemé "Palace attendant" of Yakami Kori of Inaba, who was probably the same person who had a famous affair with Aki Okimi.

Hamamari was sangi "Imperial advisor," danjo-no-suké "vice-president of justice," gyobu-kyo "minister of justice," and finally Dazai-shi "military governor of Kyushu" (781). He also wrote *Tensho*, a chronological history of Japan, and was a noted poet.

Fujiwara Tsuginawa (727-796)
Son of Toyonari. The Ebisu of Mutsu, having revolted in 780, massacred the azechi "inspector" Ki Hirozumi. Tsuginawa, having been nominated Sei-i-taishi-shogun "Commander-in-Chief," together with Ki Kosami, was ordered to reduce them to submission.

In 783 Tsunawa was appointed dainagon "grand counselor," and afterwards Dazai-shi "military governor of Kyushu," and in 790 udaijin "junior minister of state."

He is also known as Momozono no Udaijin.

Fujiwara Uchimaro (756-812)
Son of Mataté. He was a member of the Fujiwara Hok-ké "northern branch." He was successively chunagon "middle counselor," dainagon "grand counselor," and udaijin "junior minister of state."

Uchimaro is also known as Nagaoka-daijin.

Fujiwara Son'ondo (756-818)
Son of Kaedé-maro. He was Mino no kami, Yamato no kami, ukyo-tayu, kunai-kyo "minister of the Imperial Household."

Son'ondo was charged with the inspection of the San'yodo, then of the compilation of the *Shinsen Shojiroku* "Geneology of the Court Nobles." He is also known as Yamashina-daijin.

Fujiwara Tanetsugu (737-785)
Son of Kiyonari.

The Taishi "Crown Prince" Sawara having asked that Saeki Imagebito be nominated sangi "Imperial advisor," Tanetsugu opposed the nomination. In order to escape the hatred of the Prince, he retired to Nagaoka (Yamashiro), but in 785, while the Emperor Kammu (737-806) was at Nara (Yamato), the Taishi had Tanetsugu assassinated.

He received the posthumous title of sadaijin "senior minister of state," and later that of Daijo-daijin "Chancellor of the Realm."

Fujiwara Otsugu (773-843)
Son of Momokawa. In 825 he was udaijin "junior minister of state," and in 832 sadaijin "senior minister of state," during the reigns of the Emperors Saga (786-842), Junna (786-840), and Ninmyo (810-850).

Otsugu was charged with the publication of the *Nihon Koki* "Later Chronicles of Japan," the 3rd part of the *Rikkoku-shi* "Six National Histories," covering the years 792-833 in 40 volumes.

Fujiwara Asakari (8th century)
Son of Nakamaro. He was Mutsu no kami, azechi "inspector of the provinces," and Chinjufu-shogun "Defender of the North."

Asakari constructed the forts of Momono (Mutsu) and Okatsu (Dewa) against the Ebisu.

In 764, at the time of the revolt of his father, Asakari was deprived of his domains.

Fujiwara Oguro-maro (733-794)
Grandson of Fusasaki. He was Isé no kami, Mutsu no kami, dainagon "grand counselor," etc.

In 780 Oguro-maro, as a commander in the Imperial army, took a prominent part in the campaign against the Ebisu.

Fujiwara Tsunetsugu (796-840)
Son of Kadonomaro.

In 837 Tsunetsugu was made Dazai-shi "military governor of Kyushu."

In 838 Tsunetsugu was sent as ambassador to the Chinese Court, along with the Buddhist monk Ennin (793-864). He was the last Japanese ambassador to China in the Heian "Aristocratic" Period (794-1185).

Fujiwara Nakanari (774-810)
Son of Tanetsugu.

Nakanari was made sangi "Imperial advisor" by piracy with his infamous

sister Kusuko, the object of which was to restore the Emperor Heizei (773-824) to the throne by deposing the Emperor Saga (786-842), and to transfer the capital to Nara (Yamato). He was beheaded.

Fujiwara Fuyutsugu (775-826)
Son of Uchimaro. He was of the Fujiwara Hok-ké "Northern branch." He cultivated literature and the military arts, and was a poet. He was minister during the reigns of the Emperors Kammu (737-806), Heizei (773-824), Saga (786-842), and Junna (786-840). He is known by the name of Kan'in-no-daijin.

In 821 Fuyutsugu founded the Kangaku-in, a school for the education of his family.

In 825 Fuyutsugu was appointed sadaijin "senior minister of state," having been the leader of the Kurodo-dokoro, an informal Imperial secretariat.

His daughter Nobuko married the Emperor Ninmyo (810-850), and became the mother of Emperor Montoku (827-858).

Fujiwara Yoshifusa (804-872)
1st Fujiwara Regent to the Emperor. 2nd son of Fuyutsugu. His mother was Fujiwara Mitsuko.

In 814 Yoshifusa married Minamoto Kiyo-himé, daughter of the Emperor Saga (786-842). The couple had one

daughter, Akira-keiko (829-899), who became the consort to her own cousin Emperor Montoku (827-858), and was the mother of Emperor Seiwa (850-880). Montoku was the son of the Emperor Ninmyo (810-850) and his wife Junshi, who was Yoshifusa's sister.

Yoshifusa adopted his brother Nagara's 3rd son Mototsuné as heir.

Yoshifusa was minister during the reigns of the Emperors Ninmyo, Montoku, and his grandson Seiwa. In 834 he was made sangi "Imperial advisor," in 835 gon-no-chunagon "deputy middle counselor," in 840 chunagon "middle counselor," in 842 dainagon "grand counselor," and in 848 udaijin "junior minister of state."

In 857 Emperor Montoku (827-858) made him Daijo-daijin "Chancellor of the Realm," and gave him permission to wear his sword even when coming to the Palace, but Yoshifusa declined that honor.

In 859 Yoshifusa successfully ascended his grandson on the Chrysanthemum Throne as the new Emperor Seiwa, and placed himself as Sessho "Regent," the first who was not of the Imperial Household, making him the *de facto* ruler of Japan.

In 864, in order to give the young Emperor an idea of what field labor was like, Yoshifusa ordered Ki Imamori, governor of Yamashiro, to send a certain number of laborers that they might till the soil in the Emperor's presence.

In 866 Yoshifusa asked to be relieved from his function as Regent, but the Emperor never assented.

In 869 Yoshifusa, with Haruzumi Yoshitsuna, completed the *Shoku Nihon Koki* "Later Chronicles of Japan Continued*,*" the 4th part of the *Rikoku-shi* "Six National Histories," covering the years 833-850, the reign of his brother-in-law Emperor Ninmyo, in 20 volumes.

Yoshifusa is also known by the names Somé-dono-no-daijin and Shirakawa-dono.

It was with Yoshifusa that the great power of the Fujiwara house, and their line of the Sessho and the Kanpaku, began.

Fujiwara Yoshisuké (813-867)

Son of Fuyutsugu. He was sakon'é-shosho "officer of the Imperial guard."

In 857 Yoshisuké was appointed udaijin "junior minister of state."

He is also known as Nishi-sanjo-daijin.

Fujiwara Yoshikado (9th century)

Son of Fuyutsugu. He held the title Daijo-daijin "Chancellor of the Realm."

Yoshikado was the ancestor of the Uesugi, Ii, Nichiren, etc. He however adopted the surname Kanjuji which he passed on to his descendants.

Fujiwara Mototsuné (836-891)

3rd son of Nagayoshi. His mother was Otoharu, daughter of Fujiwara Tsugutada. He was adopted by his uncle Yoshifusa, who had no sons.

In 864 Mototsuné became sangi "Imperial advisor," in 866 chunagon "middle counselor," in 870 dainagon "grand counselor," and in 872 udaijin "junior minister of state." Later that year he became Sessho "Regent" to the Emperor Seiwa (850-880), and in 876 to Emperor Yozei (869-949).

In 879 Mototsuné with Sugawara Koreyoshi completed the *Montoku Jitsuroku* "True History of Montoku," the 5th part of the *Rikoku-shi* "Six National Histories,*"* covering the years 850-858, the reign of the Emperor Montoku (827-858), in ten volumes.

In 880, when Yozei attained majority, Mototsuné created for himself the position of Kanpaku "Regent during the majority of the Emperor," which allowed him to rule right through Yozei's reign. Later that year he was also elevated to Daijo-daijin "Chancellor of the Realm."

In 884, the Emperor having become uncontrollable, and giving signs of insanity, Mototsuné deposed him, and wished to replace him by the son of the Emperor Junna (786-840), Tsunesada-shinno (825-884), but who declined. So he then chose the son of Ninmyo-tenno (810-850), Tokiyasu-shinno, 55 years old, who ascended as the Emperor

Fujiwara Mototsuné
藤原基経

Koko (830-887). After Koko's death, Mototsuné raised his son Imperial Prince Sadami to the Chrysanthemum Throne as the new Emperor Uda (867-931), and continued to govern in his name.

In 890 Mototsuné retired, and died the following year at the age of 56.

Mototsuné was married to Princess Soshi, daughter of the Imperial Prince Saneyasu, son of Emperor Ninmyo. The couple had three sons, and four daughters. Two of his sons eventually became sadaijin "senior minister of state," and the other made Daijo-daijin, Sessho, and Kanpaku. His daughters all became consorts to Emperors: two to the Emperor Seiwa, one to the Emperor Uda, and their youngest daughter Onshi (885-954) to the Emperor Daigo (885-930), and was the mother of the Emperors Suzaku (923-952) and Murakami (926-967).

Mototsuné was also married to a daughter of Imperial Prince Tadara, who was a son of the Emperor Saga (809-823). That coupling produced two sons and three daughters, one of whom, Kamiko (-898), was a consort to the Emperor Koko (830-887).

He is often designated as Horikawa-daijin, as well as Shosen Ko.

Fujiwara Sugané (856-908)

Son of Yoshitoshi. He became shikibu-sho-suké "minister of ceremonies."

Sugané took part in the accusations of Fujiwara Tokihira, etc., against Sugawara Michizané (845-903), and was nominated sangi "Imperial advisor."

Fujiwara Yamakagé (824-888)

Son of Takafusa. He was chunagon "middle counselor," and minbu-kyo "minister of the interior."

Fujiwara Yasunori (825-895)

Son of Sadao. He was of the Fujiwara Nan-ké "southern branch." He was sangi "Imperial advisor," and minbu-kyo "minister of the interior."

In 855 Yasunori was appointed to a minor office in the jibu-sho "ministry of ceremonies." He held various minor offices in the minbu-sho "ministry of taxation," the hyobu-sho "ministry of war," and the shikibu-sho "ministry of civil services." In 860 he was appointed hyobu-no-dai-jo "senior staff officer of the ministry of war."

Heian Period – Fujiwara

In 866 Yasunori was appointed kokushi "governor" of Bitchu, where he improved government through a policy of promoting agriculture. He then left for Bizen, where he enjoyed great popularity for his competence in government.

In 876 Yasunori returned to Kyoto, and was appointed emon-no-suké "lieutenant of the Imperial guard," kebiishi "chief of police," and minbu-daiyu "assistant secretary of taxation."

In 878, when the Emishi of Dewa took up arms in the Gangyo Rebellion, and burnt Akita Castle, Yasunori was appointed kokushi "governor" of the province. When he arrived at his new post, he deployed soldiers, and distributed the reserve of government rice to the people. When the Emishi heard about Yasunori's good governance, they gave in without further resistance. When the Court ordered Yasunori to suppress the rebellion completely, he advised against it, and the insurrection ended without the use of force.

In 882 Yasunori was appointed kokushi of Sanuki. Afterwards he returned to Kyoto, and was promoted to minbu-kyo "minister of taxation."

In 887, having been appointed Dazai-daini "military governor of Kyushu," Yasunori feigned ill-health in order not to be obliged to go to Tsukushi (Chikuzen and Chikugo).

At the age of 70, feeling the end was near, he went to Mount Hiei (northeast of Kyoto), and died while chanting to Buddha.

Fujiwara Tokihira (871-909)

Eldest son of Mototsuné. He was successively: in 892 kebiishi "chief of police," in 897 dainagon "major counselor," and finally sadaijin "senior minister of state."

In 900, jealous of the increasing influence acquired by Sugawara Michizané (845-903), Tokihira, in concert with Minamoto Hikaru (845-913), Fujiwara Sugané, etc., accused him of plotting to dethrone the Emperor Daigo (885-930) in order to replace him by the Emperor's half-brother Tokiyo-shinno (886-927), who was Michizané's son-in-law. The Emperor, then only 17 years old, gave credit to the calumny, and in 901 Michizané was banished to Tsukushi (Chikuzen and Chikugo) with the title of Dazai-no-gon-no-sotsu "military governor of Kyushu." Tokihira then governed according to his pleasure as Kanpaku.

Also in 901 Tokihira, with Okura Yoshiyuki, presided at the redaction of the *Sandai Jitsuroku* "History of Three Reigns," part six of the *Rikkoku-shi* "Six National Histories" covering the years 858-887, the reigns of the Emperors Seiwa (850-880), Yozei (869-949), and Koko (830-887), in 50 volumes.

In 905 Daigo ordered the compilation of the *Engi-shiki*, a new set of laws. Tokihira began the task, but died before its completion, and it was eventually completed by his brother Tadahira in 927.

His nickname is Hon'in-daijin.

Fujiwara Nakahira (875-945)

Son of Motosuné, and brother to Tokihira. He was sadaijin "senior minister of state" during the reigns of the Emperors Daigo (885-930) and Suzaku (923-952). He is also known as Biwa-no-daijin.

Fujiwara Tadahira (880-949)

4th son of Mototsuné. He was married to Minamoto Junshi, daughter of the Emperor Koko (830-887), with whom he had a son, Saneyori. He was also married to Minamoto Shoshi, daughter of Minamoto Yoshiari (845-897). The couple had several children. He also had two daughters of unknown maternal parentage who became Imperial consorts. Through his younger sister Onshi (885-954) he was uncle to the Emperors Suzaku (923-952) and Murakami (926-967).

In 909 Tadahira took over as head of the Fujiwara when his elder brother Tokihira died.

Tadahira continued the compilation of the *Engi-shiki*, a compilation of a new

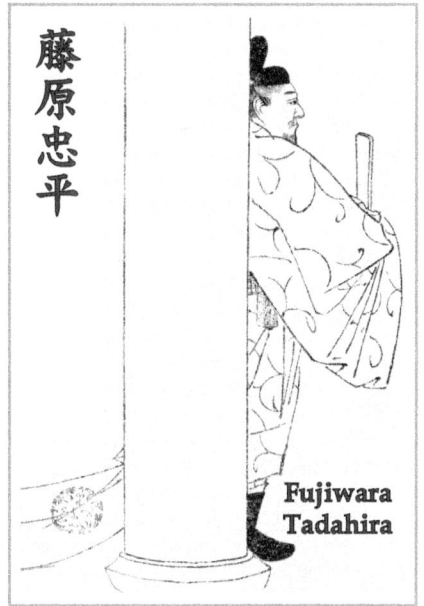

set of laws, which had been begun by Tokihira, and in 927 published it in 50 volumes.

In 924 Tadahira became sadaijin "senior minister of state."

In 931 Tadahira was made Sessho "Regent" at the accession of the Suzaku-tenno (923-952), in 936 Daijo-daijin "Chancellor of the Realm," and in 941 Kanpaku "Regent during the majority."

Towards the end of his life, Tadahira being Daijo-daijin, his eldest son Saneyori became sadaijin "minister of the left," and his 2nd son Morosuké became udaijin "minister of the right"; thus the San-ko "Three Great Ministers" were under his control.

Tadahira is also known by the names Teishin-ko and Ko-Ichijo-Daijo-daijin. He was known for his good nature and industriousness.

Fujiwara Arihira (892-970)

Grandson of Yamakagé, and adopted by Ariyori. He was a celebrated man of letters. He was first udaijin "junior minister of state," and afterwards sadaijin "senior minister of state." He is also known as Awada-no-sadaijin.

Fujiwara Tadabumi (873-947)

Son of Tsuneyoshi.

In 940 Tadabumi was appointed Sei-i-tai-shogun "Commander-in-Chief" sent against Taira Masakado (-940) who had revolted, and who he promptly suppressed. He was also chosen to reduce Fujiwara Sumitomo (-941) in Tsukushi (Chikuzen and Chikugo), but before he arrived the rebellion was at

Heian Period – Fujiwara

Fujiwara Tadabumi

an end. He was then appointed minbu-kyo "minister of taxation" and Kii no kami. He is also known as Uji-no-minbu-kyo.

Fujiwara Hidesato (10th century)

Son of Murao, who was a descendant of Fujiwara Uona.

In 939 Hidesato was governor of Shimotsuké when Taira Masakado (-940) revolted. Uniting his forces with those of Taira Sadamori, governor of Hitachi, he marched against the rebel. At Kushima (Shimosa), Masakado, having been wounded, fell from his horse, and Hidesato beheaded him with his own hand. His prayer for success before the battle is commemorated annually in the Kachiya Festival held at the Katori Shrine (Edo), where he had offered his bow and arrow after his victory. Afterwards he was appointed Chinjufu-shogun "Defender of the North," Musashi no kami, Shimotsuké no kami, etc.

Hidesato is famous for his military exploits and courage, and is the subject of many legends. He is regarded as the ancestor of the Oshu Fujiwara of Mutsu (see Hidehira, Yasuhira), as well as the Yamanouchi of Tosa, the Yuki of Shimosa and Shirakawa, the Ryuzoji of northern Kyushu, the Naito of Mikawa, the Matsuda of Bizen, the Oyama and Shimokobé of Satsuma, etc.

Fujiwara Akitada (898-965)

Son of Tokihira. He was sangi "Imperial advisor," and in 960 udaijin "junior minister of state." He is also known as Tomikoji-udaijin.

Fujiwara Atsutada (906-943)

Son of Tokihira. He was gon-chunagon "vice middle counselor."

Atsutada is especially celebrated as a poet. He is designated a member of the Sanjuroku-kasen "36 Immortal Poets" and one of his poems is included in the famous *Hyakunin-isshu* "Anthology of 100 Poets." Many of his poem written in correspondence with Court women are extant, and some are included in official poetry anthologies such as the *Gozen Wakashu* "Later Imperial Collection of Poetry."

He is also known as Hon'in-chunagon and Biwa-chunagon.

Fujiwara Saneyori (900-970)

Eldest son of Tadahira. After having been udaijin "junior minister of state," sadaijin "senior minister of state," Daijo-daijin "Chancellor of the Realm," in 967 he became Kanpaku "Regent" when Emperor Reizei (950-1011) assumed the throne, then in 960 Sessho "Regent to the Child Emperor" at the accession of En'yu-tenno (959-991). He is also known as Ono-miya-dono.

Fujiwara Morosuké (908-960)

Son of Tadahira. In 947 he became udaijin "junior minister of state."

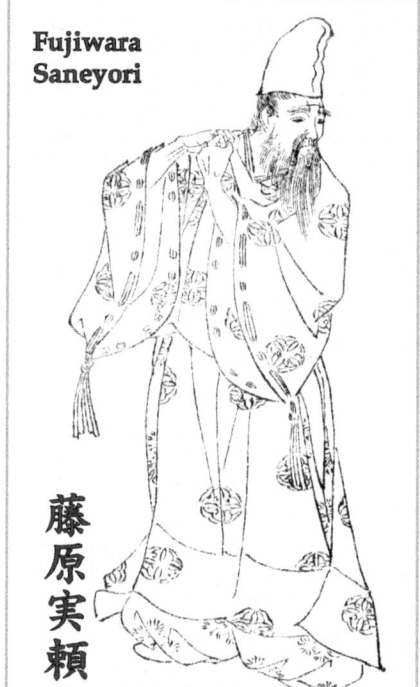
Fujiwara Saneyori

Fujiwara Hidesato

Fujiwara Atsutada

Fujiwara Morosuké

Morosuké wrote the *Kujo Nenju Gyoji*, a manual on official ceremonies.

He is also known as Kujo-dono and Hojo-udaijin.

Fujiwara Yoritada (924-989)

2nd son of Saneyori. His mother was a daughter of Fujiwara Tokihira.

In 971 Yoritada became udaijin "junior minister of state," and in 973 succeeded Koredata in the functions of Sessho "Regent to the Child Emperor" for the Emperor En'yu (959-991), and in 977 succeeded his cousin Kanemichi, who was in critical condition, as Kanpaku "Regent," which lasted until 986, through the reign of the Emperor Kazan (968-1008). In 977 he became sadaijin "sernior minister of state," and in 978 Daijo-daijin "Chancellor of the Realm," which title he held until his death.

Yoritada's two daughters were consorts of En'yu and Kazan, but they did not produce any sons.

After his death, he received the title of Suruga-ko, but he is better known by the name of Sanjo-daijin, and also as Rengi-ko.

Fujiwara Koretada (924-972)

Son of Morosuké. In 970 Koretada became udaijin "junior minister of state," and later that year, upon the death of his uncle Saneyori, he took over as head of the family. In 971 became Sessho "Regent to the Child Emperor" of Emperor En'yu (959-991), a title which he held until his death. From 971-972 he was also Daijo-daijin "Chancellor of the Realm."

Koretada is usually credited with solidifying the dominance of the Fujiwara in the Imperial Court.

He received the title of Mikawa-ko, and is also called Ichijo-Sessho.

Fujiwara Kanemichi (925-977)

2nd son of Morosuké.

In 972, at the death of his brother Koretada, Kanemichi succeeded him as Sessho "Regent to the Child Emperor" during the reign of his son-in-law Emperor En'yu (959-991), and in 974 was made Kanpaku "Regent" and Daijo-daijin "Chancellor of the Realm." In 976, when a fire destroyed the Imperial Palace, the Emperor retired to the residence of Kanemichi, his father-in-law, for more than a year.

To foil his rival younger brother Fujiwara Kaneié, Morosuké had his cousin Yoritada appointed Kanpaku when he died at the age of 51.

After his death, Kanemichi received the title of Totomi-ko. He is also called Horikawa-dono.

Fujiwara Kaneié (929-999)

3rd son of Morosuké. His mother was Moriko, daughter of Fujiwara Tsunekuni.

In 967 Kaneié was raised to the dignity of chunagon "middle counselor," then in 972 to that of gon-no-dainagon "deputy major counselor" before his brother Kanemichi, which fact excited the latter's jealousy, and was the cause of the two brother's rivalry.

In 978, after Kanemichi's death, Kaneié was made udaijin "junior minister of state." In 986, at the accession of his grandson Ichijo-tenno (980-1011), Kaneié became his Sessho "Regent to the Child Emperor." In 989, Yoritada having died, he succeeded him as Daijo-daijin "Chancellor of the Realm," and in 990 was made Kanpaku "Regent" when the Emperor attained majority.

After Kaneié's death, his house was changed into a temple under the name of Hoko-in, and Kaneié himself was called Hoko-in-daijin. He is also called Higashi-sanjo-dono by his residence.

Kaneié was married to Toki-himé, daughter of Fujiwara Nakamasa. They had five children: Michikawa, Sessho and Kanpaku to the Emperor Ichijo; Choi, consort of the Emperor Reizei (950-1011), and mother of the Emperor Sanjo (976-1017); Michikané, Kanpaku of the Emperor Ichijo; Senshi, consort of the Emperor En'yu (959-991), and mother of the Emperor Ichijo; and Michinaga, Kanpaku to the Emperor Go-Ichijo (1006-1036). He was also married to a daughter of Fujiwara Tomoyasu, who is only known by the title of Michitsuna no Haha "Mother of Michitsuna," and is the author of *Kagero Nikki* "*The Gossamer Years*," a piece of Japanese literature in the form of a diary that uses a combination of prose and waka poetry to convey the life of a Court woman during the Heian "Aristocratic" Period (794-1185). Their son Michitsuna was dainagon "major counselor."

Fujiwara Kinsué (957-1029)

5th son of Morosuké. His mother was the Imperial Princess Koshi (919-957), daughter of the Emperor Daigo (885-930). She died in Kinsué's childhood, and was brought up by his sister the Empress Anshi (927-964), consort of the Emperor Murakami (926-967), at the Imperial Palace in Kyoto.

Kinsué married a daughter of the Imperial Prince Ariakira. They had three children, one of whom, Gishi (974-1053) married the Emperor Ichijo (980-1011).

Like his brothers, Kinsué was successively: in 1017 udaijin "junior minister of state," sadaijin "senior minister of state," and in 1021 Daijo-daijin "Chancellor of the Realm."

After his death he received the title of Kai-ko. He was also referred to as Jingiko.

Kinsué is the progenitor of the Kan'in family, which later divided into the families Sanjo, Saionji, Tokudaiji, To'in, etc.

Fujiwara Sanesuké (957-1046)

4th son of Yoritada, became the adopted heir of his grandfather Saneyori, the head of the Ononomiya family, from which he inherited a vast estate.

In 1021 Sanesuké became udaijin "junior minister of state."

Sanesuké is mentioned in the *Diary of Murasaki Shikibu*, author of the *Genji Monogatari*, in which she praises him for being out of the ordinary, and describes in detail a number of occasions of his superstitious behavior. In the *Diary*, Sanesuké is described as having summoned exorcists on a number of occasions, and employed children in the beating of gongs to cure him of illness and nightmares.

Sanesuké was married to a daughter of Minamoto Koremasa, descendant of the Emperor Montoku (827-858), and

Fujiwara Kaneié

Heian Period – Fujiwara

Fujiwara Sanesuké

was also married to the Princess Enshi, daughter of the Imperial Prince Tamehira, who was a consort of the Emperor Kazan (968-1008), and married Sanesuké after the Emperor became a priest. These two marriages did not produce children, so he adopted two sons of his elder brother Kanehira: Sukehira (986-1068), who became heir of the Ononomiya, and Sukeyori; but he did have two biological children from maids later in life.

As he had a thorough knowledge of customs and rites, he was called Kenjin-ufu "Wise udaijin." He wrote the diary *Shoyu-ki* for fifty years. He died when 90 years old, and is known by the name of Go-Ononomiya.

Fujiwara Kinto (966-1041)

Son of Yoritada. He became a famous poet, calligrapher, and musician admired by his contemporaries. He is cited in works by Murasaki Shikibu (937-1014), Sei Shonagaon (966-1017), and a number of other major chronicles.

Over the course of his life, Kinto published a great many poems, as well as many poetry anthologies including the twenty-volume *Shui wakashu* "Collection of Gleanings," compiled between 1005 and 1007, and the two-book *Wakan roéishu* "Collection of Japanese and Chinese Poems for Singing," complied around 1013. He also established the Sanju-roku-kasen "36 Immortal Poets" of the Nara, Asuka, and Heian Periods of Japanese history.

Fujiwara Kinto

Kinto is also noted for his dissertations on poetry. When he criticized one of the poems by Fujiwara Nagayoshi (949-), the latter became ill and died.

Kinto is also called Shijo-dainagon. As he was nagon "counselor" at the same time as other great poets Minamoto Tsunenobu (1016-1097), Minamoto Toshikata (960-1027), and Fujiwara Yukinari (972-1027), the name Shi-nagon "Four Counselors" was given to the group.

Fujiwara Sukemasa (944-998)

Son of Yoritada. He was renowned as a calligrapher, and is honored as one of the San-seki "Three Traces," a group of three famous calligraphers of the Heian "Aristocratic" Period (794-1185).

Sukemasa was Dazai-daini "military governor of Kyushu," and afterwards usa-jinshin.

He is also known as Saseki for one of the kanji characters in his name.

Fujiwara Korenari (953-989)

Eldest son of Koretada. He was in the service of the Emperor Kazan (968-1008), and in 986 became a bonze with him at the Kazan-ji (Kyoto).

Fujiwara Yoshikané (957-1008)

2nd son of Koretada. He was a Courtier and a faithful servant to the Emperor Kazan (968-1008).

Yoshikané prevented the Emperor Kazan from committing suicide following the death of his much beloved wife Tsunéko.

In 986 Yoshikané became a bonze together with the Emperor Kazan and his elder brother Korenari.

Fujiwara Sukemasa

Fujiwara Akimitsu (944-1021)

Son of Kanemichi. He rose to the rank of sadaijin "senior minister of state."

Akimitsu's daughter Enshi was married to the Imperial Prince Atsuakira (994-1051), a son of the Emperor Sanjo (976-1017). When Atsuakira married a daughter of Fujiwara Michinaga (966-1028) as a 2nd wife, Enshi, out of spite, returned to her father, who, struck with consternation, suddenly turned grey. His daughter having died of grief soon after, Akimitsu applied to the bonze Doman to throw a spell over Michinaga. The people gave him the surname of Akuryo-safu "sadaijin with evil spirits."

Fujiwara Sumitomo (-941)

Son of Dazai-shoni "governor of Kyushu" Nagazumi.

In 939, after a secret understanding with Taira Masakado (-940), while the latter revolted in Shimosa, Sumitomo started from Iyo and invaded Harima, Bizen, and the whole San'yodo region. The Emperor Suzaku (923-952) sent Ono Yoshifuru and Minamoto Tsunemoto (894-961) against him. Sumitomo retired to Dazaifu (Kyushu), and was defeated at Hakata (Chikuzen). In 941 he fled to Iyo, where he was arrested, and put to death by Tachibana Toyasu. His head was sent to Kyoto.

Sumitomo is the ancestor of the Arima of Hizen.

Fujiwara Michitaka (953-995)

Eldest son of Kaneié. He was married to Takako, daughter of Takashina Naritada, with whom he had three sons and four daughters.

In 968 Michitaka was chunagon "middle counselor," then gon-no-dainagon "deputy grand counselor," and in 989 naidaijin "inner minister."

In 990 Michitaka succeeded his father as Sessho "Regent to the Child Emperor" for the Emperor Ichijo (980-

Fujiwara Michitaka

1011). In 993, the Emperor having performed the ceremony of the genbuku, Michitaka took the title of Kanpaku "Regent," and had Ichijo marry his eldest daughter Teishi (977-1001).

Michitaka is also called Nijo-Kanpaku and Naka-no-Kanpaku.

Fujiwara Michikané (955-995)

2nd son of Kaneié. He was a bonze at the Kazan-in when his nephew ascended the Chrysanthemum Throne as the Emperor Ichijo (980-1011). He then resumed secular life, in 994 became udaijin "junior minister of state," and the following year succeeded his brother Michitaka as Kanpaku "Regent." He died one week later.

The people called him Nanuka-no-Kanpaku "Seven-day Regent." He was replaced by his brother Michinaga: thus the three brothers, Michitaka, Michikané, and Michinaga, succeeded one another in the dignity of Kanpaku; for that reason they are called the San-michi "The Three Michi," from the first character of their names.

The Rusu, who later assumed the Daté surname in the Edo "Tokugawa" Period (1603-1868), and for a short time ruled Mizusawa, a sub-domain of Sendai (Mutsu), claimed descent from Michikané.

Fujiwara Michinaga (966-1028)

5th and youngest son of Kaneié. His mother was Toki-himé, daughter of Fujiwara Nakamasa. Among his siblings by the same mother were two Regents and two Imperial consorts. He was married to Rinshi (964-1053), daughter of sadaijin "senior minister of state" Minamoto Masanobu (920-993), with whom he had six children. He was also married to Meishi, daughter of sadaijin Minamoto Takaakira, with whom he also had six children.

In 986 Michinaga was sakyo-no-daibu, and gon-no-chunagon "deputy middle counselor." In 991 he was gon-no-dainagon "deputy grand counselor."

In 995, during the reign of Emperor Ichijo (980-1011), Michinaga's two elder brothers Michitaka and Michikané died of disease. He struggled with his nephew Fujiwara Korechika, the eldest son of Michitaka, for political power. With support of Senshi (962-1002), his sister and mother of Ichijo, Michinaga succeeded in gaining power as well as the support of majority of the Court. He was appointed nairan "Imperial inspector of documents," reviewed all documents before the Emperor himself read them, and brought the power of the Fujiwara to its zenith.

Also in 995 Michinaga became udaijin "junior minister of state," and the following year sadaijin "senior minister of state."

Though Ichijo already had an Empress, Teishi (977-1001), eldest daughter of Michitaka, Michinaga claimed there were two types of Empresshood and therefore it was legal for an Emperor to have two Empresses at the same time. Michinaga's ambitions led him to make his own daughter, Shoshi (988-1074), a 2nd Empress of Ichijo. In 1000 she was announced as a Chugu Empress, and Teishi was given the title of Kogo Empress. It was the first time an Emperor had two Empresses. A power struggle between Korechika and Michinaga was cut short with Teishi's unexpected death the following year. Shoshi would go on to become the mother of the Emperors Go-Ichijo (1006-1036) and Go-Suzaku (1009-1045).

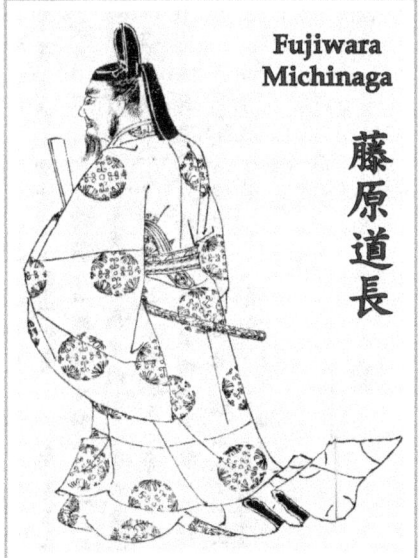
Fujiwara Michinaga

In 1006, Michinaga invited Murasaki Shikibu (973-1014) to become Shoshi's companion and tutor. It is said that he was the model for Lady Murasaki's title character in her novel *The Tale of Genji*.

In 1012, Ichijo having died, Michinaga raised the 2nd son of the Emperor Reizei (950-1011) and half-brother to the Emperor Kazan (968-1008), to the Chrysanthemum Throne as the Emperor Sanjo (976-1017), and obliged him to marry his 2nd daughter Kenshi (994-1027) as Chugu Empress. In 1016 Sanjo, having become blind, abdicated, and Michinaga replaced him by his own grandson, then only 9 years old, as the new Emperor Go-Ichijo, with Michinaga appointed Sessho "Regent to the Child Emperor." Moreover, he caused Atsunaga-shinno, his other grandson, to be declared Taishi "Crown Prince," who in 1036 ascended as the Emperor Go-Suzaku (1009-1045). Michinaga now exerted *de facto* reign over Japan.

In 1017 Michinaga gave the post of Sessho to his son Yorimichi, and received the title of Daijo-daijin "Chancellor of the Realm." The following year, having secured the welfare of his family, Michinaga became bonze at the Todai-ji (Kyoto).

In 1020 Michinaga commenced the erection of the Hojo-ji (Kyoto). For the 1022 dedication of its Golden Hall, attending were: the Emperor Go-Ichijo, who personally assisted at the ceremony; the three daughters of Michinaga, two ex-Empresses and one reigning Empress; his uncle Daijo-daijin Kinsué; his sons Kanpaku Yorimichi and naidaijin Norimichi; as well as the whole Imperial Court. According to the *Eiga Monogatari*, an epic tale written by Akazomé Emon that celebrates the life of Michinaga, the Golden Hall's pillars rested on masonry supports in the shape of elephants, the roof tiles and doors were gilded and silvered, and the foundations were of rock crystal. The interior of the hall was decorated lavishly with gold, silver, lapis lazuli, and jewels of all kinds, as well as a series of images detailing the life of the historical Buddha (563 B.C.-483 B.C.), and a central image of the Vairocana Buddha. In 1053 the temple was destroyed by fire, and not rebuilt.

Heian Period – Fujiwara

After this triumphant day, trials began for Michinaga. He lost two of his daughters successively: in 1025 Yoshiko, the wife of the Crown Prince Atsunaga (later the Emperor Go-Suzaku), and in 1027 Kenshi, the widow of the Emperor Sanjo. He himself fell ill, and the following year, notwithstanding the prayers ordered by the Empresses in all the great temples, died at the age of 62.

For thirty years Michinaga had governed the country: three Emperors were his sons-in-law, four his grandsons. After his death, he was called Hojo-ji no Kanpaku.

He is also known under the name of his residence, Mido, as the Mido-Kanpaku, so he called his diary *Mido-Kanpaku-ki*, which is a prime source for information about life at the Imperial Court during the height of the Heian "Aristocratic" Period (974-1185).

Fujiwara Tadanobu (967-1035)

Son of Tanemitsu. He was renowned as a man of letters and poet. He was dainagon "major counselor."

Fujiwara Sadayori (995-1045)

Son of Kinto. He was dainagon "major counselor," hyobu-kyo "minister of war," and renowned as a poet.

Fujiwara Korechika (974-1010)

2nd son of Michitaka. His mother was Takashina Takako, also known as Ko-no-Naishi. He was married to a daughter of gon-no-dainagon "deputy grand counselor" Minamoto Shigemitsu, with whom he had three children.

In 991 Korechika was named sangi "Imperial advisor," in 992 gon-no-chunagon "deputy middle counselor," then gon-no-dainagon "deputy grand counselor," and in 994 naidaijin "middle counselor" when only 20 years old.

In 995, at the death of his father, Korechika expected to succeed him in the dignity of Kanpaku, but his uncle Michikané supplanted him. To avenge himself, Korechika, following the custom of his time, had recourse to magic, and by that or by something else, Michikané died some days afterwards. He was however disappointed a second time, for the title of Kanpaku was given instead to his other uncle Michinaga.

In 996 Korechika become a rival of the ex-Emperor Kazan (968-1008) in a love affair, and wounded him in the side with an arrow. For that, and for performing an esoteric Shingon ceremony known as Taigen-no-ho, which was reserved solely for the Emperor, he and his younger brother Takaié was exiled to Dazaifu (Kyushu).

In 999 Korechika was pardoned, and permitted to return to Heian-kyo (Kyoto), when his sister Teishi (977-1001) bore a son, Imperial Prince Atsuyasu (999-1019), to the Emperor Ichijo (980-1011). He subsequently became jun-daijin "associate minister."

Korechika is also called Gido-sanshi or Sotsu-no-naidaijin.

Fujiwara Takaié (979-1044)

Another son of Michitaka. At the age of 18, he was chunagon "middle counselor" and Izumo no kami, and afterwards hyobu-kyo "minister of war."

In 1019 Takaié, as governor of Dazaifu (Kyushu), led an expedition against the Toi Invasion of northern Kyushu to deliver Iki and Tsushima from Jurchen pirates who often attacked those islands.

Fujiwara Yorimichi (992-1074)

Eldest son of Michinaga. In 1009 he married Taka-himé, a granddaughter of the Emperor Murakami (926-967). He was also married to Gishi (-1053), a daughter of Fujiwara Yorinari, and niece of Taka-himé.

In 1016, at the accession of the Emperor Go-Ichijo (1006-1036), Yorimichi was made naidaijin "middle counselor." In 1017 he succeeded his father to the position of Sessho "Regent to the Child Emperor," and in 1020 became Kanpaku "Regent," and governed the country for nearly fifty years. Like his father, he had his daughters married to Emperors: Genshi (1016-1039) to Go-Suzaku (1009-1045), and Kanshi (1036-1121) to Go-Reizei (1023-1068).

In 1053, at Uji (Kyoto), Yorimichi erected a splendid palace, the Byodo-in "Phoenix Hall," for himself, in which he entertained the Emperor Go-Reizei.

In 1068, with the ascension of the Emperor Go-Sanjo (1034-1073), Yorimichi resigned the office of Kanpaku in favor of his brother Norimichi, and retired to Uji, where he died at the age of 83. He is known by the name of Uji-dono.

With Yorimichi, the Fujiwara reached their highest degree of prosperity, but already signs of decline began to appear. The great military families of the Taira and the Minamoto were rising in power in the provinces, and it was evident that they would soon replace those in the government, who had learnt no other accomplishments but poetry, music, dancing, and the like.

Fujiwara Norimichi (996-1075)

5th son of Michinaga. His mother was Rinshi (964-1053), daughter of Minamoto Masanobu (920-993). His siblings by the same mother were: Kanpaku "Regent" Yorimichi; Shoshi (988-1074), consort to the Emperor Ichijo (980-1011); Kenshi (994-1027), consort to the Emperor Sanjo (976-1017); Ishi (999-1036), consort to the Emperor Go-Ichijo (1006-1036); and Kishi (1007-1025), consort of Crown Prince Atsunaga, who later ascended as the Emperor Go-Suzaku (1009-1045).

In 1012 Norimichi was married to a daughter of Fujiwara Kinto, by whom he had seven children, including Seishi (1014-1068), who in 1039 married the Emperor Go-Suzaku, and Kanshi (1021-1102), who married the Emperor Go-Reizei (1023-1068). In 1026 he was married to the Imperial Princess Shishi (1003-1048), daughter of the Emperor Sanjo, and in 1051 to the Princess Senshi (1005-1074), granddaughter of the Emperor Murakami (926-967), but neither produced children.

In 1068 Norimichi succeeded his brother Yorimichi in the functions of Kanpaku. But the Emperor Go-Sanjo

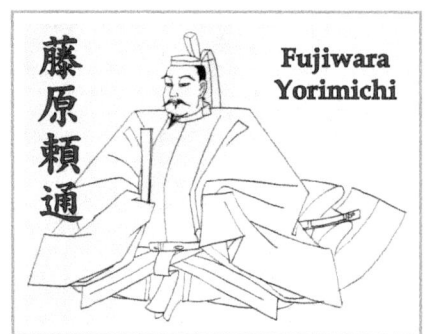
Fujiwara Yorimichi

Fujiwara Norimichi

(1034-1073), who had just ascended the throne, and was not a relative of the Fujiwara, was resolved to reign and govern, hence Norimichi could not exercise the functions of his charge. This contributed to the later decline of the clan.

In 1070 Norimichi became Daijo-daijin "Chancellor of the Realm."

The people gave him the name O-Nijo-dono.

Fujiwara Morozané (1042-1101)

3rd son of Yorimichi. His mother was Gishi (-1053), daughter of Fujiwara Yorinari. He married Reishi, who was a daughter of Minamoto Morofusa (1009-1077), a grandson of the Emperor Murakami (926-967). He had many sons and daughters, including Moromichi and Ietada.

Morozané made his adopted daughter Kenshi (1057-1084) the Chugu Empress of the Emperor Shirakawa (1053-1129). Although she died when very young, she left a son who would later ascend to the Chrysanthemum Throne as the Emperor Horikawa (1079-1107).

Morozané was appointed sadaijin "senior minister of state" by the Emperor Go-Reizei (1023-1068), but was excluded from public affairs by the Emperor Go-Sanjo (1034-1073) during the latter's reign from 1068-1073.

Morozané held the positions of Sessho "Regent to the Child Emperor" or Kanpaku "Regent" for a twenty-year period: from 1075-1086 Kanpaku during the reign of the Emperor Shirakawa (1053-1129), from 1086-1090 Sessho during the Emperor Horikawa's minority, and from 1090-1094 Kanpaku during the latter's majority. In 1094 Morozané transferred the dignity of Kanpaku to his son Moromichi, who in 1099 died without an heir.

Around 1083, during his reign, the Emperor Shirakawa seized political power, and Morozané was unable to enjoy the monopolistic power that his father and grandfather had enjoyed. Even after the Emperor Horikawa had reached adulthood, the cloistered Emperor Shirakawa governed with his betto "superintendents."

Morozané is known by the names Go-Uji-nyudo, Go-Uji-dono, Kyogoku-Kanpaku, and Kyogoku-dono. He is known as the author of the waka poetry collection *Kyogoku-Kanpaku-shu* "Anthology of Kyogoku Kanpaku," and has left memoirs bearing the title of *Kyogoku-Kanpaku-ki* "Diary of Kyogoku Kanpaku."

Fujiwara Moromichi (1062-1099)

Son of Morozané. In his youth, Moromichi studied literature under the direction of Oé Tadafusa.

In 1082 Moromichi became naidaijin "middle counselor."

In 1094 Moromichi succeeded his father as Kanpaku "Regent." Though he assisted the Emperor Horikawa (1079-1107) against the cloistered rule of the ex-Emperor Shirakawa (1053-1129), he died young at age of 38, which allowed Shirakawa to consolidate his power

Moromichi wa nicknamed Go-Nijodono and Go-Nijo-Kanpaku. He left memoirs bearing the title of *Go-Nijo-Kanpaku-ki* "Diary of Go-Nijo Kanpaku." Promoting letters and the military arts, he was respected by all, but a premature death did not allow him to realize all the good which might have been expected.

Fujiwara Mototoshi (1055-1138)

Son of Toshiié. He was renowned as a man of letters and a waka poet, and was the master to Fujiwara Toshinari.

In 1138 Mototoshi became a Buddhist monk.

Hundreds of his poems are in Imperial anthologies. Around 1010 he helped compile the anthology *Shinsen Roéi-shu*, a collection of Japanese and Chinese songs in verse.

Fujiwara Mototoshi

Fujiwara Kinzané (1053-1107)

Son of Sanesué. He was the ancestor of the Sanjo, the Tokudaiji, the Saionji, the Saga, the Kikutei, and other families.

Fujiwara Tametaka (1070-1130)

Son of Tamefusa. He was in the service of the Emperors Shirakawa (1053-1129), Horikawa (1079-1107), and Toba (1103-1156). Tametaka was sangi "Imperial advisor" and sadaiben "senior controller."

Tametaka left memoirs bearing the title of *Eisho-ki* "Diary of the Eisho Era," covering the years 1105-1129. He is the ancestor of the Bojo, the Honomi, and the Hozumi.

Fujiwara Tadazané (1078-1162)

Son of Moromichi. He was the father of Tadamichi.

In 1105 Tadazané was Kanpaku "Regent" for the Emperor Horikawa (1079-1107). In 1107, at the accession of the Emperor Toba (1103-1156), he was Sessho "Regent to the Child Emperor," then in 1113 Kanpaku on the latter attaining majority. From 1112-1113 he was also Daijo-daijin "Chancellor of the Realm."

In consequence of his disputes with the ex-Emperor Shirakawa (1053-1129), Tadazané retired to Uji (Kyoto), but in 1129, when the ex-Emperor Toba, his son-in-law, took the reins of government, he was recalled. Later he had his hair shaved, and established himself again at Uji, where he died.

Tadazané is known by the name Fuké-dono for the villa he built in 1114 at Fuké (Kyoto), north of the Byodo-in.

Fujiwara Koremichi (1093-1165)

Son of Munemichi. He was a favorite of the Emperor Sutoku (1119-1164), who successively appointed him in 1156 udaijin "junior minister of state," and in 1157 sadaijin "senior minister of state."

In 1160, after the death of Fujiwara Nobuyori, who had revolted, Koremichi became Daijo-daijin "Chancellor of the Realm."

Koremichi wrote a critique of the policies of Emperor Nijo (1143-1165) in a book called *Taikai Hisho*.

Heian Period – Fujiwara

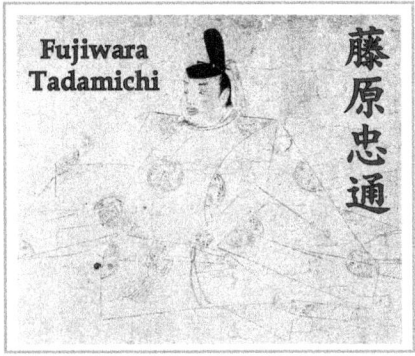

Fujiwara Tadamichi (1097-1164)

Eldest son of Tadazané.

In 1121 Tadamichi succeeded his father as Kanpaku "Regent" to the Emperor Toba (1103-1156). In 1123 he became Sessho "Regent to the Child Emperor" at the accession of the Sutoku-tenno (1119-1164), and in 1129 Kanpaku at the latter's majority.

In 1129 Tadamichi was Daijo-daijin "Chancellor of the Realm," and also from 1149-1150.

In 1130 Sutoku married Tadamichi's daughter Masako. But the ex-Emperor Toba recalled Tadazané from Uji (Kyoto), and Tadamichi was obliged to yield the title of Kanpaku to his father. In 1140, however, Tadamichi re-assumed the title when his father definitively retired from public life.

In 1141 Tadamichi was again Sessho at the accession of the Emperor Konoé (1139-1155), and in 1150 Kanpaku at his maturity. In 1155 he remained Kanpaku when Go-Shirakawa (1129-1192) became the Emperor.

During the 1156 Hogen Rebellion (Kyoto), Tadamichi sided with the victorious Go-Shirakawa.

In 1148, being a fervent Buddhist, on the site of one of the former palaces of the Emperor Shirakawa (1053-1129), Tadamichi founded the Hossho-ji (Kyoto), hence the name Hossho-ji-Kanpaku by which he is known, and the title *Hossho-ji-Kanpaku-ki* "*Diary of the Hossho-ji Kanpaku*" given to his memoirs.

Tadamichi had five sons: Motozané, Motofusa, Kanezané, Kanéusa, and Jien, who became a Buddhist monk. He had daughters Masako and Seishi; plus two that he had adopted, Ikushi and Teishi, who married Emperors, the latter to the Konoé-tenno.

Fujiwara Yorinaga (1120-1156)

Son of Tadazané. He was a scholar who kept a detailed diary called *Dai-ki* that described his studies in Indian logic and other foreign studies.

Yorinaga was successively dainagon "grand counselor," ukon'é-taisho "junior commander of the Imperial Guard," naidaijin "minister of the center," sakon'é-taisho "senior commander of the Imperial Guard," and sadaijin "senior minister of state." For the latter he was also called Uji-no-sadaijin.

In 1150, when the Emperor Konoé (1139-1155) had performed the genbuku, Yorinaga married to him his adopted daughter Masuko (1140-1201). But soon afterwards, the Emperor having also married Teishi, an adopted daughter of Tadamichi, there was disunion between the two brothers. This feud was aggravated by the fact that their father Tadazané showed preference for Yorinaga, and tried to raise him above his eldest son Tadamichi.

Yorinaga advocated the restoration of the once-powerful Fujiwara Regency, and was a dogmatic activist who displayed a great deal of courage in his actions. He made many enemies when he disapproved of the current Emperor Konoé and his cloistered puppet master Toba (1103-1156).

After the death of Konoé in 1155, Tadamichi wished to have the Imperial Prince Masahito, a son of Toba, elected. Yorinaga tried to place the ex-Emperor Sutoku (1119-1164) on the throne again, but Masahito was elected as the Emperor Go-Shirakawa (1129-1192). Furthermore Yorinaga was deprived of his charge of nairan "Imperial inspector of documents," and was refused the position of "tutor to the Crown Prince" despite his qualifications.

After these insults, Yorinaga tried to levy troops in the neighboring provinces of Kyoto to raise a revolt in the capital, but was able to gather only a few hundred soldiers. Each rival side beckoned the Minamoto and Taira clans of samurai. The head of the Minamoto, Tameyoshi (1096-1156), his 8th son Tametomo (1139-1170), and Taira Tadamasa sided with Sutoku and Yorinaga, while on the other hand the eldest son of Tameyoshi, Minamoto Yoshitomo (1123-1160), and Taira Kiyomori (1118-1181), head of the Taira

family and nephew of Taira Tadamasa, sided with Go-Shirakawa and Tadamichi.

In 1156 the fighting, known as the Hogen Rebellion, erupted in Kyoto. At night, Minamoto Yoshitomo and Taira Kiyomori, leading their cavalry, attacked Sutoku's palace, which was set aflame. The defenders fled, leaving Go-Shirakawa's allies victorious. Yorinaga was killed by an arrow during the battle, and his three sons were exiled. Both Minamoto Tameyoshi and Taira Tadamasa were executed. Minamoto Tametomo was forced to flee, and was banished to O-shima in the Izu Islands. Sutoku was banished to Sanuki (Shikoku). The Minamoto and the Taira succeeded in establishing the two warrior clans as the new major political powers in Kyoto.

Yorinaga's death symbolized the beginning of the growth of the warrior class and a war-like state that would exist within Japan for nearly 450 years, until the end of the 16th century.

Fujiwara Nobuyori (1133-1159)

Descendant of Michitaka, son of Tadataka.

Being favored by the cloistered Emperor Go-Shirakawa (1129-1192), Nobuyori was appointed kebiishi-betto "superintendent of police." He applied for a higher position, but the ex-Emperor, guided by the counsel of Fujiwara Michinori, refused to comply.

A dispute arose between the followers of the reigning Emperor Nijo (1139-1155) and those who favored the retired Go-Shirakawa. Fujiwara Michinori and the Taira clan supported Nijo, and Nobuyori and his Minamoto allies supported Go-Shirakawa's bid to retain some influence and power.

In 1160, however, when the head of the Taira, Kiyomori (1118-1181), left Kyoto for a time, Nobuyori united with

Minamoto Yoshitomo (1123-1160) against Go-Shirakawa and the Taira, and the civil war known as the Heiji Rebellion ensued. The insurgents began by burning the Sanjo Palace, abducting the Joko "retired Emperor" Go-Shirakawa, and held him and the Nijo-tenno at the Great Palace as hostages. They then moved on to the home of chief counselor Fujiwara Michinori, killing everyone there; Michinori escaped, only to be captured soon afterwards, and decapitated. Nobuyori then had Nijo, under duress, appoint him Daijo-daijin "Chancellor of the Realm." Though he still had enemies at the Court, who encouraged the Emperor to resist and to escape, overall Nobuyori's plan had succeeded.

Meanwhile Kiyomori, having been appraised of the events which had taken place in Kyoto, returned in great haste, and sent his son Taira Shigemori (1138-1197) to fight the rebels. Yoshitomo defended himself bravely, but his forces were not sufficiently prepared to defend the city, and they were defeated. The Emperor and the ex-Emperor were both freed. Nobuyori fled to Owari, but was captured and beheaded.

Fujiwara Michinori (-1159)

Son of Sanekané. He was in the service of the Emperors Toba (1103-1156), Sutoku (1119-1164), Konoé (1139-1155), and Nijo (1143-1165), and was made Hyuga no kami and shonagon "minor counselor." His wife had been nurse to the Emperor Go-Shirakawa (1127-1192), who kept no secrets from her and did nothing without her advice.

In 1145 Michinori had his hair shaved and took the name of Shinzei.

After the 1156 Hogen Rebellion (Kyoto), Michinari obtained the pardon of Fujiwara Tadazané, but that influence brought upon him the hatred of Fujiwara Nobuyori and Minamoto Yoshitomo (1123-1160), who in 1160, at the time of the Heiji Rebellion (Kyoto), tried to dispose of him. Michinori's ally Taira Kiyomori (1118-1181) had left the capital, so he fled to Nara and hid himself in a cavern, but was discovered and decapitated.

Michinori was a poet and a man of letters, and left several works. He compiled the Honcho Sei-ki "Chronicle of Imperial Reigns," an official history of Japan ordered by the ex-Emperor Toba, but it was never completed and covers only the years 935-1135.

Fujiwara Narichika (1138-1178)

Son of Ienari. He was sakon-é-chujo "senior officer of the Imperial Guard."

During the 1160 Heiji Rebellion (Kyoto), Narichika sided with Fujiwara Nobuyori, and was made prisoner by Taira Shigemori (1138-1179). Having been set free soon afterwards, he became sangi "Imperial advisor," chunagon "middle counselor," Owari no kami, and dainagon "grand counselor."

In 1177 Narichika applied for the dignity of sakon-é-taisho "senior commander of the Imperial Guard," but it was given instead to Taira Shigemori. Irritated by this, in what is known as the Shishi-ga-tani Incident, Narichika plotted against the Taira's dominance of the Imperial Court, but Minamoto Yukitsuna, one of the conspirators, revealed the plot to Taira Kiyomori (1118-1181). Narichika was exiled to Kikai-ga-shima (Satsuma), along with his son Naritsuné, Taira Yasuyori, and the monk Shunkan (1143-1179). Soon afterwards he was executed by the order of the Taira.

Fujiwara Naritsuné (-1202)

Son of Narichika. He was married to a niece of Taira Kiyomori (1118-1181). He was Tanba no kami.

In 1177 Naritsuné took part in the plot known as the Shishi-ga-tani Incident organized by his father against the Taira. When the conspiracy was discovered, he was exiled with his father to Kikai-ga-shima (Satsuma) along with Taira Yasuyori and the monk Shunkan (1143-1179).

During their time on the island, Naritsuné and Yasuyori became fervent adherents of the Kumano Shinto faith, regularly performing rituals and prayers for the kami "gods" of the Kumano Shrines.

Towards the end of the 9th lunar month of 1178, after roughly one year on the island, Naritsuné and Yasuyori received a pardon from the capital, on account of suffering experienced by the Empress being blamed on the angry spirit of the late Narichika. In the 3rd month of the following year, after visiting his father's grave, Naritsuné returned to Kyoto. He was then reunited with his young son, who had been 3 years old and another child, who had yet to be born, when he was exiled. Reinstated into the service of the retired Emperor Go-Shirakawa (1127-1192), he regained his rank, and would later be promoted to sangi "Imperial advisor."

Fujiwara Moromitsu (-1177)

Appointed saémon-no-jo through the influence of Michinori, who he succeeded, and enjoyed the confidence of the Emperor Go-Shirakawa (1127-1192). His religious name was Saiko.

In 1177, having conspired with Narichika against the Taira in the Shishi-ga-tani Incident, he was taken prisoner, tortured, and put to death with his two sons, Morotada and Morotsuné.

Fujiwara Korekata (-1125)

Son of Akiyori. He was kebiishi-betto "superintendent of police."

During the 1160 Heiji Rebellion (Kyoto), Korekata helped the ex-Emperor Go-Shirakawa (1127-1192) and the Emperor Nijo (1143-1165) to escape from the palace where Nobuyori kept them confined, and brought them to the Rokuhara (Kyoto). Later, on account of a contention between him and Go-Shirakawa, the latter charged Taira Kiyomori (1118-1181) to arrest him and put him to death, but owing to the demand of the Kanpaku "Regent" Fujiwara Tadamichi, they were content to exile him to Nagato, from whence in 1166 he was recalled.

Korekata was also known as Awada-no-betto.

Fujiwara Motozané (1143-1166)

Son of Tadamichi. In 1159 he was appointed Kanpaku "Regent" to the Em-

Fujiwara Motozané

peror Nijo (1143-1165) at the age of 15, and in 1165 Sessho "Regent to the Child Emperor" when the Emperor Rokujo (1164-1176), only 1 year old, ascended the Chrysanthemum Throne.

Motozané was a waka poet and is designated as a member of the 36 Immortal Poets. His poems are included in several Imperial poetry anthologies, including the *Shin Kokin Wakashu* "*New Collection of Ancient and Modern Poems.*" A personal poetry collection known as *Motozané-shu* also remains.

Motozané is the founder of the Konoé clan with the support from Taira Kiyomori (1118-1181). He was also called Umezu-dono.

Fujiwara Motofusa (1144-1230)

Son of Tadamichi. In 1166 he succeeded his brother Motozané in the office of Sessho "Regent to the Child Emperor" for the Emperor Rokujo (1164-1176), and later in 1168 for the Emperor Takakura (1161-1181), becoming his Kanpaku "Regent" in 1172. From 1170-1171 he was also Daijo-daijin "Chancellor of the Realm."

Though wielding great power as Regent, Motofusa was prevented from becoming the head of the Fujiwara by the political maneuvers of Taira Kiyomori (1118-1181). In 1170, while he was on his way to the Hoju-ji Palace (Kyoto), an incident further cemented his rivalry with the Taira. The Sessho, along with a large retinue, was making his way to the palace for a ceremony to which the cloistered Emperor Go-Shirakawa (1127-1192) was supposed to attend, when a young boy refused to make way for him and his retinue. As a result, the Regent's men smashed the boy's carriage and humiliated him. The boy was a son of Taira Shigemori (1138-1179) and a grandson of Kiyomori and so, after a few failed attempts at reprisal, the followers of Shigemori attacked Motofusa's men on their way to a solemn ceremony, dragging them from their horses and humiliating them. These events, while seemingly minor on the surface, led to a rift between Go-Shirakawa and the Taira, and consequently to closer relations between the Emperor and the Minamoto, enemies of the Taira.

In 1179, in concert with the ex-Emperor Go-Shirakawa, Motofusa, after the death of Shigemori, endeavored to have the latter's domain confiscated. Kiyomori, irritated, had him exiled to Tsukushi (Kyushu) with the title of Dazai-no-gon-no-sotsu. From there he went to Bizen, but in 1181 was recalled at the death of Kiyomori.

In 1183, when Minamoto Yoshinaka (1154-1184) had become master of Kyoto, Motofusa joined him against the Taira, gave him his daughter in marriage, and had his 3rd son Moroié, then 11 years old, appointed Kanpaku. In 1184, after the death of Yoshinaka, Moroié was deprived of his office, and henceforth Motofusa lived in retirement.

Motofusa is known by the names Matsudono Motofusa, as he came from the village of Matsudono (near Kyoto), and Bodai-in-no-Kanpaku.

Fujiwara Kanezané (1149-1207)

3rd son of Tadamichi. He was married to a daughter of Fujiwara Sueyuki. His brother Jien (1155-1225) was the author of the historical work *Gukan-sho* "*Notes on Bizarre Ideas,*" an analysis of Japanese history using Buddhist principles.

At the encouragement of Minamoto Yoritomo (1147-1199), Kanezané was the first that assumed the name of Kujo "9th Avenue," taken from the district in Kyoto where they resided. Among his sons, all with the family name Kujo, were Yoshimichi (1167-1188), Yoshitsuné (1169-1206), Yoshisuké (1185-1218), and Yoshihira (1185-1240). His daughter Taeko was at one point a consort to Emperor Go-Toba (1180-1239).

Kanezané was a minister during the reigns of the Emperors Go-Shirakawa (1127-1192), Nijo (1143-1165), Rokujo (1164-1176), and Takakura (1161-1181).

In 1184, after the young Emperor Antoku (1178-1185) had been carried off from Kyoto by the Taira, Kanezané prevailed upon Go-Shirakawa to replace him by the young Emperor Go-Toba (1180-1239). In 1186, at the age of 37, he was himself appointed Sessho "Regent to the Child Emperor" to the Go-Toba-tenno, and later in 1191 Kanpaku "Regent," owing to Yoritomo who supported him. From 1189-1190 he was also Daijo-daijin "Chancellor of the Realm."

Kanezané organized the compilation of the *Kitano Tenjin Engi* "*History of the Kitano Shrine.*" He also wrote the diary *Gyokuyo*, covering the years 1164-1201. He was also called Tsuki-no-wa-no-Kanpaku.

Fujiwara Moronaga (1137-1192)

2nd son of Yorinaga.

Having taken part with his father in the 1156 Hogen War (Kyoto), Moronaga was exiled to Tosa, but in 1164 was recalled.

In 1175 Moronaga became naidaijin "minister of the center," and from 1177-1179 he was Daijo-daijin "Chancellor of the Realm."

In 1179, having again been exiled to Owari by Taira Kiyomori (1118-1181), Moronaga came back the following year.

He is also called Myo-on'in-daijin.

Fujiwara Kiyohira (1056-1128)

7th generation descendant of Hidesato. He was a son of Tsunekiyo and of a daughter of Abé Yoritoki (-1057). Though the Hidesato branch of the Fujiwara was known for their fighting ability, Tsunekiyo was a mid-level bureaucrat at Fort Taga (later Sendai) when he married his Emishi wife. He left his position and went to live with his wife's family in northern Mutsu, where Kiyohira was born to an Emishi household in Emishi territory to a father who was considered a traitor by the Japanese authorities.

In 1057, during the Zen-kunen "Earlier Nine-Years" War (1051-1063),

Kiyohira lost his grandfather, Abé Yoritoki, in battle, and then in 1062 his uncle Abé Sadato (1019-1062). All of his mother's brothers were deported to Kyushu, and his own father was personally beheaded by Minamoto Yoriyoshi (998-1082) with a blunt sword.

After his father's death, Kiyohira's mother became the concubine of his enemy Kiyohara Takehira, who had helped Minamoto Yoriyoshi in the last war. He was brought up in this enemy clan as Kiyohara Kiyohira, with his elder step-brother Sanehira and younger half-brother Iehira (-1087).

The Go-sannen "Later Three-Years" War (1083-1087) involved a struggle among the three brothers in this complex relationship. In 1087 Kiyohira won the final victory in the war with aid of Minamaoto Yoriyoshi's son Yoshiié (1039-1106). He lost his wife and son during the war, however, killed by his half-brother Iehira.

After the war Kiyohira returned to his home at Fort Toyota (Iwayado Castle) in Oshu (Mutsu), to plan his future. Sometime around 1090-1100 he built a new home on Kan-zan "Barrier Mountain" in what is now Hiraizumi (Mutsu).

At about 1100 Kiyohira founded at Hiraizumi the Chuson-ji, a complex of temples, pagodas, repositories, and gardens that was to be his legacy. Its Konjiki-do "Golden Hall," covered with gold leaf decorated with imported mother-of-pearl, is considered one of the most beautiful and elaborately decorated buildings in the world.

Kiyohira eventually became o-ryoshi "provincial governor" of Mutsu and Dewa, and afterwards Chinjufu-shogun "Defender of the North."

There is evidence that Kiyohira did not use the name Fujiwara, but used the name Kiyohara until 1117, when he was more than 60 years old. But he did use it to passed it on to his children.

Kiyohira had several wives and consorts including a Taira wife from Kyoto who was the mother to several of his children. She seems to have tired quickly of life on the remote frontier, returned to Kyoto, married a policeman, and never returned. Kiyohira is also known to have had two Emishi wives, a Kiyohara and an Abé. His eldest son and rightful heir was Koretsuné. About 1105 his 2nd son and eventual successor Motohira was born, likely to one of Kiyohira's Emishi wives.

Kiyohira was the first of the great Hiraizumi or the Northern Fujiwara that ruled northern Japan from about 1100 to 1189, and whose power later on gave umbrage to Minamoto Yoritomo (1147-1199).

Fujiwara Motohira (-1157)

2nd head of the Northern Fujiwara. Son of Kiyohira.

Motohira held the same titles as his father, and maintained the glory of his family. Within the Motsu-ji in Hiraizumi (Mutsu), he build the spectacular Enryu-ji. Its main hall contained a monumental statue of Yakushi, the Buddha of Healing, with monumental statues of the Juni Shinsho "Twelve Heavenly Generals." They had been sculpted by Unkei (1151-1223) with crystal eyes, an innovation at that time. The hall itself was brightly painted and decorated with precious wood, gold, silver, and jewels. The main temple was surrounded by other buildings including a lecture hall, a circumambulation hall, a two-story main gate, a bell tower, and a sutra repository. The temple's name placard was written by Fujiwara Tadamichi, and the ornamental poem slips by Fujiwara Norinaga.

Across the road from Enryu-ji, Motohira's wife founded the Kanjizaio-in, a much plainer and simpler temple that consisted of a Large Amida Hall and a Small Amida Hall. There were bridges from the majestic entrance gate on the south to an island in the center of a lake, and to the Amida Halls on the north. The Large Amida Hall contained an Amida triad, and its walls were painted with scenes of Kyoto. The walls of the Small Amida Hall were decorated with poems written by Fujiwara Norinaga much like the walls at Enryu-ji.

Both temples were destroyed by fire in 1226 following the downfall of the Fujiwara Dynasty.

At its height Hiraizumi rivaled Kyoto in size and splendor. Its golden age lasted for nearly a century, but after the fall of the Fujiwara most of the buildings that gave the town its cultural prominence were destroyed. In 1689, when the famous poet Matsuo Basho (1644-1694) saw the state of the town, he penned his famous haiku about the impermanence of human glory:

Natsu kusa ya!
Tsuwamono-domo ga
yume no ato

Ah, summer grasses!
All that remains
Of the warriors dreams

Fujiwara Hidehira (1096-1187)

3rd ruler of the Oshu Fujiwara in Mutsu. Son of Motohira. His mother was a daughter of Abé Muneto. There is a legend that says Hidehira was raised by wolves.

In 1170 Hidehira received the title of Chinjufu-shogun "Defender of the North."

In 1174 Hidehira offered shelter in Hiraizumi (Mutsu) to Minamoto Yoshitsuné (1159-1189), who had escaped his exile from the Kurama-ji (Kyoto), and for many years he was the young Minamoto's benefactor and protector. It was from here that Yoshitsuné joined his brother at the start of the Genpei War (1180-1185), in which the

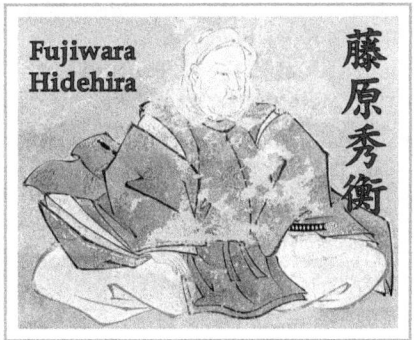

Heian Period – Fujiwara

Taira vainly appealed to Hidehira, who instead declared in favor of Minamoto Yoritomo (1147-1199).

In 1185, when Yoshitsuné incurred his brother Yoritomo's wrath, he returned to Hiraizumi. Hidehira protected him, and gave him lands at Koromogawa, where Yoshitsuné lived undisturbed for a time. In 1187, when Hidehira died, Yoshitsuné was still his guest. Before his death, Hidehira had his son Yasuhira promise to continue to shelter Yoshituné and his retainer Benkei, but in 1189 Yasuhira betrayed his father, gave into Yoritomo, and surrounded the castle with his troops, forcing Yoshitsuné to commit seppuku. During the battle, Benkei famously died standing up, which caused great fear to the attackers. Yoshitsuné's head was preserved in saké and sent to Yoritomo.

Fujiwara Yasuhira (-1189)

4th ruler of the Oshu Fujiwara in Mutsu. 2nd son of Hidehira. In 1187, after his father's death, he was governor of Mutsu and Dewa.

In 1189, having been ordered by Minamoto Yoritomo (1147-1199) to put the latter's brother Yoshitsuné (1159-1189) to death, against the exhortations of his late father, Yasuhira attacked Yoshitsuné at the Battle of Koromogawa, defeated him, and sent his head to Kyoto. This base servility however did not save him from ruin.

Later that year, wishing to become master of Mutsu and Dewa, Yoritomo marched against Yasuhira with a numerous army. Having been defeated, he tried to escape into Ezo, but was assassinated by one of his kerai, Kawata Jiro, and his immense domains were divided among Yoritomo's officers, marking the end of the Northern Fujiwara.

Fujiwara Tadahira (-1189)

3rd son of Hidehira. He is usually designated Izumi Saburo. Tadahira is the only one of Hidehira's children, who, mindful of the last words of his father, remained faithful to Minamoto Yoshitsuné (1159-1189) and died with him.

Fujiwara Motomichi (1160-1233)

2nd head of the Konoé branch of the Fujiwara. Son of Motozané. Favored by the ex-Emperor Go-Shirakawa (1127-1192), he became sadaijin "senior minister of state" at the age of 19.

In 1179 Taira Kiyomori (1118-1181), whose daughter Motomichi had married, had him appointed Kanpaku "Regent" to the Emperor Takakura (1161-1181). In 1180, at the accession of the Emperor Antoku (1178-1185), he became Sessho "Regent to the Child Emperor," but refused to follow the Taira in their flight during the Genpei War (1180-1185), and retired to Hiei-zan with Go-Shirakawa.

In 1183 Motomichi re-entered Kyoto with the army of Minamoto Yoshinaka (1154-1184), but was deposed of his position.

In 1184, at the death of Yoshinaka, Motomichi was re-established as Sessho, to the then Emperor Go-Toba (1180-1239), but was deposed anew two years later. In 1196 he was re-appointed as Kanpaku to Go-Toba, and in 1198 he became Sessho to the young Emperor Tsuchi-mikado (1196-1231).

In 1202 he resigned his functions, and became a Buddhist monk. He was also called Fugenji-dono.

Fujiwara/Kujo Yoshitsuné (1169-1206)

Son of Kujo Kanezané. He is of the Kujo branch of the Fujiwara. He came of age in 1179.

In 1188, when his elder brother died, Yoshitsuné was designated as successor to the clan.

Through his marriage to a daughter of Fujiwara Yoshiyasu, in 1190 Yoshitsuné became an ally of the Minamoto.

In 1196 a political shake-up caused Yoshitsuné to lose the Court position he was appointed a year before.

In 1199 Yoshitsuné became sadaijin "senior minister of state." From 1202 he was Sessho "Regent to the Child Emperor" to the Emperor Tsuchi-mikado (1196-1231). From 1205 he was also Daijo-daijin "Chancellor of the Realm."

When the Emperor announced that he would visit him in his residence, Yoshitsuné was assassinated the night preceding the promised meeting.

Yoshitsuné was a renowned poet, published in various Imperial anthologies. In 1205 he wrote the preface to the *Shin Kokin-shu* "*New Collection of Ancient and Modern Poems,*" in which 79 of his waka poems were included. His personal collection, *Akishi-no-Gessei-shu* "*Collection of Autumn Bamboo Grass and Moonlit Radiance,*" written around 1204, contains more than 1,600 poems.

People gave him the name Go-Kyogoku.

Fujiwara Kintsugu (1175-1227)

Son of Sanesada. In 1211 he became udaijin "junior minister of state."

Kintsugu was opposed to the design of the ex-Emperor Go-Toba (1180-1239) who desired to make war against Hojo Yoshitoki (1163-1224).

After the 1221 Jokyu War (Kyoto), Kintsugu was appointed sadaijin "senior minister of state," for which he was also called No-no-miya-sadaijin.

Fujiwara/Konoé Iezané (1180-1243)

Son of the Kanpaku "Regent" Motomichi. He is of the Konoé branch of the Fujiwara. His sons include Takatsukasa Kanehira (1228-1294), Konoé Iemichi (1204-1224), and Konoé Kanetsuné (1210-1259). In 1206 when Kujo Yoshitsuné died, he became the head of the Fujiwara.

From 1206 to 1210 Iezané was Sessho "Regent to the Child Emperor" and Kanpaku to the Emperor Tsuchi-mikado (1196-1231). From 1210-1221 he was Kanpaku to the Emperor Juntoku (1197-1242). In 1221 he was also Daijo-daijin "Chancellor of the Realm."

In the 1221 Jokyu War (Kyoto) Iezané opposed the Emperor Go-Toba (1180-1239), which cost him the Regency. But after the war he was reappointed, and from 1221-1228 he was Sessho and Kanpaku to the Emperor Go-Horikawa (1212-1234).

In 1227 Go-Horikawa raised Iezané's daughter Nagako to the rank of Chugu Empress, who was somewhat older than the Emperor, but he loved her madly.

In 1241 Iezané retired and became a priest. He died the following year.

He is the ancestor of the Konoé and the Takatsukasa.

Fujiwara/Kujo Michiié (1193-1252)

Son of Yoshitsuné. He is of the Kujo branch of the Fujiwara.

The Kujo were sponsors of the Kitano Tenman-gu (Kyoto). In 1219 Michiié offered the shrine the *Kitano Tenjin Engi Emaki* "*Illustrated Scroll of the History of the Kitano Shrine,*" and in 1223 he presented an enlarged version.

In 1219 Michiié was sadaijin "senior minister of state" when the 3rd Minamoto Shogun Sanetomo (1192-1219)

Heian Period – Fujiwara

died without an heir. The 2nd Hojo Shikken "Regent to the Shogun" Yoshitoki (1163-1224), applied to have Michiié's son Yoritsuné, at the time 2 years old, to be the 4th Kamakura Shogun.

In 1221 Michiié was Sessho "Regent to the Child Emperor" for the short-reigned Emperor Chukyo (1218-1234). From 1228-1231 he was Kanpaku "Regent" to the Emperor Go-Horikawa (1212-1234), and from 1235-1237 he was Sessho to the Emperor Shijo (1231-1242).

During 1236-1252 Michiié had the Kofuku-ji (Kyoto) built.

Michiié is the father of Kujo Norizané (1210-1235), Nijo Yoshizané (1216-1270), Kujo Yoritsuné (1218-1256), Ichijo Sanetsuné (1223-1284). He is the ancestor of the Ichijo, the Nijo, and the Kujo.

Fujiwara/Takatsukasa Kanehira (1228-1294)

4th son of Iezané. He is the founding father of the Takatsukasa branch of the Fujiwara. His sons include Takatsukasa Kanetada (1262-1301) and Takatsukasa Mototada (1247-1313). In 1252 he became head of the Fujiwara.

From 1252-1259 Kanehira was Regent to the Emperor Go-Fukakusa (1243-1304), and from 1259-1261 Kanpaku "Regent" to the Emperor Kameyama. From 1252-1253, and again in 1277, he was also Daijo-daijin "Chancellor of the Realm."

In 1290 he retired and became a priest. He was also a noted calligrapher.

Fujiwara Saneuji (1194-1269)

Son of Daijo-daijin "Chancellor of the Realm" Kintsuné. He was a minister under six Emperors.

From 1246-1247 Saneuji was Daijo-daijin.

In 1260 he shaved his head and took the name of Jikku. He is often called Tokiwai-nyudo.

Kujo/Fujiwara Yoritsuné (1218-1256)

4th Kamakura Shogun. See Kamakura Shogunate section.

Kujo/Fujiwara Yoritsugu (1239-1256)

5th Kamakura Shogun. See Kamakura Shogunate section.

Fujiwara Kanesué (14th century)

3rd son of Saionji Sanekané. From 1322-1323 he was udaijin "junior minister of state," for which he was also called Kikutei-udaijin.

In 1332 Kanesué became Daijo-daijin "Chancellor of the Realm," but resigned his office the following year.

He is the ancestor of the Imadegawa (later the Kikutei).

Fujiwara Fujifusa (1295-1380)

Son of Nobufusa. He was chunagon "middle counselor" and kebiishi-betto "superintendent of police."

In 1331, during the Genko War (1331-1333), when the Emperor Go-Daigo (1288-1339) was forced to flee from Kyoto before the troops of Hojo Takatoki (1303-1333), Fujifusa accompanied him to Kasagi-san (on the border of Yamashiro and Yamato). When the Emperor was taken prisoner, Fujifusa was exiled to Hitachi.

In 1333, during the Kenmu Restoration (1333-1336), after the downfall of the Hojo, Fujifusa returned to Heian-kyo (Kyoto).

In 1335 Fujifusa tried to prevent Go-Daigo from favoring Ashikaga Takauji (1305-1358), to whom with good reason he attributed ambitious designs, but seeing that his advice was of no avail, he became a bonze in the temple of Kitayama.

Fujiwara Toshimoto (-1331)

In 1331, during the Genko War (1331-1333), when the Emperor Go-Daigo (1288-1339) endeavored to throw off the yoke of the Hojo, Toshimoto was commissioned to gather adherents to his cause in Kinai, Sakai, etc. Hojo Takatoki (1303-1333) had him arrested, conducted to Kamakura, and assassinated.

Fujiwara Tameaki (-1364)

Son of Tamefuji. He served the Emperor Go-Daigo (1288-1339). He was also known as Nijo Tameakira.

In 1332 Tameaki accompanied Takanaga-shinno (1310-1337) in his exile to Tosa. Later, having come back to Kyoto, he received offices from the Northern Emperors Suko (1334-1398) and Go-Kogon (1338-1374).

In 1362 Tameaki started the compilation of the poetry anthology *Shinshui Waka-shu* "New Waka Collection of Gleanings," which was ordered by Go-Kogen at the request of the 2nd Ashikaga Shogun Yoshiakira (1330-1367), but he died before completing the task, and the collection was completed by the priest Ton'a (1289-1372). It consists of twenty volumes containing 1,920 poems.

Fujiwara Morokata (1300-1332)

Son of Moronobu.

In 1331, during the Genko War (1331-1333), when the Emperor Go-Daigo (1288-1339) had to flee from Kyoto, Morokata put on the Emperor's dress, and while the latter sought shelter on Mount Kasagi (on the border of Yamashiro and Yamato), he repaired to Mount Hiei (northeast of Kyoto) to recruit troops. Arrested by the emissaries of Hojo Takatoki (1303-1333), he was banished to Shimosa, the domain of Chiba Sadatané (1291-1351), where he died.

After his death, he received the postumous title of Daijo-daijin "Chancellor of the Realm." The Komikado-jinja (Shimosa) is erected in his honor. He is better known as Kanzan-in Morokata.

Fujiwara Morokata

Men of Letters, Poets

Notable Ancestors

Fujiwara Yasumasa (958-1036)

Celebrated poet and musician.

Legend tells us that, attacked at night by a robber, Yasumasa charmed him so effectually with the music of his flute, that the robber was disarmed and followed him to his house.

Fujiwara Akisué (1055-1123)

Son of Takatsuné. He was adopted by Sanesué.

Akisué was close to Emperor Shirakawa (1053-1129), both through his mother who was the Emperor's nurse, and through the influence of his foster father, who was dainagon "grand counselor" to the Emperor. Starting in 1075, Akisué held a number of local official posts, and by 1109 was appointed Dazai-daini "secretary to the administrative officer of Kyushu."

Akisué founded a school of poetry in Kyoto. As it was located at the crossing of Roku-jo and Karasuma streets, the school became to be known as the Roku-jo. As Akisué was also shuritayu, a Court title, hence the name Roku-jo-shuri-tayu by which he is also known. Members of the salon included many conservative Fujiwara poets such as Kiyosuké, Motosuké, Ariié, and his own son Akisuké.

He and the Emperor were great admirers of the esteemed poet Kaki-no-moto Hitomaro (662-710), and in his honor Akisué instituted an annual festival, which he celebrated with other poet luminaries of the time, including his son Akisuké and Minamoto Shunrai (1057-1129).

Fujiwara Akisuké (1090-1155)

Son of Akisué. He was, like his father, a celebrated poet.

In 1144, by order the retired Emperor Sutoku (1119-1164), Akisuké compiled the *Shika Waka-shu* "*Collection of Verbal Flowers*" that, despite Akisuké's ostensibly conservative nature, is rather eclectic and has a wide variety of Japanese poems.

He was also called Roku-jo Akisuké because of his membership in the Roku-jo poetry school founded by his father.

Fujiwara Yasumasa

Fujiwara Akihira (989-1066)

Held the Court position of monjo-hakasé "scholar of Chinese studies." His works, written in Chinese, were inspired by Confucianism.

About 1060 Akihira complied the *Honcho Monzui*, a 14-volume anthology of 427 poems written in Chinese by Japanese authors.

His sons Atsumoto and Atsumitsu were also renowned poets.

Fujiwara Kiyosuké (1084-1177)

Son of Akisuké. Hundreds of his poems were included in Imperial anthologies. He also wrote treatises on poetry.

Kiyosuké, with Fujiwara Toshinari and the bonze Saigyo Hoshi (1118-1190), were the most celebrated poets of their time.

Fujiwara Tamenari (12th century)

Son of Tametada. He was Izu no kami during the reign of Sutoku (1124-1141).

Fujiwara Akisuké

Fujiwara Kiyosuké

Tamenari was renowned as a poet and historian, and is sometimes attributed the writing of the epic *Eiga Monogatari*, the historical tale *O-kagami* "*Great Mirror*," and the *Kachi-zusami*.

Fujiwara Toshinari/Shunzei (1114-1204)

Son of Toshitada. He was a celebrated poet, whose poems were inspired by Chinese ideals from the late Tang Dynasty (618-907), and are mainly descriptive. His master was Fujiwara Mototoshi. He was a great favorite of the Emperors Go-Toba (1180-1239) and Tsuchi-mikado (1196-1231), the latter even deigned to assist during a feast at the waka-dokoro "poetry bureau" on the occasion of the 90th anniversary of his birth.

In 1123 Toshinari gave his name as Akihiro, but in 1167 he changed it to Shunzei, a name by which he is also well known.

In 1177, at the age of 63, Shunzei retired from the world and took Buddhist vows, taking the religious name of Shakua.

In 1187 Shunzei compiled the *Senzai Waka-shu* "*Collection of a Thousand Years*," the 7th Imperial anthology of waka poetry, at the behest of the retired Emperor Go-Shirakawa (1127-1192), who admired him.

Shunzei was also a respected judge in poetry competitions. He is also often called Gojo-san'i.

Heian Period – Fujiwara

Fujiwara Takanobu (1142-1205)

Son of Tametaka, and half-brother to the great poet Sadaié. He was born in Kyoto. He was also a distinguished poet, but is mainly known as the leading Japanese portrait artist of his day. He was of the Yamato-é school, and was the pupil of Kasuga Mitsunaga. He is credited with painting portraits of Minamoto Yoritomo (1147-1199), Taira Shigemori (1138-1179), and Fujiwara Mitsuyoshi.

In 1201 Takanobu became a lay Buddhist monk with the name Hoshoji.

His son Nobuzané (1177-1265) likewise was a renowned painter.

Fujiwara Ietaka (1158-1237)

Son of Mitsutaka. He was a pupil of Fujiwara Shunzei, and rival of Fujiwara Sadaié.

The Emperor Go-Toba (1180-1239) wishing to study poetry asked his Sessho "Regent to the Child Emperor" Kujo Yoshitsuné (1169-1206) to find a master for him. Yoshitsuné immediately proposed Ietaka, who then was called the Kaki-no-moto Hitomaro (662-710) of his century.

In 1205, with Sadaié, Ietaka compiled the *Shin Kokin Wakashu* "New Collection of Ancient and Modern Poems," in which 43 of his poems are included. His personal collection, the *Gyokugin-shu* "Collection of Jeweled Songs," includes about 3,200 poems.

Ietaka is considered the greatest poet of his time after Sadaié.

He is also known by the name Mibuni-i.

Fujiwara Sadaié/Teika (1162-1241)

Son of Shunzei. Like his father he was a poet. He was also a critic, calligra-

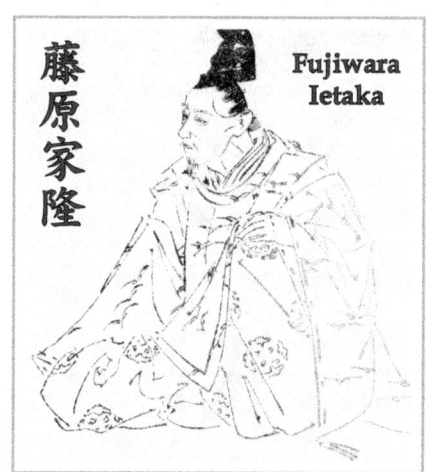

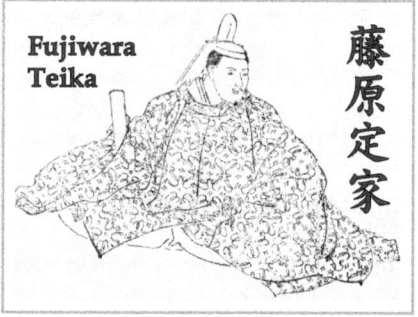

pher, novelist, anthologist, scribe, and scholar. He is more often called Teika from the Chinese reading of his name. He had 27 children by various women.

After coming to the attention of the retired Emperor Go-Toba (1180–1239), Teika began his long and distinguished career, spanning multiple areas of aesthetic endeavor.

In 1185 Teika hit a superior, was banished from the Court, and exiled. Although he was rehabilitated the next year, his career did not advance greatly until 1232 when he obtained the title gon-chunagon "deputy middle counselor." He then became a Buddhist monk under the name Myojo, and continued writing poetry.

Teika contributed to the publication of several collections of poetry, among which the best known is the *Hyaku-nin Isshu* "Poems by a Hundred Poets"; and the most important, the *Shin Kokin Waka-shu* "New Anthology of Ancient and Modern Poetry."

Teika's influence was enormous, and is today counted among the greatest of Japanese poets, and perhaps the greatest master of the waka form.

Fujiwara Tameié (1198-1275)

2nd son of Teika. He was known at the Court of the Emperor Juntoku (1197-1242) mainly as an expert in kemari, a simple cooperative sport where the objective is to keep a ball in the air.

In 1234, continuing the family tradition, Tameié began to write waka poetry.

In 1241 Tameié was gon-dainagon "deputy grand counselor," and in 1250 minbu-kyo "minister of taxation."

In 1251 Tameié completed the 10th Imperial poetry anthology *Shoku Gosen Waka-shu* "Later Poetry Collection Continued," which the retired Emperor Go-Saga (1220-1272) had asked him to compile.

In 1256 Tameié retired from public life and became Buddhist monk under the name Minbu-kyo-nyudo.

In 1265 Tameié complied the 11th Imperial poetry anthology *Shoku Kokin Waka-shu* "Poetry Collection of Ancient and Modern Times Continued."

His sons include Nijo Tameuji (1222-1286), Kyogoku Tamenori (1226-1279), and Reisei Tamesuké (-1263).

Fujiwara Seika (1561-1619)

Descendant of Tameié. Son of Tamezumi. Born in Harima, he was a member of the Reizei branch of the Fujiwara, and was a classical waka poet.

In 1580, his father having died in the service of Bessho Nagaharu (1558-1580), Seika, patronized by Hashiba (later Toyotomi) Hideyoshi (1536-1598), continued his studies, and became a bonze under the name of Myoju-in in order to be initiated in Buddhist theology and philosophy. Dissatisfied with the doctrines which were expounded to him, he resolutely separated from the Buddhists, who until then enjoyed the monopoly of teaching philosophy.

In 1598, at Fushimi Castle (Yamashiro), Seika met the Korean neo-Confucian scholar Gang Hang (1567-1618) who had been taken prisoner to Japan during the Invasions of Korea (1592-1598).

Seika devoted himself to studying the neo-Confucianism of the Chinese scholar Zhu Xi (1130-1200). Refusing all official positions, he became a hermit dedicated to studying and writing.

Seika founded a school of neo-Confucianism, Teishu-gaku-ha, and made the Chinese philosophy of the Song Dynasty (960-1279) popular under the patronage of Tokugawa Ieyasu (1543-1616), who became his student.

HEIAN PERIOD – FUJIWARA

Teika became the originator of Japanese neo-Confucianism, and left numerous disciples who continued his work, the most celebrated being Hayashi Razan (1583-1657) and Matsunaga Sekigo (1592-1657).

EMPRESSES

NOTABLE ANCESTORS

Fujiwara Miyako no Iratsumé (-754)

Daughter of Fuhito. She was the wife of the Monmu-tenno (683-707), and the mother of the Shomu-tenno (701-756). She was also called Fujiwara-kogu.

Fujiwara Kusuko (-810)

Daughter of the chunagon "middle counselor" Tanetsugu. She was married to Fujiwara Tadanushi, and afterwards was a concubine to the Emperor Heizei (774-824).

In 810, after Heizei's abdication the previous year, Kusuko, together with her brother Nakanari, tried to induce the ex-Emperor to re-ascend the Chrysanthemum Throne and re-establish the capital at Nara (Yamato). The plot was discovered, Nakanari was put to death, Heizei had his head shaved, and Kusuko took poison.

She was also called Fujiwara no Kuzushi.

Fujiwara Akira-keiko/Akiko (829-899)

Daughter of Yoshifusa. She was the wife of the Emperor Montoku (827-858), and the mother of the Seiwa-tenno (850-881) and the Imperial Princess Gishi (-879).

She was also called Akiko, and also the Somé-dono Empress.

Fujiwara Onshi I (872-907)

Daughter of Mototsuné. She was the wife of the Emperor Uda (867-931), and the mother of the Imperial Princess Kinshi (890-910).

Fujiwara Onshi II (885-954)

Another daughter of Mototsuné. She was the wife of the Emperor Daigo (885-930), and the mother of the Emperors Suzaku (923-952) and Murakami (926-967).

Fujiwara Senshi (962-1002)

Daughter of Kaneié. She was the wife of the Enyu-tenno (959-991), and the mother of the Emperor Ichijo (980-1011).

In 991, after the death of her husband, Senshi had her head shaved and became an ama "Buddhist nun" under the name Higashi-sanjo-in. It is the first instance of an Empress embracing religious life.

Fujiwara Sadako/Teishi (977-1001)

Eldest daughter of Michitaka. She was the Kogo Empress to the Ichijo-tenno (980-1011). The Imperial couple had three children.

Sadako was the patron of Sei Shonagon (966-1017).

She was also called Teishi.

Fujiwara Akiko/Shoshi (988-1074)

Daughter of Michinaga. She was the Chugu Empress to the Ichijo-tenno (980-1011), and the mother of the Emperors Go-Ichijo (1008-1036) and Go-Suzaku (1009-1045).

Akiko was the protector of the women writers Murasaki Shikibu (973-1014), Izumi Shikibu (976-), and Akazomé Emon (956-1041).

In 1026 Akiko assumed the name of Joto-mon-in, the first Empress to receive the title of mon-in, given to a widowed mother of an Emperor who had shaved her head.

She was also called Shoshi.

Fujiwara Kenshi (994-1027)

2nd daughter of Michinaga. She was the Chugu Empress to the Sanjo-tenno (796-1017).

Fujiwara Ishi (999-1036)

3rd daughter of Michinaga. She was the wife of the Go-Ichijo-tenno (1008-1036). The couple had two daughters both of whom became Chugu Empresses: Akiko/Shoshi (1026-1105) to the Emperor Go-Reizei (1023-1068), and Kaoruko/Keishi (1029-1093) to the Emperor Go-Sanjo (1034-1073).

Fujiwara Tamako/Shoko (1101-1145)

Eldest daughter of Kinzané. She was wife of the Toba-tenno (1103-1156). The couple had seven children, including the Emperors Sutoku (1119-1164) and Go-Shirakawa (1127-1192).

In 1124 Tamako had her head shaved, and received the name Taiken-mon-in. She was also called Shoko.

Fujiwara Tokuko/Nariko (1117-1160)

Daughter of Nagazané. She was wife of the retired Emperor Toba (1103-1156). The couple had four children, including the Emperor Konoé (1139-1155) and the Imperial Princess Shushi/Yoshiko (1141-1176), who became the Chugu Empress to the Emperor Nijo (1143-1165).

In 1145 Tokuko had her head shaved, and assumed the name of Bifuku-mon-in.

In 1155, when her son Konoé died under mysterious circumstances, Tokuko opposed the ascension of the son of the Emperor Sutoku (1119-1164), Imperial Prince Shigehito, to the Chrysanthemum Throne, and the 4th son of the ex-Emperor Toba (1103-1156) succeeded as the next Emperor Go-Shirakawa (1127-1192). This conflict sparked the 1156 Hogen Rebellion (Kyoto), where Go-Shirakawa prevailed with the help of Taira Kiyomori (1118-1181) and Minamoto Yoshitomo (1123-1160), and established the Minamoto-Taira rivalry.

Tokuko was also called Nariko, as well as Tokushi.

Fujiwara Masako/Seishi (1122-1182)

Daughter of Tadamichi. She was the wife of the Sutoku-tenno (1119-1164).

In 1150 Masako became a Buddhist nun under the name Koka-mon-in. She was also called Seishi.

Fujiwara Masuko/Omiya (1140-1201)

Daughter of Kin'yoshi, and later adopted by Fujiwara Yorinaga. She was the wife of the Konoé-tenno (1139-1155), and after his death she married the Nijo-tenno (1143-1165).

She was later called the Grand Empress Dowager Omiya, and is also known as Oiko, Tashi, and Tadako.

Fujiwara Yoshiko (1225-1292)

Daughter of Saneuji. She was the wife of the Go-Saga-tenno (1220-1272). The couple had five children, including the Emperors Go-Fukakusa (1243-1304) and Kameyama (1249-1305).

Fujiwara Kimiko (1232-1304)

Daughter of Saneuji. She was the wife of the Go-Fukakusa-tenno (1243-1304). The couple had two daughters.

In 1259 Kimiko took the name Higashi-Nijo-in.

Fujiwara Yasuko (1292-1357)

Daughter of Kinhira, Court lady of Go-Fushimi-tenno (1288-1336). She was the mother of the Emperors Kogon

(1313-1354) and Komyo (1322-1380) of the Northern Dynasty.

Yasuko became a Buddhist nun under the name Kogi-mon-in.

Fujiwara Renshi (1301-1359)

Adopted daughter of Kintaka. She was Court lady to the Emperor Go-Daigo (1288-1339). The couple had five children, including the Emperor Go-Murakami (1328-1368).

In 1332, during the Genko War (1331-1333), Renshi accompanied Go-Daigo in his exile to Oki.

In 1351 she became a Buddhist nun under the name Shin-Taiken-mon-in.

Fujiwara Itsuko (1351-1406)

Daughter of Kintada. She was consort to the Emperor Go-En'yu (1359-1393) of the Northern Dynasty. The couple had two children, including the Go-Komatsu-tenno (1377-1433).

In 1386 Itsuko became a Buddhist nun under the name Tsuyo-mon-in.

KIYOHARA

Territory: Dewa

Family descended from the Emperor Temmu (631-686) by his son the Toneri-shinno. The clan held the governorship of Dewa.

In the 9th century, Kiyohara Fusanori had two sons: the elder became the ancestor of the samurai branch of Dewa, the younger of the kugé "Court nobles" branch.

In the Zen-kunen "Earlier Nine-Years" War (1051-1063) the Kiyohara aided the Fujiwara governor of Mutsu and the Chinjufu-shogun "Defender of the North" Minamoto Yoriyoshi (988-1075) in their victory against Abé Yoritoki (-1057).

The Kiyohara then took over the administration of Mutsu, along with Dewa, but within twenty years, quarrels and conflicts within the family created such a disturbance that the new Chinjufu-shogun Minamoto Yoshiié (1039-1106) was appointed governor of Mutsu, and in 1083 arrived north to resolve the situation peaceably. He was soon forced to resort to gathering troops, and during the subsequent Go-sannen "Later Three-Years" War (1083-1089) Kiyohara Iehira and his uncle Kiyohara Takahira were killed, and the other Kiyohara leaders surrendered. Control of both Mutsu and Dewa then passed to Fujiwara Kiyohira (1056-1128), an ally of Yoshiié.

The Kiyohara kugé branch continued their legacy of scholarship, spawning writers, scholars, poets, and artists, including Kiyohara Motosuké (908-990) and his famous daughter Sei Shonagon (966-1017). The kugé descendants possessed hereditarily the office of daigeki "senior secretary of state." Kiyohara Yorinari (1122-1189), son of the daigeki Kiyohara Suketada, was governor of Etchu, and excelled in law, literature, and history. During the Onin War (1467-1477) the clan's Kyoto mansion, along with all the books and scrolls contained within, was destroyed.

Notable Ancestors

Kiyohara Natsuno (782-837)

Son of Prince Ogura, grandson of Toneri-shinno. He was udaijin "minister of the right," and thus is often called Narabi no Oka no Otodo.

Natsuno is the author of the ten-volume *Ryo-no-gigé*, a commentary of the Myoho "Chinese Code."

Kiyohara Fusanori (9th century)

Grandson of Natsuno. He had two sons: the elder is the ancestor of the Dewa branch; the younger, of the kugé.

Kiyohara Motosuké (908-990)

A member of the Kiyohara kugé branch. Famous for his poetry, he was one of the Sanju-roku kasen "36 Poetry Immortals." His daughter was the poet and writer Sei Shonagon, the author of *Makura no soshi* "*The Pillow Book.*"

Motosuké had a middling Court career, but eventually became governor of Higo.

One of Motosuké's poems is included in the *Ogura Hyakunin-isshu*, an anthology of 100 poems by 100 poets, compiled by Fujiwara Teika (1162-1241). He was also one of the Nashi-tsubo no go-nin "Five Men of the Pear Chamber" who compiled the *Gosen waka-shu* "*Later Collection of Japanese Poems.*"

Over the course of his long life, Motosuké was often asked by senior

Kiyohara Natsuno

KIYOHARA FAMILY TREE

TENMU-TENNO (673-686) — Toneri-shinno ┊ Natsuno (782-837) ┊ Fusanori ┊ Takenori ┬ Takesada ┬ Sanehira ┬ Narihira
                                                                                        └ Takehira └ Iehira   └ Kiyohira

Heian Period – Oba / Ono

members of the nobility to compose poems for folding screens.

His poems are included in several Imperial poetry anthologies, including the *Shui waka-shu* "Collection of Gleanings." His personal collection of poems is known as the *Motosuké-shu*.

Kiyohara Takenori (11th century)

During the Zen-kunen "Earlier Nine-Year" War (1051-1063) Takenori served in the campaign of Minamoto Yoriyoshi (998-1082) against Abé Yoritoki (-1057) and his sons. In 1062, from his residence in Yamagata (Dewa), he brought a reinforcement to Minamoto Yoshiié (1039-1106), which enabled the latter to defeat Abé Sadato (1019-1062). In return, he was appointed Chinjufu-shogun "Defender of the North."

Kiyohara Iehira (-1087)

Grandson of Takenori.

In the early 1080s, a conflict developed between Iehira and his relatives Kiyohara Narihira and Kiyohara Masahira over the leadership of the main Kiyohara branch. When violence erupted, Chinfuju-shogun "Defender of the North" Minamoto Yoshiié (1039-1106) came to the region in hopes of restoring peace and order. When diplomacy failed, Yoshiié went into battle alongside Iehira and Fujiwara Kiyohira (1056-1128), a cousin of the Kiyohara, against Kiyohara Sanehira, sparking the Go-sannen "Later Three-Year" War (1083-1089).

After Sanehira's defeat, Iehira and Yoshiié turned on one another. When the Minamoto besieged Iehira at the wooden stockade fortress of Numa, they suffered heavy losses due primarily to the cold and lack of supplies. Later, Iehira, with the aid of his uncle Kiyohara Takahira, established a warrior camp around Yoshiié's fortress at Kanezawa. Yoshiié, along with his brother Minamoto Yoshimitsu from Kyoto, besieged the encampment, and was eventually successful after they attacked Iehira with the aid of Fujiwara Kiyohira. Iehira and his uncle were both killed.

With the death of Iehira, the Dewa branch of the Kiyohara became extinct.

OBA 大庭

Territory: Sagami

Family of samurai from Sagami, descended from Taira Takamochi (late 9th century) and the legendary Kamakura Gongoro Kagemasa (1069-), the hero of the popular kabuki play *Shibaraku*.

Notable Ancestors

Oba Kageyoshi (-1210)

Inherited the domain of Oba (Sagami), and took its name. Also known as Heita.

During the Hogen Rebellion (1156), Kageyoshi sided with Minamoto Yoshitomo (1123-1160), and took part in the Siege of Shirakawa Palace (Kyoto).

During the Genpei War (1180-1185) Kageyoshi joined the party of Minamoto Yoritomo (1147-1199) against the Taira, whilst his brother Kagechicka fought on the opposite side.

After the triumph of the Minamoto, he served the Kamakura Bakufu.

Oba Kagechika (-1180)

3rd son of Kageyoshi. He was also known as Saburo.

In 1156, during the Hogen Rebellion, Kagechika fought side-by-side with his father against the army of Minamoto Yoshitomo (1123-1160), facing off against Minamoto Tametomo (1139-1170). Defeated, he was condemned to death, but was spared through the intervention of the Taira, and henceforth proved one of their most faithful partisans.

In 1180, at the Battle of Ishibashiyama (Hakoné), one of the bloodiest of the Genpei War (1180-1185), Kagechika defeated Minamoto Yoritomo (1147-1199). Two months later, after receiving reinforcements from Kai, Yoritomo counterattacked. Finding resistance impossible, Kagechika surrendered, and was decapitated.

ONO 小野

Notable Ancestors

Ono Harukazé (-899)

In 878 was appointed Chinjufu-shogun "Defender of the North," and quelled an Ebisu revolt in Dewa.

ONO 小野

Territory: Kyushu

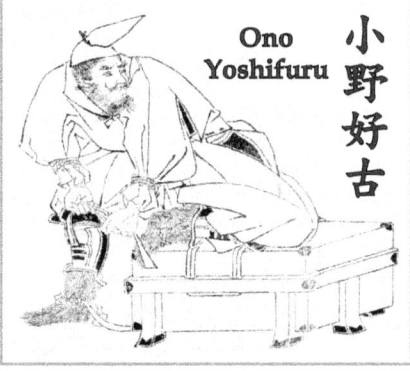

NOTABLE ANCESTORS

Ono Takamura (802-853)

Son of sangi "Imperial counselor" Kinmori. He followed his father when the latter was appointed governor of Mutsu, and became expert in all the arts of war.

Takamura was reprimanded for his ignorance by the Emperor Saga (786-842), and at once began his studies, in which he persevered to the end.

In 828 Takamura was appointed dainaiki "chief draftsman and editor" at the ministry of the center, and in 832 Dazai-shoni "vice-governor of Kyushu."

In 834 Takamura was shipwrecked by a typhoon during a mission to China. In 836 he was appointed vice-ambassador to China, but in the following year, after quarreling with Fujiwara Tsunetsugu, he feigned illness to be relived of his mission. In 838 he wrote a poem against those traditional embassies, for which reason he was exiled to the Oki by the ex-Emperor Saga (786-842), but was pardoned two years later.

In 847 Takamura was raised to the rank of sangi, hence he is also known as Sangi no Takamura, and later on to that of Daijo'osuké "official of the Supreme Council" and sadaiben "controller of the left."

Takamura was considered one of the best writers of his time. He wrote various collections of poems and prose texts in Chinese.

Ono Yoshifuru (888-968)

Son of Dazai-daini "vice governor of Kyushu" Kadotsuru, and elder brother to Michikazé.

In 939, during the revolt of Fujiwara Sumitomo (-941), Yoshifuru placed himself at the head of 200 war junks and fought the rebel in Iyo, pursued him to Tsukushi (northern Kyushu), defeated him at Hakata (Chikuzen), and made him prisoner.

In 948 Yoshifuru was appointed sangi "Imperial advisor."

Ono Michikazé (894-966)

Son of Kadotsuru, and grandson of Courtier-poet Takamura. Born in Owari, he is various called Tofu (Chinese reading of Michikazé), Yaseki Tofu, and Ono no Tofu.

Michikazé was a government official and a poet who excelled in penmanship, and is considered the founder of the Japanese style of calligraphy. He provided distinguished calligraphic service for the Emperors Daigo (reigned 897-930), Shuzaku (r. 930-946), and Murakami (r. 946-967).

When the Emperor Daigo (885-930) was building the Daigo-ji (Kyoto), he had Michikazé write an inscription for its frontispiece. In 927 Daigo ordered from him two volumes of sosho "cursive" and gyosho "half cursive" writings, and sent them to China by the bonze Kanken to have them admired there.

Towards the end of his life Michikazé was subject to palsy, yet with his trembling hand, he continued to trace characters, somewhat strange in form, which were nevertheless much admired. By the time he died, he had lost much of his sight.

Michikazé, along with Fujiwara Sukemasa (944-998) and Fujiwara Yukinari (972-1027), is considered one of the San-seki "Three Masters of Calligraphy."

SAKANOUÉ

Territory: Mutsu
Castle: Izawa (Mutsu)

Sakanoué Tamura-maro

Ancient family of warriors descended from Achi no Omi.

NOTABLE ANCESTORS

Sakanoué Karita-maro (728-786)
Son of Inukai.

In 764 Karita-maro helped repress the revolt of Fujiwara Nakamaro (706-764).

He was later Chinjufu-shogun "Defender of the North."

Sakanoué Tamura-maro (758-811)
Son of Karita-maro. He started his military career as a lieutenant of Otomo Otomaro (731-809).

In 801, after having helped to check the advance of the Ebisu, Tamura-maro was given the command of an expedition against them with the title of Sei-i-tai-shogun "Commander-in-Chief Against the Barbarians," created especially for the occasion by the Emperor Kammu (737-806). He defeated Tamo-no-kimi Aterui (-802), subdued the Ezo tribes completely, and built Izawa Castle (Mutsu) to stop their continuous incursions.

After the death of Kammu, Tamura-maro continued to serve the Emperors Heizei (773-824) and Saga (786-842) as dainagon "major counselor" and hyobu-kyo "minister of war."

Tamura-maro is considered the founder of the famous Kiyomizu-dera (Kyoto). He was buried at the village of Kurisu (Yamashiro, near Kyoto), and it is believed that it is his tomb which is known under the name of Shogun-zuka. He is the ancestor of the Tamura of Mutsu.

SATO

Territory: Mutsu

Daimyo family descended from Fujiwara Hidesato (10th century), possessing since the 11th century the fief of Shinobu (Mutsu).

NOTABLE ANCESTORS

Sato Norikiyo/Saigyo Hoshi (1118-1190)
Born Sato Norikiyo in Kyoto. Very skilful in using the bow, he became a favorite with the ex-Emperor Toba (1103-1156), who gave him rank as army captain among his Hokumen no bushi, and enjoyed his poetry.

In 1140, at the age of 23, Norikiyo was so horrified and surprised to learn of a friend's sudden death that he abandoned his wife and children, went to Saga (Yamashiro), and became a bonze under the name of En'i. Later, for his poetry, he took the pen name Saigyo "Western Journey," a reference to Amida Budda and the western paradise.

Saigyo traveled through the provinces, preached, and recited poetry. This manner of living displeased the famous monk Mongaku-Shonin, who

Saigyo Hoshi

considered him the scandal of Buddhism, went so far as to say that if ever he crossed his path, he would break his head. Hearing this, Saigyo directed his steps towards the temple at Takao-san (near Edo) and presented himself before Mongaku, who seemed quite satisfied with the interview, and, as one of his disciples expressed his surprise at this, Mongaku answered him, "Have you then not seen Saigyo? If we had fought together, I would certainly not have been victorious in the contest!"

From there Saigyo went to Kamakura (Sagami) and visited Minamoto Yoritomo (1147-1199), who took delight in speaking with him about poetry and bow shooting. At the moment of his departure, he present him with a silver cat, which Saigyo offered to the first child he met in the street. He then bent his steps towards the north, where he usually resided with one of his relatives, Fujiwara Hidehira (1122-1187).

He died at Kyoto at the age of 72. He was a good friend of Fujiwara Teika (1162-1241), and left two volumes of poetry. The great haiku master Matsuo Basho (1644-1694) greatly admired his poems.

Heian Period – Taira

Sato Tsuginobu (1158-1185)
Sato Tadanobu (1160-1185)

Sons of Motoharu. They both belonged to the Shi-tenno "Four Bodyguards" of Minamoto Yoshitsuné (1159-1189), and died in his cause.

Tadanobu is featured in the play *Yoshitsuné Senbon Zakura "Yoshitsuné and the Thousand Cherry Trees,"* which premiered in 1747 in Osaka, and is one of the three most popular and famous in the Kabuki repertoire.

佐藤忠信
Sato Tadanobu

When his hiding place at a bath house was betrayed by a former mistress, Tadanobu defended himself with a go board against a police force of more than 200 men.

– Woodblock print by Utagawa Kuniyoshi (1797-1861)

TAIRA

Territories: Shimosa, Shimotsuké, Kozuké, Isé, Mutsu

Family descended from the Imperial Prince Katsurabara (786-853), son of the Emperor Kanmu (737-806). They are often referred to as the Heishi or the Heiké, based on the Chinese readings of the family name.

The Taira were one of the four important clans that dominated Japanese politics during the Heian "Aristocratic" Period (794-1185). The others were the Fujiwara, the Tachibana, and the Minamoto.

The main branch was descended from from Imperial Prince Takamochi, a great-grandson of the Emperor Kanmu. This clan became gradually came to dominate the Kanto, and its members, among them Taira Masakado (-940) and Taira Tadatsuné (-1031), led major rebellions against the central power in 940 and 1130.

The Taira exercised great power during the 11th and 12th centuries, with Taira Kiyomori (1118-1181) eventually forming the first samurai-dominated government in the history of Japan.

The Taira's protracted struggle with the rival Minamoto covers some of the most interesting pages of Japanese history. The clan was destroyed at the end of the Genpei War (1180-1185) at the Battle of Dan-no-ura (Nagato) by the forces of Minamoto Yoritomo (1147-1199).

The Taira had many branch families, including the Hojo, the Chiba, the Miura, and the Hatekeyama. Oda Nobunaga (1534-1582) claimed descent from the Taira through Chikazané, grandson of Shigemori (1138-1179).

Notable Ancestors

Taira Takamuné (804-867)

Eldest son of Katsurabara-shinno (786-853). He was dainagon "senior counselor."

In 825 Takamuné received for himself and his descendants the family name of Taira.

Taira Takamochi (9th century)

Son of Prince Takami, nephew to Takamuné, and grandson of Katsurabara-shinno.

In 889 Takamochi received from the Emperor Uda (867-931), the name of Taira.

He is the founder of the Kanmu Heishi line of the Taira, and is the ancestor of the original Hatakeyama clan that became extinct in 1205.

Taira Kunika (-935)

Eldest son of Takamochi. He was Chinjufu-shogun "Defender of the North" and governor of Hitachi.

In 935 Kunika was put to death by his rebel nephew Masakado.

Taira Sadamori (10th century)

Son of Kunika, and grandson of Takamochi. He was also called Joheida.

In 935, whilst he was at Kyoto holding the post of sama-no-jo "deputy horseguard," Sadamori heard that his cousin Masakado had assassinated his father in an uprising. He left the city at once, and together with his uncle Yoshikané, Shimosa no suké, fought Masakado, but they were defeated.

In 940 Sadamori returned to Kyoto, levied new troops, and, with the help of Fujiwara Hidesato, again fought Masakado at the Battle of Kojima (Shimosa), who was this time defeated and killed, thus avenging his father.

Heian Period – Taira

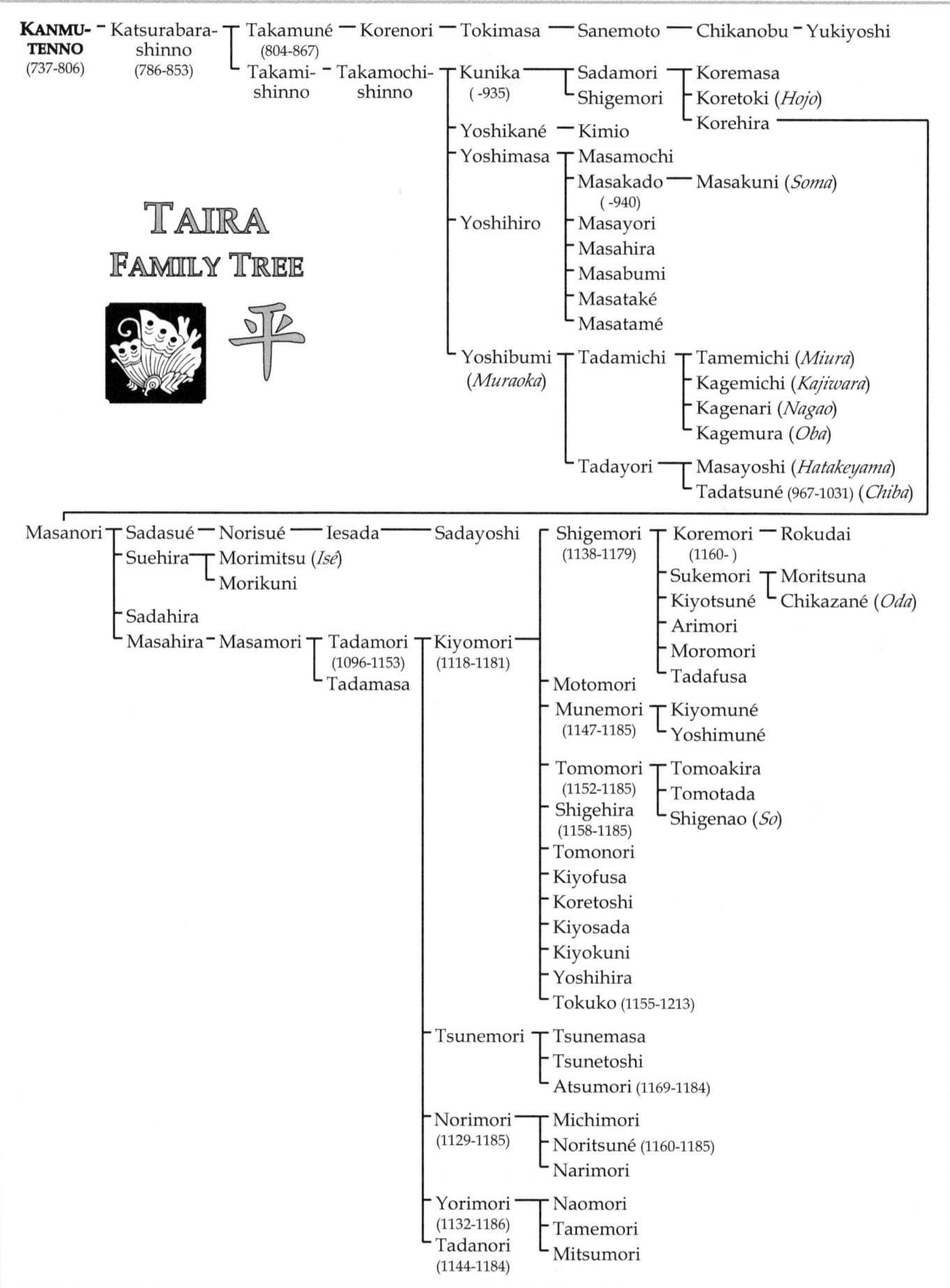

Taira Family Tree

Sadamori was awarded the 5th rank in Court for his heroism, and over the course of his life later earned the posts of Chinjufu-shogun "Defender of the North" and Mutsu no kami, as well as the 4th rank at Court.

Elements of Sadamori's life remain in the folklore volume *Konjaku Monogatari-shu* "*Tales of Past and Present*."

He was an ancestor of the Kamakura Hojo. His 4th son Korehisa was the progenitor of the Isé branch of the Taira.

Taira Masakado (-940)

Son of Yoshimasa, and grandson of Takamochi. His childhood name was Soma Kojiro.

Masakado served the Sessho "Regent to the Child Emperor" Fujiwara Tadahira (880-949), and demanded the office of kebiishi "chief of police," but was refused. In revenge he retired to Kanto, settled in the district of Toyoda (Shimosa) and began a guerrilla warfare in the surrounding country.

In 935 he attacked his uncle Taira Kunika, governor of Hitachi, and put him to death, and in 936 Taira Yoshikané, brother of Kunika, with Taira Sadamori attacked him, but were defeated and forced to take refuge in Kyoto.

In 939, after Taira Yoshikané's death, winning the support of many warriors, Masakado occupied Shimosa, Shimotsuké, and Kozuké, taking control of almost all of Kanto, which he made an autonomous state. He then assumed the title of Heishin-o "New Emperor Taira," established his Court at Ishii (Shimosa), named ministers and officials, etc. The central government in Kyoto responded by putting a bounty on his head. In the meantime, Fujiwara Sumitomo (-941), to whom Masakado had promised the Kanpaku "Regent to the Emperor" dignity, revolted in Saikaido.

Taira Masakado

In 940, Fujiwara Tadabumi (873-947), who had received the title of Sei-i-taishogun "Commander in Chief," marched against Masakado with a large army. He came too late, however, for Taira Sadamori, with the help of Fujiwara Hidesato and the o-ryoshi "provincial governor" of Shimotsuké, had already attacked the rebel, defeated and pursued him for 13 days, finally overtaking him at the Battle of Kojima (Shimosa). In the last encounter, Masakado, having wounded by an arrow, fell from his horse. Hidesato leapt to the ground, killed the wounded man, and sent his head to Kyoto. This revolt is known in history by the name Tengyo War.

Masakado's life is detailed in the *Shomon-ki*, a detailed book about his life believed to have been completed as early as the 940s by an anonymous author. Many legends were created around his life and life. It was said that he had three sons with a heavenly being who visited him in Shimosa, and that he was so brave that his enemies facing him in battle believed that he was seven warriors. Folklore attributed him with seven lives, associated with the seven stars of Ursa Major.

Taira Korehira (10th century)

Son of Sadamori. He became famous in the military arts, and gained a reputation as an outstanding swordsman. Together with Minamoto Yorinobu (968-1048), Taira Muneyori, and Fujiwara Yasumasa, he forms the Busho shi-ten "Four Great Warriors" of his epoch.

Korehira governed the provinces of Isé, Mutsu, Dewa, Izu, Shimotsuké, Sado, etc., then after some dispute, he openly made war against Taira Muneyori and was exiled to the island of Awaji.

As he spent most of the time in Isé, his descendants were called Isé Heishi "Isé Taira."

Taira Koremochi (10th century)

Educated by his uncle Sadamori. He settled in Mutsu. He was Dewa no suké and Chinjufu-shogun "Defender of the North."

Koremochi had some dispute with Fujiwara Morotané, whom he defeated and killed. This made him famous throughout all Kanto.

He died at the age of 80.

Taira Tadatsuné (967-1031)

Grandson of Yoshibumi. He lived at Muraoka (Musashi). He was governor of Shimosa.

Tadatsuné settled in Kazusa, and received the titles Kazusa no suké and Musashi o-ryoshi "provincial governor." He also managed the Grand Shrine of Isé, although he did not officially hold a title.

In 1028 Tadatsuné killed the governor of Awa, and took control of the Kanto. The Imperial Court sought to stop him, and nominated Minamoto Yorinobu (968-1048), governor of Isé, to lead the attack, but he refused. The Court then appointed Taira Naokata and Nakahara Narimichi, but they were recalled after making no progress, the Imperial troops being too weak to intervene effectively. In 1031, after being appointed governor of Kai, Yorinobu rose to the occasion and forced Tadatsuné to retreat. Knowing he could not win, Tadatsuné surrendered without a fight. He perished of disease on the way to the capital for trial.

He was also called Muraoka Goro, and is the ancestor of the Chiba.

Taira Iesada (12th century)

Served Tadamori and Kiyomori.

During the 1160 Heiji Rebellion (Kyoto) Iesada fought against Hyuga Michinaga, whom he defeated and killed in Echizen.

Taira Sadayoshi (12th century)

Son of Iesada. He was governor of Higo and Chikugo.

In 1180, at the beginning of the Genpei War (1180-1185), Kikuchi Takanao (-1185) sided with Minamoto Yoritomo (1147-1199), and levied troops in Kyushu. Sadayoshi marched against and defeated him. On his way back to Kyoto, he met up with Taira Munemori (1147-1185), who was retreating in Saikaido with the Emperor Antoku (1178-1185). He vainly attempted to induce them to return to the capital. After his arrival at Kyoto, he had the remains of Taira Shigemori (1138-1179) brought to Koya-san (Kii). He then again joined Munemori and served under him for the remainder of the war.

After the ruin of the Taira, his life was spared owning to the intercession of Utsunomiya Tomotsuna. He shaved his head, and in retirement was known by the name of Higo-nyudo.

Heian Period – Taira

Taira Tadamori (1096-1153)

Served the Emperors Shirakawa (1053-1129), Horikawa (1079-1107), and Toba (1103-1156). He governed Harima, Isé, Bizen, and Tajima, and was named kebiishi "chief of police." He married Iké Zenni.

In 1129 Tadamori was ordered to repress the wako "high-sea pirates," who infested the coasts of San'yodo and Nankaido. He also fought for his clan against the warrior monks of Nara and of Hiei-zan (Kyoto).

The ex-Emperor Toba ordered him to build the Sanjusan-gendo in the Rengé-o-in (Kyoto). In 1132, as reward, Tadamori received the governorship of Tajima. The credit he enjoyed created enemies who tried to kill him, but he escaped their snares.

Tadamori is said to be the first samurai to serve the Emperor directly at Court.

Taira Kiyomori (1118-1181)

The most renowned of the Taira. Son of the ex-Emperor Shirakawa (1053-1129), if tradition can be trusted. Taira Tadamori, having one day shown courage in presence of his master, presented Shirakawa with one of his favorite concubines, who soon after, brought forth a son, who was called Kiyomori.

In 1146 Kiyomori was made governor of Aki.

In 1153, after the death of Taira Tadamori, Kiyomori assumed control of the clan, and ambitiously entered the political realm in which he had previously only held a minor post.

During the 1156 Hogen War (Kyoto), Kiyomori with Minamoto Yoshitomo (1123-1160) aided the ex-Emperor Go-Shirakawa (1127-1192), and suppressed his uncle Tadamasa and Minamoto Tameyoshi (1096-1156), who supported the ex-Emperor Sutoku (1119-1164). This established the Taira and the Minamoto as the top warrior clans in Kyoto. Kiyomori received the titles of Harima no kami and of Dazai-daini "governor of Kyushu."

Their new strength caused the two clans to become bitter rivals. A quarrel arose between Kiyomori and Yoshitomo, and the latter, together with Fujiwara Nobuyori (-1160), devised a means of destroying the Taira. In 1160, whilst Kiyomori was at Kumano (Kii), they overpowered Go-Shirakawa, burnt his palace, and put his favorite

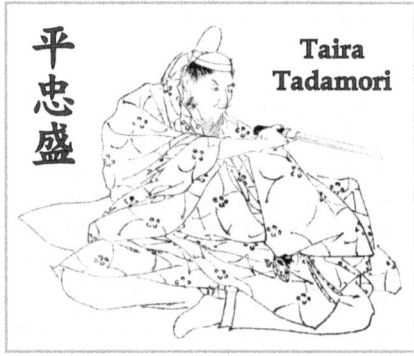
Taira Tadamori

Michinori (-1160) and others to death. Kiyomori returned in haste to Kyoto, and sent his son Shigemori against the rebels. By stratagem Shigemori succeeded in taking the ex-Emperor and the Emperor Nijo (1143-1165). He then attacked the conspirators and defeated them. Nobuyori was killed in battle, and Yoshitomo was massacred during his flight along with his two eldest sons. Thus ended the Heiji Rebellion, after which, Kiyomori was was now the head of the single most powerful warrior family in Kyoto. However, his clan's power and influence in the provinces at this time is a matter of debate. He spared the life of Yoshitomo's other children: the oldest, Minamoto Yoritomo (1147-1199), 13 years of age, was exiled to Izu; three others, including Yoshitsuné (1159-1189) and Noriyori (1156-1193), had to enter a monastery and become bonzes.

Soon after, Hyuga Michinaga revolted in Hizen, and Kiyomori sent his relative Iesada, who repressed the rebellion.

In 1165, after the death of the Emperor Nijo, his 6-month-old son ascended the Chrysanthemum Throne as the Emperor Rokujo (1164-1176). But three years later Go-Shirakawa deposed him, and replaced him by his own son, who ascended as the Emperor

Taira Kiyomori

Takakura (1161-1181). In 1167, as Takakura's mother was Kiyomori's sister-in-law, Kiyomori was named Daijo-daijin "Chancellor of the Realm," and *de facto* administrator of the Imperial government. It was the first time that a member of the military class was raised to that dignity.

In 1168 Kiyomori became ill, shaved his head, and took the name of Jokai, whilst the people called him Daijo-nyudo. Whilst living in the splendid palace he had built at Fukuhara, near Hyugo (Settsu), he governed the country as he pleased. Sixty members of his family possessed the highest offices of the land, and were at the head of more then thirty provinces. He had 300 young pages at his command who informed him of all they saw and heard.

In 1171 Kiyomori's 2nd daughter Tokuko (1155-1213), then 15 years old, married the Emperor Takakura, her junior by six years, and, as their mothers were half-sisters, her first cousin.

In 1177 Kiyomori's two sons Shigemori and Munemori were named sakon-é-taisho "senior commander of the Imperial Guard" and ukon-é-taisho "junior commander of the Imperial Guard" respectively.

In 1177 the Fujiwara, the Narichika, and the Moromitsu, for a second time, plotted the ruin of the Taira, but Tada Yukitsuna, their accomplice, revealed the whole design to Kiyomori, and Kiyomori's revenge was frightful. The principal leaders were executed, and many others were exiled. Kiyomori had even made up his mind to imprison Go-Shirakawa, who had given his approval to the plan, but on the advice of his son Shigemori, he pardoned him. This failed uprising is known as the Shishi-ga-tani Incident.

In 1178 a son, Prince Tokihito, was born to the Emperor Takakura, and Kiyomori had him at once declared heir to the throne. In 1179 Shigemori died at the age of 43. Deprived of the wise counsels, and of the firm remonstrance of his son, Kiyomori gave full vent to his tyranny: he imprisoned Go-Shirakawa in the palace of Toba, exiled the Kanpaku "Regent" and the Daijo-daijin, deposed 39 officials, and obliged his son-in-law Takakura-tenno to abdicate in favor of his 16-month-old grandson, who ascended to the Chrysanthemum Throne as the Emperor Antoku (1178-1185).

All these measures exasperated the nobles to such a pitch that a new plot was formed, headed by the Prince Mochihito (-1180), son of Go-Shirakawa. In 1180 a call to arms was sent to the warriors throughout all the provinces. The first to answer was Minamoto Yorimasa (1106-1180), who, notwithstanding his 75 years, fought bravely at the 1st Battle of Uji (Kyoto), but was overwhelmed by superior numbers of the Taira forces. This marked the beginning of the Genpei War (1180-1185). Yorimasa tried to help the Prince get away, but was struck by an arrow and committed seppuku, the first known historical incident of committing ritual suicide rather than surrendering to the enemy. Shortly afterwards, Mochihito was captured and killed at Nara (Yamato), and the bonzes who had given help to Yorimasa saw their temples burned.

To prevent a *coup-de-main*, Kiyomori took the Emperor with the whole Court to his palace in Fukuhara (Settsu). Meanwhile, the Minamoto assembled their troops in Kanto. Near Mount Fuji in the Hakoné Mountains, at the 1180 Battle of Ishibashi-yama outside Kamakura (Sagami), in Minamoto Yoritomo's first battle as commander, he was defeated by Oba Kagechika (-1180). Yoritomo, far from being discouraged, assembled a second army, and was able to rout the troops of Kiyomori's grandson Koremori. At this news Kiyomori fell sick and died after eight days. He made his sons and grandsons promise, however, to bring Yoritomo's head to his tomb, which desire was not to be fulfilled.

Kiyomori had established the first samurai-dominated administrative government in the history of Japan.

Taira Norimori (1129-1185)

Son of Tadamori, and younger brother to Kiyomori.

During the 1160 Heiji Rebellion (Kyoto), Norimori fought against Fujiwara Nobuyori (-1160), and was named Etchu no kami.

In 1161 Norimori, in concert with Taira Tokitada, tried to depose the Emperor Nijo (1143-1165), and to replace him by his brother Norihito-shinno, on which account he was deprived of all his offices. In 1169 Norihito, having be-

come the Takakura-tenno (1161-1181), named Norimori kurando "administrative official," sangi "Imperial advisor," etc.

In 1183 Norimori accompanied the Emperor Antoku (1178-1185) to Saikaido, defeated Minamoto Yukiié (-1186) at the Battle of Muroyama (Harima), and killed himself at the Battle of Dan-no-ura (1185).

Taira Yorimori (1132-1186)

Son of Tadamori, and younger brother to Kiyomori.

In 1159 Yorimori assisted his older brother Norimori, when he besieged Fujiwara Nobuyori (-1160) at the Ninna-ji (Kyoto). He was named Owari no kami, then dainagon "grand counselor." As he usually lived at Iké, he was surnamed Iké-dainagon.

In 1160, at the death of Minamoto Yoshitomo (1123-1160), Yorimori's wife Iké no Gozen pleaded for and obtained the pardon of his son Minamoto Yoritomo (1147-1199), who always showed himself very grateful.

In 1183, during the Genpei War (1180-1185), when the Taira all fled to the west, Yorimori, having nothing to fear, remained in Kyoto. The following year, Yoritomo called him together with Taira Munekiyo to Kamakura (Sagami). The latter refuge to go, but Yorimori was well treated, and returned to Kyoto.

In 1185 he became a Buddhist monk with the name Choren. He died in Kyoto.

Taira Tadanori (1144-1184)

Son of Tadamori, and younger brother to Kiyomori. He was brought

up at Kumano (Kii), received lessons from Fujiwara Shunzei (1114-1204), and became a distinguished waka poet. Later on he was Satsuma no kami.

Tadanori was one of Kiyomori's generals in the Genpei War (1180-1185) against the Minamoto, taking part in the 1180 Battle of Fujigawa (Suruga) in fighting Minamoto Yoshinaka (1154-1184). In 1184 he was killed by Okabé Tadazumi at the Battle of Ichi-no-tani (Settsu), where he had shown wonderful courage.

Taira Yasuyori (12th century)

In 1177 he took part in the Shishi-ga-tani Incident, a plot of Fujiwara Narichika (1138-1178) and the bonze Shunkan (1143-1179) against Taira Kiyomori, for which he was exiled to Kikai-ga-shima (Satsuma), but was pardoned the following year.

Taira Moritoshi (-1184)

Son of Morikuni. He was Etchu no kami.

In 1159 Moritoshi aided Taira Shigemori, and enabled him successfully to fight Minamoto Yoshihira (1140-1160) at the Rokuhara (Kyoto).

In 1181, during the Genpei War (1180-1185), Moritoshi defeated Minamoto Yukiié (-1186) and Minamoto Yoshinaka (1154-1184).

In 1184 Moritoshi perished at the Battle of Ichi-no-tani (Settsu). In 1185 his father Morikuni was taken prisoner at the Battle of Dan-no-ura (Nagato), and was taken to Kamakura (Sagami), where in captivity he starved himself to death.

Taira Tokitada (1130-1189)

Descendant of Takamuné, and son of Tokinobu. He served the Emperors Konoé (1139-1155), Go-Shirakawa (1127-1192), and Nijo (1143-1165).

In 1162 Tokitada was banished to Izumo, but in 1167 he was recalled and named chunagon "middle counselor." He eventually made gon-dainagon "deputy major counselor."

In 1177, having been involved in a plot against Taira Kiyomori, Tokitada was again exiled to Izumo. Pardoned the following year, he defeated the troops of the Hiei-zan (northeast of Kyoto) that caused disorder in the capital.

In 1183, during the Genpei War (1180-1185), Tokitada followed Taira Munemori into the western provinces.

In 1185, after the Battle of Dan-no-ura (Nagato), Tokitada was spared by the victorious Minamoto, and he allied himself with Minamoto Yoshitsuné (1159-1189). When Yoshitsuné was killed, he was banished to Noto, where he died.

Taira Tomoyasu (12th century)

Son of Tomochika. He was kebiishi "chief of police."

In 1183 the ex-Emperor Go-Shirakawa (1127-1192) ordered Tomoyasu to check the advance of the army of Minamoto Yoshinaka (1154-1184) which was threatening the capital, but frightened at the great number of his enemies, he fled without offering battle. He then went to Kamakura (Sagami) and submitted to Minamoto Yoritomo (1147-1199).

Taira Hirotsuné (12th century)

Son of Tsunetaka. He was Kazusa no suké.

Hirotsuné fought under Minamoto Yoshitomo (1123-1160) during the 1156 Hogen and 1160 Heiji Rebellions, and showed great valor.

Hirotsuné later served Minamoto Yoritomo (1147-1199), but in consequence of quarrels with some other generals, he was besieged and put to death by Kajiwara Kagetoki (1140-1200).

Taira Munekiyo (12th century)

Son of Suemuné. He served Taira Yorimori, who created him mokudai "acting provincial governor" of Owari.

In 1160, Minamoto Yoshitomo (1123-1160) having been killed, his son Yoritomo (1147-1199) fled, but was arrested by Munekiyo, who was on his way from Owari to Kyoto. Acting on orders of Taira Kiyomori, Yoritomo was kept prisoner at the house of Munekiyo, who had pity on his 13-year-old prisoner. He spoke in his behalf to the wife of Taira Yorimori, Iké no Gozen, who was Kiyomori's mother-in-law. Moved by her entreaties, Kiyomori spared Yoritomo, but exiled him to Izu.

In 1183, during the Genpei War (1180-1185), when the Taira fled to the western provinces, Munekiyo remained at Kyoto with Taira Yorimori. Minamoto Yoritomo called them both to Kamakura (Sagami), with the intention of rewarding them for the favor he had received twenty years before, but Munekiyo refused to accept the invitation and rejoined Taira Munemori in the south. It is not known what became of him after the ruin of his family.

Taira Kagekiyo (-1185)

Son of Fujiwara Tadakiyo. He was adopted by the Taira, served them loyally the rest of his life, and showed great valor.

In 1156 Kagekiyo played a role in confirming the Emperor Go-Shirakawa (1127-1192) on the Chrysanthemum Throne.

During the Genpei War (1180-1185), Kagekiyo sought unsuccessfully to

Taira Kagekiyo

have Minamoto Yoritomo (1147-1199) assassinated. He fought Minamoto Yoshinaka (1154-1184) and Minamoto Yukiié (-1186). In 1185, at the Battle of Dan-no-ura (Nagato), he was made prisoner, brought to Kamakura (Sagami), and starved himself to death.

Legends have embellished his life. They represent him taking the disguise of a bonze to assassinate Yoritomo during some ceremony, or again, plucking out his own eyes so as not to see the triumph of the enemies of his family.

He was also known as Kazusa no Shichiro.

Taira Shigemori (1138-1179)

Eldest son of Kiyomori.

Shigemori took a prominent part in the suppression of the 1156 Hogen and the 1160 Heiji Rebellions, that had been caused by the tyranny of his father.

Shigemori endeavored to moderate the impetuous character of his father. In 1177, at the time of the Shishigatani Incident, incited by Fujiwara Narichika (1138-1178), he prevented the imprisonment of the ex-Emperor Go-Shirakawa (1127-1192).

In 1177 Shigemori was appointed nai-daijin "inner minister," but two years later he resigned.

Shigemori unfortunately died before his father, of illness, and thus could not prevent the excesses that occurred in the latter days of Kiyomori's life.

Shigemori remains to the present day one of the most accomplished models of fidelity and respect due to one's sovereign.

Taira Munemori (1147-1185)

Son of Kiyomori. He became his heir at the death of his elder brother Shigemori.

Instead of moderating the excesses of his father, Munemori became the executer of of his evil designs. In 1179 he besieged the ex-Emperor Go-Shirakawa (1127-1192) in his palace, and imprisoned him at the Toba-in.

In 1181, during the Genpei War (1180-1185), at the death of his father, Munemori ascended to the leadership of the Taira. Minamoto (Kiso) Yoshinaka (1154-1184) then led an army out of Shinano, marching into Etchu, Kaga, and Echizen. At the same time, an army under Minamoto Yukiié (-1186) had been crushed in Owari, while operations in the Kanto were largely inconclusive.

In 1183 Munemori dispatched his nephew Koremori, backed by Michimori, Tadanori (1144-1184), Tomonori, Tsunemasa, and Kiyofusa, to Echizen, with the aim of rolling back Yoshinaka. The ensuing Battle of Kurikara (Etchu) ended as a crushing Taira defeat.

Yoshinaka then marched upon Kyoto. Munemori sent his brother Tadanori and his nephew Koremori against him, but they were defeated. He then summoned the bonzes of Hieizan (northeast of Kyoto) to help him, but they refused. Munemori now assembled the members of his family and the principal officers, and told them his intention of retiring into Kyushu. All opposed his project but he, taking the young Emperor Antoku (1178-1185), his mother Kenrei-mon-in (1155-1213), his brother Morisada, and others with him, started on his way south, all the vassals being obliged to follow. They had scarcely left Kyoto, when the ex-Emperor Go-Shirakawa (1127-1192), recovering power, deposed more than 200 officials of the Taira, and raised the 4th son of the ex-Emperor Takakura (1161-1181), then 3 years old, to the Chrysanthemum Throne as the Emperor Go-Toba (1180-1239).

Munemori had scarcely landed at Dazaifu (Kyushu), when he was attacked by Fujiwara (Kujo) Yoritsuné (1218-1256), Ogata Koreyoshi, etc. He retired then to Hakozaki (Chikuzen), then to Sanuki, where he built a temporary palace for the Emperor at a place called Yashima. As the Minamoto were divided into two factions, he profited of their disunion to return into San'yodo, went as far as Settsu, and built a fort at Ichi-no-tani (Settsu).

In 1184, the Minamoto brothers Noriyori (1156-1193) and Yoshitsuné (1159-

1189), after having defeated Minamoto Yoshinaka, marched against the Taira. Simultaneously attacked on both sides, Munemori was defeated, but escaped by sea to Yashima (Sanuki), leaving the following among the dead: his uncle Tadanori, his brothers Kiyosada and Kiyofusa, his cousins Tsunemasa, Tsunetoshi, Atsumori, Michimori, Narimori, his nephews Moromori, Tomo'akira, etc.

In 1185 Minamoto Yoshitsuné crossed over to Shikoku in a driving storm, and attacked the Taira at the Battle of Yashima (Sanuki). The clash was not costly in terms of blood, but it resulted in another Taira retreat. Munemori went to Shido (Sanuki), then to Hikoshima (Nagato), and returned to Hakozaki (Chikuzen), where he met Minamoto Noriyori ready to attack him. He took to sea again, and sailed to the southern tip of Honshu. Yoshitsuné followed him, and the Battle of Dan-no-ura (Nagato) ensued, in which the advantage soon was on the side of the Minamoto. When doubt as to the issue of the battle could no longer be entertained, Taira Tomomori approached the boat that bore the Imperial family, and declared that all hope of success was over. Kiyomori's widow Nii-no-ama then gathered all her children and grandchildren about her, and told them that Munemori was neither her son nor Kiyomori's: Having only one son, Shigemori, Kiyomori was becoming very anxious when hopes were entertained for an heir. A girl was born, and she was secretly exchanged for a son that had just been born to an umbrella merchant of Kitazaka, near the Kiyomizu-dera (Kyoto). "This son of an umbrella merchant," she added vehemently, "is no other than Munemori. It is then not astonishing that we do not find in him the intelligence or the courage of the Taira!" Saying this, she seized her grandson Antoku, and leapt with him into the sea. At this moment the battle became a rout, and Tomomori, Norimori, Tsunemori, Sukemori, Yukimori, Arimori, etc., were killed. The Empress Kenrei-mon-in, daughter of Kiyomori and mother of Antoku, however was saved.

Munemori shamefully would not commit suicide, and one of his own men even shoved him overboard, but he was a good enough swimmer, and was later fished out of the water by the Minamoto. He and his son Kiyomuné were made prisoners and taken to Kyoto, and then to Kamakura (Sagami), but, as Minamoto Yoritomo (1147-1199) had refused to meet with them, they were put to death on the way, at a place called Shinowara (Omi).

Munemori is infamous for his ineptness, and is seen as beneath contempt for not dying with his clan at Dan-no-ura.

Taira Tomomori (1152-1185)

4th son of Kiyomori. He fought in the Genpei War (1180-1185) against the Minamoto.

In 1180 Tomomori defeated Minamoto Yorimasa (1106-1180) at the 1st Battle of Uji (outside Kyoto), in 1180 Minamoto Yoshitsuné (1159-1189) at Mii-dera (Omi), and in 1181 Minamoto Yukiié (-1186) at Sakakura (Mino).

In 1183 Tomomori fought against Minamoto Yoshinaka (1154-1184) in Omi, but was defeated, and he retreated to Kyoto. Taira Munemori then resolved to go south, and Tomomori, who had vehemently opposed this

plan, had to follow him to Yashima (Sanuki).

In 1184, defeated at the Battle of Ichi-no-tani (Settsu), Tomomori escaped death by flight, and built a fort at Hikoshima (Nagato) against the Minamoto. In 1185 he fought bravely at the Battle of Dan-no-ura (Nagato), went to Nii-no-ama to announce to her that defeat was imminent. Hearing that Munemori had not the courage to kill himself, but had been made prisoner, he wept from very shame. Finally he with his uncle Norimori committed suicide; Tomomori tied an anchor to his feet and leapt into the sea.

Taira Shigehira (1158-1185)

Son of Kiyomori. He fought in the Genpei War (1180-1185) against the Minamoto.

In 1180 Shigehira took part in the 1st Battle of Uji (outside Kyoto) against the Imperial Prince Mochihito (-1180) and Minamoto Yorimasa (1106-1180). He then attacked the monks at the Onjo-ji in Otsu (Omi). From there he went to Nara (Yamato) and burned the Todai-ji and Kofuku-ji, temples that had given help to the Minamoto.

In 1181, after defeating Minamoto Yukiié (-1186) at the Battle of Sunomata-gawa (Owari), Shigehira was named commander-in-chief of the Taira forces.

In 1183, when the Taira went south, Minamoto Yoshinaka (1154-1184) entrusted their pursuit to Takanashi Takanobu, Ashikaga Yoshikiyo, Nishina Moriié, etc. At the Battle of Mizushima (Bitchu), the Taira, commanded by Shigehira, Michimori, and Norimori, were victorious, and Takanobu and Yoshikiyo met death in battle.

In 1184 Shigehira was made prisoner at the Battle of Ichi-no-tani (Settsu), and was taken to Kamakura (Sagami). The following year, by request of the bonzes whose temples he had burned, he was beheaded near Nara.

Taira Tokuko (1155-1213)

2nd daughter of Kiyomori. In 1171, at the age of 17, her father arranged for her to be adopted by the ex-Emperor Go-Shirakawa (1127-1192). Kiyomori then saw to it that she became the Empress consort to the 11-year-old Emperor Takakura (1161-1181). In 1178 she gave birth to the Imperial Prince Tokihito. In 1180 Kiyomori pressured Takakura to abdicate, and placed Tokihito, his grandson, on the throne as the Antoku-tenno (1178-1185).

In 1181 both Kiyomori and Takakura died, and Tokuko took the name of Kenrei-mon-in.

In 1185, at the Battle of Dan-no-ura (Nagato), when Antoku's grandmother, Tokiko, the widow of Kiyomori, leapt into the water with the young Emperor clasped firmly in her arms, Tokuko also tried to drown herself, but Minamoto warriors fished her out of the water with a rake by her long hair.

She was permitted to retire to the Choraku-ji (Izu), and shave her head as a nun. But that same year, an earthquake forced her to move to the nunnery Jakko-in (near Kyoto). After about a year, the retired Emperor Go-Shirakawa (1127-1192) visited her, wondering what had become of his adopted daughter.

After over 25 years at the lonely nunnery, praying for the spirits of her husband, her son, and the fallen Taira clan, she died of illness.

Taira Atsumori (1168-1184)

Son of Tsunemori, and nephew to Kiyomori.

In 1184, at the age of 16, Atsumori fought bravely at the Battle of Ichi-no-tani (Settsu). When the defeated Taira were obliged to take to flight, he was left behind, and to gain the boats, spurred his horse into the sea. Kumagai Naozané (1141-1208), seeing this, invited him to single combat, which challenge he accepted. Atsumori, however, was unhorsed, and the two grappled on the beach, but Naozané was too powerful. He knocked off Atsumori's helmet to deliver the finishing blow, only to be struck by the youth of the boy, who was just about the age of Naozané's own son. Naozané, wishing to spare the boy, asked for his name, but the youngster refused. He simply said that he is famous enough that Naozané's superiors will recognize his head when it is time to assign rewards. At that moment, other Minamoto war-

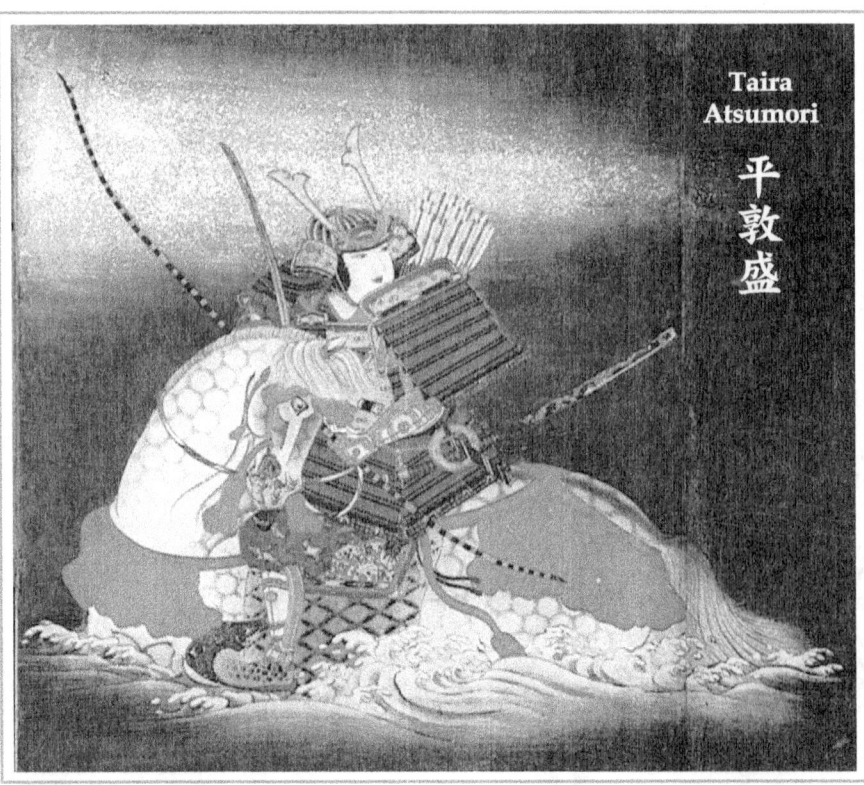

riors arrived at the scene, and believing that if he doesn't kill him, the other warriors surely will. He reasoned that it is better if he is the one to kill his noble foe, because he can offer prayers on his behalf for the afterlife. With tears and regret, Naozané beheaded the boy. Searching the body for something to wrap the head in, he came across a bag containing a flute. He realized that the youngster must have been one of the enemy soldiers playing music before the battle. It is said that the beheading of Atsumori led Naozané to take priestly vows and become a Buddhist monk. This episode has often been sung in poetry and acted on the stage.

Taira Noritsuné (1160-1185)

Son of Norimori. He was Noto no kami. He fought in the Genpei War (1180-1185) against the Minamoto.

In 1183 Noritsuné fought at the Battle of Mizushima (Bitchu), in 1184 at the battle of Ichi-no-tani (Settsu), and in 1185 at the Battle of Dan-no-ura (Nagato). In this last battle, seeing defeat inevitable, he sought out the boat of Minamoto Yoshitsuné (1159-1189) to slay him, but his men came to his rescue. Noritsuné kicked a soldier into the sea, then seizing one with each hand, he leapt into the sea.

Taira Koremori (1160-)

Eldest son of Shigemori, and grandson of Kiyomori. He fought as a general for the Imperial forces in the Genpei War (1180-1185) against the Taira.

In 1180 Koremori was sent to fight Minamoto Yoritomo (1147-1199). He went as far as Fujigawa (Suruga), when his army, hearing of the great strength of the enemy, refused to advance, thus obliging him to return to Kyoto.

In 1183 Koremori defeated Minamoto Yoshinaka (1154-1184) at Hiuchi (Echizen). He then followed Taira Munemori to Yashima (Sanuki). Soon after, however, he left the place, took to sea and landed in Kii. He caused the news to be spread that he was drowned, but in reality went to the Koya-san, and became a bonze. He was then 25 years old. To escape all search, he remained hidden at Fujigawa.

Koremori had a son called Rokudai, who after the 1185 Battle of Dan-no-ura was spared through the intercession of Mongaku-shonin (1120-1200), whose disciple he became, but in 1199, when Mongaku was exiled to Omi, he was arrested and beheaded at Tagoé (Sagami) at the age of 26 years.

Kamakura Period

Adachi

Territory: Dewa

Ancient family of Dewa, descended from Fujiwara Yamakagé (824-888).

Notable Ancestors

Adachi Morinaga (1135-1200)

Supported Minamoto Yoritomo (1147-1199) whilst he lived in exile in Izu, and sided with him against the Taira during the Genpei War (1180-1185).

After the triumph of his party, Morinaga became part of the Kamakura Bakufu of the 2nd Minamoto Shogun Yoriié (1182-1204).

Later he became a bonze under the name Rensai.

Adachi Kagemori (-1248)

Eldest son of Morinaga. From Sagami, he served under Minamoto Yoriié (1182-1204).

In 1218 Kagemori recovered the fief of Akita (Dewa), and was the first to take the title Akita-jo-no-suké.

In 1219, upon the death of Minamoto Sanetomo (1192-1219), Kagemori shaved his head, took the name of Gakuchi, and retired to Koya-san (Kii), whence the title of Koya-nyudo, by which he is commonly known.

In the 1221 Jokyu War, Kagemori marched upon Kyoto with Hojo Tokifusa (1175-1240) and defeated the Imperial army.

His daughter, who had married Hojo Tokiuji (1203-1230), became the mother of the 4th Hojo Shikken Tsunetoki (1224-1246) and the 5th Hojo Shikken Tokiyori (1227-1263), and when the latter became Shikken "Regent," the influence of Kagemori was preponderant.

In 1247 Kagemori formed an alliance with his grandson Hojo Tokiyori to battle the rival Miura.

Adachi Yoshikagé (-1255)

Son of Kagemori. He was Akita-jo-no-suké.

In 1242, after the death of the Emperor Shijo (1231-1242), Fujiwara Michiié (1193-1252) desired to have his grandson Tadanari-shinno, the 5th son of the Emperor Juntoku (1197-1242), ascend the Chrysanthemum Throne. The 3rd Hojo Shikken Yasutoki (1183-1242) opposed this, and instead sent Yoshikagé to Kyoto to enthrone the Imperial Prince Kunihito, the 2nd son of the Emperor Tsuchi-mikado (1196-1231), as the Emperor Go-Saga (1220-1272).

In 1249 Yoshikagé became the first to bear the title of Hyojo-bugyo "Chief of the Council of State."

In 1254, falling ill, Yoshikagé shaved his head and took the name Ganchi. He died the following year.

Adachi Yasumori (1231-1285)

3rd son of Yoshikagé. He succeeded to his father's title and dignities. He was an ambitious and gifted administrator as well as a scholar of Confucian classics and Buddhism.

Adachi Yasumori

His daughter married the 8th Hojo Shikken Tokimuné (1251-1284), and became the mother of the 9th Hojo Shikken Sadatoki (1271-1311), who succeeded upon the death of his father. Yasumori and his son and heir Munekagé then enjoyed great authority for a time.

Following the death of Hojo Takayori, Yasumori was named osso bugyo "appeals magistrate."

Yasumori was the go'on bugyo "chief of the rewards office," in which capacity he granted a hearing to Takezaki Suenaga (1246-1314), who had commissioned the *Moko Shurai Ekotoba* "*Mongol Invasion Scroll,*" a set of self-serving illustrations that recorded his battlefield valor and deeds.

In 1282 Yasumori left his responsibilities to his son Munekagé, and became a Buddhist monk under the name Kakushin.

In 1285, in what is known as the Shimotsuki "Frosty Moon" Incident, Taira Yoritsuna, the shitsuji "deputy Shogun" of Sadatoki, accused Yasumori of plotting against the young Shikken, and even of aspiring to the Shogunate. Sadatoki lent a willing ear to these insinuations, and authorize Yoritsuna to attack the Adachi residence, which resulted in the near extermination of the Adachi and their supporters, estimated at 500 deaths, including Yasumori, who was forced to commit suicide.

His 2nd son Morimuné replaced him as shugo "constable" of Higo.

Adachi Tokiaki (-1333)

Grandson of Yasumori's brother. He was an advisor to the last ruling Hojo Shikken Takatoki (1303-1333). He committed suicide with Takatoki and the rest of the Hojo.

Kamakura Period – Daibutsu / Hiki / Izumi / Kagami

DAIBUTSU

Residence: Kyoto

Branch of the Kamakura Shikken Hojo.

NOTABLE ANCESTORS

Daibutsu Yorimori (13th century)
Son of Hojo Tokifusa (1175-1240), and grandson of Hojo Tokimasa (1138-1215). He was the first to take the name of Daibutsu or Osaragi.

Daibutsu Sadafusa (-1306)
Grandson of Yorimori. He was a distinguished poet, and Rokuhara-tandai "governor of Kyoto."
The family became extinct at the ruin of Kamakura.

HIKI

Residence: Kamakura

NOTABLE ANCESTORS

Hiki Yoshikazu (-1203)
Originally from Musashi, rose to prominence in the Shogunal court when adopted by the nurse of Minamoto Yoritomo (1147-1199).
During the Genpei War (1180-1185) Yoshikazu accompanied Yoritomo as general in all his expeditions against the Taira. In 1189 he helped Yoritomo in his attack against Fujiwara Yasuhira (1155-1189) in Mutsu.
Yoshikazu was made kebiishi "minister of police."
Yoshikazu gave his daughter Wakasa no Tsuboné in marriage to the 2nd Minamoto Shogun Yoriié (1182-1204). In 1203, when Yoriié became seriously ill, his mother Masako of the Hojo proposed to divide the right of succession between his brother Minamoto Sanetomo (1192-1219) and eldest son Minamoto Ichiman (1198-1203). Yoshikazu found the part allotted to his grandson insufficient, and protested. The 1st Hojo Shikken Tokimasa (1138-1215) then invited Yoshikazu to his home on a pretext, and had him assassinated. His son Munetomo and grandson Ichiman tried to escape, but were killed by the 2nd Hojo Shikken Yoshitoki (1163-1224), along with a great number of the extended Hiki family.

IZUMI

Territory: Shinano

NOTABLE ANCESTORS

Izumi Chikahira (-1213)
Daimyo of Shinano, and a relative of the Minamoto. He was in the service of the 2nd Minamoto Shogun Yoriié (1182-1204).
In 1213, wishing to raise Senju-maru (1201-1214), the 3rd son of Yoriié, to the Shogunate, Chikahira revolted against the Hojo, and deputed the bonze Annen to all the provinces to recruit adherents to his cause. But Shiba Shigenané revealed the plot to the 2nd Hojo Shikken Yoshitoki (1163-1224), and an army was dispatched against Chikahira, who was defeated and killed.
Chikahira was renowned for his physical strength, and is compared to Asahina Yoshihidé, his contemporary.

KAGAMI

Territory: Omi

Ddaimyo family descended from the Sasaki.

NOTABLE ANCESTORS

Kagami Hisatsuna (-1221)
Son of Sasaki Sadashigé. He was killed in the 1221 Jokyu War (Kyoto), when fighting against the Hojo.
His descendants resided at Kagami-yama (Omi), and served the Sasaki.

Kamakura Period – Hojo

HOJO

Residence: Kamakura

Family descended from a branch of Taira Sadamori, originating around the 10th century, and adopted their family name from the small town which they controlled in Izu. They gained power by supporting the extermination of the Taira, their close relatives, and by supporting Minamoto Yoritomo (1147-1199) in the Genpei War (1180-1185).

Yoritomo's wife Masako (1156-1225) was the daughter of Hojo Tokimasa (1138-1215), who helped his son-in-law defeat the Taira forces to become Japan's 1st Shogun. After Yoritomo's death, Tokimasa became Shikken "Regent" to Yoritomo's son and successor, the child Shogun Minamoto Yoriié (1182-1204), who was also his grandson, thus usurping power, and effectively transferring control of the Kamakura Shogunate to his clan permanently.

From 1200-1333 the heads of the Hojo, under the title of Shikken, was the actual ruler of Japan. The Minamoto and even Imperial Princes became puppets and hostages of the Hojo.

In 1333 Kamakura was invaded by Nitta Yoshisada (1301-1338), and the entire Hojo clan of almost 900 killed themselves at the family temple of Tosho-ji, marking the end of the Hojo Regency and the fall of the Kamakura Shogunate.

The Hojo are known for their defiance of the Mongols, and fathering the spread of Zen Buddhism and Bushido, but also for their extreme decadence, and deciding of national policy in secret meetings at private residences.

The later Hojo of the Sengoku "Warring States" Period (1467-1573), who ruled the Kanto from Odawara (Sagami), is not related to this clan, although they did adopt the same mon "family crest."

NOTABLE ANCESTORS

Hojo Tokimasa (1138-1215)
1st Kamakura Shikken.

Hojo/Minamoto Masako (1157-1225)

Eldest daughter Tokimasa, and sister to Yoshitoki. Her mother was Maki. She was born in Kyoto when her parents were still in their teens, and was raised by many ladies-in-waiting and nannies. She was instructed in horsemanship, hunting, and fishing, and she would eat with the men rather than with the women of the household.

In 1179 Masako met the young exile Minamoto Yoritomo (1147-1199). The two fell in love, and wed later that year.

In the first year of the Genpei War (1180-1185) Masako's brother Munetoki was killed at the Battle of Ishibashiyama (Sagami), and her younger brother Yoshitoki became heir of the Hojo.

In 1182 Masako and Yoritomo had their first son Minamoto Yoriié (1182-1204). In 1192 they had another son Minamoto Sanetomo (1192-1219). Also that year Yoritomo was named Shogun by the Cloistered Emperor Go-Shirakawa (1127-1192), and set up his warrior government at Kamakura. Masako's husband was now the most powerful man in Japan.

In 1199 Yoritomo died, and was succeeded by his son Yoriié. As the latter was only 18 years old, Hojo Tokimasa proclaimed himself Shikken "Regent" to the 2nd Shogun. Masako shaved her head, accepting the tonsure from the priest Taiko Gyoyu (1163-1241), but did not take residence in a nunnery. Together with her father Tokimasa and her younger brother Yoshitoki, she created a council of regents for her son. Yoriié, however, hated his mother's family for its influences, and preferred his wife's clan, led by her father Hiki Yoshikazu (-1203).

In 1203 Masako reported to her father that Yoriié and his father-in-law were hatching a plot to kill him, and Tokimasa had Yoshikazu executed and forced Yoriié to abdicate. Suffering from illness, Yoriié retired to Izu, where in 1204 he was murdered, no doubt by Tokimasa's orders, with Masako supposedly not aware of her father's plan. During the murders and purges of the Hiki, Minamoto Ichiman (1198-1203), Yoriié's eldest son and heir, and Masako's grandson, was also executed as he was part Hiki.

When Yoriié retired, Sanetomo, Masako's other son, became the 3rd Shogun at the age of 11, with Tokimasa still Regent and now the most powerful man in Kamakura. When Masako heard rumors that Tokimasa and his 2nd wife Omaki-no-kata was planning to execute Sanetomo and replace him with their son-in-law Hiraga Tomomasa (-1205), she and her younger brother Yoshitoki ordered their father to step down and retire or they would rebel. In 1205 Tokimasa abdicated as Regent, and shaved his head at a monastery in Kamakura. Yoshitoki succeeded as the 2nd Shikken for Sanetomo.

In 1219 Sanetomo was assassinated by his nephew Minamoto Kugyo (1200-1219), 2nd son of Yoriié, who thought he should have been raised to Shogunhood instead of his uncle. Kugyo was later caught and killed by Nagao Sadakage.

Hojo Masako

Kamakura Period – Hojo

The Minamoto line was now extinct. Masako and Shikken Yoshitoki chose as the 4th Shogun, Kujo Yoritsuné (1218-1256), a member of the greater Fujiwara, and at the time an infant 2 years old.

In 1224 Yoshitoki died of a sudden illness, and his passing inspired a conspiracy by the Iga, who hoped to influence the powerful Miura Yoshimura (-1239) to topple the Hojo and replace them in Kamakura. Masako learned of the threat and personally rushed to see Yoshimura, extracting a promise that he would stand by the Hojo, effectively derailing the conspiracy before it had begun. Her brother Yasutoki safely succeeded as the 3rd Shikken.

At the age of 69 she died. The nation has surnamed her Ama-Shogun "Nun Shogun" and Ni-i no Zenni.

Hojo Yoshitoki (1163-1224)
2nd Kamakura Shikken.

Hojo Tokifusa (1175-1240)
Son of 1st Hojo Shikken Tokimasa, and younger brother to Masako and the 2nd Hojo Shikken Yoshitoki.

After the 1221 Jokyu War (Kyoto) Tokifusa was named the 1st Minamikata Rokuhara tandai "southern governor of Kyoto," while his nephew Yasutoki was the first to be named to the higher-ranking Kitakata Rokuhara tandai "northern governor of Kyoto."

In 1224, at the death of Yoshitoki, he returned to Kamakura to aid the new Shikken Yasutoki as the 1st rensho "assistant to the Regent."

He later became a Buddhist monk, and lived the rest of his life at the To-ji in Nara (Yamato), where he acquired the nickname Daibutsu "Great Buddha."

Hojo Yasutoki (1183-1242)
3rd Kamakura Shikken.

Hojo Tomotoki (1193-1245)
Son of the 2nd Hojo Shikken Yoshitoki, and brother to the 3rd Hojo Shikken Yasutoki.

At the time of the 1213 Wada Rebellion, Tomotoki fought against the famous Asahina Yoshihidé.

During the 1221 Jokyu War (Kyoto) Tomotoki brought troops from Hokurikudo "Northern Region" and led them to Kyoto. He was then appointed Hyojo-shu-betto "Chief of the Council of State."

Hojo Shigetoki (1198-1261)
Son of the 2nd Hojo Shikken Yoshitoki, and brother to the 3rd Hojo Shikken Yasutoki.

In 1230 Shigetoki replaced Tokiuji as the 3rd Kitakata Rokuhara tandai "northern governor of Kyoto" with the title of Sagami no kami.

In 1247 Shigetoki returned to Kamakura, where he was the 2nd rensho "assistant to the Regent" to the 5th Hojo Shikken Tokiyori.

He was also called Gokuraku-ji-dono.

Hojo Masamura (1205-1273)
Puppet Regent of the 5th Hojo Shikken Tokiyori.

Hojo Tokiuji (1203-1230)
Son of the 2nd Hojo Shikken Yasutoki. He took part in the 1221 Jokyu War (Kyoto) with his father. His wife was Matsushita Zenni, known for her wisdom.

In 1224 Tokiuji was sent as Kitakata Rokuhara tandai "northern governor Kyoto" with Hojo Tokimori, son of his father's uncle, as the Minamikata Rokuhara tandai "southern governor of Kyoto." The two lived in a palace separate from each other, hence the name of Ryo-Rokuhara "the Two Rokuhara," which was given to their residences.

He was expected to succeed his father as Shikken, but having become ill, he returned to Kamakura, where he died at the age of 28.

Hojo Nagatoki (1230-1264)
Puppet Regent of the 5th Kamakura Shikken Tokiyori.

Hojo Tsunetoki (1224-1246)
4th Kamakura Shikken.

Hojo Tokiyori (1226-1263)
5th Kamakura Shikken.

Hojo Tokimuné (1251-1284)
6th Kamakura Shikken.

Hojo Sadatoki (1270-1311)
7th Kamakura Shikken.

Hojo Takatoki (1303-1333)
9th Kamakura Shikken.

Hojo Tokiyuki (1322-1353)
Son of the last Hojo Shikken Takatoki.

In 1333, after the Siege of Kamakura (Sagami), and the almost complete destruction of his family, a servant helped Tokiyuki escape to the residence of Suwa Yorishigé (-1335) in Shinano, who gathered an army with which Tokiyuki can return to Kamakura and regain power. In 1335 he re-entered Kamakura and put Ashikaga Tadayoshi (1306-1352) to flight, only to be soon afterwards expelled by Ashikaga Takauji (1305-1358).

Tokiyuki then presented himself to the Emperor Go-Daigo (1288-1339), was pardoned, and formally joined the partisans of the Southern Court. He fought under the command of Kitabataké Akiié (1318-1338), and then under the Munenaga-shinno (1311-1385).

In 1352 Tokiyuki assisted at the recapture of Kamakura by Nitta Yoshioki (-1358). But afterwards, when the latter, defeated by Takauji, took refuge in Echigo, Tokiyuki hid himself in Sagami, but was discovered and beheaded at Tatsu-no-kuchi.

Hojo Tokiuji

Kamakura Period – Jo / Kudo

JO

Territory: Echigo

Ancient daimyo family of Echigo, descended from Taira Yoshikané (10th century).

NOTABLE ANCESTORS

Jo Sukenaga (-1182)

Son of Sukekuni. He was defeated and killed by Kiso Yoshinaka (1154-1184).

Jo Nagamochi (-1201)

Son of Sukekuni, brother to Sukenaga. He was also called Sukemoto.

Having been defeated with Sukenaga, Nagamochi fled to Aizu (Mutsu). Afterwards, he was nominated Echigo no kami, and in 1189 took part in the expedition of Minamoto Yoritomo (1147-1199) against Fujiwara Yasuhira (1155-1189) in Mutsu.

In the 1201 Kennin Uprising, Nagamochi revolted against the Hojo, but was defeated and killed.

Hangaku-gozen (12th-13th century)

Daughter of Jo Sukekuni, and sister to Sukenaga and Nagamochi. She is also known as Itagaki-gozen.

In the 1201 Kennin Uprising, an attempt by her brother Nagamochi to overthrow the Kamakura Shogunate, Hangaku and her nephew Sukemori raised an army for him. Under attack from Sasaki Moritsuna, Hangaku and her other brother Sukenaga took a defensive position at a fort at Torisaka-yama. Heavily outnumbered by the Hojo, ultimately she was wounded by an arrow and captured.

Hangaku was taken to Kamakura. When she was presented to the 2nd Minamoto Shogun Yoriié (1182-1204), she met Asari Yohito, a warrior of the Kai-Genji, who received the Shogun's permission to marry her. They lived in Kai, where she is said to have had one daughter.

Hangaku is said to have been exceedingly strong and beautiful. Although her use of a naginata "Japanese pole arm" in battle is debatable, she has

Hangaku-gozen

been complimented for her use of the bow.

Jo Sukemori (-1202)

Son of Sukenaga. He tried to continue the struggle after the death of his father, but was likewise defeated by Sasaki Moritsuna. With him the family became extinct.

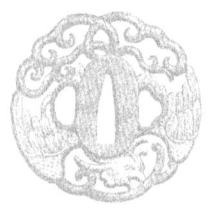

KUDO

Territory: Echigo

Family of daimyo in Izu, descended from Fujiwara Muchimaro (680-737).

NOTABLE ANCESTORS

Kudo Shigemitsu (-1181)

In 1170 Shigemitsu was commissioned to quell a revolt of Minamoto Tametomo (1139-1170), who had been exiled to Oshima (Izu) after the 1156 Hogen War (Kyoto), and was causing disturbances.

During the Genpei War (1180-1185) Shigemitsu sided with Minamoto Yoritomo (1147-1199). In 1180 he was defeated at the Battle of Ishibashi-yama (Sagami), and killed shortly afterwards.

Kudo Suketsuné (-1193)

Son of Suketsugu, and nephew to Shigemitsu. Also known as Ito Suketsuné.

Suketsuné was despoiled of his domains by his uncle Ito Sukechika and shut up in Kyoto. In 1177 he revenged himself by wounding Sukechika severely, and killing his son Sukeyasu.

In 1193 the sons of Sukeyasu, Soga Juro Sukenari (1172-1193) and Soga Goro Tokimuné (1174-1193), after having long waited for a favorable opportunity, at last succeeded in assassinating Suketsuné in the very camp of Minamoto Yoritomo (1147-1199). This is the famous vengeance of the Soga brothers.

Kumagai

Territory: Musashi

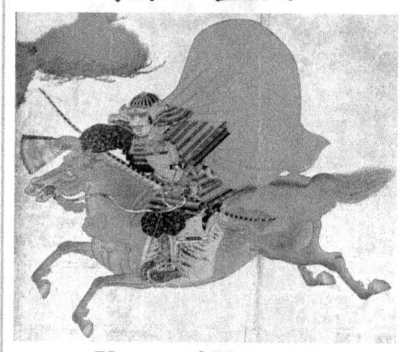

Kumagai Naozané

Family of daimyo, descended from Taira Sadamori (10th century).

Notable Ancestors

Kumagai Naosada (12th century)
Settled down at Kumagaya (Musashi) and took its name.

Kumagai Naozané (1141-1208)
Son of Naosada. Born in Kumagai (Musashi), he lost his father at a young age, and was raised by his maternal uncle Hisaka Naomitsu.

In the Genpei War (1180-1185) Naozané first served under Taira Tomomori (1152-1185), and contributed with Oba Kagechika (-1180) to the defeat of Minamoto Yoritomo (1147-1199) at the 1180 Battle of Ishibashi-yama (Sagami). Shortly afterwards, he passed over to the Minamoto, and at the 1184 Battle of Ichi-no-tani (Settsu), aided by his son Naoié and Hirayama Suéshigé, obliged the Taira to escape by sea. There it was that he pursued and killed Taira Atsumori (1169-1184). Legend has embellished this episode so far as to pretend that Naozané substituted his own son for the young heir of his former masters.

In 1192, having fallen out with Kugé Naomitsu about the limits of their respective domains, he retired to the Kurodani Komyo-ji (Kyoto), where he took the name of Rensho, and put himself under the direction of the famous Honen-bo Genku (1133-1212).

Nawa

Territories: Hoki, Inaba
Castle: Funanoé-sen (Hoki)

Family of daimyo descended from Ashikaga Suéfusa (Murakami-Genji).

Notable Ancestors

Nawa Tadafusa (12th century)
Son of Suéfusa. He established himself at Nawa (Hoki), and took that name towards the end of the 12th century.

Nawa Nagatoshi (-1336)
In 1333 received the Emperor Go-Daigo (1288-1339), who escaped from Oki where he was exiled, and installed him in his castle of Funanoé-sen (Hoki). Hearing of this, the 14th Hojo Shikken Takatoki (1303-1333) sent Sasaki Kiyotaké and Sasaki Masatsuna, to besiege the castle, but failed. Masatsuna was killed and Kiyotaké fled. After this victory Nagatoshi charged his son Yoshitaka to escort the Emperor to Kyoto. In 1334 Nagatoshi received Hoki and Inaba as recompense.

When Ashikaga Takauji (1305-1358) revolted in the Kanto, the Emperor Go-Daigo (1288-1339) sent Nitta Yoshisada (1301-1338) against him, and charged Nagatoshi and Kusunoki Masashigé (1294-1336) to defend Kyoto.

In 1335, after the defeat of Nitta Yoshisada at Hakoné (Sagami), Nagatoshi tried to hinder Ashikaga Takauji's progress, but was defeated at the bridge of Seta, and killed in trying to retake Kyoto.

Nagatoshi is considered as one of the most generous defenders of the legitimate dynasty, and a Nawa-jinja is dedicated to him at Nawa (Hoki). The family, which was hereditarily at the head of the temple, claimed descent from Nagatoshi.

Minamoto

Residence: Kamakura

Major family of warriors and statemen who dominated politics in Japan during the Heian "Aristocratic" Period (794-1185) and the Kamakura Period (1185-1333).

The Imperial Princes steadily increasing in numbers, and consequently the expenses of the Court becoming overextended, in 814 Saga-tenno (786-842) gave the name of Minamoto (Chinese: Gen) to his 7th and younger sons, effectively removing them from royal succession: it is the origin of the different Minamoto-uji, or Genji families, distinguished from one another by the name of the Emperor from whom they descended. Thus we have the four principal Minamoto families of Saga-Genji, the Seiwa-Genji, the Uda-Genji, and the Murakami-Genji. Some of these branches had offices at Court and kept their rank as kugé "nobles," but most of them entered the military career and established the lineage of the Shogun and the great daimyo.

At first the families issued from these Princes bore only the uji "patronymic name" of Minamoto; then, as their number increased, each branch, selected their own myoji "adopted name," usually taken from the district or village in which they resided: Ashikaga, Tokugawa, Matsudaira, Nitta, Takeda, Sasaki, Akamatsu, Kitabataké, etc.

Furthermore, history mentions as having received the name of Minamoto: five sons of the Emperor Ninmyo, eight of Montoku, three of Yozei, 14 of Koko, four of Daigo, four grandsons of Sanjo, and very many Princesses. Most of these branches, however, after one or several generations became extinct.

The most prominent of the Minamoto families, the Seiwa-Genji, descended from a grandson of the Emperor Seiwa (850-880), Minamoto Tsunemoto (917–961), who went to the provinces and became the founder of a major warrior dynasty. His son Minamoto Mitsunaka (912–997) loyally served several successive Fujiwara Regents by suppressing rebellions and guarding the state's borders. Thereafter the Fujiwara frequently called upon the Minamoto to restore order in the capital of Heian-kyo (Kyoto). Mitsunaka's eldest son, Yorimitsu (948–1021), became the protégé of Fujiwara Michinaga (966-1028). In 1032 another son, Yorinobu (968–1048), suppressed the rebellion of Taira Tadatsuné (-1031). Between 1051 and 1087 Yorinobu's son, Yoriyoshi (998-1075), and grandson, Yoshiié (1039-

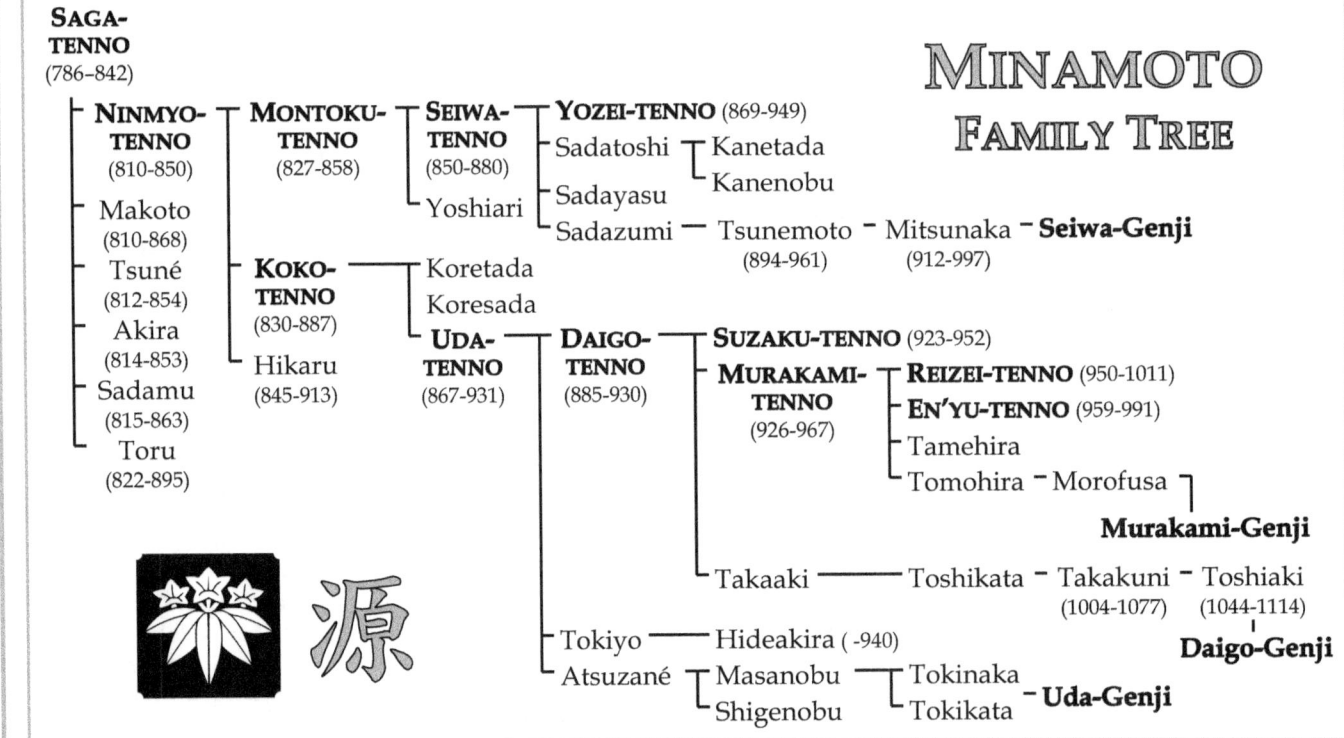

Kamakura Period – Minamoto Saga-Genji

1106), pacified most of northeastern Japan.

The Seiwa-Genji's fortunes declined in the 1156 Hogen Rebellion (Kyoto), when the Taira executed much of the line. During the 1160 Heiji Rebellion (Kyoto), the head of the Seiwa-Genji, Minamoto Yoshitomo (1123-1160), died in battle. Taira Kiyomori (1118-1181) seized power in Kyoto by forging an alliance with the retired Emperors Shirakawa (1053-1129) and Toba (1103-1156), and infiltrating the kugé. He sent the 3rd son of Yoshimoto, Minamoto Yoritomo (1147-1199), into exile. In the Genpei War (1180-1185) Yoritomo and his stepbrother, the legendary Minamoto Yoshitsuné (1159-1189), mounted a full-scale rebellion against the Taira rule, culminating in the destruction of the Taira, and the subjugation of eastern Japan.

The Seiwa-Genji proved to be the strongest and most dominant Minamoto line during the late Heian Period with Yoritomo in 1192 becoming the 1st Shogun of Japan and setting up the first Bakufu "Military Government" at Kamakura, marking the rise of the samurai class and military rule.

The line however produced only two more Shogun, and the year 1219 marked the end of the Seiwa-Genji lineage, and the decline of the Minamoto's period of historical prominence.

The struggle between the Minamoto and the Taira in the Genpei War is recounted in the epic *Heiké Monogatari "Tale of the Heiké,"* as well as in many songs, poems, and plays.

Saga-Genji

Notable Ancestors

Minamoto Makoto (810-868)

7th son of the Emperor Saga (786-842), and brother to the Emperor Ninmyo (810-850). In 814 he received the name of Minamoto. In 857 he was sadaijin "senior minister of state."

Minamoto Makoto

In 866 Makoto was accused by his political rival Ban Tomo no Yoshio of having set the blaze that destroyed the Oten-mon "main gate" of the Imperial Palace. In one of the more famous events of Court intrigues in the Heian "Aristocratic" Period (794-1185), this came to be known as the Oten-mon Conspiracy. With the help of Daijo-daijin "Chancellor of the Realm" Fujiwara Yoshifusa (804-872), Makoto was able to successfully argue his innocence. Soon afterwards, a man claiming to have witnessed the event accused Yoshio and his son of setting the fire themselves. They, along with several other members of the Ban family, as well as a few of the Ki family, were convicted and executed.

As he lived in a quarter of Kyoto called Kitabé, Makoto is often designated by the name of Kitabé-daijin.

Minamoto Tsuné (812-854)

9th son of Saga-tenno (786-842). In 840 he was udaijin "junior minister of state," and in 849 sadaijin "senior minister of state." He is often called Higashi-Sanjo-sadaijin.

Minamoto Akira (814-853)

Son of the Emperor Saga (786-842). In 832 he was daigaku-no-kami "chief education expert," and in 849 sangi "Imperial advisor."

In 850, when his brother the Emperor Ninmyo (810-850) died, Akira shaved his head and took the name Sosa. He was also called Yogawa-Saisho-nyudo.

Minamoto Sadamu (815-863)

Son of the Emperor Saga (786-842). He had great talent for music. Sadamu was also called Shigo-dainagon.

Minamoto Toru (822-895)

Son or grandson of the Emperor Saga. In 872 he was sadaijin "senior minister of state," and hence is also called Kawara-sadaijin.

Minamoto Toru

Toru built the first villa in Uji (south of Kyoto), where the Byodo-in was later built.

Toru was a noted poet, and is the author of poem 14 in the anthology *Ogura Hyakunin Isshu* "One Hundred Poems by One Hundred Poets."

Toru is sometimes considered the model for Hikaru Genji in the Japanese literary classic *The Tale of Genji* by Murasaki Shikubu.

Minamoto Hikaru (845-913)

Son of the Emperor Ninmyo (810-850).

In 901 Hikaru joined Fujiwara Tokihira (871-909) against Sugawara Michizané (845-903), who was accused of plotting against the Emperor Daigo (885-930) in order to replace him by his own son-in-law, the Imperial Prince Tokiyo (886-927). Michizané was exiled to Tsukushi, and Hikaru replaced him in the office of udaijin "junior minister of state." He is also called Nishi-sanjo-udaijin.

Minamoto Shitago (911-983)

Descendant of Sadamu. He is known as a poet and a literary man. He was one of the Sanjuroku-kasan "36 Poetic Geniuses." He received the titles of minbu-o-suké "deputy minister of taxation," Izumi no kami, and Noto no kami.

Minamoto Shitago

Between 931 and 937 Shitago compiled the *Wamyo Ruiju-sho*, the first Japanese dictionary of Chinese characters organized into semantic headings, at the request of a daughter of the Emperor Daigo (885-930). He also wrote the *Minamoto no Shitagau-shu*, a collection of his poems.

In 951 Shitago was chosen by the Emperor Murakami as one of the five compilers of the anthology *Gosen Waka-shu* "*Later Collection of Poems.*"

He became bonze under the name Anbo-hoshi.

Daigo-Genji

Notable Ancestors

Minamoto Taka'aki (914-982)

17th son of the Emperor Daigo (885-930). In 920 he received the name Minamoto. He married Yasuko (927-964), daughter of Fujiwara Morosuké (908-960). She would later marry the Emperor Murakami (926-967), and became the mother of the Emperors Reizei (950-1011) and En'yu (959-991).

In 966 Taka'aki was udaijin "junior minister of state," and in 968 sadaijin "senior minister of state."

In 969 Taka'aki, together with Minamoto Mitsunaka (912-997) and Tachibana Shigenobu, planned to dethrone the Reizei-tenno, and to replace him by his brother, the Imperial Prince Tamehira (952-1010). The plot was discovered, and Taka'aki was sent in disgrace to Tsukushi (Kyushu) with the title of Dazai-no-gon-no-sotsu "deputy constable of Kyushu." He was re-called two years after by the En'yu-tenno.

Taka'aki is usually known under the name of Nishi-no-Miya-no-sadaijin. A distinguished man of letters, he has written an autobiography.

Minamoto Toshikata (959-1027)

Son of Taka'aki. In 1005 he was chunagon "middle counselor," and in 1010 minbu-kyo "chief of police." He is one of the Shi-nagon "Four Famous Poets," all of whom had the title of nagon.

Minamoto Takakuni (1004-1077)

Son of Toshikata. He was gon-chunagon "deputy middle counselor" and dainagon "grand counselor." He was the father of the astronomer and artist Toba Sojo (1053-1140).

Takakuni was a scholar and wrote several books. He is credited with compiling the *Konjaku Monogatari-shu* "*Anthology of Tales from the Past,*" a collection of over one-thousand stories from India, China, and Japan written during the period. He is also said to have written the *Uji Dainagon Monogatari*, another collection of stories that is no longer extant, but is referenced in many other stories.

He retired to Uji (Yamashiro), and is also called Uji-no-dainagon.

Minamoto Toshiaki (1044-1114)

Son of Takakuni.

In 1087 Toshiaki was the first who received the title of betto "superintendent" of the Court of the ex-Emperor Shirakawa (1053-1129). He was also shissei-daijin, gon-dainagon "deputy grand counselor," and azechi "inspector general" of Mutsu and Dewa.

Minamoto Hiromasa (918-980)

Eldest son of the Imperial Prince Katsuakira, and grandson of the Emperor Daigo (885-930). His mother was the daughter of Fujiwara Tokihira (871-909). When Hiromasa was removed from the Imperial succession, he was granted the surname Minamoto.

In 934 the lower 4th rank was conferred upon Hiromasa. In 947 he became the senior assistant minister of the Nakatsukasa-sho "Ministry of Central Affairs." In 959 he became Captain of the Right Watch. In 965 he became the Middle Captain of the Left Palace Guards. In 974 he was promoted to the lower 3rd rank and became Provisional Master of the Palace of the Queen Mother.

Lore has it that Hiromasa attained his mastery of gagaku "elegant classical Court music" by studying vocal music with Prince Atsumi (893-967), the koto "Japanese stringed instrument" with the Emperor Daigo, the biwa "Japanese

Minamoto Hiromasa

lute" with Minamoto Osamu, the flute from O'oishi Minekichi, and the hichiriki "double-reed Japanese flute" from Yoshiminé Yukimusa. Bass hichiriki was his strong point, but he disliked song and dance.

In 951 Hiromasa played biwa at the New Year's banquet of Emperor Murakami (936-967).

There is a story that in 960 Hiromasa was called upon to participate in the so-called "4th Annual Tentoku Poetry Contest," but that he froze in front of the Emperor and accidentally gave the title of one poem but recited another.

In 966, by order of the Emperor, Hiromasa compiled the Imperial music anthology *Shinsen-gakubu*, also called *Hakuga-no-Fué-fu* "*Hiromasa's Flute Score.*" The system of notation he developed is still used today.

Hiromasa received the famous flute Ha-futatsu from a demon at the Suzaku-mon "Main Gate" of the Imperial Palace. He retrieved the famous biwa Genjou from the Rasho-mon "Main City Gate" of the Palace.

Wishing to receive lessons from the famous Semi-maru, Hiromasa went during three years, every evening, to the door of the musician's house in Osaka, without gaining audience. At last conquered by such perseverance, Semimaru accepted him as his scholar, and taught him the secret tunes "Flowing Spring" and "Woodpecker."

He is often designated by the name Hakuga-no-sanmi.

Kamakura Period – Minamoto Murakami-Genji / Uda-Genji / Seiwa-Genji

```
Morofusa ┬ Toshifusa ─ Moroyori
(1009-1077)│ (1035-1131)  (1070-1139)
           │
           └ Akifusa ─ Masazané ─ Masasada ─ Masamichi ─ Michichika
                      (1059-1127)                       (1149-1202)
```

Minamoto Murakami-Genji Family Tree

Murakami-Genji

Notable Ancestors

Minamoto Morofusa (1009-1077)

Son of Imperial Prince Tomohira. He was known as a writer and a poet. In 1020 he received the name of Minamoto. He was successively naidaijin "inner minister," ukon-é-taisho "junior commander of the Imperial Guard," udaijin "junior minister of state," sakon-é-taisho "senior commander of the Imperial Guard," and lastly, on the day of his death, he was named Daijo-daijin "Chancellor of the Realm."

Morofusa is also known under the name Tsuchi-mikado.

Minamoto Toshifusa (1035-1131)

Son of Morofusa. He occupied the highest positions including in 1083 that of sadaijin "senior minister of state," and in 1093 of sakon-é-taisho "senior commander of the Imperial Guard."

When he had his head shaved he took the name Jakushun.

Toshifusa wrote an autobiography journal called *Suisa-ki*.

The people called him Horikawa-safu.

Minamoto Moroyori (1070-1139)

Followed the steps of his ancestors and became a distinguished man of letters: he had studied under Oé Tadafusa. Moroyoshi is also called Ono-no-miya.

Minamoto Masazané (1059-1127)

In 1122 rose to the dignity of Daijo-daijin "Chancellor of the Realm," and was above the Kanpaku.

Masazané was also called Kuga, and left a diary called the *Kuga-shokoku-ki*.

Minamoto Michichika (1149-1202)

Descendant of the above nobles. He was Lord Keeper of the Privy Seal, and took part in the government during seven consecutive reigns. His adopted daughter Zaishi (1171-1257) married the Emperor Go-Toba (1180-1239), and was the mother of the Emperor Tsuchi-mikado (1196-1231).

Minamoto Michichika

Michichika is one of the authors credited with writing the *Ima Kagami* "Mirror of the Present" that recounts various events between 1025 and 1170 that have little historical value but are of literary interest.

He was also known as Fujiwara Michichika, and is the ancestor of the kugé Horikawa, Tsuchi-mikado, and Nakano-in.

Uda-Genji

Notable Ancestors

Minamoto Hidéakira (-940)

Son of the Imperial Prince Tokiyo (886-927), and grandson of the Emperor Uda (867-931). His mother was the daughter of Sugawara Michizané (845-903). He was kurodo-no-kami "head of the bureau of archivists" and sa-chujo.

Minamoto Masanobu (920-993)

3rd son of Imperial Prince Atsuzané (897-966), and grandson of the Emperor Uda (967-931). His mother was a daughter of Fujiwara Tokihira (871-909). In 978 he became sadaijin "senior minister of state."

Masanobu's daughter Rinshi married Fujiwara Michinaga (966-1028) when the latter was in a far lower position, and for this Masanobu disputed his daughter's marriage, but his wife Bokushi pushed for the marriage. Michinaga eventually entered Masanobu's residence as he successively became sakyo-no-daibu, gon-no-chunagon "deputy middle counselor," gon-no-dainagon "deputy grand counselor," nairan "Imperial inspector of documents," udaijin "junior minister of state," sadaijin "senior minister of state," and finally Sessho "Regent to the Child Emperor."

He was also called Tsuchi-mikado.

Masanobu is the progenitor of the Uda-Genji.

Seiwa-Genji

Branch issued from Sadazumi-shinno (874-916), son of the Emperor Seiwa (850-880), and from whom descend the three families of Shogun: the Minamoto, the Ashikaga, and the Tokugawa.

Notable Ancestors

Minamoto Tsunemoto (894-961)

Son of Sadazumi-shinno (873-916), and grandson of the Emperor Seiwa (850-880).

In 940 Tsunemoto took part in the campaign against Taira Masakado (-940), in 941 against Fujiwara Sumitomo (-941), and was named Chinjufu-shogun "Defender of the North."

In the year of his death, Tsunemoto received for himself and for his descendants the name Minamoto.

Minamoto Tsunemoto

Kamakura Period – Minamoto Seiwa-Genji

Minamoto Mitsunaka (912-997)

Son of Tsunemoto. His wife was the daughter of Minamoto Suguru, from the Saga-Genji branch of the family. He is the father of Yorimitsu, Yorinobu, and Yorichika.

Mitsunaka loyally served several successive Fujiwara Regents, beginning with Fujiwara Morotada (920-969). In 969 he accused Minamoto Taka'akira (914-983), Morotada's major political rival, of a plot against the throne, and Taka'akira was sent into exile, placing Mitsunaka firmly in Morotada's good graces. Later he would assist Fujiwara Kaneié (929-990) in his plot to coerce the Emperor Kazan (968-1008) into taking Buddhist vows and abdicating in favor of Kaneié's 7-year-old grandson, who ascended as the Emperor Ichijo (980-1011).

Mitsunaka's association with the Fujiwara made him one of the richest and most powerful courtiers of his day. He served as the acting kokushi "governor" of ten provinces, most notably Settsu, which became the mainstay of his military and economic power. He also inherited his father's title of Chinjufu-shogun "Defender of the North." The patron/client relationship between the Fujiwara and the Seiwa-Genji continued for nearly two hundred years after Mitsunaka's death; in-

Minamoto Mitsunaka 源満仲

Minamoto Seiwa-Genji Family Tree

- **Mitsunaka (912-997)**
  - **Yorimitsu (944-1021)** — Yorikuni
    - Yorihiro
    - Yorisuké
    - Yorizané
    - Sanekuni — Yukizané
      - Akiyuki — Koreyuki
      - Mitsuyuki — Yukiyori
    - Yoritsuna
      - Nakamasa
        - Yorimasa (1106-1180)
          - Nakatsuna (-1180) (*Tada*)
          - Hirotsuna (*Ota*)
          - Kanetsuna
          - Yorikané
        - Yoriyuki
        - Mitsushigé
      - Kuninao
    - Kunifusa — Mitsukuni — Mitsunobu
      - Mitsumoto (*Toki*)
      - Mitsunaga
  - **Yorinobu (968-1048)** — **Yoriyoshi (998-1082)**
    - Yoshiié (1041-1108)
      - Yoshichika (-1117)
        - Yoshinobu
        - Tameyoshi (1096-1156) (*See next table*) →
      - Yoshitada
      - Yoshikuni (1082-1155)
        - Yoshishigé
          - Yoshizumi (*Yamana*)
          - Yoshitoshi (*Satomi*)
          - Yoshikané (*Nitta*)
          - Yoshisué (*Tokugawa*)
        - Yoshiyasu
          - Yoshikiyo (*Hosokawa*)
          - Yoshikané (*Ashikaga*)
      - Yoshitoki (*Ishikawa*)
    - Yoshitsuna (1042 -1134) (*Ishibashi*)
    - Yoshimitsu (1045-1127)
      - Yoshinari
        - Masayoshi — Katayoshi (*Sataké*)
        - Yoshisada — Yoshitsuné (*Yamamoto*)
      - Yoshikiyo — Kiyomitsu
        - Mitsunaga (*Hemi*)
        - Nobuyoshi (*Takeda*)
        - Nagamitsu (*Ogasawara*)
        - Yoshisada (*Yasuda*)
      - Moriyoshi — Yoshinobu
        - Masayoshi (*Takenouchi*)
        - Katanobu
        - Tomonobu
        - Tomomasa (*Hiraga*)
        - Kagehira

deed, the Seiwa-Genji came to be known as the "teeth and claws" of the Fujiwara.

He retired to his manor in Tada (Settsu): for this reason he is often called Tada Manju (Chinese reading of the kanji for Mitsunaka), and one of the branches of his family bears to the present day the name of Tada.

Minamoto Yorimitsu (944-1021)

Son of Mitsunaka. He is also known as Minamoto Raiko, and is featured in a number of legends and folk tales.

Yorimitsu served the Fujiwara Regents along with his brother Yorinobu, taking the violent measures the Fujiwara were themselves unable to take. He is one of the earliest Minamoto noted for his military exploits. His loyal service earned him the governorships of Izu, Kozuké, and a number of others in turn. He also served as commander of a regiment of the Imperial Guard, and as a secretary in the Ministry of War. When his father died, Yorimitsu inherited Settsu.

Yorimitsu became famous on account of the feats he performed with his four companions known as the legendary Shi-tenno "Four Guardian Kings": Watanabé Tsuna (953-1025), Sakata Kintoki, Usui Sadamichi, and Urabé Suétaké. Kintoki is especially famous for supposedly being the Japanese folk hero Kintaro "Golden Boy," a child of superhuman strength. One story has Yorimitsu first meeting Kintaro when investigating tales of a giant skull flying through the air. Impressed by Kintaro's strength, Yorimitsu initiated him as one of his retainers. The search for the skull proved fruitless, and they retired for the night. At the house where

Minamoto Yorimitsu
Yorimitsu battling a giant spider.
– *Woodcut print by Utagawa Kuniyoshi (1797 - 1861)*

they stayed, Yorimitsu became ill, and a young servant boy brought him medicine daily, but Yorimitsu continued to grow ill, and began to suspect the boy of mischief. One day, during the daily visit, he lashed out, struck the boy, and caused him to run from the house. This broke a powerful illusion, and Yorimitsu found himself covered in a spider's web. His retainers freed him, and together they tracked the boy's trail of blood. They followed it into the mountains, and there found a huge spider, dead from a wound.

In another story, a fox having chosen the roof of the Imperial Palace for his abode, Yorimitsu shot a large arrow, and killed it on the spot.

Legend has it that Yorimitsu also killed Shuten-doji, a gigantic ruler of the oni "ogres," at Oé-yama (Tanba).

Minamoto Yorinobu (968-1048)

Son of Mitsunaka. Along with his brother Yorimitsu, he served the Fujiwara Regents, being a favorite of the Regent Fujiwara Michinaga (966-1028). He held the title, passed down from his father, of Chinjufu-shogun "Defender of the North." He also served as governor of Isé and Kai.

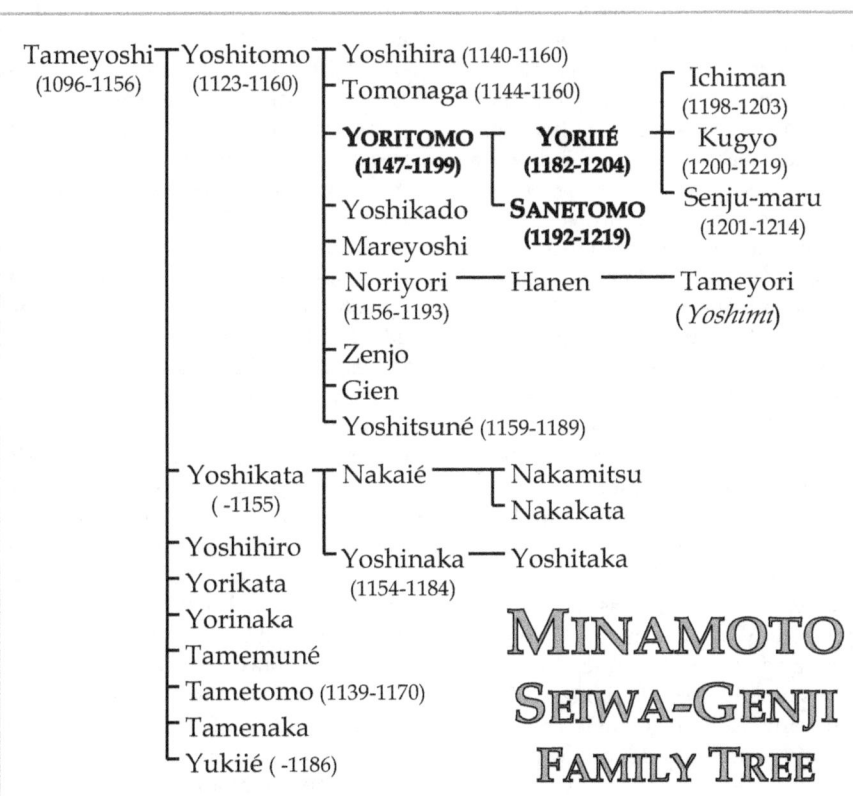

Minamoto Seiwa-Genji Family Tree

Kamakura Period – Minamoto Seiwa-Genji

Minamoto Yorinobu

In 1031 Yorinobu repressed the revolt of Taira Tadatsuné (-1031) in Shimosa, and with this he not only furthered the Court's goals and his own reputation, but created an opening for Minamoto influence in the eastern regions of the country.

Yorinobu was the progenitor of the Kawachi-Genji family line, and his son Yorisué was the ancestor of the Takanashi of Shinano.

Minamoto Yoriyoshi (998-1082)

Son of Yorinobu.

In 1031 Yoriyoshi accompanied his father to the war against Taira Tadatsuné (-1031), and was named Sagami no kami, Mutsu no kami, and Chinjufu-shogun "Defender of the North."

During the Zen-kunen "Earlier Nine Years" War (1051-1063), Yoriyoshi was ordered, along with his son Yoshiié, to fight against Abé Yoritoki (-1057), who had rebelled in Mutsu, and finished with the defeat and death of the latter and his sons. He was then named Iyo no kami. As he had his head shaved soon after this, he was also called Iyo-nyudo.

In 1063 Yoriyoshi founded Tsurugaoka Hachiman-gu in Kamakura (Sagami), which was to become, roughly a century later, the primary shrine of the Minamoto when they began their Shogunate rule.

Minamoto Yoshiié (1041-1108)

Eldest son of Yoriyoshi. In his childhood he was called Genda. At the age of 7, he performed the ceremony of the genbuku in the temple of Hachiman at Iwashimizu (Yamashiro), and was from that moment called Hachiman Taro "Son of the God of War."

Having mastered in a very short time all the branches of military art, Yoshiié made his first sojourn at arms during the Zen-kunen "Earlier Nine Years" War (1051-1063) in an expedition conducted by his father against Abé Yoritoki (-1057). The latter died of an arrow wound in 1057, and was succeeded by his capable heir Abé Sadato (1019-1062). Later that year, Yoshiié participated in the Battle of Kawasaki (Mutsu). In a snowstorm, the Minamoto assaulted Sadato's stronghold, but were driven back. The Minamoto cause was much assisted by the enlistment of Kiyohara Noritaké, a locally powerful figure whose rugged northern men swelled Yoriyoshi's ranks. In 1062 the fighting culminated in a series of actions that further enhanced Yoshiié's reputation. Sadato had attacked the Minamoto troops, but suffering a reversal, retreated into a fort by the Koromo-gawa. Yoriyoshi ordered a spirit assault, and Sadato was forced to flee. Yoshiié supposedly chased Sadato and had an impromptu renga "collaborative poetry" session with his enemy from horseback, and afterwards allowed him to escape. The war however was nearly over. Sadato continued his flight until he reached the stockade fortress at the Kuriya River, and prepared for another stand. The government troops arrived, and in the ensuing Siege of Kuriya-gawa, after a few days of fighting brought the fort down. Sadato and his son died, and his brother Muneto was captured. Yoshiié gave thanks to his namesake by establishing the Tsurugaoka Hachiman shrine near Kamakura on the way back to Kyoto. Yoshiié was named Mutsu no kami. Curiously, Abé Muneto was released into the custody of the Minamoto, lived in Iyo, and later become Yoshiié's companion. In 1081 the bonzes of Miidera came to besiege Hiei-zan (northeast of Kyoto), and Yoshiié was asked to repulse them.

Minamoto Yoshiié

During the Go-sannen "Later Three Years" War (1083-1089), Yoshiié, who was named Chinjufu-shogun "Defender of the North," took it upon himself, without orders from the Imperial Court, to bring some peace and order to the northern region. A series of disputes between Kiyohara family members Masahira, Narihira, and Iehira over leadership of the clan had turned to violence. There emerged a series of battles and skirmishes between Yoshiié's forces and those of the various Kiyohara sub-factions. Everything came to a head in 1087, at the Battle of Kanazawa, where Yoshiié, along with his younger brother Minamoto Yoshimitsu and Fujiwara Kiyohira (1056-1128), besieged the fortress held by Iehira and his uncle Takahira. In one incident that became a famous military anecdote, Yoshiié's men were approaching the fortress through a forest when a flock of cranes settled in the trees then abruptly flew off. Yoshiié suspected an ambush, and had the area surrounded, and sure enough revealed the enemy army. After many months of failed starts and skirmishes, the fortress was set aflame. The Kiyohara was defeated with Takahira and Iehira killed. The Minamoto forces suffered great losses as well, but it is said that Yoshiié was an especially skilled leader, keeping morale up and preserving a degree of discipline among the warriors. The Court was pleased with the outcome. The aristocracy held Yoshiié in near-awe, and in 1098 permitted Yoshiié to visit the Imperial Court, a rare honor for a provincial governor. Fujiwara Munetada dubbed him "the samurai of the greatest bravery under heaven."

One of the most renowned heroes of his age, Yoshiié left a powerful martial legacy, contributing to the strengthening of the Minamoto, especially those

Kamakura Period – Minamoto Seiwa-Genji

branches in the Kanto, and is considered an important ancestral kami "god" of the clan. As a cultured man of war, he established a model for future samurai that would influence generations of warriors to come.

Minamoto Yoshitsuna (1042 -1134)

Son of Yoriyoshi, and brother to Yoshiié. He made the genbuku in the temple of Kamo (north of Kyoto), and was called Kamo Jiro.

Yoshitsuna took an active part in the Zen-kunen "Earlier Nine Years" War against Abé Sadato (1019-1062). He was appointed Mutsu no kami.

In 1093 Yoshitsuna repressed in Dewa the revolt of Taira Morosuké and Taira Morosué.

In 1109 his nephew Yoshitada having been murdered, Yoshitsuna's son Yoshiaki was accused of the crime and condemned to death. Wishing to take revenge against the Court, Yoshitsuna levied an army, but he was defeated by Minamoto Tameyoshi, and banished to Sado, where he died.

Minamoto Yoshimitsu (1045-1127)

Son of Yoriyoshi, and brother to Yoshiié. He made the genbuku at the temple of Shinra Myojin, and was called Shinra Saburo.

In the Go-sannen "Later Three Years" War (1083-1087), having been informed that his brother Yoshiié found it impossible to overpower the Kiyohara, who had revolted in Mutsu, Yoshimitsu came to his help with an army, and took a prominent part in the victory.

When Yoriyoshi returned to Kyoto, Kiyohara received the Court title Gyobu-shoyu and the governorship of Kai.

Minamoto Yoshikuni (1082-1155)

Son of Yoshiié. He settled in the district of Nitta (Kozuké), and was kebi-ishi "chief of police."

In 1147 Yoshikuni repressed a sedition of Saté Masayoshi (1081-1147), and killed him in a battle in Hitachi.

After a quarrel with the udaijin "junior minister of state" Fujiwara Saneyoshi, this latter's house was burned by Yoshikuni's servants. On that account, he was obliged to retire to Ashikaga (Shimotsuké), where he died.

Yoshikuni is the forefather of the Nitta and the Ashikaga.

Minamoto Yoshichika (-1117)

Son of Yoshiié. He was governor of Tsukushi (Kyushu), and brought about troubles on account of his bad administration.

Summoned to Kyoto, Yoshichika refused to obey, and put the Imperial envoy to death. Exiled to Oki, he went into Izumo, killed its governor, and took his place. But in 1107 he was defeated by Taira Masamori (-1121), who had been sent against him.

Having become a bonze, he sought a retreat in Mutsu, tried again to raise the standard of revolt, but was defeated and put to death.

Minamoto Tameyoshi (1096-1156)

Son of Yoshichika. At first called Mutsu Shiro, he was the heir to his grandfather Yoshiié.

At the age of 13, Tameyoshi carried arms against his grand-uncle Yoshitsuna, who rebelled against the Court when his son Yoshiaki was sentenced for committing a crime.

Around 1113, the ongoing rivalry between the warrior monks of the Miidera and the Enryaku-ji of Hiei-zan (northeast of Kyoto) erupted into outright violence in the streets of Kyoto. Though the palace guard mobilized quickly to protect the Emperor, it is said that Tameyoshi, with a handful of mounted samurai, drove the mobs away himself.

In 1123 Tameyoshi was named kebi-ishi "chief of police."

During the 1156 Hogen War (Kyoto) Tameyoshi led the Minamoto, sided with the ex-Emperor Sutoku (1119-1164), was defeated, and sentenced to death by order of Taira Kiyomori (1118-1181). Tameyoshi's son Yoshitomo prayed for his father's pardon, but was ordered to execute him. He refused, and another Minamoto officer, insisting that Tameyoshi not die at the hands of a Taira, dispatched him, and then committed suicide himself.

Minamoto Yorimasa (1106-1180)

Descendant of Yorimitsu, and a son of Nakamasa. He was a warrior as well as a prominent poet whose works appeared in various anthologies. He served eight different Emperors in his long career, holding posts such as hyogo-no-kami "head of the arsenal."

In 1153 Yorimasa killed with an arrow the nué, a monster having the head of a monkey, the body of a tiger, and the tail of serpent, which had been flying over the Imperial Palace and shrieking horribly.

In the clashes between the Minamoto and the Taira that had gone on for decades, Yorimasa tried to avoid taking sides, and stayed out of politics by aligning with the ex-Emperor Go-Shirakawa (1127-1192), his protector. But he did participate in the 1156 Hogen Rebellion (Kyoto), and for a time he was even friends with Taira Kiyomori (1118-1181). During the 1160 Heiji Rebellion (Kyoto), Yorimasa leaned just enough in favor of the Taira that it allowed them to overthrow the Minamoto.

In 1178 Yorimasa was raised to san'i "3rd rank" in the Court. As he shaved his head at that time, he was called

Gan-san'i-nyudo, the name under which he is best known.

In 1179 Yorimasa officially retired from military service in Taira Kiyomori's army. By this time his connection with the Taira was becoming more and more strained, and he changed his mind about opposing his own clan. In 1180 Kiyomori forced the abdication of his son-in-law, the Emperor Takakura (1161-1181), and placed his grandson on the Chrysanthemum Throne as the Emperor Antoku (1178-1185). Yorimasa then resolved to dethrone the Taira, and to replace Antoku by Prince Mochihito (1180), son of Go-Shirakawa.

Yorimasa secured the help of the bonzes of Nara, and dispatched Minamoto Yukiié (-1186) into the provinces to recruit adherents to his cause. The plot was discovered to Taira Kiyomori, who opposed the conspirators with an army commanded by his son Tomomori (1152-1185). The Genpei War (1180-1185) began with the Battle of Uji (Yamashiro) where Yorimasa intrenched himself, and prepared to receive the enemy. He gave orders to destroy the bridge, but the assailants forded the river and began a bloody fight, in which Yorimasa's sons Kanetsuna and Nakatsuna were killed. Yorimasa was wounded by an arrow, and foreseeing certain defeat, went to the Byodo-in, and there, sitting on his fan, committed seppuku, the earliest recorded instance of a samurai's suicide in the face of defeat.

According to legend, one of Yorimasa's retainers took his head to prevent it from falling into the hands of the Taira. He then fastened his master's head to a rock and threw it into the Uji-gawa so it could not be found.

He was also called Gensanmi Yorimasa.

Minamoto Nakatsuna (-1180)

Eldest son of Yorimasa. He fought under his father against the Taira.

In 1180 Nakatsuna was killed at the Battle of Uji (Yamashiro).

He is the ancestor of the Ota.

Minamoto Yoshitomo (1123-1160)

Son of Tameyoshi. He was Shimotsuké no kami.

In 1156, when the Hogen Rebellion (Kyoto) broke out, Yoshitomo sided with Taira Kiyomori (1118-1181) in support of the Emperor Go-Shirakawa (1127-1192) and Fujiwara Tadamichi (1097-1164), while his father Tameyoshi, then head of the Minamoto, with his younger brother Tametomo and Taira Tadamasa, sided with the ex-Emperor Sutoku (1119-1164) and Fujiwara Yorinaga (1120-1156). Kiyomori prevailed, and Yoshitomo became the head of the Minamoto, establishing himself as a political power in Kyoto. Yoshitomo begged Kiyomori in vain for his father's life, but he was put to death.

When peace was re-established Yoshitomo was dissatisfied because, compared with that of Kiyomori, his reward was small. Moreover, when Fujiwara Michinori (-1160) declined to accept for his son the hand of Yoshitomo's daughter, and instead accepted the daughter of Kiyomori, war again soon broke out.

In the 1160 Heiji Rebellion (Kyoto), Kiyomori being at Kumano (Kii), Yoshitomo, in concert with the kebiishi "chief of police" Fujiwara Nobuyori (-1160), set fire to the palace of the ex-Emperor Go-Shirakawa, secured Fujiwara Michinori, and put him to death. Kiyomori hastened to Kyoto, and entrusted the repression of the insurrection to his son Shigemori. Nobuyori and Yoshitomo's two eldest sons, Yoshihira and Tomonaga, were killed, releasing Go-Shirakawa. Yoshitomo fled to Owari, where he was betrayed and murdered, while taking a bath unarmed at an onsen "hot spring," by one of his kerai, Osada Tadamuné, who sent his head to Kyoto. His wife Tokiwa

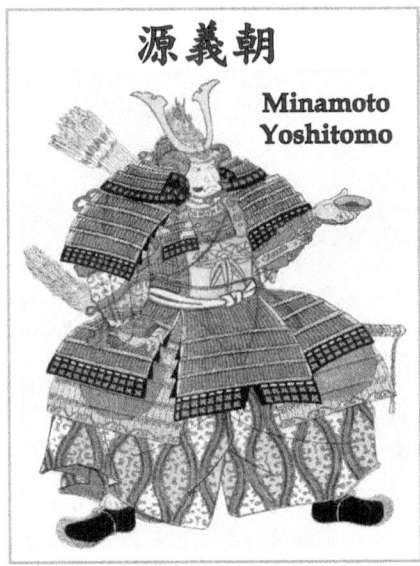

Gozen "Lady Tokiwa" fled through the snow with three of his other sons, Yoritomo, Noriyori, and Yoshitsuné, who were later captured. Kiyomori spared the children and exiled them when Lady Tokiwa agreed to become his concubine.

Tokiwa Gozen (1123-1180)

Known for her great beauty, she was at first a maid honor to the Empress, wife of Konoé-tenno (1139-1155), and then a concubine of Minamoto Yoshitomo.

When Yoshitomo perished in the 1160 Heiji War (Kyoto), Tokiwa Gozen "Lady Tokiwa" fled throught the snow with three of his sons, Yoritomo, Noriyori, and Yoshitsuné, protecting them within her robes. They hid in the village of Ryumon (Yamato). Kiyomori,

having made vain efforts to discover her, then arrested her mother. Hearing of this, Tokiwa at once surrendered herself, whereupon her mother was set free. The three children shaved their heads and were exiled after she agreed to become the concubine of Kiyomori, to whom she bore a daughter. But this union did not last long, and soon after she married Fujiwara Naganari.

She is also called Hotoké Gozen "Lady Buddha."

Minamoto Tametomo (1139-1170)

8th son of Tameyoshi, and brother to Yukiié and Yoshitomo. He is often called Chinzei Hachiro Tametomo. It is said that he was 7-feet tall and of Herculean strength. Legend has it that his left arm was about 6 inches longer than his right, enabling a longer draw of the arrow, and more powerful shots.

Being sent at the age of 13 to Kyushu, Tametomo established himself in Bungo, where in a very short time he caused disturbances.

In 1154 Tametomo returned to Kyoto, joined his father during the 1156 Hogen War (Kyoto), was forced to flee, and was banished to Oshima (Izu). Gradually he took possession of the seven islands of Izu, and again contemplated to overthrow the Taira. In 1170 Kudo Shigemitsu, Izu no suké, received orders to attack him. Seeing the fleet of the Taira coming towards him, Tametomo took an arrow, and aiming at the principal boat, shot it was such force that it pierced the hull and foundered the boat. When surrounded by his enemies, a legend says that the Taira cut the tendons of Tametomo's left arm. Thinking that he could no longer fight, he killed himself by slicing his abdomen. Tametomo may be the first warrior to have committed seppuku.

Tametomo's exploits have passed into legend, which even says that he escaped from Oshima on a small skiff that landed on Oni-ga-shima in Okinawa "Ryukyu Islands," and that he became an ancestor of the Chuzan royal family of the archipelago by siring Shunten (1166-1237), the earliest king of Okinawa for whom a name is known.

Minamoto Yoshikata (-1155)

Son of Tameyoshi, and brother to Yoshitomo and Tametomo.

Yoshikata had a contest with his nephew Yoshihira, and levied soldiers to fight him, but was defeated and killed.

Minamoto Yukiié (-1186)

10th son of Tameyoshi, brother to Yoshitomo. He was first called Yoshimori.

In 1156, after his father and brothers had been defeated by the Taira in the Hogen War (Kyoto), Yukiié retired to Shingu in the Kumano region (Kii), and was for this reason surnamed Shingu Juro.

In 1180 Yukiié was selected to carry to the provinces the invitation of Prince Mochihito (-1180) to rise against the Taira, precipitating the Genpei War (1180-1185). In 1181 he was defeated at the Battle of Sunomata-gawa (Owari) by Taira Tomomori (1152-1185), and retreated. At the Battle of Yahagi-gawa (Owari), he tried to take a stand by destroying the bridge over the river and putting up a defensive shield wall. His forces were defeated once more, but the Taira pursuit was called off when Tomomori fell ill.

Yukiié then joined his nephew Minamoto Yoritomo, the head of the clan, who was beginning his campaign. Not able to agree with Yoritomo, Yukiié left him, sided with Minamoto Yoshinaka in Shinano, and followed him in his expedition to Kyoto. He was then named Buzen no kami.

Yukiié plotted with Yoshinaka against Yoritomo. When Yoshinaka suggested kidnapping the cloistered Emperor Go-Shirakawa (1127-1192), Yukiié betrayed him, revealing his plan

Minamoto Yukiié

to the ex-Emperor, who in turn revealed it to Yoritomo.

In 1184 Yoshinaka was defeated and killed. Yukiié had to flee to Kii. The following year he sided with Minamoto Yoshitsuné against Yoritomo. In 1186 Yukiié fled to Izumi, where he was assassinated by Fujiwara Yoshiyasu, on Yoritomo's orders, on charges of high treason.

Minamoto Yoshihira (1140-1160)

Eldest son of Yoshitomo, and older brother to Yoritomo, Noriyori, and Yoshitsuné. His mother was the daughter of Miura Yoshiaki (1093-1181). He had been surnamed Kamakura Aku-genda. He married the daughter of Nitta Yoshishigé (-1202).

In 1155 Yoshihira was only 15 years old when, after a disagreement, he bore arms against his uncle Minamoto Yoshikata, whom he defeated and killed at his home in Okura (Musashi).

Minamoto Tametomo

Minamoto Yoshihira

Kamakura Period – Minamoto Seiwa-Genji

During the 1160 Heiji Rebellion (Kyoto) Yoshihira left Kamakura (Sagami) and joined his father at Kyoto. He fought bravely against Taira Shigemori (1138-1179), but was defeated, and obliged to retreat to Owari.

Yoshihira was sent by his father to recruit troops in the north, but when he learned of the death of Yoshitomo, he secretly returned to Kyoto. He was soon discovered and captured by Taira Kiyomori (1118-1181), and beheaded at Rokujo-ga-hara.

Minamoto Tomonaga (1144-1160)

Son of Yoshitomo.

In the 1150 Heiji Rebellion (Kyoto) Tomonaga accompanied his father when he fled from Kyoto after his defeat.

At Ryuka-goé (Yamashiro), in a battle against the troops of the Yokokawa bonzes, Tomonaga was wounded by an arrow. When Tomonaga arrived at Aohaka (Mino) his father ordered him to go with his brother Yoshihira to levy troops in Kai and Shinano: Yoshihira left at once, but with his wound having inflamed, it was impossible for him to go further. Irritated with this mishap, Yoshitomo dreaded to desert him and to continue his route, whereupon Tomonaga asked his father to kill him with his own hand, rather than having to waste away slowly and painfully from the infection. Yoshitomo, following in this the custom of the times, accepted and obliged, and buried his son on the spot.

Some time after, Taira Munekiyo violated Tomonaga's grave, beheaded the corpse, and sent the trophy to Kyoto.

Minamoto (Kiso) Yoshinaka (1154-1184)

Son of Yoshikata, grandson of Tameyoshi, and cousin to Yoritomo. Born in Musashi, he was brought up by Nakahara Kaneto in the mountainous district of Kiso (Shinano), hence the name Kiso Yoshinaka, under which he is often known. At the age of 13 he made the genbuku at the Iwashimizu Shrine (near Kyoto).

In 1180, obeying the orders of the Prince Mochihito (-1180), Yoshinaka levied troops in Shinano and marched against the Taira, entering the Genpei War (1180-1185). The governor of the province Ogasawara Yorinao tried to oppose him, but was defeated. Then in 1181 Jo Nagamochi, daimyo of Echigo, and Taira Tsunemasa made war against him, but they were beaten in Echigo. Yoshinaka thus remained sole master of several provinces.

In 1182 his uncle Yukiié, after a quarrel with Yoritomo, joined him, and they, with a large army, directed their steps towards Kyoto. The Taira vainly sought to oppose their progress, but in 1183 they were defeated at the Battle of Kurikara (Etchu), and when they saw the enemy approaching their city, they fled, taking with them the young Emperor Antoku (1178-1185). Yoshinaka entered Kyoto without difficulty, and was received as a liberator by the ex-Emperor Go-Shirakawa (1127-1192), who named him Iyo no kami. Yoshinaka then resolved to put the Prince Hokuroku, son of the Prince Mochihito and grandson of Go-Shirakawa on the Chrysanthemum Throne, but the ex-Emperor opposed his views. Yoshinaka, irritated at this opposition, gave full play to his anger and filled Kyoto with terror. In 1184 he burned the palace, secured the ex-Emperor, deposed the Kanpaku, replaced him by a child 12-years old, and had himself named Shogun. Yoritomo, hearing of this, placed his two brothers Noriyori and Yoshitsuné, at the head of a huge army and sent them against their cousin, who was defeated at the 2nd Battle of Uji (Yamashiro) and at Seta (Omi), and killed at the Battle of Awazu (Omi). He was 31 years old.

Yoshinaka had always been surrounded by four trusty companions-at-arms, who died with him: Imai Kanehira, Higuchi Kanemitsu, Taté Chikatada, and Nenoi Yukichika: they were called his shi-ten.

The legendary Tomoé Gozen "Lady Tomoé," famous for her physical strength, was his mistress.

Minamoto Yoritomo (1147-1199)

1st Minamoto Shogun.

Minamoto Noriyori (1156-1193)

6th son of Yoshitomo, and brother to Yoritomo and Yoshitsuné. In 1160, following his father's death, he was spared and exiled, along with his brothers, by Taira Kiyomori (1118-1181). He was educated by Fujiwara Norisué.

In 1180 Noriyori went at the head of an army, and helped Oyama Tomomasa to defeat Shida Yoshihiro in Shimotsuké.

In 1184, four years into the Genpei War (1180-1185), Noriyori was sent out from Kamakura by his elder brother Yoritomo, and made his way to the Taira strongholds of Shikoku. Later that year, Noriyori helped his younger brother Yoshitsuné defeat Minamoto Yoshinaka at the 2nd Battle of Uji (Kyoto), and then at Awazu (Omi), where the latter was struck dead by an arrow.

Noriyori then marched against the Taira, and defeated them at Ichi-no-tani (Settsu). He was in consequence named Mikawa no kami.

Two months later, Noriyori carried on the campaign to secure the Chugoku "Middle Provinces" region and then to move on into Kyushu. He played a major role in the Battle of Kojima (Suruga). He went as far as Bungo, which prevented him from taking part in the 1185 Battles of Yashima (Sanuki) and Dan-no-ura (Nagato).

After the war ended, Noriyori returned to Kamakura (Sagami). When a feud for dominance of the clan began between Yoritomo and Yoshitsuné, the former ordered Noriyori to arrest the latter. After trying in vain to talk his brother out of it, Noriyori disobeyed. The union between Noriyori and Yoritomo then became more strained, and

made worse by calumny. Finally Noriyori was banished to Shuzenji (Izu), and soon after was assassinated by his Yoritomo's warriors.

Minamoto Yoshitsuné (1159-1189)

Youngest son of Yoshitomo, half-brother to Yoritomo. His mother was Tokiwa Gozen "Lady Tokiwa." His childhood name was Ushiwaka-maru.

After the 1160 Heiji War (Kyoto), and the death of his father at the hands of Taira Kiyomori (1118-1181), Yoshitsuné was exiled to Kurama-dera at Hiei-zan (northeast of Kyoto), under the care of the learned Gakujitsu. At the age of 11, reading the annals of his family, he resolved in his mind to walk in the footsteps of his ancestors. Vainly did Gakujitsu try to inspire him with love for religious exercises, but Yoshitsuné stealthily escaped from the temple and headed north. In this journey he was accompanied by Saito Musashi-bo Benkei (1155-1189), whom he had beaten in a fencing challenge on the bridge of Gojo (Kyoto), and who became his inseparable companion. In Mutsu, they received sanctuary for many years from Fujiwara Hidehira (1122-1187) in the stronghold of Hiraizumi.

When he was 16 years of age, he made the genbuku in Omi, and chose the name Yoshitsuné, a name which he was to bring to a great celebrity.

In 1180, as soon as Yoshitsuné heard that Yoritomo had levied troops at the request of Prince Mochihito (-1180), son of the retired Emperor Go-Shirakawa (1127-1192), to march against the Taira, he hastened to join his brother. The two met near the Kiségawa (Suruga). Along with Noriyori, the three brother were now together for the first time since their exile. They then launched the Genpei War (1180-1185) against the Taira.

In 1183 their rival cousin Minamoto (Kiso) Yoshinaka (1154-1184) won a great victory over the Taira at the Battle of Kurikara (Etchu), leading the latter to abandon Kyoto, which Yoshinaka then occupied. Conflict for the overall control of the Minamoto then ensued, and Yoritomo sent his two brothers Noriyori and Yoshitsuné against him. In 1184 they defeated Yoshinaka's forces just outside Kyoto, at Uji (Yamashiro) and at Seta (Omi). Yoshinaka

Minamoto Yoshitsuné

then escaped the capital, and was finally cornered at Awazu (Omi), where he was killed.

Yoshitsuné then entered Kyoto, where he was received by Go-Shirakawa, and lodged at the Imperial Palace. After a few days' rest, he continued his campaign against the Taira, who had erected a stronghold near the sea at Suma (Settsu, west of present-day Kobé). In the ensuing Battle of Ichi-no-tani, with the help of Noriyori and Benkei, Yoshitsuné attacked the powerful Heiké army from two different sides, and completely defeated it. Those who survived fled by sea towards the west. Yoshitsuné and Noriyori returned to Kyoto, and paraded through the streets the notable Taira heads they had taken. They were received with enthusiasm, and Yoshitsuné obtained the title of kebiishi "chief of police." This increasing popularity of his younger brother bred jealousy in the mind of Yoritomo.

In 1185 Yoshitsuné was authorized to re-opened the campaign. The Taira, after their defeat at Ichi-no-tani, had carried away the young Emperor Antoku (1178-1185), and made a stronghold at Yashima on the coast of the Seto Inland Sea. In the ensuing Battle of Yashima, Yoshitsuné attacked and obliged them to retreat to Nagato. He closely pursued, and at the Battle of Dan-no-ura (Nagato) completely crushed them. The Antoku-tenno drowned with his grandmother, Kiyomori's widow. As to the Taira, most of them perished in the sea, and the prisoners put to death. This victory secured the triumph for the Minamoto.

Yoshitsuné then returned to Kyoto, and then to Kamakura (Sagami). Yoritomo's jealousy was growing all the while. A certain warrior, Kajiwara Kagetoki (1140-1200), who had previously disputed with Yoshitsuné, calumniated him before his brother. When Yoshitsuné arrived at Koshigoé, a small distance from Kamakura, Yoritomo denied him entry to the city. Yoshitsuné vainly tried to appease his brother, but after three weeks was obliged to return to Kyoto.

At the capital Yoshitsuné was named Iyo no kami, but Yoritomo forbade him to take possession of his office, and named a jito "steward" to replace him. Soon after, he was ordered to separate himself from his uncle Yukiié, and to deliver the latter to Yoritomo. Feigning some malady, he evaded the order.

Yoritomo getting always more and more irritated, ordered Noriyori to command an expedition against Yoshitsuné, but he protested on his younger brother's behalf, and refused outright, which earned him a trip into exile. Yoritomo then requested the ex-bonze Shoshun (Tosanobo Masatoshi) to go to Kyoto, and to assassinate Yoshitsuné, but he was captured and killed by Yoshitsuné's men. Yoritomo then started for Kyoto with a sizable army, and Yoshitsuné resolved to flee to Tsukushi (Kyushu), but a storm drove him back to the shore, and he hid himself in Yamato, then at the Yoshino-san (Nara), at Tabu-no-miné (Yamato), and even at the hills south of Kyoto.

Disguised as a pilgrim, and accompanied by his wife, his faithful Benkei, and some servants, Yoshitsuné wended his way towards Mutsu to be again sheltered under the hospitable roof of Fujiwara Hidehira. The latter received him cheerfully and gave him the stronghold of Koromo-gawa as a place of refuge. But in 1187 Hidehira died, and his son Fujiwara Yasuhira (1155-1189) had not the courage to resist Yoritomo's order to march against Yoshitsuné and to kill him. In 1189 Yasuhira's army laid the Siege of Koromo-gawa. Yoshitsuné, with Benkei's help, defended himself with great valor, but finding it impossible to resist such great numbers, he killed his young wife and children, and then committed suicide. He was 31 years old. Yasuhira sent his head to Kamakura, where it provoked an emotional response from those who viewed it.

According to a legend, Yoshituné did not die then. He was able to escape to the island of Ezo and is now honored by the Aino under the name of Gikyo-daimyo-jin.

According to others, who base their opinion on a similarity of name (the Japanese pronunciation of the Chinese characters of the name Minamoto Yoshitsuné would be Gen Gikyo), he emigrated to Mongolia, where he became the famous Gengis Khan (1157-1226).

At all events, Yoshitsuné is, to the present day, one of the most popular heroes of Japan. Poetry and the theater vie with each other in celebrating his legendary adventures, battles, life with his beautiful mistress Shizuka Gozen "Lady Shizuka" (1165-1211), and heroic deeds.

Minamoto Yoriié (1182-1204)

2nd Minamoto Shogun.

Minamoto Sanetomo (1192-1219)

3rd Minamoto Shogun.

Minamoto Ichiman (1198-1203)

Eldest son of 2nd Minamoto Shogun Yoriié. His mother was Wakasa Tsuboné, daughter of Hiki Yoshikazu (-1203), and was brought up by the Hiki.

In 1203, when Yoriié became seriously ill, the Hiki supported Ichiman as his father's successor, while the Hojo supported his brother Senman. The Hojo decided to get rid of the Hiki and their protegé. On a pretext, the 1st Hojo Shikken Tokimasa (1138-1215) invited Yoshikazu to his home in Kamakura (Sagami) and assassinated him. In the ensuing battle between the clans, the Hiki were defeated by a coalition of the Hojo, the Wada, the Miura, and the Hatakeyama, and exterminated along with Ichiman. The Hiki residence was destroyed by fire, and in its place now lies the Nichiren Buddhist temple of Myoho-ji.

Minamoto Yoshinari/Kugyo (1200-1219)

2nd son of 2nd Minamoto Shogun Yoriié. His childhood name was Yoshinari.

Yoshinari was only 3 years old when his father was killed, and he became his uncle Sanetomo's adopted son. His grandmother Hojo Masako (1156-1225), intending to make a bonze of him, placed him as a disciple of Songyo, who was the betto "head priest" of the Tsurugaoka Hachiman-gu in Kamakura (Sagami). After his tonsure he was given the Buddhist name Kugyo. At the age of 18 he became the 4th betto of the Hachiman-gu.

With years grew also Kugyo's hatred and jealousy against his uncle Sanetomo, who succeeded as the 3rd Minamoto Shogun in his stead, and he swore vengeance. He waited long for a good chance. In 1219 Sanetomo received the title of udaijin "junior counselor of state," and repaired to the Hachiman-gu to thank the gods. That winter evening, after the Ceremony of Celebration for his nomination was over, the Shogun descended the snow-covered steps of the shrine, when Kugyo rushed upon him and struck him with a sword, cutting off his head. He profited of the disorder which followed to make his escape, but was detected and beheaded by Nagao Sadakagé.

With the death of Sanetomo and Kugyo, the Seiwa-Genji line of the Minamoto came to a sudden end.

Minamoto Senju-maru (1201-1214)

3rd son of 2nd Minamoto Shogun Yoriié.

In 1213 Senju-maru was only 12 years old when Izumi Chikahira levied an army against the Hojo in order to raise him to the rank of Shogun. Chikahira was however defeated, and Senju-maru was obliged to become a bonze under the name Eijitsu.

In 1214, Wada Yoshimori (1147-1213) took up Chikahira's plan, but he was likewise defeated, and Senju-maru fell with his party in battle.

Miura

Territory: Sagami
Castles: Kinugasa, Arai (Sagami)

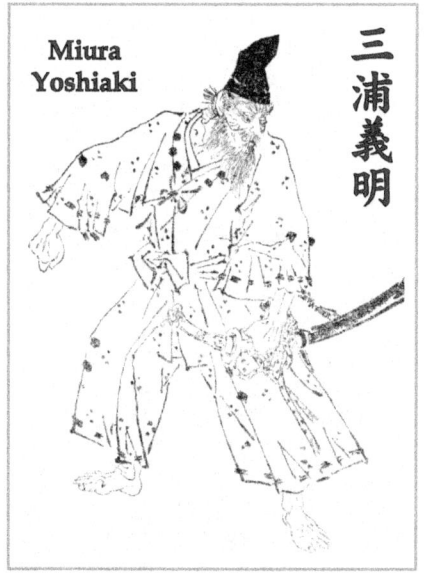

Miura Yoshiaki

Daimyo family of Sagami descended from Taira Takamochi (9th century). They held large fiefs, and great political influence. In the mid-13th century they were one of the primary opponents of the Hojo Regency.

Notable Ancestors

Miura Tamemichi (11th century)
In the 11th century settled in the district of Miura (Sagami) and took the name of the place. Towards 1060 he built the castle of Kinugasa.

Miura Yoshiaki (1093-1181)
Son of Yoshitsugu, and great-grandson of Tamemichi. He had the title of Miura-osuké and resided at the castle of Kinugasa (Sagami).

When Minamoto Yoritomo (1147-1199) began his campaign against the Taira, Yoshiaki sent his son Yoshizumi and his grandson Yoshimori to his army.

Miura Family Tree

```
Yoshitsugu
├─ Yoshiaki (1093-1181)
│   ├─ Yoshimuné ─ Yoshimori (Wada)
│   ├─ Yoshizumi (1127-1200)
│   │   ├─ Aritsugu ─ Yoshiari ┬─ Morizumi ┬─ Kazuuji ─ Tomokazu
│   │   │                       │           ├─ Kanemura ─ Kagemura
│   │   │                       │           └─ Sumitada ─ Munekané
│   │   │                       └─ Mitsuzumi
│   │   ├─ Yoshimura (-1239)
│   │   │   ├─ Tomomura ┬─ Toshimura ┬─ Tadauji ─ Kageuji
│   │   │   │            │            └─ Ieuji ─ Shigeuji
│   │   │   │            ├─ Tomouji
│   │   │   │            └─ Sadamura ┬─ Kageyoshi ─ Motomura
│   │   │   │                         ├─ Moriaki ─ Yoshitsugu
│   │   │   │                         ├─ Sadayoshi
│   │   │   │                         └─ Kanemura ─ Kaneyoshi
│   │   │   ├─ Yasumura (1204-1247) ┬─ Kagemura
│   │   │   │                         └─ Kageyasu
│   │   │   ├─ Mitsumura (-1247)
│   │   │   ├─ Iemura ─ Yoshiyuki ┬─ Yukimura
│   │   │   │                      ├─ Tomoyuki
│   │   │   │                      └─ Yukitsuné ─ Tomotsuné
│   │   │   ├─ Nagamura
│   │   │   ├─ Shigemura
│   │   │   ├─ Tanemura ─ Yorimura ┬─ Yukimura ┬─ Arimura
│   │   │   │                        │           ├─ Sadamura
│   │   │   │                        │           └─ Motomura
│   │   │   │                        ├─ Koremura
│   │   │   │                        └─ Iemura ─ Tomomura
│   │   │   ├─ Yoshisuké
│   │   │   └─ Shigetoki
│   │   ├─ Yoshiharu (Tatara)
│   │   └─ Yoshisué (Nagai)
│   ├─ Yoshiyuki (Tsukui)
│   ├─ Tamekiyo (Ashina)
│   └─ Yoshizané (Okazaki)
├─ Shigezumi ─ Shigemura
├─ Taneyoshi (-1221) ┬─ Ieyasu ─ Shigetané
│                     └─ Taneuji ┬─ Yoritané
│                                 ├─ Yasuzumi
│                                 └─ Yoshiuji
└─ Yoshitsura (Sawara)
    ├─ Kagetsura
    ├─ Moritsura ┬─ Tsunetsura
    │             ├─ Hiromori
    │             ├─ Moriyoshi
    │             ├─ Mitsumori
    │             └─ Moritoki ─ Yorimori ┬─ Yoshiyasu
    │                                      └─ Tokiaki ─ Tokitsugu
    └─ Ietsura
```

In 1180, having heard of the defeat at the Battle of Ishibashi-yama (Sagami), Yoshiaki levied other troops and routed Hatakeyama Shigetada (1164-1205), who in 1181 returned and laid siege to Kinugasa, where Yoshiaki met his death.

Miura Yoshizumi (1127-1200)

Son of Yoshiaki. He was also called Arajiro.

In 1180 Yoshizumi sided with Minamoto Yoritomo (1147-1199) against the Taira and, with the help of his brother Yoshitsura, defeated Hatakeyama Shigetada (1164-1205) at Kotsubo (Sagami).

In 1181, defeated at Kinugasa (Sagami), Yoshizumi retired into Awa, whence he returned to take part in the western expedition of Minamoto Noriyori (1156-1193), and was intrusted with the defense of Suo.

In 1185 Yoshizumi assisted at the Battle of Dan-no-ura (Nagato).

In 1189 Yoshizumi took part in the campaign against Fujiwara Yasuhira (1155-1189).

Miura Yoshitsura (12th century)

Son of Yoshiaki, and brother to Yoshizumi. He is also called Sawara Juro.

During the Genpei War (1180-1185) Yoshitsura fought for the Minamoto against the Taira: in 1180 at Kotsubo (Sagami), in 1181 at Kinugasa (Sagami), then in the campaigns against Kiso Yoshinaka (1154-1184). In 1184 Yoshitsura's achievements at the Battle of Ichi-no-tani (Settsu) made him famous.

He is said to have been 7½ feet tall, and gifted with Herculean strength.

Miura Yoshimura (-1239)

Son of Yoshizumi.

In 1213 Yoshimura helped to repress the revolt of his cousin Wada Yoshimori (1147-1213) against the Hojo.

In 1219, when Kugyo (1200-1219) had murdered his uncle and adoptive father, the 3rd Minamoto Shogun Sanetomo (1192-1219), Yoshimura had him arrested by Nagao Sadakagé, and his head sent to the 2nd Hojo Shikken Yoshitoki (1163-1224).

Miura Yoshizumi

A little before the 1221 Jokyu War (Kyoto), his brother Miura Taneyoshi, then stationed at Kyoto, pressed him to side with the ex-Emperor Go-Toba (1180-1239). Yoshimura revealed the plot to Hojo Yoshitoki, marched with him to Kyoto, and himself presented his own brother's head to his lord. By this conduct, he entirely won the Shikken's confidence, and henceforth took a large part in the government of the land.

Miura Taneyoshi (-1221)

Son of Yoshizumi, and brother to Yoshimura. He was kebiishi "chief of police."

After his quarrel with the 2nd Hojo Shikken Yoshitoki (1163-1224), Taneyoshi supported the ex-Emperor Go-Toba (1180-1239) in his designs against the Hojo. He wrote to Yoshimura to induce him to follow his steps, but his brother delivered the letter to Yoshitoki. In 1221, during the ensuing Jokyu War, Taneyoshi, after having fought with great valor, was defeated and killed by Yoshimura.

Miura Yasumura (1204-1247)

Son of Yoshimura. He is also called Suruga Jiro. He was Wakasa no kami and Hyojo-bugyo "Chief of the Council of State."

In 1221 Yasumura followed his father to the Jokyu War (Kyoto).

Yasumura enjoyed the full confidence of the 5th Hojo Shikken Tokiyori (1227-1263), but could not agree with the latter's grandfather Adachi Kagemori (-1248). In 1247 they went to war. Tokiyori sided with Kagemori, and Yasumura was defeated and killed with all his family at the Battle of Hochi.

Miura Mitsumura (-1247)

Son of Yoshimura, and brother to Yasumura. He was kebiishi "chief of police" and Noto no kami. He perished with his whole family in the war against the Hojo.

He was the last of the senior branch of the family.

Miura Yoshiatsu (-1516)

Son of Uesugi Takamasa, was adopted by Miura Tokitaka (-1496), who at the time had no heir.

Some time after, a son, Takanori, was born to Tokitaka, and he forced Yoshiatsu to become a bonze at the Sosei-ji (Sagami). Yoshiatsu at first seemed to be resigned to his fate, but in 1496 he levied troops, laid siege to Arai Castle (Sagami), where Tokitaka was staying, defeated and killed him, and took possession of his domain. He placed his son Yoshimoto at Arai, while he resided at Okazaki (Sagami).

In 1499 Yoshiatsu had his head shaved and took the name of Dosun.

In 1516, besieged in Okazaki (Sagami) by Hojo Soun (1432-1519), Yoshiatsu was defeated, took refuge in Arai Castle. The Hojo defeated Miura allies, the Ota, and left Yoshiatsu isolated. In the ensuing Siege of Arai, when defeat was inevitable, he committed seppuku. His son Yoshimoto took his own life by beheading himself.

Miura Yoshimoto (-1516)

Eldest son of Yoshiatsu. In 1496 he received Arai Castle (Sagami) at the tip of Miura Peninsula from his father.

In 1516 the Hojo laid the Siege of Arai, and after the attackers stormed the castle, his father committed seppuku, and Yoshimoto decapitated himself.

Thus ended this family, which for several centuries had been at the head of Sagami.

NIKAIDO

Territory: Mutsu, Mino
Castles: Sukagawa (Mutsu), Inaba-yama (Mino)

Ancient family of daimyo descended from Fujiwara Muchimaro (680-737).

During the Kamakura Period (1185-1333), the clan's power stretched down to Mino, where they constructed Inaba-yama Castle atop Mount Inaba between 1201 and 1204. The castle was later named Gifu Castle by Oda Nobunaga (1534-1582).

During the Sengoku "Warrings States" Period (1467-1573), the Nikaido ruled over the Iwasé domain (Mutsu), and their main residence was Sukagawa Castle.

Notable Ancestors

Nikaido Yukimasa (12th century)
Son of Yukito. He was the first to take the name of Nikaido, from his residence. He served Minamoto Yoritomo (1147-1199) and became successively shugo "constable" of Izumo, Yamashiro no kami, and shitsuji "deputy Shogun."

Nikaido Yukimori (1182-1254)
Son of Yukimitsu, and grandson of Yukimasa. He served the Shogun of Kamakura, and was a minister to the Shikken "Regent." He was one of the authors of the *Joei* (or *Goseibai*) *Shikimoku* "Formulary of Adjudication," a legal code of the Kamakura Shogunate.

Nikaido Yukifuji (1246-1302)
In 1282 was kebiishi "chief of police," in 1288 Dewa no kami, and then rensho "assistant regent" to the Shikken.

Nikaido Sadafuji (14th century)
Was kebiishi "Imperial police officer" and Dewa no kami.

During the Genko War (1331-1333) Sadafuji tried in vain to prevent the 14th Hojo Shikken Takatoki (1303-1333) from dethroning the Emperor Go-Daigo (1288-1339). He besieged Morinaga-shinno (1308-1335) at Mount Yoshino (Yamato), and defeated Murakami Yoshimitsu, whose head he sent to Kyoto.

OÉ

Territory: Higo

Ancient family of scholars, literati, and statesmen.

Notable Ancestors

Oé Otondo (811-877)
Disciple of the scholar Sugawara Koreyoshi (812-880. Otondo rose to the post of kebiishi-betto "chief of police." He is often called Koso-ko.

In 871 Otondo contributed to the *Jogan-kyakushiki*, and has left several works.

Oé Chisato (9th century)
Son of Otondo. He was a renowned poet.

Oé Asatsuna (886-957)
Grandson of Otondo. He distinguished himself as a man of letters, and published the *Shin Koku-shi* "New History of Japan." He is also called Nochino-Koso-ko.

Oé Koretoki (888-963)
Grandson of Otondo. He was a poet. He filled important functions during the reigns of the Emperors Shuzaku (923-952) and Murakami (926-967). He is also called Koso-ko.

Koretoki is the author of *Senzai-kaku*

Oé Otondo

Oé Chisato

"*Verses of a Thousand Years*," an anthology of ro-ei "folk songs" and Chinese verses.

Oé Tadahira (952-1012)
Grandson of Koretoki. He was a poet of renown.

Kamakura Period – Shimokobé

Oé Koretoki (955-1010)
Relative of Tadahira. He distinguished himself in literature.

Oé Masafusa (1041-1111)
Descendant of Tadahira. He was equally remarkable in prose and poetry, known for his knowledge of the Chinese classics. He was a famed Japanese scholar and tutor under the Emperors Shirakawa (1053-1129), Horikawa (1079-1107), and Toba (1103-1156).

Masafusa became Okura-kyo "finance minister," and from 1098 to 1102 governor of Dazaifu "Kyushu." He was also for a time acting chunagon "middle counselor."

Masafusa is the author of the famous work Goké-shidai "Ceremonial Customs," a valuable source of historic information for ceremonial and public functions of the early 12th century, commissioned by the Kanpaku "Regent" Fujiwara Moromichi (1062-1099).

Masafusa, Fujiwara Nagafusa, and Fujiwara Korefusa, who all flourished at the same time, are styled the san-bo "three bo" ('bo' is the Chinese reading of the character 'fusa').

Oé Hiromoto (1148-1225)
Son of Koremitsu, and great-grandson of Masafusa. He was adopted by Nakahara Hirosué, but in 1216 returned to the Oé. He originally served the Imperial Court in Kyoto.

At the beginning of the Genpei War (1180-1185) he served Minamoto Yoritomo (1147-1199) as soon as he rose against the Taira.

In 1184 Yoritomo invited Hiromoto to Kyoto, and appointed him as the 1st betto "superintendent" of the Kumonjo "Archives Bureau," and in 1191 that of the Mandokoro "Administrative Board."

Hiromoto had considerable influence in the Shogunate's organizational structure. In return for his services, he received the domain of Yamamoto (Higo).

In 1190 Hiromoto followed Yoritomo to Kyoto, and remained there to negotiate with the Imperial Court until 1192.

After Yoritomo's death in 1199, Hiromoto won the trust of his widow Masako (1156-1225), and assisted in the Hojo's seizure of power. He was involved in several important events in the Shogunate. Real power was moved from the 2nd Minamoto Shogun Yoriié (1182-1204) to the council of influential gokenin "vassals." In 1203 the Shogun was arrested along with his supporter Hiki Yoshikazu (-1203).

Hiromoto proved a most able administrator as counselor to both Yoriié and the 3rd Minamoto Shogun Sanetomo (1192-1219). He also helped the Hojo crush enemies as Hatakeyama Shigetada (1164-1205), Hiraga Asamasa, and Wada Yoshimori (1147-1213).

In 1217 Hiromoto became a Buddhist monk.

In the 1221 Jokyu War, Hiromoto insisted on making a sudden attack to Kyoto, and contributed to the Shogunate's overwhelming victory.

In 1224 Hiromoto backed the succession of Hojo Yasutoki (1183-1242) as the 3rd Kamakura Shikken "Regent."

The Mori of Aki are his descendants from his 4th son who took that name.

Oé Masafusa 大江匡房

SHIMOKOBÉ
下河邊

Territory: Shimosa

Ancient family descended from Fujiwara Hidesato (10th century).

NOTABLE ANCESTORS

Shimokobé Yukiyoshi (12th century)
Son of Yukimitsu. He received the domain of Shimokobé (Shimosa) in the 12th century and took the name of the place.

Shimokobé Yukihira (12th century)
Son of Yukiyoshi. He at first served the Taira, then sided with Minamoto Yoritomo (1147-1199).

In 1184, during the Genpei War (1180-1185), Yukihira took part in the western campaign of Minamoto Noriyori (1156-1193), and with Chiba Tsunetané (1118-1201) defeated and drove out the robbers that infested the environs of Kyoto.

In 1189 Yukihira accompanied Minamoto Yoritomo in his expedition to Mutsu.

He taught the art of using the bow to the 2nd Minamoto Shogun Yoriié (1182-1204).

Wada

Residence: Kamakura

Family descended from Miura Yoshiaki (-1181), and through him from the Taira. The clan was very powerful in the beginning of the 13th century.

Notable Ancestors

Wada Yoshimori (1147-1213)

Son of Sugimoto Yoshimuné, and grandson of Miura Yoshiaki (1093-1181). He took the name of Wada from the village on the Miura Peninsula where he lived.

Yoshimori joined Minamoto Yorimoto (1147-1199) in the Genpei War (1180-1185) as soon as the latter revolted against the Taira. With Minamoto Yoshitsuné (1159-1189), he undertook the campaign against Kiso Yoshinaka (1154-1184), and assisted in 1184 at the Battle of Ichi-no-tani (Settsu), and in 1185 at the Battle of Dan-no-ura (Nagato).

After the triumph of the Minamoto, Yoshimori was appointed the 1st betto "superintendent" of the samurai-dokoro "board of retainers."

In 1189 Yoshimori assisted in the expedition against Fujiwara Yasuhira (1155-1189) in Mutsu.

In 1203 Yoshimori was ordered by the 2nd Minamoto Shogun Yoriie (1182-1204) to kill the 1st Hojo Shikken Tokimasa (1138-1215), but he sided with the Hojo. Yoriié was forced to abdicate, and his younger brother Sanetomo (1192-1219) succeeded as the 3rd Minamoto Shogun.

In 1213, when Izumi Chikahira revolted against the Hojo, two of Yoshimori's sons, Yoshinao and Yoshishigé, and his nephew Tanenaga joined him and were arrested. Yoshimori, then in Shimosa, hastened to Kamakura and asked pardon for his two sons, which Sanetomo granted. Emboldened by this success he made a like request in favor of his nephew, but met with a refusal, and Tanenaga was exiled to Mutsu. Believing this to be due to the influence of the 2nd Hojo Shikken Yoshitoki (1163-1224), he conceived a violent hatred against the latter, and, levying troops, prepared to attack him. Yoshitoki, forewarned, took refuge in the Shogun's palace, which Yoshimori ventured to invest, but was repulsed and perished with his two sons.

Asahina Saburo Yoshihidé (1175-)

3rd son of Wada Yoshinori and, according to legend, of Tomoé Gozen. He later adopted the name Asahina from the area where he lived. He was renowned for his Herculean strength, which he used to accomplish a number of stunning feats.

According to one source, Yoshihidé and Minamoto Yoriié (1182-1204) were good friends, and one day, at Sagami Bay, the future Shogun challenged Yoshihidé to demonstrate his swimming prowess. The latter immediate jumped into the water and soon remerged with a shark in each fist.

The Tale of the Soga Brothers' Revenge mentions Yoshihidé has having competed for strength with Soga Goro Tokimuné (1174-1193).

Another legend tells of Yoshihidé opening the Asahina Pass, named after him, connecting Kamakura (Sagami) with Kanazawa (later part of Yokohama), in one night.

In 1213 Yoshihidé took part in the revolt of his father and Yoriié against the Hojo, and distinguished himself by his feats of prowess. It was he who raided and burned the Okura Bakufu, the seat of the Minamoto Shogunate. But his party having been defeated, he fled with 500 of his horsemen, as some say, to Kikai-ga-shima (Ryukyu), and, according to clan records, to Koma (Korea).

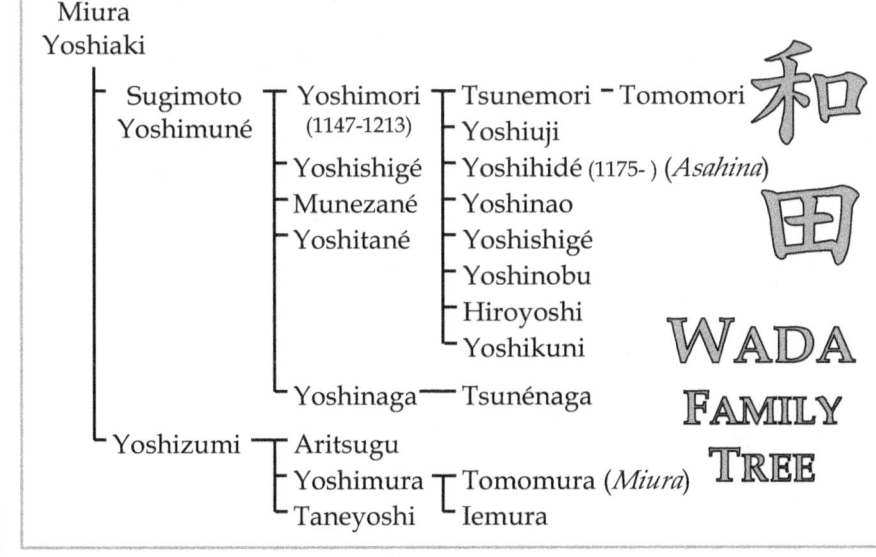

Wada Family Tree

Muromachi Period

Ashikaga

Residence: Kyoto

Descended from the Seiwa-Genji Minamoto Yoshiié (1039-1106). His son Yoshikuni (1082-1155) settled in Ashikaga (Shimotsuké). Yoshikuni's eldest son took the name Nitta, while his 2nd son Yoshiyasu (1126-1157) took Ashikaga.

The Ashikaga had many notable branch clans, including the Hosokawa, the Imagawa, the Hatakeyama (after 1205), the Kira, the Shiba, and the Hachisuka. After the head family of the Minamoto died out during the early Kamakura Period (1185-1333), the Ashikaga came to style themselves as the head of the Minamoto, co-opting the prestige which came with that name.

The Ashikaga became very wealthy under the Hojo Regents, but their defection to the Imperial cause in 1333 sealed that clan's fate.

When the subsequent Kenmu Restoration (1333-1336) proved unpopular among the military, in 1336 Ashikaga Takauji (1305-1358) overthrew the Emperor Go-Daigo, igniting the wars between the Northern and Southern Courts of the Nanboku-cho Period (1336-1392), and in 1338 he appointed himself the 1st Ashikaga Shogun, establishing his government in Kyoto.

The ensuing Muromachi "Ashikaga" Period (1336-1573) was an era of incessant warfare. The clan had many difficulties, with its members often fighting for supremacy and struggling for succession. The Ashikaga Shogun were however cultured, and developed new artistic forms such as Noh "classical Japanese musical drama," and encouraged both domestic and foreign trade.

During the 1st century of the Ashikaga Shogunate, the clan was divided in two rival branches, the Kanto Ashikaga and the Kyoto Ashikaga, the latter the Shogunate rulers of Japan. The Ashikaga of the Kanto were tasked with maintaining the authority of the Ashikaga Shogun in that region, and at first resided at Kamakura (Sagami). They were known as the Kanto-kubo "Kanto deputy Shogun," and traditionally relied on the support

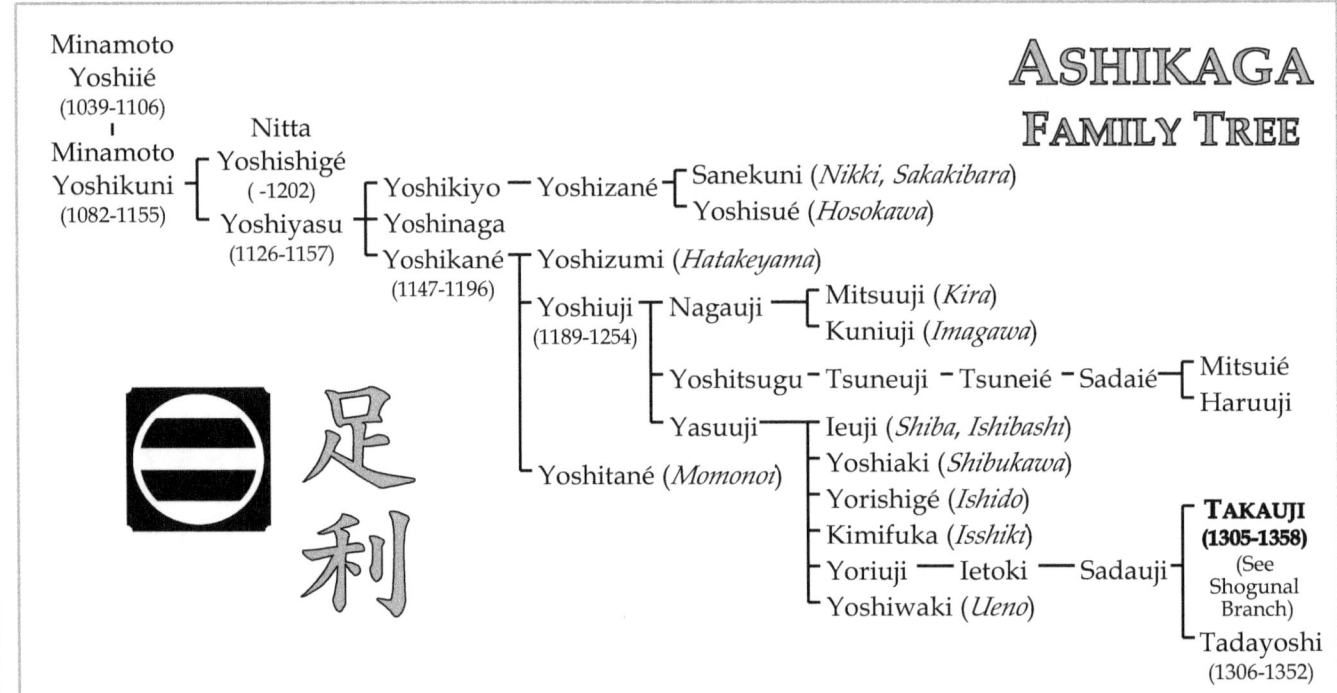

Ashikaga Family Tree

of the Uesugi, who were Kanto kanrei "Kanto governor-general."

In 1449 Ashikaga Shigeuji (1438-1531) became Kanto kubo, and had Uesugi Noritada as his deputy. Shigeuji became concerned by the influence of the Uesugi, and at length had Noritada murdered. The two main branches of the Uesugi, the Ogigayatsu and the Yamanouchi, the latter supported by the Nagao of Echigo, went to war with Shigeuji and his followers. Although Shigeuji held his own in various battles in Sagami and elsewhere, in 1455 Kamakura was taken and burned by Imagawa Noritada (1408-1461), and the Ashikaga kubo afterwards resided in Shimosa and became known as the Koga-kubo.

After the Onin War (1467-77) Kyoto was in ruins, and the clan was seriously weakened. The Ashikaga Bakufu completely fell apart, launching a century of anarchy, and the Ashikaga Shogun became puppets of the Hosokawa.

When the Odawara Hojo of Sagami began to make advances into the Kanto in the early 16th century, the Ashikaga allied with the Uesugi to challenge them. In 1554 the kubo position came to an effective end with the defeat and capture of Ashikaga Haruuji (1503-1560).

By the end of the Sengoku "Warring States" Period (1467-1573), the clan was eclipsed by Oda Nobunaga (1534-1582), who in 1573 banished the last Ashikaga Shogun Yoshiaki (1537-1597) from Kyoto, ending the Muromachi "Ashikaga" Period (1336-1573) of Japan.

Notable Ancestors

Minamoto/Ashikaga Yoshiyasu (1126-1157)

Son of Minamoto Yoshikuni (1082-1155), brother to Nitta Yoshishigé (1135-1202), and grandson of Minamoto Yoshiié (1039-1106). He was the first to bear the name of Ashikaga, from the village where his father had established residence in 1150. He was also called Saburo.

In the short 1156 Hogen Rebellion (Kyoto), Yoshiyasu was on the side of Taira Kiyomori (1118-1181), and guarded the Imperial Palace of the Emperor Go-Shirakawa (1127-1192) with Minamoto Yoshitomo (1123-1160) against those who supported the ex-Emperor Sutoku (1119-1164), whom they defeated. He was then appointed Mutsu no kami.

Yoshiyasu is the ancestor, not only of the Ashikaga, but also several families that played an important part in the events of the 14th, 15th, and 16th centuries.

Ashikaga Yoshikané (1147-1196)

3rd son of Yoshiyasu. He was Kazusa no suké. He had married a daughter of Hojo Tokimasa (1138-1215), and was thus a brother-in-law to Minamoto Yoritomo (1147-1199). For that reason he sided with the latter against the Taira.

In 1185 Yoshikané took part in the campaign of Minamoto Noriyori (1156-1193) in Kyushu, and in 1189 that of Minamoto Yoritomo in Mino. He defeated a certain Okawa Kaneto, who pretended to be Minamoto Yoshitsuné (1159-1189) escaping from the disastrous Battle of Koromo-gawa (Mutsu).

Soon afterwards he became a bonze under the name Gisho.

Ashikaga Yoshiuji (1189-1254)

He was Sama no suké.

In 1213 Yoshiuji repressed the revolt of Wada Yoshimori (1147-1213) against the Hojo. During the 1221 Jokyu War (Kyoto), he contributed greatly to the defeat of the troops of the Emperor Go-Toba (1180-1239).

He should not be confused with the later Ashikaga Yoshiuji of the Kamakura Branch, who was the last Koga Kanto kubo.

Ashikaga Ietoki (13th century)

A descendant in the 7th generation of Minamoto Yoshiié (1039-1106). He was Iyo no kami.

A writing of Yoshiié said that the Empire would be governed by his descendants in the 7th generation. Seeing that the prophecy of his ancestor was not realized, Ietoki went to the temple of Hachiman, the tutelary god of the Minamoto, and offering up his life that the oracle might be fulfilled within three generations, he committed suicide.

Shogunal Branch

Notable Ancestors

Ashikaga Takauji (1305-1358)

1st Muromachi Shogun.

Ashikaga Tadayoshi (1306-1352)

Son of Sadauji, and younger brother to Takauji. His mother was a daughter of Uesugi Yorishigé.

Tadayoshi first took part in the Kamakura Shogunate's political life in the Genko War (1131-1333) that marked the end of the Kamakura Period (1185-1333), and led to the beginning of the Muromachi Period (1336-1573), the most turbulent era in the history of Japan.

During the intervening Kenmu Restoration (1333-1336) Tadayoshi joined his brother Takauji in abandoning the Kamakura Shogunate, and sided with the Emperor Go-Daigo (1288-1339). The latter, however, wishing to rule without interference from the military, sent his 6-year-old son Prince Norinaga north, and appointed him governor-general of Mutsu and Dewa. In response, Tadayoshi, without an order from the Emperor escorted another of his sons, 11-year-old Prince Narinaga (1326-1338) to Kamakura, where he installed him as governor of Kozuké, with himself as a deputy and *de facto* ruler. The appointment of a warrior to such an important post was intended to show the Emperor that the samurai class was not ready for a purely civilian rule. Since he ruled without interference from Kyoto, and the area in itself was in effect a miniature Shogunate, this event can be considered the beginning of the Ashikaga Shogunate.

In 1335 Tadayoshi was in charge of the protection of the Shogun Narinaga-shinno, when Hojo Tokiyuki (1322-1353) came to attack Kamakura (Sagami), starting the Nakasendai Rebellion. Not being strong enough to resist him, he had to leave the city immediately. Not being able to take along his prisoner of several months, the ex-Shogun Morinaga-shinno (1308-1335), rather than letting him go, he had him beheaded. Tadayoshi retreated to Mikawa, but was soon back, accompanied by Ashikaga Takauji. They defeated Tokiyuki, and re-entered Kamakura. In 1336, turning against Go-Daigo, Tadayoshi and Takauji set up a rival Em-

Muromachi Period – Ashikaga Shogunal Branch

peror. In 1338 Takauji is appointed the 1st Ashikaga Shogun, founding the Muromachi Shogunate.

When his brother revolted, Tadayoshi marched with him against Kyoto, and took part in all the battles against the defenders of the legitimate dynasty. Unfortunately, Takauji chose as his shitsuji "deputy Shogun," Ko Moronao (-1351), who, proud of his success, soon misused his authority. Tadayoshi fell out with him, and tried to assassinated him, triggering the Kanno Disturbance (1350-1351). His design was discovered, and Moronao, to punish him, obliged him to have his head shaved and to become a bonze under the name Keishin.

In 1351 Tadayoshi rebelled and joined his brother's enemies, the supporters of the Southern Court at Yoshino (southern Yamato), whose Emperor Go-Murakami (1328-1368) appointed him general of all his troops. Later that year he defeated Ashikaga Takauji, occupied Kyoto, and entered Kamakura. In the same year his forces killed the Ko brothers, Moronao and Moroyasu, at Mikagé (Settsu). In 1352 he was defeated by Takauji at Satta-yama (Suruga). The brothers reconciled, but it proved to be brief, and Tadayoshi fled to Kamakura pursued by Takauji's army. After an ostensible 2nd reconciliation, in the winter of 1351-52, Tadayoshi was captured and killed, perhaps by poison, on Takauji's order.

Tadayoshi is considered a military and administrative genius, and the true architect of many of his elder brother's successes. He is mostly referred to as Daikyu-ji-dono from the name of his family temple in Kamakura, where he had died. His posthumous name is Kozan Keigen.

Ashikaga Tadafuyu (ca. 1327-1400)

Illegitimate eldest son of Takauji, and adopted by his uncle Tadayoshi. His mother was the concubine Echizen no Tsuboné.

From 1349-1352 Tadafuyu was tandai "governor" of Chugoku (far western Honshu).

In 1351, when Tadayoshi joined the Southern Court, Tadafuyu also revolted against Takauji. Having been defeated by Ko Moronao (-1351), he fled to Kyushu, where he married the daughter of Shoni Yorihisa.

In 1352, after the death of Tadayoshi, Tadafuyu fought under the command of Yamana Tokiuji, and forced Takauji from Kyoto.

In 1355 Tadafuyu entered Kyoto, from whence Takauji had fled; but soon afterwards he was obliged to retreat to Iwami.

In 1363 Tadafuyu lost Bingo.

In 1376 Tadafuyu submitted to the 3rd Ashikaga Shogun Yoshimitsu, and received the title of Iwami no kami.

Ashikaga Yoshiakira (1330-1368)
2nd Muromachi Shogun.

Ashikaga Yoshimitsu (1358-1408)
3rd Muromachi Shogun.

Ashikaga Yoshimochi (1386-1428)
4th Muromachi Shogun.

Ashikaga Yoshikazu (1407-1425)
5th Muromachi Shogun.

Ashikaga Yoshinori (1394-1441)
6th Muromachi Shogun.

Ashikaga Yoshikatsu (1433-1443)
7th Muromachi Shogun.

Ashikaga Yoshimasa (1435-1490)
8th Muromachi Shogun.

Ashikaga Yoshihisa (1465-1489)
9th Muromachi Shogun.

Ashikaga Masatomo (1436-1491)

3rd son of the 6th Ashikaga Shogun Yoshinori, and brother to Yoshikatsu, Yoshimasa, and Yoshimi.

Masatomo was a bonze at the Kogon-in (Kyoto) when the Kanto kanrei "Kanto governor-general" Ashikaga Shigeuji was expelled from Kamakura by Uesugi Fusaaki (1432-1466). In 1455 Masatomo's brother Yoshimasa sent him to take Shigeuji's place; but, although supported by the troops of Kai and Isé, he was repulsed by Ashikaga Yoshiuji. He then established his residence at Horigoé Castle (Izu), from whence he tried to govern Kanto, and became known as the Horigoé-kubo. Shigeuji settled in Koga (Shimosa) and attempted to rule Kanto from there. Neither prevailed and the region was essentially in the hands of the Uesugi.

Putting aside his eldest son Chachamaru, Masatomo selected his 2nd son Yoshizumi as his heir. Chacha revolted against this decision, assassinated his

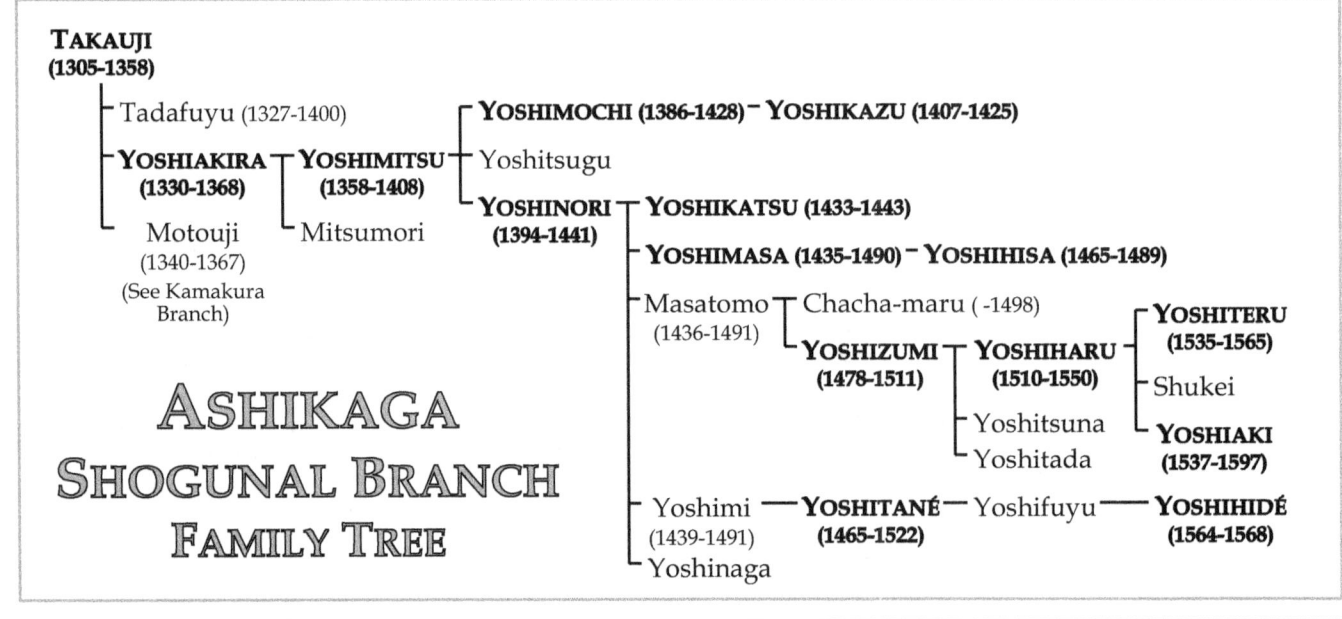

Ashikaga Shogunal Branch Family Tree

father, and took his inheritance. Two years later he was himself deposed and killed by Hojo Soun (1432-1519).

Ashikaga Yoshimi (1439-1491)

The 4th son of Yoshinori, and brother to Yoshikatsu and to the 8th Ashikaga Shogun Yoshimasa.

He was the abbot of a Jodo monastery, under the name Gijin, when Hosokawa Katsumoto (1430-1473) approached him to succeed his brother Yoshimasa, who was childless, as the next Shogun, but he initially declined. In 1464 Gijin was persuaded to join his brother as deputy, with the understanding that he will in time succeed to the Shogun's office. He then took the name Yoshimi. In the following year, however, Yoshimasa's wife Hino Tomiko (1440-1496) produced a son, Yoshihisa, which caused friction between the two brothers, and eventually led to a succession dispute that ignited the disastrous Onin War (1467-1477), and which initiated the Sengoku "Warring States" Period (1467-1573).

The Ashikaga tried to prevent the outbreak of war over the next heir, but the succession dispute became a pretext for a struggle for military supremacy between Hosokawa Katsumoto, who supported Yoshimi, and Yamana Sozen (1404-1473), who supported the infant Yoshihisa. In 1467 fighting broke out, and Kyoto's northern parts were in ruins from looting and incendiarism by undisciplined troops. By the end of the year, both forces were exhausted, and withdrew.

During the hostilities, Yoshimi established himself first at Sakamoto (Omi), afterwards he applied for an asylum to Kitabataké Noritomo in Isé. Finally he settled on Hiei-zan (northeast of Kyoto). Peace having been concluded, he retired to Mino.

In 1489 Yoshihisa died, and Yoshimasa summoned Yoshimi to Kyoto. The brothers reconciled, and Yoshimasa adopted Yoshimi's son Yoshitané, who became the 10th Ashikaga Shogun.

Yoshimi returned to priesthood at the Tsugen-ji in Sanjo (Kyoto), and died two years later at the age of 53.

Ashikaga Yoshitané (1465-1522)
10th Muromachi Shogun.

Ashikaga Yoshizumi (1478-1511)
11th Muromachi Shogun.

Ashikaga Yoshiharu (1510-1550)
12th Muromachi Shogun.

Ashikaga Yoshiteru (1535-1565)
13th Muromachi Shogun.

Ashikaga Yoshihidé (1564-1568)
14th Muromachi Shogun.

Ashikaga Yoshiaki (1537-1597)
15th Muromachi Shogun.

Kamakura Branch

Notable Ancestors

Ashikaga Motouji (1340-1367)

1st Kanto-kubo "Kanto deputy Shogun." 4th son of Takauji.

After his revolt against the Emperor Go-Daigo (1288-1339), having again set up the Shogunate in his own person, Takauji installed himself at Kamakura. He soon perceived that the situation was not the same as in the time of Minamoto Yoshitomo (1123-1160), and that Kyoto was the right residence of the Shogun. On the other hand, the difficulty of governing the turbulent eastern provinces from the capital, suggested to him the thought of not abandoning Kamakura entirely. In 1349, reserving the succession to the Shogunate for his eldest son Yoshiakira, Takauji intrusted the government of the eastern provinces to his 4th son Motouji with the title of Kanto-kubo. However, as Motouji was yet a child, the administration was put in the loyal hands of Uesugi Noriaki and Ko Morofuyu (-1351) with the title of shitsuji "deputy Shogun."

In the Kanno Disturbance (1350-1351), however, Uesugi Noriaki, together with Takauji's brother Tada-

Ashikaga Motouji

yoshi, defected and joined the Southern Court of the Emperor Go-Murakami (1328-1368), leaving Kamakura for Kozuké. Ko Morofuyu, remaining faithful to Motouji, marched against his colleague, but was killed in Kai. Takauji repaired then to Kamakura and defeated the troops of his brother, who was made a prisoner, and later assassinated.

In 1352 the Nitta brothers, Yoshioki (-1358) and Yoshimuné (1335-1368), with their cousin Wakiya Yoshiharu, took Kamakura and ousted Motouji. Soon after Takauji came back and defeated Yoshimuné, who retired to Echigo. Having returned to Kyoto, Takauji sent Hatakeyama Kunikiyo to Kamakura as shitsuji.

In 1358, after the death of Takauji, Yoshioki returned to the countryside of Kozuké and Musashi. He continued to fight for some time and was going to attack Kamakura again, but he was captured by Takezawa Nagahira. Kunikiyo sentenced Yoshioki to death, and he was drowned in the the Rokugogawa (Musashi).

Peace was then restored in the Kanto, and Motouji sent troops commanded by Hatakeyama Kunikiyo to help his brother, the 2nd Ashiakaga Shogun Yoshiakira (1330-1368), to invest the Yoshino region, where the Emperor of the South had entrenched himself. Kunikiyo, however, disobeyed orders, and went to attack Nikki Yoshinaga. Motouji marched in person against his deputy, whom he defeated without difficulty.

In 1364 Motouji reconciled with Uesugi Noriaki, and reinstalled him in the office of shitsuji. He died three years later, during an epidemic, while firmly in power, at the age of 28.

Ashikaga Ujimitsu (1359-1398)

2nd Kanto-kubo. Son of Motouji.

In 1367 Ujimitsu succeeded his father as the Kanto deputy Shogun when he was only 9 years old. Uesugi Noriaki continued his functions as shitsuji "deputy," and the Rinzai Zen priest Gido Shushin (1325-1388) was his tutor.

Uesugi Noriaki died the following year, and was replaced by his son Yoshinori (-1378), who, soon afterwards, had to lead an expedition against Nitta Yoshimuné (1335-1368) and Wakiya Yoshiharu: Yoshimuné was killed in an engagement with Ue-

Muromachi Period – Ashikaga Kamakura Branch

Ashikaga Ujimitsu

sugi Norimasa, and Yoshiharu fled into Shinano.

As Ujimitsu advanced in years, ambition entered the heart of the young kubo. In 1379, while Yoshiakira was subduing Kyushu, Ujimitsu conceived the project of making himself master of Kyoto and having himself nominated Shogun. Uesugi Noriharu, to whom he spoke of his plan, first tried to dissuade him from that foolish enterprise, but seeing that his advice was of no avail, he committed suicide by seppuku. This tragic death made Ujimitsu reflect, and he abandoned his design.

In 1382 Ujitmisu sent Uesugi Norikata (1335-1394) to defeat and kill Oyama Yoshimasa, a partisan of the Southern Court, who caused troubles in Shimotsuké.

In 1391, when the Shogun Yoshimitsu fought against the Yamana, Ujimitsu was going to join him but the campaign was finished before he could take part in it. His jurisdiction was nevertheless extended to Mutsu and Dewa.

Ashikaga Mitsukané (1378-1409)

3rd Kanto kubo. Eldest son of Ujimitsu. He was 21 years old when his father died and succeeded him as the Kanto deputy Shogun. Uesugi Tomomuné (1339-1414) was his shitsuji "deputy."

In the year after taking power, Mitsukané dispatched his sons Mitsunao and Mitsusada to Sasagawa Gosho and Inamura Gosho to stabilize the situation in Mutsu.

In 1399, when Ouchi Yoshihiro (1356-1399) revolted in Izumi in favor of the Southern Court, Mitsukané conceived the project, known as the Oei Rebellion, of joining him and taking the place of the 4th Ashikaga Shogun Yoshimochi (1386-1428); but the revolt was promptly put down and he could not realize his plan.

In 1400 Mitsukané swore fidelity to the retired 3rd Ashikaga Shogun Yoshimitsu (1358-1408), and peace between Kamakura and Kyoto lasted until Mitsukané's death.

In 1402 Mitsukané sent Uesugi Zenshu (-1417) to quell the revolt of Daté Masamuné, ancestor of the more famous Tokugawa tozama daimyo with the same name, who, with some allies, had rebelled in southern and central Mutsu against Kamakura.

He died at the age of 32 of natural causes.

Ashikaga Mochiuji (1398-1439)

4th Kanto kubo. Son of Mitsukané. He was 11 years old when he succeeded his father as the Kanto deputy Shogun. Uesugi Norisada ruled for him at the beginning as his shitsuji "deputy," and in 1411, at his death, was replaced by his son Uesugi Zenshu (-1417).

In 1415, after a disagreement, Mochiuji rebuked and forced his shitsuji to resign. Zenshu then plotted to replace Mochiuji by the latter's brother Mochinaka. Mochiuji immediately asked Uesugi Norimoto (1383-1418) for help, and took refuge first in Izu, then in Suruga, whence Imagawa Noritada (1408-1461) conducted him to Kyoto. In 1417 the 4th Ashikaga Shogun Yoshimochi (1386-1428) ordered all the daimyo of Kanto to support Mochiuji. Norimoto, who had been levying troops in Echigo, came back with great forces, and Zenshu fled to the Tsurugaoka Hachiman-gu (Kamakura), where he committed seppuku. Mochinaka also committed suicide, and Mochiuji returned to Kamakura.

In 1428, at the death of Yoshimochi, Mochiuji tried in vain to be nominated Shogun, but Yoshinori (1394-1441) succeeded as the 6th Ashikaga Shogun. Convinced that Uesugi Norizané (1410-1466) was the cause of his failure, he tried to get rid of him. As however Norizané was as powerful as he was popular in Kanto, the attempt was difficult.

In the meantime, Mochiuji attacked the Oda, the Takeda, and the nobles of Musashi. The Ashikaga disapproved, and the Shogun Yoshinori ordered him to stop, but he disobeyed.

In 1438 Mochiuji concerted measures with Isshiki Naokané and Uesugi Narinao, inciting the Eikyo Rebellion; but the plot was discovered, and the kubo was obliged to apologize to Uesugi Norizané, and exile both his accomplices. New attempts having been directed against him, Norizané retired to his castle of Hirai (Kozuké), and thence informed the Shogun Yoshinori of the events. The answer was to put to death Mochiuji, who, besieged in the Yoan-ji (west of Kamakura), committed seppuku. He was 42 years old. His uncle Mitsusada and his eldest son Yoshihisa did the same at the Hokoku-ji (Kamakura).

The three younger sons of Mochiuji, however, succeeded in fleeing to Nikko (Shimotsuké). In 1440 Yuki Ujitomo, daimyo of Koga (Shimosa), led them to his castle and took up their party; but his castle was besieged, and he lost his life. Two of his protégés were caught in

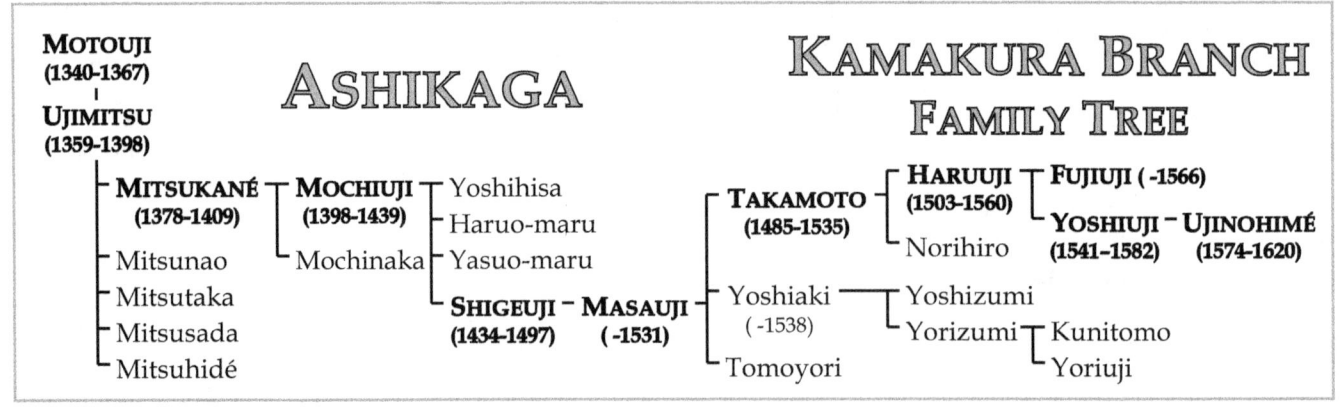

Ashikaga Kamakura Branch Family Tree

their flight, and put to death in Mino. Haru-maru, Mochiuji's 2nd son, was 13, and Yasuo-maru, the 3rd, was 11 years old. The youngest, Shigeuji, was taken to Shinano, into his mother's family.

The events in Kamakura caused widespread resentment among the Shogun Yoshinori's generals, and in 1441 one of them, Akamatsu Mitsusuké (1381-1441), murdered him in revenge.

Ashikaga Shigeuji (1434-1497)

5th Kanto kubo. 4th son of Mochiuji. His childhood name was Eijuo-maru. After his father's death at the age of 5, he was taken to his mother's family in Shinano.

In 1449 Eijuo's uncle Oi Mochimitsu managed to have him appointed to the post of Kanto deputy Shogun, the first Ashikaga to hold the post since his father's death ten years earlier. On the occasion, the 11-year-old boy reached manhood, and received the character shigé for the adult name from the 8th Ashikaga Shogun Yoshimasa (1436-1490) himself (who took it from his former name, Yoshinari), and he became Shigeuji. Yoshimasa, not trusting Shigeuji, nominated his ally Uesugi Noritada, a son of Norizané (1410-1466), as shitsuji "deputy," with the task of keeping him informed of developments in Kamakura. The relationship between the two men, already difficult because of the role the Uesugi had had in Mochiuji's death, was therefore strained from the beginning.

Tensions culminated when Yuki Shigetomo, a son of Ujitomo, came from Mutsu to join Shigeuji at Kamakura, and both prepared to revenge the deaths of their fathers and brothers. In 1454 Shigeuji invited Uesugi Noritada to his mansion, and there assassinated him, setting in motion the Kyotoku Rebellion (1454-1482). At the news of this crime, all the vassals of the Uesugi rose in arms against Shigeuji, and civil war re-commenced. In 1455 Imagawa Noritada (1408-1461) defeated Shigeuji, and Uesugi Fusaaki, Noritada's brother, established himself at Kamakura. Shigeuji fled to Koga (Hitachi), and took refuge there; hence the name of Koga kubo, by which the people designated him and his successors.

Meanwhile Uesugi Fusaaki sent a report on the events to Kyoto, and asked

Ashikaga Shigeuji

the Shogun to designate someone to replace Shigeuji. Yoshimasa sent his own brother Masatomo as the new Kanto kubo. But as many daimyo and samurai had remained faithful to Shigeuji, Masatomo was unable to enter Kamakura, and was obliged to establish himself at Horigoé (Izu); on that account he was called Horigoé-gosho. Thus there were two rulers in the Kanto: on the one side, Masatomo was supported by the whole clan of the Uesugi; on the other, Shigeuji was supported by the Chiba, the Utsunomiya, the Oyama, etc.

In 1471 the Uesugi came to besiege Koga, and Shigeuji was compelled to escape to Chiba (Shimosa).

In 1482, by the intervention of the Shogun, peace was concluded between the two parties, and Shigeuji was able to return to Koga, where he founded a dynasty and ruled until his death at the age of 63.

Ashikaga Masauji (-1531)

Son of Shigeuji. Like his father, he lived in Koga as the Koga Kanto kubo.

In 1506 Masauji's son Takamoto tried to revolt against him, but peace was restored owing to the intervention of Nagao Kageharu.

Ashikaga Yoshiaki (-1538)

3rd son of Masauji, and grandson of Shigeuji.

Around 1525, after some disagreement having arisen between him and his father, the Takeda of Kazusa set up Yoshiaki at Oyumi Castle (Mutsu), hence the name of Oyumi gosho that was given him.

In 1538 Satomi Yoshihiro (1530-1578), after having submitted to him, joined Yoshiaki against Hojo Ujitsuna (1487-1541) at the 1st Battle of Konodai (Musashi). They suffered a crushing defeat, and Yoshiaki perished in the battle.

He should not be confused with the last Ashikaga Shogun Yoshiaki (1537-1597).

Ashikaga Haruuji (1503-1560)

Son of Takamoto, and grandson of Masauji. He married the daughter of Hojo Ujitsuna (1487-1541), and was Koga Kanto kobu.

In 1545 Haruuji joined Ogigayatsu Tomosada (1525-1546) and Uesugi Norimasa (1523-1579) at the Battle of Kawagoé (Musashi) against the Hojo brothers Tsunanari (1515-1587) and Ujiyasu (1515-1571). After being informed by ninja spies that the besiegers, especially Haruuji, had relaxed their vigilance due to their overconfidence, the Hojo forces coordinated a successful and decisive night attack.

In 1554, after another defeat at the hands of the Hojo, Haruuji was captured at Koga (Hitachi), and forced to accept Hojo rule.

In 1560 he died of illness.

Ashikaga Yoshiuji (16th century)

Son of Haruuji. He was the 5th Koga Kanto kubo.

Yoshiuji had a daughter known by the name of Koga-himegimi, for whom he adopted Kunitomo, who established himself in 1590 at Kitsuregawa (Shimotsuké), where his descendants resided with a revenue of 10,000 koku.

He should not be confused with the earlier Ashikaga Yoshiuji (1189-1254).

AKAMATSU

Territories: Harima, Bizen, Mimasaka, Inaba, Tajima
Castle: Shirahata (Harima)

Akamatsu Norimura

Ancient daimyo family from Harima, descended from Minamoto Morifusa (-1077) of the Minamoto Murakami-Genji branch.

The Akamatsu were patrons of Sesson Yubai (1290-1348), a Zen Buddhist monk of the Rinzai sect, who became the founder of a number of provincial temple monasteries in Japan, including the Houn-ji and the Horin-ji in Harima. Prominent among Yubai's followers were Akamatsu Norimura (1277–1350) and his son Norisuké (1314–1371).

The Akamatsu became powerful during the Muromachi "Ashikaga" Period (1336-1573). By the time of the 3rd Ashikaga Shogun Yoshimitsu (1358-1408), they were shugo "constables" for Harima, Bizen, and Mimasaka, as well as one of the four families that provided members of the Bakufu's samurai-dokoro "board of retainers."

In 1441 the assassination of Ashikaga Yoshinori (1394-1441) by Akamatsu Mitsusuké resulted in a damaging response by the Yamana and others, and by the Sengoku "Warring States" Period (1467-1573), the Akamatsu's power had waned. In 1521 the clan lost their properties when they were defeated by their rivals, the Uragami. At length, weakened by rebellions, they became vassals of the Toyotomi.

NOTABLE ANCESTORS

Akamatsu Suéfusa (12th century)

Descendant of Morifusa in the 6th generation.

Towards 1110 Suéfusa was the first to take the name of Akamatsu, from a village of Harima, where he settled and built the castle of Shirahata.

Akamatsu Norimura/Enshin (1277-1350)

Son of Shigenori. A fervent member of the Zenshu sect, he shaved his head while still young, and took the name of Enshin, by which he is mostly known.

In 1333, by order of Morinaga-shinno (1308-1335), Norimura levied troops, marched on to Kyoto with Kitabataké Akitada, defeated Hojo Takatoki (1303-1333), and totally destroyed the Rokuhara (Kyoto), where the representatives of the Kamakura Hojo Regency resided.

In 1336, during the Kenmu Restoration (1333-1336), the Emperor Go-Daigo (1288-1339) rewarded Norimura by bestowing upon him the title of Harima no shugo "constable" and giving him the province in fief. But shortly after, he was stripped of his province, and limited to the shoen "estate" of Sayo (Harima). Incensed at this, Norimura passed over to the Ashikaga and became the implacable adversary of the Southern Dynasty. While Ashikaga Takauji (1305-1358) went to levy troops in Kyushu, he stayed the progress of Nitta Yoshisada (1301-1338). In 1336, returning towards the east with Takauji, he fought victoriously at the Battle of Minato-gawa (Settsu).

Norimura constructed the Shomyo-ji at the base of Mount Himeji (Harima), which later became the site of Himeji Castle.

He was a patron of the Zen Buddhist monk Sesson Yubai (1290-1348), who with the help of the Akamatsu was able to found a number of provincial Bud-

AKAMATSU FAMILY TREE

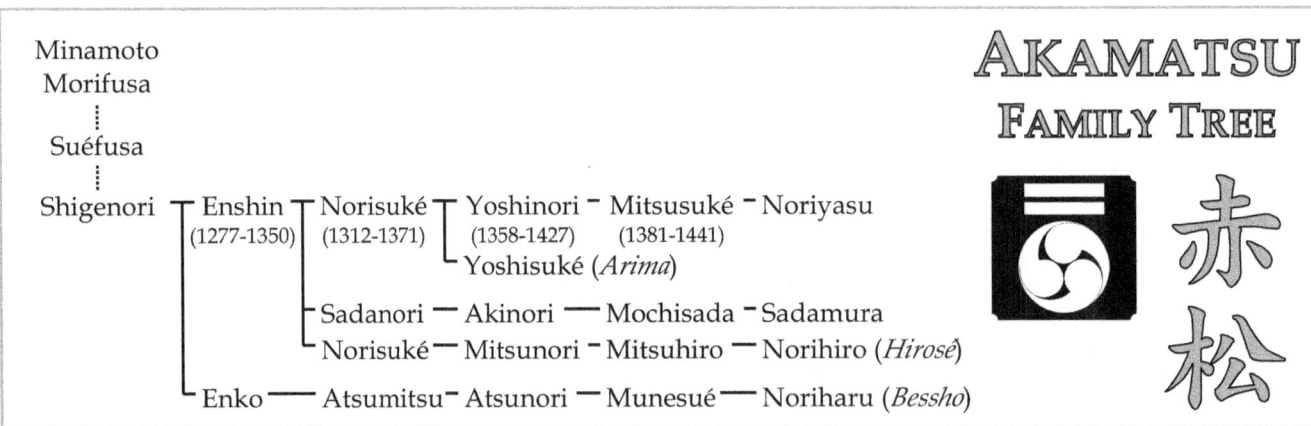

dhist temple monastaries, including the Houn-ji and the Horin-ji in Harima.

Akamatsu Norisuké (1312-1371)

Son of Norimura. He was a Tendai Buddhist monk at Hiei-zan (northeast of Kyoto) under the name Jiten.

In 1333, in answer to the appeal of Morinaga-shinno (1308-1335), Norisuké threw off his religious garb, and with his father, levied troops against the Hojo. Afterwards he followed Norimura to the camp of the Northern Dynasty.

He was governor of Harima, Bizen, and Mimasaka.

Akamatsu Yoshinori (1358-1427)

Was in great favor with the 3rd Ashikaga Shogun Yoshimitsu (1358-1408), who numbered him among his ministers.

In 1391, after the overthrow of the Yamana, Yoshinori annexed Mimasaka and several districts of Inaba and Tajima to his domain.

Later on he shaved his head and took the name Shosho. Being of very small stature, he was surnamed the Sanshaku-nyudo "Three-Foot Tall Monk."

Akamatsu Mitsusuké (1381-1441)

Son of Yoshinori.

In 1427 Mitsusuké's relative Akamatsu Mochisada intrigued at the court of the 4th Ashikaga Shogun Yoshimochi (1385-1428) to obtain his domain. Hearing that the Shogun was about to consent, Mitsusuké returned to Harima and began to fortify his castle of Shirahata (Harima). Yoshimochi sent Hosokawa Mochimoto and Yamana Tokinori against him, but with the majority of the daimyo having declared in favor of Mitsusuké, the Shogun yielded, and Mochisada, who was rumored to be the Shogun's lover, was invited to commit sepukku. Mitsusuké returned to Kyoto, where he shaved his head and took the name Shogu.

In 1440 Akamatsu Sadaura, son of Mochisada, recommenced the intrigues of his father to dispossess Mitsusuké at the court of the new Ashikaga Shogun Yoshinori (1394-1441). In 1441 Mitsusuké, informed of this by his son Noriyasu, invited the Shogun to a feast at his residence in Kyoto, during which he had him assassinated. Thereupon Mitsusuké fled to Shirahata (Harima), where he was soon besieged by Hosokawa Mochiyuki (1400-1442), Akamatsu Sadaura, Takeda Nobukata, Yamana Mochitoyo (1404-1473), etc. He killed himself, and his son followed his example.

Akamatsu Sadamura (15th century)

Son of Mochisada. He conspired to have himself chosen as leader of the Akamatsu by the 6th Ashikaga Shogun Yoshinori (1394-1441), of whom Sadamura was suspected of being a lover.

Akamatsu Yoshisuké (-1576)

Son of Harumasa.

In 1554 Yoshisuké captured Akashi Castle (Harima) from Hosokawa Harumoto (1519-1563).

In 1569 Yoshisuké was defeated by Kuroda Kanbei (1546-1604), and within a few years was so weakened that he lived in Himeji Castle (Harima) under the Akamatsu's former vassals, the Odera.

Akamatsu Masanori (-1577)

Son of Masamoto, and cousin to Yoshisuké. He had a reputation as a discerning and proud general.

Masanori held Kozuké Castle (Harima), which in late 1577 came under the attack of the Oda forces, led by Toyotomi Hideyoshi (1536-1598). He resisted stoutly, but when a relief force sent by the Ukita was defeated, and Kozuké became isolated, the Oda army launched an all-out attack. With the battle lost, Masanori killed his family, committed seppuku, and died along with many of his men.

Akamatsu Norifusa (1559-1598)

Son of Yoshisuké. He served as the shugo "constable" of Harima.

Norifusa was defeated during 1576 the Chugoku Offensive of Toyotomi

Hideyoshi (1536-1598). He then became the latter's vassal, and eventually was given Itano (Awa -- 10,000 koku) in fief.

Norifusa assisted Hideyoshi in 1583 at the Battle of Shizugataké (Omi), in 1584 at the Battle of Komaki (Owari), in 1585 for the Invasion of Shikoku, and in 1592 for the 1st Invasion of Korea.

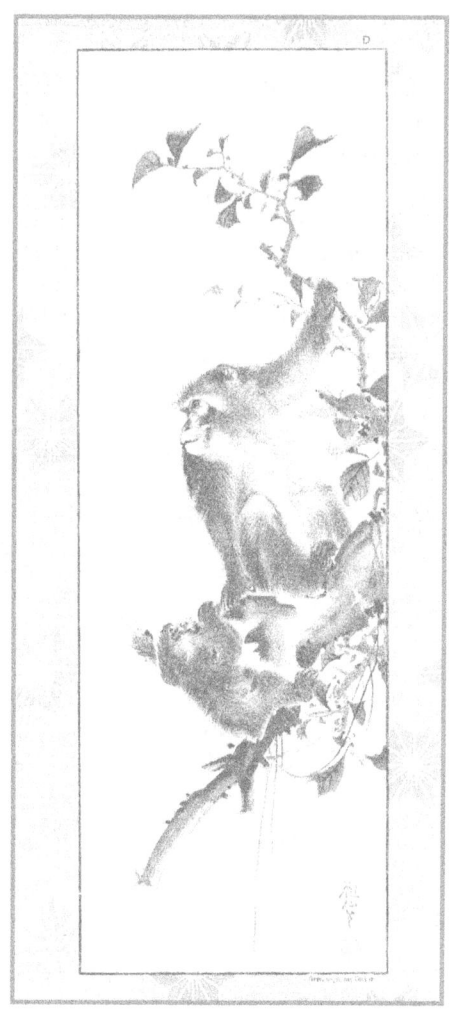

HOSOKAWA

Residence: Kyoto

Daimyo family descended from the Emperor Seiwa (850-880), Minamoto Yoshiié (1039-1106), his grandson Minamoto (later Ashikaga) Yoshiyasu (1126-1157), and thence his great-grandson Ashikaga Yoshisué, who was the first to take the Hosokawa name.

In the late Kamakura Period (1185-1333), Hosokawa Yoriharu (1299-1352), great-grandson of Yoshisué, fought for the Ashikaga clan against the Kamakura Shogunate. Another, Hosokawa Akiuji (-1352), defeated Nitta Yoshisada (1301-1338) and helped establish the Ashikaga Shogunate.

The Hosokawa were thus very powerful from the 14th to the 16th century, producing many prominent officials in the Ashikaga Shogunate's administration. The 1st Hosokawa Kyoto kanrei "Kyoto deputy Shogun" Yoriyuki (1329-1392), son of Yoriharu, acted as guardian and counsel to the 3rd Ashikaga Shogun Yoshimitsu. The lineage of the 2nd Hosokawa Kyoto kanrei Yorimoto (1343-1397), Yoriyuki's brother, was one of the san-kan "three families" from which the Kyoto kanrei had to be chosen. Over the centuries the family moved from Shikoku, to Kinai, thence to Kyushu. Members of the clan were shugo "constables" of Awa, Awaji, Bitchu, Izumi, Sanuki, Settsu, Tanba, Tosa, and Yamashiro.

A conflict between the 5th Hosokawa Kyoto kanrei Katsumoto (1430-1473) and his father-in-law Yamana Sozen over the Shogunate's succession sparked the Onin War (1467-1477), which led to the fall of the Ashikaga Shogunate, and ignited a century of war known as the Sengoku "Warring States" Period (1467-1573). Following the fall of the Ashikaga Shogunate, which was based in Kyoto, control of the city, and thus ostensibly the country, fell into the hands of the Hosokawa, who held the Kyoto kanrei post for a few generations.

Katsumoto's son, Hosokawa Masamoto, held power in this way at the end of the 15th century, but in 1507 was assassinated. After his death, the clan became divided and was weakened by internecine fighting. What power they still had, however, was centered in and around Kyoto. This gave them the leverage to consolidate their power to some extent, and came to be strong rivals with the Ouchi, both politically, and in terms of dominating trade with China. This lasted until 1558, when Miyoshi Nagayoshi (1522-1564) and Matsunaga Hisahidé (1510-1577) ousted Hosokawa Harumoto (1519-1563) from Kyoto, and the lineage died out soon thereafter.

One branch of the family decended from Hosokawa Yorimochi, son of Yoriharu and brother to Yoriyuki and Yorimoto, survived to much success under Hosokawa Fujitaka (1534-1610) and his son

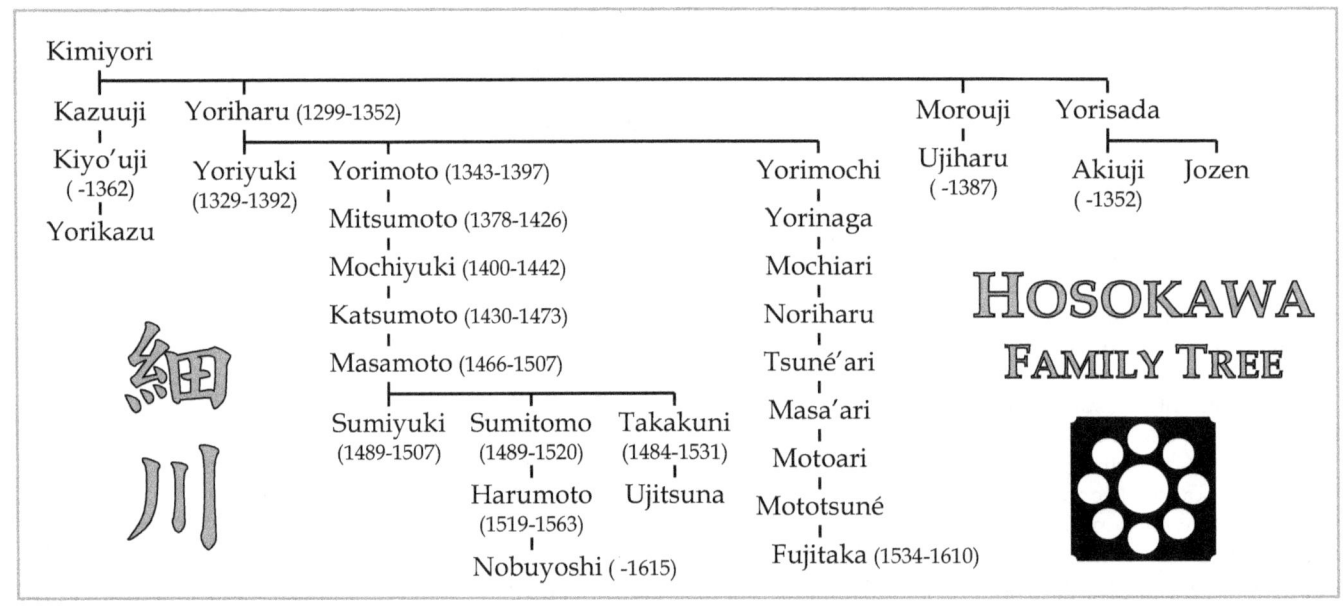

HOSOKAWA FAMILY TREE

Tadaoki (1564-1645). Thanks to their efforts, the Hosokawa family would endure as daimyo to the end of the Edo Period (1603-1868). This branch is chronicled in *Daimyo of 1867* (Different Worlds Publications 2010).

NOTABLE ANCESTORS

Hosokawa Yoriharu (1299-1352)

Was Sanuki no kami.

From the beginning, Yoriharu joined the party of Ashikaga Takauji (1305-1358), who was likewise a descendant of the Minamoto, and fought for the Northern Court during the wars of the Nanboku-cho Period (1336-1392).

In 1337 Yoriharu besieged and took Kanasaki Castle (Echizen), and killed Takanaga-shinno (1310-1337), Nitta Yoshiaki, Doi Michiharu, with the rest of the garrison.

In 1340 Yoriharu took Seta Castle (Iyo), and brought the whole of Shikoku under the rule of the Ashikaga.

In the years 1348-1351 Yoriharu, with Ko Moronao (1351), fought against Kusunoki Masanori (-1390).

Hosokawa Kiyo'uji (-1362)

Son of Kazuuji. He was Sagami no kami.

Kiyo'uji took part in the 1348 Battle of Shijo-nawaté (southern Yamanto) against Kusunoki Masatsura (1326-1348), and in all the campaigns against the partisans of the Southern Dynasty.

In 1361, on account of disputes with the 2nd Ashikaga Shogun Yoshiakira (1330-1368), Kiyo'uji offered his services to the Emperor Go-Murakami (1328-1368) and the Southern Court.

In 1362 Kiyo'uji and Kusunoki Masanori (-1390) drove the Shogun Yoshiakira and the Emperor Go-Kogon (1338-1374) of the Northern Court out of Kyoto, but was compelled to leave the capital just twenty days later when Yoshiakira returned with a numerous army. Kiyouji retired into Kawachi, thence into Sanuki, where he built the castle of Shiraminé, and prepared again to take Kyoto. He was however besieged by his cousin Yoriyuki, who defeated and killed him in battle. Kiyo'uji's sons took refuge in Awaji.

Hosokawa Yoriyuki (1329-1392)

Son of Yoriharu. He was shugo "constable" of Sanuki, Tosa, and Settsu.

By order of Ashikaga Takauji (1305-1358), Yoriyuki went into Bitchu and pacified San'yodo.

In 1362 Yoriyuki passed into Shikoku, besieged his cousin Hosokawa Kiyouji in the castle of Shiraminé (Sanuki) and, having defeated and killed him, subjected the whole island to the Ashikaga.

In 1367, on his deathbed, the 2nd Ashikaga Shogun Yoshiakira (1330-1368) named Yoriyuki as Kyoto kanrei "Kyoto deputy Shogun," the first to hold this post, essentially as guardian for the young Yoshimitsu (1358-1408), who the next year became the 3rd Ashikaga Shogun when only 10 years old.

The government under Yoriyuki was the first time since the fall of the Hojo that laws were enforced and order maintained. He organized administrative procedures and governmental operations to a significant degree. To cultivate discipline and loyalty among the samurai, and to suppress forces of dissent, he established property rights of the hereditary landlords, religious groups, and Imperial lands, and promulgated sumptuary laws. When the Shogun Yoshimitsu came of age, he took issue with the latter policy, and would reject notions of frugality. In 1372, when Yoriyuki realized the young Shogun was beginning to chafe under his counsel, he retired to the Saiho-ji (Kyoto).

In 1374 Yoriyuki took part in the Kyushu Campaign.

In 1379, having been calumniated by jealous adversaries, the Shogun Yoshimitsu asked Yoriyuki to resign as kanrei, and banished him to Sanuki.

In 1391 Yoshimitsu, seeing himself threatened by the ever increasing power of the Yamana, recalled his kanrei. Yoriyuki then took the field, and soon afterwards the Yamana were defeated.

Yoriyuki died the following year. Being childless, he had adopted his two brothers Yorimoto and Mitsuyuki.

Yoriyuki is little known, but he epitomized the soldier-statesman ideal so cherished during the early- to mid-Muromachi Period.

Hosokawa Yorimoto (1343-1397)

Brother to Yoriyuki.

From 1391 to 1393 Yorimoto was Kyoto kanrei "deputy Shogun" to the 3rd Ashikaga Shogun Yoshimitsu (1358-1408), succeeding Shiba Yoshimasa (1350-1410).

Hosokawa Ujiharu (-1387)

Son of Morouji. He was shugo "constable" of Awaji.

In 1361 Ujiharu followed his cousin Kiyouji, who had joined the party of the Southern Court, entered Kyoto with him, and accompanied him to Sanuki.

In 1362, when Kiyo'uji was defeated and slain by their cousin Yoriyuki, Ujiharu returned to the Ashikaga.

Hosokawa Akiuji (-1352)

Son of Yorisada. He was Mutsu no kami.

In 1338 Akiuji was sent by Ashikaga Takauji (1305-1358) to assist in the defense of Kuromaru (Echizen), a fortress belonging to the shugo "constable" Shiba Takatsuné (1305-1367). His men clashed with horsemen under the command of one of the more famous commanders of the rival Southern Court, Nitta Yoshisada (1301-1338), who was mortally wounded by an arrow in this exchange.

Akiuji was later made shugo "constable" of the seven provinces on Shikoku and in central Honshu.

In 1347 Akiuji faced Kusunoki Masatsura (1326-1348) at Sakai-no-ura (Izumi). He was greatly outnumbered, and so he broke off his attack. Kusunoki followed, and in a night attack defeated Akiuji at Kawachi, causing numerous casualties. Akiuji fell back to Tenno-ji (Settsu), and was defeated again, despite the aid of Yamana Tokiuji. At the 1348 Battle of Shijo-nawaté (southern Yamato) Masatsura was defeated and killed, but Akiuji did not take part in this event.

In the Kanno Disturbance (1350-1351) Akiuji followed Ashikaga Tadayoshi (1306-1352) when the latter quar-

Hosokawa Yoriyuki

reled with his brother Takauji, and abandoned the cause of the Northern Court.

In 1352 Akiyoshi was killed with Hosokawa Kiyo'uji when they fought against the troops of Ashikaga Yoshiakira (1330-1368).

Hosokawa Jozen (14th century)

Son of Yorisada, and brother to Akiuji.

In 1335, when Hojo Tokiyuki (1322-1353) attacked Kamakura, Jozen, with Ashikaga Tadayoshi (1306-1352), fled to Musashi, and afterwards retired into Sanuki, where he raised troops for Ashikaga Takauji (1305-1358) and the Northern Court. Later he fought against Nitta Yoshisada (1301-1338), Wakiya Yoshisuké (1305-1340), etc.

In 1336, at the Battle of Minatogawa (Harima), Jozen helped Ashikaga Tadayoshi and Shoni Yorihisa defeat the Imperial army of Nitta Yoshisada, Wakiya Yoshisuké, and the Kusunoki brothers Masashigé (1294-1336) and Masasué.

Hosokawa Mitsumoto (1378-1426)

Son of Yorimoto. From 1412 to 1421 he was Kyoto kanrei "Kyoto deputy Shogun."

Hosokawa Mochiyuki (1400-1442)

Son of Mitsumoto. He was shugo "constable" of Settsu, Tanba, Tosa, and Sanuki.

In 1432 Mochiyuki succeeded Shiba Yoshiatsu (1397-1434) in the office of Kyoto kanrei "Kyoto deputy Shogun," which he held till 1442.

In 1441, after the assassination of the 6th Ashikaga Shogun Yoshinori (1394-1441), Mochiyuki secured the right of succession to the Shogun's son, the 7th Ashikaga Shogun Yoshikatsu (1434-1443), and sent troops to punish the murderer Akamatsu Mitsusuké (1381-1441).

Hosokawa Katsumoto (1430-1473)

Son of Mochiyuki. He inherited the domain of his ancestors, i.e., nearly all of Shikoku. He married the daughter of Yamana Sozen (1404-1473).

In 1445 Katsumoto was made Kyoto kanrei "Kyoto deputy Shogun" at the age of 15, and served until he was replaced in this office by Hatakeyama Norimoto in 1449. He recovered it in 1452 and served again until 1464. From 1468 to 1473 he again held the post.

In 1452 the strife between the Shiba cousins, Yoshitoshi (1430-1490) and Yoshikado (-1480), for the succession of their clan commenced. In 1455 Hatakeyama Yoshinari raised troops to fight against his brother Masanaga in a succession dispute.

In 1464 the 8th Ashikaga Shogun Yoshimasa (1436-1490) adopted his brother Ashikaga Yoshimi as his successor, with Katsumoto appointed as his shitsuji "deputy." The following year, however, a son, Yoshihisa (1465-1489), was born to Yoshimasa, and Yamana Sozen was called upon to support his rights.

The question of succession exploded into the disastrous Onin War (1467-1477) that put much of Kyoto in flames. On one side, we find Katsumoto supporting Ashikaga Yoshimi, Hatakeyama Masanaga, and Shiba Yoshitoshi; on the other, Yamana Sozen defending the interests of Ashikaga Yoshihisa, Hatakeyama Yoshinari, and Shiba Yoshikado. The other daimyo were divided between the two camps.

Katsumoto, at the head of a large army, was posted on the east of Muromachi, in order to guard the residence of Ashikaga Yoshimi; and Yamana Sozen, having assembled another large army, established himself on the west of Muromachi. Over the next several months Kyoto was looted and pillaged, and much of the north was was reduced to rubble and ash. Fighting was intense, but over time both sides were exhausted and entrenched themselves. The Hosokawa and the Yamana forces glared at each other between the trenches, and a stalemate continued for years.

In 1473 both Katsumoto and Yamana Sozen died, but the ex-Shogun Yoshimasa did nothing to halt the war, instead spending his time in leisure and overseeing the construction of the Ginkaku-ji "Temple of the Silver Pavilion" (Kyoto). By 1477, when the fighting finally ended, the Ashikaga Shogunate had become mere puppets of the Hosokawa.

Katsumoto is famous for his involvement in the creation of the Ryoan-ji "Temple of the Dragon at Peace" (northwest Kyoto), a Zen Buddhist temple of the Rinzai branch, famous for its rock garden.

Hosokawa Masamoto (1466-1507)

Son of Katsumoto.

In 1486 Masamoto was Kyoto kanrei "Kyoto deputy Shogun." After a brief interval when Hatakeyama Masanaga held the post, he was again kanrei in 1487, 1490, and then from 1495 until his death in 1507.

In 1489, when the 9th Ashikaga Shogun Yoshihisa (1465-1489) died, Masamoto supported the nomination of Ashikaga Yoshizumi (1480-1511), a son of Ashikaga Masamoto and grandson of the 6th Ashikaga Shogun Yoshinori (1394-1441), as successor. But Yoshitané (1466-1523) prevailed as the 10th Ashikaga Shogun.

In 1493 Masamoto assisted Hatakeyama Yoshitoyo, who was attacked by Hatakeyama Masanaga and the Shogun Yoshitané. The latter were defeated at the Shokoku-ji (Kawachi); Masanaga killed himself during battle, and Yoshitané fled to Etchu, but was captured, held prisoner at Kyoto, and then exiled.

In 1495 Masamoto then placed as puppet the 11th Ashikaga Shogun Yoshizumi. Also that year he led a campaign against his opponents in Yamashiro.

Masamoto established himself at Kyoto, and named Miyoshi Nagateru

Hosokawa Katsumoto

Hosokawa Masamoto

(-1520) and Kosai Motonaga/Motochika to replace him in the government of Awa and Sanuki, but disputes arose between them and troubles ensued. Masamoto, who may have been an homosexual, being childless had adopted three sons: Sumiyuki, son of Kujo Masamoto (1445-1516); Sumimoto, a son of Hosokawa Yoshiharu of Awa; and Takakuni. During a succession dispute Nagateru sided with Sumimoto, whilst Motonaga was a partisan of Sumiyuki. Originally Masamoto had decided on Sumiyuki, the 1st adoptee, to succeed him, but this caused dissension in the clan due to Sumiyuki's noble blood. In 1504 he had to put down the rebellious Yakushiji Motoichi (1475-1504), a supporter of Sumimoto, and in 1506 he was threatened by an army led by Nagateru.

In 1507, after Masamoto had changed his mind for successor in favor of Sumimoto, Kosai Motonaga, along with Sumiyuki, broke into his residence, and assassinate him in his bath.

Hosokawa Sumimoto (1489-1520)

Son of Yoshiharu, was adopted by Masamoto.

In 1507, when his adoptive father died, Kosai Motonaga/Motochika declared against him, and Sumitomo took refuge in the castle of Rokkaku Takayori (-1520) in Koga (Omi). Sumimoto, with support from Miyoshi Nagateru (-1520), raised troops in Settsu, and killed his rival Sumiyuki and Motonaga. He then took possession of his Shikoku domain, and was nominated Kyoto kanrei "Kyoto deputy Shogun." But his adoptive brother Takakuni prevailed, and in the following year entered Kyoto with Ouchi Yoshioki (1477-1528) and the 10th Ashikaga Shogun Yoshitané (1466-1523), whence Sumimoto fled to Awa (Shikoku).

In 1511, supported by the Akamatsu, Sumimoto defeated Takakuni and re-entered the capital, but was driven from it after being defeated by Takakuni and Ouchi Yoshioki at the Battle of Funaoka-yama (Kyoto).

In 1518 Yoshioki left the capital to maintain his own domain in Suo, and seeing this as a chance, in the following year Sumimoto allied himself with Miyoshi Motonaga, and again defeated Takakuni. The latter, aided by Rokkaku Sadayori (1495-1552), vanquished him in turn, and Sumimoto again fled to Awa, where he died some months later.

Hosokawa Sumiyuki (1489-1507)

Son of the Kanpaku "Regent" Kujo Masamoto (1445-1516), adopted by Hosokawa Masamoto. The latter, having chosen him as his heir, afterwards preferred Sumimoto, and instead gave Sumiyuki some domain in Tanba.

In 1507, after the death of his adoptive father, Kosai Motonaka/Motochika supported Sumiyuki against Sumimoto; but having been attacked near Kyoto by the latter and Miyoshi Nagateru (-1520), they were defeated and killed in the battle.

Hosokawa Takakuni (1484-1531)

Son of Masaharu, adopted by Masamoto like Sumimoto and Sumiyuki.

In 1508, when Ouchi Yoshioki (1477-1528) desired to re-establish the 10th Ashikaga Shogun Yoshitané (1466-1523) in the office of the Shogun, the antipathy of Takakuni for his adopted father was such that he joined the party, which Masamoto had always opposed. They defeated Hosokawa Sumimoto, who fled into Awa, and the 11th Ashikaga Shogun Yoshizumi (1480-1511) retired to Omi. Yoshitané was reinstalled as Shogun, and Takakuni took over as head of the Hosokawa, taking the titles of Kyoto kanrei "Kyoto deputy Shogun" and shugo "constable" of Settsu, Tanba, Sanuki, and Tosa.

Hosokawa Takakuni

In 1511 Takakuni assisted Ouchi Yoshioki at the Battle of Funaokayama, where Hosokawa Sumimoto and Hosokawa Masataka suffered a defeat.

In 1519, having been defeated by Hosokawa Sumimoto, Takakuni retired into Omi to ask Rokkaku Sadayori (1495-1552) for assistance. He returned with an army and obliged Sumimoto to again flee into Awa.

Takakuni then built a castle at Amagasaki (Settsu), and assumed so much authority that the Shogun Yoshitané appointed Hatakeyama Tanenaga as kanrei. In 1521 Takakuni revolted against the Shogun, whom he had always supported, obliged him to flee into Awaji, and installed as the 12th Ashikaga Shogun Yoshiharu (1510-1550), a son of the ex-Shogun Yoshizumi.

As his wakashu "young lover" Takakuni took Yanagimoto Kenji, the younger brother of Hosokawa karo "chief vassal" Kanishi Motomori. The two swore eternal love to each other, and Kenji, even after reaching adulthood, remained a favorite. However, as a result of a calumny, Takakuni felt obliged to have Motomori killed. Though initially appeased, Kenji shortly joined with another brother to avenge Motomori's death.

In 1527 Miyoshi Motonaga (-1532), with Hosokawa Harumoto, son of Sumimoto, attacked Kyoto. Takakuni again fled to Omi, to apply to the Rokkaku and the Asakura for aid, and re-entered the capital.

In 1531 Miyoshi Motonaga and Hosokawa Harumoto defeated Takakuni at Amagasaki (Settsu). He retired toward Awa, but was caught hiding in a saké storeroom, and committed suicide.

Hosokawa Harumoto (1519-1563)

Son of Sumimoto. His childhood name was Somei-maru. He was only 2 years old at the death of his father, and was supported by his caretaker Miyoshi Motonaga (-1532) of Settsu.

In 1527, when Miyoshi Motonaga marched into Kyoto with Harumoto, the 12th Ashikaga Shogun Yoshiharu (1510-1550) and his Kyoto kanrei "Kyoto deputy Shogun" Hosokawa Takakuni fled into Omi. But soon afterwards Motonaga and Harumoto were driven from the capital.

Muromachi Period – Isé

In 1531 Miyoshi Motonaga returned and defeated Hosokawa Takakuni, who was killed.

In 1532, having disputed with Miyoshi Motonaga, Harumoto, with the help of the Ikko-shu of Ishiyama Hongan-ji (later Osaka), trapped him at the Kenpon-ji in Sakai (Izumi), and forced him to commit suicide.

In 1533, having parted ways with the Ishiyama Hongan-ji, the Hosokawa attacked the warrior monks there. After that, Harumoto ruled the whole of Kinai: Yamashiro, Yamato, Kawachi, Izumi, and Settsu.

In 1534 Harumoto reconciled with the Shogun Yoshiharu, who then in 1536 appointed him Kyoto kanrei.

In 1546 Yuza Junsei having sided with Hosokawa Ujitsuna, the foster son of Takakuni, raised an army. Harumoto sent Miyoshi Nagayoshi/Chokei (1522-1564), the eldest son of Motonaga, against him, but he was defeated.

In 1547 Yoshiharu abdicated in favor of his eldest son, the 13th Ashikaga Shogun Yoshiteru (1536-1565), who was then 11 years old.

In 1548 Miyoshi Nagayoshi, having had some quarrels with Harumoto, became a partisan of Hosokawa Ujitsuna, and made himself master of the castles of Nakajima, Miyaké, and Eguchi.

In 1549 Yoshiharu opened negotiations with Hosokawa Ujitsuna, and proposed terms of peace, promising him the title of Kyoto kanrei in return. Harumoto was ousted from the capital, but later re-entered, forcing the Shogun and his son Yoshiteru to flee to Sakamoto (Omi).

In 1550 peace was made, and Harumoto was made Kyoto kanrei, while Hosokawa Ujitsuna returned to Awa. Miyoshi Nagayoshi then attacked, defeated Harumoto at Otsu (Omi), and the latter, with Yoshiharu and the Shogun Yoshiteru, were compelled to flee to Kuchiki (Omi).

In 1553 the Shogun negotiated for peace and returned to Kyoto. Harumoto then attacked Kyoto, burning much of it, and re-entered. He then attempted unsuccessfully to convince Hosokawa Yoshiharu to come out of retirement.

Finally in 1558, Miyoshi Nagayoshi and Matsunaga Hisahidé (1510-1577) again made themselves masters of the capital. Harumoto and the Shogun Yoshiteru fled to Sakamoto (Omi), and thence opened negotiations. Peace was signed, and the Shogun returned to Kyoto.

In 1559 Harumoto was captured, and was allowed to retire, as prisoner, to a temple at Akutagawa (Settsu), where in 1563 he died from a disease.

He was the last of the Hosokawa Kyoto kanrei. The family had occupied that office for 180 years.

Hosokawa Nobuyoshi (-1615)

Son of Harumoto. He remained a prisoner at Akutagawa (Settsu) with his father.

In 1568 Oda Nobunaga (1534-1582), after having seized Settsu, gave Nobuyoshi two kori "districts" in Tanba, but he was deprived of them by Toyotomi Hideyoshi (1536-1599), and died in obscurity.

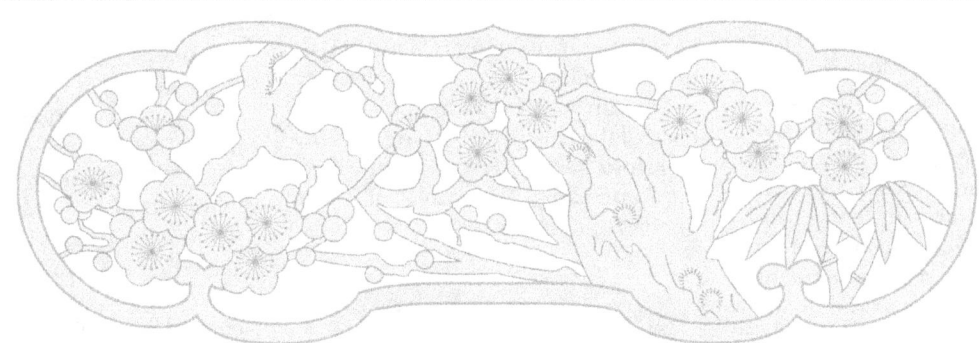

Daimyo family descended from Taira Masanori, whose 8th descendant Toshitsugu, Buzen no kami, was the first that took the name Isé.

Notable Ancestors

Isé Sadayuki (14th-15th century)

Isé no kami. He served the 3rd Ashikaga Shogun Yoshimitsu (1358-1408).

Isé Sadachika (1417-1473)

Son of Sadakuni. He was tutor to the 8th Ashikaga Shogun Yoshimasa (1436-1490).

In 1460 Sadachika was appointed leader of the Mandokoro "Administrative Board" of the Bakufu.

During the Onin War (1467-1477) Sadachika sided with Hosokawa Katsumoto (1430-1473).

He wrote the *Isé Sadachika Kyokun*, a short work on moral percepts.

Imagawa

Territories: Suruga, Totomi

Daimyo family that claimed descent from the Emperor Seiwa (850-880), and hence the Minamoto Seiwa-Genji branch.

In the 13th century Ashikaga Kuniuji (1243-1282) established himself at Imagawa (Mikawa) and took its name.

In the 14th century the Imagawa split into two branches when Norikuni died, with the eldest son Noriuji keeping Suruga and the 2nd son Sadayo taking Totomi.

After the death of Imagawa Yoshimoto at the 1560 Battle of Okehazama (Owari), many Imagawa officers defected to other clans. Within a decade the clan had lost all of its land holdings to the Takeda and the Tokugawa.

During the Edo Period (1603-1603) the Imagawa held the hereditary position of koké "masters of ceremonies" in the service of the Tokugawa.

Notable Ancestors

Imagawa Kuniuji (1243-1282)
Son of Ashikaga Nagauji (1211-1290), and grandson of Ashikaga Yoshiuji (1189-1254). He established himself at Imagawa (Mikawa) and took its name.

Imagawa Norikuni (1295-1384)
A relation to Ashikaga Takauji (1305-1358), who gave him Totomi, and later that of Suruga. He took part in the 1348 Battle of Shijonawaté (southern Yamato).

Imagawa Noriuji (1316-1365)
Eldest son of Norikuni. He inherited Suruga from his father, served Ashikaga Takauji (1305-1358) and Ashikaga Yoshiakira (1330-1367), and was Kazusa no suké.

Imagawa Sadayo/Ryoshun (1326-1420)
2nd son of Norikuni. His childhood name was Sadayo. During his early years he was taught Buddhism, Confucianism, and Chinese. Under Reizei Tamehidé (-1372) he studied poetry, which became one of his greatest passions. His Father taught him archery and the military arts such as strategy and horseback riding. From his father he inherited Totomi, with his brother Noriuji keeping Suruga.

In 1359, during the wars of the Nanboku-cho Period (1336-1392), Sadayo accompanied the 2nd Ashikaga Shogun Yoshiakira (1330-1368) in his campaign against the Emperor Go-Murakami (1328-1368) of the Southern Court in Yoshino (southern Yamato).

In 1361, when Hosokawa Kiyouji joined the party of the Southern Court, Sadayo marched against and defeated him. Afterwards he had his head shaved and took the name Ryoshun, by which he is often known.

In 1371 the 3rd Ashikaga Shogun Yoshimitsu (1358-1408) nominated Ryoshun as Chinzei tandai "military governor of Kyushu" after the failure of the previous post holder to quell the rebel uprisings in the region, which were largely instigated by Southern Court partisans who supported the Imperial Prince Kanenaga (1326-1383), a son of the late Emperor Go-Daigo (1288-1339). At first defeated by Kikuchi Takemitsu (1319-1373), in 1372 Ryoshun vanquished him in turn with the aid of Ouchi Yoshihiro (1356-1399). The Southern Court then went on the defensive, leading to a stalemate. In 1373 Takemitsu died, leaving Kanenaga's military with no strong leader. Ryoshun seized the opportunity and planned a final attack. He met with three of the most powerful families on Kyushu, the Shimazu, the Otomo, and the Shoni, to gain their support in the attack. Things seemed to be going well

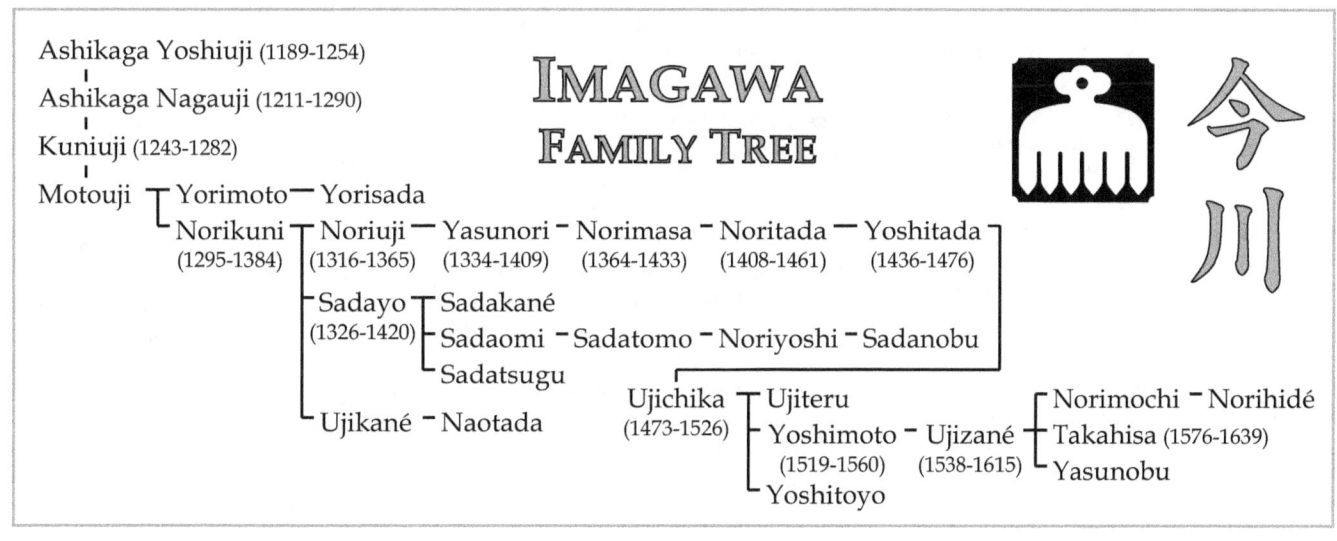

until 1375 when Ryoshun suspected the Shoni chieftain Fuyusuké of treachery, and had him killed at a drinking party. This outraged the Shimazu, who had originally been the ones to convince the Shoni to throw their lot with Ryoshun, and they returned to Satsuma to raise a force against him. This gave the Kanenaga-shinno time to regroup, and he forced the Imagawa back North, prompting Ryoshun to request assistance from the Bakufu. But help never arrived, forcing him to take matters in to his own hands, and he continued to push the loyalists forces. In 1383 Kanenaga died, and the resistance ended. In 1385 the death of Shimazu chieftain Ujihisa also helped ease tensions between Ryoshun and the Shimazu for a time.

In 1395 the Ouchi and the Otomo calumniated against Ryoshun, informing the Bakufu that he was plotting against the Shogun, a move that was likely an attempt to restore the governorship of Kyushu to the Shibukawa, who had held it prior to Ryoshun. In addition Ryoshun had acted fairly independently in his negotiations with the Shimazu, the Otomo, and the Shoni, and also in negotiations with Korea. Ryoshun's enemies in the Shogun's court used these causes against him, and he was recalled to Kyoto by the Shogunate.

In 1400 Ryoshun was once again questioned by the Bakufu, this time in relation to the Imagawa's province of Totomi's failure to respond to a levy issued by the Bakufu, a negligence interpretable as treason and rebellion. This charge saw Ryoshun stripped of his post as constable of Suruga and Totomi, and gave him reason to believe he might be assassinated. With this in mind he fled the capital for a time, though was later pardoned and returned to the capital, spending the rest of his days pursuing religious devotions and poetry until his death.

In 1400 Ryoshun had become the tutor of classical Court poetry and other areas of literature to Shotetsu (1381-1459), who would go on to become one of the finest waka poets of the 15th century. Ryoshun himself displayed his poems most effectively in his fairly popular and influential travel diary *Michiyukiburi* "Travelings." He also wrote a number of renga "collaborative poetry."

Imagawa Ryoshun

He cultivated literature and history, and published several works, among which was the *Nan Taiheiki* "Commentary of the Taihei-ki," the *Imagawa-soshi*, the *Kyushu-kassen-ki*, etc. He also wrote the *Imagawa-jo*, a manual for students attending terakoya "temple schools."

Imagawa Yasunori (1334-1409)

Son of Noriuji. He fought against Yamana Ujikiyo.

Imagawa Norimasa (1364-1433)

Son of Yasunori.

In 1396 Norimasa was sent by the Shogunate to combat Uesugi Ujinori (-1417), whom he defeated. Afterwards he was surnamed Fuku-Shogun "Vice-Shogun."

Imagawa Noritada (1408-1461)

Son of Norimasa.

In 1439 Noritada was sent by the 6th Ashikaga Shogun Yoshinori (1394-1441) to combat Yuki Ujitomo (1398-1441) in Kanto, and defeated him. He then received the name Fuku-Shogun "Vice Shogun."

In 1455 Noritada drove Ashikaga Shigeuji (1438-1497) out of Kamakura (Sagami), where he reinstalled Uesugi Fusa'aki (1432-1466).

Imagawa Yoshitada (1436-1476)

Son of Noritada.

In 1476 Yoshitada invaded Totomi, and defeated the Katsumada and the Yokota. On the return to Suruga, however, he was waylaid at Shiokaizaka, and was attacked and killed by the remnants of the two families he had just defeated.

Imagawa Ujichika (1473-1526)

Son of Yoshitada. His childhood name was Tatsuo-maru. He was only 3 years old at the time of his father's death. He was brought up in his mother's family, and obtained possession of his domain owing to Isé Shinkuro Nagauji (later Hojo Soun, 1432-1519).

In 1476, upon the death of his father, a succession dispute developed between Tatsuo's supporters and that of his cousin Oshika Shingoro Norimitsu. Nagauji proposed that until Tatsuo has his coming-of-age ceremony, Norimitsu act as a regent in his name. This averted armed conflict within the Imagawa, at least temporarily. In 1490, however, when Tatsuo turned 17 and took the name Ujichika, Norimitsu would not relinquish control of the clan to him, and hostilities ensued. Nagauji, on Ujichika's behalf, attacked Norimitsu's mansion, and once his rival was defeated, Ujichika assumed leadership of the Imagawa.

In 1491 Ujichika gave asylum to Ashikaga Yoshizumi (1481-1511) after the latter fled Kyoto, and afterwards escorted him back.

A capable leader, Ujichika spent much time campaigning in Totomi and Mikawa, strengthening the position of the Imagawa along the provinces of the Tokaido.

In 1525 Ujichika built Nagoya Castle (Owari).

In 1526, just before he died of illness, Ujichika composed the *Imagawa Kana Mokuroku* "Imagawa House Code." Clauses included such stipulations as the punishment for trespassing in another's residence, the imposition of capital punishment in violent quarrels between retainers, the accountability of the parents of children (of retainers) involved in fights, regulations concerning the private sale and leasing of land, debt repayment, and forbidding retainers to arrange marriages outside the Imagawa domain. It was widely imitated by other families that established estates, notably the Takeda.

Imagawa Yoshimoto (1519-1560)

3rd son of Ujichika. Born in Sunpu (Suruga), his mother was a daughter of Naka-mikado Nobutané. As he was not the eldest, he was sent as a youth to the Zentoku-ji (Bungo) where he became a bonze and took the name Baigaku Shoho.

In 1526 his father Ujichika died and was succeeded by his eldest son Ujiteru. When in 1536 Ujiteru died suddenly of illness without children, a succession dispute broke out between Baigaku Shoho and his older half-brother Genko Etan. As the latter's mother was a concubine, many supported Baigaku Shoho as the rightful heir. In the ensuing Hanagura Disturbance, with aid from Taigen Sessai (1496-1555), military assistance from Hojo Ujitsuna (1487-1541) of Sagami, and the support of Takeda Nobutora (1493-1574) of Kai, he defeated and killed his rival. He then changed his name to Yoshimoto, and succeeded the clan.

In 1537 Yoshimoto cemented an alliance with the Takeda by marrying the daughter of Nobutora. He also acted as a go-between for the arranged marriage of the latter's eldest son Takeda Harunobu (later Shingen, 1521-1573) to the daughter of court noble Sanjo Kimiyori.

Up until this time, the Imagawa and the neighboring Hojo were allies, with both at odds with the Takeda. Yoshimoto's rise to power, and his subsequent alliance with the Takeda, offended Hojo Ujitsuna, and a period of hostilities between them commenced. In 1540, concerned by the proximity of Kai to his own domain, Yoshimoto sought to influence the Takeda, and was apparently involved in Harunobu's takeover of his clan from his father. Relations between the Takeda and the Imagawa then remained stable for the remainder of Yoshimoto's life.

In 1542 Yoshimoto began his advance into Mikawa in an effort to fight the growing influence of Oda Nobuhidé (1510-1551) in that region. He was initially defeated at the 1st Battle of Azukizaka (Mikawa), but in campaigns over the course of the ensuing decades, he succeeded in bringing Mikawa, Totomi, and Suruga under his authority.

In 1544 Yoshimoto, with help from Harunobu, defeated Hojo Ujitsuna's

Imagawa Yoshimoto

son Ujiyasu (1515-1571) at the Kitsunébashi (Suruga).

In 1548 Oda Nobuhidé led his men against the Matsudaira's Okazaki Castle (Mikawa), prompting Yoshimoto to dispatch Taigen Sessai with a relief army. In return the castle lord Matsudaira Hirotada (1526-1549) was obliged to send his young son Takechiyo (later Tokugawa Ieyasu, 1543-1616), reluctantly, as a hostage to Suruga, but the boy was kidnapped on the way by Nobuhidé and confined to Kowatari Castle (Owari). The subsequent clash, the so-called 2nd Battle of Azukizaka, ended with an Imagawa victory.

In 1549 Taigen Sessai pressed his advantage to put Anjo Castle (Mikawa) under siege. Oda Nobuhiro (-1574) was forced to surrender, but in a deal arranged by his brother Nobunaga (1534-1582) he was returned to his clan in return for Takechiyo, who finally arrived in Sunpu (Suruga) after a year's delay.

In 1552 Yoshimoto's daughter married Shingen's son Takeda Yoshinobu (1538-1567). In 1554 Yoshimoto and the Hojo reached a peace agreement with the marriage of his son Ujizané to the daughter of Hojo Ujitsuna.

In the early summer of 1560, after forming a three-way alliance with the Takeda and the Hojo, Yoshimoto set forth on a march to Kyoto with Matsudaira Motoyasu (formerly Takechiyo, and later Tokugawa Ieyasu) and his Mikawa contingent in the vanguard.

Yoshimoto sought to force Nobunaga's submission, and two Oda forts near Kyoto, Maruné and Terabé, were reduced. At the onset of the Battle of Okehazama (Owari), the Imagawa faction, with its many victories, had let its guard down, celebrating with song, dance, and saké. Although outnumbered 10-to-1, following a terrific thunderstorm, Oda Nobunaga led a surprise attack that left the Imagawa forces in complete disorder. Two Oda samurai, Mori Shinsuké and Hattori Koheita, ambushed the retreating army, and beheaded Yoshimoto in the village of Dengaku-hazama.

Imagawa Ujizané (1538-1615)

Eldest son of Yoshimoto. He was born in Sunpu (Suruga).

In 1554 Ujizané married the daughter of Hojo Ujiyasu (1515-1571) to cement a three-way alliance between the Imagawa, the Hojo, and the Takeda.

In 1558 Ujizané became head of the clan when his father retired in order to focus his attention on the Imagawa advance into Totomi and Mikawa.

In 1560, after the death of his father, Ujizané lost a great number of his samurai, who joined Matsudaira Motoyasu (later Tokugawa Ieyasu, 1543-1616), who was then established at Okazaki (Mikawa). He then relied on the Asahina to maintain order in his troubled domain. Between 1561 and 1565 he felt compelled to execute or quell a number of his men, including Ii Naochika (1506-1562) and Iio Tsuratatsu (-1565).

In 1568, although Ujizané was his nephew, Takeda Shingen (1521-1573) invaded Suruga, while Tokugawa Ieyasu (formerly Matsudaira Motoyasu) attacked Totomi.

As Ujizané was married to a daughter of Hojo Ujiyasu, the clan offered assistance, but could not prevent Sunpu from falling to the Takeda. By then Ujizané had fled and taken up with the Asahina at Kakegawa Castle (Totomi). He was surrounded by Ieyasu's troops and surrendered, giving up control of the province in exchange for safe passage to Hojo territory. Since the Takeda had burned Sunpu, Ujizané went on to Sagami to await developments. Since the Takeda had firmly established themselves in Suruga, and in 1571 the last Hojo troops had been ejected, in 1575 Ujizané retired to Kyoto.

In 1582, when the Takeda were destroyed, Ujizané hoped that Sunpu might be returned to him. Ieyasu supported his case, but Oda Nobunaga (1534-1582) refused.

Eventually Ujizané joined the Tokugawa in Edo, and was bestowed a small pension. Later he went to Kyoto, had his head shaved, and took the name of Sokan.

He died at the family estate in Shinagawa (Edo) at the age of 77.

Although remembered as a poor ruler, Ujizané was culturally refined, and his descendants, who served the Tokugawa Shogun, were among the families who held the post of koké "master of ceremonies."

Shinagawa Takahisa (1576-1639)

Son of Imagawa Ujizané. He was an hatamoto who served the Tokugawa.

Imagawa Norinobu (1829-1887)

3rd son of Yoshiyori. He was an hatamoto who headed one of the families holding the position of koké "master of ceremonies."

A direct descendant of the famed Imagawa Yoshimoto and his son Ujizané, Norinobu was influential in the last days of the Tokugawa Shogunate, being appointed a waka-doshiyori "junior elder" shortly before its demise, and working for the new government to show clemency to the Tokugawa family.

As his son Yoshihito died young without an heir, the direct line of descent in the Imagawa family came to an end.

ISHIBASHI

Territory: Wakasa

Daimyo family descended from the Seiwa-Genji.

NOTABLE ANCESTORS

Ishibashi Kazuyoshi (14th century)

Sided with Ashikaga Takauji (1305-1358) and fought against the Southern Dynasty.

At Mitsuishi Castle (Bizen) Kazuyoshi was delivered by Takauji when he was besieged by Wakiya Yoshisuké (1305-1340).

In 1361 Kazuyoshi received the province of Wakasa in fief.

ISHIDO

Residence: Kyoto

Daimyo family descended from the Seiwa-Genji.

NOTABLE ANCESTORS

Ishido Yorishigé

Was the first that took the name of Ishido.

Ishido Yoshifusa (14th century)

Son of Yorishigé. He sided with his relative Ashikaga Takauji (1305-1358), and was Chinjufu-shogun "Defender of the North" of Mutsu.

When Takauji fell out with his brother Ashikaga Tadayoshi (1306-1352) Yoshifusa followed the latter to the Southern Court.

After the death of Ashikaga Tadayoshi, Yoshifusa, with Nitta Yoshioki (-1358), fought against the Northern Court, and contributed to the taking of Kamakura (Sagami). The army of the Southern Court having been repulsed soon afterwards, he retired into Suruga.

When Ashikaga Yoshiakira (1330-1368) had vanquished Wada Masatada, Yoshifusa, seeing the precarious situation of the legitimate Southern Dynasty, again submitted to the Ashikaga.

Ishido Yorifusa (14th century)

Son of Yoshifusa. He continued to serve Ashikaga Tadayoshi after his father's quarrel with Ashikaga Takauji (1305-1358).

Yorifusa inflicted several defeats on the troops of the Northern Court in Settsu and Harima. After being defeated by Takauji in Omi, Yorifusa retired to the Kannon-ji (Osaka).

In 1352, when the Shogun Takauji had retaken Kamakura (Sagami), Yorifusa submitted to him, and hence sided with the Northern Court.

ITAGAKI

Territories: Kai, Shinano
Castles: Ina (Shinano)

NOTABLE ANCESTORS

Itagaki Nobukata (1489-1548)

Daimyo of Kai. He was governor of the Sua district and resided at Ina Castle (Shinano). He served both Takeda Nobutora (1493-1574) and Takeda Shingen (1521-1573).

In 1541, when Shingen drove Nobutora from the headship of the Takeda, Nobukata served as a general for Shingen, often leading the troops into a battle when the latter could not.

In 1545 Nobukata successfully captured Takato Castle (Shinano) from Takato Yoritsugu (-1552).

In 1546 Nobukata defeated Uesugi Norimasa (1523-1579) at Usui-togé "Usui Pass" (between Shinano and Kozuké).

With these victories Nobukata proved himself a skilled tactician, and they were instrumental in his gaining control of Shinano. He is renowned as one of the celebrated "24 Generals of Takeda Shingen." He was also known to have fielded one of the units in Shingen's extensive spy network.

In 1547 Nobukata and his troops were almost completely wiped out in a battle against the Murakami, but was saved by a timely rescue by Hara Toratané (1497-1564).

In 1548, at the Battle of Uedahara (Shinano) against Murakami Yoshikiyo (1501-1573), Nobutaka, as the eldest of Shigen's retainers, led the vanguard. The battle was the first defeat suffered by Shingen, and the first field battle in Japan at which firearms were used. Nobutaka was killed when he charged head-on into the enemy vanguard. Hundreds of Takeda men lost their lives, including two other generals, Amari Torayasu and Hijkano Den'-émon.

ITAMI

Territory: Settsu
Castles: Itami (Settsu)

Daimyo family of Settsu, which in the 16th century resided at Itami.

NOTABLE ANCESTORS

Itami Chikaoki (16th century)

Minor daimyo of Settsu, controlled Itami Castle.

In 1568 Chikaoki submitted to Oda Nobunaga (1534-1582), and in the next year he defeated a Miyoshi army at Katsura-gawa on his behalf.

In 1574 Chikaoki was accused of having consorted with the last Ashikaga Shogun Yoshiaki (1537-1597), and had his castle besieged by Araki Murashigé. He surrendered, and was deprived of his lands.

NAGOSHI

Branch of the Hojo family, descended from Tomotoki, the 2nd son of the 2nd Hojo Shikken "Regent" Yoshitoki (1163-1224).

NOTABLE ANCESTORS

Nagoshi Takaié (-1333)

Son of Sadaié, descended in the 5th generation from Hojo Tomotoki.

In 1331 Takaié was charged by the 14th Hojo Shikken Hojo Takatoki (1303-1333) to march against Kyoto with Ashikaga Takauji (1305-1358), and depose the Emperor Go-Daigo (1288-1339).

Takaié was killed in a combat against Akamatsu Enshin at Kuganawaté (Yamashiro).

Nagoshi Takakuni (14th century)

Son of Takaié. He served Ashikaga Takauji (1305-1358), and aided him in the fight against the Southern Dynasty.

Muromachi Period – Jinbo

Jinbo

Territory: Etchu
Castle: Toyama (Etchu)

Family of Etchu, at one time possible retainers of the Hatakeyama. They were almost constantly at war with local rivals such as the Shiina and the Ikko-ikki. Defeated by Nagao Tamekagé (1489-1542) in 1520, they enjoyed a brief period of local power under Jinbo Nagamoto, but when Uesugi Kenshin (1530-1578), sided with the Shiina they lost their castle at Toyama (Etchu), and at length became Uesugi vassals.

During the Edo "Tokugawa" Period (1603-1868), one branch of the Jinbo would enter the service of the Matsudaira of Aizu, and another would become hatamoto in the service of the Shogun.

Notable Ancestors

Jinbo Yoshimuné (-1520)

In 1501 became the head of his family. He was Echizen no kami.

Yoshimuné was a rival of the Nagao of Echigo and fought a number of battles with them. In 1520 Yoshimuné was defeated by Nagao Tamekage (1489-1542) after setting out to attack the latter's Shinjo Castle (Echigo). With his army broken, Yoshimuné retreated to Futagami-yama Castle (Etchu), and committed suicide there.

After Yoshimuné's death, the leadership of the weakened Jinbo clan appears to have passed to his younger brother Yoshiaki, and then to Yoshimuné's son Nagamoto.

Jinbo Nagatsuna (-1511)

Cousin to Yoshimuné. He was Mikawa no kami.

Nagatsuna fought in a number of battles against the Nagao of Echigo in support of his cousin Yoshimuné. However, in 1510, Nagatsuna and his brother Nagakiyo conspired with Nagao Tamekagé (1489-1542). They were at length discovered and put to death along with most of their families. This is considered to have weakened the Jinbo.

Jinbo Nagakiyo (-1511)

Younger brother to Nagatsuna. Reputed to be both a playboy and an alcoholic, he was known to hold raucous parties at his estate in Etchu to celebrate victories in battle.

Nagakiyo conspired with Nagao Tamekagé (1489-1542) against his cousin Yoshimuné, and is reputed to have pressured his brother Nagatsuna to do the same. As a result, in 1511 they were both put to death, an event that severely weakened the Jinbo.

Jinbo Nagamoto (-1572)

Son of Yoshimuné. He ruled from Toyama Castle (Etchu), and was the last lord of the Jinbo clan.

Nagamoto is most remembered for his almost constant warfare with Shiina Yasutané (-1576), and their rivalry has been compared to that of Takeda Shingen (1521-1573) and Uesugi Kenshin (1530-1578). Much like those two, in 1554 Nagamoto and Yasutané met once in personal armed combat during the Battle of Imizu (Etchu), where Nagamoto struck Yasutané across the jaw with his sword, permanently disfiguring him. When the Shiina generals ordered Nagamoto chased down and captured, he was assisted in his escape from the battlefield by his page Chiba Kazusa. A Chiba family legend states that Kazusa donned Nagamoto's distinctive helmet and rode into the ranks of the pursuing Shiina, calling out that he was Nagamoto and daring the pursuers to try to take his head. He is said to have killed over twenty of the enemy before being shot from his horse by an arrow.

In 1559 Nagamoto attacked Shinna Yasutané's Matsukura Castle (Etchu). Yasutané called on the assistance of Uesugi Kenshin of Echigo, who in 1560 captured Toyama Castle. Nagamoto fled to Masuyama Castle (Etchu) and continued to resist the Shiina from his remaining holdings.

In 1562 Nagamoto again attacked the Shiina, and once again Uesugi Kenshin led an army into Etchu and defeated him.

After 1566, when Takeda Shingen became involved in Etchu's fortunes, Uesugi Kenshin sided with Nagamoto for a time, though internal strife within the Jinbo clan at length brought about the demise of the family as daimyo. The Jinbo were afterwards Uesugi vassals.

Jinbo Kiyoshigé (-1554)

Grandson and only surviving descendant of Nagakiyo. Unlike his grandfather, who was executed for betraying the clan, he was a valuable asset to the Jinbo as a general and advisor to Nagamoto.

Kiyoshigé was fearless on the battlefield, often leading charges and covering retreats. In 1554 he was killed while covering a retreat during the Battle of Imizu (Etchu). His distinctive blue armor was returned to the Jinbo later that year by the enemy general Shiina Yasutané (-1576) as both a tribute to Kiyoshige's bravery during the battle, and as a peace offering to assist in smoothing over differences between the two clans.

Jinbo Yoshikata (-1581)

Vassal of Uesugi Kenshin (1530-1578). He was the lord of Yoita Castle (Echigo) for a time until it was given to Naoé Nobutsuna (-1581).

After Kenshin's death, Yoshikata fought for Uesugi Kagekatsu (1556-1623). In 1581 however he was killed alongside Naoé Nobutsuna at Kasugayama Castle (Echigo).

Jinbo Ujiharu (1528-1592)

Became a retainer of Uesugi Kenshin (1530-1578) following the Jinbo's submission.

Ujiharu later joined Sassa Narimasa (1536-1588), but became a ronin after 1587 when the Sassa moved to Higo.

KIKUCHI

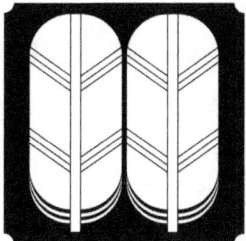  

Territory: Higo

Powerful daimyo family of Kyushu, descended from Dazaigon-no-sotsu "Kyushu governor" Fujiwara Takaié (979-1044).

The Kikuchi lineage was renowned for its valiant service in defense of the Emperor and against foreign invaders. The clan first distinguished itself during the 1019 Jürchen invasion of northern Kyushu.

Many famous warriors have come from this family such as Kikuchi Takanao, Kikuchi Takefusa, whose heroism helped drive back the 1281 Mongol Invasions of Japan, Kikuchi Taketoki, and Kikuchi Takemitsu. Their stories have become some of the most colorful in the history of Japan.

The family also was active in the Kenmu Restoration (1333-1336), an attempt by the Emperor Go-Daigo (1288-1339) to reassert Imperial authority against the Kamakura Shogunate.

Along with the Otomo, the Ouchi, the Shoni, and the Shimazu, the Kikuchi would write the history of the island.

In the middle of the 16th century the Kikuchi was taken out of power when the Ouchi took control over Kyushu. Many of the members of the clan went into hiding either by moving or entering another family. A notable descendant of the Kikuchi is Hayashi Narinaga (1517-1606), a general for Toyotomi Hideyoshi (1536-1598) and Mori Motonari (1497-1571).

NOTABLE ANCESTORS

Kikuchi Noritaka (11th century)

1st head of the Kikuchi clan. Son of Masanori, and grandson of Chikanori. He was the first to take the name Kikuchi. He held a high position in the Dazaifu "Kyushu" government, and worked for Fujiwara Takaié (979-1044).

In 1070, when Takaié went back to Kyoto, Noritaka retired and built a villa in Kikuchi. In 1071 he became master of Kikuchi (Higo), where he established a castle town.

Kikuchi Jiro Takanao (-1185)

7th head of the Kikuchi clan. He was Higo gon no Kami.

In 1180, at the beginning of the Genpei War (1180-1185), Takanao sided with Minamoto Yoritomo (1147-1199) and began levying troops in Kyushu. Taira Sadayoshi, governor of Higo and Chikugo, marched against him and defeated him.

In 1181 Takanao joined Ogata Koreyoshi of Bungo, another important local warlord, and rebelled against the Taira. The rising was crushed by Harada Tanenao.

Towards the end of the Genpei War the Kikuchi chose to align themselves with the Taira. In 1185, at the Battle of Dan-no-ura, along with the Harada, the Yamaga, and the Itai, Takanao was defeated by the Minamoto. After the battle he was turned over to Minamoto Yoshitsuné (1159-1189) by Ogata Koreyoshi. He was taken to the Rokujo riverbed in Kyoto and beheaded.

With the Minamoto victory, the center of military power tilted decidedly toward the east and against the west, which had profound consequences for the island's future.

Kikuchi Yoshitaka (13th century)

8th head of the Kikuchi clan. Greatgrandson of Takanao. During the Genpei War (1180-1185) he was fighting together with the Taira, and even though the Kikuchi were on the losing side, the Minamoto permitted them to keep their land.

During the Jokyu Disturbance (1221) Yoshitaka was oban'yaku "Imperial Palace guard" in Kyoto. He had two uncles that followed the retired Emperor Go-Toba (1180-1239). This displeased the Kamakura Shogunate, and when Yoshitaka dispatched them both to Kyoto, the Kikuchi were rewarded with additional lands.

Kikuchi Jiro Takefusa (1245-1285)

10th head of the Kikuchi clan. 2nd son of Takayasu, and grandson of Yoshitaka.

In 1274, during the 1st Mongol Invasion of Japan, Takefusa fought with his brother Aritaka and was rewarded.

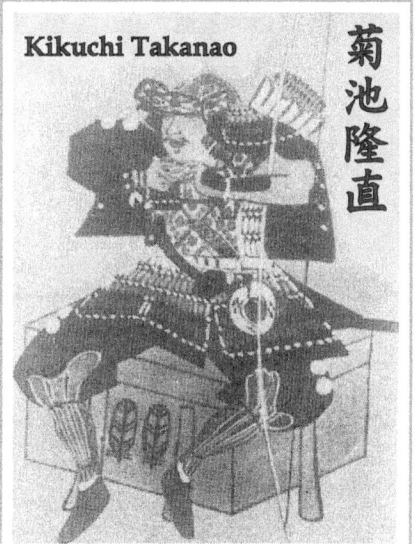

Kikuchi Takanao

Kikuchi Takefusa

Muromachi Period – Kikuchi

In 1281 the Kikuchi rose to prominence during the 2nd Mongol Invasion, when the heroism of Takefusa helped drive back the invaders. He gained fame for all the heads of the enemy that he collected.

Kikuchi Jiro Tokitaka (1287-1304)

11th head of the Kikuchi clan. Eldest son and heir of Takamori, and grandson of Takefusa. He died very young when he was only 17 years old so his younger brother Taketoki, 2nd son of Takamori, became the next head of the family.

Kikuchi Taketoki (1293-1334)

12th head of the Kikuchi clan. 2nd son of Takamori, and younger brother to Tokitaka. His childhood name was Shoryu-maru. He was also known as Jakua. When his father died, his uncle Takenori and his brother Tokitaka fought each other for power, and both ended up dying. Therefore Taketoki became the next head of the Kikuchi.

In 1333 Taketoki was asked by the Emperor Go-Daigo (1288-1339) for his help. He gathered supporters in Kyu-

Kikuchi Taketoki
菊池武時

KIKUCHI FAMILY TREE

菊地

Chikanori
|
Masanori
|
1 NORITAKA (11th century)
|
2 TSUNETAKA (11th century) (*Hyodo*)   Yoritaka (*Kojima*)   Masataka (*Saigo*)
|
3 TSUNEYORI (12th century)
|
4 TSUNEMUNÉ (12th century)
|
5 TSUNENAO (12th century)
|
6 TAKANAO (-1185)   (*Akahoshi*)
|
7 TAKATADA (13th century)
|
Takatsugu (13th century)
|
8 YOSHITAKA (13th century)
|
9 TAKAYASU (13th century)   Takatsune (*Jo*)   Takayori (*Jo*)
|
10 TAKEFUSA (1245-1285)   Naotaka   Yoritaka   Aritaka (*Akahoshi*)   (*Wakamiya*)   Takafuyu   Yasunari
                                                                                                Shigemuné
|
Takamori   Michitaké   Takemoto   Takenari   Taketsuné   Takekado   Takemura
|
11 TOKITAKA (1287-1304)   **12 TAKETOKI** (1292-1333)

13 TAKESHIGÉ | **14 TAKEHITO** | Taketoshi | **15 TAKEMITSU** (1319-1373)   Takezumi   Takenao (*Takasé*)   Taketoyo
(1307-1338)   (1321-1401)   (-1341)   **16 TAKEMASA** (1342-1374)   Takemoto   Takekuni
     Yoritaka   Takeyoshi   **17 TAKETOMO** (1363-1407)   Moritaké   Takenaga (adopted by the Hayashi)
                                                 18 KANETOMO (1383-1444)   Yasuharu   Hayashi Naringa
                                                 19 MOCHITOMO (1409-1446)   Takeyasu
                                                 20 TAMEKUNI (1430-1488)   **25 TAKEKANÉ** (-1532)
                                                 21 SHIGETOMO (1449-1493)   武邦   重安
                                                 22 YOSHIYUKI (1482-1504)   **23 MASATAKA** (1491-1509)
                                                 24 TAKETSUNÉ (1480-1537) (adopted from the Asa)
                                                 25 TAKEKANÉ (-1532) (from the Takezumi line)
                                                 26 YOSHITAKÉ (formerly Ōtomo Shigeharu) (1505-1554)

shu and was planning to attack Chinzei tandai "military governor of Kyushu" Hojo (Akahashi) Hidetoki, but they found out about his plan and attacked first. Taketoki and his son Yoritaka died in this attack.

Kikuchi Takeshigé (1307-1338)

13th head of the Kikuchi clan. Eldest son of Taketoki. He was Higo no kami.

When Takeshigé's father attacked the Hojo, the Shoni and the Otomo betrayed and killed him. Takeshige ran back to the castle, and was awarded Higo by the Emperor Go-Daigo (1288-1339), whom his father followed.

In 1335, when Ashikaga Takauji (1305-1358) attacked Go-Daigo, Takeshigé went with his brother Takeyasu to join Nitta Yoshitada (1301-1338) against the Ashikaga. The latter was defeated and ran back to Kyoto. Takeshigé was captured by Takauji when the latter came back to Kyushu, but was released.

In 1337 Takeshigé returned to Kyushu when Isshiki Noriuji invaded Higo. With the aid of Uji Korezumi, chief of the temples of Mount Aso, he defeated Noriuji and the army of the Northern Court at Otsukahara.

Kikuchi Takehito (1321-1401)

14th head of the Kikuchi clan. Son of Taketoki, and younger brother to Takeshigé. He succeeded his older brother when he died without offspring. He had other older brothers but he was the only one born from the head wife.

Takehito ruled weakly and so his older half-brothers Takeshigé and Toketoshi helped him with the clan. When the Kikuchi were attacked by the Otomo, Takehito was not able to handle the military situation so another of his older half-brother Takemitsu took over the family and pushed him out. He then became a priest and died at an old age.

Kikuchi Taketoshi (-1341)

8th son of Taketoki, and older brother to Takemitsu. Early in the Nanbokucho Period (1336-1392) he fought against the Ashikaga and the Northern Court with his father and his brothers.

Early in 1336 a number of Kyushu clans, anticipating the movements of the Shogun's army against them, made efforts to unite and present a formidable resistance. A number of skirmishes were fought against the clans loyal to the Shogun on the island, including a siege of the stronghold at Dazaifu (Chikuzen), held by Shoni Sadatsuné. Taketoshi succeeded in reducing the fort and driving out Sadatsuné, who made a stand in the neighboring hills, but was thoroughly defeated and committed suicide with several of his kinsmen. When Ashikaga Takauji (1305-1358) arrived in Munakata, a short distance away, he heard of the death of Sadatsuné. Gathering forces, he marched to meet the opposing army under the command of Taketoshi, consisting primarily of warriors of the Kikuchi, the Aso, the Mihara, and the Kuroki. In the ensuing Battle of Tatarahama, the Kikuchi forces were chased by Ashikaga Tadayoshi (1306-1352) to Dazaifu, at which point they fled into the hills. The Aso and the Akizuki commanders committed suicide, and the other commanders simply surrendered. Takauji rewarded his commanders for their bravery and service, but offered pardon to his opponents and to several clans not participating in the battle but who had joined him in its aftermath. Kyushu thus became united under the Shogunate and the Northern Imperial Court.

Kikuchi Takemitsu (1319-1373)

15th head of the Kikuchi clan. 9th son of Taketoki. He succeeded his brother Takeshigé, who had died without offspring. He supported the Kanenaga-shinno (1326-1383), son of the Emperor Go-Daigo (1288-1339), in his efforts to maintain Kyushu under the authority of the Southern Dynasty.

In 1358 Takemitsu defeated Isshiki Naouji in Chikuzen, in 1359 Hatakeyama Kunihisa in Hyuga, and in 1360 Shoni Yorihisa in Chikugo.

In 1361 Takemitsu again defeated Shoni Yorihisa and, with him, Otomo Ujitoki and Matsuura Yasumasa, and captured Dazaifu. Afterwards he fought against Shiba Ujitsuné, sent by the 2nd Ashikaga Shogun Yoshiakira (1330-1367).

In 1372 the armies of Ashikaga Yoshinori (1394-1441), Ashikaga Takasaki, and Ashikaga Tadaaki enveloped Dazaifu, and it fell into their hands. Takemitsu had to retreat and escape to Chikugo with Prince Kanenaga. When Takemitsu died he left the loyalist defense without a really tested leader, and his heir Takemasa, a promising soldier, died in 1374.

Kikuchi Jiro Takemasa (1342-1374)

16th head of the Kikuchi clan. Eldest son of Takemitsu. He fought with his father in Kyushu against the Northern Dynasty, and had great success.

In 1366 Takemasa mustered an army of men and defeated Ouchi Hiroyo of Suo.

In 1371 Takemasa fought against Imagawa Sadayo (1326-1420), who was appointed Kyushu tandai "governor," and won many battles against Takemasa, who subsequently asked Aso Koretaka for help.

In 1374, when the 3rd Ashikaga Shogun Yoshimitsu (1358-1408) came with an army to subdue Kyushu, Takemasa, notwithstanding a stubborn resistance, had to declare himself vanquished; but he later took the field again and defeated Otomo Chikayo.

Kikuchi Taketomo (1363-1407)

17th head of the Kikuchi clan. Eldest son and heir of Takemasa. He was present when only 13 at the Battle of Mizushima (Bizen and Bitchu), where Imagawa Sadayo (1326-1420) was defeated.

In 1377 Taketomo was vanquished by Ouchi Yoshihiro, but in 1378 was victorious again over Imagawa Sadayo. That was his last success. Exhausted, he retreated to Higo.

In 1397 Taketomo tried to provoke a fresh rising, which was at once quelled.

Taketomo shows up in *The Tale of Genji*, where Lady Murakami (10th-11th century) calls him Chuwa-mono "powerful leader of the wilderness."

Kikuchi Mochitomo (1409-1446)

19th head of the Kikuchi clan. Son of Kanetomo, and grandson of Taketomo.

In 1441 Mochitomo joined forces with Ouchi Masayo and defeated Shoni Sukeyori.

Muromachi Period – Momonoi / Oimi

Kikuchi Yoshiyuki

Kikuchi Yoshiyuki (1482-1504)
22nd head of the Kikuchi clan. Along with his brother, Masataka, the 23rd head of the family, they were the last of the actual Kikuchi bloodline to rule. The 24th head, Taketsuné, was adopted from the Asa clan.

Kikuchi Takekané (-1532)
25th head of the Kikuchi clan. Son of Takeyasu, who was 4th in descent from Kikuchi Takezumi, one of the sons of Taketoki. When the main line of Takemitsu had problems with succession Takekané was adopted from the branch family and became the next head of the Kikuchi.

Kikuchi Yoshitaké (1505-1554)
26th and last head of the Kikuchi clan. Younger brother to Otomo Yoshiaki. He was originally Otomo Shigeharu when his brother placed him as the head of the Kikuchi. He then took the name Kikuchi Yoshitaké.

Yoshitaké did not act as a puppet. He placed his bets on the Ouchi to prevail in northern Kyushu, and took up arms against his older brother, who brushed him aside.

In 1550, when Yoshiaki died and his eldest son Yoshishigé (later Otomo Sorin) became head of the Otomo, Yoshitaké declared his independence. In 1554 Yoshishigé marched against his uncle and destroyed him, ending the long line of the Kikuchi clan.

MOMONOI

Old daimyo family descended from Ashikaga Yoshikané (1154-1199).

Notable Ancestors

Momonoi Yoshitané (13th century)
Son of Ashikaga Yoshikané (1154-1199). He established himself at Momonoi (Kozuké) and took the name of the place.

Momonoi Naotsuné (14th century)
Great-grandson of Yoshitané. He was named shugo "constable" of Etchu by the 1st Ashikaga Shogun Takauji (1305-1358).

In 1337 Naotsuné was defeated by Kitabataké Akiié (1318-1338) at Kamakura and at Aono-ga-hara (Mino). In 1338 Naotsuné in his turn defeated Akiié at Nara (Yamato). He likewise defeated Akiié's brother Akinobu at Otoko-yama (near Kyoto).

In 1350, when disunion set in between Ashikaga Takauji (1305-1358) and his brother Ashikaga Tadayoshi (1306-1352), Naotsuné sided with the latter, passed with him to the side of the Emperor Go-Daigo (1288-1339), and went into Etchu to recruit his troops. In 1351 he returned and occupied Hieizan (northeast Kyoto), but was dislodged by Takauji and Ko Moronao (-1351).

In 1354 Naotsuné joined Shiba Takatsuné, and marched on to Kyoto, whence Ashikaga Takauji had to flee into Omi. Being in want of provisions, he returned into Etchu, where he had soon to defend himself against Takatsuné and his son Shiba Yoshimasa (1350-1410), who, having passed to the cause of the Northern Court, had received orders to combat him.

In 1369, and again in 1370, Naotsuné was defeated by Shiba Yoshimasa. After this date, history no longer mentions his name. It is certain that his whole family was destroyed in the struggle against the Ashikaga.

OIMI

Territory: Shimosa

Ancient family of daimyo in Shimosa, destroyed in the 16th century by the Hojo of Odawara (Sagami).

KIRA

Territory: Mikawa

Family of daimyo descended from the Emperor Seiwa (850-880) and the Seiwa-Genji Minamoto Yoshiuji (1189-1254). Ashikaga Mitsuuji, grandson of Ashikaga Yoshiuji (1189-1254), was the first to take the name of Kira.

The Kira were a minor branch of the Minamoto that never held the rank of shugo "constable," nor possessed any important domains, and never represented a real power, in comparison with other great Seiwa-Genji clans.

In the Edo "Tokugawa" Period (1603-1868), the descendants of this family did not possess the title of daimyo, but ranked below them, numbering among the koké "masters of ceremony."

NOTABLE ANCESTORS

Kira Mitsusada (14th century)

Sided first with his relative Ashikaga Takauji (1305-1358), then passed over to the Southern Dynasty.

In 1352 Mitsusada defeated Hosokawa Kiyouji. In 1360 he was defeated by Hatakeyama Kunikiyo, shugo "constable" of Kawachi, and submitted again to the Ashikaga.

Kira Yoshinaka (1641-1703)

Eldest son of Kira Yoshifuyu. His mother was a member of the high-ranking Sakai, and his wife was from the Uesugi. He was a Tokugawa hatamoto with a stipend of 4,200 koku, and served for about 40 years as koké "master of ceremonies" in the Shogun's Edo Palace. His court title was Kozuké no suké. Based on recent findings, the real pronunciation of his name should be Yoshihisa.

In 1663, at the age 22, Yoshinaka, being highly regarded, was given the duty of congratulating the Emperor Reigen (1654-1732) on his succession, for which he was praised by the Shogunate, and bestowed with the lower 4th Court rank by the Emperor.

In 1664, when Yoshinaka's brother-in-law Uesugi Tsunakatsu, the head of the Yonezawa domain (Dewa), died without an heir, his one-year-old son was adopted to take the latter's place. He was further honored when his son, now Uesugi Tsunanori, was permitted to marry Sakaé-himé, the sister of Tokugawa Tsunanori, the successor of the house of Kii, who would later became the son-in-law of the 5th Tokugawa Shogun Tsunayoshi (1646-1709), giving Yoshinaka family relations with the Shogun, a rather demanding ruler, whom Yoshinaka successfully served for twenty years.

In 1668, on the death of his father, Yoshinaka became the 17th head of the Kira.

Yoshinaka was remembered fondly by many in his hometown as he was responsible for building many public works.

In 1701 Yoshinaka was commissioned to receive and treat the envoys of the Emperor Higashiyama (1675-1710) and the ex-Emperor Reigan, and assigned to tutor Asano Naganori (1667-1701), daimyo of Ako (Harima), in matters of protocol. On the day when the envoys were scheduled to meet the 5th Tokugawa Shogun Tsunayoshi (1646-1709) at Edo Castle, Yoshinaka, who had a reputation for arrogance, reprimanded his charge, and Naganori in anger drew his short sword and, attempting to kill his tutor, struck him in the forehead, causing a minor wound. For this Naganori was ordered to commit seppuku that very evening, and his domain was confiscated by the Bakufu. In 1703, in what is known as "The Incident of the 47 Ronin," Naganori's ex-samurai, after waiting over a year for a good occasion, avenged their lord and assassinated Yoshinaka in his mansion in Edo.

In the aftermath, the Tokugawa Shogunate condemned Kira Yoshichika, Yoshinaka's grandson by Tsunanori, whom he had adopted as a son and heir, for not fighting to the death. The Kira lost the rank of koké, and were dispossessed of their lands.

Ko 高

Family of warriors of the 14th century, in the service of the Ashikaga.

Notable Ancestors

Ko Moronao (-1351)

Along with his brother Moroyasu and cousin Morofuyu, he was one of the most important generals of the 1st Ashikaga Shogun Takauji (1305-1358) during the early Nanboku-cho Period (1336-1392). He was appointed by Takauji as the 1st shitsuji "Shogun's deputy."

In 1333 Moronao helped Takauji destroy the Rokuhara "office of the Kamakura Regency" in Kyoto.

In 1338 Moronao fought against Kitabataké Akiié (1318-1338), defeating and killing him at Sakai-ura (Izumi).

In 1348, at the Battle of Shijo-nawaté (Yamato), Moronao, leading a large army of men, defeated Kusunoki Masatsura (1326-1348), who was struck by an arrow and committed seppuku.

In 1351 Moronao triumphed at Kyoto over Takauji's kinsman Momonoi Naotsuné (1307-1371) of Shimotsuké.

In March of that year, Takauji and his younger brother Ashikaga Tadayoshi (1306-1352) agreed to a truce arranged by Zen master Muso Soseki (1275-1351), who was close to both brothers. One of the condition was that the Ko brothers would retire from politics forever and shave their heads, which they did, and Moronao became a Zen monk. They left Hyogo for Kyoto accompanied by Takauji, but were captured by Uesugi Akiyoshi (-1351), and executed with many dozens of their family at the Mokugawa (Hyogo) in revenge for their killing Akiyoshi's father Uesugi Shigeyoshi (-1349).

Moronao was an iconoclast with no intention of following tradition, especially insofar as the Emperor was concerned. He once said, "What is the use of a King? Why should he live in a Palace? And why should we bow to him? If for some reason a King is needed, let us have one made of wood or metal, and let all the live Kings be banished."

He and his brother Moroyasu are often depicted as avid villains, with Moronao particularly violent, greedy, and lewd.

Ko Morofuyu (-1351)

Cousin to Moronao, who adopted him as a son. He was Mikawa no kami, shugo "constable" of Musashi, and Kanto kanrei "Shogun's deputy in the east." Along with his cousins Moronao and Moroyasu, he was one of the most important generals of the 1st Ashikaga Shogun Takauji (1305-1358) during the early Nanboku-cho Period (1336-1392).

In 1336 Morofuyu took part in the attack on Hiei-zan (Kyoto).

In 1338, together with his cousin Moronao, Morofuyu went to fight against the Southern Court forces in Ao-no-hara (Mino) to help contain Kitabataké Akiié (1318-1338), who was threatening Kyoto.

Morofuyu fought for several years in Hitachi against Kitabataké Chikafusa (1293-1354), and in 1343 succeeded in expelling him.

In 1347 Morofuyu was sent to Isé as shugo "contable," in which role he fought several battles.

In 1349, when Ashikaga Motouji (1340-1367) was appointed Kanto kanrei when just a child, Morofuyu became his shitsuji "deputy" with Uesugi Noriaki, who was his political enemy.

In 1350, during the Kanno Disturbance, Morofuyu remained with Takauji, while Noriaki defected and went with Ashikaga Tadayoshi (1306-1352). In 1351 he left Motouji in Kamakura (Sagami) to attack Noriaki. Defeated and pursued by Sua Takashigé, he committed seppuku at Suzawa Castle (Kai).

Ko Moroyasu (-1351)

Brother to Moronao. He was Echigo no kami.

In 1335 Moroyasu defeated Hojo Tokiyuki (1322-1353). In 1337 he besieged Nitta Yoshisada (1301-1338) at Kanasaki (Echizen). In 1340 he captured Ii Castle (Totomi). In 1348 he was at the Battle of Shijo-nawaté (Yamato) with his brother Moronao.

In 1351 Moroyasu besieged Ishido Yorifusa in the Komyo-ji (southwest of Kyoto), when he was assassinated along with his son Moroyo.

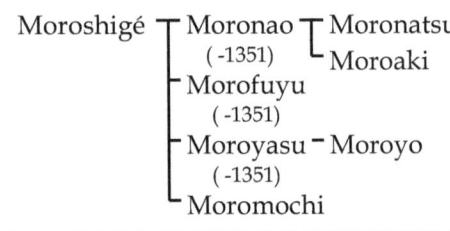

Ko Family Tree

Kusunoki

Territories: Settsu, Kawachi, Izumi
Castle: Akasaka (Kawachi)

Kusunoki Masashigé

Family of daimyo, descended from Tachibana Moroé (683-757), an influential nobleman and scholar.

Notable Ancestors

Kusunoki Masashigé (1294-1336)

Resided east of the temple of Kongozan (Kawachi).

In 1331, when the Emperor Go-Daigo (1288-1339) was expelled from Kyoto by Hojo Takatoki (1303-1333), and fled to Mount Kasagi (Kyoto), he appealed to Masashigé and commissioned him to defend his cause. Masashigé levied troops, fortified Mount Kongo (near Osaka), built the castles of Akasaka and Chihaya (Kawachi), and began the struggle with the Hojo. He was joined by Prince Morinaga (1308-1335), who had fled from the Enryaku-ji (Kyoto).

At the Siege of Akasaka, Masashigé was greatly outnumbered by the Bakufu forces, but his forces fought gallantly, and held on for about three weeks. The enemy finally managed to cutoff the garrison's water supply, and he ordered the castle torched, faked his own death, and slipped out under cover of night. Morinaga then left Masashigé and went into hiding at Yoshino (southern Yamato).

In 1332 Go-Daigo was exiled to Oki, but resistance to the Hojo continued in the Yamato. Masashigé assembled another band of men and began a campaign of harassment against the Bakufu forces in the Kinai, while Morinaga appealed to other landowners and warriors to rally against Kamakura (Sagami).

At the 1333 Siege of Chihaya, Masashigé had prepared a defense that demonstrated a high level of siegecraft, which included an internal water supply, movable bridges, dummy troops, surprise raids, rockslides, boiling water, pitfalls, rolling logs, etc. The Hojo forces suffered great bloodshed, and the siege came to an abrupt end when Ashikaga Takauji (1305-1358) revolted and marched into Kyoto in the name of the Emperor Go-Daigo.

After the subsequent capture of Kamakura by Nitta Yoshisada (1301-1338), Masashigé defeated the bonze Kenbo at Iiyama (Shinano), and pacified the region. In reward he received Settsu, Kawachi, and Izumi, and the title of Kawachi no kami.

Kusunoki Family Tree

Muromachi Period – Kusunoki

In 1335, during the Kenmu Restoration (1333-1336), when Ashikaga Takauji revolted in the Kanto, Nitta Yoshisada went to fight against him, whilst Masashigé remained to protect Kyoto. In 1336, Yoshisada having been defeated at Hakoné (Sagami), Takauji marched upon the capital. Masashigé advanced to check him, but was defeated at Uji, and Go-Daigo had to seek shelter in Hiei-zan (northeast of Kyoto). Yoshisada then returned to attack Takauji at Kyoto, put him to flight, and re-installed the Emperor at the capital.

In 1336 Ashikaga Takauji returned from Kyushu with a numerous army. Masashigé suggested to Go-Daigo that they take refuge in Hiei-zan, and allow Takauji to take Kyoto, but the Emperor was unwilling to leave Kyoto and ordered him to meet Takauji's superior forces. He obediently accepted his Emperor's foolish command, and knowingly marched his army into almost certain death. At the Battle of Minatogawa (Harima), the forces of Masashigé, Nitta Yoshisada, and Nitta Yoshisuké (1305-1304) attacked the forces of Takauji, Shoni Yorihisa, Hosokawa Jozen, and Ashikaga Tadayoshi (1306-1352). After prodigies of valor, they yielded to overwhelming odds, and Masashigé, covered with numerous wounds, committed seppuku with his brother Masasué. After his death, the Emperor conferred on him the title of sakon'é-chujo "middle commander of the Imperial guard" and the rank of sho-san'i.

Masashigé has remained as the paragon of loyalty and devotion to the Imperial Southern Dynasty. He stands as a soldier of the first order, brave and unselfish, with honorable intentions, and a steadfast determination. Along with Minamoto Yoshitsuné (1159-1189), Oda Nobunaga (1534-1582), Toyotomi Hideyoshi (1536-1598), and Tokugawa Ieyasu (1543-1616), he is considered one of the greatest generals and strategists in Japanese history.

Kusunoki Masaié (-1348)

Relative of Masashigé, succeeded him as the head of the Kusunoki forces during the minority of Kusunoki Masatsura (1326-1348), supporting the Emperor Go-Daigo (1288-1339) against the Kamakura Shogunate.

In 1336, after the Battle of Minatogawa (Settsu), Masaié repaired to Urizura (Hitachi). He was attacked there by the Ashikaga troops of the Northern Court, but put them to flight, killing their two generals, Satoké Yoshifuyu and Goto Motoaki.

In 1337 Masaié accompanied Kitabataké Akiié (1318-1338) in his expedition to Kyoto.

In 1347, when Masatsura came of age and took the field, Masaié willingly relinquished command and served under his orders. In 1348 he was defeated and killed with him at the Battle of Shijo-nawaté (Yamato).

Kusunoki Masatsura (1326-1348)

Eldest son of Masashigé. He was only 10 years old at his father's death.

In 1347 Masatsura took the leadership of the Southern Imperial Court partisans, and rose against the Ashikaga. He led an attack on Northern Court sympathizers in Kii and ended up attracting supporters from that province, as well as from Izumi and Settsu.

When the Shogunate sent Hosokawa Akiuji (-1352) to stop him, Masatsura defeated him in the Battle of Sakai-no-ura (Izumi). He also defeated Yamana Tokiuji, who had come to the rescue of Akiuji.

In 1348 Ashikaga Takauji (1305-1358) sent Ko Moronao (-1351) and Ko Moroyasu (-1351) with a large army of men to attack Masatsura. At the Battle of Shijo-nawaté (Yamato) Masatsura, with his brother Masatoki and his cousin Wada Takahidé, defended himself valiantly, but as his army was quite inferior to that of his enemies, he was overwhelmed and perished with all his partisans. He was only 22 years old. A shrine was erected on the spot where he died.

Kusunoki Masanori (-1390)

Youngest son of Masashigé, and brother to Masatsura. He became the head of the Kusunoki after the death of his brothers. He fought for the Southern Court in the Nanboku-cho Period (1336-1392), and is famed for his skills as a leader and military strategist.

In 1348, following the death of his brother Masatsura at the Battle of Shijo-nawaté (Yamato), Masanori continued to oppose the armies of the Northern Court pretenders. In 1353 he and Yamana Tokiuji managed to seize Kyoto, but the 2nd Ashikaga Shogun Yoshiakira (1330-1368) escaped, and a month later, they were driven from the capital.

In 1360, after regrouping, Masanori and Yamana Tokiuji fought Ashikaga Yoshiakira again at Kaminami (Harima), where both sides suffered heavy losses, and they were eventually forced to retreat.

In 1362 Masanori took the field, defeated the Sasaki, and then, joining sides with Hosokawa Kiyouji, who had just embraced the cause of the Southern Court, became master of Kyoto, whence he was expelled one month later by Ashikaga Yoshiakira. Then joining forces with Wada Masataké, he won a victory over the Shogun's army, and reappeared in Kawachi.

In 1368, upon the death of the Emperor Go-Murakami (1328-1368), departing from his family traditions, Masanori entered into a parley with Hosokawa Yoriyuki (1329-1392) and submitted to the Ashikaga. He was then attacked by his former companion-in-arms Wada Masataké, but with the aid of Yoriyuki, he succeeded in repelling him.

In 1373 Masanori himself besieged the Southern Emperor Chokei (1343-1394) in his stronghold of Kongo-zan (Mino).

In 1378 Masanori undertook a new campaign with his son Masakatsu.

In 1381 Masanori submitted to the Emperor Go-Kameyama (1347-1424), who was then confined to Mount Yoshino (Yamato).

Kusunoki Masatsura

In 1392 Masanori's castle of Akasaka (Kawachi) was captured by Yamana Ujikiyo.

Kusunoki Masakatsu (late 14th century)

Eldest son of Masanori. He continued, even after the fusion of the two parties, to struggle against the Ashikaga.

In 1399 Masakatsu revolted in Izumi with Ouchi Yoshihiro (1356-1399), but they were defeated.

Kusunoki Masamoto (-1402)

Son of Masanori, and brother to Masakatsu.

In 1402 Masamoto conceived the project of assassinating the 3rd Ashikaga Shogun Yoshimitsu (1358-1408), but he was found out and put to death by Urakami Yukikagé.

Kusunoki Mitsumasa (-1429)

Descendant of Masanori.

In 1429 Mitsumasa attempted to assassinate the 6th Ashikaga Shogun Yoshinori (1394-1441) and to raise to the Chrysanthenum Throne a Prince of the Southern Dynasty, but he was arrested and beheaded at Rokujo-ga-hara (Kyoto).

Kusunoki Masatora (16th century)

Descendant of Masanori. He was Kawachi no kami.

Masatora served the 15th and last Ashikaga Shogun Yoshiaki (1537-1597), and was shitsuji "deputy" of Oda Nobunaga (1534-1582). He shaved his head and received the title of shiki-bugyo-hoin.

In 1588, by order of Toyotomi Hideyoshi (1536-1598), Masatora wrote a narrative of the visit of the the Emperor Go-Yozei (1572-1617) and the ex-Emperor Ogimachi (1517-1593) to the Jurakudai (Kyoto).

NIKKI

Territories: Mikawa, Isé
Castle: Nagano (Isé)

Family of daimyo descended from Minamoto Yoshikiyo (-1183) (Seiwa-Genji).

The Sakakibara descended from a family of the same name.

NOTABLE ANCESTORS

Nikki Sanekuni (13th century)

Grandson of Minamoto Yoshikiyo (-1183). He was the first to take the name Nikki, from the village of Nikki (Mikawa), where he fixed his residence.

Nikki Yoriaki (1299-1359)

Descendant of Sanekuni, served the 1st Ashikaga Shogun Takauji (1305-1358), and fought for the Northern Dynasty. He became Suo no kami, Iga no kami, and shitsuji "Shogun's deputy."

Nikki Yoshinaga (-1367)

Brother to Yoriaki. He distinguished himself by his bravery in the campaigns against the Southern Dynasty.

Having become an object of jealousy for his companions-in-arms, who attempted to take his life, Yoshinaga left the service of the Ashikaga and fortified himself in the castle of Nagano (Isé), where he was besieged in vain.

Yoshinaga later reconciled with the 2nd Ashikaga Shogun Yoshiakira (1330-1368), and was killed while fighting against Kitabataké Akitoshi.

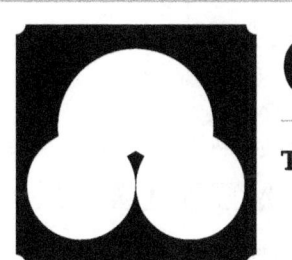  

ODA

Territory: Hitachi

Ancient family of daimyo, descended from Hatsuda Tomoié, son of the Seiwa-Genji Minamoto Yoshitomo (1123-1160).

During the Sengoku "Warring States" Period (1467-1573) the Oda were active in the on-going struggle between the Hojo and the Satomi. The clan lost their lands around 1574 to the Ota.

NOTE: This is not the family of Oda Nobunaga (1534-1582), whose family uses a different character for the first kanji.

NOTABLE ANCESTORS

Oda Tomoshigé (12th century)

Son of Tomoié. He fixed his residence towards the end of the 12th century at Oda (Hitachi) and took its name.

Oda Haruhisa (-1352)

At first a vassal of the Hojo, In 1333 he rallied to the Imperial cause after the fall of Kamakura (Sagami).

Haruhisa fought against Ashikaga Takauji (1305-1358), and afforded shelter to Kitabataké Chikafusa (1293-1354).

Haruhisa later passed over to the Ashikaga party, and in 1352 defeated Nitta Yoshimuné (1335-1368).

In 1573 the family was dispossessed by Ota Sukemasa (-1591).

MIYOSHI

Territories: Settsu, Awa, Kawachi, Tosa, Iyo, Sanuki, Awaji, Harima, Tanba, Yamashiro, Yamato

Castles: Iimori Castle (Kawachi), Takaya Castle (Kawachi), Wakaé Castle (Kawachi)

Daimyo family issued from the Ogasawara, and through them from the Emperor Seiwa (850-880) and the Minamoto Seiwa-Genji.

At the beginning of the 14th century Ogasawara Nagafusa settled in Shikoku. His descendant from the 8th generation came to the district of Miyoshi (Awa), took the name of the place, and served the Hosokawa, who was then all-powerful in Shikoku.

During the Sengoku "Warring States" Period (1467-1573), the Miyoshi controlled several provinces, including Settsu and Awa, reaching their zenith under Nagayoshi/Chokei. Following his death, the Miyoshi Sannin-shu "Miyoshi Triumvirate" dominated the Kyoto region from their base in Sakai (Izumi). They were Miyoshi Nagayuki, Miyoshi Masayasu, and Iwanari Tomomichi, and competed with their erstwhile retainer Matsunaga Hisahidé (1510-1577). In 1565 the Miyoshi and the Matsunaga briefly joined forces to destroy the 13th Ashikaga Shogun Yoshiteru (1536-1565). In 1568 they placed a child as the 14th Ashikaga Yoshihidé Shogun (1564-1568). Later that year, driven from Yamashiro by Oda Nobunaga (1534-1582), the Miyoshi were next forced from their strongholds in Settsu, and retired to Awa. There the remaining Miyoshi were eventually overcome by Chosokabé Motochika (1538-1599).

NOTABLE ANCESTORS

Miyoshi Nagateru/Yukinaga (-1520)

Was Chikuzen no kami. He served the Hosokawa, and held land in Awa.

Upon the death of Hosokawa Masamoto (1466-1507), a succession dispute arose between his two adopted sons Sumiyuki (1489-1507) and Sumimoto (1489-1520). Nagateru supported Sumimoto, and took arms against Sumiyuki, defeating him near Kyoto.

In 1508 Ouchi Yoshioki (1477-1528) marched to Kyoto with the dispossessed 10th Ashikaga Shogun Yoshitané (1466-1523). Nagateru vainly tried to stop him, but he was defeated, and retreated to Awa with Hosokawa Sumimoto.

In 1511 he had his head shaved and took the name Kiun.

In 1519, having gathered an army, Nagateru marched against Kyoto and entered the city, but was defeated by Asakura Takakagé when help from Hosokawa Sumimoto never arrived. Attacked a second time, he was again defeated, and killed himself in the Chion-in.

Miyoshi Masanaga (1508-1549)

Brother to Nagateru, and cousin to Chokei. He was Echizen no kami. He became a bonze and took the name of Sosan.

With Ikeda Nagamasa (1519-1563) as his son-in-law, Masanaga had strong relations with the Ikeda. For this Chokei considered his cousin a threat. In 1549 the two engaged in a major battle, and having been defeated together with Hosokawa Harumoto (1519-1563), Masanaga was murdered by rovers.

Miyoshi Motonaga/Nagamoto (-1532)

Eldest son of Nagateru. He was Chikuzen no kami. He was originally a retainer of the Hosokawa.

In 1520 Motonaga entered Kyoto with the Hosokawa army, and the 10th Ashikaga Shogun Yoshitané (1466-1523) fled to Awa. The latter was re-

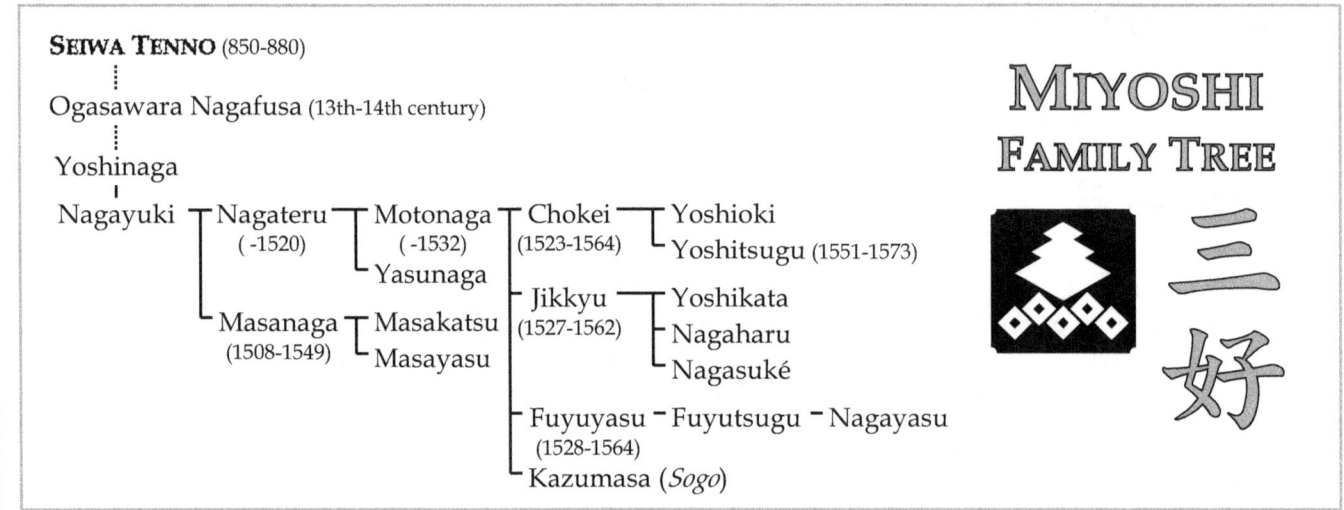

MIYOSHI FAMILY TREE

placed with the 12th Ashikaga Shogun Yoshiharu (1510-1550).

In 1521 Motonaga completed work on the Miyoshi stronghold at Saki (Settsu), which he named the Mandokoro.

In 1532 he had his head shaved and took the name Kai-un.

Motonaga acted on behalf of Hosokawa Harumoto (1519-1563) and Ashikaga Yoshitsuna in their bid for power, and lodged them in Sakai (Izumi), but Motonaga and Harumoto soon grew hostile to each other. In 1532, with the help of the Ishiyama Hongan-ji (later Osaka), Harumoto suddenly attacked Motonaga at the Kenpon-Ji in Sakai, and forced him to kill himself. More than 70 of his servants committed suicide on the same occasion.

Miyoshi Nagayoshi/Chokei (1523-1564)

Eldest son of Motonaga. His childhood name was Norinaga. He was Chikuzen no kami.

In 1532, following the death of his father, Nagayoshi struggled with his uncle Masanaga for power.

In 1539, at the age of 17, with the help of of Matsunaga Hisahidé (1510-1577) and his relative Miyoshi Masanaga, Nagayoshi invaded the Kinai, entered Kyoto, and made an alliance with the Hosokawa, initially accepting the orders of Hosokawa Harumoto (1519-1563).

In 1543 Nagayoshi was dispatched to defeat Hosokawa Ujitsuna (1514-1564), who was driven from Sakai (Izumi), where Nagayoshi placed his brother, Sogo Kazunari, in charge of its administration.

In 1546 Nagayoshi was compelled to defend Sakai against an advance by Hosokawa Ujitsuna, and was successful through political aid on the part of the Sakai city members and his brothers on Shikoku.

In 1548 he took the name Chokei.

In 1549, having had some dispute with Masanaga, Chokei asked his lord Hosokawa Harumoto for authorization to levy troops in Settsu, Izumi, and Kawachi, but instead of giving the required permission, Harumoto sided with Miyoshi Masanaga. Chokei, irritated, then sided with Hosokawa Ujitsuna, and at once attacked and defeated Masanaga. Then, establishing Ujitsuna as chief of the Hosokawa, he went and besieged Harumoto in his cas-

tle of Miyaké. He did not dare however to go so far as to oblige his former lord to kill himself, and, raising the siege, he again turned his arms against Masanaga, whom he again defeated. Harumoto fled into Omi, and asked the 13th Ashikaga Shogun Yoshiteru (1536-1565) for help.

In 1550 Chokei entered Kyoto, and intrusted the city into the hands of Matsunaga Hisahidé. Chokei extended Miyoshi power into the Yamato, and was then the most powerful man in the Kinai, actively playing a role in Kyoto politics.

In 1552 Chokei returned to Kyoto, forced Ashikaga Yoshiteru to submit, and had himself made shobanshu "Shogun's private guard" and shuri-tayu.

In 1557 Chokei had built in Sakai the Nanshu-ji, a notable temple that was destroyed in 1615, and later rebuilt by the renowned priest Takuan Soho (1573-1645).

In 1558 Chokei recaptured Hosokawa Harumoto.

In 1562 Chokei besieged Hatakeyama Takamasa (1527-1576), took his castle of Iimori (Kawachi), and installed himself there. Takamasa went into Kii, levied new troops, and returned to attack Chokei, but was again defeated, and at last peace was restored in the Kinai.

In 1563 Chokei's son Yoshioki died from the effects of poison given him by Matsunaga Hisahidé. Chokei then adopted Yoshitsugu (1551-1573), a son of his younger brother Sogo Kazumasa (1532-1561), but there never reigned great harmony between them.

In 1564 Matsunaga Hisahidé had Chokei's brother Atagi Fuyuyasu (1528-1564) put to death. Shortly after Chokei himself fell sick, and died at the age of 42.

An avid poet, Chokei is also remembered in part for his patronage of the famous renga "collaborative poetry" composer Satomura Joha (1524-1602).

Miyoshi Yoshikata/Yukiyasu/ Yukitora/Jikkyu (1527-1562)

2nd son of Motonaga. He was Buzen no kami, and resided at Miyoshi Castle (Awa). He gave support to his elder brother Chokei, who was based in Settsu.

In 1552 Jikkyu put Hosokawa Mochitaka to death and seized his possessions. The latter's vassal Hisamitsu Yoshioki, in revenge, levied troops against Jikkyu, but failed and was killed.

In 1562 the 13th Ashikaga Shogun Yoshiteru (1536-1565) sent an army into Awa, and Jikkyu died on the battlefield.

Miyoshi/Atagi Fuyuyasu (1528-1564)

3rd son of Motonaga. He was a distinguished poet, and lord of the castle at Araki (Settsu). He commanded ships for his elder brother Chokei.

In 1562 Fuyuyasu and his older brother Yoshikata (1527-1562) were defeated in battle by Hatakeyama Takamasa (1527-1576) in Izumi, and he was forced to flee to Awaji. Later that year however Takamasa was destroyed in Kawachi.

Fuyuyasu is thought to have been murdered on the orders of Matsunaga Hisahidé (1510-1577) while visiting Iimori Castle (Awaji) as part of the latter's efforts to undermine the Miyoshi.

Muromachi Period Otaté

Miyoshi Yoshitsugu (1551-1573)

Son of Sogo Kazunari (1532-1561), and nephew to Chokei. He was initially known as Sogo Shigemasa.

After his father died, Shigemasa was reared by his uncle Chokei. In 1563 when the latter's son Yoshioki died, he was adopted and changed his name to Miyoshi Yoshitsugu. In 1564, when Chokei died, he succeeded as head of the clan.

In 1565 Yoshitsugu, influenced by Matsunaga Hisahidé (1510-1577), assisted the latter in the assassination of the 13th Ashikaga Shogun Yoshiteru (1536-1565) and his brother Shuko, cooperating to nominate the young Ashikaga Yoshihidé (1564-1568).

In 1566 Yoshitsugu established in Kyoto the Juko-in, a temple that would later be the burial place of the tea master Sen Rikyu (1520-1591).

Installed at Takaya Castle (Kawachi), Yoshitsugu soon fell out with Matsunaga Hisahidé, and they went to war. In 1568 Oda Nobunaga (1534-1582) restored peace, and confirmed Yoshitsugu in the possession of half of Kawachi, including Wakaé Castle.

In 1572 Yoshitsugu, hearing that a quarrel had arisen between the 15th Ashikaga Shogun Yoshiaki (1537-1597) and Nobunaga, sided with the Shogun. Nobunaga then besieged Wakaé Castle, and Yoshitsugu killed himself.

With him the clan disappears from history. Its last representatives were defeated in Shikoku by the Chosokabé.

OTATÉ

Family of daimyo descended from the Seiwa-Genji Minamoto Yoshishigé (1135-1202).

NOTABLE ANCESTORS

Otaté Ieuji (13th century)

Son of Nitta Masayoshi. Was the first to take the name of Otaté, his elder brother Masauji keeping that of Nitta.

Otaté Muneuji (14th century)

Son of Ieuji. Fought under Nitta Yoshisada (1301-1338), and in 1333 entered Kamakura with him.

Otaté Ujiaki (-1341)

Son of Muneuji. Fought under Kitabataké Akiié (1318-1338) for the Southern Dynasty.

Ujiaki defeated Akamatsu Norimura (1277-1350) at Muroyama (Harima), and was appointed governor of Iyo. He joined forces with Wakiya Yoshisuké (1305-1340) to conquer the province.

In 1340, upon the death of Wakiya Yoshisuké, Ujiaki was besieged in Seta Castle (Omi) and committed suicide.

Otaté Ujikiyo (1337-1412)

Son of Ujiaki.

In 1361 fought under Kitabataké Akiyoshi (-1383), and captured Sekioka Castle (Iga).

In 1373 Ujikiyo defeated Nikki Yoshinaga (-1367), and received the title of Iga no kami. Later on he changed his name to Sekioka.

MUROMACHI PERIOD – NITTA

NITTA

Territories: Kozuké, Harima

Nitta Yoshisada

Daimyo family of Kozuké descended from the Seiwa-Genji Minamoto Yoshishigé (1135-1202), grandson of Minamoto Yoshiié (1039-1106). They numbered among the chief enemies of the Ashikaga Shogunate, and later the Hojo Regency.

The Nitta rose to importance in the early 13th century. They controlled Kozuké, but had little influence in the Kamakura Shogunate because their ancestor Yoshishigé had not joined his fellow clansmen in the Genpei War (1180-1185), a century earlier. In the 1330s however Nitta Yoshisada led the clan and a number of other Minamoto vassals against the Hojo Regency. In 1333 they succeeded in destroying the Bakufu's buildings in Kamakura.

During the Nanboku-cho Period (1336-1392), the Nitta played an important role once again, allying with the Daté and the Southern Court, but were almost completely annihilated by the Ashikaga Shogunate.

NOTABLE ANCESTORS

Minamoto Yoshishigé/Nitta Taro (-1202)

Eldest son of Minamoto Yoshikuni, and grandson of Minamoto Yoshiié (1039-1106). Received the name Nitta Taro.

When Minamoto Yoritomo (1147-1199) began the Genpei War (1180-1185) against the Taira, Yoshishigé sided with him, and accompanied him to Kamakura.

In 1611, four centuries after his death, the 2nd Tokugawa Shogun Hidetada (1579-1632), whose ancestor he was, had the title Chinjufu-shogun "Defender of the North" posthumously conferred upon him.

Nitta Yoshisada (1301-1338)

At first served in the army of the 14th Hojo Shikken Takatoki (1303-1333) against Kusunoki Masashigé (1294-1336) in Kawachi. But in 1331 he was induced by Imperial Prince Morinaga (1308-1335) and the Emperor Go-Daigo (1288-1339) to embrace the cause of the Southern Dynasty, and so he retired to Kozuké to levy troops.

In 1333 Yoshisada, at the head of a large army, marched upon Kamakura (Sagami). Judging it impossible to enter the city by land, he decided to try by sea. He threw his sword into the surf and prayed to the dragon god Ryujin, who parted the waters for him. Taking advantage of the low tide, he moved through the beaches to capture the Shogun's capital, and put an end to the Hojo domination. As a reward, he received the titles sa-chujo and Harima no kami, and Kozuké and Harima as fiefs. Moreover he courted the Emperor's secretary Koto-Naishi, and married her through the Emperor's mediation.

In 1335, during the Kenmu Restoration (1333-1336), when Ashikaga Takauji (1305-1358) revolted against Go-Daigo, Yoshisada was sent against him. He defeated the rebel on the banks of the Yahagi-gawa (Mikawa), and then again in Suruga, but he was defeated in his turn at the Battle of Také-no-shita near Hakoné (Sagami). Yoshisada was recalled to Kyoto, but could not prevent Takauji from getting possession of the city. But shortly afterwards, aided by Kitabataké Akiié (1318-1338), he expelled Takauji, and defeated him at Hyogo (Settsu).

In 1336, having recruited a fresh army in Kyushu, Ashikaga Takauji re-entered the field, and at the Battle of Minato-gawa (Settsu), won a signal victory over Yoshisada and Kusunoki Masashigé, in which the latter committed suicide. Taking the Princes Tsune-

---

Minamoto Yoshiié (1039-1106)
|
Minamoto Yoshikuni (1082-1155)
|
Minamoto Yoshishigé/Nitta Taro (1135-1202)

┌ Yoshikané – Yoshifusa – Masayoshi ┬ Ieuji (*Otaté*)
├ Yoshinori (*Yamana*)   └ Masauji – Motouji – Tomouji
├ Yoshitoshi (*Satomi*)
└ Yoshisué (*Tokugawa*)

Yoshisada (1301-1338) ┬ Yoshiaki (-1337)
                     ├ Yoshioki (-1358)
                     └ Yoshimuné (1335-1368) – Sadakata (-1410)

Yoshisuké (-1340) (*Wakiya*)

NITTA FAMILY TREE

naga (1324-1338) and Takanaga (1310-1337) with him, Yoshisada sought refuge in Kané-ga-saki Castle (Echizen). Besieged shortly after, he fled to Somayama (Echizen) where he collected fresh troops.

At the 1338 Battle of Fujishima (Echizen), Yoshisada and 50 horsemen were on their way to attack Shiba Takatsuné (1305-1367) at Kuromaru "Black Fortress" (Echizen), when they encountered Hosokawa Akiuji (-1352), who, by order of Ashikaga Takauji, was on his way to reinforce Takatsuné. During the ensuing battle Yoshisada's horse suffered five arrow wounds, collapsed, and pinned Yoshisada's left leg under its body. An arrow pierced his helmet and into his forehead, but he was still conscious, and with his sword, decapitated himself. Several of Yoshisada's commanders performed junshi seppuku in a show of allegiance, and to follow their lord in death.

Yoshisada is considered as one of the staunchest supporters of the legitimate Southern Dynasty. He is honored in the Fuji-shima-jinja, erected on the very spot where he died.

Nitta/Wakiya Yoshisuké (-1340)

Brother to Yoshisada. He fought by his brother's side.

In 1336 Yoshisuké helped drive Ashikaga Takauji (1305-1358) from Kyoto, and when the Emperor Go-Daigo (1288-1339) returned, he made him musha-dokoro and governor of Suruga.

In 1337, defeated by Ashikaga Takauji at Yamazaki (Yamashiro), Yoshisuké fled to Hiei-zan (northeast of Kyoto), then returned to Kyoto. He afterwards accompanied Yoshisada to Somayama Castle (Echizen), and later to Kanegasaki (Echizen).

In 1338, after the death of his brother Yoshisada, Yoshisuké fled to Mino, then to Owari, and finally went to Yoshino (southern Yamato), thus living near the Emperor Go-Murakami (1328-1368).

In 1340 Yoshisuké was sent to Iyo, which he nearly conquered, but he fell sick and died soon after.

Nitta Yoshiaki (-1337)

Eldest son of Yoshisada. He fought in all the campaigns of his father for the Emperor Go-Daigo (1288-1339) against the Ashikaga.

In 1337, at the Siege of Kané-ga-saki (Echizen), his father fled to Somayama (Echizen), and Yoshiaki remained to keep the enemy at bay, but when he saw that all further resistance was fruitless, he put an end to his life and Prince Takanaga (1310-1337) followed his example. Prince Tsunenaga (1324-1338) escaped, but was captured on his way to seek shelter at Somayama, and taken to Kyoto, where he was given poison by Ashikaga Takauji (1305-1358).

Nitta Yoshioki (-1358)

2nd son of Yoshisada.

In 1333 Yoshioki aided in the Siege of Kamakura (Sagami), and battled alongside Kitabataké Akiié (1318-1338) against the Hojo.

In 1334 Yoshioki fought with Kitabataké Akinobu. Yoshioki fortified Mount Otoko, but was defeated, and obliged to seek refuge on Mount Yoshino (southern Yamato).

In 1352, together with his brother Yoshimuné and his cousin Wakiya Yoshiharu, Yoshioki expelled Ashikaga Motouji (1340-1367) from Kamakura and took possession of the city, but soon after he was dislodged by Ashikaga Takauji (1305-1358). Yoshioki repaired to Echigo, and retook the field in Kozuké and Musashi.

In 1358 Yoshioki was captured by Takezawa Nagahira, and Hatakeyama Kunikiyo, minister of Ashikaga Motouji, condemned him to death. He was drowned in the Rokugo-gawa at Yaguchi-no-watari (Musashi), where a shrine stands in his honor.

Nitta Yoshimuné (1335-1368)

3rd son of Yoshisada. On the death of his elder brother Yoshiaki, he was chosen to inherit his father's domain.

Yoshimuné fought at first against Ashikaga Yoshiakira (1330-1367) on Mount Yoshino (Yamato).

In 1352 Yoshimuné, with a strong force from Echigo, attacked Ashikaga Takauji (1305-1358) and defeated him in several short engagements, but he was at last driven back at Kotesashi-gahara (Musashi), and withdrew to Fuéfuki-togé "Fluteplayers' Pass" with Imperial Prince Munenaga (1311-1385), but he was besieged by Takauji, and forced to seek shelter in Echigo, where he conquered half the province and built a castle.

Yoshimuné was killed in an engagement with Uesugi Norimasa (1523-1579).

Nitta Sadakata (-1410)

Son of Yoshimuné. He continued till the end to fight for the Southern Court

Nitta Yoshioki

Wakiya Yoshisuké

Muromachi Period – Nagao

even after 1395, when it had surrendered its rights to its Northern Court rival.

In 1395 Sadakata was defeated and fled to Mutsu. In 1396 he defeated the Yuki and the Ashina, and established himself at Shirakawa (Mutsu).

In 1410, in a final attempt against Kamakura (Sagami), Sadakata was made prisoner, and was put to death at Shichi-ri-ga-hama.

NAGAO

Territory: Echigo
Castle: Kasugayama (Echigo)

Family of Echigo daimyo, descendants of Taira (Muraoka) Yoshibumi.

The Nagao were for several centuries vassals of the Uesugi till Nagao Kagetora (1530-1578), adopted by Uesugi Norimasa (1523-1579), took the name Uesugi Kenshin, and became the head of that family.

Notable Ancestors

Nagao Kageharu (15th century)

Vassal of Uesugi Akisada (1454-1510), revolted against him and defeated him in what is known as the Nagao Kageharu Rebellion (1476-1480).

After they made peace he shaved his head and took the name Igen.

Nagao Tamekagé (-1542)

Son of Yoshikagé (1459-1506). He was Shinano no kami. He served as shugo-dai "deputy constable" to shugo "constable" Uesugi Fusayoshi (-1507).

From 1500-1505, in a series of conflicts, Tamekagé led his lord's Yamanouchi Uesugi forces to victory against the Ogigayatsu Uesugi.

One of a number of upstarts during the Sengoku "Warring States" Period (1467-1573), Tamekagé dared to reproach his master for his negligence in directing his clan. In 1507 Uesugi Fusayoshi, wishing to be rid of him, attacked Tamekagé at Nishihama (Etchu), but was overcome, and later killed when Tamekagé laid siege to him at Matsu-no-yama (Echigo). A large number of Uesugi vassals then rallied to his cause, and Tamekagé went on to pursue a number of campaigns, gathering territory and power.

In 1510 Tamekagé plotted to overthrow Jinbo Yoshimuné (-1520) of Etchu, and ally with the Uesugi. In 1511 he arranged for the execution of the Jinbo brothers Nagakiyo and Nagatsuna, which weakened the clan.

In 1510 Fusayoshi's successor, the new shugo Uesugi Akisada (1454-1510), came in his turn to fight Tamekagé, now allied with Hojo Soun (1432-1519), but was likewise defeated and killed. Within a few years the Uesugi collapsed completely.

In 1513 Tamekagé fought with Jojo Sadanori.

In 1520 Tamekagé attacked Etchu, and defeated the Shiina. Soon afterwards he was attacked at Shinjo Castle (Dewa) by Jinbo Yoshimuné, who was defeated and committed suicide at Fukagami-yama.

Usami Sadamitsu/Sadayuki (1489-1564), a vassal of the Uesugi, continued the war against Tamekagé, and it was not till 1538 that peace was concluded.

In 1536, at the Battle of Sendanno (Etchu), Tamekagé was defeated by Enami Kazuyori and the anti-samurai Ikko-ikki of Kaga. It was said that he died in battle, but there is evidence that he survived to live longer.

His son Kagetora became the famous Uesugi Kenshin. His wife, the mother of Kagetora, was Tora Gozen (-1568), who lived in Kasuga-yama Castle (Echigo).

Nagao Masakagé (-1564)

Brother-in-law to Uesugi Kenshin (1530-1578). He was Echizen no kami.

Masakagé initially fought against Kenshin in support of Nagao Harukagé (-1553), but later became his retainer. He may have been assassinated on Kenshin's orders.

Masakagé was the father of Uesugi Kagekatsu (1555-1623).

Nagao Harukagé (-1553)

Son of Tamekagé. He was Shinano no kami. He succeeded his father as governor of Echigo.

Harukagé became involved in a civil war with a number of Echigo warlords who supported his younger brother Kagetora (later Uesugi Kenshin).

Harukagé was reputedly a sickly and weak character who allowed himself to be influenced by his retainers.

In 1547, following the defeat of his allies, including Kuroda Hidetada (1492-1546), Harukagé was replaced by Kagetora.

His fate is unclear. The popular view is that Harukagé committed suicide, while another, somewhat more reliable, version has him forced to adopt Kagetora to succeed him.

Nagao Kageyasu (-1545)

Son of Tamekagé. He was killed at Kasuga-yama Castle (Yamato) on orders by Kuroda Hidetada (1492-1546).

Nagao Kagenao (16th century)

Adopted son-in-law of Shiina Yasutané (-1576), and cousin to Uesugi Kenshin (1530-1578), who named him hatamoto.

Nagao Fujikagé (16th century)

Served under Uesugi Kenshin (1530-1578). He was counted among the illustrious "28 Generals of Kenshin."

In 1561 Fujikagé fought on the left flank at the 4th Battle of Kawanakajima (Shinano).

OGIGAYATSU

Territory: Musashi

Castles: Kawagoé (Musashi), Edo (Musashi), Kandai-ji (Musashi)

Branch of the Uesugi established toward the middle of the 15th century at Ogigayatsu (Sagami). The clan controlled the heart of the Kanto plain, and fought against the encroaching Hojo until their defeat at the 1545 Battle of Kawagoé (Musashi) which broke their strength, and eventually led to their elimination.

NOTABLE ANCESTORS

Ogigayatsu Akisada (14th century)

Grandson of Uesugi Shigéaki. He settled at Ogi-ga-yatsu (Sagami) and took the name of the place.

Ogigayatsu Mochitomo (1416-1467)

Great-grandson of Akisada.

In 1438, during the Eikyo Rebellion, Mochimoto sided with his relative Uesugi Norizané (1410-1466) against Ashikaga Mochiuji (1398-1439).

In 1449, when Ashikaga Shigeuji (1438-1497) had been made Kanto kubo "Shogun's Deputy in the Kanto," Mochimoto shaved his head, took the name of Docho, resigned his domains in favor of his son Akifusa, and retired to Kawagoé (Musashi).

In 1454, when Ashikaga Shigeuji murdered Uesugi Noritada (1433-1454), Mochimoto joined Uesugi Fusaaki (1432-1466), marched against Shigeuji, and obliged him to seek refuge in Koga.

In 1457 Mochitomo built the castle of Kawagoé, supported Ashikaga Masatomo against Ashikaga Shigeuji, and maintained the struggle for several years. At that epoch, the Yamanouchi branch of the Uesugi was in the height of its power and Nagao Masakata, its principal kerai "vassal," served it with intelligence and energy, and maintained its authority in Echigo, Kozuké, Musashi, and Izu.

In the meantime Ota Dokan (1432-1486), principal vassal of the Ogigayatsu, was engaged in extending the influence of his own lord, and rivalry soon became so intense between the two families that war broke out. In 1462 the 8th Ashikaga Shogun Yoshimasa (1436-1490) commanded his brother Masatomo and the Uesugi to begin another campaign against Ashikaga Shigeuji. Mochitomo, contrary to expectations, sided with Shigeuji. Masatomo and Fusasada marched against him, and he died during the war.

Ogigayatsu Sadamasa (1443-1494)

Son of Mochitomo. He continued the war in which his father had been engaged.

Sadamasa was especially aided by Ota Dokan (1432-1486). In 1486 two servants jealous of the favor enjoyed by Dokan, and probably bribed by the Yamanouchi Uesugi, calumniated him to his master, and he was put to death.

Disorder having broken out in the domains of the two clans, Uesugi Akisada (1454-1510) took up arms to restore peace. Sadamasa asked Ashikaga Shigeuji (1438-1497) for help, who sent his son Masauji with some troops, and the Uesugi were defeated. The Ashikaga and the Ogigayatsu party gained the ascendancy for some time, especially when Hojo Soun (1432-1519) joined it.

In a later battle against Uesugi Akisada, Sadamasa fell from his horse, and was killed.

Ogigayatsu Tomoyoshi (-1518)

Son of Tomomasa. He was chosen heir by his uncle Sadamasa. He was among the first to oppose the Odawara Hojo's rise to power.

In 1494, when Tomoyoshi heard that Hojo Soun (1432-1519) had occupied Odawara, he levied troops and marched against him. Soun, fearing to begin war prematurely, acknowledged, for the time being at least, the suzerainty of the Ogigayatsu.

Tomoyoshi then turned against Uesugi Akisada (1454-1510). After having fought several battles in Musashi, despite the support of Hojo Soun and Imagawa Ujichika (1473-1526), he was defeated.

Tomoyoshi retired to Kawagoé (Musashi), where he was obliged to capitulate. In 1504 he was transferred to Edo Castle (Musashi).

Ogigayatsu Tomo'oki (1488-1537)

Son of Tomoyoshi. He was lord of Edo Castle (Musashi).

In the 1516 Siege of Arai (Sagami) by Hojo Soun (1432-1519), Tomo'oki attempted to relieve Miura Yoshiatsu (-1516) and his eldest son Yoshimoto (-1516), but was defeated.

In the 1524 Siege of Edo, Tomo'oki was betrayed by Ota Suketaka, and lost the castle to Hojo Ujitsuna (1487-1541).

In the 1530 Battle of Ozawahara, Tomo'oki was defeated by Hojo Ujiyasu (1515-1571).

Ogigayatsu Tomosada (1525-1546)

Eldset son of Tomo'oki. He fortified Kandai-ji (Musashi) as a castle to resist the Hojo of Odawara (Sagami).

In 1537 Hojo Ujitsuna (1487-1541) took Kawagoé Castle (Musashi) from Tomosada's uncle Uesugi Tomonari, and Tomosada was obliged to take refuge in Matsuyama (Musashi).

In the 1545 Battle of Kawagoé, Tomosada, allied with Uesugi Norimasa (1523-1579), Ashikaga Haruuji, and Imagawa Ujichika (1473-1526), tried to recover the castle. Hojo Tsunanari (1515-1587), with relief by his brother Hojo Ujiyasu (1515-1571), foiled the siege, and Tomosada was killed in battle. With him, the Ogiyayatsu branch of the Uesugi ended.

OUCHI

Territories: Suo, Nagato, Iwami, Buzen, Izumi, Kii, Aki

Castles: Yamaguchi (Suo), Saijo (Aki), Kagami-yama (Aki)

Major family of daimyo descended from the Rinsei-taishi, a royal Prince of the Baekje Dynasty (Korea), who emigrated to Japan in 611.

The Ouchi was one of the most powerful and important families in Japan during the Muromachi "Ashikaga" Period (1336-1573). In 1363 they were appointed shugo "constable" in Suo and Nagato. At their height, their domains, ruled from the castle town of Yamaguchi (Suo), comprised six provinces, including Iwami and Aki, which they had to hold against the Amako.

During the Nanboku-cho Period (1336-1392) the clan played a major role in supporting the Ashikaga against the Imperial Court.

Based towards the western end of Honshu, the Ouchi were among the primary families to be involved in foreign trade and relations, particularly with China. Following the Onin War (1467-1477), a strong rivalry developed between the Ouchi and the Hosokawa, who were now in power. In 1523 the two clashed at Ningbo (China), and as a result the Ming Dynasty closed the port to Japanese traders. By the time the Ouchi were again allowed to send a ship a few years later, the trade was dying out. The family's trade with China fully came to an end by 1548, their monopoly broken by merchants from the seaport of Sakai (Izumi).

In 1551 the Ouchi housed the Portuguese Jesuit missionary Francis Xavier (1506-1552) for a time.

The Ouchi remained powerful up until the 1560s, when they were eclipsed by their vassals, the Mori.

As a result of their wealth and trading contacts, the Ouchi gained renown in the worlds of art and culture. They possessed countless items of cultural significance and artistic beauty from throughout Japan, China, and further abroad.

NOTABLE ANCESTORS

Ouchi Morifusa (late 12th century)

Towards 1180 installed at Ouchi (Suo). He was the first to take the title of Ouchi no suké, and was admitted to the military class.

Ouchi Hiroyo (14th century)

Descendant of Morifusa in the 8th generation. He governed Suo, where he built Yamaguchi Castle, and resided there.

At first Hiroyo supported the Southern Dynasty, then in 1364 passed over to the Ashikaga, and received Nagato and Iwami.

Ouchi Yoshihiro (1356-1399)

2nd son of Hiroyo. He was also known as Ouchi Sakyo-no-tayu. Along with his military endeavors, Yoshihiro worked to secure Ouchi dominance in the trade with China.

In 1374 Yoshihiro served in the Kyushu expedition of the 3rd Ashikaga Shogun Yoshimitsu (1358-1408), led by Imagawa Sadayo (1326-1420), against the Kikuchi, and received as reward Buzen.

In 1379, when his father died, Yoshihiro was involved in a power struggle with one of his brothers, who in 1380 he defeated at Sakari-yama.

In 1391 Yoshihiro defeated the Southern Dynasty adherent Yamana Ujikiyo (1345-1392) at Kyoto, and annexed Izumi and Kii to his domain, which then comprised six provinces.

In 1392, after having defeated Yamana Yoshisato in Kii, Yoshihiro advanced to Mount Yoshino (southern Yamato), the last refuge of the Southern Court, and opened negotiations with Kitabataké Akinori, a delegate of the Emperor Go-Kameyama (1347-1424). He skillfully brought about the fusion of the two Dynasties to close the Nanboku-cho Period (1336-1392).

In the 1399 Oei Rebellion, Yoshihiro revolted against the Bakufu due to what he considered unfair demands on his resources, including an order by the Shogun Yoshimitsu to build for him a villa at Kitayama (Kyoto). He was supported by many other shugo "constables," so he moved his forces from Kyoto to Sakai (Izumi). Yoshimitsu then gathered the armies of the Kyoto kanrei "Kyoto deputy Shogun" Hatakeyama Motokuni (1352-1406), Shiba Yoshishigé, and the Hosokawa, and moved on Sakai. It did not go well for Yoshihiro: the Inland Sea pirates, whose support he had been counting on, created a naval blockage against him; his Iwami and Izumi troops proved to be generally incompetent; and the promised aid from his supporters, including that of the Kanto kanrei "governor-general of Kanto" Ashikaga Mitsukané (1378-1409), who aspired to the Shogunate, did not materialize. Though his forces resisted stubbornly, the Bakufu troops managed to set fire to Sakai, and Yoshihiro ended up committing suicide.

Ouchi Mochiyo (1395-1442)

Son of Yoshihiro. He was only 5 years old at his father's death. His uncle Morimi governed his extensive domain, but in 1431 he was killed in Chikuzen in an engagement with the Shoni.

Mochiyo then took the title of Ouchi no suké and entered Yamaguchi (Suo).

After the assassination of the 6th Ashikaga Shogun Yoshinori (1394-1441), Mochiyo served in the campaign against the assassin, Akamatsu Mitsusuké (1381-1441), and contributed to the elevation of Ashikaga Yoshikatsu (1434-1443) to the Shogunate.

After that Mochiyo marched against Shoni Sukeyori, who had sided with Akamatsu Mitsusuké, and wrested Chikuzen from him.

He died the following year without issue, and was succeeded by Norihiro, the son of his brother Mochimori.

Muromachi Period – Ouchi

Ouchi Norihiro (-1465)

Nephew of Mochiyo, bore after him the title of Ouchi no suké.

In an expedition headed by Hosokawa Katsumoto (1430-1473) to quell some troubles in Iyo, he died of illness.

Ouchi Masahiro (1446-1495)

Son of Norihiro. He was at first called Taro, and worked to increase the Ouchi domination of trade with China.

In the Onin War (1467-1477) Masahiro served Yamana Sozen (1404-1473), defeated Akamatsu Masanori, and entered Kyoto. But he had to return in all haste to Kyushu, where Shoni Noriyori had mustered troops in Tsushima, and, embracing the party of Hosokawa Katsumoto (1430-1473), tried to recover his domain in Chikuzen.

In 1473 both Yamana Sozen and Hosokawa Katsumoto died, but Masahiro refused to lay down his arms until the Shogunal succession was decided. Finally in 1475, after most of the other daimyo had submitted to the rule of the Shogunate, Masahiro did the same, and returned to his Kyoto residence. There he destroyed his own house, blaming it in his diary on ashigaru "foot-soldiers," left the capital, returned to his family's ancestral domains of Yamaguchi (Suo), and sought to recreate there the depth of Kyoto culture. He decorated his castle lavishly with artwork, including many imported from China and Korea, and invited a number of famous artists there, including in 1486 the famous painter Sesshu Toyo (1420-1506).

Ouchi Yoshioki (1477-1528)

Eldest son of Masahiro. He ruled from Yamaguchi (Suo), and was married to a daughter of Otomo Yoshiaki (1502-1550).

In 1499 Yoshioki gave hospitality to 10th Ashikaga Shogun Yoshitané (1466-1523), who was expelled from Kyoto by Hosokawa Masamoto (1466-1507).

The 11th Ashikaga Shogun Yoshizumi (1480-1511), who was appointed by Hosokawa Masamoto over Yoshitané, gave orders to the Kyushu daimyo to unite their forces against Yoshioki, but fearing the power of a man who ruled over six provinces, they did not dare to obey.

In 1507, having mustered a powerful army, Yoshioki set out from Suo to reinstate the former Shogun Yoshitané. Hosokawa Sumimoto (1489-1520) intended to check him in Settsu, but on ascertaining the strength of his adversary did not dare to risk an engagement and fled to Awa with Miyoshi Nagateru (-1520), whilst Yoshizumi sought refuge in Omi with Sasaki Takayori (-1520). In 1508 Yoshioki entered Kyoto, and, after an absence of 15 years, reinstalled Yoshitané as Shogun. He was then awarded the 4th rank in the Imperial Court.

Shortly afterwards, he was defeated by Hosokawa Masakata, a relative of Hosokawa Sumimoto, and left Kyoto for Tanba to raise fresh troops. In 1511 he returned with Hosokawa Takakuni (-1531), and defeated Masakata and Sumimoto at Funaoka-yama (north of Kyoto). After that, Yoshioki applied himself to restore order in the state with the assistance of the Rokkaku.

In 1518 Amako Tsunehisa (1458-1541) of Izumo invaded Bizen and Hoki, and Yoshioki returned to Suo to defeat him at Aki and Iwami. In 1519 he crossed over to Kyushu and defeated successively Shoni Masasuké and Otomo Yoshinori (-1550) of Bungo.

In 1522 Yoshioki invaded Aki, and built the castles of Saijo (Iyo) and Kagami-yama (Omi). Tsunehisa resorted to arms once more, but was again defeated.

In 1528 he died of illness.

Ouchi Yoshitaka (1507-1551)

Eldest son of Yoshioki. His mother was the daughter of Naito Hironori. He became the head of the Ouchi upon his father's death.

In 1522 Yoshitaka fought with his father against the Amago to win the control of Aki.

Ouchi Yoshitaka

In 1534 Yoshitaka quelled the disturbances raised in Chikuzen by Shoni Sukemoto (1497-1532) and Hoshino Chikatada. Seeing his authority secure, he then began to neglect military affairs, and gave his time to literature, art, and pleasure.

In 1540 Yoshitaka sent Sué Harukata (-1555) to lift the Siege of Koriyama (Aki) laid by Amago Haruhisa (1514-1562). By the next year the Ouchi completely controlled the province. Then in 1542 Yoshitaka marched into Izumo against Haruhisa, but was repulsed at Gassan-Toda Castle, losing a large number of Ouchi and Mori troops, along with his adopted son Harumochi.

Yoshitaka then returned to Yamaguchi (Suo) and indulged more than ever to the arts and culture introduced into his castle by the kugé, who had resorted thither, owing to the troubled condition of Kyoto, attracting a large number of artists such as Sesshu Toyo (1420-1506) and Sogi (1421-1502). In 1543 he paid the expenses of the coronation of the Emperor Go-Nara (1495-1557), and was appointed Dazai shoni "vice-governor of Kyushu."

In 1551 Yoshitaka was on his way to Kyoto, and intended to stay only a few days at Yamaguchi, but he prolonged his visit by six months, and entertained the Spanish Jesuit priest Francis Xavier (1506-1552), who formed a Christian community there, which soon numbered 500 members. Yoshitaka received the foreign preacher kindly, and listened to his instructions with interest, but went no further. The Jesuits called him "King of Yamaguchi."

Yoshitaka's kerai "vassals" Sué Harukata and Mori Motonari (1497-1571) endeavored to draw him away from his effeminate life. Sagara Taketo (1498-1551), on the other hand, wanted the clan to simply do nothing more than maintain the control of their current domain. Disunion then broke out among his subjects. Harukata intrenched in his castle of Wakayama (Suo), came to a secret understanding with the Otomo of Bungo and prepared for revolt.

In 1551, hearing of the treacherous designs of Sué Harukata, Yoshitaka called his retainers to arms against the rebel, but most disregarded his appeal. He then left his castle, where he felt too unsafe, and retired to the Hosen-ji (Sagami), which he too soon left, and fled towards Nagato. A storm however diverted his boat, and he landed in the village of Fukawa (Aki), where he was soon besieged by Harukata, and committed suicide along with his son Yoshihiro.

A younger branch, descended from Mochimori, grandson of Yoshitaka, had taken the name of Yamaguchi.

Ouchi Yoshinaga (1532-1557)

Younger brother to Otomo Sorin (1530-1587). His mother was a daughter of Ouchi Yoshioki (1477-1528). He was chosen by Sué Harukata (-1555), who had just taken control of the Ouchi, to serve as the puppet head of the clan.

In 1554 Yoshinaga, with the help of Sué Harukata, quelled a revolt of Yoshimi Masayori in Iwami.

In 1555 Mori Motonari (1497-1571) revolted too, and Yoshinaga again sent Sué Harukata, who was this time defeated and killed at the Battle of Miyajima (Aki).

In 1557 Motonari invaded Suo and was joined by a large number of samurai. Yoshinaga fled to Chofu (Nagato), where he was soon overtaken by Fukuhara Hiroyoshi, the commander of Motonari's vanguard. He sought refuge in the Chofuku-ji, where he committed suicide. The family became extinct thereafter.

Ouchi Teruhiro (-1569)

Son of Takahiro, and cousin to Yoshitaka.

In 1557, when the Ouchi were brought down by Mori Motonari (1497-1571), Teruhiro fled and continued to resist their rule, eventually aided in this by Amago loyalist Yamanaka Yukimori (1545-1578).

In 1569 Teruhiro and Yamanaka Yukimori attacked Izumo while the Mori were preoccupied with events on Kyushu. Motonari's son Kikkawa Motoharu (1530-1586) destroyed Teruhiro at Cha-usu-yama (Settsu).

OYAMA

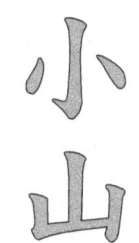

Territory: Shimotsuké
Castle: Oyama (Shimotsuké)

Family of daimyo descended from Fujiwara Hidesato (10th century).

NOTABLE ANCESTORS

Oyama Masamitsu (12th century)

Descended from Hidesato in the 11th generation. Towards the middle of the 12th century he was the first to take the name of Oyama from the castle in Shimotsuké, occupied by his ancestors for three centuries.

Oyama Tomomasa (1155-1238)

Son of Masamitsu.

At the onset of the Genpei War (1180-1185), Tomomasa sided with Minamoto Yoritomo (1147-1199) as soon as he rose in arms against the Taira, and as reward received some land in Hitachi. In 1184 he fought at the Battle of Ichino-tani (Settsu), and in 1187 in the campaign against Fujiwara Hidehira (1122-1187).

In 1190 Tomomasa accompanied Minamoto Yoritomo to Kyoto, and was appointed kebiishi "chief of police" and Shimotsuké no kami, then in 1199 shugo "constable" of Harima.

In 1203 Tomomasa, with Hatakeyama Shigetada (1164-1205), quelled the uprising of Hiki Yoshikazu (-1203) against the Hojo.

Oyama Hidetomo (-1335)

Descendant of Tomomasa in the 6th generation. He fought under the Hojo against the Emperor Go-Daigo (1288-1339), and besieged Akasaka Castle (Kawachi).

Hidetomo rallied to the standard of Nitta Yoshisada (1301-1338), defeated Kanazawa Sadamasa at Tsurumi (Musashi), and took part in the 1333 Siege of Kamakura. He was then appointed Shimotsuké no kami.

He was killed in Musashi while fighting against Hojo Tokiyuki (1322-1353).

Oyama Yoshimasa (-1382)

Grandson of Hidetomo.

In 1380 Yoshimasa raised an army to defend the cause of the Southern Dynasty, and defeated Utsunomiya Mototsuna at Mobara, but was obliged to fall back when Uesugi Norikata (1335-1394) was sent against him by the the Kanto-kubo "Shogun's Kanto deputy" Ashikaga Ujimitsu (1359-1398). Rallying his troops, he soon took the field again, but was defeated by Uesugi Tomomuné (1339-1414), and committed suicide. His family afterwards became extinct.

ROKKAKU

  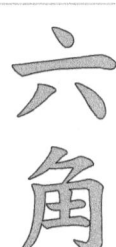

Territory: Omi
Castles: Kannon-ji (Omi)

Family of shugo "constables" descended from the Minamoto Uda-Genji founded by Sasaki Yasutsuna (13th century) of Omi. The name was taken from their residence in Kyoto. Family members faithfully served the Ashikaga, and were powerful in the province into the 16th century.

In the wake of the Onin War (1467-1477) the Rokkaku played a role in the struggle for power around Kyoto, competing with the Asai.

In 1568 Oda Nobunaga (1534-1582) took Kannon-ji Castle (Omi) from them on his march to Kyoto. In 1570 Shibata Katsuié (1522-1583) defeated them absolutely, felling the clan from daimyohood.

During the Edo Period (1603-1868), the descendants of Rokkaku Yoshisuké (-1612) were considered a koké "high family."

NOTABLE ANCESTORS

Rokkaku Yasutsuna (13th century)

Son of Sasaki Nobutsuna. He was the first to take the name Rokkaku.

Yasutsuna possessed the full confidence of the Hojo Regency, was kebiishi "chief of police," Omi no shugo "constable," Iki no kami.

Rokkaku Ujiyori (1326-1370)

Great-grandson of Yasutsuna. He was Omi no shugo "constable" and kebiishi "chief of police." He resided at Kannon-ji Castle (Omi), built by his ancestors.

Ujiyori sided with the Northern Dynasty, and fought under the Ashikaga Shogun Takauji (1305-1358) and Yoshiakira (1330-1368).

Rokkaku Mitsutaka (-1413)

Son of the 2nd Ashikaga Shogun Yoshiakira (1330-1368). He was adopted by Ujiyori and succeeded him in all his titles and possessions.

At the time of the reconciliation of the two Imperial Houses, it was Mitsutaka who came to Kyoto with the three sacred emblems, until then in the hands of the Southern Court Emperor Go-Kameyama (1347-1424), and handed them to the Northern Court Emperor Go-Komatsu (1377-1433).

Rokkaku Takayori (-1520)

Son of Masayori.

In the Onin War (1467-1477) Takayori sided with Yamana Sozen (1404-1473), and conquered the whole of Omi from the Kyogoku (another Sasaki branch).

After the war, Takayori seized land and manors owned by the nobles of the Imperial Court, temples, and shrines. In 1487 Takayori was besieged in Kannon-ji Castle (Omi) by the 9th Ashikaga Shogun Yoshihisa (1465-1489). He fled, and sought refuge on Koga-zan (Omi). Yoshihisa died during the siege and was replaced by the 10th Ashikaga Shogun Yoshitané (1466-1523).

In 1492 Takayori was attacked by the Shogun Yoshitané. He was defeated, and was again compelled to flee.

On the death of the Emperor Go-Tsuchi-mikado (1442-1500), Takayori paid all the expenses of the funeral, and in reward was allowed to add to his arms the kiku "chrysanthemum" and the kiri "paulownia" of the Imperial family.

In 1508 Takayori sheltered the 11th Ashikaga Shogun Yoshizumi (1480-1511) when he was expelled from Kyoto by his rival Ashikaga Yoshitané.

Rokkaku Sadayori (1495-1552)

2nd son of Takayori. He was first a bonze at the Sokoku-ji (Kyoto), but when his elder brother Chikatsuna died, he inherited the successionhood of the Rokkaku, and resided at Kannon-ji Castle (Omi), where he stimulated mercantile activity.

In the 1511 Battle of Funaoka-yama (Kyoto) Sadayori contributed to the victory won by Ouchi Yoshioki (1477-1528) over Hosokawa Masakata, and was then appointed kanryo "deputy Shogun" and danjo-sho-suké.

In 1518 Sadayori besieged in vain Asai Sukemasa (1491-1546) in Odani Castle (Omi).

In 1520, mustering fresh troops, Sadayori marched upon Kyoto, and expelled Miyoshi Yukinaga/Nagateru (-1520), who committed suicide when cornered, and Hosokawa Sumimoto (1489-1520).

In 1523 Sadayori intervened in an internal struggle between his retainers, the Gamo brothers Takasato and Hideyuki, and forced the latter to abandon Otowa Castle.

He was killed during a fight against the Miyoshi.

Rokkaku Yoshikata (1521-1598)

Son of Sadayori. He was shugo "constable" and later daimyo of an area of southern Omi, and was lord of Kannon-ji Castle. He learned archery from Yoshida Shigekata and horsemanship from Saito Jogen, and founded the Sasaki-ryu, a school to teach the arts of war.

In 1549 Yoshikata aided Hosokawa Harumoto (1519-1563) against Miyoshi Chokei (1522-1564).

In 1552, upon his father's death, Yoshikata succeeded as head of the Rokkaku.

In 1555, coveting a part of Isé, Yoshikata laid siege to the castle of Chikusa, but Chikusa Tadaharu negotiated a peace.

In 1558 Yoshikata fought against Matsunaga Hisahidé (1510-1577) at Nyoi-ga-miné (Yamashiro), and entered Kyoto with the 13th Ashikaga Shogun Yoshiteru (1536-1565).

In 1559 Yoshikata officially retired in favor of his son Yoshiharu, shaved his head, took the name Shotei, and was ranked among the shobanshu "Shogun's private guard."

In the 1560 Battle of Norada, Yoshikata led his clan's forces to battle against Asai Nagamasa (1545-1573) of northern Omi, seeking to maintain his control over their territory. Despite a reportedly two-to-one advantage, he was defeated, and this marked the beginning of the decline of the Rokkaku.

In 1562 Yoshikata made peace with Miyoshi Nagayoshi/Chokei (1522-1564).

In 1563 Yoshikata executed one of his vassals Goto Tajima no kami Katatoyo for killing someone within Kannon-ji Castle, creating dissension within the ranks of their retainers, leading to the Kannon-ji Disturbance. Yoshikata and Yoshiharu were driven from the castle, but they returned soon afterwards through the mediation of Gamo Sadahidé and Gamo Katahidé (1534-1584).

In 1565 the Rokkaku were again attacked by the Asai, but the invading forces were contained.

In 1567 Yoshikata promulgated the *Rokkaku-shi shikimoku* "*Rokkaku house code of conduct*," laws that placed a legal framework on the authority of the daimyo.

In 1568 the Rokkaku were asked by Oda Nobunaga (1534-1582), who was in the service of Ashikaga Yoshiaki (1537-1597), who aspired to succeed as Shogun, to join his army, but Yoshikata refused. Nobunaga then took Kannonji Castle on his way to Kyoto, effectively eliminating the clan as daimyo. They settled in Koka (Omi) and continued to contest Nobunaga's activities from Namazué Castle.

In the 1570 Siege of Choko-ji (Omi) by the Rokkaku, Shibata Katsuié (1522-1583) successfully sallied from the temple to defeat the besiegers.

Yoshikata eventually submitted to Oda Nobunaga, who imprisoned him in Ishibé Castle, held by Sakuma Nobumori (1528-1582). But in 1574 he escaped, fleeing to Shigaraki (Omi), where he lived in seclusion, aiding local movements and the Ikko-ikki against Nobunaga in the Ishiyama Hongan-ji War (1570-1580).

After the war, Oda Nobunaga allowed him to retire to Omi. He was baptized at Azuchi (Omi) the very year of his death.

Rokkaku Yoshiharu/Yoshisuké (1545-1612)

Eldest son of Yoshikata.

In 1559, when his father abdicated, Yoshiharu took in hand the administration of the Rokkaku domain, with Gamo Katahidé (1534-1584) as counselor.

In the 1560 Battle of Norada against the Asai, Yoshiharu shared defeat with his father.

In 1565, after the assassination of the 13th Ashikaga Shogun Yoshiteru (1536-1565), his brother Yoshiaki (1537-1597) implored Yoshiharu to help him recover his rights to the Shogunate, but he did not dare risk a war with the powerful Miyoshi. In 1568 Yoshiaki turned to Oda Nobunaga (1534-1582), who enthusiastically accepted the mission, raised an army, and marched on to Kyoto. On his way, in Omi, he captured several castles of the Sasaki, and compelled Yoshiharu to seek shelter on Koka-san (Omi).

In 1572 Yoshiharu was besieged by Shibata Katsuié (1522-1583) in Namazué Castle (Omi). Forced to surrender, he lost all his domains.

Yoshiharu then allied with the Asai, but in 1573 fled when that clan was destroyed.

Yoshiharu then took up with the Takeda, and hid in the Erin-ji (Kai). He later became a retainer of Toyotomi Hideyoshi (1536-1598), and served Toyotomi Hidetsugu (1568-1595). At Osaka Castle he was an instructor of archery for Toyotomi Hideyori (1593-1615).

Lastly he entered the service of Tokugawa Ieyasu (1543-1616), and his descendants received the title of koké "high family."

SHIBUKAWA

Territory: Musashi

Castle: Warabi (Musashi)

Daimyo family descended from Ashikaga Yasuuji (13th century) of the Seiwa-Genji branch of the Minamoto.

Notable Ancestors

Shibukawa Yoshiaki (13th century)
Son of Yasuuji. In the 13th century he took the name Shibukawa.

Shibukawa Yoshiyuki (14th-15th century)
Descendant of Yoshiaki. He was governor of Musashi and built Warabi Castle (Musashi).

Shibukawa Mitsuyori (-1446)
Son of Yoshiyuki.

In 1395 Mitsuyori was named Kyushu tandai "governor of Kyushu" to replace Imagawa Sadayo (1326-1420). He later shaved his head and took the name Dochin.

Shibukawa Yoshikané (15th century)
Son of Mitsuyori.

In 1457 Yoshikané was named Kyushu tandai "governor of Kyushu," defeated Ashikaga Shigeuji (1438-1497), and secured the office of Kanto kanrei "deputy Shogun of the east" to the Uesugi. He continued to govern Musashi, which his descendants were deprived by the Hojo of Odawara (Sagami).

Saito

Territories: Musashi, Mino

Ancient daimyo family coming from Echizen and descending from the Chinjufu-shogun "Defender of the North" Fujiwara Toshihito (9th century).

Throughout the earlier years of the Sengoku "Warring States" Period (1467-1573), the Saito ruled as one of the most powerful clans in Japan.

Notable Ancestors

Saito Sanemori (1111-1183)

Left Echizen and established himself at Nagai (Musashi).

Sanemori served Minamoto Yoshitomo (1123-1160), but after the latter's death he attached himself to Taira Munemori (1147-1184).

At the Battle of Shinohara (Kaga) during the Genpei War (1180-1185), Sanemori was killed fighting against Kiso Yoshinaka (1154-1184).

In his old age he is said to have dyed his hair and beard so that he could continue to fight.

Saito Dosan/Toshimasa (1494-1556)

Of unclear origins, he was either born in Yamashiro as an illegitimate son of Matsuda Motomuné, or in Kyoto as son of Shinzaémon-jo, a monk at the Myo'ukaku-ji, who had given up the

Saito Sanemori

Saito Dosan

priesthood and married the daughter of an oil merchant.

He was eventually adopted by the Nishimura and took the name of Hidemoto. He then entered the service of Nagai Nagahiro of Mino, murdered him, and changed his name to Nagai Toshimasa.

Toshimasa used his power and influence to become a retainer of the daimyo of Mino, Toki Yorinari (1502-1582). In 1526, owing to the disruptions that Toshimasa was causing in the province, Yorinari gave him one of his concubines in hopes of appeasing him. According to another story, Toshimasa had in fact won the concubine through a wager: he bet Yoshinari that he could put a spear through the eye of tiger painted on a sliding door, and succeeded. Toshimasa later married Omi-no-kata, a daughter of Suruga no kami Akechi Mitsutsugu.

Toshimasa eventually succeeded in becoming the magistrate of Mino, and settled in Inaba-yama Castle. In 1544, using his power and wealth, he drove Toki Yorinari out of Mino in a *coup d'état*, and claimed the Mount Kinka region as his own, becoming a daimyo in his own right, and changed his name to Saito Dosan.

Toki Yorinari then allied with Oda Nobuhidé (1510-1551) of Owari, south of Mino. At the 1547 Battle of Kanoguchi (Mino) Dosan defeated Nobuhidé, who made peace, and in 1549 arranged a political marriage between his son Nobunaga (1534-1582) and Dosan's daughter No-himé, to end hostilities.

As Dosan's eldest son Yoshitatsu was born in less than nine months to the concubine from when Yoshinari had given her to him, his parentage was unclear. In 1555 Dosan decided to name Kiheiji, one of his other sons, heir. Yoshitatsu, who was living in Sagiyama Castle (Mino) at the time, in response, killed two of his brothers, and went to war against his father. In the 1556 Battle of Nagara-gawa (Mino) Dosan was heavily outnumbered, and his head was taken by Komaki Genta, a retainer of Yoshitatsu's son Tatsuoki.

Oda Nobunaga desired to revenge the death of his father-in-law, but did not dare to enter into conflict with Yoshitatsu.

Dosan is known for having a large number of pseudonyms and for frequently changing his name. They include Minemaru, Horenbo, Matsunami Shokuro, Nishimura Kankuro Masatoshi, Shinkuro, Nagai Yorihide, Saito Hidetatsu, and Saito Sakon-dayu Toshimasa. For his ruthless tactics, reputation for cruelty, and a highly unsavory character, he is nicknamed Mino-no-mumushi "Serpent of Mino."

Saito Yoshitatsu (1527-1561)

Eldest son of Saito Dosan. Born in Mino, his biological father may have been Toki Yorinari (1502-1582) by a concubine he had given Dosan less than nine months before his birth.

In 1555 Dosan decided to deprive Yoshitatsu of succession, and name as heir Kiheiji, one of his other sons. Yoshitatsu rebelled and, with the help of Nagai Michitoshi (-1571), put two of his younger brothers to death in the family residence at Inaba-yama (Mino). In 1556, after a stiff fight, he defeated his father at the Battle of Nagara-gawa (Mino), and declared himself the 2nd head of the Saito and took control of Mino.

He proved a capable commander, but suffered from leprosy, and died of his illness.

Muromachi Period – Shoni

Saito Nagatatsu (-1582)

Younger son of Dosan.

In 1555 Nagatatsu was taken from Mino to avoid the fate of his elder brothers, slain by Saito Yoshitatsu, and entered the protection of Oda Nobunaga (1534-1582).

Nagatatsu was later married to a daughter of a certain Sato Kii no kami, and was given a fief in Mino, which in 1567 was taken by the Oda.

Nagatatsu served in various campaigns for Oda Nobunaga, and was killed alongside Oda Nobutada (1557-1582) at Nijo Castle (Kyoto) following Nobunaga's death at the hands of Akechi Mitsuhidé (1528-1582).

Saito Tatsuoki (1548-1573)

3rd-generation head of the clan. Son of Yoshitatsu, and grandson of Dosan. He was also the nephew of No-himé, the 1st wife of Oda Nobunaga (1534-1582).

In 1564 Tatsuoki was defeated by Oda Nobunaga, and fled. From that time, the name of his family is no more mentioned in history.

SHONI

Territory: Chikuzen

Ancient daimyo family of Fujiwara Hidesato (10th century).

One of the descendants of Hidesato received the title Dazai shoni "vice-governor of Kyushu" from Minamoto Yoritomo (1147-1199), settled there, and took Shoni as the family name.

During the Mongol Invasions of Japan in 1274 and 1281 members of the clan played an important role in commanding the defense.

During the Nanboku-cho Period (1336-1392), after initially supporting the Emperor Go-Daigo (1288-1339) of the Southern Court, the Shoni later allied with Ashikaga Takauji (1305-1358) and the Northern Court.

In the 14th and 15th centuries the Shoni were repeatedly defeated by the Ouchi, and they gradually lost their territories.

In the Sengoku "Warring States" Period (1467-1573) they recovered their domain with the help of the Otomo, but in 1553 their erstwhile vassal Ryuzoji Takanobu (1530-1584) rebelled, and by 1559 the clan was entirely eliminated.

Notable Ancestors

Shoni Sukeyori (12th century)

Descendant of Hidesato in the 9th generation. In 1189 he received the title of Dazai shoni from Minamoto Yoritomo (1147-1199), settled at Dazaifu (Chikuzen), and took the name Shoni.

Shoni Kagesuké (-1285)

In 1285 was on duty at the time of the Mongols' expedition against Kyushu. He organized the defense, fought gallantly, and when the tempest had dispersed the invaders' fleet, pursued them as far as to Takashima, and massacred all those who had sought shelter there.

Shoni Sadatsuné (-1336)

Sided at first with the Emperor Go-Daigo (1288-1339), but hearing of the success of the Ashikaga he went over to their side, and fought for the Northern Dynasty.

In 1334 Sadatsuné defeated and killed Kikuchi Taketoki (1292-1333).

In 1336 Dazaifu (Chikuzen) was besieged and taken by a force of Kyushu clans fighting against those loyal to the Shogun. Sadatsuné fled, but was defeated soon afterwards by Kikuchi Taketoki's son Taketoshi (-1341), and committed suicide along with a number of his retainers.

Shoni Yorihisa (14th century)

Son of Sadatsuné.

In 1336, after defeating Kikuchi Taketoshi (-1341), Yorihisa led an army of men to help Ashikaga Takauji (1305-1358), and fought in the battles of Minato-gawa (Settsu) and Amida-ga-miné, where the Southern Army was defeated.

After returning to Kyushu, Yorihisa fought against Kikuchi Takemitsu (1319-1373), but was defeated on the Chikugo-gawa.

Shoni Fuyusuké (-1375)

Son of Yorihisa. He at first served Imagawa Sadayo (1326-1420), and was nominated Kyushu tandai "governor of Kyushu."

After some contention with Imagawa Sadayo, Fuyusuké turned against him, but was defeated and killed.

Shoni Yorizumi (14th century)

Son of Yorihisa, and brother to Fuyusuké, whom he succeeded. He served Prince Yasunaga, who named him Kyushu tandai "governor of Kyushu" and Echigo no kami.

Shoni Masasuké (-1506)

Descendant of Yorizumi. He was killed whilst fighting against Ouchi Yoshioki (1477-1528), who came to despoil him of his domain.

Shoni Sukemoto (1497-1532)

Son of Masasuké. He tried to regain the inheritance of the family.

Sukemoto married the daughter of Otomo Masachika, who in 1529 helped him defeat the encroaching army of the Ouchi.

Shoni Tokinao (-1556)

Son of Sukemoto.

In 1554 Tokinao was defeated by his vassal Ryuzoji Takanobu (1530-1584), and took refuge in Chikugo. In 1556 he levied a second army, and again took the field, but being defeated a second time, he killed himself. With him ended the Shoni.

The Shoni are ancestors of the Nabeshima.

SASAKI

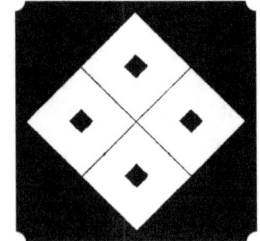

Territories: Omi, Bizen

Daimyo family descended from Uda-Genji Minamoto Masanobu (920-993), grandson of the Emperor Uda (867-931).

NOTABLE ANCESTORS

Sasaki Nariyori (11th century)

Great-grandson of Minamoto Masanobu (920-993). He is the first to take the name Sasaki from his domain in Omi.

Sasaki Hideyoshi (1112-1184)

Descendant of Nariyori. He was adopted by Minamoto Tameyoshi (1196-1156) when 13 years old.

During the Hogen War (1156) Hideyoshi fought under the command of Minamoto Yoshitomo (1123-1160), and besieged Shirakawa (Kyoto), burning the palace to the ground, incurring the ire of the rival Taira.

At the time of the Heiji War (1159) Hideyoshi helped Minamoto Yoshihira (1140-1160), and withstood Taira Shigemori (1138-1179), but after the defeat of Minamoto Yoshitomo, he fled.

Hideyoshi intended to ask his uncle Fujiwara Hidehira (1122-1187) to give him shelter in Mutsu, but he stopped on his way thither at Sagami, where Shibuya Shigekuni took an interest in him, gave in marriage his daughter, who would become the mother of Yoshikiyo, and named him heir to his lands. He remained at that place for 20 years.

In 1180 when Minamoto Yoritomo (1147-1199) rose in revolt against the Taira, Hideyoshi with his four sons sided with him in the Genpei War (1180-1185).

He was killed at Ohara (Omi) in a battle fought against Hirata Ietsugu, a Taira partisans.

Sasaki Sadatsuna (12th century)

Son of Hideyoshi.

In 1180 Sadatsuna entered the Genpei War (1180-1185) with Minamoto Yoritomo (1147-1199), and under the orders of Hojo Tokimasa (1138-1215) attacked the governor of Izu, Taira Kanetaka, and defeated him.

After the 1181 Battle of Ishibashiyama (Sagami), Sadatsuna asked shelter from Taira Shigekuni at Shibuya (Sagami), where he lived a long time with his father.

When Yoritomo attacked Saté Hideyoshi, Sadatsuna joined him and came to besiege Kanasa Castle (Hitachi). As reward he was reinstated in the fief of Sasaki (Omi), of which his father had been deprived, and obtained in addition the government of the whole province, which his descendants kept for more then three centuries.

In consequence of a quarrel in reference to the Hié-jinja (Musashi), Sadatsuna was banished to Satsuma, and recalled after four years in exile.

Sadatsuna is the ancestor of the Rokkaku, the Kuroda, the Kyogoku, and the Amako.

Sasaki Saburo Moritsuna (12th century)

Son of Hideyoshi.

In the Genpei War (1180-1185) Moritsuna sided with Minamoto Yoritomo (1147-1199) against the Taira.

In 1184 Moritsuna accompanied Minamoto Noriyori (1156-1193) in his expedition to the west. When the Minamoto army arrived at Fujito (Bizen), it found Taira Yukimori entrenched in the peninsula. In the ensuing Battle of Kojima, Moritsuna found a ford, spur-

Sasaki Moritsuna

SASAKI FAMILY TREE

- **Uda-Tenno** (867-931)
  - Minamoto Masanobu (920-993)
    - Nariyori (11th century)
      - Hideyoshi (1112-1184)
        - Sadatsuna — Nobutsuna (-1242) — Yasutsuna — Yoritsuna — Tokinobu — Ujiyori (*Rokkaku*)
          - Ujinobu — Mitsunobu — Munemitsu — Munenobu (*Kuroda*)
            - Munetsuna — Takauji (1306-1373) — Takahidé — Taka'aki (*Kyogoku*)
              - Takahisa (*Amako*)
        - Tsunetaka
        - Moritsuna
        - Takatsuna (1160-1214)
        - Yoshikiyo — Yasukiyo — Yorikiyo — Yasunobu — Kimikiyo — Yoshitsuna (*To*)

red his horse into it, and inducing his samurai to follow his example, decided the success of the battle. In reward he received the district of Kojima in fief, and the title of Iyo no shugo "constable."

In 1199, after the death of Minamoto Yoritomo, Moritsuna shaved his head and took the name of Sainen.

In 1201 he defeated Jo Sukemori (-1202) in Kozuké.

Sasaki Takatsuna (1160-1214)

Son of Hideyoshi. He grew up with an aunt in Kyoto. He fought in the Genpei War (1180-1185) for the Minamoto.

In the bloody 1180 Battle of Ishibashi-yama (Sagami), Takatsuna saved the life of Minamoto Yoritomo (1147-1199), and was made shugo "constable" of Nagato.

In 1184, at the 2nd Battle of Uji (near Kyoto), in a legendary race, Takatsuna, mounted atop Yoritomo's white horse Ikezuki, was the first to cross the river, beating Kajiwara Kagesué, who was mounted atop Yoritomo's black horse Surusumi.

Takatsuna took a prominent part in the campaign of Minamoto Noriyori (1156-1193) against Kiso Yoshinaka (1154-1184). He was named governor of Bizen and Aki.

In 1195 he shaved his head, took the name Ryochi, and retired to Koya-san (Kii).

His military feats became the stuff of legend.

Sasaki Nobutsuna (-1242)

Son of Sadatsuna.

During the Jokyu War (1221) Nobutsuna fought on the side of the 3rd Kamakura Shikken Hojo Yasutoki (1183-1242), and was named kebiishi "chief of police," Omi no shugo "constable," etc. He retired to Koya-san (Kii).

Sasaki Takauji/Doyo (1306-1373)

Great-grandson of Nobutsuna. He was born in Omi. He briefly served the last ruling Kamakura Shikken Hojo Takatoki (1303-1333), then aided Ashikaga Takauji (1305-1358) in overthrowing the Kenmu Restoration (1333-1336), and establishing the Muromachi Shogunate.

During the Nanboku-cho Period (1336-1392) Takauji assisted at the 1348 Battle of Shijo-nawaté (southern Yamato) against Kusunoki Masatsura (1326-1348), at the 1356 investment of Mount Yoshino by Ashikaga Yoshiakira (1330-1367), and at all the campaigns against the Southern Dynasty.

Starting in 1354 Takauji directed the Mandokoro "Administrative Board."

Takauji served as shugo "constable" of six provinces, and held a number of other important positions. He was known for his waka and renga "collaborative" poetry. He is portrayed in the epic *Taiheiki* as a paragon of elegance and luxury, and as the quintessential military aristocrat.

Toward the end of his life he became a Buddhist monk with the name Doyo.

He is the ancestor of the Kyogoku and the Amako.

SUZUKI

Territory: Mikawa

Daimyo family, which in the 16th century lived at Asuké (Mikawa). They were dispossessed in 1571 by Takeda Shingen (1521-1573).

UENO

Ancient daimyo family descended from Ashikaga Yasuuji (13th century). It ceased to exist towards the end of the 14th century after faithfully serving the Ashikaga.

SHIBA

Territories: Echizen, Kozuké, Owari

Castles: Kanagasaki (Echizen), Takanosu (Kozuké), Somayama (Echizen), Kiyosu (Owari)

Daimyo family descended from the Seiwa-Genji Minamoto Yasuuji (13th century). Also called Bué from the district in Kyoto where the family resided.

During the Muromachi "Ashikaga" Period (1336-1573) the Shiba was one of the san-kan "three families" from which the Kyoto kanrei "Kyoto deputy Shogun" could be chosen. They held influence and territory in Echizen and Owari, to which they were shugo "constables."

At beginning of the Sengoku "Warring States" Period (1467-1573) the Shiba lost Echizen to the Asakura. By 1550 they were represented by Shiba Yoshimuné (1513-1554) of Kiyosu Castle (Owari), a figurehead behind which the Iwakura branch of the Oda ruled. When he was killed by Oda Nobumoto (1516-1555), the clan effectively came to an end.

Notable Ancestors

Shiba Ieuji (13th century)

Son of Yasuuji. At the end of the 13th century, he was the first to adopt the name Shiba.

Shiba Takatsuné (-1367)

Great-grandson of Ieuji. During the Nanboku-cho Period (1336-1392), he was Echizen no shugo "constable."

In 1335 Takatsuné joined the party of Ashikaga Takauji (1305-1358), aided in the defeat of the Imperial army at Také-no-shita (Suruga), and entered Kyoto.

In 1336 Takatsuné defeated Nitta Yoshiaki (-1338) and Wakiya Yoshisuké (1305-1340) at Uryu (Settsu).

In 1337, after the Siege of Kané-gasaki (Echizen), where Nitta Yoshisada (1301-1338) had intrenched himself, Takatsuné occupied the castle. In 1338 he also occupied Takanosu Castle (Kozuké), which was defended by Hata Tokiyoshi, who was slain there.

In 1338 Takatsuné was ordered by Ashikaga Takauji to attack Uryu Tamotsu at his fortress at Somayama (Echizen), but failed. Then, at the Siege of Kuromaru (Echizen), he was attacked by Nitta Yoshisada, but Hosokawa Akiuji (-1352), sent by Takauji, and the warrior-monks from the Heisen-ji came to his rescue, and Yoshisada was mortally wounded by an arrow in the battle.

In 1339 Takatsuné was again besieged at Kuromaru when the new Emperor Go-Murakami (1328-1368) sent Yoshisada's brother Wakiya Yoshisuké to lead another attack on the fortress. The siege succeeded, and he was forced to surrender.

In 1354 Tadatsuné, after his quarrels with Ashikaga Takauji, supported Ashikaga Tadafuyu (-1400), who having been defeated, took refuge in Echizen.

In 1362 Takatsuné reconciled with the 2nd Ashikaga Shogun Yoshiakira (1330-1367), and his son Yoshimasa was named shitsuji "deputy Shogun."

Peace did not last long: Takatsuné quarreled with Sasaki Takauji (1306-1373) and Akamatsu Norisuké (1314-1371). The Shogun Yoshiakira sent against him Sasaki Ujiyori (1326-1370) and Hatakeyama Yoshito (1331-1379), who besieged him in his castle of Somayama (Echizen). He held out for more than one year, but finally died of sickness during the siege.

Shiba Yoshimasa (1350-1410)

Son of Takatsuné. He is also known as a poet.

In 1362 Yoshimasa received the title of shitsuji "deputy Shogun." In 1379 the 3rd Ashikaga Shogun Yoshimitsu (1358-1408) changed it into that of Kyoto kanrei "Kyoto deputy Shogun," a position which he held until 1391, and again from 1393-1398. Favorite of the 4th Ashikaga Shogun Yoshimochi (1386-1428), he received the government of Echizen, Etchu, Noto, Shinano, Sado, and Wakasa.

Yoshimasa was firmly opposed to re-opening diplomatic relations with China.

Shiba Yoshitaké (-1452)

Died without an heir. His succession was disputed by Yoshikado and Yoshitoshi.

Shiba Yoshikado (-ca. 1480)

Son of Shibukawa Yoshino.

At the death of Yoshitaké, who passed without an heir, his cousin Shiba Yoshitoshi was appointed to succeed him, but the great vassals of the Shiba, the Kai, the Asakura, and the Oda refused to sanction this choice, and named Yoshikado to lead the clan. A war of succession ensued between the two rivals and their partisans.

In 1459 the 8th Ashikaga Shogun Yoshimasa (1435-1490) approved the nomination of Yoshikado, and gave orders that all the lands of the Shiba should be restored to him, whence Shiba Yoshitoshi, without relinquishing his claims, fled to Suo. In 1466 his cause came before the Court of Kyoto, and the Shogun, repealing his first decision, recognized Yoshitoshi as the legitimate heir to Yoshitaké. Yoshikado refused to submit, and appealed to his father-in-law Yamana Sozen (1404-1473). Yoshimasa alarmed, again abandoned Yoshitoshi and named Yoshikado Kyoto kanrei "Kyoto deputy Shogun."

When the Onin War (1467-1477) broke out, Yoshikado naturally sided with Sozen. After peace was restored, he retired to Kiyosu Castle (Owari).

Shiba Yoshitoshi (1430-1490)

Son of Ono Yoshikané. He had been adopted by Shiba Mochitané, uncle to Yoshitaké.

In 1452, at the death of Yoshitaké, the family named Yoshitoshi as his successor, but the great vassals refused to acknowledge him, and began to divide the large domain of their lord among themselves: the Oda took Owari; the Asakura, Echizen; the Kai, Totomi; etc. Shiba Yoshikado appealed to the 8th Ashikaga Shogun Yoshimasa (1436-1490), to whom the rebel vassals deputed Isé Sadachika (1417-1473) to explain their conduct, based, they said, on the incapacity of Yoshitoshi. The

Shogun accepted their reasons, and their candidate Yoshikado.

Yoshitoshi now went to Suo to ask help of Ouchi Norihiro (-1465). Isé Sadachika, having married the sister of Yoshitoshi's wife, returned to the Shogun to plead the cause of his new ally. In 1466 Yoshitoshi's rights were admitted. Shiba Yoshikado, helped by his father-in-law Yamana Sozen (1404-1473), levied an army and marched against Kyoto. Yoshitoshi fled to the north, and when the Onin War (1467-1477) broke out, he naturally sided with Hosokawa Katsumoto (1430-1473), Sozen's adversary.

In 1475 he retired to Owari, but the Oda had already occupied the greater portion of the province, of which they had been shugo-dai "deputy constable" for several generations, and Yoshitoshi, finding himself powerless to regain his domain, fled to Echizen, where he died.

Shiba Yoshisato (-1521)

Grandson of Yoshikado. He tried in vain to regain authority over his vassals, of whom three had gradually become independent in the domains which had been confided to them.

Shiba Yoshimuné (1513-1554)

Son of Yoshisato. He was the final head of the clan. He was nominally shugo "contable" of Owari, and resided at Kiyosu Castle, but Oda Nobutomo (1516-1555) ruled behind him.

Following the death of Oda Nobuhidé (1510-1551), his son Nobunaga (1534-1582) was appointed heir to his late father's position. Nobutomo, who was of the Iwakura Oda faction of the clan, and was Nobunaga's uncle, planned to assassinate him. Yoshimuné learned of these designs, and reported them to Nobunaga, with whom he had a secret relationship. Nobutomo caught wind of this hidden activity of Yoshimuné, and subsequently attacked and took Kiyosu Castle. Yoshimuné then killed himself.

Shiba Yoshikané (1540-1580)

Son of Yoshimuné.

In 1554, after the death of his father, Yoshikané asked the help of Oda Nobunaga (1534-1582) against the latter's uncle Oda Nobutomo (1516-1555), who had taken Kiyosu Castle (Owari) from his father. In 1555 Nobunaga retook the castle and captured his uncle, forcing him to commit suicide. Yoshikané then resided at Kiyosu.

Soon after Yoshikané tried to shake off the authority of Nobunaga, but was obliged to leave Owari, passed into Isé, and afterwards into Kawachi, where he died, almost in misery.

With him, the Shiba, which for over two centuries had been so powerful, disappears from history.

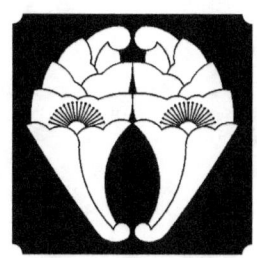

TAWARA

Territory: Bungo

Daimyo family which from the 13th to the 16th century resided at Aki (Bungo), but was eventually dispossessed by Otomo Sorin (1530-1587).

NOTABLE ANCESTORS

Tawara Chikataka (16th century)

At the 1578 Battle of Mimigawa (Hyuga) Chikataka led the army of his brother-in-law Otomo Sorin (1530-1587) against Shimazu Yoshihisa (1533-1611) and his brother Iehisa (1547-1587). Chikataka sent the Otomo army in a frontal attack that was repulsed after some bitter fighting. The Otomo were quickly routed, with thousands killed and thousands of others scattered, heralding the decline of that clan.

Takeda (Aki)

Territory: Aki
Castle: Kanayama (Aki)

A cadet branch of the Takeda of Kai, descended from the Emperor Seiwa (850-880) and the Seiwa-Genji Minamoto. The Takeda of Wakasa was a cadet branch of the Takeda of Aki.

Their principal fortress was Kanayama Castle (Aki) on Mount Takeda, a castle built by Takeda Nobumuné in the late Kamakura Period (1185-1333) near Hiroshima.

Nobutaké (-1362) was the last Takeda shugo "constable" of the three provinces of Kai, Aki, and Wakasa. His elder son Nobunari received Kai, and the younger Ujinobu received Aki and Wakasa.

During the Muromachi "Ashikaga" Period (1336-1573) the clan supported the Ashikaga against the Southern Dynasty, and sided the Hosokawa during the Onin War (1467-1477)

In the early Sengoku "Warring States" Period (1467-1573) they were allied first with the Ouchi, and then with the Amako.

Their fortunes declined after the 7th lord of the clan Motoshigé was killed fighting the Mori at the 1517 Battle of Arita-Nakaidé (Aki). In 1535 his heir Mitsuo died suddenly. In 1541 Mitsuo's adopted son Nobuzané quit Kanayama when it was threatened by the Mori and Ouchi in the wake of the Amako's defeat at the Siege of Yoshida-Koriyama (Aki). Nobuzané fled to Izumo, and Kanayama surrendered.

Notable Ancestors

Takeda Motoshigé (-1517)

7th lord of the Takeda of Aki. He held Kanayama Castle (Aki).

At the end of the 15th century the Takeda had suffered a period of internal unrest and as a result were forced to accept the authority of the encroaching Ouchi. In 1508 Motoshigé was himself married to an adopted daughter of Ouchi Yoshioki (1477-1528), and joined his expedition to Kyoto in support of the deposed 10th Ashikaga Shogun Yoshitané (1466-1523).

Motoshigé later returned to Aki and cut his ties with Ouchi Yoshioki, who remained in Kyoto with the bulk of his army. He divorced Yoshioki's daughter, and married a daughter of Amako Hisayuki, thus sealing an alliance with that family.

In 1517 Motoshigé took advantage of Ouchi Yoshioki's involvement in Kyoto, and the death of Mori Okimoto (1492-1516), to attack Arita Castle (Aki) of the Kikkawa. A few weeks later he dispatched a raid into Mori territory, and set fire to houses in Tajihi.

Mori Motonari (1497-1571) then allied with the Kikkawa and the Kobayakawa, and moved to relieve Arita with support from the Awaya, the Fukuhara, the Inoué, the Kuchiba, the Watanabé, and his younger brother Mototsuna. They force marched towards Arita Castle and on the way encountered the Takeda vanguard, commanded by Kumagai Motonao, who was struck and killed by an arrow.

Motoshigé himself brought the remainder of his army to attack Mori Motonari, and, at the Battle of Arita-Nakaidé (Aki), encountered the Mori and the Kikkawa. Motoshigé was pressing his enemy forces hard, but was struck by an arrow, and fell dead from his horse. The Takeda broke and retreated, leaving Motonari the victor.

TOGASHI

Territory: Kaga
Castle: Takao (Kaga)

Ancient daimyo family descended from the Chinjufu-shogun "Defender of the North" Fujiwara Toshihito (10th century).

NOTABLE ANCESTORS

Togashi Tadayori (11th century)
Great-grandson of Toshihito. He received the title of Kaga no suké.

Togashi Iekuni (11th century)
Son of Tadayori. He built Takao Castle at Togashi (Kaga). He was also known under the title of Kaga no suké or Togashi no suké, which he transmitted to his descendants.

Togashi Ienao (late 12th century)
Great-grandson of Iekuni. He served Minamoto Yoritomo (1147-1199).

Togashi Takaié (early 14th century)
Sided with Ashikaga Takauji (1305-1358) and aided the Northern Dynasty.

Togashi Yasutaka (-1504)
Uncle to Masachika.
In 1487 Yasutaka lent his support to the Ikko uprising against Masachika from Kyoto, and was allowed to act as nominal shugo constable" of Kaga. Nonetheless he did not actually go to live in the province until 1493, when he was forced to flee the capital by Hosokawa Masamoto (1466-1507).
Yasutaka attempted to aid the ousted 10th Ashikaga Shogun Yoshitané (1466-1523) in his bid to reclaim the capital, and to this end clashed with the Asakura on a number of occasions.

Togashi Masachika (-1488)
Was Kaga no shugo "constable."
At the time of the Onin War (1467-1477) Masachika sided with Hosokawa Katsumoto (1430-1473).
Masachika worked to reassert Togashi authority in Kaga, which had been lost in 1447 to two vassal families, the Moto'ori and the Yamagawa. In 1473 he reclaimed Kaga with the assistance of Asakura Toshikagé (1428-1481) and Kaga's Ikko sects, defeating his younger brother Kochiyo. Within a year Masachika and the Ikko had grown hostile, although all initial Ikko uprisings fizzled.
In 1487 Masachika chose to honor a call by the 9th Ashikaga Shogun Yoshihisa (1465-1489) to give battle to Rokkaku Takayori (-1520). He led an army out of Kaga, and in his absence the Ikko rebelled once again, this time drawing on support from Togashi house members. In 1488 he returned and, despite some initial victories, was besieged in his castle of Togashi (Kaga) and ultimately forced to flee to Etchu, where he killed himself.
He was the last scion of that family which had governed Kaga for four centuries.

WADA

Territory: Izumi

Ancient daimyo family of Izumi, related to the Kusunoki.

NOTABLE ANCESTORS

Wada Masauji (-1336)
Junior brother of Kusunoki Masashigé (1294-1336), who he fought with for the Southern Dynasty, and died at the Battle of Minato-gawa (Settsu).

Wada Sukehidé/Kenshu (14th century)
Son of Masauji. He was companion-in-arms to his cousin Kusunoki Masatsura (1326-1348).

Wada Masatomo (-1352)
Brother of Sukehidé. He distinguished himself by his wars against the Ko brothers Moronao (-1351) and Morofuyu (-1351).

Wada Masataké (14th century)
In 1360 Masataké supported the cause of the Emperor Go-Murakami (1328-1368), and fought against the 2nd Ashikaga Shogun Yoshiakira (1330-1368) and Sasaki Hidéaki, whom he defeated and killed.
In 1369, when Kusunoki Masanori (-1390) joined the Northern Dynasty, Masataké fought against him, remaining faithful to the Southern Dynasty.

Wada Masatada (14th century)
In 1352 Masatada, with Kusunoki Masanori (-1390) and Hosokawa Akiuji (-1352), became master of Kyoto and reinstalled the Emperor Go-Murakami (1328-1368), but soon after the 2nd Ashikaga Shogun Yoshiakira (1330-1368) returned with a large body of men, whom he levied in Omi, and attacked him on the Otoko-yama (Kyoto). Masatada died during the battle. He was then only 17 years old.

URAKAMI

Territories: Harima, Mimasaka, Bizen

Ancient daimyo family descended from Ki Kosami (late 8th century).

During the Sengoku "Warring States" Period (1467-1573) they settled in Bizen.

The death of Urakami Norimuné in 1502 resulted in Matsuda Motokatsu seizing the opportunity to lead a full-scale assault on the clan. One of their major retainers at the time was Ukita Yoshiié (-1534), who led an attack against the Matsuda.

Notable Ancestors

Urakami Norimuné (-1502)

Was a vassal of the Akamatsu.

In 1468, during the Onin War (1466-1477), Norimuné sided with Yamana Sozen (1404-1473), but was defeated by the Hosokawa.

Norimuné then went to Kyoto, where his lord Akamatsu Masanori (-1494), who was at the head of the samurai-dokoro "board of retainers," made him shoshidai "deputy governor."

In 1494, when Akamatsu Masanori died, he was succeeded by his son Masamura, who was then only a child, and Norimuné administrated his domain.

Urakami Muramuné (-1524)

Son of Munesuké, and grandson of Norimuné. At the time of the ruin of the Akamatsu, he received Harima and Mimasaka.

Urakami Masamura vainly tried to regain possession of his domain, but in 1505 he was defeated, and in 1522 put to death by Muramuné.

In 1523 some former kerai "vassals" of the Akamatsu attempted to revolt, but were subjugated by Ukita Yoshiié (-1534). Later that year Muramuné assisted Hosokawa Takakuni (1484-1531), besieged and took Takamatsu Castle (Sanuki) from Hosokawa Harumoto (1519-1563), and gave it to Takakuni.

In 1524 Hosokawa Harumoto returned with a large army and defeated Hosokawa Takakuni at the Battle of Imamiya (Settsu), where Muramuné was killed.

Urakami Munekagé (mid-16th century)

Son of Muramuné. He nominally held much of Bizen and ruled from Tenjin-yama.

As rival of the Akamatsu to the west and the Amako to the north, to maintain order in Bizen, Munekagé was compelled to rely on Ukita Naoié, who grew in strength and began to find pretexts to eliminate the clan's other retainers. Munekagé was ultimately forced to flee his lands to Sanuki, and the Ukita assumed control of Bizen. Henceforth the Urakami disappears from history.

WAKIYA

Territories: Suruga, Iyo

Branch of the Nitta family, which during the Nanbokucho Period (1336-1392) distinguished itself by its fidelity to the Southern Dynasty.

Notable Ancestors

Wakiya Yoshisuké (-1340)

See Nitta Yoshisuké.

Wakiya Yoshiharu (mid-14th century)

Son of Yoshisuké. He was taught the use of arms under his father's direction.

In 1337, at the age of 13, Yoshiharu assisted at the Battle of Také-no-shita (Suruga), where his father was defeated by Ashikaga Takauji (1305-1358).

Yoshiharu fought in Echizen against Shiba Takatsuné (-1367), and in 1340, after the death of his father, fixed his abode in Shimotsuké.

In 1345 Yoshiharu joined Kojima Takanori to be able to take the field again, but was defeated and fled to Shinano.

In 1352, with the help of his cousins Nitta Yoshioki (-1358) and Nitta Yoshimuné (1332-1368), Yoshiharu took Kamakura (Sagami), but was soon after expelled from that place by Ashikaga Takauji. He then retired to Echigo.

In 1368, being again defeated, he retired to Dewa, and from that time he and his family is lost to history.

Momoyama Period

AKECHI

Revenues: 100,000 koku
Castles: Akechi (Mino), Sakamoto (Omi), Yakami (Tanba)

Ancient family descended from Toki Yorimoto, who was descended from the Seiwa-Genji Minamoto Yorimitsu (944-1021).

The Akechi thrived around the latter part of the Sengoku "Warring States" Period (1467-1573). Until 1540 they served under the Toki, when that clan fell to the Saito.

The Akechi became powerful under the leadership of Oda Nobunaga (1534-1582), who Akechi Mitsuhidé (1528-1582) served as general. Mitsuhidé however betrayed his master, trapping him at the Honno-ji (Kyoto), and forcing him to commit suicide. Twelve days later, Mitsuhidé was slain at the Battle of Yamazaki (Yamashiro) by Hashiba (later Toyotomi) Hideyoshi (1536-1598), and the clan fell from prominence.

Notable Ancestors

Akechi Mitsukuni/Mitsutsuna (-1538)

Son of Mitsutsugu. Served as senior retainer under the Toki, and resided at Akechi Castle (Mino).

Akechi Mitsuyasu (-1552)

Son of Yorihisa. Held Akechi Castle (Mino), and served the Toki. His daughter was married to Saito Dosan (1494-1556).

Akechi Mitsuhidé (1528-1582)

Son of Mitsukuni. Born in Mino. Middle named Jubei. Also called Koreto Hyuga no kami from his title. He at first served the Saito of Mino, and then Asakura Ujikagé (1449-1486) of Echizen. He was the father of Tama, who married Hosokawa Tadaoki (1563-1646), and in 1587, when she was baptized, received the Christian name Gracia. A cultured man, Mitsuhidé was a great lover of cha-no-yu "tea ceremony," and a poet of note.

As the head of his kerai "vassals," Mitsuhidé entered the service of Ashikaga Yoshiaki (1537-1597), who was later the 15th and last Muromachi Shogun, and Asakura Yoshikagé (1533-1573), and then that of Nagaoka (Hosokawa) Fujitaka (1534-1610).

In 1566 Mitsuhidé retired to Gifu (Mino), offered his services to Oda Nobunaga (1534-1582), and took rank among his officers.

In 1571 Mitsuhidé received from Nobunaga two districts and Sakamoto-jo (Omi) in fief, with a revenue of 100,000 koku, and the title of Hyuga no kami. He also defeated the Isshiki of Tango, and received Kamiyama Castle and Tanba.

In 1575 Mitsuhidé received the mission to pacify Tanba. He besieged Hatano Hideharu (1541-1579) in Yakami Castle, but as the siege was protracted, in 1579 he took Hideharu's mother as a hostage, upon which the latter surrendered, only to be crucified by order of Nobunaga. To avenge their lord, the retainers of Hideharu kidnapped Mitsuhidé's mother and executed her. Mitsuhidé then destroyed the castle and put all its inmates to death. Moreover he conceived a mortal hatred against Nobunaga, on whom he swore to wreak vengeance. The situation was fueled when Nobunaga directed several public insults at Mitsuhidé.

Mitsuhidé waited five years for a favorable occasion. In 1582 Hashiba (later Toyotomi) Hideyoshi (1536-1598), who was fighting in the San'yodo against Mori Terumoto (1553-1625), asked Nobunaga for reinforcements. Before he personally started, Nobunaga sent orders to Mitsuhidé to muster his men, and to lead them in all haste to Hideyoshi. Mitsuhidé assembled his troops, but instead of directing them towards Hideyoshi, he marched them upon Kyoto, entered the city and, with his cousin Akechi Mitsuharu (1537-1582), besieged Nobunaga in the Honno-ji. Wounded by an arrow, and judging that resistance was useless, Nobunaga set fire to the temple and committed seppuku. His eldest son Nobutada (1557-1582), cut off from all help in the Nijo Palace (Kyoto), met the same fate. Thence Mitsuhidé hastened to Azuchi Castle (Omi), which he gave up to plunder and put to flame.

Mitsuhidé then returned to Kyoto, where he obtained an audience with the Emperor, who received him warmly. He styled himself Shogun, and appointed a shoshidai "deputy Shogun," a machi-bugyo "city magistrate," etc. To secure for himself the public sympathy, he exempted the citizens of Kyoto from taxes, and made liberal grants to the principal temples.

Meanwhile Hideyoshi, on hearing of these events, immediately made peace and disengaged with the Mori, and forced march towards the capital at a rapid pace, catching Mitsuhidé off guard. At the Battle of Yamazaki (border of Settsu and Yamashiro), he was completely beaten, and he fled to Sakamoto-jo, which was held by his cousin Akechi Mitsuyasu. The castle

Akechi Mitsuhidé

was soon reduced by Hori Hidemasa (1553-1590), and two days later he was massacred by a mob in the village of Ogurusu, reportedly by a peasant warrior. Only 13 days had elapsed from the time he began to muster troops against Nobunaga, hence he is known as the Jusan-kubo "13-day Shogun."

Akechi Mitsuharu (1537-1582)

Son of Mitsuyasu, and cousin to Mitsuhidé. He followed the fortune of the latter. He was also known as Hidemitsu or Mitsutoshi.

Mitsuharu endeavored to deter Mitsuhidé from plotting against Oda Nobunaga (1534-1582), and although his advice was not heeded, in 1582 he entered Kyoto with his cousin, besieged the Honno-ji (Kyoto), and himself buried the head of Nobunaga.

During the Battle of Yamazaki (border of Settsu and Yamashiro), Mitsuharu was at Azuchi Castle (Omi), and arrived too late to prevent disaster and save his cousin Mitsuhidé.

At Uchidé-hama, near Otsu (Omi), Mitsuharu met the troops of Hori Hidemasa (1553-1590) and was defeated. He escaped by famously crossing the narrow southern neck of Lake Biwa alone on his illustrious horse Okagé. He then returned to Sakamoto-jo (Omi), where he was besieged by the Hori. Mitsuharu slaughtered his whole family as well as the wife and children of Mitsuhidé, and set fire to the castle. He then nobly committed seppuku while writing a poem on a door with blood from his abdomen.

Akechi Mitsutada (1540-1582)

Cousin and retainer of Mitsuhidé. In 1577 he was given Yakami Castle (Tanba) after the destruction of the Hatano.

In 1582, when Mitsuhidé treacherously attacked Oda Nobunaga (1534-1582) at the Honno-ji (Kyoto), Mitsutada participated in the assault on Nijo Palace (Kyoto), where Nobunaga's heir Nobutada (1557-1582) was holed up. During the battle he was wounded by gunfire and was put under medical attention at a nearby temple. He committed seppuku when he learned of Mitsuhidé's defeat at the Battle of Yamazaki (border of Settsu and Yamashiro).

Akechi Mitsuyoshi (1569-1582)

Eldest son of Mitsuhidé.

In 1582 Mitsuyoshi was defeated at the Battle of Yamazaki (border of Settsu and Yamashiro) by Nakagawa Kiyohidé (1556-1583) and Dom Justo Takayama (1552-1615), and committed seppuku.

AKAZA

Revenues: 20,000 koku
Territory: Imajo (Echizen)

Notable Ancestors

Akaza Shichiroémon (-1582)

At first a vassal of Saito Tatsuoki (1548-1573) of Mino, and when he died Shichiroémon passed his loyalties onto Oda Nobunaga (1534-1582).

In 1569 Shichiroémon served with distinction in the battles waged against the Miyoshi, and was awarded lands in Echizen.

In 1582, at the time of the Incident at Honno-ji (Kyoto) where Oda Nobunaga lost his life, Shichiroémon was killed at Nijo Gosho (Kyoto).

Akaza Naoyasu (-1606)

Also known as Kyubei, and also Yoshiié. He held the title of Bingo no kami, and served Toyotomi Hideyoshi (1536-1598).

During the 1590 Siege of Odawara, Naoyasu took part in capturing Iwatsuki Castle (Musashi) and Oshi Castle (Musashi), and was given 20,000 koku. After that, based in Imajo (Echizen), he supported Kobayakawa Hideaki (1577-1602) and Horio Yoshiharu (1542-1611).

At the 1600 Battle of Seki-ga-hara (Mino), Naoyasu served under the command of Otani Yoshitsugu (1559-1600), who led a part of the force of Ishida Mitsunari (1560-1600). However, taking advantage of the betrayal of Kobayakawa Hideaki (1577-1602), he switched sides with Wakisaka Yasuharu (1554-1626), Kutsuki Mototsuna (1549-1632), and Ogawa Suketada (1549-1601). Together, they defeated Yoshitsugu's force. After the battle Tokugawa Ieyasu (1543-1616) did not give Naoyasu credit, and seized his domain. Naoyasu then became a retainer of Maeda Toshinaga (1562-1614) with a stipend of 7,000 koku.

In 1606, looking over the flooded Daimon River (Etchu), he fell off a horse, and drowned.

Naoyasu was survived by his son Takaharu, who changed his family name to Nagahara, and became a retainer of the Maeda of Kaga, where they remained.

Amako

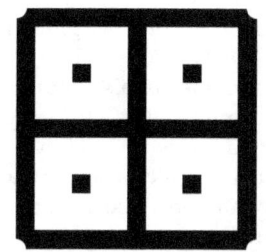

Territories: Inaba, Hoki, Izumo, Iwami, Oki, Harima, Mimasaka, Bizen, Bitchu, Bingo, Aki

Castles: Gassan-Toda Castle (Izumo)

Family of daimyo descended from the Emperor Uda (868-897) through the Rokkaku branch of the Sasaki.

The Amako became powerful during the Muromachi "Ashikaga" Period (1336-1573) when in 1486 Amako Tsunehisa conquered Izumo and Oki.

During the Sengoku "Warring States" Period (1467-1573), the clan, from their headquarters at Gassan-Toda Castle (Izumo), challenged with mixed results the Ouchi, and later the Mori, who had been among their vassals. In 1566 they were destroyed as daimyo by Mori Motonari (1497-1571) when they lost their castle.

Amako Katsuhisa later tried to bring back the glory of his clan by joining Oda Nobunaga (1534-1582), but besieged in Kozuki Castle (Harima), he committed suicide, and the Amako faded from history.

The clan name is also often pronounced Amago.

Notable Ancestors

Amako Takahisa (14th century)

Grandson of Sasaki Takauji (1306-1373), was the first to take the name of Amako "nun's child," because, having lost his parents at the age of 3, he was brought up by an ama "nun."

Takahisa took Tomita Castle (Izumo) for the shugo "constable" Kyogoku.

Amako Tsunehisa (1458-1541)

Eldest son of Kiyosada, grandson of Mochihisa, and great-grandson of Takahisa. He inherited from his father the office of Izumo no shugo "constable," and resided at Gassan-Toda Castle. At the time of the Onin War (1467-1477) he started as a vassal of the Kyogoku, and secured the Amako's status as daimyo.

In 1484 Tsunehisa, along with his father, was expelled from Gassan-Toda by Kyogoku Masatsuné, and was forced to wander while he gained the support of Yamanaka Katsushigé and other Amako allies.

Meanwhile Gassan-Toda Castle came into the possession of the Enya.

Amako Tsunehisa

During the 1486 New Year's celebration, Tsunehisa snuck in a handful of men, killed the lord of the castle and his family, and reclaimed the place as his own.

In 1508, with Ouchi Yoshioki (1477-1528) of Suo heading to Kyoto, Tsunehisa secretly communicated with the koku-jin "regional clans" to counter the powerful Ouchi.

In 1513, as the Amako were moving against the Hoki, Tsunehisa's eldest son and successor Masahisa was killed by an arrow while besieging Sakurai Soteki, who had rebelled. Tsunehisa was overcome by grief, and thought of retiring in favor his brother Hisayuki, but gave up the notion when the latter refused to consider it.

In 1518 Tsunehisa marched against Ouchi Yoshioki, but in 1522 the 12th Ashikaga Shogun Yoshiharu (1510-1550) brought about peace.

In 1522 Ouchi Yoshioki invaded Aki, and the war recommenced. In 1524 Tsunehisa had Kagami-yama Castle (Omi), held by Kurata Fusanobu, besieged by Mori Motonari (1497-1571), who recaptured the place, but he himself was repulsed before Kanayama Castle (Aki) by Ouchi Yoshitaka (1507-1551).

In 1528, when Ouchi Yoshioki died, Tsunehisa took the opportunity to expand Amako influence eastward into Iwami and its valuable silver mines. By this time, Tsunehisa ruled eleven provinces: Inaba, Hoki, Izumo, Iwami, Oki, Harima, Mimasaka, Bizen, Bitchu, Bingo, and Aki.

In 1532, encouraged by retainers, Tsunehisa's 3rd son Okihisa rebelled over the clan succession. He was defeated by an army led by his uncle Haruyuki, and was obliged to flee to Bingo, where he committed suicide. In 1538, left without a successor, Tsunehisa handed over the Ouchi clan lead-

---

Amako Family Tree

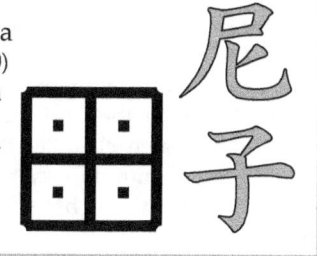

Uda-tenno (867-931)
: Minamoto Masanobu (920-993)
: Sasaki Takauji (1306-1373)
: Sasaki Takahidé
: Takahisa (14th century) — Mochihisa — Kiyosada — ┬ Tsunehisa (1458-1541) ┬ Masahisa (1488-1518) — Haruhisa (1514-1561) ┬ Yoshihisa (1536-1610)
                                                                                                                                  └ Hidehisa
                                                                  ├ Kunihisa (1492-1554) — Masahisa (-1554) — Katsuhisa (1553-1578)
                                                                  └ Okihisa (1497-1534)
                                                  └ Hisayuki (-1541)

ership to his grandson Haruhisa, the son of Masahisa, but continued to make the most important decisions.

In 1540 Tsunehisa attacked Mori Motonori, hitherto a loyal retainer of the Amako who had passed over to the Ouchi, but was defeated. In the next year he died of illness.

Tsunehisa was a noted strategist and a competent ruler who was overshadowed by later warlords. He left as legacy the Kitsugi Grand Shrine (Izumo), which he had built in the 1530s.

Amako Hisayuki (-1541)

2nd son of Kiyosada, and younger brother to Tsunehisa. He was Shimotsuké no kami. He was considered a capable, if cautious, leader.

In 1486, when Tsunehisa was banished from Gassan-Toda Castle (Izumo) after plotting to split from the Kyogoku, Hisayuki, who had not yet come of age, was at length placed under the protection of the Takeda at Kanayama Castle (Aki), where he was given his manhood ceremony. When Tsunehisa retook Gassan-Toda Castle, Hisayuki returned and went on to become a valuable asset to his brother.

In 1516 Hisayuki married the daughter of Takeda Motoshigé when the latter broke off ties to the Ouchi and allied with the Amako.

In 1525 Hisayuki led a force to assist the Takeda when they were threatened by the Ouchi.

In 1540, after Tsunehisa had retired in favor of his grandson Haruhisa, the latter conceived of a great campaign to destroy the Mori of Aki. When a council of the Amako retainers was called to discuss the plan, all favored the attack except Hisayuki, who considered the risks to be too great, arguing that a more methodical approach was needed to defeat the enemy leader Mori Motonari (1497-1571). For his troubles he was derided by Tsunehisa as a coward and publicly humiliated. He and his nephew Kunihisa were dispatched against the Shishido of Aki in what was a secondary operation of the coming campaign. After the long Siege of Koriyama, the Amako was forced to retreat, and as they were withdrawing, they were attacked by the Mori and the Ouchi, causing such chaos in the ranks that Haruhisa himself became threatened. Hisayuki threw himself into the fray and was killed.

Amako Masahisa (1488-1518)

Son of Tsunehisa. He was slain attacking the castle of rebellious Amako retainer Sakurai Soteki.

Amako Kunihisa (1492-1554)

Son of Tsunehisa. Known in his youth as Magoshiro. He married the daughter of Amako retainer Tako Tadashigé. He was Kii no kami.

Kunihisa was a principle Amako general while his father was alive, leading a force that came to be nicknamed the Shingu Army after the valley to the northeast of Gassan-Toda (Izumo) where his mansion was located.

In 1518 Kunihisa acted as the guardian for Amako Haruhisa after his father Masahisa was killed.

During the 1520s Kunihisa fought under his father's campaigns in Aki and Bingo.

In 1540 Kunihisa fought alongside Haruhisa at the Siege of Koriyama (Aki). He also joined his nephew Haruhisa to fight against Takeda Tsunenobu.

In 1544 Kunihisa defeated a Mori army.

In 1546, at the hard-fought Battle of Hashizu-gawa, Kunihisa lost his 2nd son Toyohisa fighting against Takeda Kuninobu of Inaba.

Despite his many services, Kunihisa came to be distrusted by Haruhisa, his nephew and the daimyo after Tsunehisa's death. In 1554 Kunihisa was executed at Gassan-Toda by Haruhisa on the suspicion of treason, along with his eldest son Sanehisa and two grandsons, as well as a number of his associates. His 3rd son Takahisa committed suicide the next day. His death was a contributing factor in the eventual fall of the Amako.

Kunihisa was known for his arrogance, often looking down on those who did not do well on the battlefield, and was obnoxious from time to time.

He was the grandfather of Amako Katsuhigé.

Amako Okihisa (1497-1534)

3rd son of Tsunehisa. At first called Genshiro. He received in fief Enya (east Izumo) and used Mount Yogai for his castle. He also called himself Enya Okihisa for the domain he ruled. Like his elder brother Kunihisa, he was skilled in warfare.

In 1532, not satisfied with the size of domain, Okihisa revolted against his father, suspecting Kamei Hidetsuna, his father's chief advisor, of plotting against him. The Amako split into two factions, and Hidetsuna's younger brother Toshitsuna died fighting for Okihisa, who was driven out of Enya.

He committed seppuku when he realized that he would never be able to return to his clan.

Amako Masahisa (-1554)

Son of Kunihisa.

NOTE: There are two Amako Masahisa: one is Tsunehisa's son, the other is his grandson by Kunihisa.

Amako Akihisa/Haruhisa (1514-1561)

Eldest son of Masahisa, and grandson of the legendary Tsunehisa. Initially named Akihisa. When his father died, he was placed in the care of his uncle Kunihisa, who acted as his guardian until he came of age.

In 1536 Akihisa invaded the domains of Ouchi Yoshitaka (1507-1551) when the latter, having been appointed Dazai-daini "deputy governor of Kyushu," crossed over to the island, but he was repelled by Sué Takafusa (later Sué Harukata).

In 1537 Akihisa became the head of the Amako after his grandfather stepped down in the wake of the revolt and death of his uncle Okihisa.

Akihisa then took the silver mines of Iwami from the Ouchi. In 1539 he lost them, and in 1541 retook them.

Akihisa expanded Amako influence eastward, launching a series of invasions to expand his domain. In 1538 he marched as far as Harima, and fought the Akamatsu at Ojio and Akashi castles.

The 1540 Siege of Koriyama (Aki) against Mori Motonari (1497-1571), however, ended in a humiliating de-

Amako Akihisa

Azuchi-Momoyama Period – Amako

feat, and many of his retainers defected and passed over to the service of the Ouchi, believing that Akihisa's days were numbered. His grandfather died the next year, and Ouchi Yoshitaka (1507-1551) launched a counterattack to finish the Amako. Haruhisa recruited those retainers who had defected earlier, and after gathering enough troops, managed to repel the invasion. From this point, Akihisa worked to secure his footing and control of Izumo, Hoki, Mimasaka, and Oki.

In 1541 he changed his name to Haruhisa when the 12th Ashikaga Shogun Yoshiharu (1510-1550) offered to let him use a kanji from his name.

In the 1542-1543 Siege of Gassan-Toda (Izumo), Haruhisa was able to resist the Ouchi efforts to bring down the castle.

In 1552, after Yoshitaka was killed when Sué Harukata (1521-1555) rebelled, the Muromachi Shogunate offered Haruhisa lordship over eight domains: Izumo, Bingo, Bizen, Bittchu, Hoki, Inaba, Mimasaka, and Oki. It was during this period that the Amako enjoyed their widest influence.

In 1553, however, the Eda of Bingo surrendered to Mori Motonari. Haruhisa led a force to assist them, but arrived too late.

In 1554 Haruhisa captured Mimasaka and 17 castles in Harima.

To solidify his control of the clan, Haruhisa killed his uncle Kunihisa, as well as those retainers under him, which resulted in a serious shortage of battle-proven leaders.

When Sué Harukata lost against Mori Motonari, dying in the 1555 Battle of Itsuku-shima (Aki), Haruhisa saw an opportunity to claim Iwami, and making an alliance with the Ogasawara of Iwami, moved to claim the Omori Silver Mine. Motonari launched a counterattack, and both clashed in a string of battles with Motonari seizing the eastern part of the province. In 1561 Haruhisa collapsed in Gassan-Toda Castle while engaged in a battle and died.

Amako Katsuhisa (1553-1578)

Youngest son of Masahisa, and grandson of Kunihisa. As his father, grandfather, and two elder brothers were executed on orders by Amako Haruhisa when he was still an infant, he was spirited away, and at length became a Buddhist monk in Kyoto.

Katsuhisa struggled incessantly against the Mori, conquered Tajima, and, with the aid of Ukita Naoié (1529-1582), subdued all of the San'indo.

In 1568, after the Amako were overthrown by Mori Motonari (1497-1571), Katsuhisa was supported by the legendary clan vassal Yamanaka Yukimori (1544-1578) in the Izumo-Bitchu area against the Mori, but failed to make any lasting gains.

In 1570 Katsuhisa was defeated by Mori Terumoto (1553-1625) at Nunobé-yama (Izumo) and fled to Oki. On his return to Izumo he expelled Yamanaka Yukimasu and Yamana Toyokuni (1548-1626), who had invaded the province, and reconquered Tajima and Inaba.

Katsuhisa next allied with Oda Nobunaga (1534-1582), who by 1577 was at war with the Mori and pressing westward.

In 1578, entrusted with the guard of Kozuki Castle (Harima) against the Mori by Hashiba (later Toyotomi) Hideyoshi (1536-1598), Katsuhisa was besieged and defeated by Kikkawa Motoharu (1530-1586) and Kobayakawa Takakagé (1533-1597), and put an end to his own life in exchange for the lives of his men. The Amako thereafter disappeared from the political map.

Amako Yoshihisa (1536-1610)

2nd son of Haruhisa. His childhood name was Saburo-shiro.

In 1561, when his father died, Yoshihisa became the head of the clan, and continued the fight against the Mori.

In 1563 Yoshihisa listened with joy to the overtures of Otomo Sorin (1530-1587), who proposed to conquer and divide between themselves the domain of the Mori. He attacked Mori Motonari (1497-1571) at once but was defeated. He then lost Shiga Castle (Omi).

In 1565 Yoshihisa was besieged by a powerful Mori army in his castle of Gassan-Toda (Izumo), but held out valiantly. In 1566, having executed his bravest officer Uyama Hisakané, erroneously accused of conniving with the enemy, he estranged the affections of his remaining troops, and many deserted. Faced with starvation, and perceiving that further resistance was impossible, he surrendered to Mori Motonari.

Yoshihisa was held captive at the Enmei-ji (Aki), where in 1566 he shaved his head and took the name Yurin. He remained under confinement with his younger brothers Tomohisa and Hidehisa for the following 16 years.

When Mori Terumoto (1553-1625) succeeded as head of his clan, Yoshihisa became his retainer. He was allowed an income of some 570 koku, and later moved to Nagato, where his his income was increased to around 1,300 koku.

He was very fat and short, had long hair, and wore ragged clothes; but looked very young when he died.

With him the Amako family disappeared from history.

Azuchi-Momoyama Period – Asai

ASAI

Territory: Omi
Castle: Odani (Omi)

Family descending from the Fujiwara. They were at first vassals to the Kyogoku (Sasaki) in Omi, and after some time made itself independent.

In 1516 the Asai rebelled against the Kyogoku. The clan struggled to expand their domain in Omi at the expense of the Rokkaku, and came to eclipse the Kyogoku. In the process they forged close ties with the Asakura of Echizen.

In 1570 the clan broke an alliance with Oda Nobunaga (1534-1582), and was defeated at the Battle of Anegawa (Omi). In 1573 they were all but eliminated when their home castle of Odani was taken.

The family name is often pronounced and spelled Azai.

Notable Ancestors

Asai Sukemasa (1495-1546)

1st Asai daimyo. Son of Naotané. He succeeded Naomasa.

Sukemasa was a vassal under Kyogoku Takaié, but he revolted. He gradually increased his power, and eventually became daimyo, mading himself master of northern Omi, which Rokkaku Takayori (-1520) in vain tried to reconquer.

In 1516 Sukemasa built Odani Castle (Omi) for the Asai to rule from.

In 1518 Sukemasa successfully defended Odani Castle against Rokkaku Sadayori (1495-1552).

Sukemasa was later completely overrun and forced to retreat into Echizen, but he managed to maintain his independence with the help of the Asakura, whose alliance would later prove to be a curse for the Asai.

Asai Hisamasa (1524-1573)

2nd Asai daimyo. Son of Sukemasa. In 1542 he became head of the clan when his father died, but unlike Sukemasa he was not a strong leader.

In 1558, after losing territory against the Rokkaku (Sasaki), Hisamasa became their retainer, leading to a dissatisfaction among his kerai "vassals." When his son Nagamasa, at the 1560 Battle of Norada, defeated a force led by Rokkaku Yoshikata (1521-1598) that was twice his size to win back independence for his clan, the principal Asai vassals forced Hisamasa into retirement in favor of his son.

Hisamasa then retired to the clan's Odani Castle (Omi), but managed to hold some sway within the family. In 1570, after Oda Nobunaga (1534-1582), who was allied with Nagamasa, attacked Asakura Yoshikagé (1533-1573), who in the past had supported the Asai against enemies like the Rokkaku, Hisamasa, who hated Nobunaga for his personality, demanded that the clan repay the Asakura for their past support, and forced a war with Nobunaga, breaking that alliance. It is thought that Nagamasa opposed him and believed that the alliance could somehow be mended over time since he refused to divorce his wife, Oichi (1547-1583), who was Nobunaga's younger sister, but he failed to gain enough support to overturn Hisamasa.

In 1573 Oda Nobunaga's forces laid the Siege of Odani, and facing a loss, Hisamasa committed seppuku. The downfall of the castle was the ruin of the clan.

Despite his lackluster reputation, Hisamasa seemed to have been a competent enough administrator, and, among other endeavors, mediated a dispute over irrigation in his fief, and strengthened the foundations of the Asai house in northern Omi.

One of his daughters married Saito Yoshitatsu (1527-1561) of Mino, and she became the mother of Saito Tatsuoki (1548-1573), the lord of that province from 1561 to 1567.

Asai Nagamasa (1545-1573)

3rd Asai daimyo. Son of Hisamasa. Born at Odani Castle (Omi). He was initially a retainer of the Rokkaku.

At the 1560 Battle of Norada, Nagamasa's army, with generals Dodo Kuranosuké, Anyoji Ujihidé, Imai Ujinao, and the forces of the Dodo, the Isono, the Yono, the Imamaru, the Yugé, the Hongo, and other clans, faced the army of Rokkaku Yoshikata (1521-1598), with generals Gamo Katahidé (1534-1584), Nagaharu Nagaoki, Shindo Shikatamori, and a contingent from the Ikeda as part of the vanguard, with the Narazaki, the Tanaka, the Kido, the Wada, the Yoshida, and other clans in the second line, and the Goto, the Miura, the Yamada, the Tazaki, and other clans bringing up the rear. Kuranosuké was the first to engage in battle, and was killed, but when an elite Asai force attacked the Rokkaku main force directly, Yoshikata withdrew despite outnumbering his enemy two-to-one. Nagamasa then declared independence from the Rokkaku, and went on to take several of their castles.

After Norada, Nagamasa inherited the clan leadership from his father, who had previously submitted to the Rokkaku (Sasaki) and was subsequently forced to retire by the vassals of his clan.

In 1564 the Rokkaku laid siege to Sawayama Castle (Omi), but Nagamasa saved the castle when he promptly dispatched Isono Kazumasa (1534-1583) with a relief force.

Nagamasa then vanquished Saito Tatsuoki (1548-1573), besieging him in Ogaki (Mino), and was going to make himself master of a part of his domain, when he was opposed by Oda Nobunaga (1534-1582), who made war against him. In 1568, after a protracted struggle, peace was signed and alliance was made between the two warlords. To seal the arrangement Nagamasa married Nobunaga's sister Oichi (1547-1583).

Hostilities however recommenced. In 1570, when Oda Nobunaga attacked the Asakura, the Asai decided to support their long-time allies, and broke their alliance with the Oda. Nagamasa is thought to have opposed this move, and refused to divorce Oichi, but most of his retainers supported aiding the Asakura, with Endo Naotsuné (1531-1570) among the few dissenters. For this treachery Nobunaga marched with Tokugawa Ieyasu (1543-1616) to take Odani Castle (Omi). Nagamasa called for help from Echizen, and Asakura Yoshikagé (1533-1573) came with an army; their combined force marched to confront Nobunaga. At the ensuing Battle of Anegawa (Omi) the superior Oda forces, which included Inaba Yoshimichi (1515-1589), Shibata Katsuié (1522-1583), Hashiba (later Toyotomi) Hideyoshi (1536-1598), Sakuma Nobumori (1528-1582), and Mori Yoshinari (1523-1570), defeated the Asai forces, which included Isono Kazumasa, Atsuji Sadahidé, Miyabé Tsugimasu (1528-1599), and Endo Naotsuné, who died in battle, along with thousands of Asai and Asakura soldiers. The battle, however, saved Odani Castle for the time being, as Nobunaga withdrew his weary army. Later that year Nagamasa and his Asakura allies replied with a victory near Otsu (Omi) that cost Nobunaga a younger brother. By the intervention of the Emperor Ogimachi (1517-1593) and the 15th Ashikaga Shogun Yoshiaki (1537-1597), a truce was concluded. It was of short duration, and the final struggle was not slow to begin.

In 1571 Oda Nobunaga again attempted to bring down Odani Castle, but was thwarted.

In 1572, in what is known as the 4th Siege of Odani, Oda Nobunaga led a large army, including his son and heir Nobutada (1557-1582), his first battle, to the castle. The first Oda attack breached the outer defenses, and Nagamasa's own residence went up in flames. Further Oda efforts stalled however, thanks in part to the staunch resistance of the garrison commander Atsuji Sadahidé. Asakura Yoshikagé came down from Echizen to relieve Nagamasa, and a retainer of Asakura Kagemori named Takeuchi Sannosuké led an undercover attack during a rainstorm, causing fiasco in the Oda camp. Soon after Nobunaga departed the field.

In 1573, with the death of Takeda Shingen (1521-1573), the full attention of the Oda turned to Omi and Echizen. Oda Nobunaga laid siege to Sawayama Castle, which was defended by Isono Kazumasa, who held out for months, but in the end surrendered. Nobunaga then besieged Odani Castle again. The Asakura again sent a relief force, but this time Nobunaga ambushed and routed them before they could reach Nagamasa. Now isolated and seeing that all was lost, Nagamasa returned his wife and three daughters to his brother-in-law, set fire to the castle, and, together with his father and his two sons, committed suicide.

Nagamasa is remembered as being a capable leader of troops on the battlefield. The Asai had as retainer clans the Isono, the Atsuji, the Shinjo, the Akao, the Amemori, and the Imai. Although of relatively small size, their success in battle was due in part that they had a somewhat higher number of rifles then one might find in a clan of the Asai's means; this was because during the 1560s they and the Asakura collaborated on a gun-making workshop at Kunimoto (Omi).

Of his three daughters, who were Nobunaga's nieces, the eldest, Yodogimi (1569-1615), was married to Toyotomi Hideyoshi; the 2nd, Ohatsu (1570-1633), to Kyogoku Takatsugu (1560-1609); the 3rd, Oeyo (1573-1626), to the 2nd Tokugawa Shogun Hidetada (1579-1632): she was the mother of the 3rd Tokugawa Shogun Iemitsu (1604-1651) and of the dainagon "grand counselor" Tokugawa Tadanaga (1606-1633).

Asai Inori (-1573)

Son of Itomo. A relative of Nagamasa, he served in his campaigns.

Upon the fall of Odani Castle (Omi), Inori surrendered and was executed under orders of Oda Nobunaga (1534-1582).

Asai Manpuku-maru (1563-1573)

Nagamasa's only son and heir, and half-brother to Nagamasa's three daughters. Oda Nobunaga (1534-1582) killed him after the fall of Odani Castle (Omi).

With him the clan ended.

ASAKURA

Territory: Hokuriku region
Castle: Ichijo-ga-dani (Echizen)

Family of daimyo descending from Crown Prince Kusakabé-oji (662-689), a son of Temmu-tenno (631-686).

The clan settled in Tajima during the Heian "Aristocratic" Period (794-1185), and took the name Asakura.

In 1338, during the Muromachi Period (1336-1573), the Asakura supported the Ashikaga Shogun against Nitta Yoshisada (1301-1338).

The clan later moved to Echizen, and served the Shiba shugo "constable," which Asakura Toshikagé (1428-1481) usurped at the dawn of the Sengoku "Warring States" Period (1467-1573).

In the late 16th century the Asakura were powerful in the Hokuriku "Northern" region, and allied with the Asai to oppose Oda Nobunaga (1534-1582). The clan was defeated by him at the Battle of Anegawa (1570), and all but eliminated when their home castle of Ichijo-ga-dani (Echizen) was taken three years later, after which surviving members became vassals of first the Oda, then the Toyotomi.

The Asakura are well-known in part for their *Toshikagé Jushichikajo "House Code of Asakura"* (c.1480).

Notable Ancestors

Asakura Hirokagé (1255-1352)

Helped the Ashikaga in their struggle against Nitta Yoshisada (1301-1338).

In 1338 Hirokagé was charged with the guard of Kuromaru Castle (Echizen) in the service of the Shiba.

Asakura Toshikagé (1428-1481)

Descendant of Hirokagé. He was one of the three roshin "principal vassals" of the Shiba, and occupied the castle of Ichijo-ga-dani (Echizen).

In 1467 Toshikagé defeated Kyogoku Mochikiyo of Kaga.

In 1470 the 8th Ashikaga Shogun Yoshimasa (1436-1490) made him shugo "constable" of Echizen.

At the start of the Onin War (1467-1477) Toshikagé initially supported Yamana Sozen (1404-1473), but in 1471 he switched his loyalties to the Hosokawa, a move that was coupled with a break from his nominal lords, the Shiba shugo.

In 1472 Toshikagé defeated the Kai of Echizen, and became the *de facto* ruler of that province.

In 1473 Toshikagé aided Togashi Masachika in his efforts to restore his clan's authority in the politically confused Kaga.

In 1479 Toshikagé's hold on Echizen was cemented with his defeat of the Shiba at the Kofuku-ji in Nara (Yamato).

Toshikagé composed the *Toshikagé Jushichi-kajo "Toshikagé's 17 House Codes,"* one of the earlier and most straightforward house codes of the Sengoku "Warrings States" Period (1467-1573). He established the Asakura capital at Ichijo-ga-dani, which in some ways foreshadowed the castle towns of the Edo "Tokugawa" Period (1603-1868).

Asakura Ujikagé (1449-1486)

8th head of the Asakura. Son of Toshikagé. His childhood name was Kumagimi.

In 1481, after the death of his father, Ujikagé took control of the clan.

Asakura Norikagé (1477-1555)

8th son of Toshikagé. He was also called Kotaro, and later Soteki.

In 1503, upon the rise of his nephew Sadakagé to the position of daimyo, a faction of the Asakura retainers formed a plot against him, and Norikagé helped to suppress the short-lived rebellion.

In 1506 Norikagé defeated an Ikko army at Kuzuryu-gawa (Echizen), one of a number of battles he would fight against them.

In 1517 and 1526 Norikagé commanded an expedition into Tango.

In 1526 Norikagé led an army to support the Asai against the Rokkaku, cementing the alliance between the Asakura and the Asai.

In 1531 Norikagé marched against the Ikko of Kaga. In 1555 he attack them again, storming the Daisho-ji-omoté. He afterwards fell ill and returned to Ichijo-no-dani (Echizen), leaving the army in the hands of his grandnephew Kagetaka.

Norikagé was a pillar of the Asakura, and was arguably the most talented general the Asakura ever produced, and his writings on various military matters have provided a valuable historical record. Numerous sayings attributed to Norikagé survive, including "The warrior may be called a beast or a dog; the main thing is winning."

He had adopted the name Soteki after entering the priesthood. He hewed to his religious beliefs, producing no children of his own, and adopted his grandnephew Kagetoshi.

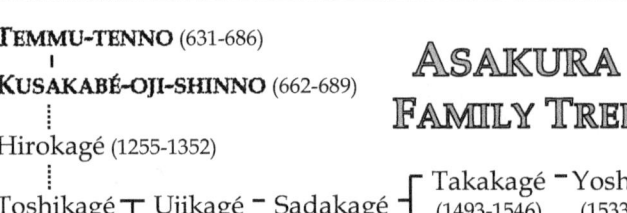

ASAKURA FAMILY TREE

TEMMU-TENNO (631-686)
|
KUSAKABÉ-OJI-SHINNO (662-689)
⋮
Hirokagé (1255-1352)
⋮
Toshikagé (1428-1481) — Ujikagé (1449-1486) — Sadakagé (1473-1512)
— Kageyoshi
— Norikagé (1477-1555)

Takakagé (1493-1546) — Yoshikagé (1533-1573)
Kagetaka (1495-1543) — Kagé'akira (1529-1574)
Kagetoshi (1505-1572) — Kagenao

Azuchi-Momoyama Period – Asakura

Asakura Sadakagé (1473-1512)

9th head of the Asakura. Son of Ujikagé.

In 1503, upon his ascension to daimyohood, Sadakagé, assisted by his uncle Norikagé, had to contend with a short-lived rebellion.

Sadakagé worked to expand the Asakura domain, clashing with the Togashi of Kaga (1494 and 1504), the Ikko-ikki of Echizen, and the Rokkaku of Omi.

Asakura Takakagé (1493-1546)

Son of Sadakagé. He succeeded his father upon his death.

In 1518 Takakagé sent troops to aid the struggling Toki of Mino. He also aided the Asai of Omi in their bid to throw off the authority of the Kyogoku, and supported them against the Rokkaku.

Takakagé was a successful daimyo, expanding Asakura influence while enhancing Echizen's growing culture status. He is said to have formally enacted the famous *Toshikagé Jushichi-kajo "Toshikagé's 17 House Codes."*

Asakura Kagetaka (1495-1543)

Son of Sadakagé, and younger brother to Takakagé.

Kagetaka excelled in diplomacy, and was considered generally capable, but discord developed with Takakagé. Feeling his life was in danger, he fled to Wakasa and took up with the Takeda.

Asakura Kagetoshi (1505-1572)

Son of Sadakagé, adopted by Norikagé. He fought alongside his adoptive father in many campaigns against the Ikko-ikki, and held Tsuruga Castle.

In 1565 Kagetoshi tended to the needs of Ashikaga Yoshiaki (1537-1597) when he came to Echizen after the death of the 13th Ashikaga Shogun Yoshiteru (1536-1565).

Asakura Kagetaka (1508-1570)

Distant cousin to Yoshikagé.

In 1555 Kagetaka took over the army of Norikagé when he fell ill and died during the campaign against the Ikko-ikki.

In 1564 Kagetaka was a commander in a campaign against the Ikko-ikki of Kaga.

Asakura Yoshikagé (1533-1573)

Eldest son of Takakagé. Born in Ichijo-ga-dani (Echizen). Ascended as head of the Asakura upon his father's death.

As Yoshikagé had a weak constitution, and was not well-suited for campaigning, in 1555, after the death of Norikagé, the Asakura army was commanded by Kagetaka and his cousin Kagé'akira.

In 1555 and 1564 Yoshikagé defeated the Ikko-ikki of Kaga.

In the 1560s Yoshikagé lent nomial support to the Saito during their war with the Oda.

In 1562 Yoshikagé defeated the troops of Ikko-ikki of Echizen, forcing them to accept peace, and gave his daughter in marriage to the chief bonze of the Hongan-ji (Kyoto), who was to be content with the single province of Kaga as his fief.

During the late 1560s Yoshikagé moved into neighboring Wakasa and absorbed that province at the expense of the Takeda.

Yoshikagé proved to be adept at political and diplomatic management, as demonstrated by his negotiations with the Ikko-ikki in Echizen. As a result of the negotiations, and his effective governance, Echizen enjoyed a period of relative domestic stability compared to the rest of Japan during the Sengoku "Warring States" Period (1467-1573). Consequently, Echizen became a site for refugees fleeing the violence in the Kansai region.

It is said that Yoshikagé's tragic flaw was indecision. In 1566 Ashikaga Yoshiaki (1537-1597) asked for Asakura aid in order to acquire the inheritance of his brother the 13th Ashikaga Shogun Yoshiteru (1536-1565), but Yoshikagé declined that difficult task. In 1568 Yoshiaki then applied to Oda Nobunaga (1534-1582), who accepted the mission and installed him as the 15th Ashikaga Shogun at Kyoto.

It is said that Yoshikagé resented Oda Nobunaga's presumption as both of

their clans had once served the Shiba. In 1570 he was summoned to the capital, but refused to go. Immediately Nobunaga took the field with Tokugawa Ieyasu (1543-1616), and invaded Echizen. At the Siege of Kanagasaki, Hashiba (later Toyotomi) Hideyoshi (1536-1598) led the attack, and due to Yoshikagé's lack of military skills, they were successful, leaving the Asakura domain open to invasion. The Oda forces then marched to besiege Ichijoga-dani (Echizen), but Yoshikagé applied for help to his brother-in-law Asai Nagamasa (1545-1573), and Nobunaga, conscious that he was not strong enough, returned to Kyoto.

Soon afterwards Oda Nobunaga issued from the capital with a more numerous army and defeated his adversaries at the Battle of Anegawa (Omi), at which Yoshikagé was not present. By the intervention of the Emperor Ogimachi (1517-1593), peace was concluded.

In 1573 however war recommenced. Yoshikagé escaped the siege at Ichijoga-dani, but his whereabouts were betrayed by his own cousin Kagé'akira, and he killed himself with all his family at the Rokubo Kensho-ji. His weak character had by then disenchanted a number of his senior men, and this greatly contributed to his downfall.

Asakura Kagetsura (-1570)

A senior Asakura retainer. He was an expert in diplomacy.

An interesting anecdote survives about him. In 1561, when Asakura Yoshikagé held a dog-hunting gathering at Okubo, Kagetsura is said to have dressed so nicely that those in attendance mistook him for the lord of the clan, causing him much embarrassment.

Asakura Kagé'akira (1529-1574)

Son of Kagetaka. He held Ino Castle (Echizen).

After the battles of 1570 Kagé'akira commanded the Asakura army at various times, but in 1573 he went over to Oda Nobunaga (1534-1582) when he invaded Echizen. Nobunaga granted Kagé'akira a fief in Echizen, and changed his name to Tobashi Kagé'akira.

He died fighting the Echizen Ikko, who had rebelled and was supported by the forces of Kaga commanded by Shimotsuma Raisho (-1575).

Asakura Kagetaké (1529-1574)

In 1570 Kagetaké lost to the Oda and the Tokugawa at the Battle of Anegawa (Omi) while commanding the Asakura army for Yoshikagé.

In 1573 Kagetaké surrendered to Oda Nobunaga (1534-1582), and was given a fief in Echizen. When the Ikko of the province rebelled, Kagetaké surrendered to them. As a result, the following year Nobunaga sent an army to destroy him.

Asakura Nobumasa (1583-1637)

Nephew of Yoshikagé. He served Toyotomi Hideyoshi (1536-1598) and Tokugawa Ieyasu (1543-1616).

In 1625 Nobumasa received in fief the castle of Kakegawa (Totomi -- 25,000 koku).

In 1632 Nobumasa was implicated in the plot of dainagon "grand counselor" Tokugawa Tadanaga (1606-1633), of whom he was a counselor. He was dispossessed of his fief, and banished to Koriyama (Yamato), where he died.

ANEGAKOJI

Territory: Hida
Castles:
Matsukura, Takayama (Hida)

Cadet branch of a family of kugé descending from Fujiwara (Sanjo) Sanefusa (1146-1224). The clan became figures of note by the 14th century, when they governed Hida for two centuries.

In 1585 the Anegakoji were destroyed by the forces of Toyotomi Hideyoshi (1536-1598) for supporting Sassa Narimasa (1536-1588). The clan was in fact led by men of Mitsugi blood by the mid-Sengoku "Warring States" Period (1467-1573).

NOTABLE ANCESTORS

Anegakoji Tadatsuna (-1411)

2nd son of Takamoto. He was the first to receive the title of Hida no koku-shi "administrator." He fought for the Emperor Go-Kameyama (1347-1424).

Anegakoji Yoshiyori (1520-1571)

Son of Mitsugi Naoyori.

In 1562 Yoshiyori assumed control of the clan and resided at Matsukura Castle (Hida).

In 1564 incursions by Takeda Shingen (1521-1573) into Hida from Shinano forced Yoshiyori to agree to a peace treaty.

Anegakoji Koretsuna (1540-1587)

Son of Yoshiyori. Resided at Takayama Castle (Hida). He was Hida no kami. An ally of Oda Nobunaga (1534-1582), he first defeated Kiso Yoshimitsu.

In 1582 Koretsuna defeated the Ema, and secured control of all Hida. Around this time, believing that his eldest son Nobutsuna and a younger brother were plotting against him, he ordered their deaths.

In 1584-1585 Koretsuna supported Sassa Narimasa (1536-1588) when the latter defied Hashiba (later Toyotomi) Hideyoshi (1536-1598). As a result he was attacked by the latter's forces under Kanamori Nagachika (1524-1608). Koretsuna surrendered and retired to Kyoto, while his 2nd son Hidetsuna committed suicide.

ASHINA

Territory: Mutsu

Castles: Kurokawa (Aizu-Wakamatsu), Mukai-haguro-yama

Family of daimyo descending from the Miura, and by them from the Taira.

Sawara Yoshitsuru, the last son of Miura Yoshiaki (1093-1181), received the district of Aizu (Mutsu) in fief. His grandson took the name of Ashina from the area in Yokosuka (Sagami). Morimasa was his great-grandson.

In 1333 Ashina Naomori built a mansion at Wakamatsu that would form the basis of the later Kurokawa Castle (Mutsu), later known as Aizu-Wakamatsu Castle, which served as the Ashina's home.

During the Muromachi "Ashikaga" Period (1336-1573) the clan was powerful in Mutsu, and was shugo "constable" of Aizu.

In 1589 the clan suffered a severe loss against Daté Masamuné (1567-1636) at the Battle of Suri-agé-hara (Iwashiro), leading to the demise of the clan.

NOTABLE ANCESTORS

Ashina Morimasa (1386-1432)

Son of Norimori. Resided at Kurokawa Castle (Mutsu), and was shuritayu.

In 1416 Morimasa joined the Uesugi in a war against the 4th Kanto-kubo "Kanto deputy Shogun" Ashikaga Mochiuji (1398-1439).

Ashina Morihisa (-1444)

10th lord of the Ashina. Was shuritayu and Shimosa no kami.

Ashina Morinori (1431-1466)

Was Shimosa no kami.

Ashina Moritaka (1448-1517)

13th head of the Ashina. Son of Moriakira. He was Shimosa no kami and Totomi no kami. In 1473 he married the daughter of Daté Ujimuné.

In 1478 a contention arose between Moritaka and his son, and war broke out between them, which lasted till 1506.

Ashina Morikiyo (1490-1553)

15th head of the Ashina. He was Totomi no kami. He succeeded his brother Moritaka, whose son had died.

In 1528 Morikiyo assisted Daté Tanemuné (1488-1565) in an attack on the Kasai.

In 1534 Morikiyo allied with the Daté, the Ishikawa, and the Iwasé against the Shirakawa.

In 1547 Morikiyo tried with Daté Harumuné (1519-1578) to seize the domain of the Soma, but was defeated.

Ashina Moriuji (1521-1580)

Eldest son of Morikiyo. He was shuritayu. He ruled Kurokawa Castle (Mutsu) and its environs.

Moriuji was constantly at war with Satake Yoshishigé (1547-1612), Hojo Ujiyasu (1515-1571), etc. He expanded the Ashina domain in the face of the Uesugi and the Satake resistance and came into conflict with the Daté.

Moriuji was renowned as a good and wise leader, doing much to improve the economic condition of the Ashina domain, while expanding its borders. For this reason, his reign is considered the Ashina's golden age.

Moriuji also built Mukai-haguro-yama Castle, completed in 1561, which he used as a residence when in retirement.

Ashina Moritaka (1560-1583)

18th lord of the Ashina. Son of Nikaido Moriyoshi (1544-1581), lord of Sukagawa Castle (Mutsu). He was sent to the Ashina clan as a hostage, but was later adopted by Morioki to succeed Moriuji, whose eldest son had died of illness, and married Morioki's daughter.

In 1579, having sent presents to the Emperor Ogimachi (1517-1593) and to Oda Nobunaga (1534-1582), Moritaka was appointed Totomi no kami.

Moritaka waged war against Daté Masamuné (1567-1636) and Tamura Kiyozumi.

Although a skilled warrior, Moritaka, for unknown reason, became unpopular with his retainers, and was assassinated by Oba Sanzaémon, one of his kerai "vassals."

Moritaka, whose own son Kiomaru had died at the age of 2, was succeeded by Satake Morishigé, who had married his daughter, and was adopted by the Ashina upon his murder.

Ashina Morishigé/Yoshihiro (1575-1631)

2nd son of Satake Yoshishigé (1547-1612).

Prior to Morishigé's adoption by the Ashina, at the 1585 Battle of Hitadori (Mutsu) Daté Masamuné (1567-1636) faced the combined forces the Ashina, the Satake, the Hatakeyama, the Soma, and the Satake, led by Hatakeyama (Nihonmatsu) Yoshitsugu (1552-1586). In the battle, Daté retainer Oniwa Yoshinao (1513-1585) was killed by

---

Miura Yoshiaki (1093-1181)
|
Sawara Yoshitsuru
⋮
Norimori
|
Morimasa — Morihisa — Morinori ┬ Moritaka (1448-1517)
(1386-1432)   (-1444)   (1431-1466) └ Morikiyo — Moriuji ┬ Moritaka — Morishigé
(1490-1553) (1521-1580) │ (1560-1583) (1575-1631)
└ Morioki

ASHINA FAMILY TREE

Kobuta Juro. Heavily outnumbered, the Daté retreated to Motomiya Castle. The castle was saved when Morishigé's father Satake Yoshishigé suddenly departed for his own lands in Hitachi, which were being attacked. The remaining allies did not feel that they had the necessary strength to bring down the castle, and retreated.

In 1587 Morishigé married the daughter of Moritaka, and was adopted as successor upon his father-in-law's murder. He was then 12 years old. Many kerai "vassals" of the Satake accompanied him to his new domain, which caused discontent within the Ashina, and a number of their retainers passed over to the Daté, who had also offered to provide an heir.

The failure of the Hitadori campaign and the internal problems within the Ashina eventually allowed Daté Masamuné, who was only waiting for an opportunity, to invade Ashina territories.

In 1589 Daté Masamuné laid the Siege of Kurokawa (Mutsu), took the castle with little effort, and defeated Morishigé at the Battle of Suri-agé-hara (Iwashiro). Morishigé escaped to Edosaki (Hitachi), where he lived in seclusion.

Thus ended the Ashina family, after having been for two centuries one of the most powerful daimyo in the north.

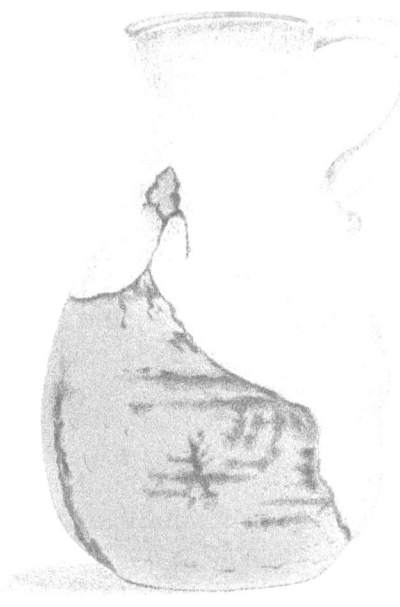

Aso

Revenues: 300,000 koku

Castle: Yabé (Chikugo)

Kyushu family descending from Kamu-ya-i-mimi no mikoto, a son of Jimmu-tenno (711-585 B.C.). Asotsu-hiko no mikoto, a son of Kamu-ya-i-mimi, was nominated Aso-kuni no miyatsuko, and his descendants assumed the name of Aso.

During the reign of the Emperor Keiko (reigned 71-130), the clan was charged with performing rites and ceremonies at the Aso-jinja (Higo).

During the Nanboku-cho Period (1336-1392), the Aso sided with the Southern Court against Ashikaga Takauji (1305-1358).

Notable Ancestors

Aso Korezumi (14th century)

Son of Korekuni. Resided at Yabé Castle (Chikugo). He sided with the Southern Court during the Nanboku-cho Period (1336-1392).

In 1336 Korezumi was defeated at the Battle of Tatara-hama (Chikuzen) by Ashikaga Takauji (1305-1358), but continued to support the Yasunaga-shinno.

Aso Korenao (-1336)

Was killed at the Battle of Tatara-hama (Chikuzen).

Aso Koretoyo (1543-1584)

Descendant of Korenao. Possessor of Yabé Castle (Chikugo -- 300,000 koku).

Koretoyo allied with the Otomo, which resulted in an attack by the Shimazu.

Aso Koremitsu (1582-1593)

Son of Koretoyo. He was but a child when his father died.

In 1588, when Higo was divided between Konishi Yukinaga (1555-1600) and Kato Kiyomasa (1562-1611), Koremitsu took refuge with the latter.

When Koremitsu was 11 years old Toyotomi Hideyoshi (1536-1598) ordered him killed for reasons unknown.

CHIBA

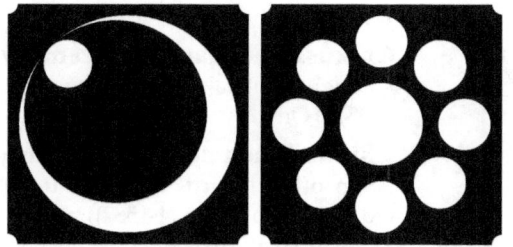

Territory: Shimosa
Castles: Ichikawa, Sakura (Shimosa)

Daimyo family descended from Taira Tadatsuné (-1031). The Chiba were very powerful in Shimosa from the 12th to the 16th century.

Historically, the clan controlled the city of Chiba (near Edo), and also an area called Soma, which included the Grand Shrine of Isé.

During the 1140s the Chiba clashed with Minamoto Yoshitomo (1123-1160) over rights to certain Chiba estates, but in 1156 they supported him in the Hogen Rebellion (Kyoto).

In the Genpei "Minamoto-Taira" War (1180-1185), the Chiba, along with the other Taira branch families of the Hojo, the Miura, and the Doi, were allies of the Minamoto, opposing the greater 'core' Taira clan. While they were valued allies to Minamoto Yoritomo (1147-1199), they were however not always trusted.

The Chiba remained powerful during the Kamakura Period (1185-1333), but saw their power decline during the Muromachi "Ashikaga" Period (1336-1573). In the mid-16th century they became vassals of the Hojo.

Notable Ancestors

Chiba Tsunetané (1118-1201)

Son of Tsuneshigé. Was Chiba no suké.

In the 1156 Hogen Rebellion (Kyoto), Tsunetané sided with the victorious Emperor Go-Shirakawa (1127-1192).

In 1180 Tsunetané joined the party of Minamoto Yoritomo (1147-1199) as

Chiba Tsunetané

soon as the latter rose against the Taira, becoming a general famous for his military exploits.

Tsunetané took part in the campaign of Minamoto Noriyori (1156-1193) against Minamoto Yoshinaka (1154-1184).

In 1184 Tsunetané fought at the Battle of Ichi-no-tani (Settsu).

In 1187 Tsunetané pacified the Kyoto region.

In 1189 Tsunetané joined in Yoritomo's northern expedition against Fujiwara Yasuhira (1155-1189), and in 1190 entered Kyoto with him.

Chiba Sadatané (1291-1351)

He at first supported the Hojo. In 1333, after the capture of Kamakura, Sadatané joined the Southern Court of the Emperor Go-Daigo (1288-1339), but he later followed the party of the Northern Court.

Chiba Kanetané (early 15th century)

In 1416 he supported Uesugi Ujinori (-1417) against the 4th Kanto kubo "Kanto deputy Shogun" Ashikaga Mochiuji (1398-1439).

Chiba Tanenao (-1455)

Son of Kanetané. He remained faithful to Uesugi Norizané (1410-1466), but when Ashikaga Shigeuji (1438-1497) became the 5th Kanto kubo "Kanto deputy Shogun," he gave him his support.

In 1455, having been defeated conjointly with Ashikaga Shigeuji, Tanenao, along with his son Tanenobu, committed seppuku. The Uesugi chose his brother Sanetané as his successor.

Chiba Sanetané (15th century)

At the death of his brother Tanenao he was governor of Ichikawa Castle (Shimosa), and became Chiba no suké.

In 1456 being besieged at Ichikawa, Sanetané was compelled to surrender, and was replaced as governor by his nephew Takatané.

Chiba Takatané (15th century)

Son of Yasutané.

Assisted by his father, Takatané supported the 5th Kanto kubo "Kanto deputy Shogun" Ashikaga Shigeuji (1438-1497), and fought against the Uesugi and their general Ota Dokan (1432-1486), who in 1479 finally triumphed over him.

Chiba Toshitané (1528-1559)

Grandson of Takantané.

In 1559 Toshitané fought against Uesugi Kenshin (1530-1578), was defeated, and killed.

Chiba Shigetané (16th century)

Vassal of the Odawara Hojo.

In 1590, during the Odawara Campaign of Toyotomi Hideyoshi (1536-1598), being besieged in his castle at Sakura (Shimosa) by Honda Tadakatsu (1548-1610) and Sakai Ietsugu (1564-1619), Shigetané surrendered and was dispossessed.

After this the family disappears from history.

CHIKUSA

Territory: Isé
Castle: Chikusa (Isé)

 ancient family of daimyo in Isé.

NOTABLE ANCESTORS

Chikusa Takamichi (14th century)
Built Chikusa Castle (Isé) towards 1350.

Chikusa Tadaharu (16th century)
Fought Rokkaku Yoshikata (1521-1598) of Omi.

Chikusa Tadamoto (16th century)
Son of Tadaharu. He submitted to Oda Nobunaga (1534-1582), and was killed in a battle in Mino.

DAIDOJI

Revenues: 180,000 koku
Territories: Kawagoé (Musashi), Matsuida (Kozuké)
Castle: Kawagoé (Musashi)

Samurai family descending from the Taira. The clan became important retainers of the Hojo, and served as senior advisors until the fall of Odawara Castle in 1590.

NOTABLE ANCESTORS

Daidoji Shigetoki (15th century)
Formerly his name was Isé Taro. He lived in Daido-ji (Yamashiro), and in 1471 he took that name. His younger brother Isé Shinkuro later became the famous Hojo Soun (1432-1519), to whose fortune Shigetoki attached himself.

Daidoji Shigéoki/Kanekatsu (15th or 16th century)
Was Suruga no kami. He was charged by the Hojo with the guard of Kawagoé Castle (Musashi).

Daidoji Masashigé (1533-1590)
Son of Shigeoki. Was Suruga no kami. He was one of the chief advisors of Hojo Ujimasa (1538-1590). He came to hold authority over both Kawagoé in Musashi and Matsuida in Kozuké, and had his revenues raised to 180,000 koku.

In 1582 Masashigé was present at the Battles of Mimasé-togé (Sagami) and Kanagawa (border between Kozuké and Musashi).

Masashigé was among those that urged Hojo Ujinao (1562-1591) to avoid an open battle with Toyotomi Hideyoshi (1536-1598).

In 1590 Masashigé was vanquished by Maeda Toshiié (1539-1599) to whom he surrendered. After the capture of Odawara (Sagami), as a consequence of his advice, he was forced to commit seppuku.

Masashigé's 4th son Naotsugu eventually became a retainer of the 3rd Tokugawa Shogun Iemitsu (1604-1651).

Daidoji Naoshigé (1573-1628)
Son of Masashigé. Served successively Maeda Toshinaga (1562-1614) of Kaga, Matsudaira Tadayoshi, and Tokugawa Yoshinao (1601-1650) of Owari.

Daidoji Shigehisa (17th century)
Followed the fortunes of Matsudaira Tadateru (1592-1683).

Daidoji Shigesuké (1639-1730)
Published some works on military art.

HIRATSUKA

Territory: Mino

NOTABLE ANCESTORS

Hiratsuka Tamehiro (late 16th century)
Daimyo of Mino (50,000 koku).
At the 1600 Battle of Seki-gahara (Mino) Tamehiro fought against Tokugawa Ieyasu (1543-1616), and afterwards was despoiled of his domains.

HASEBÉ

Territory: Noto
Castle: Anamizu (Noto)

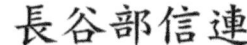

Hasebé Nobutsura

Family descended from Ki no Haseo.

NOTABLE ANCESTORS

Hasebé Nobutsura (-1217)

Son of Tametsura. He was a military commander between the end of the Heian "Aristocratic" Period (794-1185) and the beginning of the Kamakura Period (1185-1333). His father was an uma-no-jo "stable master."

Brave and fearless, Nobutsura earned a reputation for capturing robbers getting into the Inner Palace of the Heian Palace (Kyoto), and was promoted to sayoé-no-kami "officer of the palace guard."

Later Nobutsura was attached to the Prince Mochihito (-1180). In 1180 the Prince, together with Nobutsura and Minamoto Yorimasa (1106-1180), plotted to ruin the Taira. The plot having been divulged, Taira Kiyomori (1118-1181) had Mochihito besieged in his palace of Takakura-no-miya (Kyoto), but Nobutsura helped him to escape disguised as a woman to Mii-dera (Omi). Nobutsura fought tremendously, but was captured. Although cross-examined by Taira Munemori (1147-1185), he did not divulge the Prince's location. Taira Kiyomori (1118-1181) admired his braveness, and exiled him to Hino (Hoki).

After the fall of the Taira, Minamoto Yoritomo (1147-1199) recalled him and gave him Noto in fief, which his descendants governed for twenty generations.

Hasebé Tsunatsura (-1576)

In 1576 Tsunatsura was besieged in his castle at Anamizu (Noto) by Uesugi Kenshin (1530-1578). He escaped to Nanao (Noto), but was defeated and killed. He was the last of his family.

A descendant of the clan adopted the Cho name from the first kanji of the Hasebé name, and that family became prominent retainers to the Maeda. In the late Azuchi-Momoyama Period (1573-1603) Cho Hisatsura was counted among the high-ranking retainers to Maeda Toshiié (1539-1599). The Cho continued to serve the Maeda during the Edo "Tokugawa" Period (1603-1868).

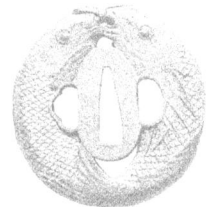

ISHIKAWA

Revenues: 12,000 koku
Territory: Owari
Castle: Inuyama (Owari)

NOTABLE ANCESTORS

Ishikawa Sadakiyo (-1625)

Son-in-law of Ishida Mitsunari (1560-1600). He was Bizen no kami.

Sadakiyo was in the service of Toyotomi Hideyoshi (1536-1598), and received in fief Inuyama Castle (Owari -- 12,000 koku), as well as being named daikan "administrator" of Kiso (Shinano).

In 1600 Sadakiyo was present at the Siege of Tanabé (Tango). After the castle fell, he shut himself at Inuyama. When Ishida Mitsunari was defeated at the Battle of Seki-ga-hara, he was deprived of his domain. He then shaved his head, made his way to Kyoto, where he died in obscurity, it is said, as a moneylender.

HASHIBA

Territories: Koriyama (Yamato), Kameyama (Tanba)

Patronymic name adopted originally by Toyotomi Hideyoshi (1536-1598) in 1575, which he formed by borrowing two characters from the names of two generals, his friends Niwa (ha) and Shibata (shiba). Ten years later he changed it for that of Toyotomi, but some members of his family who had adopted the name of Hashiba, retained it.

NOTABLE ANCESTORS

Hashiba Hidenaga (1540-1591)

Half-brother to Toyotomi Hideyoshi (1536-1598), whose chief retainer he was. He was formerly known as Koichiro, and is often referred to as Toyotomi Hidenaga. He accompanied his half-brother in all his campaigns.

In 1573 Hidenaga joined Hideyoshi's staff when the latter took up in Omi.

In 1582, following the death of Oda Nobunaga (1534-1582) and the defeat of Akechi Mitsuhidé (1528-1582), Hidenaga was given the fief of Koriyama (Yamato), which was confiscated from the Tsutsui, and was appointed Mino no kami.

In 1585, after participating in and helping Hideyoshi win the battle at Kii, Hidenaga oversaw the construction of

Hashiba Hidenaga

Wakayama Castle (Kii), appointing Todo Takatora (1556-1630) as chief engineer. Later that year, with Toyotomi Hidetsugu (1568-1595), he commanded an expedition into Shikoku against Chosokabé Motochika (1538-1599).

In 1587 Hidenaga led Hideyoshi's vanguard into Satsuma. At the Battle of Sendai-gawa (Satsuma) they engaged the Shimazu, led by Niiro Tadamoto (1526-1611). Despite being vastly outnumbered, Tadamoto charged the Toyotomi army, even engaging Kato Kiyomasa (1562-1611) in personal combat, before retreating under cover of night. After the conquest of the island, Hidenaga was rewarded with Kii, Izumi, and Yamato, reaching a governance of one-million koku, and was appointed gon-dainagon "acting grand counselor."

In 1591, when Hideyoshi's infant son Tsurumatsu died, Hidenaga stood as the likely heir to the now childless Taiko. Unfortunately Hidenaga died later that year in Koriyama (Yamato), of an illness that had plagued him for a number of years, despite the fervent prayers of Hideyoshi and Kyoto's temples.

Hidenaga was regarded as Hideyoshi's brain and right arm.

Hashiba Hidetoshi (1577-1594)

Nephew and adopted son of Hidenaga. His mother was the eldest sister of Toyotomi Hideyoshi (1536-1598).

Hashiba Hidekatsu (1567-1594)

4th son of Oda Nobunaga (1534-1582). Born in Owari.

In 1582 Hidekatsu was adopted by Toyotomi Hideyoshi (1536-1598). He became daimyo of Kameyama (Tanba) and Tanba no kami. Shortly after the death of Nobunaga, he assisted his adoptive father during the Battle of Yamazaki (Yamashiro).

In 1584 Hidekatsu served Hideyoshi at the Battle of Komaki and Nagakuté (Owari); in 1587 took part in an expedition to Kyushu against the Shimazu; and in 1590 participated in the campaign against the Hojo of Odawara.

He died in Korea.

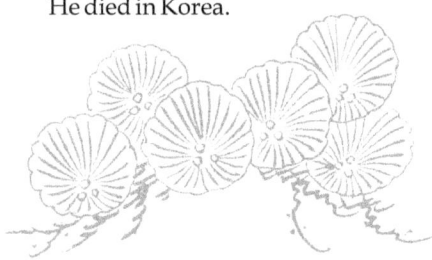

KAGAÉ

Daimyo family native of Owari.

NOTABLE ANCESTORS

Kagaé Shigemuné (-1584)

Was Suruga no kami. Served Oda Nobunaga (1534-1582) and was killed in the fight against Toyotomi Hideyoshi (1536-1598).

Kagaé Shigemochi (-1600)

Son of Shigemuné. He submitted to Toyotomi Hideyoshi (1536-1598), joining the party against Tokugawa Ieyasu (1543-1616), and fought against Mizuno Tadashigé (1541-1600), whom he defeated and killed. He himself lost his life soon afterwards.

HATAKEYAMA

Territories: Musashi, Yamashiro, Kawachi, Kii, Etchu, Noto, Mutsu

Castles: Takaya (Kawachi), Nihonmatsu (Mutsu), Nanao (Noto)

Daimyo family of Musashi, originally descended from Taira Takamochi (late 9th century).

In 1205 the clan fell victim to political intrigue when Hatakeyama Shigeyasu and his father Shigetada (1164-1205) were killed in battle by Hojo forces in Kamakura. That lineage now being extinct, the son of Ashikaga Yoshizané (1154-1199), Yoshizumi, was chosen by the 1st Kamakura Shikken Hojo Tokimasa (1138-1215) to revive the name of Hatakeyama. Yoshizumi married Tokimasa's daughter, the widow of Shigeyasu, and inherited the Hatakeyama domain. Thus the new family descended from the Minamoto (Seiwa-Genji).

During the wars of the Nanbokucho Period (1336-1392) the Hatakeyama were an ally of the Ashikaga Shogunate against the Imperial Southern Court, and afterwards were rewarded with the hereditary position of shugo "constable" of Yamashiro, Kii, Kawachi, Etchu, and Noto.

During the 15th century, the Hatakeyama were one of the san-kan "three families" from which the Kyoto kanrei "Kyoto deputy Shogun" was selected, holding great influence over the Imperial Court.

Around the mid-15th century a feud arose between Hatakeyama Masanaga and Hatakeyama Yoshinari over succession to the kanrei position. The internal conflict quickly grew, as each side gained allies, and weakened the clan as a whole, causing them to lose the position to the Hosokawa. It was one of the sparks that ignited the Onin War (1467-1477).

In the aftermath of the war, the Hatakeyama were much diminished, and were now represented by a number of scattered branches, the most notable of which resided in Kawachi, Noto, and Mutsu.

NOTABLE ANCESTORS

Hatakeyama Shigetada (1164-1205)

Son of Shigetoshi. His ancestors, who for several generations were in possession of Hatakeyama (Musashi), took its name.

In 1180, when Minamoto Yoritomo (1147-1199) started his campaign, Shigetada, although descended from the Taira, joined his party, and under the command of Minamoto Noriyori (1156-1193) and Minamoto Yoshitsuné (1159-1189), fought against Minamoto (Kiso) Yoshinaka (1154-1184).

In 1184, at the 2nd Battle of Uji (Kyoto), Shigetada competed with a number of other warriors to be the first to cross the Uji River. When his horse was shot in the head with an arrow, he used his bow as a staff to help himself across. Just as he was about to climb the bank, however, his godson Okushi Shigechika asked for help, and Shigetada grabbed and threw him ashore, whereupon Shigechika proclaimed himself the first to cross the river.

Hatakeyama Shigetada

HATAKEYAMA FAMILY TREE

```
Ashikaga Yoshikané (1154-1199)
│
Nariyori (early 13th century)
⋮
Iekuni (14th century)
├─ Kunikiyo ( -1364)
└─ Yoshito (1331-1379)
    └─ Motokuni ┬ Mitsuié ─ Mochikuni ┬ Masanaga ─ Naonobu ┬ Tanenaga ┬ Takamasa ─ Masayoshi
       (1352-1406) │ (1372-1433)  (1397-1455) │ (1442-1493)  ( -1534) │ Masakuni │ (1527-1576)
                   │                          │ Yoshinari ─ Yoshitoyo ─ Yoshihidé ├ Terutaka
                   │                          │ (1454-1493)  ( -1499)   ( -1532)  └ Masayori ─ Sadamasa
                   │                                                                           ( -1584)
                   └ Mitsunori ─ Masakuni ─ Yoshimuné ─ Yoshitsuna ─ Yoshinori ─ Yoshitaka ─ Yoshiharu
                                             ( -1480)
```

GAMERS GUIDE TO FEUDAL JAPAN — SHOGUN & DAIMYO

Later that year Shigetada distinguished himself at the Battle of Ichi-no-tani (Settsu).

In 1185, at the Battle of Dan-no-ura (Nagato), Shigetada ended the Genpei War on the winning side.

In 1189 Shigetada accompanied Minamoto Yoritomo in his expedition against Fujiwara Yasuhira (1155-1189) of Mutsu.

In 1199, after the death of Minamoto Yoritomo, Shigetada became a counselor to Minamoto Yoriié (1182-1204).

In 1205 Shigetada and his eldest son Shigeyasu, having been calumniated with the 1st Kamakura Shikken Hojo Tokimasa (1138-1215), who held a neighboring fief, were summoned to Kamakura, but refused to go. In consequence Tokimasa sent troops to arrest them. After Shigeyasu was killed at his residence at Yui-ga-hama (near Kamakura), Shigetada was killed at Futamata-gawa (Musashi).

Shigetada's heroic actions became the stuff of legend, and in literature he is known for his bravery and strength.

This was the end of the 1st line of the Hatakeyama.

Hatakeyama Shigeyasu (-1205)

Eldest son of Shigetada.

In 1204 Shigeyasu was one of the samurai who was chosen to go to Kyoto to pick up the wife of the 3rd Minamoto Shogun Sanetomo (1192-1219), and it was in that occasion that, at a feast, he had a verbal fight with Hiraga Tomomasa (-1205), who was responsible for the capital's defenses. Tomomasa then calumniated with his father-in-law, the 1st Kamakura Shikken Hojo Tokimasa (1138-1215). Tokimasa himself held a grudge against his son-in-law Shigetada, who had protected the 2nd Minamoto Shogun Yoriié (1182-1204), the heir to the 1st Minamoto Shogun Yoritomo (1147-1199), and was looking for a pretext to kill them. Having obtained from the Shogun an order to arrest the Hatakeyama, he surrounded Shigeyasu's residence at Yui-ga-hama (near Kamakura) with his soldiers. Shigeyasu fought well, but in the end was killed. The next day his father was killed at Futamata-gawa (Musashi).

Hatakeyama Yoshizumi (early 13th century)

Son of Minamoto (Ashikaga) Yoshikané (1154-1199).

In 1205 Yoshizumi was chosen by the 1st Kamakura Shikken Hojo Tokimasa (1138-1215) to revive the name of Hatakeyama after the deaths of Hatakeyama Shigetada (1164-1205) and his son Shigeyasu (-1205). He married the widow of Shigeyasu, a daughter of Tokimasa, and inherited the Hatakeyama domain.

Hatakeyama Kunikiyo/Dosei (-1364)

Son of Iekuni, and a 6th-generation descendant of Yoshizumi.

In 1335 Kunikiyo accompanied Ashikaga Tadayoshi (1306-1352) in his campaign against Nitta Yoshisada (1301-1338), followed Ashikaga Takauji (1305-1358) into Kyoto, and was made Kii no shugo "constable."

From 1336-1337 Kunikiyo was Izumi no shugo.

In 1349, when Ashikaga Motouji (1340-1367) was sent to Kamakura as the 1st Kanto kubo "Kanto deputy Shogun," Kunikiyo became his shitsuji "deputy" and Kawachi no shugo. He then shaved his head and took the name Dosei.

In 1358 Dosei was ordered to put Nitta Yoshioki (-1358) to death, and accordingly had him drowned in the Rokugo-gawa (Musashi).

In 1360 Dosei defeated Kira Mitsusada, who then submitted to the Ashikaga.

Dosei took part in the expedition of the 2nd Ashikaga Shogun Yoshiakira (1330-1368) against the Kusunoki and the Wada of the Southern Court.

Later, on account of differences with the Shogun, he lost favor, fled to Shuzen-ji (Izu), then to Kyoto, where he died.

Hatakeyama Yoshito (1331-1379)

Son of Iekuni. He shared the fortune of his brother Kunikiyo.

When his brother lost favor, however, Yoshito replaced him, and vanquished Shiba Takatsuné (-1367).

Kawachi-Hatakeyama

The Kawachi-Hatakeyama were represented at the start of the 16th century by two main branches issuing from Hatakeyama Mochikuni, with the more powerful of the two deriving from Masanaga, who had been adopted by Mochikuni, who had despaired of having any natural sons. When Mochikuni did in fact a sire a son, Yoshinari, he sought to disinherit Masanaga. A civil war ensued and the two branches were often at odds thereafter.

Their descendants served Toyotomi Hideyoshi (1536-1598) and Tokugawa Ieyasu (1543-1616), and during the Edo Period (1603-1868) the clan held the hereditary position of koké "master of ceremonies."

Notable Ancestors

Hatakeyama Motokuni (1352-1406)

Son of Yoshito. In 1392 he received Yamashiro, then in 1394 Kawachi.

In 1398 Motokuni was made Kyoto kanrei "Kyoto deputy Shogun," and was the first of his family to bear that title. Soon afterwards he had his head shaved and took the name Tokugen.

Hatakeyama Mitsuié (1372-1433)

Son of Motokuni.

In 1399 Mitsuié repressed the Oei Rebellion of Ouchi Yoshihiro (1356-1399) in Izumi, and received Kii.

In 1408 Mitsuié was appointed Kawachi no shugo "constable."

In 1410 Mitsuié became Kyoto kanrei "Kyoto deputy Shogun," shaved his head and took the name Dosui. After having been replaced as kanrei by Hosokawa Mitsumoto (1378-1426) in 1412, in 1421 Mitsuié was again invested with this office.

In 1428 Mitsuie was appointed Yamashiro no shugo.

In 1429 Mitsuie had the honor of drawing from lot the name of Ashikaga Yoshinori (1394-1441) as the 6th Kamakura Shogun in the sanctuary of the Iwashimizu-Hachiman Shrine (Kyoto). It was believed that Hachiman's influence had affected this auspicious choice.

Hatakeyama Mochikuni (1397-1455)

Son of Mitsuié. In 1441 he had his head shaved and took the name Tokuhon.

From 1442-1445 Mochikuni was Kyoto kanrei "Kyoto deputy Shogun."

Mochikuni, having no children, adopted his nephew Masanaga; but in 1454 a son, Yoshinari, was born to him. A succession dispute was set off when Masanaga applied to Hosokawa Katsumoto (1430-1473), who set fire to Mochikuni's house. He fled to Kawachi, and Masanaga took possession of his domain.

In 1455 Mochikuni raised troops in retaliation, but the 8th Ashikaga Shogun Yoshimasa (1436-1490) succeeded in reconciling them.

Hatakeyama Masanaga (1442-1493)

Son of Mochitomi. Was Owari no kami.

Masanaga was adopted by his uncle Mochikuni, who had no children; but in 1454 a son, Yoshinari, was born to him, and he sought to disinherit Masanaga. The latter set off a succession dispute, but in 1455 the 8th Ashikaga Shogun Yoshimasa (1436-1490) succeeded in reconciling them. The Hatakeyama were thus divided into two camps.

In 1460 the struggle began anew: Masanaga defeated the supporters of Yoshinari, who fled to Yoshino.

In 1464 Masanaga was made Kyoto kanrei "Kyoto deputy Shogun."

In the Onin War (1467-1477) Masanaga fought on the side of Hosokawa Katsumoto (1430-1473), and Yoshinari fought on that of Yamana Sozen (1404-1473). The two parties were alternately victorious and defeated. The hostilities ceased in 1485, but they recommenced in 1493, when Masanaga attacked Yoshitoyo, a son of Yoshinari, in Kawachi, but he was defeated and committed suicide.

Masanaga is sometimes credited for inventing the horo, a stiffened cloak used by messengers and bodyguards to improve their visibility on the battlefield, and to act as an arrow catcher.

Hatakeyama Yoshinari (1454-1493)

Son of Mochikuni.

Before Yoshinari's birth, his father had adopted his nephew Masanaga, who revolted when he was deprived of his succession. The whole life of Yoshinari was one long struggle against his rival cousin and adoptive brother.

In 1454 Hosokawa Katsumoto (1430-1473) and Yamana Sozen (1404-1473) having joined the party of Masanaga, Yoshinari was taken to Iga.

After a short period of peace, in 1460 the war recommenced, and Yoshinari retired to Kawachi, then to Koya-san (Kii).

During the Onin War (1467-1477) Yoshinari was supported by Yamana Sozen (1404-1473).

He fought till his death.

Hatakeyama Naonobu (-1534)

Son of Masanaga. He followed the 10th Ashikaga Shogun Yoshitané (1466-1523) in his campaign against Rokkaku Takayori (-1520). Afterwards in 1492 he retired to Kii.

In 1504 Naonobu transferred his castle of Takaya (Kawachi) to his son Tanenaga, and shaved his head.

In 1534 Naonobu tried to create trouble, but was arrested, and exiled to Awaji, where he soon afterwards died.

Hatakeyama Yoshitoyo (-1499)

Son of Yoshinari.

In 1493 the 10th Ashikaga Shogun Yoshitané (1466-1523), together with his uncle Masanaga, warred against him in Kawachi. Yoshitoyo, aided by Hosokawa Masamoto (1466-1507), defeated the Shogunal army and killed his uncle, but in turn perished in a battle.

Hatakeyama Yoshihidé (-1532)

Son of Yoshitoyo. He resided in Takaya Castle (Kawachi).

In 1507 Yoshihidé was besieged by Hatakeyama Naonobu, resisted for a whole year, but finally fled to Izumi.

In 1511 Yoshihidé sided with the Miyoshi and Hosokawa Sumimoto (1489-1520), and was able to re-entered Takaya Castle.

In 1532 Yoshihidé, allying with Miyoshi Motonaga (-1532), was attacked by Hosokawa Harumoto (1519-1563), and committed suicide.

Hatakeyama Takamasa (1527-1576)

Son of Masakuni. He inherited Kawachi, and resided at Takaya Castle. He was Kii no kami, Harima no kami, and Owari no kami.

In 1559 Takamasa was defeated by Miyoshi Chokei (1522-1564), who took Takaya Castle. In the following year he was more fortunate in his campaign against Miyoshi Yoshikata (1527-1562).

In 1568 the 15th Ashikaga Shogun Yoshiaki (1537-1597) again put him in the possession of Takaya Castle.

In 1573 Yusa Nobunori, one of his kerai "vassals," seized Takaya Castle, and slew Takamasa's son Terutaka. Takamasa raised troops and tried to take revenge, but without success. Then Oda Nobunaga (1534-1582) came, defeated Nobunori, and kept Takaya Castle for himself.

Takamasa lived three years more, almost in a state of destitution. In 1575 he received baptism.

Hatakeyama Sadamasa (-1584)

Son of Masayori, and nephew to Takamasa.

In 1577 Sadamasa was encouraged by Kennyo Kosa (1543-1592), the 11th head of the Hongan-ji (Kyoto) and the chief abbot of the Ishiyama Hongan-ji (later Osaka), in conjunction with Matsunaga Hisahidé (1510-1577), to revolt against Oda Nobunaga (1534-1582).

In 1584 Sadamasa joined the alliance headed by Tokugawa Ieyasu (1543-1616) against Toyotomi Hideyoshi (1536-1598), but was killed in the fighting.

His descendants went on to serve the Tokugawa.

Hatakeyama Yukishigé (late 16th century)

Served Toyotomi Hideyoshi (1536-1598). In 1587 he was given Hiji Castle (Bungo).

During the Seki-ga-hara Campaign (1600) Yukishigé sided with Ishida Mitsunari (1560-1600), and was afterwards deprived of his fief by Tokugawa Ieyasu (1543-1616).

NOTO-HATAKEYAMA

In 1398, Hatakeyama Mitsunori, Noto no shugo "constable," built Nanao Castle there. The branch was weakened by internal strife that finally brought about its ruin as an independent daimyo house. In the 1577 Siege of Nanao, Uesugi Kenshin (1530-1578) attacked Hatakeyama Yoshitaka, who sent for assistance from Oda Nobunaga (1534-1582), but before the latter could respond, the castle fell, and Yoshitaka lost his life.

AZUCHI-MOMOYAMA PERIOD – KAKIMI

NOTABLE ANCESTORS

Hatakeyama Yoshimuné (-1480)
Son of Masakuni.

Yoshimuné first served Yamana Sozen (1404-1473), then, by the order of the 8th Ashikaga Shogun Yoshimasa (1436-1490), he joined the party of Hosokawa Katsumoto (1430-1473).

Hatakeyama Yoshifusa (1495-1545)
In 1514 succeeded Yoshimoto (-1514). He was lord of Noto.

In 1526, to consolidate his power, Yoshifusa reinforced Nanao Castle (Noto), where he established himself.

Yoshifusa was best known for acting as a patron to scholars, and invited various scholars from Kyoto to come and lecture at Nanao. A capable leader, the Noto-Hatakeyama enjoyed a period of relative stability under his rule.

Hatakeyama Yoshitsuna (1536-1594)
Succeeded Yoshitsugu at the age of 16.

The Noto-Hatakeyama was governed by a council of seven clan retainers, and these men endeavored to use Yoshitsuna as a puppet, but he and his father worked quietly to create rifts within the council. They found an ally in Igawa Mitsunobu, whom they had appointed to the council in 1554, following the death of an original member. Civil war erupted again at around the same time and the effect was to enhance Yoshitsuna's position. He was unable to maintain control over his troublesome retainers, however, and in 1566 was finally forced to flee to Omi.

In 1574 Yoshitsuna's son Yoshitaka was overthrown by those same retainers, prompting Uesugi Kenshin (1530-1578) to later attack Noto.

His brother Yoshiharu served the Uesugi, and became better known as Jojo Masashigé (1545-1643).

Hatakeyama Yoshitaka (1557-1577)
2nd son of Yoshitsuna. In 1574 he assumed control as the 11th head of the Noto-Hatakeyama, but was overthrown from Nanao Castle by their retainers, the Cho, and others.

In the 1577 Siege of Nanao, Uesugi Kenshin (1530-1578) attacked Yoshitaka, who sent a message to Oda Nobunaga (1534-1582) seeking his assistance, but he did not have time to respond. Yoshitaka was poisoned and murdered by one of his kerai "vassals," Yusa Yoshifusa. A traitor among the Hatakeyama opened the gates, and the castle fell.

From this epoch the branch disappears from history.

MUTSU-HATAKEYAMA

The Mutsu-Hatakeyama held Nihonmatsu Castle (Mutsu), built by Hatakeyama Mitsuyasu, and saw its power gradually diminish over the course of the Sengoku "Warrings States" Period (1467-1573) until they were looked upon by their neighbors, the Ashina, as essentially vassals. Nonetheless, allied to the Kasai, they clashed frequently with the Daté. In 1586 the branch was largely destroyed at the hands of Daté Masamune (1567-1636).

NOTABLE ANCESTORS

Hatakeyama Yoshikuni (1521-1580)
Son of Yoshiuji. In 1547 he succeeded as the 13th lord of the Mutsu-Hatakeyama.

At various times Yoshikuni came into conflict with the Ashina.

Hatakeyama Yoshitsugu (1552-1586)
Son of Yoshikuni. He was head of the Nihonmatsu Hatakeyama of Mutsu.

Yoshitsugu was hard-pressed by Daté Masamuné (1567-1636), so in 1585 called on Masamuné's retired father, Daté Terumuné (1543-1585), to intercede and make peace. When Terumuné and Yoshitsugu met, however, Yoshitsugu kidnapped Terumuné at swordpoint. When Masamuné heard of this double-cross, he rode hard after Yoshitsugu.

In 1586 Daté Masamuné attacked Nihonmatsu Castle (Mutsu), and the Hatakeyama accepted an offer of surrender brokered by the Soma. Yoshitsugu's life however was forfeit, and Masamuné had his head exposed.

KAKIMI

Revenues: 20,000 koku
Territory: Bungo
Castle: Tomiku (Bungo)

NOTABLE ANCESTORS

Kakimi Iezumi (-1600)
Entered the service of Toyotomi Hideyoshi (1536-1598), who bestowed on him the castle of Tomiku (Bungo -- 20,000 koku).

In the Invasions of Korea (1592-1598) Iezumi took part.

In 1600 Iezumi sided with Ishida Mitsunari (1560-1600) against Tokugawa Ieyasu (1543-1616) during the latter's Seki-ga-hara Campaign, and was killed at Ogaki Castle (Mino).

HATANO

Territory: Tanba
Castles: Kameyama, Yakami (Tanba)

Family of Tanba daimyo descended from Fujiwara Hidesato (10th century). Eight generations later, Tsunenori settled in Tanba, and was the first to take the name of Hatano.

After the Onin War (1467-1477) a branch settled at Yakami (Tanba) and was called Higashi-Hatano; another at Hikami (Tanba), the Nishi-Hatano.

NOTABLE ANCESTORS
Hatano Hideharu (1541-1579)

Eldest son of Harumichi, and grandson of Tanemichi. He was originally a retainer of Miyoshi Nagayoshi/Chokei (1522-1564). His brother Hidetoshi occupied the castle of Kameyama (Tanba).

In 1565, after Miyoshi Nagayoshi died, Hideharu became independent, capturing Yakami Castle (Tanba), which he took as his place of residence.

Nagayoshi later sided with the 15th Ashikaga Shogun Yoshiaki (1537-1597) when the latter was estranged with Oda Nobunaga (1534-1582).

In 1576 Oda Nobunaga ordered Akechi Mitsuhidé (1528-1582) to invade Tanba, but Hideharu managed to hold Yakami-jo for three years.

In 1579 Akechi Mitsuhidé offered his mother as a hostage to let Hideharu surrender with dignity. The latter complied, knowing he could not hold out indefinitely. When he arrived at Azuchi Castle (Omi) to submit, Oda Nobunaga executed him. After hearing of this, the troops at Yakami killed Mitsuhidé's mother. This incident strained the relationship between Mitsuhidé and Nobunaga, eventually culminating in Mitsuhidé killing Nobunaga at the Honno-ji (Kyoto) in 1582.

With Hideharu's death, no one rose to hold together the clan and it disappeared completely.

KASAI

Territories: Musashi, Mutsu

Family descended from the Taira, who originally settled in Musashi.

In the late 12th century they moved to Mutsu, where they were powerful locally and clashed with the Hatekayama in the Kurihara area.

The Kasai later allied with the Daté, but suffered internal disturbances, such as the Tenmon no Ran (1532-1536), riots that took place in Kyoto between the followers of the Nichiren sect and the followers of the Ikko-ikki and Tendai-shu sects. The Kasai were later invaded by their erstwhile allies and badly defeated at Tasuku. After this defeat a number of retainers began to drift away and the power of the family waned as it accepted Daté control.

In 1590 the Kasai were dispossessed by Toyotomi Hideyoshi (1536-1598) for tardiness in attending the Siege of Odawara.

In 1591 former Kasai retainers and farmers rioted against Kimura Hidetoshi and his son Shigemasa, whom Toyotomi Hideyoshi had placed in control of the Kasai lands, and had to be suppressed by Daté Masamuné (1567-1636).

NOTABLE ANCESTORS
Kasai Kiyoshigé (12th-13th century)

During the Genpei War (1180-1185) Kiyoshigé joined the party of Minamoto Yoritomo (1147-1199), and accompanied Minamoto Noriyori (1156-1193) in his campaign against the Taira.

In 1189 Kiyoshigé accompanied Yoritomo in his expedition against Fujiwara Yasuhira (1155-1189). He was then appointed governor of Mutsu.

In 1213 Kiyoshigé contributed to the suppression of the revolt of Wada Yoshimori (1147-1213) against the Hojo, and received the title Iki no kami.

In 1215 he had his head shaved, and the people gave him the name Ikinyudo.

His descendants, for several generations, continued to govern Mutsu.

ISHIDA

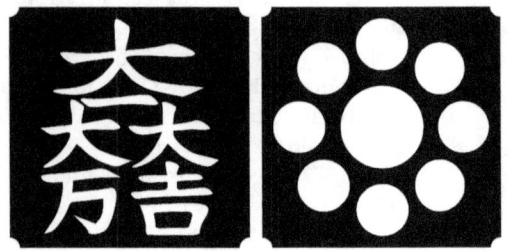

Territory: Omi
Castles: Ishida, Sawayama (Omi)

Family descended from the Fujiwara.

NOTABLE ANCESTORS

Ishida Masatsugu (-1600)

Son of Seishin. Held Ishida Castle (Omi).

Masatsugu served the Asai, and in 1573 retired after that clan's defeat.

In 1600 he committed suicide when he heard of the defeat of his son Mitsunari at the Battle of Seki-ga-hara (Mino).

Ishida Kazushigé/Mitsunari (1560-1600)

2nd son of Masatsugu. Born at Ishida (Omi). His childhood name was Sakichi. The Ishida were retainers of the Asai until that clan's defeat in 1573.

Around 1578 Mitsunari was recruited into the service of Hashiba (later Toyotomi) Hideyoshi (1536-1598), in part due to his cultural acuity. When Hideyoshi engaged in a campaign in the Chugoku "middle provinces" region, Mitsunari assisted in the 1581 Siege of Tottori (Inaba), the 1582 Siege of Takamatsu (Bitchu), and others. After Hideyoshi seized power, Mitsunari became known as a talented financial manager due to his knowledge and skill at calculation.

In 1585 Mitsunari was made jibushosuké. He was the administrator of Sakai (Izumi), a role he took together with his elder brother Masazumi, and received in fief Sawayama Castle (Omi -- 186,000 koku).

Mitsunari became distrusted and disliked by many, in part due to his rigid character, and in part to the power he wielded within the Toyotomi government. He issued numerous orders in Toyotomi Hideyoshi's name, and often acted as his representative. Though he had many friends, he was on bad terms with some daimyo that were known as good warriors, including Hideyoshi's relative Fukushima Masanori (1561-1624).

In 1592 Mitsunari took part in the 1st Invasion of Korea as a member of the staff to the commander-in-chief Ukita Hideié (1573-1655).

In 1597, during the 2nd Invasion of Korea, Mitsunari was dispatched there as inspector of forces. In the course of carrying out his duties he earned the hatred of both Kuroda Yoshitaka (1546-1604) and Kobayakawa Hideaki (1577-1602), whom he reported as being lax in their conduct.

In 1598, right before he died, Toyotomi Hideyoshi named Mitsunari as one of the go-bugyo "five commissioners," responsible with maintaining the civil affairs of the realm while his son Hideyori (1593-1615) came of age. Mitsunari was outspoken, and at times tactless, but held enough support to challenge Tokugawa Ieyasu (1543-1616), the most powerful of the Go-Tairo "Five Regents." He argued, with some cause, that Ieyasu was undermining both the legacy of the late Taiko and his final wishes. Ieyasu countered by painting Mitsunari, also with some validity, as an unscrupulous schemer. In 1599 Mistunari went so far as to attempt the assassination of Ieyasu, and narrowly avoided his own death at the hands of several Tokugawa loyalists.

In 1600 Mitsunari persuaded Uesugi Kagekatsu (1556-1623) to be the first to take the field against Ieyasu, and, whilst they were combating, he formed his party, predominantly from the western provinces: Mori Terumoto (1553-1625), Ukita Hideié, Kobayakawa Hideaki, Shimazu Yoshihiro (1535-1619), Nabeshima Katsushigé (1580-1657), Tachibana Muneshigé (1567-1642), Konishi Yukinaga (1555-1600), Kikkawa Hiroié (1561-1625), Chosokabé Morichika (1575-1615), etc., declared for Toyotomi Hideyori, raised a large army of men, and marched against Tokugawa Ieyasu who, in haste, came southward. The two armies met at the Battle of Seki-ga-hara (Mino), where the defection of some of the allies caused the defeat of Mitsunari, who fled to Mount Ibuki (Omi). His father, brother, and son Shigeié took refuge at Sawayama, but being pursued by the victorious army, they put their wives and children to death, and committed suicide. Mitsunari was arrested six days later at the village of Iguchi, conducted to Kyoto, and, along with Konishi Yukinaga and Ankokuji Ekei (1539-1600), decapitated at Rokujo-ga-hara.

Christian missionaries gave him the name Gibo-no-chio.

Ishida Shigenari (1589-1641)

Son of Mitsunari. He was also known as Sugiyama Gengo.

Shigenari served as a retainer of the Tsugaru of Hirosaki (Mutsu).

ISSHIKI

Territories:
Mikawa, Wakasa, Tango

Daimyo family descended from the Seiwa-Genji.

During the Muromachi "Ashikaga" Period (1336-1573) it was one of the shi-shoku "four families" in which the shitsuji "minister" of the Kyoto kanrei "Kyoto deputy Shogun" was chosen.

The family lost its domain during the civil wars of the 16th century.

Notable Ancestors

Isshiki Kimifuka (late 13th century)

7th son of Minamoto Yasuuji. Towards the end of the 13th century he established himself at Isshiki (Mikawa), and took that name.

Isshiki Akinori (-1406)

In 1392 defeated and killed Yamana Ujikiyo (1345-1392) of Izumi, and received the fief of Imatomi (Wakasa).

Isshiki Yoshitsura (1400-1440)

Son of Mitsunori (-1414), and grandson of Akinori.

In 1411 Yoshitsura divided his domain with his brother Mochinori, who received Tango, and kept Wakasa for himself. Thus the family was divided into two branches.

In 1440 Yoshitsura revolted against the 6th Ashikaga Shogun Yoshinori (1394-1441), but was defeated and killed by Takeda Nobukata.

Isshiki Yoshinao (-1483)

Son of Yoshitsura.

During the Onin War (1467-1477) Yoshinao sided with Yamana Sozen (1404-1473). In 1467 he was defeated by Hosokawa Katsumoto (1430-1473).

Isshiki Yoshiharu (late 15th century)

Son of Yoshinao.

In 1488 Yoshiharu accompanied Ashikaga Yoshimi (1439-1491) in his flight into Omi, and remained there till 1490 when Yoshitané (1466-1523) was nominated as the 10th Ashikaga Shogun.

Isshiki Yoshimichi (-1579)

Son of Yoshiyuki. In 1558 he became head of the clan. He opposed Oda Nobunaga (1534-1582).

In 1578 Yoshimichi suffered the invasion of his lands by Hosokawa Fujitaka (1534-1610) and Hosokawa Tadaoki (1563-1646). He was initially successful against the former, but was defeated when Akechi Mitsuhidé (1528-1582) arrived, and the Nuta betrayed him.

In 1579, after his castle fell to Hosokawa Fujitaka, Yoshimichi was forced to commit suicide, but his son Yoshisada continued to resist.

Isshiki Yoshisada (-1582)

Son of Yoshimichi. In 1579 took over as head of the clan when his father was forced to commit suicide by the Hosokawa.

Yoshisada continued to resist until he accepted a truce with Hosokawa Fujitaka (1534-1610), and married one of his daughters.

In 1582 Yoshisada was overthrown and killed by his uncle Isshiki Yoshikiyo, who was in turn destroyed by the Hosokawa.

Isshiki Yoshikiyo (-1582)

Governor of Yumigi Castle (Tango).

After Yoshikiyo overthrew and killed his nephew Yoshisada, he was in turn killed by the Hosokawa.

KASUYA

Revenues: 12,000 koku
Territory: Harima
Castle: Kakogawa (Harima)

Notable Ancestors

Kasuya Takenori (1562-1607)

2nd son of Tadayasu. He was naizen-no-kami "1st cupbearer to the Emperor."

Following the 1576 Chugoku "middle provinces" Campaign, at the recommendation of Kuroda Yoshitaka (1546-1604), Takenori became a page of Toyotomi Hideyoshi (1536-1598).

In 1583 Takenori achieved notoriety with his distinguished combat at the Battle of Shizu-ga-také (Omi), where he was known as one of the Seven Spears of Shizu-ga-také, and for this distinction he received a stipend of 3,000 koku from Toyotomi Hideyoshi.

For his service in the Invasions of Korea (1592-1598), Takenori received Kakogawa Castle (Harima -- 12,000 koku).

After the death of Toyotomi Hideyoshi, Takenori joined the party of Ishida Mitsunari (1560-1600) against Tokugawa Ieyasu (1543-1616), and joined in the 1600 Siege of Fushimi Castle (Kyoto).

After the Battle of Seki-ga-hara (Mino) Takenori's holdings were confiscated, but his family was later allowed a 500 koku stipend, and was given the status of hatamoto under the Tokugawa. Soon after Takenori's death, however, the Kasuya line ended.

Takenori's brother was fellow Sengoku-era warrior Kasuya Tomomasa, and his nephew was the famed archer and Aizu domain retainer Kasuya Takenari.

KATATA

Revenues: 20,000 koku
Territory: Katata (Omi)

Daimyo family that resided at the village of the same name towards the end of the 16th century (Omi -- 20,000 koku).

NOTABLE ANCESTORS

Katata Horozumi (-1600)

He was hyobu-sho-suké "deputy minister of war."

In 1600, having joined the party against Tokugawa Ieyasu (1543-1616), Horozumi was dispossessed and condemned to commit seppuku.

KIMURA

Revenues: 300,000 koku
Territory: Mutsu
Castles: Toyoma (Mutsu), Furukawa (Mutsu)

NOTABLE ANCESTORS

Kimura Hidetoshi (late 16th century)

A samurai who served first Akechi Mitsuhidé (1528-1582), then Toyotomi Hideyoshi (1536-1598).

After the 1590 Siege of Odawara, Hidetoshi received a revenue of 300,000 koku in Mutsu. He thereupon established himself in the castle of Toyoma, and his son Shigemasa in that of Furukawa.

In 1591 their poor administration touched off a revolt by the farmers and former Kasai and Ozaki retainers that had to be put down by Daté Masamuné (1567-1636). Soon afterwards Hidetoshi and his son Shigemasa were dispossessed.

KODERA

Residence: Himeji Castle (Harima)

Family of daimyo who were entrusted with the guard of the Himeji Castle (Harima), first for the Akamatsu, and then for the Yamana, before finally becoming independent.

NOTABLE ANCESTORS

Kodera Norimoto (mid 16th century)

In 1557 was dispossessed by Toyotomi Hideyoshi (1536-1598).

Kitabataké

Territory: Northern Mutsu

Kitabataké Chikafusa

Daimyo family of northern Mutsu, related to the Kitabataké of Isé, and like them descended from Naka-no-in Michikata (Murakami-Genji).

This branch, also known as the Namioka-Kitabataké, was descended from Kitabataké Akiié (1317-1338), a son of the famous Kitabataké Chikafusa (1293-1354).

During the 16th century the clan competed with the neighboring Daikoji and Oura (later Tsugaru) families. Following a damaging internal disturbance in 1562, the power of the family waned, and in 1578 Kitabataké Akimura was attacked by Tsugaru Tamenobu (1550-1608) and committed suicide, ending the clan as daimyo.

A cousin of Akimura named Kitabataké Akinori became a retainer of the Nanbu, and assumed the name Namioka. Later, his descendants would restore the Kitabataké name.

Notable Ancestors

Kitabataké Chikafusa (1293-1354)

Son of Moroshigé. Was a noble of the Imperial Court and a writer. He was successively chunagon "middle counselor" (1319), dainagon "grand counselor" (1323), then daijin (1333).

Chikafusa was tutor to Prince Tokinaga, and when the latter died, he became a Buddhist monk with the name Sogen.

Chikafusa disliked and opposed the 1st Ashikaga Shogun Takauji (1305-1358), who he felt was a "greedy soldier of no great merit, and not of a really good family." He supported the Southern Court in Yoshino (southern Yamato), and over the span of his career served five Emperors: Go-Fushimi (1288-1336), Go-Nijo (1285-1308), Hanazono (1297-1348), Go-Daigo (1288-1339), and Go-Murakami (1328-1368).

Some of Chikafusa's greatest and most famous works were performed during the reign of Go-Daigo, under whom he proposed a series of reforms, amounting to a revival or restoration of political and economic systems of several centuries earlier. He authored a number of works defending the right of Go-Daigo's line to the throne,

Chikafusa was sent by Go-Daigo to Mutsu as governor, and worked to drum up support there for the cause of the Southern Dynasty.

In 1335 Chifusa was hard-pressed by Ishido Yoshifusa, whom Takauji had dispatched as a counter to Chikafusa, and captured Taga, which was the Loyalist's seat in Mutsu.

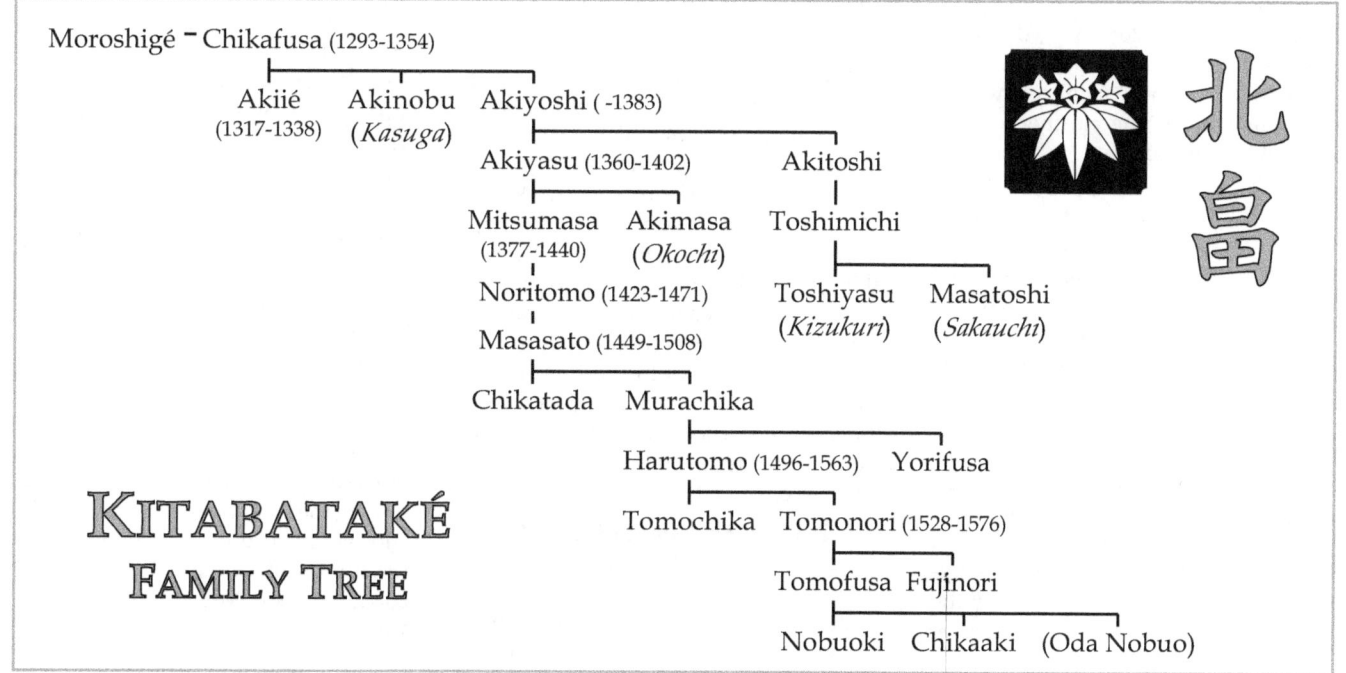

Kitabataké Family Tree

In 1339, when Go-Daigo died, at the Siege of Hitachi, Chikafusa defended himself against Yuki Chikatomo. The siege lasted four years, but when the fortress ultimately fell to the forces of the Ashikaga Bakufu, he was forced to flee to Yoshino, where he advised the Emperor until his death.

Along with Ashikaga Takauji, Chikafusa is considered one of the greatest men of his time. He sought to abolish the system of land tenure and tax collection that supported the power of the bushi, who he viewed as enemies of the Throne. His works, though heavily biased by his personal and political motives, are some of the most detailed accounts available on the history of Japan's feudal government and Imperial line. His *Jinno-shoto-ki* "*Chronicles of the Authentic Lineages of the Divine Emperors*" is a Japanese historical book that addressed the chaotic and unbalanced distribution of land, which he blamed on the government, and the officials and feudal lords who claimed the land. He wrote that seeking rewards was not part of proper behavior, and that it was a warrior's place to give up land and even his life for duty. His Shokugen-sho describes the origins and organization of government officials and structure, as well as his opinion on the promotion and appointment of officials.

Kitabataké Akiié (1317-1338)

Eldest son of Chikafusa.

In 1333 Akiié was ordered to accompany the 6-year-old 8th son of the Emperor Go-Daigo (1288-1339), the Noriyoshi-shinno (1328-1368), to Taga-jo (Mutsu), where the Prince became governor-general of the northern provinces of Mutsu and Dewa.

In 1334 Akiié was appointed Chinjufu-shogun "Defender of the North." Under his direction, a number of families formed a league supporting the Southern Court: they included the Yuki, the Daté, the Nanbu, the Soma, and the Tamura. Later, however, the Soma and several other daimyo were convinced to change sides by Ashikaga Takauji (1305-1358).

In 1336 Akiié led an army, nominally under the command of the Prince Noriyoshi, to reinforce the forces of Nitta Yoshisada (1301-1338) against Ashikaga Takauji. They were aided by the monks from the Enryaku-ji to defeat Takauji at Mii-dera (Omi), which was burned to the ground. The victory allowed the Emperor Go-Daigo to re-enter Kyoto, and Akiié traveled to Kyushu to gather support there for the Southern Court.

In 1337 Akiié returned to Mutsu with the Noriyoshi-shinno to raise troops. Despite facing opposition in the north, he was ordered by the Emperor Go-Daigo to come to the aid of his army to the south of Kyoto. Akiié led his forces slowly south, fighting the Northern Court in many battles. He was defeated at Tonegawa (Kozuké) before pushing south and occupying Kamakura, the capital of the Ashikaga Shogunate, and making his way to Nara (Yamato), fighting at Iga and Seki-ga-hara (Mino). In Nara, while trying to rest and reorganize his forces, he was set upon by Ko Moronao (-1351), and barely escaped to Kawachi. He recouped and pushed through enemy forces at Tenno-ji (near Osaka), but was eventually defeated and killed at Sakai-no-ura (Izumi).

Kitabataké Akinobu (early 14th century)

Son of Chikafusa. Also called Kasuga-shosho. At first he fought under his brother Akiié, and in 1338 succeeded him as Mutsu no kami and Chinjufu-shogun "Defender of the North."

After several campaigns in Hitachi, Shimosa, etc., Akinobu repaired to Kyushu with Prince Yasunaga, and was killed in battle fought against Shoni Yorihisa at Ohara (Chikuzen).

Kitabataké Akiyoshi (-1383)

Son of Chikafusa. He fought first in Mutsu, then in Isé, of which he was appointed koku-shi "governor."

In 1352, joining forces with Wada Masatada and Kusunoki Masayoshi, Akiyoshi defeated Ashikaga Yoshiakira (1330-1367) and entered Kyoto.

Obliged to retreat before overwhelming odds, Akiyoshi remained until his death in the camp of the Southern Dynasty on Mount Yoshino (southern Yamato), and received the titles udaijin "junior minister of state," sangi "counselor," etc.

Kitabataké Akiyasu (1360-1402)

Son of Akiyoshi. He was, like his father, governor of Isé.

After the 1392 fusion of the two Imperial Dynasties, Akiyasu rallied round the 3rd Ashikaga Shogun Yoshimitsu (1358-1408).

In 1399 Akiyasu helped to quell the revolt of Ouchi Yoshihiro (1356-1399), and received from the Shogun the district of Koga (Omi).

Kitabataké Mitsumasa (1377-1440)

Son of Akiyoshi, and brother to Akiyasu, who adopted him as his heir.

In 1414, seeing that contrary to the convention of 1392, the successor to the Emperor Go-Komatsu (1377-1433) was taken from the Northern Dynasty, Mitsumasa conceived the project of marching on Kyoto, and raising to the Chrysanthemum Throne the Prince Ogura, a son of the Emperor Go-Kameyama (1347-1424), but he could not execute his design.

In 1429, a second attempt at the time of the accession of the Emperor Go-Hanazono (1419-1471) did not succeed better: Mitsumasa was defeated by Toki Tokiyori.

Kitabataké Noritomo (1423-1471)

Son of Mitsumasa. Was koku-shi provincial "governor" of Isé.

In 1462 Noritomo repressed an attempt by Hatakeyama Yoshinari (-1493) to revolt against the 8th Ashikaga Shogun Yoshimasa (1436-1490).

At the time of the Onin War (1467-1477), Noritomo gave hospitality to Ashikaga Yoshimi (1439-1491) who was obliged to flee from Kyoto.

Kitabataké Masasato (1449-1508)

Son of Noritomo. Was koku-shi "governor" of Isé.

In 1488 Masasato had to proceed with vigor against one of his officers, Enokura Ujinori, who behaved badly towards those going on pilgrimages to Isé.

Kitabataké Harutomo (1496-1563)

Son of Murachika, and grandson of Masasato. His former name was Chikahira. He supported the 12th Ashikaga Shogun Yoshiharu (1510-1550) and was allowed to change his name to Harutomo as a result.

Harutomo sent troops to assist the Rokkaku fight the Kyogoku while suppressing the Nagano within his own domain. He also repressed the revolt of the samurai of Tamaru (Isé) who had massacred their lord, Tamaru Tomotada.

He was known for his interest in cultural pursuits, which he shared with his father-in-law, Hosokawa Takakuni (1484-1531).

Kitabataké Tomonori (1528-1576)

Son of Harutomo. 8th generation lord of the clan. He used Anotsu Castle (Isé) as his central domain of power.

As time passed Tomonori found himself forced to deal with strife that had evolved itself within his clan, and in 1566 he had to ward off a subsequent invasion by the Miyoshi.

In 1569 this detriment further expanded itself with threats instigated by Oda Nobunaga (1534-1582), who invaded Isé, captured the castles of Kanbé and Kuwana, and surrounded Anotsu. Preparations had been made by Iwami no kami Toriyao, who had reinforced their defenses and stocked enough rice, against such an incursion, but with the defection of Tomonori's younger brother Kotsukuri Tomomasa, and Nobunaga's offer for peace that obliged Tomonori to submit and adopt his 2nd son Nobukatsu (1558-1630) as his heir, Tomonori elected for surrender, and became a monk.

In 1576 Tomonori fell ill, and was assassinated by his samurai.

Tomonori was a swordsman of note who had studied the Kashima Shinto-ryu style of swordsmanship under the famous fencing instructor Tsukahara Bokuden (1489-1571).

Kitabataké Nobuoki (late 16th century)

Eldest son of Tomofusa. He was obliged to cede his hereditary rights to Oda Nobukatsu (1558-1630), son of Nobunaga (1534-1582), who had taken Isé. Dissension broke out between the two, and Nobuoki shut himself up at Nagashima (Isé).

Later on Nobuoki dwelt in Kawachi, then Owari, and at last died in Kyoto.

KONISHI

Revenues: 240,000 koku
Territory: Udo (Higo)
Castle: Udo (Higo)

NOTABLE ANCESTORS

Konishi Yukinaga (1555-1600)

Son of Ryusa, a wealthy apothecary of Sakai (Izumi). He was adopted by a samurai of Ukita Hideié (1573-1655), daimyo of Okayama (Bizen).

In 1577, when Ukita Hideié had to submit to Hashiba (later Toyotomi) Hideyoshi (1536-1598), he chose Yukinaga to negotiate the peace. The young man impressed Hideyoshi, who convinced him to join in his service, and granted him a revenue of 10,000 koku, with the title of Takumi no suké, then that of Settsu no kami.

In 1583 Yukinaga was baptized Augustine, and is spoken of in the letters of the ancient missionaries as Dom Augustinho.

In 1587, after quelling a local uprising in Higo during Toyotmi Hideyoshi's Kyushu Campaign, Yukinaga received as fief, half of the province (240,000 koku), and settled down at Udo Castle, the other half going to his rival Kato Kiyomasa (1562-1611). The two neighbors came to be at odds over the issue of Christianity, which Yukinaga embraced and which Kiyomasa persecuted.

Konishi Yukinaga

In 1592, at the 1st Invasion of Korea, Yukinaga, with Kato Kiyomasa, led the vanguard, and was the first to land at Pusan. He captured Busan and Seoul, whence the king fled with all his Court. Yukinaga pursued him as far as Heijo (Pyongyang), on the frontiers of China, but without being able to overtake him. Shortly after, attacked by a numerous Chinese army, and due to poor supplies, he had to fall back on Seoul.

In 1595, Yukinaga accompanied to Japan the Chinese embassy that came to treat of peace. In 1597, after the rupture of the negotiations, he led the 2nd Invasion of Korea, again with Kato Kiyomasa. He defended the Japanese castle of Suncheon, and repelled the Ming China and the Joseon allied forces.

In 1598, after Toyotomi Hideyoshi's death, Yukinaga returned to Japan.

In 1600 Yukinaga sided with Ishida Mitsunari (1560-1600) against Tokugawa Ieyasu (1543-1616), and was one of the vanquished at the Battle of Sekiga-hara (Mino). He fled into Mount Ibuki (Omi), but was captured by Takenaka Shigekado (1573-1631) and surrendered to Kuroda Nagamasa (1568-1623). He was condemned to death, but being Christian, refused to commit suicide, and was beheaded at Rokujo-ga-hara (Kyoto) along with Mitsunari, Ankokuji Ekei (1539-1600), etc. His domain in Udo (Higo) was given to his rival Kato Kiyomasa, who had supported Ieyasu.

KOBAYAKAWA

Revenues: 520,000 koku

Territories: Bingo, Bizen, Mimasaka, Iyo, Chikuzen

Castles: Mihara (Bingo), Najima (Chikuzen), Okayama (Bizen)

Descended from Doi Sanehira, a notable figure in the Genpei War (1180-85). Sanehira's grandson Kagehira, the adopted son of Doi Tohira, assumed the name Kobayakawa, and lived in the Nuta area of Aki.

By 1260 the Kobayakawa had split into three branches: the Nuta, the Shinjo, and the Takehara. By the mid-15th century the Nuta and Shinjo branches had essentially reformed, while being at increasing odds with the Takehara branch. By the mid-16th century, the Nuta and the Takehara had reconciled to the extent that they reformed under the 3rd son of Mori Motonari (1497-1571), Kobayakawa Takakagé. The Kobayakawa grew in influence due to Takakagé's close relationship with Toyotomi Hideyoshi (1536-1598).

At the end of the 16th century the clan had holdings in Kyushu, and served under the Mori and Toyotomi Hideyoshi. The Kobayakawa fought alongside the Kikkawa, the Mori, the Toyotomi, and the Otomo against the Shimazu, for control of Kyushu. They were awarded Chikuzen as fief following the Shimazu's defeat, but the clan came to an end only a generation later when Kobayakawa Hidéaki died without a successor.

NOTABLE ANCESTORS

Kobayakawa Takakagé (1532-1597)

3rd son of Mori Motonari (1497-1571). He was adopted by the head of the Kobayakawa, who was a vassal of Ouchi Yoshitaka (1507-1551), and in 1545 succeeded his adoptive father following his death.

Takakagé served in all the campaigns of his brother Kikkawa Motoharu (1530-1586), a pillar of the Mori clan, and their reputation became such that they were commonly called Ryo-kawa "Two Rivers."

At the 1555 Battle of Miyajima (Aki) Takakagé defeated Etchu no kami Miura, a general of Sué Harukata (1521-1555).

In 1562 Takakagé defeated Otomo Sorin (1530-1587) in Kyushu.

In 1582, after a long struggle against the armies of Oda Nobunaga (1534-1582) and Toyotomi Hideyoshi (1536-1598), Takakagé had a large share in the conclusion of the peace between Hideyoshi and the Mori following the Siege of Takamatsu (Bitchu).

In 1587, after playing significant roles in the Shikoku and Kyushu campaigns, Takakagé was awarded by Toyotomi Hideyoshi an estate in Iyo and Chikuzen totaling 350,000 koku, and built a castle in Najima (Chikuzen).

In 1592, as Takakagé had no children, Hideyoshi, with whom he had become close friends, gave him as an adopted son and heir, his nephew Hidéaki (1577-1602).

In 1593, during the 1st Invasion of Korea, Takakagé led a division of Kyushu troops, and defeated a Chinese force at the Battle of Byokchekwan (near Pyongyang), distintinguishing himself by his valor. Later that year however he was harried by Korean guerillas in Chollado province, and was forced to retreat.

In 1595 Takakagé was named one of the original Regents for Toyotomi Hideyori (1593-1615), son of Hideyoshi, who gave him the title chunagon "middle counselor."

He then retired to his castle of Mihara (Bingo), where he died after two years there.

Often depicted as being the most intelligent of Motonari's sons, Takakagé was one of the great figures of the latter half of the Sengoku "Warring States" Period (1467-1573).

Kobayakawa Hidekané (1566-1601)

9th and last son of Mori Moronari (1497-1571). He was adopted when a child by Ota Hidetsuna, and was later brought to Kyoto by Toyotomi Hideyoshi (1536-1598) and allowed to use the name Toyotomi.

Around 1587 Hidekané became a Christian, and was baptized as Simon. He married the Christian daughter of Otomo Sorin (1530-1587), Maxentia.

In 1587 Hidekané served in Toyotomi Hideyoshi's Kyushu Campaign, and was afterwards given a large fief at Kurumé (Chikugo).

During the 1600 Seki-ga-hara Campaign, Hidekané commanded troops for the Western Army against the forces of Tokugawa Ieyasu (1543-1616), and fought under Tachibana Muneshigé (1567-1642) at the Siege of Otsu (near Kyoto). After the battle he was deprived of his Chikugo holdings, and was given a small fief in Nagato.

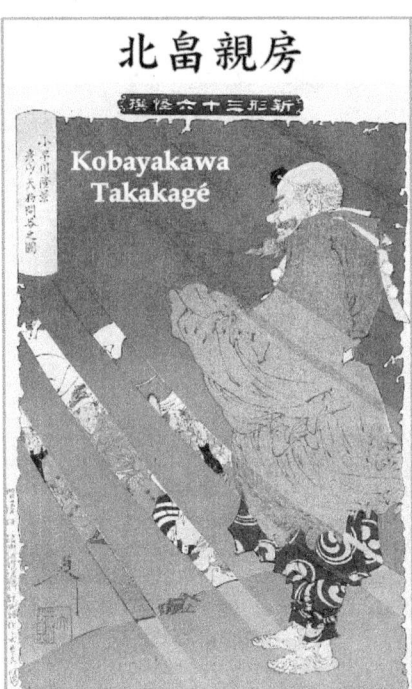

Kobayakawa Takakagé

Azuchi-Momoyama Period – Maki

Kobayakawa Hidéaki (1577-1602)

5th son of Kinoshita Iesada (1543-1608). He was adopted first by his uncle Hashiba (later Toyotomi) Hideyoshi (1536-1598), but in 1592 he became the adopted son and heir to Takakagé. He held the title of chunagon "middle counselor."

For Toyotomi Hideyoshi's 2nd Invasion of Korea (1597), although only 20 years old, Hidéaki was nominally appointed gensui "commander-in-chief" of the expedition by his uncle, with Kuroda Yoshitaka (1546-1604) assigned to assist him with his counsel. During the Battle of Keicho he led reinforcements to rescue Ulsan Castle from the Ming army. Fighting on the front line with a spear, he managed to capture an enemy commander, and successfully broke the siege. The campaign was ultimately unsuccessful, but the cause of the failure should be traced to the rivalry and jealousy of the generals, rather than to the incapacity of the commander-in-chief. Hidéaki was nevertheless denounced as incompetent by the inspector of forces Ishida Mitsunari (1560-1600). The Taiko was displeased, and ordered him to yield the command to another, but he refused to obey. Relations became strained between uncle and nephew, but Tokugawa Ieyasu (1543-1616) succeeded in reconciling them. Hidéaki could forget neither the proceedings of Mitsunari, nor the good offices of Ieyasu.

After the 1598 death of Toyotomi Hideyoshi, Ishida Mitsunari and Otani Yoshitsugu (1559-1600), in order to win Hidéaki over to their side, offered him two additional estates and the tutorship of Hideyoshi's young heir Hideyori (1593-1615) until the age of 15, if he would help them to victory. Nor was Ieyasu slow in making him brilliant offers.

Hidéaki, although rather late, initially embraced the cause of Toyotomi Hideyori. In 1600 he lent his strength to the Siege of Fushimi (Kyoto). However, at the subsequent Battle of Seki-ga-hara (Mino), he remained towards the evening a simple spectator of the doubtful struggle. Then, suddenly abandoning his party, he sent his samurai against the troops of Otani Yoshitsugu (1559-1600), and put them to flight. He then attacked the flank of Ukita Hideié (1573-1655), and secured the victory to Ieyasu. On the very morrow, he besieged the castle of Sawayama (Omi), where Ishida Mitsunari's whole family met their fate.

Although Tokugawa Ieyasu clearly kept Hidéaki at an arm's length, he proved grateful to the defector, and gave him in fief Bizen and Mimasaka, formerly of Ukita Hideié, and headquartered at Okayama Castle (Bizen), raising his revenue to 520,000 koku. But he died less than two years later, aged only 26, after supposedly going mad. As he had no heir, his clan disbanded, and his fiefdoms were absorbed by the neighboring Ikeda.

Kobayakawa Hidéaki

MAKI

Revenues: 100,000 koku
Territory: Kazusa

Anicent family of daimyo that resided at Maki (Kazusa -- 100,000 koku) in the 16th century. In 1590 the clan was deprived of its possessions by Toyotomi Hideyoshi (1536-1598).

Notable Ancestors

Maki Shumé (late 16th century)

Captain of the uma-mawari "mounted guard" of Toyotomi Hidetsugu (1568-1595).

In 1595, when Hidetsugu was forced to commit seppuku, Shumé apparently became a ronin.

KONO

Territory: Iyo

Daimyo family descended from Iyo-shinno, son of the Emperor Kanmu (737-806).

Powerful in Iyo for centuries, in the Genpei War (1180-85) the Kono supported Minamoto Yoritomo (1147-1199), and in the 13th-century Mongol Invasions played a notable role.

During the Nanboku-cho Period (1336-1392) the Kono at first supported the Ashikaga, then shifted their loyalty to the Southern Court.

During the early Sengoku "Warring States" Period, the clan's hold on Iyo was steadily weakened, and at length their domain fell to the Chosokabé of Tosa.

In 1600 an ill-fated attempt by Kono loyalists to restore their clan to Iyo with Mori support ended in defeat at the hands of the Kato.

It is from this family that the Inaba and the Hitotsuyanagi descend.

Notable Ancestors

Kono Michinobu (1156-1223)

In 1180 Michinobu sided with Minamoto Yoritomo (1147-1199) when he rose against the Taira. At first victorious, he afterwards was obliged to flee to Aki. There the Numata furnished him with troops, and in 1184 he re-entered Iyo, but was defeated by Taira Michimori, and fled again.

In 1185, when Taira Munemori (1147-1185), bringing along with him the young Emperor Antoku (1178-1185), arrived at Yashima (Sanuki), he summoned Michinobu to join them and fight against the Minamoto, but he refused, and was again forced to flee. When during his flight he met Minamoto Noriyori (1156-1193) and Minamoto Yoshitsuné (1159-1189), who were coming to fight against the Taira, he joined them, contributed to their victory, and was re-instated in Iyo.

In 1189 Michinobu accompanied Yoritomo in his campaign to Mutsu against Fujiwara Yasuhira (1155-1189).

In the 1221 Jokyu War (Kyoto), Michinobu sided against the Hojo, and was exiled to Hiraizumi (Mutsu), where he died.

Kono Michiari (late 13th century)

Grandson of Michinobu. He was Tsushima no kami.

In 1281 Michiari won fame in fighting against the Mongolian fleet that came to attack Chikuzen Castle. He performed with prowess and captured an enemy admiral. His exploits are captured in the *Moko Shurai Ekotoba* "*Illustrated Account of the Mongol Invasion*," an emakimoto "picture scroll" commissioned by Takezaki Suénaga (1235-1314).

Kono Michimori (-1362)

Son of Michiari. He supported Hojo Takatoki (1303-1333) and Ashikaga Takauji (1305-1358), who confirmed him in the possession of Iyo.

Kono Michitaka (-1374)

Son of Michimori. He abandoned the cause of the Ashikaga, and offered his services to Prince Yasunaga.

Joining forces with Kikuchi Takemitsu (1319-1383), Michitaka fought against Hosokawa Yoriyuki (1329-1392), and had at first some success, but afterwards was defeated, and committed suicide.

Kono Michinao (-1572)

Son of Michihisa. In 1519 he became head of the Kono.

Michinao suffered the revolt of a number of retainers in 1523 and 1530.

In 1539 Michinao repulsed an attack by Hosokawa Harumoto (1519-1563). Michinao's difficulties continued with two Ouchi attacks on Iyo's coastal areas in 1541 at Omi-shima and in 1544 at Kutsuna-shima, though these were also repulsed.

Michinao apparently considered turning over the leadership of the clan to his relative Kono Naomasa, but abandoned the idea when his retainers began to fight amongst themselves.

Michinao died of illness. He was known to be skilled in waka poetry.

Kono Michinobu (-1581)

Younger son of Kono Omi no kami Michiyoshi (-1579). He succeeded Michinao, and was Iyo no kami.

In 1554 Michinobu suffered the abortive rebellion of his vassal Wada Michioki.

In 1565 Michinobu suffered an Otomo campaign against him, which was evidently inspired by his alliance with Mori Motonari (1497-1571).

In 1568 Michinobu took ill, and was forced to give up his duties as lord, handing them to his son Michinao.

Kono Michinao (-1587)

Son of Michinobu. He was danjo-shosuké.

In 1568 Michinao was attacked by Utsunomiya Toyotsuna, who had the support of the Chosokabé of Tosa, and implored the help of Mori Motonari (1497-1571). At the Battle of Torisaka (Iyo), Kobayakawa Takakagé (1533-1597) and Kikkawa Motoharu (1530-1586) came to his rescue, whereupon Toyotsuna was defeated and forced to sue for peace, and Michinao was re-instated in his domain. The victory was afterwards reported to the Bakufu, and a note of congratulations was sent from the 15th Ashikaga Shogun Yoshiaki (1537-1597).

In 1580 Michinao was attacked by Chosokabé Motochika (1538-1599), who conquered Iyo. He fled to Aki, where he died.

MARUMO

Revenues: 20,000 koku
Territory: Fukuzuka (Mino)
Castle: Fukuzuka (Mino)

NOTABLE ANCESTORS

Marumo Chikayoshi (16th-17th century)

Daimyo of Fukuzuka (Mino -- 20,000 koku).

In 1600 Chikayoshi took the side against Tokugawa Ieyasu (1534-1616). He was besieged in his castle by Ichibashi Nagakatsu, deprived of his possessions, and banished to Kaga.

MIYABÉ

Territory: Miyabé (Omi), Inaba, Tajima
Castle: Tottori (Inaba)

Daimyo family of the 16th century.

NOTABLE ANCESTORS

Miyabé Tsugimasu/Keijun (1528-1599)

First a bonze of Enryaku-ji at Hiei-zan (northeast of Kyoto). He followed Asai Nagamasa (1545-1573), who gave him the domain of Miyabé (Omi), which name he took.

At the 1570 Battle of Anegawa (Omi) Tsugimasu fought for Asai Nagamasa and Asakura Yoshikagé (1533-1573) against Oda Nobunaga (1534-1582), but they were defeated.

In 1573, when Isono Kazumasa (1534-1583) was forced to surrender Sawayama Castle (Omi) to Oda Nobunaga, Asai Nagamasa crucified Kazumasa's mother for his failure. Tsugimasu, enraged at the backstabbing qualities of Nagamasa, defected to Nobunaga, and assisted him in the downfall of the Asai.

Tsugimasu served Oda Nobunaga until the latter's death in 1582. He then served Toyotomi Hideyoshi (1536-1598) as an agricultural daikan "administrative official," and was eventually rewarded with Tottori Castle (Inaba).

In 1587 Tsugimasu took part in Toyotomi Hideyoshi's Kyushu Campaign against the Shimazu, and was at the Battle of Taka-jo (Hyuga). After the campaign he obtained an increase of revenues.

In 1596 he retired in favor of his son Nagafusa.

Miyabé Nagafusa/Nagahiro (1581-1634)

Son of Tsugimasu. In 1596 he succeeded his father, and held a sizable fief in Inaba and Tajima.

At the 1600 Siege of Otsu (Kyoto) Nagafusa served under the Kakiya against the garrison of Kyogoku Takatsugu (1560-1609) and forces loyal to Tokugawa Ieyasu (1543-1616). Although the siege was successful, Ieyasu won the concurrent Battle of Seki-ga-hara (Mino). Afterwards Nagafusa was dispossessed of his holdings, and placed in the custody of Nanbu Toshinao (1576-1632).

NAGATSUKA

Revenues: 50,000 koku
Territories: Omi
Castles: Minakuchi (Omi)

NOTABLE ANCESTORS

Nagatsuka Masaié (-1600)

At first kerai "vassal" of Niwa Nagahidé (1535-1585), he passed into the services of Toyotomi Hideyoshi (1536-1598), who gave him the fief of Minakuchi (Omi -- 50,000 koku), and appointed him as one of the go-bugyo "five commissioners."

After the death of Toyotomi Hideyoshi, he opposed Tokugawa Ieyasu (1543-1616), and with Chosokabé Morichika (1575-1615) besieged Anotsu Castle (Isé).

In 1600, vanquished at the Battle of Seki-ga-hara (Mino), Masaié fled to his castle of Minakuchi, which soon after was invested by Ikeda Terumasa (1565-1613).

Masaié hid himself for some time at Sakurai-dani (Settsu), but was found out and committed suicide.

MATSUNAGA

Territories: Kawachi, Yamato
Castle: Shigi-san (Kawachi)

NOTABLE ANCESTORS

Matsunaga Hisahidé (1510-1577)

Was since childhood a companion of Miyoshi Chokei (1522-1564). Since 1541 he appears in documents as a Miyoshi retainer.

In 1549 Hisahidé entered Kyoto with Miyoshi Chokei, and became governor of that city.

In 1558 Hisahidé fought against the Sasaki, who supported the 13th Ashikaga Shogun Yoshiteru (1536-1565).

In 1560 Hisahidé pacified Izumi, and constructed Shigi-san Castle (Kawachi), from which place he governed Yamato and Kawachi. He then received the title of danjo-sho-suké, hence he is also surnamed Danjo.

Between 1561 and 1564, three of Miyoshi Chokei's brothers and his heir died: Miyoshi Yoshikata (1527-1562) and Sogo Kazumasa (1532-1561) passed on under what may be considered mysterious circumstances, while Atagi Fuyuyasu (1528-1564) was assassinated, some say due to Hisahidé framing him, and goading Chokei into having him killed. In 1563 Chokei's son and heir Yoshioki also died under what was probably an unnatural death, rumored to be due to Hisahidé poisoning him.

When Miyoshi Yoshioki died, Miyoshi Chokei adopted his nephew Yoshitsugu (1551-1573) as his heir. In 1564, when Chokei died, his domain essentially came under the independent rule of Hisahidé, and Yoshitsugu came under the guardianship of the so-called Miyoshi triumvirate: Miyoshi Nagayuki, Miyoshi Masayasu, and Iwanari Tomomichi (1519-1578), who held Miyoshi headquarters in Sakai (Settsu). While animosity existed between the guardians and Hisahidé, for the time being they acted in unison.

In 1565 the Shogun Yoshiteru attempted to rid himself of the pervasive Miyoshi influence he had been saddled with for years. The Matsunaga and the Miyoshi sent troops to Nijo Palace (Kyoto), and after a heroic struggle forced Yoshiteru to commit suicide. Yoshiteru's brother Ashikaga Yoshiaki (1537-1597) fled to seek out a patron, and Hisahidé placed the infant Yoshihidé (1564-1568) as the 14th Ashikaga Shogun.

In the meantime Hisahidé and Miyoshi Yoshitsugu came to a parting of ways, and the two clans began fighting. In 1566 the Matsunaga warriors were defeated outside Sakai (Izumi), and Hisahidé himself failed in attempts to reduce the Miyoshi presence in Kawachi. When Hisahidé was attacked at the same time by Rokkaku Yoshikata (1521-1598), a truce was arranged that allowed Hisahidé to leave the Sakai area, and fighting continued further inland. In the course of the conflict, Hisahidé is reputed to have burned down the Daibutsu-den "Great Buddha Hall" of the Todai-ji (Nara), to this day considered a needless act of near-villainy.

In 1568 Oda Nobunaga (1534-1582), with the figurehead Ashikaga Yoshiaki, captured Kyoto, and placed him as the 15th Ashikaga Shogun. Hisahidé cannily decided to submit, and as a token of his sincerity, sent Nobunaga, a bit of a tea enthusiast, a renowned item of tea known as Tsukumogami. He was allowed to keep his lands in Yamato, and was named its shugo "military governor."

For a while Hisahidé served Oda Nobunaga in his extended campaigns against the Miyoshi, the Asai, and the Asakura.

In 1573 Hisahidé briefly allied with Miyoshi Yoshitsugu, and revolted against Oda Nobunaga, but when defeated, he returned to him, and contributed to the destruction of the Miyoshi.

Hisahidé then became involved with the long Siege of Ishiyama Hongan-ji (1570-1580). In 1577 Hisahidé rebelled once again, and with his son Hisamichi abandoned their positions around the fortress temple, and returned to Yamato. Oda Nobunaga sent his son Nobutada (1557-1582) and Tsutsui Junkei (1549-1584) to besiege him in his castle of Shigi-san. The castle was burned, and Hisahidé killed himself. Before his death he defiantly destroyed a priceless tea kettle called Hiragumo that Nobunaga coveted, and ordered his own head destroyed to prevent it becoming a trophy. Hisahidé's other son Kojiro is said to have grabbed his head, and jumped off the castle wall with his sword through his own throat. Hisamichi was captured, taken to Kyoto, and executed.

Although Hisahidé stands out in Japanese history as an infamous schemer, and is portrayed in fictional works as a shriveled old villain, he was in fact a tall handsome educated man, and a patron of tea and the arts.

Matsunaga Hisamichi (-1577)

Son of Hisahidé.

In 1565 Hisamichi assisted his father in forcing the suicide of the 13th Ashikaga Shogun Yoshiteru (1536-1565).

In 1577 Hisamichi joined his father in rebelling against Oda Nobunaga (1534-1582), but was captured, and later executed in Kyoto.

Matsunaga Hisahidé

MUNAKATA

Territory: Chikuzen
Castle: Shira-yama (Chikuzen)

Family descended from the Minamoto. They were the hereditary heads of the Shintoist temple of Munakata-jinja, situated in the district of Munakata (Chikuzen), between the villages of Tashima and Oshima.

NOTABLE ANCESTORS

Munakata Kiyouji (early 10th century)
In 914 Kiyouji was named daiguji "chief" of the Munakata-jinja (Chikuzen), from which he took his name.

Munakata Ujikuni (late 12th century)
Descendant of Kiyouji. He was daiguji "chief" of the Munakata-jinja (Chikuzen).
In 1182 Ujikuni built a castle on Shirayama to protect the temple and its dependencies.
In 1216 Ujikuni adopted Ujitoshi, son of Otomo Toshinao, and transmitted him his charge.

Munakata Ujihiro (mid 15th century)
In 1444 Ujihiro became daiguji "chief" of the Munakata-jinja (Chikuzen).
In 1469 Ujihiro defeated Shoni Noriyori, who had intended to strip him of his domain, and obliged him to escape to Tsushima.

Munakata Okiuji (early 16th century)
Son of Ujihiro.
In 1506 Okiuji joined Ouchi Yoshioki (1477-1528) in order to repulse a new attack of Shoni Noriyori.

Munakata Ujio (-1551)
Sided with Ouchi Yoshitaka (1507-1551).
When Ouchi Yoshitaka was attacked by his vassal Sué Harukata (1521-1555), and committed seppuku, Ujio was likewise defeated, and killed himself at the Dainei-ji at Fukagawa (Suo).

Munakata Ujisada (-1586)
Was constantly at war with his neighbors. After his death the family disappears.

NANJO

Revenues: 60,000 koku
Territory: Hoki
Castle: Hané'ishi (Hoki)

Family of daimyo, who in the 16th century occupied the castle of Hané'ishi (Hoki -- 60,000 koku), and were deprived of it by Tokugawa Ieyasu (1543-1616) in 1600.

OGAWA

Revenues: 70,000 koku
Territory: Iyo
Castle: Imabaru (Iyo)

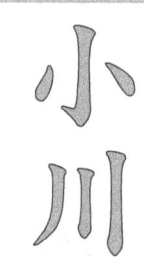

Daimyo family, who at the end of the 16th century occupied the castle of Imabaru (Iyo -- 70,000 koku). They were dispossessed by Tokugawa Ieyasu (1543-1616) in 1600.

NOTABLE ANCESTORS

Ogawa Suketada (1549-1601)
Initially served Akechi Mitsuhidé (1528-1582), and then Shibata Katsutoyo (1556-1583). After Katsutoyo died, he served Toyotomi Hideyoshi (1536-1598), was given Imabari (Iyo -- 70,000), and became a daimyo.
At the 1600 Battle of Seki-ga-hara (Mino), Suketada initially sided with Ishida Mitsunari (1560-1600). During the battle he switched sides to join Tokugawa Ieyasu (1543-1616) along with Kobayakawa Hideaki (1577-1602), Wakisaka Yasuharu (1554-1626), Kutsuki Mototsuna (1549-1632), and Akaza Naoyasu (-1606). Ieyasu won the battle and became the *de facto* ruler of Japan. After the battle Ieyasu seized Suketada's domain.

NISHINA

Territory: Shinano
Castle: Takato (Shinano)

Family descended from Taira Sadamori (10th century). From the 12th century they were established in Shinano.

NOTABLE ANCESTORS

Nishina Morito (-1221)

Having gone to Kumano one day with his son, Morito met the ex-Emperor Go-Toba (1180-1239), who took him into his service. The 2nd Kamakura Shikken Hojo Yoshitoki (1163-1224), apprised of the fact, deprived him of his estates. Go-Toba tried in vain to have them restored to him, but the Shikken remained inflexible. The Emperor was highly incensed at this, and appealed to arms against the Hojo.

In 1221, during the ensuing Jokyu War (Kyoto), Morito passed over into Etchu to support the Imperial cause, but was defeated and killed at Tonami-yama.

Nishina Morinobu (1557-1582)

4th son of Takeda Shingen (1521-1573). His mother was Lady Yukawa, and his childhood name was Takeda Harukiyo. In 1561 he was adopted by the Nishina family of Shinano as part of Shingen's plan to cement his control over the province. He was Satsuma no kami.

In 1582, after the defeat of his brother Takeda Katsuyori (1546-1582), Morinobu fortified himself in the castle of Takato (southern Shinano), and prepared for resistance with his ally Oyamada Masayuki (-1582). Oda Nobutada (1557-1582) sent a bonze to negotiate surrender. Morinobu, miffed at this, had the unfortunate monk's nose and ears cut off, and sent him back to his master. Attacked shortly after, he resisted valiantly. When the castle was about to fall, Morinobu informed the Oda soldiers of his prediction of the coming downfall of Oda Nobunaga (1534-1582), then committed suicide.

OKAMOTO

Revenues: 20,000 koku
Territory: Isé
Castle: Kameyama (Isé)

NOTABLE ANCESTORS

Okamoto Shigemasa (1542-1600)

Native of Owari. He served Oda Nobunaga (1534-1582), then Toyotomi Hideyoshi (1536-1598), who in 1587 gave him the castle of Kameyama (Isé -- 20,000 koku).

In 1590 Shigemasa served in Toyotomi Hideyoshi's Odawara Campaign against the Hojo, and in 1592 the 1st Korean Invasion.

After Toyotomi Hideyoshi's death, he sided against Tokugawa Ieyasu (1543-1616), and was condemned to perform seppuku.

ONOKI

Revenues: 18,000 koku
Territory: Tanba
Castle: Fukuchi-yama (Tanba)

NOTABLE ANCESTORS

Onoki Shigekatsu (-1600)

At first a samurai from Tanba.

In 1579, after the ruin of the Hatano, Shigekatsu received the castle of Fukuchi-yama (Tanba -- 18,000 koku).

After the death of Oda Nobunaga (1534-1582), Shigekatsu served Toyotomi Hideyoshi (1536-1598). In 1587 he accompanied Hideyoshi in his Kyushu Campaign, and had his possessions doubled.

In 1600 Shigetkatsu was on the losing side against Tokugawa Ieyasu (1543-1616). He asked for pardon through the assistance of Ii Naomasa (1561-1602), but was nevertheless invited to take his life by seppuku at the Jodo-ji at Kameyama (Tanba).

His wife was the daughter of Saionji Kintomo. She had been baptized by the name of Joanna in 1583.

ONODERA

Territory: Senboku (Dewa)
Castle: Omori Castle (Dewa)

Family of daimyo, who in the 15th and 16th centuries possessed the district of Senboku (Dewa). They were dispossessed in 1600.

NOTABLE ANCESTORS

Onodera Terumichi (-1598)

Son of Onodera Izu no kami Masumichi (-1546). In his youth, he was sent to Kyoto to serve as page for the 13th Ashikaga Shogun Yoshiteru (1536-1565), from whom he received the 'teru' character in his name. He eventually returned to Dewa, and proved a capable leader.

Onodera Yoshimichi (1566-1645)

2nd son of Terumichi. He held Omori Castle in Ogachi (Dewa), and held the title Totomi no kami.

In 1594 Mogami Yoshiaki (1544-1614), an old enemy of Yoshimichi, is said to have deceived him into punishing one of his chief retainers, and greatly damaged the unity of the Onodera retainers.

In 1599 Yoshimichi resisted attempts by Otani Yoshitsugu (1559-1600) to conduct land surveys in his domain, and as a result was besieged at Omori-jo, but he was able to hold out until winter forced Yoshitugu to retreat.

During the 1600 Seki-ga-hara Campaign, Yoshimichi supported Uesugi Kagekatsu (1556-1623), and afterwards was deprived of his lands.

In 1601 he was exiled to the Chugoku "middle provinces" region.

OTANI

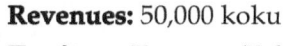

Revenues: 50,000 koku
Territory: Tsuruga (Echizen)

Family that may have been former retainers of the Otomo of Bungo.

NOTABLE ANCESTORS

Otani Yoshitaka/Yoshitsugu (1559-1600)

Born in Bungo. His father was said to be a retainer of either Otomo Sorin (1530-1587) or Rokkaku Yoshikata (1521-1598).

Around 1574, at the age of 15, Yoshitaka was recommended, some say by Ishida Mitsunari (1560-1600), to Hashiba (later Toyotomi) Hideyoshi (1536-1598), who resided then at Himeji Castle (Harima). He quickly rose through the ranks.

In Toyotomi Hideyoshi's 1583 Shizuga-také Campaign, Yoshitaka attacked Takigawa Kazumasu (1525-1586). After Hideyoshi's defeat of Shibata Katsuié (1522-1583), he received the fief of Tsuruga (Echizen -- 50,000 koku), and the title of gyobu-shosuké.

In Toyotomi Hideyoshi's 1587 Kyushu Campaign, Yoshitaka assisted in its logistics. In 1590 he was present at the Siege of Odawara.

For Tomoyoshi Hideyoshi's Invasions of Korea (1592-1598), Yoshitaka served as one of the "Three Bureaucrats" with Ishida Mitsunari and Mashita Nagamori (1545-1615). Yoshitaka and Mitsunari were known for their legendary friendship, which may have been formed in Korea.

Yoshitaka was later dispatched to the northern provinces as a land survey officer. While there he was forced to deal with the resistance of Onodera Yoshimichi (1566-1645), who in 1599 Yoshitaka besieged at Omori Castle (Dewa).

In 1600 Yoshitaka sided at first with Tokugawa Ieyasu (1543-1616), and leaving Tsuruga with his samurai, made ready to join him in his campaign against Uesugi Kagekatsu (1556-1623). At Sawayama (Omi), he met his friend Ishida Mitsunari, who succeeded in winning him over to his party. At the Battle of Seki-ga-hara he was at the head of a force commanded by Toda Shigemasa (1557-1600), Hiratsuka Tamehiro, his son Yoshikatsu, and Kinoshita Yoritsugu. Though suffering from now-advanced leprosy, making him nearly blind and unble to standup, he directed his troops from within a palanquin. After the defection of Kobayakawa Hideaki (1577-1602) to Ieyasu's side, he ordered a retainer to cut off his head, and spirit it away.

His daughter was married to Sanada Yukimura (1567-1615).

Ryuzoji

Revenues: 350,000 koku
Territory: Hizen
Castle: Saga (Hizen)

Family of daimyo originating in Hizen, claiming descent from Fujiwara Hidesato (mid-10th century). It was founded in 1186 by Fujiwara Sueié, who was jito "steward" of Hizen.

In 1336 the Ryuzoji sided with Ashikaga Takauji (1305-1358), but they were defeated in an attempt to conquer the territories of the Otomo and the Shimazu, and their estate was taken over by neighbors.

They came to prominence in the Sengoku "Warring States" Period (1467-1573) in the fight in northern Kyushu.

They were retainers of the Shoni until 1553 when Ryuzoji Takanobu overthrew them. While Takanobu was able to secure most of Hizen, his defeat and death at the 1584 Battle of Okita-na-waté greatly weakened his clan, and they were effectively supplanted by the Nabeshima.

The clan's descendants became retainers of the Matsudaira of Aizu.

Notable Ancestors

Ryuzoji Iekané (1454-1546)

5th son of Yasuié. He was Yamashiro no kami. He succeeded to the head of his family by outliving his elder brothers. He was a vassal of Shoni Masasuké, and fought with him against Ouchi Yoshioki (1477-1528) of Bungo.

In 1506, when Masasuké was defeated and killed, Iekané raised fresh troops, and defeated the Ouchi. In 1530 he again defeated the Ouchi at the Battle of Chikugo-gawa.

Iekané gradually drew away from the Shoni and grew in power within Hizen, although he had long since officially retired. In 1544 however another Shoni retainer, Baba Yorichika (-1545), concerned by Iekané's power, sprung a trap on him. Although he lost many members of his family in the attack, he escaped to Chikugo, and took up with Kamachi Akimori (-1578), lord of Yanagawa Castle.

In 1545, although he was by then nearly 90, Iekané led an army back into Hizen, and defeated and killed Baba.

Ryuzoji Tanehidé (1524-1548)

18th lord of the Ryuzoji. Eldest son of Tanehisa.

In 1545 Tanehidé lent support to Iekané when he counterattacked the Baba.

He died of natural causes.

Ryuzoji Takanobu (1530-1584)

19th head of the Ryuzoji. Eldest son of Chikaié, and great-grandson of Iekané. In 1544 his father was killed by Baba Yorichika (-1545). He was at first a bonze under the name of Engetsu, but at the age of 18, he returned to secular life. He was Yamashiro no kami.

In 1548, upon the death of Ryuzoji Tanehidé (1524-1548), Takanobu became the head of the clan, despite doubts of his ability to rule by certain retainers, who supported Tanehidé's son Ienari instead.

In 1554 Takanobu rebelled against Shoni Tokinao (-1556), and in the following year he took Saga Castle (Hizen), where he established residence, and drove Tokinao to Chikugo. In 1556 Takanobu pursued and killed him. Takanobu then expanded his power throughout Hizen, struggling in the Sonogi region with the Omura and the Arima.

Takanobu soon came into conflict with the Otomo of Bungo. At the 1570 Battle of Iyama (Hizen) he with Nabeshima Naoshigé (1537-1619) dealt a major defeat to Otomo Chikasada (-1570), who was slain in battle.

After the Otomo's defeat at the 1578 Battle of Mimigawa (Hyuga) at the hands of the Shimazu, Takanobu expanded into Higo and east of Hizen at their expense. In 1579 he defeated an Otomo army in Chikugo. Around the same time he attacked the lands of the Omura, and in the following year forced the submission of Omura Sumitada (1533-1587).

In 1579 Takanobu, a ruthless schemer, tricked Kamachi Shigenami into coming to a party, and had him murdered, thus acquiring his powerful Yanagawa Castle (Chikugo). Given the Kamachi's service to Ryuzoji Ienari during the war with Baba Yorichika back in 1544-1545, this was seen as especially underhanded, and disturbed the Ryuzoji retainers.

Takanobu soon came into conflict with the Shimazu over Higo, while gradually wearing down the flagging Arima of Hizen's Shimabara area. In 1584 he assembled an army, and marched against Arima Harunobu (1567-1612), whose own meager forces were reinforced by Shimazu Iehisa (1547-1587). At the Battle of Okina-waté, Shimazu swordsmen burst into Takanobu's command post, and was cut down by Kawakami Tadakata, triggering a general rout of the Ryuzoji forces. After Takanobu's death, his son Masaié submitted to the Shimazu.

Takanobu's nickname was Hizen no kuma "Bear of Hizen," at least in part a reference to his habit of wearing bearskin on his armor. He is said to have heavily indulged in alcohol, and by

Ryuzoji Takanobu

1580 was showing signs of advanced alcoholism, including a dulling of his mental capabilities, and an increasing girth. At Okinawaté he was physically incapable of riding, and was carried to his last battle in a palanquin.

Ryuzoji Nobuchika (-1608)

2nd son of Chikaié, and younger brother to Takanobu. He was Awa no kami and Bungo no kami. He assisted his brother in various military endeavors, including war with the Matsuura.

After Takanobu's death Nobuchika assisted his nephew Masaié in matters of administration.

Ryuzoji Naganobu (-1603)

3nd son of Chikaié, and younger brother to Takanobu. He was Izumi no kami. He was given the 'naga' in his name from the lord of Yamaguchi (Suo) Ouchi Yoshinaga (1532-1557).

Naganobu was the founder of the Taku.

Ryuzoji Masaié (1556-1607)

Eldest son of Takanobu.

In 1584, following his father's defeat and death at the hands of the Shimazu, Masaié agreed to a truce with them. He was physically weak, and a poor leader, and so in short order suffered the defection of a number of his retainers. He relied on Nabeshima Naoshigé (1537-1619), who was himself maneuvering towards independence.

In 1587 Masaié transferred his allegiance to Toyotomi Hideyoshi (1536-1598), and served in his Kyushu Campaign against the Shimazu. He was then confirmed in six districts of Hizen (350,000 koku), headquartered in Saga, but in 1590 his lands were transferred to his former vassal Nabeshima Naoshigé.

During the Invasions of Korea (1592-1598) Masaié was present at Toyotomi Hideyoshi's headquarters.

Ryuzoji Ietané (-1593)

2nd son of Takanobu.

In 1584 Ietané fought at the Battle of Okita-na-waté, and when he learned that his father had been struck down, he grabbed a handful of spears and plunged into the enemy ranks. He fought valiantly before being forced to fall back with the rest of the army.

He later became a retainer of Nabeshima Naoshigé (1537-1619), and died in Korea.

Ryuzoji Ienobu (1563-1622)

3rd son of Takanobu. He was Hoki no kami.

Ienobu took an interest in Christianity, and was baptized, provoking his father's intense displeasure. He accordingly renounced his new religion until 1584 when his father died, after which he was again baptized. This in turn created friction between himself and his elder brother Masaié.

In 1598 Ienobu was part of the relief effort that broke the long Siege of Ulsan in the 2nd Invasion of Korea.

He was eventually adopted by Goto Taka'aki.

SAKAZAKI 坂崎

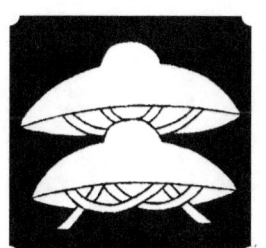

Revenues: 20,000 koku
Territory: Iwami

Family descended from the Ukita.

Notable Ancestors

Sakazaki Tadaié (-1609)

Younger brother of Ukita Naoié (1529-1582). He was Dewa no kami. He assisted his elder brother in all his campaigns.

In 1582 Tadaié was active in the campaign of Toyotomi Hideyoshi (1536-1598) in Bitchu, and assisted in the taking of Kanmuri-yama and Takamatsu Castles.

He took the family name of Sakazaki.

Sakazaki Naomori/Narimasa (1563-1616)

Son of Tadaié. He served Ukita Hideié (1573-1655), then Maeda Gen'i (1539-1602). He took part in the attack against the Uesugi of Aizu (Mutsu).

At the 1600 Battle of Seki-ga-hara (Mino) Naomori left the Ukita army and joined Tokugawa Ieyasu (1543-1616). After the battle he was given an estate in Hamada (Iwami).

In 1615 Naomori assisted at the Siege of Osaka, and was awarded Tsuwano (Iwami -- 20,000 koku). In 1616 he killed himself.

SASSA

Revenues: 100,000 koku
Territories: Komaru (Echizen), Etchu, Higo

NOTABLE ANCESTORS

Sassa Magosuké (-1556)

Son of Morimasa, and elder brother to Narimasa.

In 1542 Magosuké distinguished himself at the 1st Battle of Azukizaka (Mikawa) fighting for Oda Hobunidé (1510-1551) against Imagawa Yoshimoto (1519-1560), and was named one of that battle's 'Seven Spears.'

At the Battle of Inabu-ga-hara, Magosuké was killed fighting the forces of Oda Nobuyuki (1536-1557).

Sassa Narimasa (1539-1588)

Son of Morimasa, and younger brother to Magosuké. He was born of a family vassal to the Oda, and served Oda Nobunaga (1534-1582) throughout his career.

In 1570 Narimasa was present at the Battle of Anegawa (Omi) against the Asai and the Asakura forces, where he was in the rear guard. In 1575 he fought at the Battle of Nagashino (Mikawa) against Takeda Katsuyori (1546-1582). He was later given Komaru (Echizen), where he had recently helped put down the rioting Ikko-ikki, and became a member of the so-called Sanninshu "Echizen Triumvir" along with Maeda Toshiié (1539-1599) and Fuwa Mitsuharu (-1580).

In 1580 Narimasa, a veteran of fights against the Kaga monto "lay followers," was tasked with helping to fight the Uesugi and their vassals in Etchu. He was officially given the province the following year, settled at Toyama (100,000 koku), and immediately conducted a land-survey, as well as improving the province's poor flood control system.

In 1582, taking advantage of the year-long feud within the Uesugi, Narimasa and Shibata Katsuié (1522-1583) spearheaded the Siege of Uozu (Etchu), which was the Uesugi's last major stronghold in the province. Uesugi Kagekatsu (1556-1623) dispatched a number of his important retainers to help hold the place, but the Oda forces nonetheless prevailed, and the taking of the castle opened the way for an invasion of Echigo.

Oda Nobunaga's death at the hands of Akechi Mitsuhidé (1528-1582), however, sent all the Oda generals involved in the war against the Uesugi onto the defensive, with Narimasa adopting a wait-and-see stance while Shibata Katsuié hurried to Owari to be heard in the naming of an heir for Nobunaga. When Katsuié and Hashiba (later Toyotomi) Hideyoshi (1536-1598) came to blows towards the end of the year, Narimasa supported Katsuié, although with little impact on the outcome of the 1583 Battle of Shizu-ga-také (Omi). In 1584 Narimasa threw in his lot with Tokugawa Ieyasu (1543-1616), the next man to challenge Toyotomi Hideyoshi. The Sassa clashed with Maeda Toshiié at Kanazawa (Kaga), and attempted the Siege of Suémori (Noto), but failed. Narimasa submitted to Hideyoshi, and was spared his life.

In 1587 Toyotomi Hideyoshi transferred Narimasa to Kumamoto (Higo), along with careful instructions regarding how it should be governed. Narimasa evidently ignored Hideyoshi's injunctions, and within a year the Higo samurai were in a state of rebellion. Hideyoshi ordered Narimasa to commit seppuku as a result. His sons Nobuharu and Nariharu killed themselves as well.

While in the service of Oda Nobunaga, Narimasa had been considered something of an expert in gunnery tactics, and consequently commanded arquebus troops in many of the engagements he fought in. Regarding his suicide, some have speculated that Toyotomi Hideyoshi assigned Narimasa to Higo expecting that trouble would arise there, giving him an excuse to dispose of Narimasa, which is at any rate what occurred.

His daughter married the kugé Takatsukasa Nobufusa (1565-1657), with whom she had their son Nobuhisa.

Sassa Narimasa

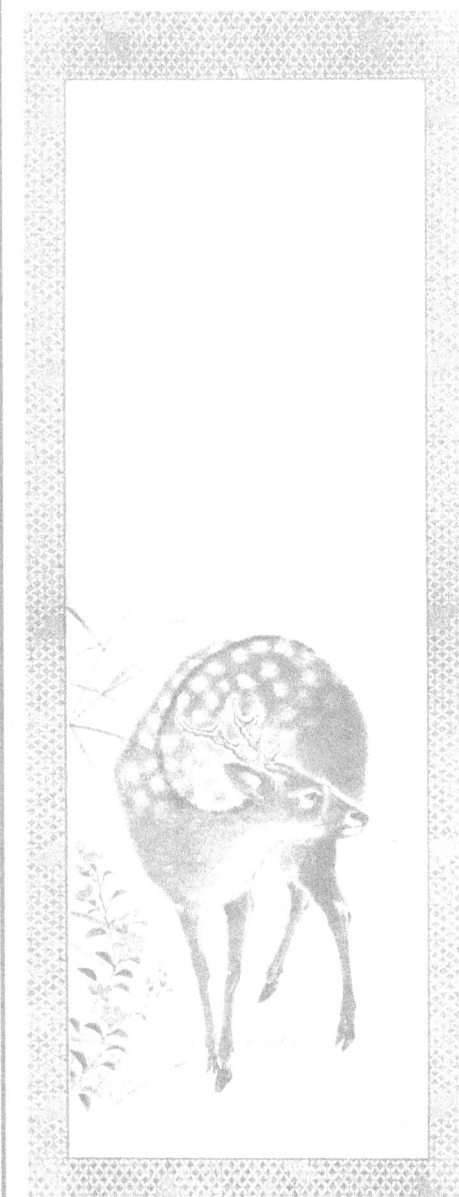

Shibata (Owari)

Territories: Echizen, Kaga, Omi
Castles: Choko-ji (Omi), Kita-no-sho/Fukui (Echizen), Nagahama (Omi)

Daimyo family from Owari descended from the Minamoto (Seiwa-Genji).

The Shibata of Owari became well known owing to the exploits of Shibata Katsuié, a senior retainer of Oda Nobunaga (1534-1582). After Katsuié committed suicide in 1583, they faded from history.

The clan was related to the Shibata of Echigo.

Notable Ancestors

Shibata Katsuié (1530-1583)

In 1557 Katsuié Joined in the plot formed by Hayashi Michikatsu to replace Oda Nobunaga (1534-1582) by his younger brother Nobuyuki (1536-1557). Ikeda Nobuteru (1536-1584), having been sent against them, defeated them at the Battle of Ino. Nobunaga had Nobuyuki executed, but spared Michikatsu and Katsuié, who henceforth showed Nobunaga unquestionable loyalty. He married Nobunaga's younger sister Oichi (1547-1583), and was a key asset to the Oda in their days as simple lords of Owari.

At the 1560 Battle of Okehazama (Owari) Katsuié served Oda Nobunaga against the Imagawa

From 1561 to 1563 Katsuié served in the Oda's war with the Saito of Mino.

In 1563 Oda Nobunaga had Katsuié divorce his wife Oichi so that she can marry Asai Nagamasa (1545-1573) to form a political alliance.

In 1567 Katsuié led an army into Settsu, and defeated the allied forces of the Miyoshi and the Matsunaga near Sakai (Izumi), while Oda Nobunaga secured his position in Kyoto.

In 1570 Katsuié distinguished himself again at the Siege of Choko-ji (southern Omi). Entrusted to guard the castle while Oda Nobunaga was campaigning against the Asai and the Asakura, he found himself besieged by Rokkaku Yoshikata (1521-1598). The situation at the garrison became grim, and things were made only worse when the enemy managed to cut their aqueduct. Knowing the Rokkaku planned to sit them out, Katsuié launched raids into the enemy lines with the object of keeping morale up and keeping the Rokkaku off-balance. Before too long however the Rokkaku discovered that the castle's water supply was very short, and planned an all-out assault. That night Katsuié gathered his men, and to their amazement smashed the last remaining pots of water, declaring, "Sooner a quick death in battle than a slow death from thirst!" Katsuié then led a desperate final charge that proved so ferocious that the Rokkaku retreated.

In 1573, following the defeat of Asai Nagamasa (1545-1573) and Asakura Yoshikagé (1533-1573), Katsuié received Echizen and Kaga in fief, and established himself in Kita-no-sho (Echizen) and built a castle there. He also re-married Oichi, Nagamasa's widow, and received their three daughters. His first years in the new province were occupied quelling local Hongan-ji adherents.

In 1575 Katsuié assisted Oda Nobunaga at the Battle of Nagashino (Mikawa).

After 1576, with the help of Maeda Toshiié (1539-1599) and Sassa Narimasa (1536-1588), Katsuié pushed further north and into Kaga, a campaign short in glory but long in difficulty. Theoretically a part of Shibata's fief since 1573, Kaga was in fact under the sway of the Ikko-ikki, and required strenuous effort to subdue them, particularly since the Uesugi of Echigo were openly hostile to the Oda.

In 1577 Katsuié was present for the Battle of Tedori-gawa (Kaga), in which Uesugi Kenshin (1530-1578) defeated Oda Nobunaga, and pushed Uesugi influence well into Kaga. Fortune shined on the Oda however, for in 1578 Kenshin died, plunging the Uesugi house into a virtual civil war. When Uesugi Kagekatsu (1556-1623) finally emerged as the new daimyo, Katsuié had spearheaded an Oda advance all the way into Etchu.

In 1581 Maeda Toshiié was sent to rule Noto, and Sassa Narimasa received Etchu. It is of some note and rather interesting that Shibata was never transferred from Echizen after 1573, the only major Oda retainer not to be shuffled around from province to province. It may well be that Oda Nobunaga considered him the best man to guard the dangerous northern front against the Uesugi. Despite later events, there is no reason to believe that Katsuié was overly ambitious, and a solid, loyal man was just what Echizen required.

In 1582 Katsuié invaded Noto, but the three daimyo of the province, the Yuza, the Miyaké, and the Nukui, appealed to Uesugi Kagekatsu (1556-1623). Katsuié had made preparations to fight the powerful daimyo of Echigo, taking part in the Siege of Uozu (Etchu) with Sassa Narimasa along the way, but when he heard of the death of Oda

Nobunaga, he at once marched against Akechi Mitsuhidé (1528-1582), but arrived only after his defeat.

Afterwards the Oda retainers met at Kiyosu (Owari) to discuss the succession issue, and Hashiba (later Toyotomi) Hideyoshi (1536-1598) won the day with the election of Oda Nobunaga's 2-year-old grandson Hidenobu (1580-1605) as successor of the clan. Katsuié, skeptical of Hideyoshi's intentions, and chagrined at having to treat a low-born junior as an equal, did not, at least, walk away from Kiyosu a complete loser, picking up Hideyoshi's Nagahama Castle (northern Omi).

Jealous of the ever-growing influence of Hideyoshi, Katsuié resolved to get rid of him, and when a dispute occurred between Oda Nobutaka (1558-1583) and the future Taiko, he sided against the latter. War ensued, and in 1583 the army of Katsuié was defeated at the Battle of Shizu-ga-také (Omi), owing to the imprudence of Sakuma Morimasa (1554-1583), and Toyotomi Hideyoshi laid siege to Kita-no-sho. Not being able to resist such a powerful foe, Katsuié implored his wife to escape with her children, but she decided to remain, and after entrusting her three daughters to a faithful servant who led them to a place of safety, he set fire to the castle, and killed himself together with his wife and some 30 servants.

Shibata Katsutoyo (-1583)

Son of Shibukawa Hachizaémon, was adopted by his uncle Katsuié.

In 1582 Katsutoyo was entrusted with the keeping of the castle of Nagahama (Omi), but in the following year he was forced to surrender to Hashiba (later Toyotomi) Hideyoshi (1536-1598). Soon after he died in Kyoto from a disease.

Shibata Katsumasa (1557-1583)

Son of Sakuma Moritsugu, was adopted by his uncle Katsuié. He was killed at the Battle of Shizu-ga-také (Omi) fighting under the command of his brother Sakuma Morimasa (1554-1583).

Shibata Katsuhisa (1568-1583)

Nephew of Katsuié, who adopted him.

In 1583 Katsuhisa fought at the Battle of Shizu-ga-také (Omi) and, after the defeat, fled into the mountains where he was pursued and killed.

SHIBATA (ECHIGO)

Territory: Echigo

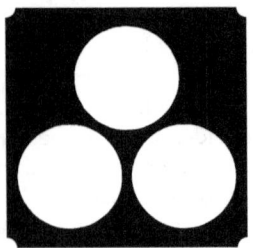

Descended from Sasaki Moritsuna, a supporter of Minamoto Yoritomo (1147-1199) and a son of Sasaki Hideyoshi (1112-1184). The clan later became retainers of the Nagao, and served Uesugi Kenshin (1530-1578).

After 1578 the clan attempted to break away from the Uesugi, but when Shibata Shigeié died in 1587, the Shibata of Echigo became extinct.

The clan was related to the Shibata of Owari, but note that their kanji are different.

NOTABLE ANCESTORS

Shibata Naganori/Nagaatsu (-1580)

Son of Tsunasada, and elder brother to Shigeié. He was Owari no kami. He served under Uesugi Kenshin (1530-1578) from his earliest campaigns.

During the 1579 Otaté no Ran (Echigo), the succession struggle that followed Kenshin's death, Naganori supported Kenshin's son Kagekatsu (1556-1623), but he died the following year of illness.

Shibata Shigeié (-1587)

Son of Tsunasada, and younger brother to Naganori. He was Inaba no kami.

During the 1579 Otaté no Ran (Echigo) Shigeié served Uesugi Kagekatsu (1556-1623), but was afterwards dissatisfied with his reward, and joined Oda Nobunaga (1534-1582). In 1587 Kagekatsu led an army out, and destroyed Shigeié.

TAGAYA

Revenues: 60,000 koku
Territory: Hitachi
Castle: Shimotsuma (Hitachi)

Daimyo family that in the 16th century possessed the Shimotsuma Castle (Hitachi -- 60,000 koku). In 1600 they were dispossessed.

TAKAHASHI

Revenues: 50,000 koku
Territories: Mikaya (Bungo), Miyazaki (Hyuga)
Castles: Iwaya (Bungo)

Ancient daimyo family of Kyushu. During the 15th and the 16th centuries they were vassals of the Otomo of Bungo.

NOTABLE ANCESTORS

Takahashi Shigetané/Shoun (1544-1586)

Governed Mikawa (Bungo), and resided at Iwaya Castle. He was a pillar of the Otomo. In 1567 he shaved his head and took the name Shoun.

In 1586 a Shimazu drive into Otomo territory resulted in the Siege of Iwaya by Shimazu Yoshihisa (1533-1611). Shigetané bravely resisted against enormous odds. Right in the middle of battle, a commanding officer of the Shimazu stopped the attack and asked Shigetané, "Why do you serve the unjust Otomo that makes light of Buddism and has faith in Christianity? Your bravely has been proved, please surrender." He answered, "A lot of men serve hard when their lords are powerful, but few men try to protect their lords at the risk of their lives when their lords become weaker. Do you also abandon your lord when your lord become weaker? Samurai who are ungrateful are worse than animals." It was said that all men in the battlefield, including Shimazu's soldiers, admired him. After heroically holding out for over two weeks, in the end, seeing the situation was far beyond salvation, he killed himself. When the Shimazu heard of his end, they are said to have prayed for his spirit, so impressed were they by his bravery.

His eldest son Muneshigé (1567-1642) was adopted by Tachibana Dosetsu (1513-1585), married his daughter Ginchiyo (1569-1602), and succeeded as the head of the Tachibana.

Takahashi Mototané (late 16th century)

Adopted son of Shigetané.

In 1587 Mototané received Miyazaki (Hyuga -- 50,000 koku) in fief from Toyotomi Hideyoshi (1536-1598).

During Hideyoshi's Invasions of Korea (1592-1598) Mototané served under Kuroda Nagamasa (1568-1623).

In 1600 Mototané fought against Tokugawa Ieyasu (1543-1616) and protected Ogaki Castle (Mino). Owing to the influence of Mizuno Katsushigé (1564-1651), he was allowed to retain his domain, but having been implicated in the plot of Tomita Motonobu, he was dispossessed, and banished to Tanakura (Mutsu), where he died.

TAKAYAMA

Territories:
Settsu, Yamato
Castles:
Takatsuki (Settsu),
Sawa (Yamato)

Ancient family of daimyo from Settsu.

NOTABLE ANCESTORS

Takayama Tomoteru (1531-1596)

Hida no kami. He was a retainer of Matsunaga Hisahidé (1510-1577).

In 1564 Tomoteru was baptized as Darie, and was henceforth a fervent Christian, though previously he had been an ardent foe of Christianity, and had attempted to convince Matsunaga Hisahidé to expel the foreign missionaries from Kyoto.

In 1565 Matsunaga Hisahidé murdered the 13th Ashikaga Shogun Yoshiteru (1536-1565), and then became involved in a war with the Miyoshi. In the course of the feud, Tomoteru lost his castle in Sawa (Yamato), forcing the Takayama to flee. In 1568, through the good offices of Wada Koremasa (1536-1571), a friendly acquaintance of Tomoteru, the Takayama came under the banner of Oda Nobunaga (1536-1582), and took up service with the Wada.

In 1571 the Wada came to blows with Araki Murashigé (-1579), a powerful vassal of Ikeda Katsumasa (1539-1578), who in turn served the Miyoshi, Oda Nobunaga's enemies. Murashigé besieged Tomoteru's castle, and Wada Koremasa came up to the front with a relief force. In the ensuing confrontation, Koremasa was killed. Murashigé was nonetheless unable to bring the castle down, and retreated, allowing Tomoteru to become advisor to Koremasa's successor, Korenaga. Relations between the young lord and the Takayama were sour, and word came to Tomoteru that Korenaga plotted to have him and his son Ukon killed.

Tomoteru decided to act first. In 1573 he called upon Korenaga, and had him visit his home, where waited fifteen samurai, including his son Ukon. Korenaga arrived with an armed escort, but in the ensuing melee he was killed. The Takayama took over the Wada's castle in Takatsuki (Settsu), a move backed by the troops of Murashigé, whose support Tomoteru had gained prior to the assassination. As Murashigé had just sided with Nobunaga, this affair was not quite treason, rather being an internal matter which Nobunaga seems to have had no comment.

In 1578, when Araki Murashigé rebelled against Oda Nobunaga, the Takayama followed suit. Besieged at Takatsuki, Ukon was convinced to abandon the castle, to his father's chagrin. In the following year, after Murashigé fled to the west, Tomoteru retired to Kita-no-sho (Echizen), where he died.

Takayama Shigetomo/Ukon (1552-1615)

Son of Tomoteru. His childhood name was Hikogoro. He had the title of ukon-tayu "junior officer of the Imperial guard."

In 1564 he was baptized at the age of 12, at the same time as his father, and received the name of Justo. For this he is mentioned in the writings of the old missionaries under the name of Justo Ukon-dono. At his coming-of-age ceremony, he was named Shigetomo. The Japanese called him Takayama Ukon.

In the Ishiyama Hongan-ji War (1570-1580) of Oda Nobunaga (1534-1582) Ukon served under Araki Murashigé (-1579).

In 1573 Ukon killed Wada Korenaga and took over his estate at Takatsuki (Settsu).

In 1578 Araki Murashigé rebelled against Oda Nobunaga, who then had the Takayama's castle at Takatsuki surrounded by the forces of Fuwa Mitsuharu (-1580), Kanamori Nagachika (1524-1608), and others. Knowing the Takayama were devout Christians, Nobunaga asked the Jesuit Padre Gnecchi-Soldo Organtino (1530-1609) to convince them to surrender, promising that such an outcome would benefit the Church, and hinting that failure to submit would lead to an unfortunate persecution. Unwilling to allow harm to come to his religion, Ukon abandoned Takatsuki in the night. His father was furious, and went to Murashigé to apologize, hoping to save a number of hostages that had earlier been sent to the Araki. Murashigé took no action against the hostages, and in the end released them.

Oda Nobunaga rewarded Ukon for his decision, especially after he was able to convince Nakagawa Sebei (1542-1583) to surrender Ibaraki Castle (Settsu) to the Oda. Both the Takayama and the Nakagawa kept their castles, and Ukon set about converting the people in his fief, where eventually 18,000 of Takatsuki's population of 25,000 became Christian, an achievement much lauded by the Jesuits, but scorned by many Japanese as an example of forced conversion. Many temples were reportedly torn down or converted to churches.

In 1582, after Oda Nobunaga was killed, Ukon helped Hashiba (later Toyotomi) Hideyoshi (1536-1598) by commanding vanguard troops at the Battle of Yamazaki (Yamashiro) to defeat the traitorous Akechi Mitsuhidé (1528-1582).

In the ensuing warfare between Toyotomi Hideyoshi and Shibata Katsuié (1530-1583) sparked by the Oda succession dispute, Hideyoshi dispatched Ukon to the fort at Iwasakiyama (Omi) to help block Katsuié's movement from Echizen. The fort was attacked by Sakuma Morimasa (1554-1583), and Ukon was forced to retreat to nearby Tagami.

In 1585, after Toyotomi Hideyoshi's victory over Shibata Katsuié, Ukon went on to serve in the Invasion of Shikoku, and was transferred to Akashi (Harima -- 60,000 koku), where, as at Takatsuki, he set about converting the population, which enraged the local Buddhist monks, but drew no immediate attention from Hideyoshi.

From 1585 to 1585 Ukon assisted Toyotomi Hideyoshi in breaking the power of the armed monks in Yamato.

In 1587 Ukon went on to serve in Toyotomi Hideyoshi's Kyushu Campaign. After that victory Hideyoshi became the *de facto* ruler of Japan.

Toyotomi Hideyoshi then ordered the expulsion of missionaries. While many daimyo obeyed this order, and discarded Catholicism, Ukon proclaimed that he would maintain his religion, and rather give up his land and property. He was thus deprived of his fief, and forced to find shelter under Konishi Yukinaga (1555-1600), a much more powerful Christian lord who was awarded a substantial fief in Hyuga. Ukon ended up wandering all the way to the Hokuriku "northern provinces" region, where he sought service with the Maeda in Kaga.

In 1588 Maeda Toshiié (1539-1599) accepted him as a retainer, an interesting turnaround in Ukon's career. It is believed that in 1590 Toshiié took Ukon to the Siege of Odawara in the hope that his valor would obtain the favor of Toyotomi Hideyoshi, but this was in vain.

Over the next decade Toyotomi Hideyoshi gradually stepped up persecution against Christianity in Japan that was only temporarily halted by the Taiko's death in 1598.

In 1614 however an edict of Tokugawa Ieyasu (1543-1616) banished all the missionaries from Japan, as well as those samurai who refused to recant their faith, and Ukon was among them. Though Maeda Toshitsuné (1594-1658) feared that he would fight rather than leave the country, Ukon peacefully left Kanazawa (Kaga) to go to Nagasaki (Hizen), and from there sailed for Manila with his whole family. The junk in which his family embarked carried 300 Japanese Christians, including 30 missionaries, Naito Joan (1549-1626) and his family, and several Christian women, among whom was a daughter of Otomo Sorin (1530-1587).

In Manila the exiles were received with great honor by the Spanish Jesuits and the local Filipinos. The Spanish Philippines suggested overthrowing the Japanese government with an invasion to protect Japanese Catholics, but Ukon declined to participate, and died less than 40 days after his arrival in Manila from a short illness.

The Spanish government interred him with a Christian burial in a Jesuit church with full military honors as a daimyo, the first daimyo to be buried in Philippine soil.

Ukon was a noted tea man, practicing that art with Sen no Rikyu (1522-1591).

TAKIGAWA

Territories: Owari, Isé, Kozuké, Shinano
Castle: Umabayashi (Kozuké)

The origins of the Takigawa of Owari are unclear. They rose to some prominence in the 16th century thanks to Takigawa Kazumasu, a general for Oda Nobunaga (1534-1582) and Toyotomi Hideyoshi (1536-1598). With Kazumasu's death, the Takigawa faded into obscurity.

NOTABLE ANCESTORS

Takigawa Kazumasu (1525-1586)

Son of Kazukatsu. He was originally from Omi. He was Iyo no kami, saburohei, and sakon "senior officer of the Imperial guard," for which he was also known as Sakon-shogen.

Around 1558 Kazumasu entered the service of Oda Nobunaga (1534-1582), and became one of his staunchest supporters.

Oda Nobunaga appointed Kazumasa as Kanto kanrei "Shogun's Deputy in the East." In this post, with a portion of Kozuké as his domain, he was assigned to keep an eye on the powerful Hojo of Odawara (Sagami).

In 1569 Kazumasu received five districts of Isé as fief, and supported Oda Nobukatsu (1558-1630), heir to the Kitabataké.

Under Oda Nobunaga, he took part in a great many battles, including the 1570 Battle of Anegawa (Omi), and the 1571-1574 campaigns against the Ikko-ikki of Nagashima (Owari).

Kazumasu's battle record was mixed, as he fled from the 1573 Battle of Mikata-ga-hara (Totomi), and in 1579 acted poorly during the 1st Invasion of Iga.

Kazumasu also rendered service to the Oda through domestic affairs: in 1578 he assisted in the construction of Azuchi Castle (Omi), and in 1580 he conducted land surveys with Akechi Mitsuhidé (1528-1582) in Yamato.

In 1579 Kazumasa besieged Araki Murashigé (1535-1586) in Itami.

Kazumasa aided in the campaign against Takeda Katsuyori (1546-1582), and, at the end of which, in 1582 he received Kozuké, establishing himself at Umabayashi Castle, and the districts of Chiisagata and Saku in Shinano.

In 1582, shortly after the death of Oda Nobunaga, Kazumasu was defeated by the Hojo at the Battle of Kanagawa (area between Kozuké and Musashi), and fled to Isé.

Following the Kiyosu Conference (Owari), Kazumasu was given a domain in Isé.

In 1583 Kazumasu supported Shibata Katsuié (1522-1583) when the latter opposed Toyotomi Hideyoshi (1536-1598), but submitted to Hideyoshi after he was besieged in Kamegawa Castle.

In 1584 Kazumasa assisted Toyotomi Hideyoshi during the Komaki Campaign by laying the Siege of Kanié (Owari) along with Kuki Yoshitaka (1542-1600). When he performed badly in this campaign, he shaved his head and retired in shame to Echizen, where he died.

TAKEDA

Territories: Kai, Aki, Wakasa, Shinano, Suruga; parts of Kozuké, Totomi, Hida

Castle: Yogai-yama (Kai)

Daimyo family descended from the Seiwa-Genji Minamoto Yoshimitsu (1056-1127), brother to the Chinjufu-shogun "Defender of the North" Yoshiié (1041-1108), who had loyally served Minamoto Yoritomo (1147-1198).

In the 12th century the Takeda controlled Kai. In the 1221 Jokyu War (Kyoto) Takeda Nobumitsu helped the Hojo, and in reward received the governorship of Aki. Until the Sengoku "Warring States" Period (1467-1573) the Takeda were shugo "military governors" of Kai, Aki, and Wakasa.

In 1415 the Takeda helped to suppress the rebellion of the Uesugi, beginning a rivalry between the two families, which would last roughly 150 years.

The rebellion of Atobé Kageié in 1465 was the initial punctuation to a period of internal unease within the clan. In 1472 Takeda Nobumasa defeated an army led by allied Shinano warlords, and this reestablished the authority of the Takeda as rulers of Kai. The Takeda however would be forced to contend with the numerous warlords of Shinano for many years. By 1519 Takeda Nobutora had quelled all resistance within Kai to Takeda leadership, and under his son Shingen the family enjoyed its height, extending its control over Shinano and Suruga, as well as parts of Kozuké, Totomi, and Hida. After Shingen's son Katsuyori suffered a crushing defeat at the 1575 Battle of Nagashino (Mikawa), the offensive potency of the Takeda was drastically reduced. Oda Nobunaga (1534-1582) and Tokugawa Ieyasu (1543-1616), the victors at Nagashino, invaded the Takeda domain in 1582, and the Takeda were destroyed as daimyo.

The *Koshu Hatto*, composed at some point in the 15th century, is the code of laws of the Takeda family, while the *Koyo Gunkan*, composed largely by Kosaka Masanobu (1527-1578), is an epic recording the family's history and Shingen's innovations in military tactics.

Certain collateral branches of the Takeda survived into the Edo Period (1603-1868), though none enjoyed significant power. They were the Matsumaé of Ezo, the Nanbu of Mutsu, The Yanagisawa of Yamato and Echigo, the Goto of Hizen, and the Ogasawara of Buzen, Harima, Hizen, and Echizen. Two branches named Takeda were also ranked among the koké "high families."

SUCCESSION

1. Minamoto Yoshimitsu (1045-1127)
2. Minamoto Yoshikiyo (1075-1149)
3. Minamoto Kiyomitsu (1110-1168)
4. Takeda Nobuyoshi (1128-1186)
5. Takeda Nobumitsu (1162-1248)
6. Takeda Nobumasa (-1265)
7. Takeda Nobutoki (-1289)
8. Takeda Tokitsuna
9. Takeda Nobumune (-1330)
10. Takeda Nobutaké (1292-1359)
11. Takeda Nobunari (-1394)
12. Takeda Nobuharu (-1413)
13. Takeda Nobumitsu (-1417)
14. Takeda Nobushigé (1386-1450)
15. Takeda Nobumori (-1455)
16. Takeda Nobumasa (1447-1505)
17. Takeda Nobutsuna (1471-1507)
18. Takeda Nobutora (1494-1574)
19. Takeda Harunobu/Shingen (1521-1573)
20. Takeda Katsuyori (1546-1582)
21. Takeda Nobukatsu (1567-1582)

NOTABLE ANCESTORS

Minamoto/Takeda Yoshikiyo (1075-1149)

Son of Minamoto Yoshimitsu (1045-1127). He was the 2nd head of the clan, his father being the 1st. He was the first to take the name of Takeda.

Takeda Nobuyoshi (1128-1186)

4th head of the Takeda. Grandson of Yoshikiyo.

In 1180 Nobuyoshi sided with Minamoto Yoritomo (1147-1199) and levied troops for his support in Kai and Shinano. In 1184 he accompanied Minamoto Noriyori (1156-1193) in his campaign against the Taira.

Takeda Nobumitsu (1162-1248)

5th head of the Takeda. Son of Nobuyoshi. He assisted at the campaign against Minamoto (Kiso) Yoshinaka (1154-1184), and against the Taira. Being a favorite of Minamoto Yoritomo (1147-1199), he obtained Suruga in fief.

In 1213 Nobumitsu repressed the revolt of Wada Yoshimori (1147-1213).

In 1221, at the time of the Jokyu War (Kyoto), Nobumitsu did not even reply to the offers made him by the ex-Emperor Go-Toba (1180-1239), but helped the Hojo, and entered Kyoto. In reward he was made governor of Aki.

Soon after he shaved his head and took the name Koren.

Nobumitsu was famous for his skill in horsemanship and archery.

Takeda Nobumitsu (-1417)

13th head of the Takeda. Descendant of Nobuyoshi in the 9th generation. He inherited Kai and Aki.

Defeated at Tokusa (Kai) whilst fighting against Uesugi Norimuné, Nobumitsu killed himself.

Takeda Nobushigé (1386-1450)

14th head of the Takeda. Son of Nobumitsu.

In 1417, at the death of his father, Nobushigé became a bonze at the Koya-san (Kii), but upon the death of his uncle Nobumoto, governor of Kai, he returned to succeed the latter.

Takeda Nobumasa (1447-1505)

16th head of the Takeda. Grandson of Nobushigé.

Azuchi-Momoyama Period – Takeda

Nobumasa repressed the revolt of one of his most powerful vassals, Atobé Kageié, whose aim was nothing less than to become master of the whole of Kai. In 1465 he attacked Kageié at Ishizawa, where he defeated and killed him and his son Atobé Kagetsugu. Nobumasa was then but 19 years old.

Takeda Nobutora (1493-1574)

Eldest son of Nobutsuna, and grandson of Nobumasa. His childhood name was Nobunao. His mother was of the Iwashita. He held the titles Mutsu no kami and sakyo-daibu.

In 1507, upon his father's death from illness, Nobutora succeeded.

In 1508 Nobutora's authority was challenged by his uncle Nobué, and fighting broke out between the two factions, in which Nobué and his his ally Oyamada Nobutaka were killed. However, other important families within Kai, including the Oi and the Oyamada, now led by Oyamada Nobuari, continued to oppose him.

In 1510 Nobutora forced the submission of the Oyamada, and the following year married a daughter to Oyamada Nobuari. However, the Oi of southern Kai were supported by the Imagawa of Suruga, and proved more formidable.

In 1517, however, Imagawa Ujichika (1473-1526) withdrew his troops from Kai, and Oi Nobutatsu was compelled to come to terms with Nobutora, who married his daughter. This union would produce four of Nobutora's many sons: Katsuchiyo (later Harunobu, then Shingen), Nobushigé, Nobutomo, and Nobukado.

In 1519 Nobutora established the center of the clan at Yogai-yama (Kai). This moated mansion complex would remain the center of the Takeda for the next sixty years, until Takeda Katsuyori moved the family to Nirayama (Izu). In 1521 Oi Nobutatsu again defied his authority, and war broke out. Imagawa Ujichika came to Nobutatsu's support once more, and ordered his retainer Kushima Masanari to launch an attack into Kai. Nobutora defeated Imagawa general Fukushima Masashigé at Iida-ga-wara, and afterwards Nobu-

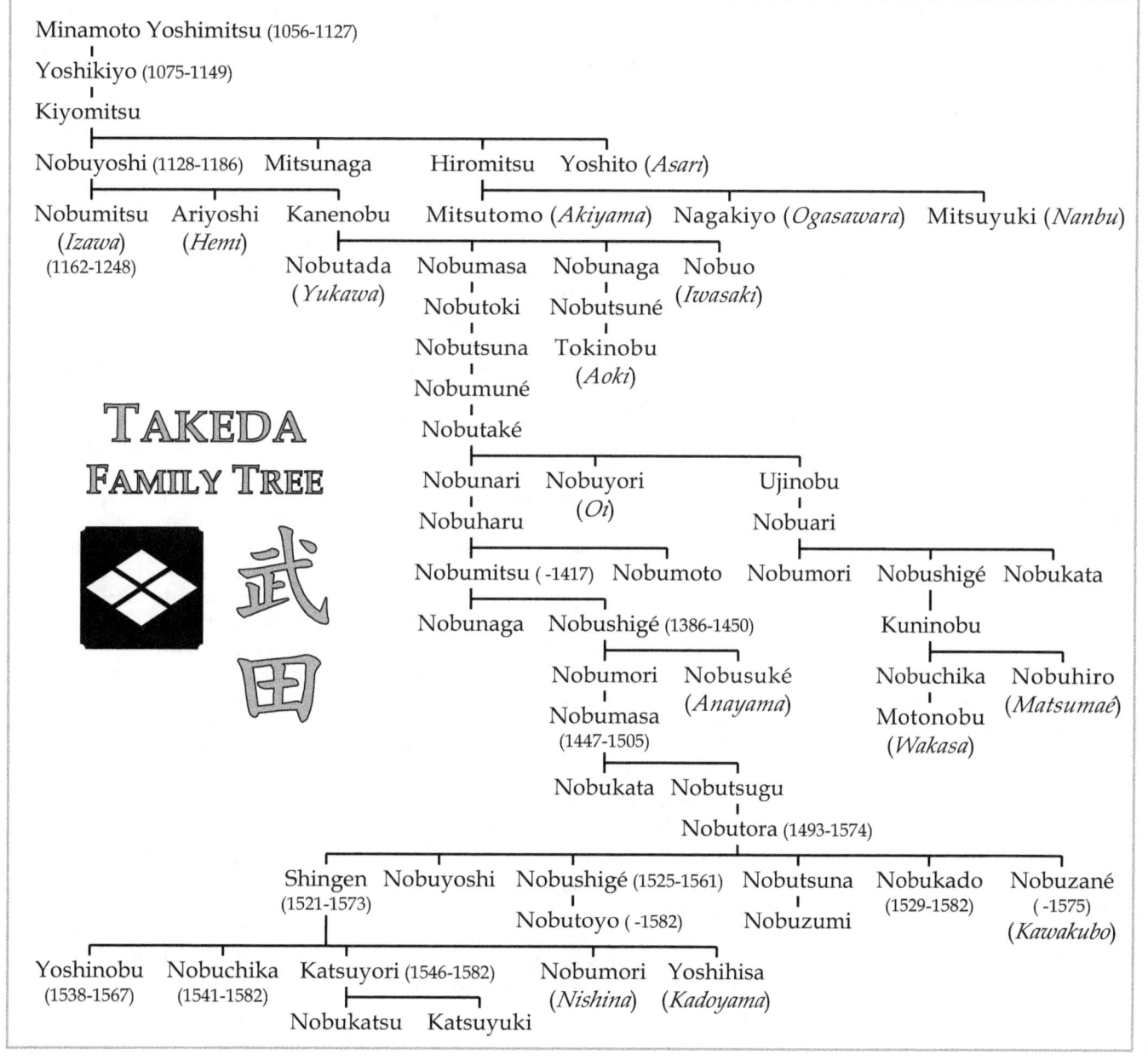

tatsu submitted, retired, and became a monk. Around this time Nobutora's eldest son Katsuchiyo, was born.

Over the course of the next decade, Nobutora was at odds with the Imagawa, the Hojo, and a number of Shinano daimyo. The latter at length banded together in an anti-Nobutora coalition that included the Suwa, the Imai, the Hiraga, and others. The Suwa, being at this time the strongest of them, was Nobutora's main antagonist.

In 1530 Nobutora took the widow of Uesugi Norifusa as concubine. Additionally, he would maintain concubines from the Imai, the Kudo, the Kusuura, and the Matsuo.

In 1531 Nobutora defeated a coalition army near present-day Nirasaki (Kai), but in 1535 found himself pressed on his southern borders by the Imagawa and the Hojo.

In 1536 Nobutora was granted a reprieve by the death of Imagawa Ujichika, and their resulting battle for power within the clan. Nobutora supported the bid of Imagawa Yoshimoto (1519-1560) for leadership, and when Yoshimoto emerged as the new daimyo he married Nobutora's eldest daughter. In return Yoshimoto acted as a go-between to arrange the marriage of Nobutora's eldest son, now Harunobu (later Shingen), to the daughter of the Court noble Sanjo Kimiyori. Although the Takeda and Hojo made peace, Nobutora's alliance with Yoshimoto split the Hojo-Imagawa union, and those two clans began fighting.

Later that year, with his southern borders secure, Nobutora attacked the domain of Hiraga Genshin (-1537), and surrounded his castle of Umi-no-kuchi (Shinano). The defenders resisted stoutly, and when winter snows began to fall, Nobutora withdrew. According to legend, it was his eldest son Harunobu, commanding the rear guard, who opted to make a countermarch that caught the Hiraga men by surprise, which led to Genshin's death, and the destruction of the Hiraga.

In 1540, following the surrender of Imai Nobumoto, the Suwa and the Takeda reconciled, and Suwa Yorishigé (1516-1542) married another of Nobutora's daughters, Nené. At the same time, a treaty was made with the Murakami, and, along with the Suwa, the two clans defeated the Unno at the Battle of Unnotaira.

Nobutora came to favor his 2nd son Nobushigé over Harunobu, and contemplated naming him heir. Perhaps as importantly to the coming events, Nobutora had alienated his retainers with his arbitrary style of leadership, and burdened the people of Kai with heavy taxes and forced labor for his seemingly endless campaigns.

In 1541 Nobutora was overthrown by Harunobu and his chief retainers, perhaps most notably Amari Torayasu (1498-1548) and Itagaki Nobutaka (1489-1548), although the manner in which this played out is not entirely clear. According to one version of the so-called 'bloodless coup,' Nobutora departed for Suruga to visit his daughter, the wife of Imagawa Yoshimoto, and Harunobu seized power in his absence, possibly with the secret understanding of Yoshimoto. The people of Kai in any event celebrated his fall, and the Takeda retainers accepted Harunobu's rule without incident. Nobutora afterwards shaved his head, and lived quietly in Sunpu (Suruga) until 1560 when Yoshimoto died at the Battle of Okehazama (Owari).

Nobutora's relationship with his grandson, Imagawa Yoshimoto's heir Ujizané (1538-1615), was not good, and at length Nobutora migrated to Isé, and took up with Kitabataké Tomonori (1528-1576), who gave him property in Shima. In return Nobutora assisted Tomonori in his conflict with Kuki Yoshitaka (1542-1600).

In 1573, after the death of Shingen, Katsuyori, the new lord of the Takeda, allowed Nobutora to return to the east, and he took up with his 4th son Nobukado at Takato Castle (Shinano).

Nobutora was regarded as an intemperate, and even unstable, man who was not well-liked by his retainers, though he was an aggressive warrior of obvious ability. Katsuyori was said to have been taken aback at how fearsome his grandfather looked even at 80 years of age.

Takeda Harunobu/Shingen (1521-1573)

Eldest son of Nobutora. He was born in Yogai-yama Castle (Kai). His mother was a daughter of Oi Nobutatsu. His childhood name was Katsuchiyo. In his youth he was an accomplished poet. He held the Court title of daizen-tayu "minister of the Imperial Household."

In 1533 Katsuchiyo's father arranged for him to marry the daughter of Uesugi Tomo'oki (1488-1537), who held considerable territory in the Kanto. The bride later died however attempting to deliver their first child. Imagawa Yoshimoto (1519-1560) of Suruga then arranged the marriage of Katsuchiyo to a daughter of the kugé Sanjo Kimiyori.

At his genbuku "coming-of-age ceremony," the 12th Ashikaga Shogun Yoshiharu (1511-1550) bestowed on him the character 'haru' from his name, and he was formally renamed Harunobu, along with the honorific title Shinano no kami.

Harunobu is thought to have seen his first campaign in 1536, when his father led an army against Hiraga Genshin (-1537) of Shinano. Nobutora surrounded and attacked Genshin's Umi-no-kuchi Castle, but found the defenders unwilling to give, and withdrew with the onset of heavy winter snows. According to tradition, Harunobu, who commanded the rearguard, decided to double back and launch a surprise attack. This took the seemingly victorious Hiraga men by surprise, and the battle went to the Takeda.

In 1540 Nobutora and Harunobu went on a campaign together to Shinano, joined by the Suwa and the Murakami, to attack Unno Munetsuna, who lost and fled the province.

In 1541, Nobutora having planned to disinherit him in favor of a younger brother Nobushigé, Harunobu suddenly revolted, supported by a great many of the Takeda retainers, and placed his father in custody with Harunobu's brother-in-law Imagawa Yoshimoto in Suruga Castle, and assumed the government of Kai in a bloodless coup. Nobushigé, for his part, seems to have borne his brother no ill will, and became a valued retainer. Subsequently an alliance was forged between the Imagawa and the Takada.

In 1542 a number of major daimyo in Shinano marched on the border of Kai hoping to neutralize the power of the still-young Harunobu before he had a chance to expand into their lands. At the Battle of Sezawa (Shinano) however Harunobu was able to score a quick victory, which set the stage for his drive into Shinano. The young warlord made considerable advances into the province, conquering the Suwa headquarters in the Siege of Kuwabara (Shinano) from Suwa Yorishigé (1516-1542) before moving into central Shinano. With the help of his strategist Yamamoto Kansuké (1501-1561), Harunobu defeated both Tozawa Yorichika and Takato Yoritsugu (-1552), taking the strategic Takato Castle from the latter.

In 1544 the Takeda marched into Suruga in support of the Imagawa and faced Hojo Ujiyasu (1515-1571), but no actual fighting occurred as a result of this confrontation.

In 1548 Murakami Yoshikiyo (1510-1573), perhaps the most formidable of Harunobu's Shinano enemies, defeated the Takeda at the Battle of Uedahara in a bitter clash which saw the use, on the part of the Murakami, of a number of Chinese arquebuses, the first such weapons ever deployed in a Japanese battle. The Takeda lost generals Itagaki Nobukata (1489-1548), Amari Torayasu (1498-1548), and Hajikano Den'-émon. It was Harunobu's first defeat, and he himself suffered a spear wound to his side. He quickly rebounded with a string of victories against his Shinano rivals starting at the Battle of Shiojiri-togé, where he launched a surprise attack against Ogasawara Nagatoki (1519-1583). By 1552 the Murakami and the Ogasawara had fled Shinano outright to Echigo, and took refuge with Uesugi Kenshin (1530-1578).

In 1551 he shaved his head and took the name of Shingen, by which he is generally known, and adopted a monk's habit. By this time he was already known for his taste for women, penetrating judgment, skill at calligraphy, and wise government.

A war began between Shingen and Kenshin that became legendary. It lasted for twenty years, and they faced each other on the battlefield five times at the Battles of Kawa-naka-jima (northeast Shinano), where they both distinguished themselves by skillful strategy. The battles took place in 1553, 1555, 1557, 1561, and 1564, and they were generally confined to controlled skirmishes, neither daimyo willing to devote himself entirely to a single all-out attempt. The conflict between the two that had the fiercest fighting, and

Takeda Shingen

might have decided victory or defeat for one side or the other, was the 4th battle in 1561, during which the famous tale arose of Uesugi forces clearing a path through the Takeda troops, and Kenshin engaging Shingen in single combat. The tale has Kenshin attacking with his sword, while Shingen defending with his iron tessen "war fan." Both sides lost many men in this fight, and Shingen in particular lost two of his main generals, his younger brother Nobushigé and Yamamoto Kansuké.

In 1554 the leader of the Imagawa, the Hojo, and the Takeda met at the Zentoku-ji (Suruga) to establish a peace treaty, called Kousousun-sangoku-doumei "Kai-Sagami-Suruga Three Provinces Alliance," moderated by the monk Taigen Sessai (1496-1555). The attending daimyo agreed to not attack each other, as well as to send each other support and reinforcements if necessary. The agreement was cemented by three marriages: Hojo Ujimasa married Shingen's daughter Obai-in; Imagawa Ujizané (1538-1615) married a daughter of Hojo Ujiyasu; and Shingen's son Yoshinobu had previously married a daughter of Imagawa Yoshimoto in 1552. The treaty allowed the Imagawa to focus on the Oda in Owari, and to attempt a move on Kyoto; the Hojo were able to expand their influence in the Kanto; and Shingen was able to focus on his invasion of Shinano.

Internally the Takeda suffered two grim incidents. In 1560 Shingen's cousin Katanuma Nobumoto led a plot against him, and was made to commit seppuku. In 1565 Shingen's own son Yoshinobu, with Obu Toramasa (1504-1565), was accused of plotting against him. Toramasa was made to commit seppuku, while Yoshinobu was confined to the Toko-ji (Shinano), where two years later he died. Shingen then designated his 4th son Katsuyori as the acting leader of the clan after himself until Katsuyori's son came of age.

By 1564 Shingen had subdued all of Shinano, and shifted his attention to Kozuké, where he took a number of castles from the Uesugi. For the next five years, he limited himself to raids and local conquests, including land grabs in mountainous Hida, and concentrated on internal affairs. During this time Shingen's greatest achievement was the Fuji River damming project, the largest and most ambitious of his many innovative domestic endeavors. The benefit of the dam far-outlived its mastermind, and is ranked as one of the greatest domestic initiatives of the 16th century.

By 1567, after he had successfully kept the Uesugi forces out of the northern boundaries of Shinano, had taken over a strategically-important castle in western Kozuké, and had suppressed internal objection to his plans to take advantage of the weakened Imagawa, Shingen was ready to carry out his planned Suruga invasion.

Shingen is believed to have made a pact with Tokugawa Ieyasu (1543-1616) to share the remaining Imagawa lands in Totomi and Suruga between them, and in 1568 they both moved against the late Imagawa Yoshimoto's incompetent son and heir Ujizané that resulted in the downfall of the Imagawa. The alliance however quickly fell through.

The formidable Hojo Ujiyasu of Sagami took a dim view to this shift in the balance of power, and sent troops to defy Shingen, which they did with varying degrees of success for a year or so. In 1569 Shingen responded by invading Sagami. After failing to take Hachigata and Takiyama Castles, he attacked the Hojo capital and laid the Siege of Odawara, but stayed only three days, after which the Takeda forces burned the town to the ground and left, leaving the castle still standing. On their way back to Kai, the Takeda army was ambushed at the Battle of Mimasé-togé by Hojo forces led by the brothers Ujiteru (1540-1590) and Ujikuni (1541-1597). Shingen and his commanders Baba Nobuharu (1514-1575) and Yamagata Masakagé (1524-1575) inflicted heavy casualties, and the Hojo were forced to retreat north.

By 1570 the Takeda lands now included Kai, Shinano, Suruga, and pieces of Kozuké, Totomi, and Hida. Shingen at age 49 was the most important warlord east of Mino, and the one who was in a position to derail the march of Oda Nobunaga (1534-1582) to national hegemony. Shingen alone possessed the necessary army and strategic position. That year Hojo Ujiyasu died, and his heir Ujimasa (1538-1590) quickly made peace with Shingen.

In 1572 Shingen joined the Asai, the Asakura, and the bonzes of Hiei-zan to answer the summons of the 15th Ashikaga Shogun Yoshiaki (1537-1597), who was trying to rid himself of Oda Nobunaga. Late that year he launched an attack into Totomi, and laid the Siege of Futamata, taking the fortress from the Tokugawa garrison.

In early 1573 Shingen returned to Totomi, and at the Battle of Mikata-ga-hara conducted a near-complete defeat of the combined forces of the Tokugawa and the Oda in one of the best demonstrations of his cavalry-based tactics, forcing Ieyasu to retreat to his headquarters at Hamamatsu Castle (Totomi).

Shingen then pushed further into Mikawa, laid the Siege of Noda, and took the castle from Suganuma Sadamichi.

At this time Shingen fell ill, and died two months later at Kobama (Shinano). His last request was to keep his death under wraps for as long as possible to discourage his enemies from attacking Kai. Although this was not a well-kept secret for long, he was not buried until three years afterwards in the Eirin-ji at Matsuzato (Kai).

Upon hearing of Shingen's death, Uesugi Kenshin reportedly cried aloud at the loss of one of his strongest and most deeply respected rivals. He ordered that no music be played at his headquarters at Kasuga-yama Castle (Echigo) for a span of three days, and vowed to never attack Takeda lands.

For his martial prowess, Shingen is known as Kai-no-tora "the Tiger of Kai," and Uesugi Kenshin was known as "the Dragon of Echizen." In Chinese mythology the tiger and the dragon are bitter rivals who try to defeat the other, but neither is ever able to gain the upper hand.

One of the most lasting tributes to Shingen's legacy was that of Tokugawa Ieyasu himself, who is known to have borrowed heavily from the old Takeda leader's governmental and military innovations after he had taken leadership of Kai during the rise of Toyotomi Hideyoshi (1536-1598). Many of these designs were put to use in the Tokugawa Shogunate.

Shingen also profoundly influenced many lords with his law, tax, and administration systems, and many tales were told about him. Although aggressive towards military enemies he was probably not as cruel as other warlords.

The Takeda war banner contained the famous phrase Fu-Rin-Ka-Zan "Wind, Forest, Fire, Mountain," taken from Sun Tzu's *Art Of War* (5th or 6th century B.C.), referring to the ideal of "swift as the wind, silent as a forest, fierce as fire, and immovable as a mountain." This motto applied to Shingen's policies and his military strategy.

Takeda Nobushigé (1525-1561)

Son of Nobutora, and younger brother to Shingen. He held the titles Sama no suké and tenkyu, the latter for which he is also known as Takeda Tenkyu.

Nobushigé held the favor of his father, and was meant to inherit the Takeda lands, wealth, and power, to become head of the clan. In 1541 his older brother Shingen however rebelled, and seized the lands and power for himself. Nobushigé nevertheless fought alongside his brother, who relied on him for support.

Nobushigé became an important Takeda general and led large forces on several occasions. In 1544 Shingen sent Nobushigé to lay the Siege of Kojinyama (Shinano), a fortress defended by Tozawa Yorichika.

In 1553, at the Siege of Katsurao (Shinano), the main castle of Murakami Yoshikiyo (1501-1573), fell to Nobushigé and Shingen's son Yoshinobu (1538-1567). This drove Yoshikiyo to Uesugi Kenshin (1530-1578), and was really the last significant act before the start of the Kawa-naka-jima campaigns proper.

In 1561, at the 4th Battle of Kawa-naka-jima (Shinano), Nobushigé fell in the melee against Kakizaki Kageié (1513-1575). His head was later recovered by one of Shingen's warriors Yamadera Nobuaki, killing the man who had taken it.

Nobushigé is famous not only for his strategic insight, but also his wisdom. He wrote among other things the *Kyujukyu-kakun*, a set of 99 short rules for Takeda clan members, some of which are erroneously attributed to Shingen himself from time to time.

The real name of Sanada Yukimura (1567-1615), a loyal vassal of the Takeda, was Nobushigé, named after this very person.

Takeda Nobukado (1529-1582)

Son of Nobutora, and younger brother to Shingen. While not known as a great captain, he was an avid painter and a man of learning. He also acted as his brother's double from time to time. After Shingen's death, he served as an advisor to his heir Katsuyori.

At the 1575 Battle of Nagashino (Mikawa), Nobukado commanded the Takeda central company as an adviser under Katsuyori.

Nobukado held Takato Castle (Shinano) until his nephew and son-in-law Nishina Morinobu (1557-1582) came of age.

Azuchi-Momoyama Period – Takeda

In 1582, when Oda Nobunaga (1534-1582) invaded the Takeda lands, Nobukado attempted to flee but, was captured and beheaded by Oda troops at the Zenko-ji (Shinano), along with many other Takeda retainers.

Takeda Nobuzané (-1575)

Son of Nobutora, and younger half-brother to Shingen. He was adopted by the Kawakubo, and his name became Kawakubo Nobuzané. He was Hyogo no suké. He occasionally acted as a double for Shingen.

At the 1575 Battle of Nagashino (Mikawa) Nobuzané was killed in an attack led by Sakai Tadatsugu (1527-1596) and Kanamori Nagachika (1524-1608).

Takeda Yoshinobu (1538-1567)

Eldest son of Shingen. His mother was a daughter of the kugé Sanjo Kimiyori. In 1550 he came of age, and took the name Yoshinobu, formally receiving the 'yoshi' from the 13th Ashikaga Shogun Yoshiteru (1536-1565). He was Izu no kami.

In 1552, to further Takeda-Imagawa ties, Yoshinobu married a daughter of Imagawa Yoshimoto (1519-1560).

In 1561 Yoshinobu argued with his father over the conduct of the 4th Battle of Kawa-naka-jima (Shinano), where he was wounded, as well as disagreed on what to do about the Imagawa in Suruga after the death of his father-in-law. He went so far as to lobby his position to Shingen's generals behind his back, and relations between father and son soured after this.

In 1565 Yoshinobu, with Obu Toramasa (1504-1565), was accused of conspiring against Shingen, the alleged plot being brought to light by Yamagata Masakagé (1524-1575). Toramasa was made to commit seppuku, while Yoshinobu was confined to the Toko-ji (Shinano), where two years later he died. Shingen then designated Yoshinobu's half-brother Katsuyori as the acting leader of the clan after himself until Katsuyori's son Nobukatsu came of age.

Takeda Nobuchika (1541-1582)

2nd son of Shingen. He was born completely blind and therefore could not become a retainer of the Takeda. Shingen named him heir to the Unno of Shinano in order to further expand his influence, hence he was named Unno Nobuchika.

In 1582, when the Oda-Tokugawa alliance invaded Kai, Nobuchika committed suicide by taking hemlock. Tokugaway Ieyasu (1543-1616), who had felt sympathy towards Nobuchika, protected the latter's son Nobumitsu from harm.

Takeda Katsuyori (1546-1582)

3rd son of Shingen. His mother was a daughter of Suwa Yorishigé (1516-1542). He was adopted by his mother's clan, and in 1562 succeeded as its head. He resided at Takato Castle (Ina district of Shinano) as the seat of his domain.

In 1563 Katsuyori campaigned with his father and Hojo Ujiyasu (1515-1571) in the successful Siege of Musashi-Matsuyama, taking the castle from Uesugi Norikatsu (-1575).

In 1565 Shingen and Oda Nobunaga (1534-1582) of Owari established friendly ties, and Katsuyori wedded Nobunaga's niece and adopted daughter Toyama-hujin.

In 1567, after Katsuyori's elder brother Yoshinobu died, Shingen had to select a new heir. As his 2nd son Unno Nobuchika had been born blind, and 3rd son Nobuyuki had died earlier in 1553, Shingen selected Katsuyori's son Nobukatsu, who had been adopted by Shingen's younger brother Nobukato, as his heir, with Katsuyori acting as his guardian. In 1570 Katsuyori was ordered to move his household from Suwa to Tsutsuji-ga-seki (Kai).

Takeda Katsuyori

In 1573, upon the death of his father, Katsuyori assumed leadership of the Takeda, but soon made enemies of Shingen's companions in arms by refusing to take their advice in important matters, and by deciding all affairs according to his own pleasure.

In 1574, at the 1st Siege of Takatenjin (Totomi), Katsuyori defeated Ogasawara Ujisuké (-1590), who was under the command of Tokugawa Ieyasu (1543-1616). His taking of the castle, which even his famous father could not, marked the height of Takeda power, and gained him the support of his clansmen.

In 1575 Katsuyori planned to capture Ozaki Castle (Mikawa), assisted by a treacherous minister who promised to throw open the gates when the Takeda arrived. This would have isolate Tokugawa Ieyasu at Hamamatsu (Totomi), cutting him off from Oda reinforcements, and possibly led to his surrender or death. Unfortunately the plot was uncovered by the Tokugawa, and Katsuyori called off the attack, deciding instead to invest Nagashino Castle (Mikawa). The siege failed as one of the defenders, Torii Suné'émon, managed to escape, and call for reinforcements. At the ensuing Battle of Nagashino, Katsuyori and his army commanded by Anayama Nobukimi (1541-1582), his uncle and Shingen's brother Nobukata, and his cousin and Nobushigé's son Nobutoyo, faced the forces of Oda Nobunaga, Tokugawa Ieyasu, and Okudaira Sadamasa (1555-1615). Nobunaga's arquebusiers were able to fire continuously on the formidable Takeda cavalry when it had to slow down to cross a stream 50 meters from the enemy. The Oda army's rotating volleys of fire led to a complete rout of the Takeda forces, and a decisive victory for Nobunaga's troops. Katsuyori suffered terrible losses, losing a large part of his army as well as a number of his generals, including his uncle and Shingen's brother Takeda Nobuzané, Baba Nobuharu (1514-1575), Yamagata Masakagé (1524-1575), Naito Masatoyo (1522-1575), Hara Masatané (1531-1575), Sanada Nobutsuna (1537-1575), Sanada Masateru, Kasai Mitsuhidé, Wada Narishigé, and Yonekura Shigetsugu. From this point the glory of the Takeda declined rapidly.

In 1577 Katsuyori married the sister

of Hojo Ujimasa (1538-1590). Uesugi Kenshin (1530-1578) of Echigo, in honor of his long-time rival Shingen, and to focus on the Oda's advance into Kaga, made peace with the Takeda.

In 1578 Katsuyori gave help to Uesugi Kagekatsu (1556-1623) against his rival Uesugi Kagetora (1552-1579), who was the 7th son of Hojo Ujiyasu (1515-1571), adopted by and heir to Uesugi Kenshin. The Ujimasa was furious at Katsuyori, and canceled their alliance. The Hojo took up arms to defend their relative, and Katsuyori found himself simultaneously at war with the Oda, the Tokugawa, and the Hojo. As the Uesugi were involved with their succession stuggle, the Takeda were thus effectively isolated. After having taken Numata Castle (Kozuké) from the Hojo, Katsuyori built forts at Numazu (Suruga), and at Sanmai-bashi (Suruga).

In 1581, at the 2nd Siege of Takatenjin, Oda Nobunaga sent Mori Nagahidé to retake the fortress from the Takeda garrison commanded by Okabé Naganori. The siege succeeded after four months, and the loss of the castle led to retainers like Kiso Yoshimura (1540-1595), Anayama Nobukimi (1532-1582), and Katsuyori's uncle Nobukado to withdraw their support.

In 1582, at the Battle of Tenmoku-zan (Kai), the forces of Katsuyori and Oyamada Nobushigé (1545-1582) were completely destroyed by the forces of Oda Nobunaga and Tokugawa Ieyasu. Katsuyori then burned his castle at Shinpu, and fled into the mountains to the stronghold at Iwadono held by an old Takeda retainer Oyamada Nobushigé, but they were denied entry. Pursued by enemy troops under Takigawa Kazumasu, and while they were held at bay by his last few retainers, the three Tsuchiya brothers, Katsuyori, his son Nobukatsu, and his wife killed themselves. Katsuyori's death marked the end of the Takeda.

Oda Nobunaga is rumored to have had great pleasure in seeing Katsuyori's decapitated head, as the Takeda had always been his biggest rival.

Takeda Harukiyo (1557-1582)
5th son of Shingen. See Nishina Morinobu.

Kensho-in (-1622)
2nd daughter of Shingen. Her mother was Lady Sanjo. She married her cousin Anayama Nobukimi (1541-1582).

Takeda Nobutoyo (-1582)
2nd son of Nobushigé. He held Komoro Castle (Shinano). He was Sama no suké.

In 1569 Nobutoyo assisted his cousin Katsuyori at the Siege of Kanbara (Suruga), where the Takeda forces took the castle from Hojo Tsunashigé (1515-1587).

At the 1575 Battle of Nagashino (Mikawa) Nobutoyo played an important role in the attack, and also in 1579 in the action around Numazu (Suruga) against the Hojo.

He was killed in the Oda-Tokugawa invasion of the Takeda lands.

Takeda Nobuyoshi (1583-1603)
Son of Tokugawa Ieyasu (1543-1616). He was born Tokugawa Fukumatsumaru. His mother is believed to have been Otoma, the daughter of the Takeda retainer Akiyama Torayasu. As Ieyasu took pity on the destroyed Takeda, he changed his son's name to Takeda Manchiyo-maru, and then to Takeda Shichiro Nobuyoshi. He entrusted the boy to the care of the Anayama of Kai.

After Ieyasu's move into the Kanto region, Nobuyoshi was granted a fief centered around Kogané Castle (Shimosa -- 30,000 koku). From Kogané he was moved to Sakura Castle (Shimosa -- 100,000 koku). In 1600, for his service as rusui-yaku "guard" for the western enceinte of Edo Castle, Ieyasu, victorious in the wake of the Seki-ga-hara Campaign, gave his son the fief of Mito (Shimosa -- 250,000 koku). However, as Nobuyoshi had been sickly from birth, he soon died at the young age of not yet 20. With his death, the Takeda of Kai came to a second end.

TSUKUSHI

Territories: Tsukushi (Chikuzen)
Castle: Yamashita (Chikuzen)

An ancient daimyo family descended from Shoni Sukeyori (late 12th century), who took his name from the village in Chikuzen, where he resided.

Notable Ancestors

Tsukushi Korekado (1531-1567)
Held land in Chikuzen. He was at first a retainer of the Shoni.

After the Shoni lost their domain to the Ryuzoji, Korekado served the 13th Ashikaga Shogun Yoshiteru (1536-1565) and the Ouchi.

In 1557, joining Akizuki Fumitané, Korekado sided with Mori Motonari (1497-1571), but lost his domain to Otomo Sorin (1530-1587), and had to seek refuge in Yamaguchi (Suo).

Tsukushi Hirokado (1548-1615)
2nd son of Korekado. He held Tsukushi (Chikuzen).

In 1567 Hirokado was defeated by Takahashi Joun, a general of Otomo Sorin (1530-1587), then by Shimazu Yoshihisa (1533-1611).

In 1572 Hirokado was compelled to surrender to Ryuzoji Takanobu (1530-1584).

In 1587 Hirokado joined Toyotomi Hideyoshi (1536-1598) in his Kyushu Campaign, and as a result had Tsukushi restored to him, settling in Yamashita Castle.

From 1592-1598 Hirokado took part in Toyotomi Hideyoshi's Invasions of Korea under Kobayakawa Takakagé (1532-1597).

In 1593 Hirokado and his son Harukado were baptized.

In 1600, during the Battle of Seki-ga-hara (Mino), Hirokado sided against Tokugawa Ieyasu (1543-1616), and fought at Otsu Castle (Omi). Afterwards he was dispossessed, but was allowed to become a retainer of Kato Kiyomasa (1562-1611).

UJIIÉ

Revenues: 25,000 koku
Territories: Shimotsuké, Mino, Isé, Omi
Castles: Ujiié (Shimotsuké), Ogaki (Mino)

An ancient daimyo family native of Shimotsuké, and descended from the Fujiwara.

Notable Ancestors

Ujiié Kinyori (12th-13th century)

At the end of the 12th century, settled at Ujiié (Shimotsuké), where he built a castle.

Ujiié Naomoto/Bokuzen (-1571)

Son of Yukikuni. He was Hitachi no suké. He shaved his head and took the name Bokuzen.

Naomoto was one of the three chief retainers of the Saito of Mino, the famed Nishi Mino Sannin-shu "Western Mino Triumvirate," along with Inaba Yoshimichi (1515-1589) and Ando Morinari (1503-1582), and commanded Ogaki Castle.

Around 1564 Naomoto lost faith in Saito Tatsuoki (1548-1573), and defected to the Oda.

In 1570 Naomoto fought at the Battle of Anegawa (Omi).

Naomoto died at the 1st Siege of Nagashima (Owari), while under the command of Shibata Katsuié (1522-1583), fighting against the Ikko-ikki.

Ujiié Yukihiro (1546-1615)

2nd son of Naomoto. He was also known as Ogino Douki. He served Hashiba (later Toyotomi) Hideyoshi (1536-1598), and was given in fief Kuwana (Isé -- 25,000 koku).

In 1582, after the death of Oda Nobunaga (1534-1582), the Ujiié at first supported Nobunaga's 3rd son Nobutaka (1558-1583), but when he opposed against Hashiba Hideyoshi, they sided with the latter.

In 1583, upon the death of his elder brother Naomasa, Yukihiro became the head of the clan.

During the 1600 Seki-ga-hara Campaign, Yukihiro fought for Ishida Mitsunari (1560-1600), and afterwards was dispossessed.

In 1614 Yukihiro joined the defenders of Osaka Castle in support of Toyotomi Hideyori (1593-1615), and in the aftermath of the Summer Campaign was ordered to commit seppuku.

Ujiié Yukitsugu (16th-17th century)

Son of Naomoto, and brother to Yukihiro. He was Shima no kami.

Yukitsugu was the daimyo of Moriyama (Omi -- 15,000 koku), but in 1600 he was dispossessed.

YAMAGATA

Territories: Suruga, Shinano
Castle: Ejiri (Suruga)

Notable Ancestors

Yamagata Masakagé (1524-1575)

Lord of Eijiri Castle (Suruga). He was a personal friend of Takeda Shingen (1521-1573). He was one of the Takeda Nijushi-sho "24 Generals of the Takeda," and was considered one of its fiercest warriors, famous for his red armor and skill on the battlefield.

Masakagé was the younger brother of Obu Toramasa (1504-1565), who was also a retainer of Takeda Shingen, and led the famous Red Fire Unit, the name of which was derived from Shingen's slogan Fu-Rin-Ka-Zan. After Toramasa committed seppuku as a cover for the failed rebellion of Takeda Yoshinobu (1538-1567), Masakagé adopted the Red Fire Unit name, and outfitted his cavalry in bright red armor. It was said that his cavalry always charged first in battle, sowing confusion and panic in the enemy ranks.

Masakagé fought for Takeda Shingen in many battles, and was awarded a fief in Shinano. In 1569 he fought the Hojo at the Battle of Mimasé-togé (Sagami). In 1572 he captured Yoshida Castle (Mikawa), a Tokugawa possession. In 1573 he faced the Tokugawa at the Battle of Mikata-ga-hara (Totomi).

In 1575 Masakagé tried twice to persuade Takeda Katsuyori (1546-1582) to call off the attack of Nagashino (Mikawa) as he was sure there was an ambush waiting for them, but Katsuyori would not listen. In the ensuing ill-fated Battle of Nagashino, Masakagé was shot down from his horse while charging with his Red Fire Unit, who all died with him.

Ii Naomasa (1561-1602) of the Tokugawa was inspired by Masakagé's red armor, and made tribute to him by naming his army the Red Devil Brigade.

According to legend, Takeda Shingen called out to Masakagé from his deathbed, and ordered him to plant his banners at the Seta Bridge, the traditional eastern gateway of Kyoto.

UKITA

Revenues: 575,000 koku
Territories: Bizen, Bitchu, Mimasaka
Castles: Okayama (Bizen)

Ancient daimyo family descended from Kojima Takanori (early 14th century), who was himself descended from the venerable Miyaké of Bizen, and hence from the Seiwa-Genji Minamoto.

The 16th century opened with the Ukita led by Yoshiié, and vassals to the Urakami. Yoshiié's grandson Naoié would come to usurp the Urakami and rule all of Bizen.

Under Toyotomi Hideyoshi (1536-1598), the Ukita became very powerful in western Honshu but lost their domain following the 1600 Battle of Seki-ga-hara (Mino).

Notable Ancestors

Ukita Yoshiié (-1534)

Was Izumi no kami and heiza'émon-no-jo. He was a vassal of the Urakami of Mimasaka.

In 1502 Urakami Norimuné died of illness, and Matsuda Motokatsu seized the opportunity to lead a full-scale assault on the Urakami domain. That winter Yoshiié crossed the Yoshii River with the Urakami army, which inflicted a reverse on the Matsuda.

In 1503 the Urakami and the Ukita entered Bizen's Uemichi district, while the Matsuda advanced to the Ono district, and established themselves at Kasai-yama. The two sides confronted one another across the dry river bed of the Asahi River. Yoshiié helped Urakami Muramuné (-1524) to score a victory for the Urakami and the Ukita, with the Matsuda retreating from the field.

Yoshiié continued to clash with the Matsuda until 1524, when he retired in favor of his son Okiié.

He had displeased Urakami Munekagé, son of Muramuné in some way, and was executed.

Ukita Okiié (-1536)

Eldest son of Yoshiié. In 1524 he succeeded his father. He was lord of Toishi Castle (Bizen), and served the Urakami.

Okiié was not considered a competent leader, and accomplished little during his tenure as daimyo.

Ukita Naoié (1530-1582)

Son of Okiié. He was born in Bizen. In 1536, after his father's death, he succeeded to the family headship. He at first served Urakami Munekagé, who ruled from Tenjin-yama Castle (Bizen).

In 1545 Naoié received a small fort on the shore of the Inland Sea, together with a small garrison. From there he began his expansion of his lands through conquest and alliance, helping Urakami Munekagé along the way in the 1550s to reach the height of his power.

In 1566 Naoié had the Endo brothers, Matajiro and Yoshijiro, assassinate Mimura Iechika (1517-1566), lord of Matsuyama Castle (Bitchu).

By 1568 Naoié had destroyed the Matsuda, and was the most powerful of the Urakami vassals.

In 1573 Naoié rebuilt Okayama Castle (Bizen), and made it his capital.

When an internal dispute broke out at Tenjin-yama, Naoié attacked and removed the Urakami from power, forcing Munekagé to flee to Sanuki, thus bringing all of Bizen under his banner.

Naoié went on to struggle with the Akamatsu of Harima and the Miyoshi of Shikoku, while expanding his authority into Mimasaka and Bitchu.

By this time the expansion of the powerful Mori had brought them to Bizen's borders, and Naoié signed an alliance with them. This placed the Ukita as one of the first lines of defense against Oda Nobunaga (1534-1582).

By 1576 the Mori and the Oda opened hostilities between them. Naoié led Ukita forces into Harima, and clashed with the Oda soldiers. In 1578 he recaptured Kozuki Castle (Harima), which in the previous year the Mori had lost to the Oda troops, but it was subsequently lost again to Yamanaka Shika no suké Yukimori (1545-1578) of the Amako.

A relief effort in 1579 ended in a defeat for the Ukita, and in 1580 Naoié signed a treaty with the Oda. He sent his son Hideié as a hostage to Hashiba (later Toyotomi) Hideyoshi (1536-1598), and in return was confirmed as lord of Bizen, as well as a fair amount of Mimasaka.

He was ultimately succeeded by his son Hideié.

Naoié's senior retainers included his brother Tadaié (-1609), Hanabusa Masayuki (1524-1605), Osafuné Kii no Kami Sadachika, Togawa Higo no Kami Hideyasu (1538-1597), and Oka Bungo no kami Toshikatsu (-1592).

Ukita Yoshiié

Ukita Naoié

Azuchi-Momoyama Period – Wada

Ukita Tadaié (-1609)

Son of Okiié, and younger brother to Naoié. Dewa no kami. He assisted his elder brother in all his campaigns.

In 1582 Tadaié was active in the campaigns of Hashiba (later Toyotomi) Hideyoshi (1536-1598) in Bitchu, and assisted in the taking of Kanmuri-yama and Takamatsu Castles.

Ukita Hideié (1572-1662)

Son of Naoié. In 1582, when his father died, he became the head of the clan, but being still a child, he was brought up by Hashiba (later Toyotomi) Hideyoshi (1536-1598) as something of a protegé. He was chunagon "middle counselor" and sangi "Imperial advisor."

In 1582, after the assassination of Oda Nobunaga (1534-1582), Hashiba Hideyoshi immediately made peace with the Mori, and raced back to Kyoto, leaving Naoié in charge of Bizen, Mimasaka, and the newly taken parts of Bitchu, as well as to keep watch on Mori Terumoto (1553-1625) to the west.

In 1585 Hideié joined Hashiba Hideyoshi's Invasion of Shikoku, and in 1586 the Invasion of Kyushu.

In 1586 Hideié married Go-himé, a daughter of Hashiba Hideyoshi that he had adopted from Maeda Toshiié (1539-1599).

In 1590 Hideié served Toyotomi (formerly Hashiba) Hideyoshi at the Siege of Odawara (Sagami).

From 1597-1598 Hideié served in Toyotomi Hideyoshi's 2nd Invasion of Korea as gensui "chief field commander."

In 1594 Hideié received the title of chunagon "middle counselor."

In 1598 Hideié was appointed to the council of Go-Tairo "Five Elders" along with Maeda Toshiié, Uesugi Kagekatsu (1556-1623), Mori Terumoto, and Tokugawa Ieyasu (1543-1616) by Toyotomi Hideyoshi for the minority of his son Hideyori (1593-1615). By this time Hideié ruled Bizen, Mimasaka, and parts of Bitchu from Okayama Castle, yielding an income of around 575,000 koku.

After the death of Toyotomi Hideyoshi, Hideié opposed Tokugawa Ieyasu. In 1600 he helped lay the Siege of Fushimi (near Kyoto), and stormed the castle. When the armies met at the Battle of Seki-ga-hara (Mino), Hideié advised a night attack, but Ishida Mitsunari (1560-1600) refused. After the defeat of his party Hideié fled to seek refuge with the Shimazu in Satsuma. Okayama Castle and surrounding Ukita territories were granted as spoils of war to Kobayakawa Hidéaki (1577-1602), one of the defectors during the battle.

In the beginning of 1603 Shimazu Tadatsuné (1576-1638) revealed the retreat of Hideié to Tokugawa Ieyasu, and the Shogun at first condemned him to death, but commuted this penalty to perpetual exile to the island prison of Hachijo-jima (Izu), wither he was transported with several supporters, including his two sons and their nurses. Upon arrival he shaved his head, and took the name Raifu. His wife Go-himé returned to the Maeda, her birth family, and from there sent correspondences and gifts of rice, saké, and clothing to her husband and sons. Upon Ieyasu's death, he was offered a conditional pardon, but declined, and never returned to the mainland. He died at an advanced age of more then 90 years old, possibly the last of the Toyotomi-era daimyo to die.

Ukita Hideié

WADA

Territories: Settsu
Castles:
Akutagawa (Settsu),
Takatsuki (Settsu)

Notable Ancestors

Wada Koremasa (1536-1571)

Son of Koresuké (-1546). He was a vassal of the Sasaki of Omi. He was Iga no kami.

In 1565 Koremasa gave shelter to the future 15th Ashikaga Shogun Yoshiaki (1537-1597), after the murder of his brother, the 13th Ashikaga Shogun Yoshiteru (1536-1565).

In 1568, after the ruin of the Sasaki, Koremasa offered his services to Oda Nobunaga (1534-1582), who entrusted Akutagawa Castle (Settsu) to him.

In 1569 Koremasa defeated Miyoshi Yoshitsugu (1551-1573), and was made governor of Kyoto. That same year he helped secure the Portuguese Jesuit missionary Luis Frois (-1597) an audience with Oda Nobunaga in Kyoto.

Koremasa supported the Takayama of Settsu, and was later killed fighting with Araki Murashigé (1535-1586) in their defense.

Wada Korenaga (-1573)

Son of Koremasa. In 1571 he succeeded his father upon his death. He held Takatsuki Castle (Settsu).

Korenaga planned to destroy the Takayama, but when they learned of his intentions, they lured him into a dark room, and murdered him in a brief but vicious swordfight.

Azuchi-Momoyama Period – Yamana

YAMANA

Territories: Inaba, Mimasaka, Bizen, Bitchu, Tanba, Hoki, Izumo, Oki, Tajima, Harima, Izumi

Castle: Tottori (Inaba)

An anicent daimyo family, descended from the Seiwa-Geji Minamoto Yoshishigé (1135-1202). Originally from Kozuké, and later centered at Inaba, they were valued retainers under Minamoto Yoritomo (1147-1199), and counted among his go-kenin "Shogunal vassals."

The Yamana were among the chief clans in fighting for the establishment of the Ashikaga Shogunate, and was one of the most powerful of the Muromachi "Ashikaga" Period (1336-1573). Thanks in large measure to the efforts of Yamana Tokiuji, a staunch Ashikaga supporter, they were valued and powerful under the new government. By 1363 they were shugo "military governors" of five provinces, and a short time later of eleven.

In 1391 however members of the Yamana rebelled against the Shogunate, and lost most of their land. In 1441 Yamana Sozen, the most famous member of the clan, regained these lands. Through all of this the Yamana managed to somehow retain a great degree of reputation and power within the Bakufu. Along with the Hosokawa and the Hatakeyama, they served as agents of the Ashikaga in resolving various disputes. In 1467 Sozen would then become embroiled in a conflict with Hosokawa Katsumoto (1430-1473) over naming the Shogun's successor. This conflict grew into the Onin War (1467-1477), which destroyed much of Kyoto, and led to the fall of the Shogunate, and the beginning of the Sengoku "Warring States" Period (1467-1573). In the end this cost the Yamana much of their former influence and land.

By the end of the 16th century the Yamana had been reduced to holding the better part of Inaba, which they held until the end of the Edo "Tokugawa" Period (1603-1868).

Notable Ancestors

Yamana Yoshinori (12th-13th century)

Son of Yoshishigé. He was the first to take the name of Yamana.

Yamana Tokiuji (-1372)

Descendant of Yoshinori in the 8th generation.

In 1336 Tokuji sided with Ashikaga Takauji (1305-1358), and assisted at the Battle of Takenoshita (Suruga) and in the Kyushu Campaign.

In 1340 Tokiuji put Enya Takasada to death in Izumo. At that time he was made betto "superintendent" of the samurai-dokoro and governor of Inaba and Hoki.

In 1347 Tokiuji was sent by Ashikaga Takauji to rescue Hosokawa Akiuji

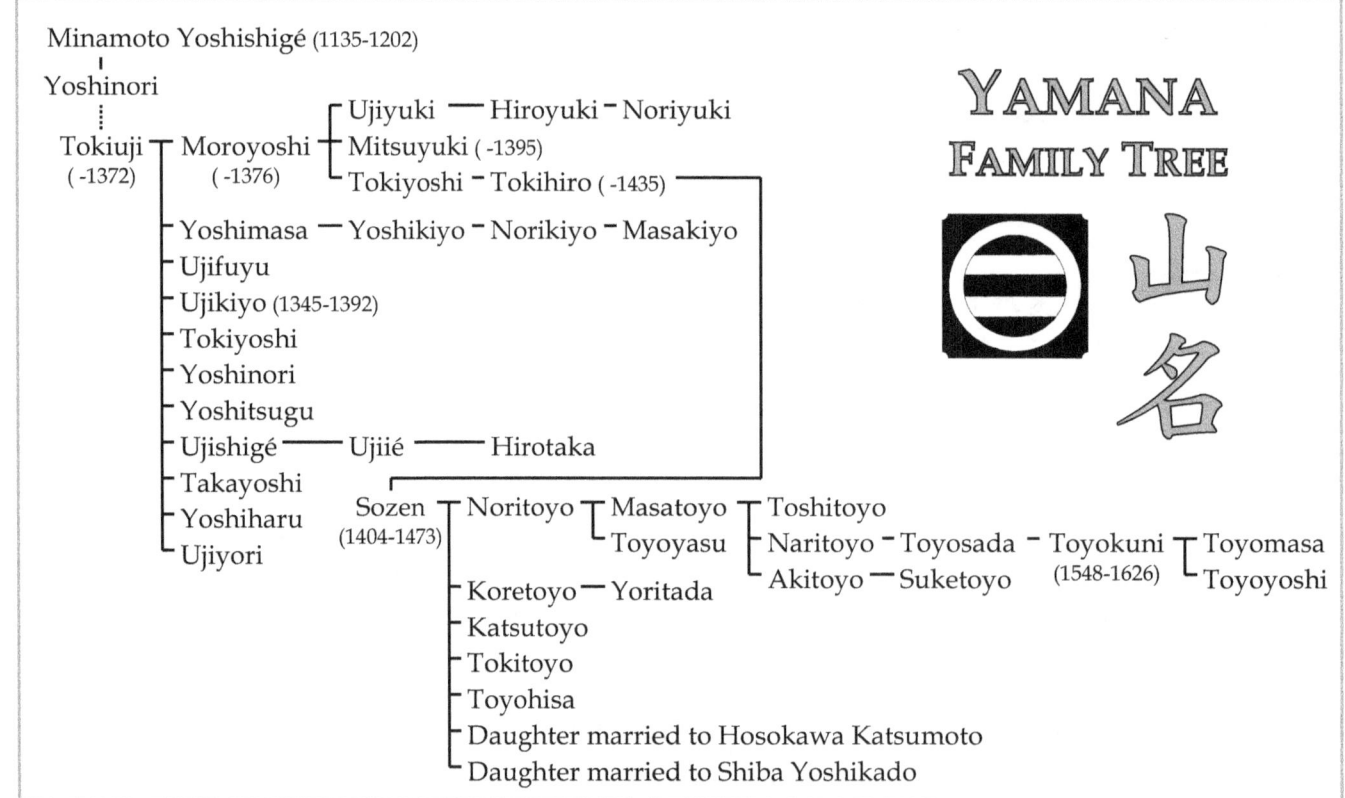

Yamana Family Tree

(-1352), but was defeated by Kusunoki Masatsura (1326-1348), and was completely defeated at Uriuno (Settsu), receiving seven wounds in the battle.

In 1352 Tokiuji sided with the Southern Dynasty, due to a territorial dispute, and fought against the 2nd Ashikaga Shogun Yoshiakira (1330-1367).

In 1362 Tokiuji conquered Mimasaka, Bizen, Bitchu, Inaba, and Tanba. He renewed his allegiance to the Northern Dynasty, and the Shogun allowed him to retain the five provinces in fief.

He then shaved his head, and took the name Dojo. He left eleven sons.

Yamana Moroyoshi (-1376)

Eldest son of Tokiuji. At the age of 14 he took part in the campaigns of his father.

In 1352 Moroyoshi induced his father to join the join the Southern Dynasty when the clan did not received the promised territory of Wakasa from the Ashikaga.

In 1353 Moroyoshi defeated the 2nd Ashikaga Shogun Yoshiakira (1330-1367) at Kyoto, but in 1355 was in turn defeated.

After conquering Mimasaka, Bizen, etc., Moroyoshi returned to the party of the Ashikaga, and became betto "superintendent" of the samurai-dokoro.

He then shaved his head, and took the name Doko.

Yamana Yoshimasa (late 14th century)

2nd son of Tokiuji, and brother to Moroyoshi. He occupied Izumi and Kii in the name of the Ashikaga.

Having quarreled with the 3rd Ashikaga Shogun Yoshimitsu (1358-1408), Yoshimasa ventured to attack him, but was defeated in a battle where his brother Ujikiyo was slain. He submitted to the victors, and was condemned to shave his head, taking the name Soko, and retiring to Kokoku-ji.

Yamana Ujikiyo (1345-1392)

4th son of Tokiuji. He was governor of Tanba, then of Izumi.

Ujikiyo opposed the Ashikaga, but was defeated and killed by Isshiki Akinori (-1406).

Yamana Ujiyuki (late 14th century)

Son of Moroyoshi.

In 1390 Ujiyuki revolted against the 3rd Ashikaga Shogun Yoshimitsu (1358-1408), but was defeated, and made his submission.

In 1392, at the partition of his family's domain, Ujiyuki received Hoki.

Yamana Mitsuyuki (-1395)

Son of Moroyoshi, and brother to Ujiyuki. In 1384 he was made governor of Izumo and Tanba.

In 1390 Mitsuyuki, together with his uncle Ujikiyo, was ordered to repress the rebellion of his brother Ujiyuki and his nephew Tokihiro.

Some time after, Ujiyuki resigned his possession to Mitsuyuki, and thus he governed Hoki and Oki, in addition to his own.

By this time the Yamana possessed eleven provinces, i.e., one-sixth of the whole country, for which reason the people had called them Roku-no-bunno-ichi-dono "the lords of one-sixth." The 3rd Ashikaga Shogun Yoshimitsu (1358-1408) became jealous of such power, and resolved to crush it. Mitsuyuki furnished a pretext when he dared to appropriate some lands in Izumo that belonged to the ex-Emperor. The Shogun at once recalled his exiled minister Hosokawa Yoriyuki (1329-1392), and with him prepared an expedition against the Yamana. Mitsuyuki did not wait to be attacked, and with his uncle Ujikiyo came to invest Kyoto. Yoshimitsu, aided by Isshiki Akinori (-1406), Hatakeyama Motokuni (1352-1406), etc., defeated them. Ujikiyo was killed, and Mitsuyuki escaped to Kyushu.

In 1392 the Yamana's large estates were divided, but the family was allowed to retain Taijma and Hoki.

Three years later Mitsuyuki was assassinated.

Yamana Tokihiro (-1435)

Son of Tokiyoshi. In 1392 he received Tajima.

In 1393 Tokihiro rebelled, but was suppressed, despoiled of his domain, and ordered to shave his head.

Yamana Mochitoyo/Sozen (1404-1473)

Son of Tokihiro. He was originally named Mochitoyo. In 1435 he inherited the domain of his family, which at the time consisted of Tajima, Inaba, and Hoki.

In 1441 Mochitoyo assisted at the Siege of Shirahata, which completed the ruin of the Akamatsu, and in reward received Harima.

In 1450 he shaved his head and took the name Sozen, by which he is especially known. Due to his red complexion, he was sometimes known as Akanyudo "Red Monk."

In 1454, having offended the 8th Ashikaga Shogun Yoshimasa (1435-1490), Sozen retired to Tajima, and sent his son Noritoyo to replace him at Kyoto.

In 1455 Akamatsu Norinao entered Harima, but Sozen marched against him, defeated and put him to death. He then continued his march to Kyoto.

At the time of the division of the Hosokawa, Sozen sided with Yoshinari.

In 1464 a succession dispute erupted over the Shogunate. Sozen supported the rights of Ashikaga Yoshihisa (1465-1489), son of Yoshimasa, against Ashikaga Yoshimi (1439-1491), who was supported by Sozen's rival Hosokawa Katsumoto (1430-1473). All the great daimyo then divided into two factions, and a civil war known as the Onin War (1467-1477) broke out, but before its end Katsumoto died, and two months later so did Sozen. The result of the war was then yet undecided.

Yamana Koretoyo (15th century)

Son of Sozen.

In 1462 Koretoyo defeated Hosokawa Yoshinari at the Kintai-ji (Kawachi).

During the Onin War (1467-1477) Koretoyo left his father, and fought on the side of his brother-in-law Hosokawa Katsumoto (1430-1473).

Yamana Masatoyo (15th century)

Son of Noritoyo.

In 1487 Masatoyo took part in the campaign of the 9th Ashikaga Shogun Yoshihisa (145-1489) in Omi against Sasaki Takayori (-1520).

Yamana Toyokuni (1548-1626)

Son of Toyosada, and great-grandson

Yamana Toyokuni

of Masatoyo. He was governor of Inaba, and resided at Tottori Castle. He clashed with the Hatano and the Akamatsu, and made a pact with the Mori.

At the 1581 Siege of Tottori, Toyokuni fled the castle rather than face the Oda armies commanded by Hashiba (later Toyotomi) Hideyoshi (1536-1598), and left it to be defended by Kikkawa Tsuneié (1547-1581) in one of the most vicious engagements of the Sengoku "Warring States" Period (1467-1573).

Hideyoshi allotted to him two districts of Tottori as his domain, but Toyokuni divided them among his servants, and preferred to wander about till his death.

During the Edo "Tokugawa" Period (1603-1868) his descendants remained at Muraoka (Inaba).

UTSUNOMIYA

Territories: Shimotsuké
Castle: Utsunomiya (Shimotsuké)

A nicent daimyo family descended from the Kanpaku "Regent to the Emperor" Fujiwara Michikané (955-995). A great-grandson of Michikané became a bonze under the name Soen, and was placed at the head of the temple of Futara (now Nikko). His son Munetsuna built the castle of Utsunomiya (Shimotsuké) and took his name from that place.

The Utsunomiya at first supported the Southern Court in the Nanboku-cho Period (1336-1392), but eventually submitted to the Ashikaga. In the 1380s they became involved in a dispute with the Oyama that escalated into war.

The clan was weakened in the Sengoku "Warring States" Period (1467-1573) by outside perils, and came to rely first on the Yuki, and later the Saraké.

In 1597 the Utsunomiya lost their lands to Toyotomi Hideyoshi (1536-1598), and from 1607, with the death of Kunitsuna, drifted into obscurity.

NOTABLE ANCESTORS

Utsunomiya Kintsuna (1302-1356)

Son of Sadatsuna. He was governor of Bizen.

In 1332, sent by Hojo Takatoki (1303-1333) to defend the Rokuhara (Kyoto), Kintsuna joined the Imperial cause after the capture of Kamakura (Sagami), and fought under Nitta Yoshisada (1301-1338). Seeing his party defeated everywhere, he returned to Utsunomiya.

In 1337 Kintsuna re-entered the field, and defeated Ashikaga Yoshiakira (1330-1367), Uesugi Noriaki (1306-1368), etc.

When his lord Kitabataké Akiié (1318-1338) had suffered defeat, Kintsuna returned to Utsunomiya, shaved his head, and took the name Riren.

Utsunomiya Ujitsuna (-1370)

Son of Kintsuna.

Ujitsuna continued the war against the Ashikaga, and defeated Ashikaga Tadayoshi (1306-1352) and Momonoi Naoyoshi. He afterwards surrendered to the 1st Kanto kubo Ashikaga Motouji (1340-1367).

Utsunomiya Toshitsuna (1437-1477)

Son of Mochitsuna. He sided with the 5th Kanto-kubo Ashikaga Shigeuji (1438-1497) against the Uesugi, but was defeated, obliged to shave his head, and confined to Shirakawa (Mutsu).

Utsunomiya Tadatsuna (15th-16th century)

In 1499, Tadatsuna's domain being invaded by Saraké Yoshiaki and Iwaki Shigekata, Yuki Masatomo (1477-1545) came to his aid. Instead of being grateful for the favor received, Tadatsuna plotted against his benefactor. Masatomo therefore returned, deposed him, and replaced him by his uncle Okitsuna.

Utsunomiya Hisatsuna (1519-1546)

Son of Okitsuna. He was killed at Saotomé (Shimotsuké) in a war against his neighbor, the Nasu.

Utsunomiya Hirotsuna (1543-1590)

Son of Naotsuna. Following his father's death, owing to a strife within Shimotsuké led by Nasu Takasada, he was forced to flee to the Saraké of Hitachi as a child, whence he eventually married a daughter of Saraké Yoshiaki (1531-1565), who helped him recover his domain.

Utsunomiya Kunitsuna (1568-1607)

Eldest son of Hirotsuna. He succeeded his father.

Kunitsuna initially submitted to the Hojo, but in turn gave his support to Toyotomi Hideyoshi (1536-1598) when he laid the 1590 Siege of Odawara (Sagami).

In 1597 Toyotomi Hideyoshi deprived Kunitsuna of his domain, and following the Taiko's death, was unable to regain it.

Edo Period

Chosokabé

Territory: Shikoku
Castles: Oko, Toyo'oka, Nagahama (Tosa)
Legacy: *Chosokabé-shi Okitegaki* "100 Article Code of the Chosokabé"

Family of samurai believed to have descended from the Chinese Emperor Qin Shi Huang (295 B.C.-210 B.C.).

From the 12th century they were respected jito "stewards" of Tosa. They served successively the Hosokawa, the Miyoshi, and finally the Ichijo.

By 1584 Motochika, the 21st head of the Chosokabé, had conquered all of Shikoku, but in the following year submitted to Hashiba (later Toyotomi) Hideyoshi (1536-1598) when he invaded the island, but was allowed to keep Tosa.

After the 1600 Battle of Seki-ga-hara (Mino), defeated by Tokugawa Ieyasu (1543-1616), the clan lost Tosa to the Yamauchi.

In 1615 the clan sided with Toyotomi Hideyoshi's son Hideyori (1593-1615), and were annihilated by Tokugawa Ieyasu during the Siege of Osaka.

Among the retainers of the Chosokabé were Tani Tadasumi (1533-1600), Hisataké Chikanao, Yoshida Takayori (1494-1563), Yoshida Shigetoshi, and Yoshida Masashigé.

The 19th century missionary Shiro Sokabé was a descendant of this clan.

Notable Ancestors

Chosokabé Kunichika (1504-1560)

Son of Kanetsugu. His childhood name was Senyu-maru. He was Shinano no kami.

In 1508, right before his father was killed by the Motoyama while attempting to flee from Oko Castle, Kunichika, then 4 years old, was placed in the care of the kugé Ichijo Fusaié (1445-1511) of Tosa.

According to a storybook, about three years later Ichijo Fusaié is said to have offered his young ward a deal. After a bit of drinking, he proposed that if Kunichika jumped off the side of the castle they were presently sitting in, he would help retake Oko for him. To his great surpirse, Kunichika promptly leapt off the edge, an act of fearlessness that moved the Ichijo men who saw it.

Around 1518 the Ichijo secured Oko, and handed it over to Kunichika.

Nominally a vassal of the Ichijo, Kunichika built a castle at Toyo'oka (Tosa), and strengthened his position on the Kochi Plain through alliances, timely aggression, and adoptions into other families.

In 1560 Kunichika captured Nagahama Castle (Tosa) from his long-time rivals, the Motoyama. In response Motoyama Shigetoki departed Asakura Castle (Tosa) to take the castle back. Kunichika, with his son Motochika, intercepted the army near the castle. In the ensuing Battle of Tonomoto, Shigetoki was completely routed, and fled to Urado Castle (Tosa), where Kunichika held him in siege until he was forced to withdraw due to illness, from which shortly afterwards he died.

Chosokabé Motochika (1539-1599)

21st head of the Chosokabé. Eldest son of Kunichika. Born at Oko Castle at Nagaoka (Tosa). His mother was of the Saito of Mino. He was at first a vassal to the Ichijo of western of Tosa.

In 1560 Motochika took part in his first engagement at the Battle of Tonomoto against the Motoyama, in which he fought bravely, greatly impressing his father and his retainers.

Motochika later defeated the Motoyama at the Battle of Asakura.

By forming alliances with local families, Motochika built his power base in the Kochi Plain. By 1569 Motochika was strong enough to march on the rival Aki of east Tosa, and brought them to bear.

In the course of the decade he was awarded a Court rank of Kunai-sho "2nd assistant to the chief of the Imperial Household," and was sufficiently confident after the reduction of the Aki to finally turn on the Ichijo.

While still lord of the Hata district of Tosa, Ichijo Kanesada (1542-1585) was unpopular, and had already suffered the defection of a number of important retainers. In 1573, seizing the opportunity, Motochika marched on the Ichijo's headquarters at Nakamura, and defeated Kanesada, who fled to Bungo. In

---

Qin Shi Huang (295 BC-210 BC)
⋮
Kanetsugu – Kunichika ┬ Motochika ┬ Nobuchika (1565-1587)
        (1504-1560) │ (1539-1599) ├ Chikakazu (1567-1587)
                         ├ Chikayasu ├ Chikatada (1572-1600)
                         ├ Chikasada ├ Morichika ┬ Moritaka
                         └ Chikamasu │ (1575-1615) ├ Morinobu
                                   └ Yasutoyo   └ Moriyasu

Chosokabé Family Tree

1575 the Otomo supplied Kanesada with a fleet, but his return in an expedition was easily crushed at the Battle of Watari-gawa (Tosa) by the Chosokabé. The twice-defeated Ichijo daimyo then submitted, and was allowed to go into exile on an island off Iyo, only to be assassinated in 1585, presumably on Motochika's orders.

Motochika, now sole ruler of Tosa, transferred his residence to Nagahama Castle, and his ambition propelled him towards domination of the whole island. He turned north, and invaded Iyo, ruled by Kono Michinao. In 1579 the Chosokabé army, commanded by Hisataké Chikanobu, attacked the strongest fortress in southern Iyo, held by Doi Kiyoyoshi. During the ensuing Siege of Okayama, Chikanobu was shot and killed by an arquebus, and his army was defeated. The loss however proved little more than an unfortunate delay. In 1580 Motochika led his men into Iyo, and forced Michinao to flee to Bungo.

With little interference from either the Mori or the Otomo, the Chosokabé was free to press onwards. In 1582 Motochika stepped up ongoing raids into Awa, and defeated the Sogo. By 1583 Chosokabé troops had subdued both Awa and Sanuki, making Motochika's dream of ruling all of Shikoku a reality.

In 1585 Hashiba (later Toyotomi) Hideyoshi (1536-1598) invaded Shikoku with Ukita Hideié (1573-1655), Kobayakawa Takagé (1533-1597), Kikkawa Motonaga (1548-1587), Hashiba Hidenaga (1540-1591), and Hashiba Hidetsugu (1568-1595). Despite the overwhelming size of Hideyoshi's army, and the suggestions of his advisors, Motochika chose to defend his territories. The battles culminated in the Siege of Ichi-no-miya (Awa), which lasted for 26 days. Motochika made a half-hearted attempt to relieve his castle, but surrendered in the end. He was allowed to keep Tosa, but the rest of Shikoku was divided among Hideyoshi's generals.

In 1587 Motochika was called upon for Toyotomi Hideyoshi's Kyushu Campaign, becoming part of an advance force alongside Sengoku Hidehisa. Their mission was to relieve the besieged Otomo of Bungo, whose request for assistance had provided Hideyoshi

Chosokabé Motochika

with the pretext for the invasion. Despite Motochika's sage advice, the Otomo and the Sengoku ignored their orders to adopt a defensive stance, and attacked the encroaching Shimazu forces in the Battle of Hetsugi-gawa (Bungo). The allied troops were soundly defeated, and in the process Motochika suffered the death of his beloved son and heir Nobuchika (1565-1587). Hideyoshi praised Motochika's sober thinking, and offered him Osumi as compensation for his loss, which Motochika respectfully declined.

After Nobuchika's death, Toyotomi Hideyoshi suggested that Motochika's 2nd son Chikakazu be named heir of the Chosokabé, but Motochika decided instead on his 4th son Morichika. Chikakazu withdrew from public life deeply embittered, and died of illness later that year. Motochika's 3rd son Chikatada, also passed over, openly objected. Morichika's ally Hisataké Chikanao agitated against him, and in 1599 Chikatada was confined to a temple under guard. The following year Chikatada was accused of colluding with the Tokugawa, and was put to death.

In 1590 Motochika led a fleet in support of the Siege of Odawara (Sagami) against the Hojo. In 1592 he took part in Toyotomi Hideyoshi's 1st Invasion of Korea, where he distinguished himself by his courage, and received the title Tosa no kami.

After his return, he transmitted his domain to Morichika, had his hair shaved, and died at his mansion in Fushimi (Yamashiro).

Motochika is remembered for his *Chosokabé-shi Okitegaki* " 100 Article Code of the Chosokabé," written in 1596, which was later used as the foundation for the Yamauchi rule in Tosa after the Chosokabé were dispossessed.

The Chosokabé were served by the Kosokabé, the Kira (both of whom were led in Motochika's time by his brothers), the Yoshida, the Kumu, the Kagawa (into which Motochika had adopted his 2nd son Chikakazu), the Yumioka, and others.

Chosokabé Chikataké (-1589)

Son of Kuniyasu, and cousin and retainer to Motochika.

Chikataké was active in Motochika's wars to conquer Shikoku, and in 1570 was given Tonami Castle, which was taken from the Ichijo, the name of which he assumed.

In 1584 Chikataké was given Sogo Castle (Sanuki).

In 1585 Chikataké attempted to resist the Invasion of Shikoku by Hashiba (later Toyotomi) Hideyoshi (1536-1598) at Ueda Castle.

His eventual fate is unclear.

Chosokabé Nobuchika (1565-1587)

Eldest and favorite son of Motochika. He was popular with the Chosokabé retainers owing to his warm and genial nature. At his genbuku "coming-of-age ceremony" Oda Nobunaga (1534-1582) himself provided the 'nobu' in Nobuchika, along with a sword and his ceremonial headgear.

Nobuchika was killed during the retreat from the defeat at the Battle of Hetsugi-gawa (Bungo). The Shimazu honored Motochika by sending his son's body to him, and allowing him to flee to Shikoku.

Chosokabé Chikakazu (1567-1587)

2nd son of Motochika.

In 1581 he succeeded Kagawa Nobukagé as the head of that family, and was given Amagiri Castle (Sanuki).

In 1587, when his elder brother Nobuchika died, Chikakazu was a potential heir to the Chosokabé, and in fact Toyotomi Hideyoshi (1536-1598) gave his approval for him to be named as successor to Motochika, who instead selected his 4th son Morichika to succeed him. Despondant and bitter, Chikakazu withdrew from active life, and died later that year. One story goes however that it was specifically because of Chikakazu's weak constitution that Motochika had him given to another house, and not kept on as a possible heir.

Chosokabé Chikatada (1572-1600)

3rd son of Motochika. He was adopted by Tsuno Katsuoki.

Following the 1585 conquest of Shikoku, Chikatada was sent as a hostage to Hashiba (later Toyotomi) Hideyoshi (1536-1598).

Following the death of his elder brother Nobuchika in 1587, Chikatada was passed over as heir to the Chosokabé. In 1599 his lingering displeasure, combined with slanderous attacks by Hisataké Chikanao, who favored Motochika's 4th son Morichika as heir, compelled Motochika to have him confined to a temple.

Following the 1600 Battle of Seki-ga-hara (Mino), Chikatada was accused of colluding with the Tokugawa, and was murdered on orders by his younger brother Morichika. Tokugawa Ieyasu (1543-1616) harshly judged Morichika for this, and used it as a basis to deprive the Chosokabé of their domain.

Chosokabé Morichika (1575-1615)

4th son of Motochika. In 1587, after the death of his elder brother Nobuchika, he was named heir to the clan. He ruled Tosa, and was a vassal of Toyotomi Hideyoshi (1536-1598).

In 1590 Morichika fought alongside his father at the Siege of Odawara (Sagami) against the Hojo. From 1592-1593 he and his father took part in Toyotomi Hideyoshi's 1st Invasion of Korea.

In 1596 Morichika assisted his father with the preparation of the *Chosokabé-shi Okitegaki* "100 Article Code of the Chosokabé."

In 1600 Morichika sided with Ishida Mitsunari (1560-1600) at the Battle of Seki-ga-hara (Mino), where he saw little action. Afterwards he sent Tokugawa Ieyasu (1543-1616) an apology, but was later deprived of his fief, which was granted to Yamauchi Kazutoyo (1545-1605). Later that year he ordered the execution of his elder brother Chikatada, who had questioned his right to be Motochika's heir. He then became a bonze, and retired to Kyoto.

In 1614 Morichika joined the Toyotomi forces to defend the Siege of Osaka by the Tokugawa, arriving there the same day as Sanada Yukimura (1567-1615). The Chosokabé contingent fought well in both the Winter and Summer Campaigns. Following their defeat at the Battle of Tenno-ji, he fled to Hachiman-yama, but was captured by the Hachisuka, conducted to Kyoto, and beheaded at the Rokujo-ga-wara with many of his sons.

BESSHO

Revenues: 20,000 koku
Territories: Harima, Tanba
Castles: Miki (Harima), Ayabé (Tanba)

Daimyo family of Harima descended from Akamatsu Enshin (1277-1350), a staunch supporter of Ashikaga Takauji (1305-1358).

In 1580 they were defeated by Hashiba (later Toyotomi) Hideyoshi (1536-1598).

NOTABLE ANCESTORS

Bessho Nagaharu (1558-1580)

Eldest son of Yasuharu. He married a daughter of Hatano Hidemichi of Tanba.

Nagaharu initially aligned himself with Oda Nobunaga (1534-1582), but following the rebellion of Araki Murashigé, he allied with his brother-in-law Hatano Hideharu (1541-1579) of Tanba.

Nagaharu fought for four years against Hashiba (later Toyotomi) Hideyoshi (1536-1598), commissioned by Oda Nobunaga to subjugate the San'yodo. In 1578 Hideyoshi began the Siege of Miki (Harima). Nagaharu initially repelled the Oda force with the help of the Mori, and by the revolt of Araki Murashigé that temporarily diverted Hideyoshi's attention. In 1580 Hideyoshi returned, and this time, instead of launching a direct assault, he launched multiple sieges against smaller castles like Kamiyoshi and Shigata to cut off the support from the Mori. This led to a rapid depletion of food, and with no hope of another reinforcement from the Mori, Nagaharu committed seppuku with his brother Tomoyuki in exchange for the lives of his troops.

Bessho Harusada (1561-1579)

Son of Yasuharu, and younger brother to Nagaharu.

Harusada defended Hirayama Castle (Harima) against Hashiba (later Toyotomi) Hideyoshi (1536-1598), and committed suicide when the garrison could no longer resist.

Bessho Toyoharu (1578-)

Son of Nagaharu. In 1580, when his father died, he was only 2 years old. Following the fall of Miki Castle (Harima), he was spared by Hashiba (later Toyotomi) Hideyoshi (1536-1582). He later obtained the title of Bungo no kami, and the castle of Ayabé (Tanba -- 20,000 koku).

In 1628 he was dispossessed by the Tokugawa Bakufu for misconduct.

Edo Period – Fukushima

FUKUSHIMA

Revenues: 498,000 koku
Territories:
  Imabari (Iyo),
  Kiyosu (Owari),
  Hiroshima (Aki),
  Kawanaka-jima (Shinano)
Castle: Kiyosu (Owari)

Samurai family native of Owari. The clan reached its apex with Masanori in the Momoyama Period (1573-1603), and later served the Tokugawa Shogunate as hatamoto.

Notable Ancestors

Fukushima Masanori (1561-1624)

Adopted son of Masamitsu. Born in Owari. His childhood name was Ichimatsu. He first served Hashiba (later Toyotomi) Hideyoshi (1536-1598).

In 1578 Masanori participated in his first engagement at the Siege of Miki (Harima), which lasted until 1580, when Bessho Nagaharu (1558-1580) finally surrendered the castle to Oda forces commanded by Hashiba Hideyoshi.

Following the 1582 Battle of Yamazaki (Yamashiro), Masanori was granted a 500 koku stipend.

At the 1583 Battle of Shizu-ga-také (Omi) near Lake Biwa, Masanori had the honor of taking the first head in the battle, that of the enemy general Ogasato Ieyoshi. He gained recognition as one of the Seven Spears of Shizu-ga-také, which also included Kato Kiyomasa (1562-1611), Kato Yoshiaki (1563-1631), and others. For his bravery in the battle he was rewarded with a 5,000 koku increase in his stipend, while the other six "Spears" each received 3,000. Hashiba Hideyoshi also appointed him Saémon-no-suké.

After the 1587 Kyushu Campaign, Masanori was made daimyo, receiving the fief of Imabari (Iyo -- 110,000 koku).

During the 1590 Kanto Campaign, Masanori took part in the Siege of Nirayama (Izu), though the Tokugawa forces to which he was assigned failed to reduce it.

Fukushima Masanori

In 1592, during the 1st Invasion of Korea, Masanori once again received distinction at the Battle of Ch'ungju.

In 1595 Masanori was involved with the death of Toyotomi Hidetsugu (1568-1595), surrounding the Seigan-ji (near Kyoto), until he had committed suicide. Masanori afterwards received Hidetsugu's former fief of Kiyosu (Owari -- 200,000 koku).

After the death of Toyotomi Hideyoshi in 1598, in order to attach Masanori to his party, Tokugawa Ieyasu (1543-1616) gave an adopted daughter in marriage to Masanori's son Masayuki.

At the 1600 Battle of Gifu Castle (Mino) Masanori and Ikeda Terumasa (1565-1613) led the Tokugawa forces to victory over the Toyotomi forces commanded by Oda Hidenobu (1580-1605). At the Battle of Seki-ga-hara (Mino) he routed the troops of Ukita Hideié (1573-1655), and received as reward the daimyoate of Hiroshima (Aki -- 498,000 koku).

In 1610 Masanori was charged by Tokugawa Ieyasu with the reconstruction of Nagoya Castle (Owari). Masanori did all he could to evade that ruinous corvée, but it was in vain. From that time the relations with the Shogun became continually more strained.

At the time of the 1615 Osaka Campaign, Masanori asked to join the Shogunal army, but Tokugawa Ieyasu obliged him to remain in Edo.

In 1619 Masanori was accused by the 2nd Tokugawa Shogun Hidetada (1579-1632) of bad administration and of being a Christian sympathizer. His Hiroshima daimyoate was taken from him, and he was transferred to Kawanaka-jima (Shinano -- 45,000 koku).

Fukushima Masayori (16th-17th century)

Younger brother to Masanori. Kamon-no-suké "1st assistant inspector of housekeeping." Daimyo of Nagashima (Isé -- 12,000 koku).

In 1600 Masayori was transferred to Uda (Yamato -- 30,000 koku), but in 1615 he was deprived of his possessions.

EDO PERIOD – FURUTA / HINENO

FURUTA

Revenues: 60,000 koku
Territories: Matsuzaka (Isé), Hamada (Iwami)
Castle: Matsuzaka (Isé)

Tozama daimyo family of the 16th and 17th centuries.

NOTABLE ANCESTORS

Furuta Shigenari/Oribé (1545-1615)

Born in Mino. At first a retainer of Oda Nobunaga (1534-1582), who gave him the title Oribé (near Kyoto) no kami with a revenue of 35,000 koku; then of Toyotomi Hideyoshi (1536-1598), for whom he was Oribé-no-sho "deputy tax collector of manufacturers and dyers."

In 1600 Shigenari fought at the side of Tokugawa Ieyasu (1543-1616) at the Battle of Seki-ga-hara (Mino), and afterwards received an income of 10,000 koku. But during the 1615 Siege of Osaka, he plotted in Kyoto against the Tokugawa and the Emperor on behalf of the Osaka defenders. For this he was dispossessed, and forced to commit suicide along with all of his sons.

He is more familiarly known in Japanese culture history as Furuta Oribé, a celebrated master of tea ceremony. His

Furuta Oribé

teacher was the famous Sen no Rikyu (1522-1591), after whose death Oribé became the foremost tea master in the land. The tea ceremony he established is known as Oribé-ryu. He taught the art to the 2nd Tokugawa Shogun Hidetada (1579-1632), and among his famous students were Kobori Enshu (1579-1647) and Hon'ami Koétsu (1558-1637).

As a potter he created a unique style called Oribé, or Mino, ware.

He also designed the garden of Nanshu-ji in Sakai (Izumi), and invented stone lanterns for tea gardens known as Oribé-doro.

Furuta Shigekatsu (1561-1600)

Was hyobu-shosuké "deputy minister of war."

Shigekatsu served Toyotomi Hideyoshi (1536-1598), who gave him the castle of Matsuzaka (Isé -- 37,000 koku).

After the 1600 Battle of Seki-ga-hara (Mino) Shigekatsu's revenue was raised to 60,000 koku. He died the same year.

Furuta Shigeharu (early 17th century)

Was Daizen-tayu "chief steward of the Imperial Household."

In 1619 Shigeharu was transferred to Hamada (Iwami -- 54,000 koku) as the 1st Furuta daimyo of that domain.

Furuta Shigetsuné (1598-1648)

2nd Furuta daimyo of Hamada (Iwami -- 54,000 koku). He was hyobu-shosuké "deputy minister of war."

In 1648 Shigetsuné was dispossessed on account of the tyranny he exercised over his kerai "vassals."

HINENO

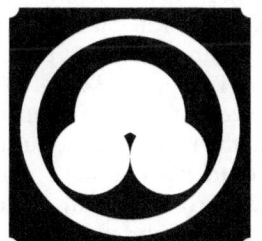

Revenues: 28,000 koku
Territories:
Takashima (Shinano),
Mibu (Shimotsuké),
Funai (Bungo)
Castle: Takashima (Shinano)

Daimyo family native of Mino.

NOTABLE ANCESTORS

Hineno Hironari (1518-1602)

Was a vassal of Saito Yoshitatsu (1527-1561), and then Saito Tatsuoki (1548-1573).

In 1567, when Saito Tatsuoki was completely vanquished by Oda Nobunaga (1534-1616), Hironari had his head shaved, and took the name Jibukyo-hoin.

Hineno Takayoshi (1539-1600)

Son of Hironari. He served the Toyotomi.

In 1590 Takayoshi took part in the Odawara Campaign against the Hojo, and as a reward received the castle of Takashima (Shinano -- 28,000 koku).

Hineno Yoshitomo (1588-1658)

Son of Takayoshi.

In 1601 Yoshitomo was transferred to Mibu (Shimotsuké), and in 1634 to Funai (Bungo -- 20,000 koku).

He died without an heir, and his domain was confiscated.

Gamo

Revenues: 1 million koku
Territories: Hino (Omi), Matsusaka (Isé), Aizu (Mutsu), Utsu-no-miya (Shimotsuké), Matsuyama (Iyo)
Castles: Hino (Omi), Aizu-Wakamatsu (Mutsu)

Daimyo family of Omi descended from Fujiwara Hidesato (10th century), governor of Shimotsuké, who clashed with Taira Masakado, and in 940 beheaded him.

Fujiwara Hidesato's descendant Narutoshi settled in Gamo (Omi), and took its name.

During the Genpei War (1180-1185), Narutoshi's son Toshitaka served Minamoto Yoritomo (1147-1199). The Gamo would later support Ashikaga Takauji (1305-1358).

They came to be retainers of the Rokkaku and served them into the Sengoku "Warring States" Period (1467-1573). In 1523 an internal struggle broke out between the Gamo brothers Takasato and Hideyuki, prompting Rokkaku Sadayori (1495-1552) to intervene, and force Hideyuki to abandon his castle, an action on Sadayori's part which is sometimes described as foreshadowing the later shiro-wari "one castle" policy.

The Gamo joined Oda Nobunaga (1534-1582) in 1568, and would grow powerful in his service, and later with Toyotomi Hideyoshi (1536-1598).

The clan survived into the Edo "Tokugawa" Period (1603-1868), but in 1634 died out with the passing of Tadatomo.

Notable Ancestors

Gamo Katahidé (1534-1584)

Eldest son of Sadahidé. He was sa-hyo-é-tayu.

Katahidé was at first a retainer of Rokkaku Yoshikata (1521-1598), and held Hino Castle (Omi). Around 1568 he joined Oda Nobunaga (1534-1582).

Gamo Ujisato (1557-1596)

Son of Katahidé. Born in the Gamo district of Hino (Omi). His childhood name was Tsuruchiyo. He studied Zen and the arts of tea and pottery.

In 1568, when Oda Nobunaga (1534-1582) was en route to Kyoto, he defeated the Rokkaku, who were his father's masters. Katahidé then pledged his loyalty of Nobunaga, and gave up as hostage his son Tsuruchiyo, who was taken to Oda headquarters in Gifu (Mino). Tsuruchiyo impressed Nobunaga with his sagacity, and had his manhood rite in Gifu, taking the name Utahidé.

In 1569, at the age of 13, Utahidé took part in the taking of Okochi Castle (Isé) during Oda Nobunaga's subjugation of Kitabaké Tomomasa of Kizukuri Castle (Isé). For his distinction in battle, he received Nobunaga's daughter Fuyu-himé (1561-1641) in marriage, and was allowed to return to his father's castle in Hino.

In 1570 Utahidé fought at the Battle of Anegawa (Omi) against the Asai of Omi and the Asakura of Echizen. Later that year he joined his father in the Oda assault on Echizen, led by Shibata Katsuié (1522-1583). When Asai Nagamasa (1545-1573) came to support the Asakura, Utahidé assisted Oda Nobunaga's withdrawal by taking him into Hino Castle, facilitating his escape to Gifu. For this Nobunaga increased the stipend of Utahidé and his father. In 1573 the Gamo would see further action against the Asakura.

In 1575, upon Shibata Katsuié's posting to Kita-no-sho Castle (Echizen), the Gamo came under Oda Nobunaga's direct command, serving as hatamoto. That year Utahidé fought at the Battle of Nagashino (Mikkawa) against Takeda Katsuyori (1545-1573).

In 1582, when Oda Nobunaga was assassinated in the Incident at Honno-ji (Kyoto), Utahidé was with his father, who had been posted as warden of Azuchi Castle (Omi). Together the two sheltered Nobunaga's widow and children in Hino Castle, saving their lives. After the death of Akechi Mitsuhidé (1528-1582) at the Battle of Yamazaki (Settsu), Utahidé submitted to Hashiba (later Toyotomi) Hideyoshi (1536-1598).

In 1583 Utahidé joined Hashiba Hideyoshi's attack on Takigawa Kazumasu (1525-1586), as well as the victorious Battle of Shizu-ga-také (Omi) against the loyal forces of the Oda, and received the title of Hida no kami. That year his son Hideyuki was born.

In 1585, following his siege of Oda Nobukatsu (1558-1630) during the Battles of Komaki and Nagakuté (Owari), Utahidé received Matsusaka (Isé -- 120,000 koku) in fief. After taking part in the subjugation of Kii, Utahidé took the name of Ujisato. Soon after, due to the influence of Takayama Ukon (1552-1615), he received a Christian baptism in Osaka, and the name of Leo, but in 1587 returned to his old faith after Toyotomi (formerly Hashiba) Hideyoshi edicted his anti-Christian laws.

In 1587 Ujisato served in Toyotomi Hideyoshi's Kyushu Campaign.

In 1588 construction on Matsu-ga-shima Castle in Matsusaka was completed, whereupon Ujisato immediately moved therein.

Gamo Ujisato

In 1590 Ujisato took part in Toyotomi Hideyoshi's Odawara Campaign against the Hojo. Afterwards he was transferred to Aizu (Mutsu -- 420,000 koku), with the object of pacifying Oshu (Mutsu and Dewa). In 1591 Kunohé Masazané resisted, and Ujisato, assisted by Asano Nagamasa (1546-1610), besieged him in his castle of Kunohé (Mutsu), where he was defeated and killed.

In 1591 Ujisato took control of Shiomatsu (Mutsu), and held Obama Castle through one of his vassals Gamo Chuzaémon.

After this Ujisato's revenues were raised to 1 million koku, making him one of the most powerful daimyo in Japan. He then went to Kyoto where he was appointed sangi "Imperial advisor."

At the time of the Korean Campaign (1592-1598), Ujisato accompanied Toyotomi Hideyoshi to Nagoya (Hizen), where in 1593 he fell ill, coughing up blood. He then returned to Aizu to see the completion of the redesigned Kurokawa Castle (Mutsu), and changed its name to Tsuruga Castle (now more popularly known as Aizu-Wakamatsu Castle). He then went to Fushimi (Kyoto) to see the completion of the Gamo family mansion, where Hideyoshi himself would twice visit him. Ujisato died at Fushimi Castle. Several have accused Hideyoshi of having poisoned him.

Gamo Hideyuki (1583-1612)

Son of Ujisato. He was Bitchu no kami, and a Christian.

In 1598 Hideyuki was deprived of the immense daimyoate of Aizu (Mutsu), and in return received that of Utsu-no-miya (Shimotsuké -- 180,000 koku). The reasons are unclear, but Toyotomi Hideyoshi (1536-1598) may have hoped that moving the experienced Uesugi Kagekatsu (1555-1623) to Aizu would offset the regional supremacy of Tokugawa Ieyasu (1543-1616).

In 1600 Hideyuki supported the Tokugawa during the Seki-ga-hara Campaign (Mino), and while he saw little fighting, nonetheless received Wakamatsu (Mutsu -- 600,000 koku) as reward.

Gamo Tadasato (1603-1627)

Eldest son of Hideyuki. He succeeded to the daimyoate of Aizu (Mutsu), but died without an heir.

Gamo Tadatomo (1605-1634)

2nd son of Hideyuki, and brother to Tadasato. He was chosen as the heir to his brother, after he had died without issue.

In 1627 Tadatomo was transferred from Aizu (Mutsu) to Kamino-yama (Dewa -- 40,000 koku), and then to Matsuyama (Iyo -- 240,000 koku).

He died without an heir, and was the last of the Gamo.

HIRAIWA

Revenues: 100,000 koku

Territories: Mikawa, Kai, Kozuké, Owari

Castles: Umayabashi (Kozuké), Inuyama (Owari)

Hiraiwa Chikayoshi

Family of Mikawa claiming descent from the ancient Mononobé. They came to be retainers of the Imagawa, but later joined the Matsudaira (Tokugawa).

NOTABLE ANCESTORS

Hiraiwa Chikayoshi (1542-1611)

Was brought up with Tokugawa Ieyasu (1543-1616), who intrusted him with the education of his eldest son Nobuyasu (1559-1579), who was later made to committed suicide.

In 1575 Chikayoshi fought at the Battle of Nagashino (Mikawa) against the Takeda of Kai.

After the downfall of the Takeda in 1582, Chikayoshi was made governor of Kai.

In 1585 Chikayoshi took part in the failed expedition against the Sanada.

In 1590 Chikayoshi received the castle of Umayabashi (Kozuké -- 30,000 koku).

Having been appointed guardian of Tokugawa Ieyasu's 9th son Yoshinao (1601-1650), Chikayoshi returned to Fuchu (Kai). In 1607 he followed his ward to Kiyosu (Owari), and in 1610 to Nagoya (Owari), where he possessed the castle of Inuyama (Owari -- 100,000 koku), from where he governed the whole province.

He died without an heir.

EDO PERIOD – INA / ITAMI / KOBORI

INA

Revenues: 20,000 koku
Territory: Konosu (Musashi)

Daimyo family descended from the Seiwa-Genji.

NOTABLE ANCESTORS

Ina Tadatsugu (1551-1607)
Was in the service of Tokugawa Ieyasu (1543-1616), who in 1590, when he established himself in the Kanto, gave Tadatsugu the fief of Konosu (Musashi -- 13,000 koku).
After the 1600 Battle of Seki-ga-hara (Mino), Tadatsugu's revenue was raised to 20,000 koku.
Tadatsugu was remarked for his zeal in developing agriculture, digging canals, draining rice fields, etc.

Ina Tadamasa (16th-17th century)
Son of Tadatsugu. He was dispossessed for participating in the conspiracy of Okubo Nagayasu (1545-1613).

ITAMI

Revenues: 12,000 koku
Territories: Suruga, Kai
Castle: Tokumi (Kai)

Daimyo family native of Suruga.

NOTABLE ANCESTORS

Itami Yasukatsu (1571-1649)
Harima no kami. Served Tokugawa Ieyasu (1543-1616).
In 1632 Yasukatsu was intrusted with the guard of the Kofu Castle at Tokumi (Kai -- 12,000 koku).

Itami Katsunaga (1601-1662)
Son of Yasukatsu. Assassinated by Isshiki Kurano-suké.

Itami Katsumori (-1698)
Grandson of Katsunaga. Killed himself in a fit of insanity, and his domain returned to the Shogun.

KOBORI

Revenues: 10,000 koku
Territory: Omi

Family of daimyo in Omi during the 17th and the 18th centuries.

NOTABLE ANCESTORS

Kobori Masakazu/Enshu (1579-1647)
Born in Omi. Vassal of Toyotomi Hideyoshi (1536-1598), then Tokugawa Ieyasu (1543-1616).
In 1600 Masakazu received Komuro (Omi -- 10,000), with the title of Totomi no kami. In 1623 he was appointed Fushimi bugyo "Fushimi city magistrate."
Masakazu won fame in all the branches of Japanese art, painting, poetry, flower arrangement, etc. His accomplishments include numerous garden designs, including that of the Sento Imperial Palace (Kyoto), Katsura Imperial Villa (Kyoto), the Kodai-ji (Kyoto), Sunpu Castle (Suruga), the Nagoya Castle keep (Owari), Matsuyama Castle, and the central baileys of Fushimi (Kyoto), Nijo (Kyoto), and Osaka Castles.
To teach the solemn preparation of tea, Masakazu founded a school, which, from his title Totomi no kami, was called Enshu-ryu, Enshu being the Chinese name for Totomi, for which he is commonly called Kobori Enshu. He was chosen to teach the tea ceremony to the 3rd Tokugawa Shogun Iemitsu (1604-1651). In this role, he designed many tea houses including the Bosen-seki in the sub-temple of Koho-an at the Daitoku-ji (Kyoto), and the Mittan-seki at the Ryuko-in of the same temple. He also sponsored the kilns of potters making pieces for the tea ceremony.

Kobori Masakazu

Kobori Masakata (18th century)
Descendant of Masakazu. He was Izumi no kami and Fushimi bugyo "Fushimi city magistrate."
In 1788 Masakata was dispossessed on account of his bad administration.

KANAMORI

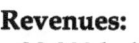

Revenues: 20,000 koku
Territories: Hida, Mino
Castles: Matsukura, Takayama (Hida)

Ancient daimyo family descended from the Fujiwara, and through the Seiwa-Genji Minamoto to the Toki of Hida. A son of Toki Sadayori moved to the village of Kamanori in nearby Omi, and his son took the name of the village.

SUCCESSION

1. Nagachika (1524-1607)
2. Arishigé
3. Shigeyori   6. Yoritoki
4. Yorinao   7. Arihiro
5. Yorinari   8. Yorikané

NOTABLE ANCESTORS

Kanamori Nagachika (1524-1607)

Izumo no kami and Nagato no kami. He first served the Saito of Mino. After their demise he became a retainer of Oda Nobunaga (1534-1582), and fought in a number of his battles.

In 1575 Nagachika fought at the Battle of Nagashino (Mikawa) against the Takeda of Kai.

In 1582, following Oda Nobunaga's death, Nagachika first sided with Shibata Katsuié (1522-1583), then gave his loyalty to Hashiba (later Toyotomi) Hideyoshi (1536-1598).

In 1585 Hashiba Hideyoshi dispatched Nagachika to sieze Hida, where he defeated and killed Anenokoji Koretsuna (1540-1587), wherefore he received the province in fief, and ruled the castles of Matsukura and Takayama, where he resided.

In 1591, after Toyotomi (formerly Hashiba) Hideyoshi ordered the death of Sen no Rikyu (1522-1591), Nagachika sheltered his son Sen Doan (1546-1607).

During the 1600 Seki-ga-hara Campaign, Nagachika supported Tokugawa Ieyasu (1543-1616), and fought at the Battle of Seki-ga-hara (Mino).

Kanamori Yoshishigé (1559-1616)

Son of Nagao Kagenaga, was adopted by Nagachika. He served Oda Nobunaga (1534-1582), and afterwards Toyotomi Hideyoshi (1536-1598). In 1600 he joined the party of Tokugawa Ieyasu (1543-1616).

During the 1615 Osaka Campaign, Yoshishigé defended the castle of Kishiwada (Izumi), and fought so well that he secured the heads of 208 enemies slain by himself as trophies.

Yoshishigé was renowned for his skill in performing the tea ceremony, which he had learned from Sen no Rikyu (1522-1591).

In 1697 his descendants were transferred to Yawata (Mino -- 20,000 koku). In 1759 the last one, Yorikané, was dispossessed on account of bad administration, and exiled to Nanbu (Kai).

KIMURA

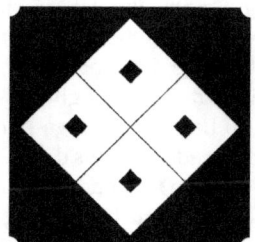

Territory: Yamashiro

Family of daimyo of the 16th century.

NOTABLE ANCESTORS

Kimura Shigekoré (-1595)

Vassal of Toyotomi Hideyoshi (1536-1598).

In 1582 Shigekoré served at the Battle of Yamazaki (Settsu) against Akechi Mitsuhidé (1528-1582). In 1590 he served in the Odawara Campaign against the Hojo.

In 1592 Shigekoré took part in the 1st Korean Campaign, and received a fief in Yamashiro.

In 1595 Shigekoré was implicated in the conspiracy of Toyotomi Hidetsugu (1568-1595). He was dispossessed, and committed seppuku.

Kimura Shigenari (1594-1615)

Son of Shigekoré. Nagato no kami. He was educated by his mother, who, after the death of her husband, sought refuge with a Christian family, whose religion she embraced, which supposes that Shigenari, then quite an infant, was baptized with her.

When Shigenari came of age, he enlisted in the army of Toyotomi Hideyori (1593-1615), and perished during the Osaka Summer Campaign at the Battle of Wakaé (Kawachi), fighting against Todo Takatora (1556-1630) and Ii Naotaka (1590-1659).

He was said to be have been a strikingly handsome man, and was famed for his bravery.

KATO

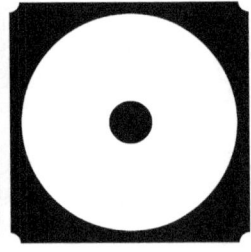

Revenues: 520,000 koku
Territories: Hizen, Higo
Castle: Kumamoto (Hizen)

Daimyo family that resided at Kumamoto (Hizen) from 1588 to 1632.

NOTABLE ANCESTORS

Kato Kiyomasa (1562-1611)

Son of Kiyotada, a blacksmith. He was born at Nakamura (Owari), a village that supposedly also produced Toyotomi Hideyoshi (1536-1598). He was called Tora-no-suké in his childhood, and his mother Ito was a cousin to the mother of Hideyoshi. He lost his father when he was 3 years old, and Hideyoshi took upon himself to educate the boy in his castle at Nagahama (Omi).

In 1576 Kiyomasa was granted a revenue of 170 koku.

In 1582 Kiyomasa fought in Hashiba (later Toyotomi) Hideyoshi's army at the Battle of Yamazaki (Yamashiro) against Akechi Mitsuhidé (1528-1582).

In 1583, at the Battle of Shizu-ga-také against Shibata Katsuié (1522-1583), Kiyomasa distinguished himself, and became known as one of the Shichi-hon'yari "Seven Spears" of Shizu-ga-také. Afterwards Hashiba Hideyoshi rewarded him with an increased revenue of 3,000 koku.

In 1585, when Hashiba Hideyoshi became the Kanpaku "Regent to the Emperor," Kiyomasa received the Court title of Kazué no kami and ju-go-i-no-gé "junior 5th Court rank, lower grade."

In 1587 Kiyomasa participated in Toyotomi (formerly Hashiba) Hideyoshi's Kyushu Campaign, and fought at the Battle of Sendai-gawa (Satsuma) against the Shimazu, during which he unhorsed and defeated Niiro Tadamoto (1526-1610) in a one-on-one duel, but spared his life. Afterwards, when the governor of Higo, Sassa Narimasa (1536-1588), was dispossessed, he received in fief half of this province, with residence at Kumamoto (250,000 koku). Almost immediately, Kiyomasa, who was fanatically Nichiren, began a relentless persecution of Christians in his domain. At the Battle of Hondo, he ordered his men to cut open the bellies of all pregnant Christian women, and cut off their babies' heads. This brought him into conflict with his neighbor in the other half of Higo, the Christian Konishi Yukinaga (1555-1600).

In 1592 Kiyomasa and Konishi Yukinaga commanded the vanguard of Toyotomi Hideyoshi's 1st Korean Expedition, and captured Seoul, Busan, and many other crucial cities, the Josean king Seonjo (1552-1608) abandoning Seoul in fear of Kiyomasa. His bravery and victories led the enemies to surname him Kisho-kan "Demon General." Kiyomasa held as hostages two Korean princes who had deserted, and used them to force lower-ranking Korean officials to surrender. When he killed a tiger while hunting in the forest, he presented its skin to Hideyoshi.

Kiyomasa was an excellent architect of fortifications, and built several Japanese-style castles in Korea to better defend the conquered lands. When Ishida Mitsunari (1560-1600), Konishi Yukinaga (1555-1600), and others proposed peace, Kiyomasa opposed the measure, and was recalled to Japan by Toyotomi Hideyoshi.

In 1597 Kiyomasa returned for the 2nd Korean Expedition. At the Siege of Ulsan, he and Asano Yukinaga (1576-1613) offered noble resistance, suffering heavy losses against a numerous Sino-Korean army led by Ming commanders Yang Hao (-1629) and Ma Gui (1543-1607), and Korean commander Gwon Yul (1537-1599), but after ten long days was at last delivered by Kobayakawa Hideaki (1577-1602) and Mori Hidemoto (1579-1650), with heavy rain helping to rout the retreating forces. His brave defense however was not reported to Toyotomi Hideyoshi by his rival Konishi Yukinaga's overseer Ishida Mitsunari, setting up a rivalry between them.

In 1598, after the death of Toyotomi Hideyoshi, Kiyomasa returned to Japan. Both Tokugawa Ieyasu (1543-1616) and Ishida Mitsunari courted his support, but as Kiyomasa was a rival of both Mitsunari and Konishi Yukinaga, who had sided with the Ishida, he sided with Ieyasu, who then gave him in marriage the daughter of Mizuno Tadashigé, whom he had brought up.

After the 1600 Battle of Seki-ga-hara (Mino), Kiyomasa added to his domain the other half of Higo that had been till then the property of Konishi Yukinaga. His revenues thus rose to 520,000 koku.

In his later years, Kiyomasa tried to work as a mediator for the increasingly complicated relationship between Tokugawa Ieyasu and Toyotomi Hideyoshi's son Hideyori (1593-1615). In 1611, en route by sea to Kumamoto after one such meeting, he fell ill, and died shortly after his arrival. He was buried in Kumamoto at the Honmyo-ji, a temple of the Nichiren sect, under the religious name Seisho-ko, Seisho being

Kato Kiyomasa

the Chinese pronunciation of Kiyomasa's kanji characters. When he died, Ieyasu was suspected of having had a hand in his death, fearing that Kiyomasa might side with Hideyori.

Contemporary accounts describe him as awe-inspiring, yet not unfriendly, and a natural leader of men, but he was a ferocious fighter, and often a ruthless warrior. Later in life he wrote to his followers that poetry and dancing were shameful pastimes for a samurai, and ordered anyone who engaged in the latter to commit suicide.

Kato Tadahiro (1597-1653)

Son of Kiyomasa. He was Higo no kami.

Tadahiro was accused of having entered into a conspiracy to replace the 3rd Tokugawa Shogun Iemitsu (1604-1651) with the latter's brother. For this he was dispossessed, and banished to Tsuru-ga-oka (Dewa), where he died. At the same time his son Mitsuhiro was exiled to Takayama (Hida), where he died the following year.

HORIO

Revenues: 235,000 koku

Territories: Wakasa, Totomi, Echizen, Izumo, Aki

Castles: Takahama (Wakasa), Hamamatsu (Totomi), Matsué (Izumo), Hiroshima (Aki)

Family Temple: Shuko-in at Hanazono (Yamashiro)

Daimyo family of Owari.

SUCCESSION

1. Yoshiharu
   (1543-1611, daimyo 1600-1604)
2. Tadauji (1578-1604, daimyo 1604)
3. Tadaharu
   (1596-1633, daimyo 1604-1633)

NOTABLE ANCESTORS

Horio Yoshiharu (1543-1611)

Son of Yoshihisa. Also known as Mosuké. He occupied the castle of Takahama (Wakasa).

From the early 1560s Yoshiharu served Kinoshita (later Hashiba, then Toyotomi) Hideyoshi (1536-1598).

In 1567 Yoshiharu served Kinoshita Hideyoshi in the capture of Inabayama (later Gifu) Castle (Mino) by Oda Nobunaga (1534-1582) from the Saito.

In 1574 Yoshiharu accompanied Hashiba (formerly Kinoshita) Hideyoshi to Omi when the latter received a fief there.

In 1582, when Hashiba Hideyoshi attacked Takamatsu Castle (Bitchu), Yoshiharu conducted an inquest into the death of Shimizu Muneharu (1537-1582). He next led a contingent of troops at the Battle of Yamazaki (Yamashiro) against Akechi Mitsuhidé (1528-1582).

In 1590, for his part in the Siege of Odawara (Sagami), Yoshiharu was awarded Hamamatsu (Totomi -- 60,000 koku).

Yoshiharu, along with Nakamura Kazuuji (-1600) and Ikoma Chikamasa (1526-1603), was appointed by Toyotomi (formerly Hashiba) Hideyoshi in his later years as one of the three churo, and participated in the Toyotomi administration.

After the death of Toyotomi Hideyoshi, Yoshiharu switched his allegiance to Tokugawa Ieyasu (1543-1616).

In 1599 Yoshiharu transferred responsibility as head of the family to his son Tadauji, and was given Fuchu (Echizen -- 50,000 koku) to live after retirement.

In 1600, during Tokugawa Ieyasu's Seki-ga-hara Campaign, Yoshiharu killed Kaganoi Shigemochi (1561-1600) at Chiryu (Mikawa), but was injured by him. Due to this he could not take part at the Battle of Seki-ga-hara (Mino), and Tadauji substituted for him. Afterwards, Ieyasu gave him Matsué (Izumo -- 235,000 koku) for having killed Shigemochi, and for Tadauji's exploits in battle.

In 1604 Tadauji died, and Yoshiharu's grandson Tadaharu succeeded him. As he was only 9 years old, Yoshiharu ruled as his guardian until his own death.

Yoshiharu was popular for his good nature and calmness, and was nicknamed Hotoké "Buddha."

Horio Tadauji (1575-1604)

2nd Horio daimyo of Matsué (Izumo -- 235,000 koku). Son of Yoshiharu. He was Izumo no kami.

In the 1600 Battle of Seki-ga-hara (Mino), acting as a substitute for his father, who had been injured in the run up to the battle, Tadauji took part in the force of Tokugawa Ieyasu (1543-1616). Afterwards Ieyasu praised Tadauji, and awarded his father Matsué domain.

He died before his father from disease.

Horio Tadaharu (1596-1633)

3rd Horio daimyo of Matsué (Izumo -- 235,000 koku). Son of Tadauji, and grandson of Yoshiharu.

In 1604, upon the death of his father, Tadaharu but due to his youth his grandfather acted as regent.

From 1607-1611 Tadaharu completed the construction of Matsué Castle.

In 1611 Tadaharu received Hiroshima Castle (Aki) when the domain of Fukushima Masanori (1561-1624) was seized.

He died childless, and his domain reverted to the Shogunate.

After the Matsudaira took over Matsué in 1638, a branch of the Horio became their retainers.

KORIKI

Revenues: 40,000 koku

Territories: Mikawa, Musashi, Totomi, Hizen

Castle: Iwatsuki (Musashi)

Family of daimyo originating in Mikawa.

Dduring the Sengoku "Warring States" Period (1467-1573) the Koriki became prominent as retainers of the Tokugawa.

SUCCESSION

1. Kiyonaga (1530-1608)
2. Masanaga (1558-1599)
3. Tadafusa (1583-1655)
4. Takanaga (1604-1676)

NOTABLE ANCESTORS

Koriki Kiyonaga (1530-1608)

Native of Mikawa. He married a daughter of Abé Michikané.

In 1552 Kiyonaga first entered the service of Tokugawa Ieyasu (1543-1616). In 1560 he transported provisions to Otaka Castle at the Battle of Okehazama (Owari). In 1564 he helped suppress the Ikko-ikki of Mikawa. He also joined in the pacification of Totomi.

In 1565 Kiyonaga was named one of Ieyasu's san-bugyo "three magistrates" for Mikawa with Amano Yasukagé (1537-1613) and Honda Shigetsugu (1529-1596). Of the three, Yasukagé was known for his patience, Shigetsugu for his fortitude, and Kiyonaga for his leniency, for which he earned the nickname of Hotoké "Buddha" Koriki.

In 1584 Kiyonaga took part in the Battle of Komaki and Nagakuté (Owari).

In 1586 Kiyonaga received the title of Kawachi no kami. In 1590 he received the fief of Iwatsuki (Musashi -- 20,000 koku). In 1592 he was named as commissioner for warships built to accompany a Tokugawa army assigned to Kyushu during the 1st Korean Invasion of Toyotomi Hideyoshi (1536-1598).

As he was preceded in death by his son Masanaga, Kiyonaga retired after the 1600 Seki-ga-hara Campaign, and passed down family headship to his grandson Tadafusa.

Koriki Masanaga (1558-1599)

Son of Kiyonaga. Like his father, he served the Tokugawa.

Koriki Tadafusa (1583-1655)

Eldest son of Masanaga. He was born in Hamamatsu (Totomi). As his father died when he was young, he was raised by his grandfather Kiyonaga. In 1600 he inherited the lordship of Iwatsuki (Musashi -- 20,000 koku) from his grandfather. He was married to a daughter of Sanada Nobuyuki (1566-1558) of Shinano.

During the 1600 Seki-ga-hara Campaign, Tadafusa was in the army of Tokugawa Hidetada (1579-1632). Afterwards he was entrusted with the care of Mashita Nagamori (1545-1615).

In 1609 Iwatsuki Castle was destroyed by fire.

In 1614 Tadafusa oversaw the transfer of Odawara (Sagami) from the disgraced Okubo Tadachika (1553-1628) to Abé Masatsugu (1569-1647).

In 1615 Tadafusa took part in the Siege of Osaka, and pursued the remnants of Toyotomi forces led by Doi Toshikatsu (1573-1644) into Yamato.

In 1619 Tadafusa was transferred to Hamamatsu (Totomi -- 35,000 koku) with the title sakon-daiyu "senior officer of the Imperial guard" and Court rank of lower 5th.

In 1639 the 3rd Tokugawa Shogun Iemitsu transferred Tadafusa to Shimabara (Hizen -- 40,000 koku), which in the wake of the 1637-1638 Shimabara Rebellion was a wasteland devastated by years of warfare. Within a year, Tadafusa was able to restore the domain to its former productivity through tax exemptions, pardons to surviving rebels, and encouraging immigration of farmers from other areas of Japan. Tadafusa was also assigned the security of the foreign trade port of Nagasaki (Hizen) for the Tokugawa Shogunate.

Koriki Takanaga (1604-1676)

Son of Tadafusa. In 1668 he was dispossessed and exiled to Sendai (Mutsu) on account of his maladministration. He died heirless.

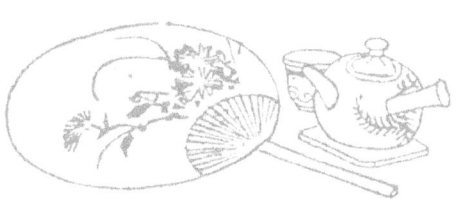

KUWAYAMA

Revenues: 30,000 koku

Territories: Kii, Yamato

Castle: Wakayama (Kii)

Family of daimyo originating in Kuwayama (Owari).

Eldest branch, which from 1600 resided at Shinjo (Yamato -- 16,000 koku), in 1682 was dispossessed.

Younger branch, which in 1600 settled at Gosé (Yamato -- 26,000 koku), in 1629 became extinct.

NOTABLE ANCESTORS

Kuwayama Shigeharu (1524-1606)

Served Toyotomi Hideyoshi (1536-1598). In 1585 he built a castle at Wakayama (Kii -- 30,000 koku).

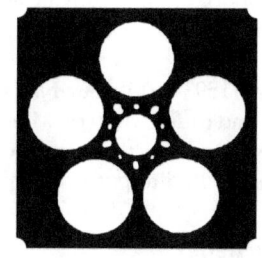

MAEDA 前田

Revenues: 50,000 koku
Territory: Tanba

Ancient daiimyo family issued from the Fujiwara, or, according to others, from the Sugawara, and allied to the Maeda of Kaga.

Notable Ancestors

Maeda Munehisa/Gen'i (1539-1602)

Also called Munehisa. Was first a bonze of the Hiei-zan (northeast of Kyoto). He was variously called Gen'i, Genki Hoin (hence the name of Ghenifoin or Guenifoin, which was given him in the letters of the old missionaries), Minbu-kyo Hoin, Tokuzen'in Gen'i.

Sometime before 1570 Gen'i entered the service of Oda Nobunaga (1534-1582).

In 1582 Gen'i was appointed Kyoto shoshidai "Shogunal representative to the Imperial Court."

When Oda Nobutada (1557-1582), after the death of this father Nobunaga, was attacked at Nijo Palace (Kyoto) by Akechi Mitsuhidé (1528-1582), he confided his eldest son Hidenobu (1580-1605) to Gen'i, who conducted him to Gifu (Mino), and then to Kiyosu (Owari).

Afterwards Gen'i went to serve under Hashiba (later Toyotomi) Hideyoshi (1536-1598). In 1585, when the latter became Kanpaku "Regent to the Emperor," Gen'i received the fief of Yakami (Tanba -- 50,000 koku).

Maeda Gen'i

In 1588, when the Emperor Go-Yozei (1572-1617) and the ex-Emperor Ogimachi (1517-1593) came to visit Toyotomi (formerly Hashiba) Hideyoshi in his lavish new palace of Juraku-dai (Kyoto), Gen'i had to regulate and prepare all the details of the reception. He studied with the utmost care the rules of the ceremony adopted when the Emperors Go-Komatsu (1377-1433) and Go-Hanazono (1419-1471) formerly visited the Ashikaga Shogun, adapted it to the present circumstances, and succeeded to the satisfaction of everybody. Gen'i embellished the city, and at the same time rendered it more healthy.

Being obliged to search for Christians in the capital, Gen'i endeavored to arrest only as few as possible, say the Jesuits; whilst the Japanese attribute to him the first idea of obliging those arrested to tread under foot the holy images in order to identify those who belonged to the forbidden religion, a process that was used with much rigor under the Tokugawa.

In 1592 Gen'i laid the groundwork for Fushimi Castle (Kyoto).

In 1595 Toyotomi Hideyoshi chose Gen'i as one of the go-bugyo "five magistrates." As a member of this council he was to concern himself with national affairs, and was subordinate only to Hideyoshi.

In 1600, feigning sickness, Gen'i was able to abstain from rejoining Tokugawa Ieyasu (1543-1616) without entering openly into the party of Ishida Mitsunari (1560-1600), and thus keep his domain.

Maeda Hidenori Sakon (1577-1602)

Eldest son of Gen'i. In 1595 he was baptized under the name of Paul.

Maeda Munetoshi (16th-17th century)

2nd son of Gen'i. In he 1595 was baptized under the name of Constantine. He inherited the fief of Yakami (Tanba -- 50,000 koku), but in 1608 he showed signs of insanity, and was deposed.

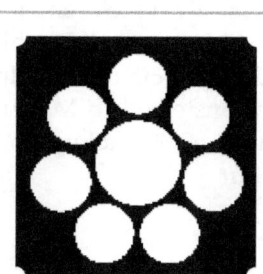

MAITA 蒔田

Revenues: 10,000 koku
Territory: Bitchu

Daimyo family which resided at Asao (Bitchu -- 10,000 koku).

MASUDA

Revenues: 200,000 koku
Territory: Yamato
Castle: Koriyama (Yamato)

NOTABLE ANCESTORS

Masuda Nagamori (1545-1615)

Born at Masuda (Owari). He served Toyotomi Hideyoshi (1536-1598), who chose him as one of the go-bugyo "five magistrates."

In 1594 Toyotomi Hideyoshi gave Nagamori the fief of Koriyama (Yamato -- 200,000 koku).

In 1600, having sided against Tokugawa Ieyasu (1543-1616), Nagamori was banished to Koya-san (Kyoto), then to Iwatsuki (Musashi).

In 1615, before besieging Osaka Castle, Tokugawa Ieyasu wished to entrust him with a threatening letter for Toyotomi Hideyori (1593-1615), but Nagamori refused, and thus, as his son Moritsugu had enlisted in the army of Osaka, he was invited to perform seppuku.

Masuda Moritsugu (17th century)

In the 1615 Siege of Osaka he sided with Toyotomi Hideyori (1593-1615). He was allowed to escape, and became a kerai "vassal" of Todo Takatora (1556-1630) of Tsu (Isé).

MATSUSHITA

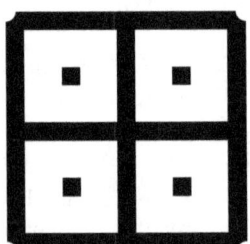

Revenues: 30,000 koku
Territories: Totomi, Mutsu

Daimyo family descended from Sasaki Yasutsuna (13th century), and which took its name from a village in Mikawa where it was at first stationed.

NOTABLE ANCESTORS

Matsushita Yukitsuna (1538-1598)

Son of Naganori. Iwami no kami. He at first served the Imagawa at Zudai-ji Castle (Totomi).

Yukitsuna was the first master of Kinoshita (later Hashiba, and then Toyotomi) Hideyoshi (1536-1598), who would abscond with a sum of money entrusted into his care. Hideyoshi would not forget Yukitsuna's kindness however, and when he later became Kanpaku "Regent to the Emperor" he bestowed favors to Matsushita descendants.

Matsushita Yoshitsuna (16th-17th century)

Son of Yukitsuna. He served Toyotomi Hideyoshi (1536-1598), who bestowed on him Kuno (Totomi -- 10,000 koku), with the title of Iwami no kami.

Matsushita Shigetsuna (1580-1628)

Resided at Nihonmatsu (Mutsu -- 30,000 koku).

Matsushita Nagatsuna (17th century)

Son of Shigetsuna. In 1628, at the death of his father, he was transferred to Miharu (Mutsu -- 30,000 koku).

In 1645 Nagatsuna was dispossessed on account of his excesses.

MIZUNOYA

Revenues: 50,000 koku
Territories: Hitachi, Bitchu

Daimyo family which remained at Shimodaté (Hitachi) from the end of the 16th century. In 1639 it was transferred to Matsuyama (Bitchu -- 50,000 koku), and in 1693 died out.

SUCCESSION

1. Katsutaka
2. Katsumuné
3. Katsuyoshi

Edo Period

Matsukura

Revenues: 60,000 koku
Territories:
Harima, Yamato, Hizen
Castles: Futami (Harima), Gojo-Futami (Yamato), Honoé, Hara, Shimabara (Hizen)

Daimyo family from Yamato, descended from the Fujiwara.

Notable Ancestors

Matsukura Nobushigé (1522-1586)
Served the Tsutsui of Iga.

Matsukura Shigemasa (1574-1630)
Son of Shigenobu. He was Bingo no kami, and held the rank of ju-go-i-no-gé "junior 5th, lower grade." He was initially a retainer of Tsutsui Sadatsugu (1562-1615) of Yamato.

Following the death of Tsutsui Junkei (1549-1584), the Tsutsui was moved to Iga, but the Matsukura remained in Yamato, and came under the supervision of Hashiba (later Toyotomi) Hideyoshi (1536-1598), who in 1587 gave Shigemasa the castle of Futami (Harima).

In 1600 Shigemasa fought at the side of Tokugawa Ieyasu (1543-1616) at the Battle of Seki-ga-hara (Mino), and for his merits was awarded lordship over the castle of Gojo-Futami (Yamato -- 25,000 koku), the former estate of his suzerain Tsutsui Sadatsubu, who had fallen into disgrace.

In 1616, for his meritorious actions at the Domyo-ji just prior to the Osaka Summer Campaign, Shigemasa was transferred to Hinoé (Hizen -- 60,000 koku), a domain formerly belonging to Arima Harunobu (1567-1612).

In 1618, as per the Ikkoku-ichi-jo "one province, one castle" order established by the Tokugawa Shogunate, Shigemasa dismantled his two castles of Hara and Hinoé, and began construction on the new Shimabara Castle, also known as Moritaké Castle. The castle was on a scale much grander than the domain could afford, and so Shigemasa taxed the commoners outrageously.

In 1621 the persecutions of Christians began, with mutilation and branding being practices ordered by the ever-tightening restrictions of the 3rd Tokugawa Shogun Iemitsu (1504-1651). Beginning in 1627, the Matsukura tortured the Shimabara Christians by boiling them alive in the infamous Unzen Volcanic Springs. In 1629 Shigemasa approached the Nagasaki magistrate Takenaka Danjo-no-sho Shigeyoshi, and offered to do the same for all the Christians in Nagasaki, to which he agreed.

In 1624 some of his ships were carried by the wind toward the south, and landed at Luzon (Philippines). The sailors entered into communication with the inhabitants of the island, and made some exchanges, then returned to Hizen, and gave an account of it to Shigemasa, who told them to return to Luzon and obtain all the information they could on these islands. Several years later he asked Edo for permission to lead an expedition against the Philippines, boasting that he would be as successful as the Satsuma daimyo, Shimazu Tadatsuné (1576-1638), who some twenty years before conquered the Ryukyu. The 3rd Tokugawa Shogun Iemitsu (1604-1651) seems to have given his consent to this foolish enterprise, and Shigemasa further taxed his citizens, but his death hindered its realization.

He died at the Obama Hot Springs, some say from poisoning by the Shogunate, which did not entirely approve of his iron rule.

Matsukura Shigeharu/Katsuié (-1638)
Son of Shigemasa. Nagato no kami. He continued his father's draconian measures. He was hated for his cruelty, and was renowned for dressing disobedient peasants in straw raincoats and setting them on fire.

In 1637 over-taxation by the Matsukura of the local peasants for the construction of Shimabara Castle (Hizen), and the religious persecution of the local Christians, ignited the Shimabara Rebellion. As the insurrection spread, it was joined by ronin "masterless samurai" who once had served families such as the Amakusa and the Shiki who had once lived in the area, as well as former Arima and Konishi retainers. The rebels plotted the assassination of the local daikan "tax official" Hayashi Hyozaémon. The charismatic 16-year-old youth Amakusa Shiro (1621-1638) was soon chosen as the revolt's leader. After a couple of setbacks the rebels gathered at the site of Hara Castle (Hizen), where they built up palisades. The allied armies of the local domains under the command of the Tokugawa Shogunate began their Siege of Hara, the first massive military effort since the 1615 Siege of Osaka. The rebels resisted for months, and caused heavy losses on the besiegers. They slowly ran out of food, ammunition, and other provisions, however, and were eventually routed. After the castle fell, the Shogunate forces beheaded an estimated 37,000 rebels and sympathizers. Shiro's severed head was taken to Nagasaki (Hizen) for public display. Subsequently Portuguese trader were driven out of the country, the seclusion policy was made more strict, and the existing ban on Christianity was enforced more stringently, forcing Japanese Christian to go underground.

Although the rebellion was successfully put down, for his mismanagement of the situation, Katsuié was was dispossessed, and banished to Tsuyama (Mimasaka), where a message from the Shogun came to invite him to commit seppuku.

Matsukura Shigetoshi (17th century)
Son of Shigeharu. In 1638, upon the seppuku of his father, he was banished to Takamatsu (Sanuki).

Edo Period – Minagawa / Mori / Nakamura

MINAGAWA

Revenues: 40,000 koku
Territories: Shimotsuké, Shinano, Hitachi

Daimyo family from Shimotsuké descended from the Fujiwara.

Notable Ancestors

Minagawa Hiroteru (-1625)
Son of Hirokatsu (1548-1576). At first he fought for the Hojo of Odawara.
In 1590 Hiroteru joined Toyotomi Hideyoshi (1536-1598), who confirmed his fief at Minagawa (Shimotsuké -- 30,000 koku).
In 1603 Hiroteru was named preceptor of the 6th son of Tokugawa Ieyasu (1543-1616), Matsudaira Tadateru (1592-1683), and was transferred to Iiyama (Shinano -- 40,000 koku).
In 1616 Hiroteru was dispossessed as a result of his association with the Okubo of Odawara, who were disgraced and fell from power.

Minagawa Takatsuné (-1645)
Son of Hiroteru.
In 1623 Takatsuné received the fief of Fuchu (Hitachi -- 15,000 koku). The family became extinct with his son Narisato.

MORI

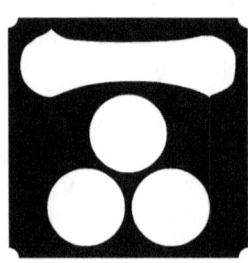

Revenues: 60,000 koku
Territory: Buzen

Daimyo family of the 16th century.

Notable Ancestors

Mori Katsunobu (-1601)
Served Toyotomi Hideyoshi (1536-1598), who gave him the fief of Kokura (Buzen -- 60,000 koku).
From 1592-1598 Katsunobu assisted in Toyotomi Hideyoshi's Invasions of Korea.
In 1600, having taken sides against Tokugawa Ieyasu (1543-1616), Katsunobu was banished to Tosa, where he died soon after.

Mori Katsunaga (-1615)
Son of Katsunobu.
In 1600 Katsunaga fought at the Battle of Seki-ga-hara (Mino), but met with defeat, and was exiled with his father to Tosa.
At the time of the 1615 Siege of Osaka, Katsunaga secretly fled from Tosa with his son Katsuié and came to offer their services to Toyotomi Hideyori (1593-1615). At the final Battle of Tenno-ji they fought with desperate abandon alongside Sanada Yukimura (1567-1615). Katsunaga personally defeated Honda Tadatomo (1582-1615), but he and his son both killed themselves when the castle fell.

NAKAMURA

Revenues: 175,000 koku
Territories: Izumi, Omi, Suruga, Hoki

Family of daimyo of the 16th and the 17th centuries.

Notable Ancestors

Nakamura Kazuuji (-1600)
Served Toyotomi Hideyoshi (1536-1598), who gave him successively the fiefs: in 1577 Kishiwada (Izumi), in 1585 Minakuchi (Omi), and in 1590 Fuchu (Suruga -- 140,000 koku).
He died just as he had made preparations to accompany Tokugawa Ieyasu (1543-1616) in his campaign against Uesugi Kagekatsu (1556-1623).

Nakamura Tadakazu (1590-1609)
Son of Kazuuji. He was transferred to Yonago (Hoki -- 175,000 koku), but died at the age of 19 without an heir.

Edo Period – Mogami

MOGAMI

Revenues: 570,000 koku
Territory: Dewa, Omi
Castle: Yamagata (Dewa)

Mogami Yoshiaki

Ancient daimyo family of Dewa, and a branch of the Ashikaga. It was founded by a son of Shiba Iekané (14th century), Kaneyori, who around 1360 built Yamagata Castle (Dewa), and took the name Mogami from the town where he settled.

The clan increased their influence during the Sengoku "Warring States" Period (1467-1573). In the early 16th century the Mogami became dominated by the Daté, but when an internal war broke out in that clan, they succeeded in getting independence.

The Mogami reached their peak after the 1600 Battle of Seki-ga-hara (Mino), when the clan received increased revenue in their domain at Yamagata (Dewa -- 570,000 koku), making their fief the 5th largest in Japan, excluding that of the Tokugawa.

NOTABLE ANCESTORS

Mogami Yoshimori (1521-1590)

Son of Yoshiharu, and cousin to the head of the clan Yoshisada (-1523). When the latter died without an heir, Yoshimori, then 2 years old, was chosen to succeed him.

Yoshimori ruled from Yamagata Castle (Dewa). He clashed with the Uesugi, the Daté, and numerous local houses to expand the Mogami domain.

During the Tenbun no Ran (1542 to 1548), a succession feud between Daté Tanemuné (1488-1565) and his son Harumuné (1519-1578), Yoshimori supported the former, but the latter eventually took control of the clan. His daughter Yoshiko would later marry Harumuné's son Daté Terumuné (1543-1585), and become the mother of the famous Masamuné (1566-1636).

In 1571 Yoshimori indicated that he wished to bypass his eldest son Yoshiaki as his successor, and name a younger son as heir. A faction of retainers loyal to Yoshiaki intervened to place Yoshimori in confinement, and force the succession of Yoshiaki.

Mogami Yoshiaki (1546-1614)

Eldest son of Yoshimori. He succeeded his father as daimyo of the Yamagata domain in Dewa. He was Dewa no kami, and held the rank of ukyo-daibu. He took advantage of the general confusion of his neighbors to increase his domain at their expense. He clashed repeatedly with the Daté and the Uesugi to expand Mogami influence in Dewa, and became known as a capable leader.

In 1590 Yoshiaki submitted to Toyotomi Hideyoshi (1536-1598).

In 1595, in hopes of securing his clan's future, Yoshiaki sent his daughter Koma-himé as concubine to Toyotomi Hideyoshi's nephew Hidetsugu (1568-1595), but as soon as she arrived in Kyoto, Hidetsugu was accused of plotting a coup, and was ordered to commit seppuku. Yoshiaki in vain tried to intercede for his daughter's life, but she was beheaded at the same time as her husband. Yoshiaki was outraged and greatly saddened by the turn of events, and henceforth held a deep resentment against the Toyotomi.

After Toyotomi Hideyoshi's death, Yoshiaki came to support Tokugawa Ieyasu (1543-1616), and sent his 2nd son Iechika as a hostage to the Tokugawa.

At the 1600 Siege of Shiroishi (Mutsu) Yoshiaki, with his nephew Daté Masamuné (1567-1636), despite their earlier feuds, captured the castle from a retainer of Uesugi Kagekatsu (1556-1623), who was a chief supporter of Ishida Mitsunari (1560-1600). At the Battle of Seki-ga-hara (Mino) Yoshiaki and Masamuné supported Tokugawa Ieyasu. Afterwards, for his loyal service, the clan income was increased from 330,000 to 570,00 koku, making their fief the 5th largest in Japan, excluding that of the Tokugawa.

Yoshiaki was later compelled to order his eldest son Yoshiyasu to commit suicide by Tokugawa Ieyasu, who perhaps desired Iechika to succeed as head of the Mogami.

Yoshiaki laid out and developed Yamagata, bringing the culture of Kyoto and Osaka to the castle town. He brought to control the Mogami River, making navigation from the Japan Sea to the inland safer. His dam-building projects at Kitadaseki, Inabazeki, and other places, and other irrigation control measures helped develop rice cultivation in the Shonai Plain.

He died at Yamagata Castle.

Mogami Yoshitoshi (-1631)

Grandson of Yoshiaki. He was dispossessed of his large estate on account of misgovernment, and was transferred to Omori (Omi -- 10,000 koku). He died without leaving any heir.

MURAKAMI

Revenues: 95,000 koku
Territories: Shinano, Echigo
Castles:
  Katsurao (Shinano),
  Nechi, Honjo (Echigo)

Daimyo family descended from Tamehira-shinno (952-1010), son of the Emperor Murakami (926-967).

During the Genpei War (1180-1185) the clan supported the Minamoto. During the Nanboku-cho Period (1336-1392) they supported the Southern Dynasty.

During the first half of the Sengoku "Warring States" Period (1467-1573) the Murakami were powerful in Shinano.

The clan became involved in a long war with the Takeda, and by 1553 were driven from their lands. They took up with the Uesugi in Echigo, and served that family into the Edo "Tokugawa" Period (1603-1868).

Notable Ancestors

Murakami Yorikiyo (11th century)

Son of Chinjufu-shogun "Defender of the North" Minamoto Yorinobu (948-1048). He was adopted by Norisada, a son of Tamehiro-shinno (952-1010), and was the first to take the name Murakami.

Murakami Yoshiteru (-1333)

Descendant of Yorikiyo. Also called Hikoshiro. He was an ardent defender of the Southern Dynasty, and was killed while defending Prince Moriyoshi (1308-1335) in the Yoshino Mountains (southern Yamato). His son Yoshitaka died before him at the age of 18.

Murakami Yoshikiyo (1501-1573)

Son of Akikuni. Suo no kami. Born at Katsurao Castle (Shinano). His mother was a daughter of Shiba Yoshishiro, and he was married to the daughter of Ogasawara Hagamuné. Sometime in the early 1520s, upon his father's death, he succeeded him.

Yoshikiyo contested for local power with the Takanashi and the Unno. In 1541 he joined with the Suwa and the Takeda in bringing down Iiyama Castle (Shinano), and forcing Unno Munetsuna and Takanashi Masayori (-1581) to flee to Echigo, and Sanada Yukitaka (1512-1574) to flee to Kozuké.

Shortly thereafter, Takeda Nobutora (1493-1574) was exiled from Kai, and the Takeda-Suwa-Murakami alliance became nullified. Yoshikiyo extended his power in Shinano, and became increasingly at odds with Takeda Shingen (1521-1573), who was expanding into the province.

In 1548 the Takeda and the Murakami clashed at the Battle of Uedahara (Shinano). Yoshikiyo emerged the victor in a clash that claimed a number of senior Takeda retainers, and with Takeda Shingen himself wounded. Four months later however Shingen recovered to defeat Yoshikiyo's ally Ogasawara Nagatoki (1519-1583) at the Battle of Shiojiri-togé (Shinano).

Yoshikiyo's position thus became more difficult. In 1551 the Sieges of Toishi (Shinano) came to an end when the Takeda captured the castle.

In 1553 Takeda Shingen laid the Siege of Katsurao (Shinano), took the castle, and then lost it again. When Shingen returned later that year with an army too large for Yoshikiyo to contest, he abandoned his territories, and fled north to Echigo, where he become a retainer of Uesugi Kenshin (1530-1578), and fought for him against Shingen and his father Takeda Nobutora (1493-1574).

From 1553-1564 Yoshikiyo fought in the center division of the Uesugi army at the five Battles of Kawanaka-jima (Shinano) against Takeda Shingen. In 1561, at the 4th Battle, he fought in the Uesugi vanguard, and some accounts credit him with the defeat and death of Takeda Nobushigé (1525-1561).

In 1565 Yoshikiyo was given Nechi Castle (Echigo), and resided there.

In 1569 Yoshikiyo had his head shaved, and ceded his domain to his son Kunikiyo, who likewise served the Uesugi as a retainer. In 1582 Kunikiyo was able to recover the Murakami's Shinano lands.

Murakami Yoshiakira (-1624)

Grandson of Yoshikiyo. He served Niwa Nagahidé (1535-1585), and later Toyotomi Hideyoshi (1536-1598), who in 1596 gave Yoshiakira the castle of Honjo (Echigo -- 95,000 koku).

After the 1600 Battle of Seki-ga-hara (Mino) Yoshiakira was one of the counselors to the 6th son of Tokugawa Ieyasu (1536-1598), Tadateru (1592-1683). In 1618, when Tadateru was charged with aspiring to the Shogunate, Yoshiakira was deprived of his domain, and banished to Sasayama (Tanba), where he died.

NAITO

Revenues: 200,000 koku
Territory: Tanba

Family of daimyo of the 16th century, native of Tanba.

NOTABLE ANCESTORS

Naito Genzaémon (16th century)
Served Oda Nobunaga (1534-1582), and received from him the fief of Kameyama (Tanba -- 200,000 koku).

Naito Yukiyasu/Joan (1549-1626)
Son of Genzaémon. Hida no kami. His mother was the daughter of Naito Sadafusa of Yagi Castle (Tanba). He succeeded his father in the fief of Kameyama (Tanba -- 200,000 koku). He was also called Tokuan.

In 1565 Yukiyasu heard about Christianity from the Christian woman Constance of Tanba. He visited Kyoto, and was baptized there by the name of Joan.

In 1573, having sided with the 15th Ashikaga Shogun Yoshiaki (1537-1597), Yukiyasu was dispossessed by Oda Nobunaga (1534-1582). He then lived for a while in Aki with Yoshiaki.

Around 1588 Yukiyasu started serving Konishi Yukinaga (1555-1600) of Higo. During the 1592-1598 Korean Expedition, Yukiyasu fought under his command, and in 1593 was chosen, on account of his knowledge of Chinese writing, to treat for peace at Beijing. The Emperor of China having proposed to confer on Toyotomi Hideyoshi (1536-1598) the title of King of Japan, Yukiyasu was told that his mission had ended in failure, and he retired to Yukinaga's domain in Higo.

After the 1600 Battle of Seki-ga-hara, Konishi Yukinaga was executed, and Yukiyasu accepted the invitation of the new lord of Higo, Kato Kiyomasa (1562-1611), to serve him.

About 1602 Kato Kiyomasa tried to force the Christians to join the Nichiren-shu, but Yukiyasu refused, and was forced to live in the mountains. In 1603, doubtless through the influence of Takayama Ukon (1552-1615), the Naito were invited to settle in Kaga by Maeda Toshinaga (1562-1614), who gave Yukiyasu a revenue of 4,000 koku.

In 1613 Tokugawa Ieyasu (1543-1616) promulgated a national anti-Christian edict, and in 1614 Yukiyasu was banished to Manila with his family, sister Julia, Takayama Ukon, Ukita Hisayasu, Shinagawa Uhei, Shinagawa Gonbei, etc. The Spanish Philippines welcomed the party warmly, and provided for their support. There Joan worked at translating Christian and medical books from Chinese into Japanese.

He died after 12 years of exile, and his wife died a number of years later.

NIGAO

Revenues: 10,000 koku
Territories: Dewa, Hitachi
Castle: Nigao (Dewa)

Ancient family of daimyo that in the 16th century occupied the castle of Nigao (Dewa).

In 1602 Tokugawa Ieyasu (1543-1616) transferred them to Takeda (Hitachi -- 10,000 koku).

NOTABLE ANCESTORS

Nigao Takanobu (1560-1623)
Upon his death, his children became simple samurai.

NASU

Revenues: 20,000 koku
Territory: Shimotsuké
Castle: Karasu-yama (Shimotsuké)

Ancient daimyo family of Shimotsuké descended from Fujiwara Michinaga (966-1027).

The clan was founded in the 12th century, and became more and more influential. Under the Ashikaga the Nasu became one of the Kanto-hakké "eight great families of Kanto."

During the Sengoku "Warring States" Period (1467-1573), the clan vanquished their neighbor, the Utsunomiya, took their domain, and built a castle at Karasu-yama (Shimotsuké).

Notable Ancestors

Nasu Sukeié (12th century)
In 1125 installed himself in the district of Nasu (Shimotsuké), and took that name.

Nasu Takasuké (-1551)
Eldest son of Masasuké. He clashed with the Utsunomiya.

In 1551 Takasuké was tricked out of Karasu-yama Castle (Shimotsuké) by Utsunomiya Hirotsuna (1543-1580), and was murdered.

Nasu Suketané (-1583)
Younger son of Masasuké. In 1551 he succeeded his murdered elder half-brother Takasuké, and held Karasu-yama Castle (Shimotsuké).

Starting in 1560 Suketané clashed with the allied forces of the Ashina, the Saraké, and the Utsunomiya.

In 1561 Suketané fought at the Siege of Odawara (Sagami) on the side of Uesugi Kenshin (1530-1578) against the Hojo.

Nasu Sukeharu (1546-1609)
Son of Suketané. He held the Court title of shuri-daibu. He inherited a rivalry with the Utsunomiya and the Saraké, and defeated the local Senbon family.

In 1590 Sukeharu was transferred by Toyotomi Hideyoshi (1536-1598) to Fukuwara (Shimotsuké -- 20,000 koku).

During the 1600 Seki-ga-hara Campaign, Sukeharu supported Tokugawa Ieyasu (1543-1616).

Nasu Sukefusa (17th century)
In 1685 was dispossessed for having disinherited his son Suketoyo in favor of Sukenori, son of Tsugaru Nobumasa (1646-1710), whom he had adopted.

OKUBO

Revenues: 30,000 koku
Territory: Musashi

Notable Ancestors

Okubo Nagayasu (1545-1613)
Son of Konparu Shichiro, an actor of noh for the Takeda of Kai. He became a minor administrator for the Takeda, and was raised to the rank of samurai. He was later adopted by Okubo Tadachika (1553-1628), from whom he adopted his surname.

Around 1590 Nagayasu joined the party of Tokugawa Ieyasu (1543-1616), to whom he rendered great pecuniary services by working the mines of Izu. In return he received the title of Iwami no kami and the domain of Hachioji (Musashi -- 30,000 koku).

In 1606 Nagayasu was made daikan of Izu, handling tax collection and finances in general for that province. Such was his importance that he was nicknamed tenka no sodaikan "Great Administrator of the Realm." He became involved in a bitter feud with Honda Masazumi (1566-1637) that worsened the fortunes of the Okubo in general.

After his death, from discoveries made in his dwelling, Nagayasu's illegal activities came to light, which included a plot formed with the Christians and the Spaniards to overthrow the 2nd Tokugawa Shogun Hidetada (1579-1632). His son Tojuro was arrested on the spot, and put to death with six supposed accomplices.

Otomo

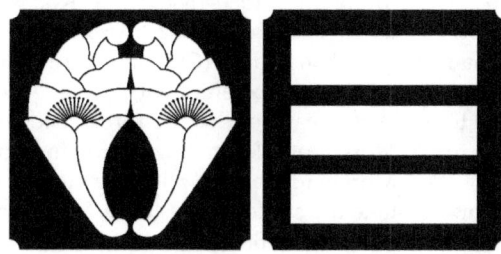

Territory: Northern Kyushu
Castles: Niyushima, Tachibana (Chikuzen)

Family of daimyo descended from Fujiwara Nagaié (1005-1064).

Following the establishment of the Kamakura Shogunate in 1185, members of the clan were granted the posts of shugo "military governor" of Bungo and Buzen.

As the Otomo were one of the major clans of Kyushu, along with the Shoni and the Shimazu, they played a central role in organizing the efforts against the 1274 and 1281 Mongol Invasions of Japan.

At the beginning of the Muromachi Period (1336-1573) the clan played an important role in the establishment of the Ashikaga Shogunate. Otomo warriors fought alongside Ashikaga Takauji (1305-1358), and enabled him to win a number of key battles, including the Battle of Sanoyama (Suruga). This helped to ensure the clan powerful government positions in the new Shogunate.

In 1501 tensions with the Ouchi of Suo and Nagato brought a war, which resulted in a victory for the Otomo at Uma-ga-také (Buzen). Feuds with other local clans followed, and at various points over the next five decades the Otomo clashed with the Shoni, the Tawara, and the Tachibana, the last two eventually becoming Otomo vassals. The Hoshino of Chikuzen also submitted, but later revolted; their bid for independence dragged Otomo Yoshinori/Yoshiaki into a bitter civil war.

A powerful clan throughout the Sengoku "Warring States" Period (1467-1573), the Otomo are especially notable as one of the first clans to make contact with Europeans, and to establish a trade relationship with them. In or around 1542 three Portuguese, including the explorer Fernão Mendes Pinto (1509-1583), were carried by a typhoon to the island of Tané-gashima, just south of Kyushu. Within ten years, trade with the Portuguese was fairly regular and common in Kyushu.

In 1549 the Jesuit missionary Francis Xavier (1506-1552) arrived in Japan, and soon afterwards met with Otomo Sorin (1530-1587), shugo of Bungo and Buzen, who would later be described by Xavier as a "king," and in 1578 converted to Roman Catholicism. Sorin was eager to secure for his clan further trade and contact with the Portuguese, seeing the technological and, more importantly perhaps, economic benefits that could be derived. In 1552 Otomo emissaries traveled to Goa (India) with Xavier, to meet with the Portuguese governor there. Xavier and other Jesuit missionaries would return to Kyushu, traveling and proselytizing. The Otomo were always well-disposed towards them, and they saw some success in Bungo as a result, converting many Japanese to Christianity.

By 1568 Sorin had extended the influence of the Otomo over Bungo, Buzen, northern Hyuga, Chikuzen, and Chikugo. However, defeats at the hands of the Ryuzoji in 1570 at Imai, and the Shimazu in 1578 at the Battle of Mimigawa (Hyuga), combined with internal dissension, weakened the Otomo. They were on the verge of being destroyed by the Shimazu when Toyotomi Hideyoshi (1536-1598) invaded Kyushu in 1587. Although this preserved the Otomo domain for a time, it was lost owing to cowardice on the part of Sorin's heir Yoshimuné during Hideyoshi's 1st Korean Invasion of 1592.

Towards the end of the 16th century, the Otomo fought both the Shimazu and the Mori, of whom the latter were expert sailors. Although the Otomo did not play a major role in the campaigns of Tokugawa Ieyasu (1543-1616), which ended the Sengoku Period, they did retain their domain into the Edo Period (1603-1868).

Notable Ancestors

Otomo Yoshinao (late 12th century)

Descendant of Fujiwara Hidesato (10th century), lord of Funai (Bungo). He was adopted by Nakahara Chikayoshi, and was the first to take the name Otomo.

During the Genpei War (1180-1185) Yoshinao served Minamoto Yoritomo (1147-1199) against the Taira, and in 1189 he fought in the Mutsu campaign against Fujiwara Yasuhira (1155-1189).

In 1193 Yoshinao was appointed shugo-shoku of Buzen and Bungo, and Chinzei bugyo "Kyushu administrator." Thenceforth his family acquired great influence in Kyushu.

Otomo Sadamuné (early 14th century)

Descendant of Yoshinao in the 5th generation. He sided with the Ashikaga, and fought against the Kikuchi in Kyushu.

In 1336, under the orders of Ashikaga Takauji (1305-1358), Sadamuné besieged Kyoto, and fought against Nitta Yoshisada (1301-1338).

Edo Period – Otomo

Otomo Sadanori (-1336)

Son of Sadamuné. He was the first to take the name Tachibana.

He was killed whilst fighting against Yuki Chikamitsu (-1336).

Otomo Chikayo (14th century)

Great-grandson of Sadamuné.

During the Nanboku-cho Period (1336-1392) Chikayo fought against the Kikuchi, supporters of the Southern Dynasty, and got possession of the six provinces of Buzen, Bungo, Chikuzen, Chikugo, Hizen, and Higo.

During the war Chikayo assisted the Chinzei tandai "military governor of Kyushu" Imagawa Sadayo (-1429), but once the fighting ended, he banded with the Ouchi to have him removed, and he himself became Chinzei tandai.

Otomo Yoshinori/Yoshiaki (1502-1550)

Descendant of Chikayo in the 9th generation, and son of Yoshinaga. He was married to a daughter of Ouchi Yoshioki (1477-1528).

Yoshiaki inherited a troubled retainer band, and had to contend with his independent-minded brother Yoshitaké. He worked to secure Otomo influence over Bungo, and clashed with the Ouchi and the Shoni. He fought a long time against Hoshino Chikatada, who attempted to become independent in Chikuzen.

In 1542, on learning that some Europeans had landed at Tané-ga-shima (Osumi), Yoshiaki invited them to his court. Portuguese explorer Fernão Mendes Pinto (1509-1583) then repaired to Funai (Bungo), and caused profound stupefaction by showing the use of arquebuses, which were then unknown in Japan.

Yoshiaki indicated that he wished to name as heir his 2nd son Shioichi-maru, who was a bastard. This prompted a group of retainers who supported the rights of the eldest son Yoshishigé (later Sorin) to attack Yoshiaki's residence. Led by Irida Chikazané (1510-1550), Tsukumi Mimasaka mortally wounded Yoshiaki, and Shioichi-maru and his mother were killed.

Otomo Yoshishigé/Sorin (1530-1587)

21st head of the Otomo. Eldest son of Yoshiaki. Saémon no kami. He inherited the domain Funai (Bungo) from his father.

In 1551 Yoshishigé gave hospitality to Francis Xavier (1506-1552) for two months, and was deeply impressed by the truths of Christianity, although he embraced the faith only many years afterwards. In the same year, he triumphed over Kikuchi Yoshimuné, who had revolted in Higo.

In 1552 Otomo emissaries traveled to Goa (India) with Francis Xavier, to meet its Portuguese governor.

In 1556 Yoshishigé quelled the troubles caused by the priests of the great Usa Hachiman-gu (Buzen).

In 1557 Yoshishigé defeated Akizuki Kiyotané in Chikuzen, and took possession of his domain.

In 1559 Yoshishigé led an assault that recaptured the strategic Moji Castle, which had been lost to the Mori in the previous year, but the Mori soon took it back. In 1561 Yoshishigé laid the Siege of Moji in alliance with the Portuguese, whose bombardment is said to be the first by foreign ships on Japan. The defending Mori however were able to break the siege lines, and reinforce the castle.

In 1562, leaving Funai to his son Yoshimuné, yet quite a child, Yoshishigé built a castle for himself at Niyushima, shaved his head, and took the name Sanbisai Sorin. It is by the name Sorin that he is best known. Shortly afterwards, in alliance with the Amako, he invaded Buzen, and prepared to cross over to Suo, where Mori Takamoto (1523-1563) was preparing to resist him, but the 13th Ashikaga Shogun Yoshiteru (1536-1565) intervened and made peace. His daughter was then betrothed to Takamoto's son Terumoto (1553-1625).

In 1564 Sorin led another expedition into Chikuzen, and defeated Akizuki Tanezané (1548-1596), who had rebelled.

In 1568 the Otomo moved against the Ryuzoji of Hizen, which prompted the

Otomo Sorin

interference of the Mori. In 1569 Hetsugi Akitsura, a notable vassal of the Otomo, was defeated at the Battle of Tatarahama (Chikuzen) by Kikkawa Motoharu (1530-1586) and Kobayakawa Takakagé (1532-1596), and lost Tachibana Castle (Chikuzen) to a powerful Mori expeditionary force. After Sorin heard of this, he threatened the Mori foothold in Buzen, forcing the Mori to retreat, and allowing him to retake the castle. By this time, Sorin was in control of Bungo, most of Buzen, Chikuzen, Chikugo, and had influence over Higo and Hizen. Otomo banners even flew over forts in Iyo, taken from the hostile Kono. The Otomo soon became known as the Otomo shichi-kakoku no zei "Seven-Province Host of the Otomo."

In 1576 Sorin retired, and handed over the reins of government to his son Yoshimuné, who in 1574 had been Christened Constantinho. In 1578 he divorced his wife, who was an ardent opponent of Christianity, and was labeled Jezebel by the Jesuits. He then had himself baptized, taking the name of Francisco.

In 1578 Sorin and his son Yoshimuné led an enormous host into Hyuga, intent on recapturing lands that the Shimazu had taken from Ito Yoshisuké (1512-1585), who had taken shelter with the Otomo. They first overwhelmed Tsuchimochi Chikanari (-1578), lord of Matsu Castle, who had earlier betrayed Yoshisuké and joined the Shimazu. While they set about destroying all the Buddhist temples and Shinto shrines in the Tsuchimochi lands, Sorin's brother-in-law Tawara Chikataka led the bulk of the army to besiege Shimazu Iehisa (1547-1587) in Taka Castle. Shimazu Yoshihisa (1533-1611) then hastily rallied his kinsmen. His brother Shimazu Yoshihiro encountered and scattered an advance Otomo force, and destroyed an enemy fort at Matsuyama. In the ensuing Battle of Mimigawa (Hyuga), Chikataka sent the Otomo in a frontal attack that was repulsed after some bitter fighting. They were quickly routed, and the Shimazu won an amazing victory, with Sorin and his son returning crestfallen to Bungo. The defeat heralded the decline of the Otomo.

By 1579 the Otomo were largely driven from Chikugo by the Ryuzoji, and in that year they suffered another rebellion by Akizuki Tanezané. In Bungo dissension was rife, in many cases as a result of Sorin's continued support Christianity. The Shimazu, no longer worried about the Otomo, called for a cease fire so Yoshihisa can freely fight "the Bear of Hizen" Ryuzoji Takanobu (1530-1584), which he considered a more dangerous opponent.

In 1582 Sorin sent ambassadors, later known as the Tensho Embassy for the nengo "era" in which it took place, to the Pope and the kings of Europe. It was led by Ito Mancio (1570-1612), the son of Ito Shuri-no-suké, a close relative of Sorin. This first official Japanese embassy to Europe was also sponsored by Christian daimyo Omura Sumitada (1532-1587) and Arima Harunobu (1567-1587). After visiting Macau, Cochin, and Goa, they arrived in Lisbon in 1584. From there they went on to Rome where Mancio became an honorary citizen, and taken into the ranks of European nobility with the title Cavaliere di Speron d'oro "Knight of the Golden Spur." During their stay in Europe, they met with the Spanish King Philip II (1527-1598), the Grand Duke of Tuscany Francesco I de' Medici (1541-1587), Pope Gregory XIII (1502-1585), and his successor Pope Sixtus V (1520-1590). After an eight-year voyage, the ambassadors arrived back in Japan in 1590.

Meanwhile, in 1586, after defeating the Ryuzoji, the Shimazu returned their attention to Bungo, which prompted Sorin to leave his place of retirement in Usuki, and travel to Osaka to plead with Toyotomi Hideyoshi (1536-1598) for assistance against Shimazu Yoshihisa. Hideyoshi called for peace in the Kyushu, but Yoshihisa refused to agree, and seized Toshimitsu and Funai Castles from the Otomo. Late that year the first Toyotomi troops landed on the island, and with them, the Otomo, the Sengoku, and the Chosokabé were defeated at the Battle of Hetsugi-gawa by the Shimazu. In 1587 however, once Hideyoshi's massive army arrived, the Shimazu were swept all the way back to Satsuma. Peace was restored, but the Otomo retained only Bungo.

Sorin died just when Toyotomi Hideyoshi returned to his castle of Osaka.

Otomo Chikasada (-1570)

Son of Yoshikai, and younger brother to Sorin. He led the Otomo army in various campaign in Buzen, Chikugo, and elsewhere.

In 1570 Sorin assembled a massive army, led by Chikasada, that included allied men from the Arima, the Imayama, the Oda, the Usuki, the Kumashiro, and the Hetsugi, to crush "the Bear of Hizen" Ryuzoji Takanobu (1530-1584), who Chikasada surrounded at Saga Castle. In the ensuing Battle of Iyama, somewhat northwest of the castle, Takanobu's retainer Nabeshima Naoshigé (1537-1619) attacked the much larger army under cover of darkness, and in a violent charge they drove into Otomo headquarters, where Chikasada was killed by Ryuzoji warrior Narimatsu Nobukatsu (1540-1584). The Otomo army fell into chaos, and withdrew.

Otomo Yoshimuné (1558-1605)

Eldest son of Sorin. In 1574 he was baptized as Constantinho. In 1576 he officially succeeded his father.

In 1580 Yoshimuné carried war into Chikuzen, where Tawara Chikazané had revolted.

In 1584 Yoshimuné defeated Ryuzoji Masaié (1556-1607) of Hizen.

In 1586, when the Shimazu of Satsuma invaded Bungo, Toyotomi Hideyoshi (1536-1598) sent an expeditionary force, led by Chosokabé Motochika (1538-1599) and Sengoku Hidehisa (1552-1614), to relieve Funai. Yoshimuné, against the advice of Motochika, insisted on taking the field to relieve Toshimitsu Castle, then under attack by Shimazu general Niiro Tadamoto (1526-1611). The result of this ill-conceived undertaking was the Battle of Hetsugi-gawa, where Shimazu Yoshihiro (1535-1619) and his brother Iehisa (1547-1587) fooled them into attacking by a feigned retreat, and the allies were routed after a bloody fight.

In 1587, after Toyotomi Hideyoshi's massive army arrived and subjugated the Shimazu, Yoshimuné saw his domain reduced to the single province of Bungo.

In 1592, for Toyotomi Hideyoshi's 1st Invasion of Korea, Yoshimuné led his Otomo samurai, and fought under the orders of Kuroda Nagamasa (1568-1623). After some easy successes over the Koreans, the situation became more serious, especially when the Japanese found themselves in presence of a strong Chinese army. Konishi Yukinaga (1555-1600), besieged in Heijo (Pyongyang), asked for assistance from Yoshimuné, who, frightened by the number of the enemies, retreated in haste towards Seoul. In 1593 Hideyoshi, on hearing of this cowardice, deprived him of his possessions, and banished him to the domain of Mori Terumoto (1553-1625) in Aki.

In 1600 Yoshimuné sided with Ishida Mitsunari (1560-1600) against Tokugawa Ieyasu (1543-1616), and after the loss at the Battle of Seki-ga-hara (Mino) returned to Bungo, and fortified himself at Ishitaté Castle, where he was besieged, made prisoner by Kuroda Yoshitaka (1546-1604), and exiled to Hitachi.

Otomo Chikaié (1561-1641)

2nd son of Sorin. Owing to his bad nature he was sent into priesthood, and after he had mended his behavior he was allowed to return to secular life.

In 1575 Chikaié was baptized. In 1579 he was adopted as heir by the Tawara.

Around 1586 Chikaié feuded with his elder brother Yoshimuné, and was accused of colluding with the Shimazu of Satsuma, enemies of the Otomo. Toyotomi Hideyoshi (1536-1598) wanted him executed, but Sorin convinced him to deprive him of his domain instead.

Otomo Chikamori (1567-1643)

3rd son of Sorin. In 1580 he was baptized as a Christian, and in 1581 he was adopted by Tawara Chikakata.

In 1587 Chikamori was present at the Battle of Hetsugi-gawa (Bungo). In 1592 he led troops in the 1st Invasion of Korea of Toyotomi Hideyoshi (1536-1598).

After his elder brother Yoshimuné was deprived of his domain in 1593, Chikamori became a retainer of Hosokawa Tadaoki (1564-1645), and gave up Christianity.

Otomo Yoshinobu (-1639)

Son of Yoshimuné. He was baptized in his childhood by the name of Fulgentius. He served the Tokugawa as a simple samurai, and distinguished himself at the 1615 Siege of Osaka.

Otomo Yoshitaka (16th-17th century)

Grandson of Yoshimuné. In 1589, at the request of Prince Ninnaji no Miya, he was raised to the rank of koké, which his descendants kept throughout the Edo Period (1603-1868).

SAIGO

Revenues: 10,000 koku
Territories: Shimosa, Awa
Castle: Tojo (Awa)

Daimyo family coming from Mikawa.

NOTABLE ANCESTORS

Saigo Masakatsu (-1561)
At first a vassal of the Imagawa. In 1561 he became a partisan of Tokugawa Ieyasu (1543-1616).

Besieged in his castle by Asahina Yasunaga, general of Imagawa Ujizané (1538-1615) of Suruga, Masakatsu set fire to it, and perished therein with his son Motomasa.

Saigo Iezané (-1597)
Grandson of Masakatsu.
In 1590, after having fought on the side of Tokugawa Ieyasu (1543-1616) in all his campaigns, Iezané followed him to the Kanto, and received a small fief in Shimosa.

Saigo Masakazu (1593-1638)
In 1615 he received the castle of Tojo (Awa -- 10,000 koku), and the title of Wakasa no kami.

Saigo Nobukazu (1614-1697)
In 1693 was dispossessed.

SANO

Territory: Shimotsuké

Ancient family of daimyo, who during the 12th century resided at Sano (Shimotsuké).

NOTABLE ANCESTORS

Sano Masatsuna (16th-17th century)
In 1614, having been implicated in the Okubo plot, was dispossessed and banished to Shinano.

SUGANUMA

Revenues: 40,000 koku
Territories: Isé, Omi, Tanba

Ancient daimyo family coming from Mikawa and descended from the Fujiwara.
The family became extinct in 1647.

NOTABLE ANCESTORS

Suganuma Sadamitsu (1542-1604)
Nominally served the Imagawa of Suruga. In 1560 the clan transferred their loyalties to the Tokugawa.
In 1570 Sadamitsu served Tokugawa Ieyasu (1543-1616) at the Battle of Anegawa (Omi) against the Asai and the Asakura, and in 1575 at the Battle of Nagashino (Mikawa) against the Takeda.
In 1601 Sadamitsu received the fief of Nagashima (Isé -- 20,000 koku).

Suganuma Sadayoshi (16th-17th century)
Son of Sadamitsu.
In 1619 Sadayoshi was transferred to Zezé (Omi -- 31,000 koku), then in 1634 to Kameyama (Tanba -- 40,000).

Sakuma

Revenues: 30,000 koku
Territories:
Omi, Kaga, Shinano
Castles:
Nagahama (Omi),
Oyama (Kaga),
Iiyama (Shinano)

Daimyo family descended from the Miura of Sagami. They settled at Yamazaki (Owari), and came to serve the Oda.

Notable Ancestors

Sakuma Nobumori (1528-1582)

Son of Nobuharu. Born in Owari. Dewa no suké and Uémon no jo. He initially served Oda Nobuhidé (1510-1551), and was entrusted with the care of his 2nd son Nobunaga (1534-1582).

In 1557 Nobumori briefly supported Oda Nobuyuki (1536-1557) in his abortive attempts at rebellion, but came to be one of Oda Nobunaga's most loyal and important retainers, and fought in every important battle under his command. Nobumori was known for his cautious tactics, and came to be called Noki Sakuma "Retreating Sakuma."

Nobumori was successful in the campaign against the Rokkaku, and helped to suppress rebellions caused by Buddhist sects in Echizen. In 1570, having the custody of Nagahama Castle (Omi), he defeated the Sasaki. That year he also commanded troops at the Battle of Anegawa (Omi).

In 1573 Oda Nobunaga dispatched Nobumori and his men to reinforce Tokugawa Ieyasu (1543-1616) against Takeda Shingen (1521-1573). At the resulting Battle of Mikata-ga-hara (Totomi) he joined Takigawa Kazumasa (-1586) in retreating after a preliminary engagement.

In 1576, during the Ishiyama Hongan-ji War (1570-1580), Nobumori was chosen to replace Harada Naomasa (-1576), who had died during the campaign, and was given the largest army among the Oda retainers. However, unlike his colleagues, who won battles on fronts to which they were assigned, he made no progress against the Buddhist zealots. Immediately after the war, Oda Nobunaga drafted a scathing 15-point accusation against Nobumori, censuring him for his incompetence and negligence, including past failures with those at the Hongan-ji, and ordered him to shave his head, and give up his lands in Yamato. Nobumori and his son Jinkuro was banished to Mount Koya (Kii), where they were forced to spend their days in the monk lifestyle as beggars.

Nobumori died of starvation or disease at Totsugawa (Yamato).

Sakuma Masakatsu (late 16th century)

Eldest son of Nobumori. In 1580 he shared in his father's disgrace at the hands of Oda Nobunaga (1534-1582), and was banished along with him to Mount Koya (Kii). He was later allowed to return to public life.

Sakuma Genba Morimasa (1554-1583)

Son of Moritsugu, who was a cousin to Nobumori. His mother was the elder sister to Shibata Katsuié (1522-1583), to whom he became one of his top generals, and accompanied him on most of his campaigns while serving the Oda. After several battles, owing to his aggressive spirit, he was nicknamed Oni Genba "Demon Genba," Genba being his middle name.

In 1575 Oda Nobunaga (1534-1582) gave Oyama Castle (Kaga), which he had taken from the Ikko-shu bonzes, to Morimasa.

After the death of Oda Nobunaga in 1582, a succession dispute split the Oda retainers into two main factions led by Shibata Katsuié and Hashiba (later Toyotomi) Hideyoshi (1536-1598). In 1583, when war came with Hideyoshi,

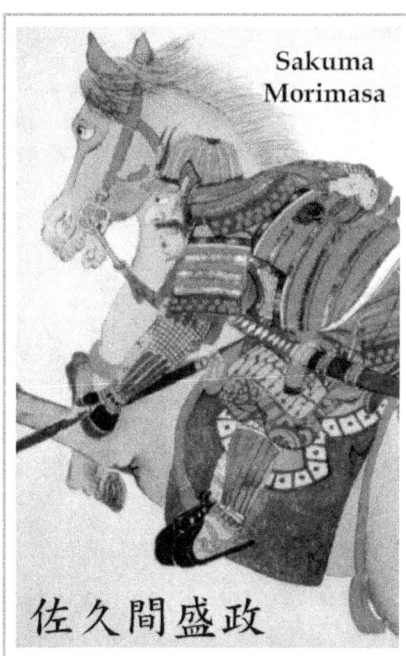

Morimasa led the Shibata army into northern Omi. In the course of the campaign he captured Iwasaki-yama from Takayama Ukon (1552-1615). He then defeated and killed Nakagawa Kiyohidé (1556-1583), but at the ensuing Battle of Shizu-ga-také, his army was routed by Hideyoshi. He then fled, but was captured, and beheaded at the Rokujo-ga-hara (Kyoto).

Sakuma Yasumasa (1555-1627)

Son of Moritsugu, and brother to Morimasa. He was initially adopted into the Hoda. He was Bizen no kami. He served Shibata Katsuié (1522-1583), and after his death, served Oda Nobuo (1558-1630). After peace was struck between Nobuo and Toyotomi Hideyoshi (1536-1598), he served Hojo Ujiyasu (1515-1571). After the fall of Odawara Castle (Sagami), he served Gamo Uji-

sato (1557-1596). At this point he changed his name from Hoda back to Sakuma. After Ujisato's death he served Tokugawa Ieyasu (1543-1616), and was given a fief in Omi (7,000 koku).

In 1615 Yasumasa was granted Iiyama Castle (Shinano -- 30,000 koku).

Sakuma Yasutsugu (1556-1638)

In 1583, after the ruin of his party at the Battle of Shizu-ga-také (Omi), he submitted to Hashiba (later Toyotomi) Hideyoshi (1536-1598).

In 1632 Yasutsugu became lord of Iiyama Castle (Shinano -- 30,000 koku). With his death the family became extinct.

TAKENAKA

Revenues: 20,000 koku
Territories: Iwaté, Bungo

Daimyo family descended from the Seiwa-Genji Minamoto's Toki branch. It was founded by Iwaté Shigeuji (15th-16th century), who was the first to take the name Takenaka, and held land in the Fuwa district of Mino.

Takenaka Shigeharu enjoyed the favor of Toyotomi Hideyoshi (1536-1598), and as a result, at the start of the Edo "Tokugawa" Period (1603-1868), the clan came to hold the status of daimyo.

In 1593 the clan resided at Takata (Bungo), then in 1600 at Funai (Bungo -- 20,000 koku).

NOTABLE ANCESTORS

Takenaka Shigemoto (1498-1560)

Eldest son of Shigeuji. Totomi no kami. He was at first a retainer of Saito Dosan (1494-1556), but in 1556 joined Saito Yoshitatsu (1527-1561) when he destroyed Dosan.

In 1558 Shigemoto took control of Iwaté by winning the Battle of Urushihara.

Takenaka Shigeharu/Hanbei (1544-1579)

Son of Shigemoto. Son-in-law to Ando Morinari (1503-1582). At first a retainer of Saito Yoshitatsu (1527-1561).

Shigeharu plotted an uprising and attacked his brother Saito Tatsuoki (1548-1573) at Inaba-yama Castle (Mino), which he took when his brother fled. He later returned the castle to his brother, but Tatsuoki had lost much reputation and honor due to his per-

Takenaka Shigeharu

ceived cowardly flight. In 1567, when Oda Nobunaga (1534-1582) attacked the castle, many of Tatsuoki's men defected, and Nobunaga easily took the castle.

Shigeharu so impressed Hashiba (later Toyotomi) Hideyoshi (1536-1598) that the latter invited him to join his forces as a strategist.

In 1570 Shigeharu participated in the Oda campaign against the Asai and the Asakura.

Shigeharu was given temporary custody of the young son of Kuroda Yoshitaka (1546-1604), who in 1578 was captured and imprisoned by the Araki. This prompted Oda Nobunaga to suspect that Yoshitaka was in fact colluding with his captors, and therefore ordered that Yoshitaka's son be put to death. Shigeharu is said to have put off carrying out this command until Nobunaga at length dropped the matter, and his ward, the future Kuroda Nagamasa (1568-1623), was spared.

He died of illness during Hashiba Hideyoshi's attack against the Mori in the Chugoku "middle provinces" region, while Miki Castle (Harima) was being besieged.

Takenaka Shigekado (1573-1631)

Son of Shigeharu. Like his father, he served Toyotomi Hideyoshi (1536-1598).

In 1584 Shigekado saw his first action at the age of 12, taking part in the Battle of Komaki (Owari).

At the 1600 Battle of Seki-ga-hara (Mino) Shigeharu sided with Tokugawa Ieyasu (1543-1616).

During his life the Takenaka became kotai-yoriai hatamoto, a class of Tokugawa retainers who held provincial fiefs with high income, but not at a daimyo level, and had sankin-kotai "alternate attendance" duties.

Shigekado studied Chinese and Japanese philosophy with Neo-Confucian scholar Hayashi Razan (1583-1657), and was known for his skill in calligraphy and poetry.

He died in Edo, and was succeeded by his son Shigetsuné.

Takenaka Shigetsuku (-1634)

In 1632 was made Nagasaki-bugyo "city magistrate." He was accused of debauchery and extortions, and condemned to kill himself, and his domain returned to the Shogunate.

Edo Period – Satomi

SATOMI

Revenues: 120,000 koku
Territories:
  Kozuké, Awa, Kazusa, Hoki
Castles: Shirahama, Tateyama (Awa), Kururi (Kazusa)

Daimyo family descended from Nitta Yoshishigé (-1202) of the Seiwa-Genji.

In the mid-15th century the clan moved from Kozuké to Awa, and remained there into the Edo "Tokugawa" Period (1603-1868).

In 1539 the Satomi were forced to submit to Hojo Ujitsuna (1487-1541). The remainder of the Sengoku "Warring States" Period (1467-1573) saw the clan battle the Hojo, the Takeda, and the Imagawa on a number of occasions.

At the beginning of the Edo Period the clan's holdings amounted to 120,000 koku; however in 1622 the clan died out.

Notable Ancestors

Satomi Yoshitoshi (12th-13th century)

Son of Nitta Yoshishigé (-1202). He was the first to take the name of Satomi from his domain in Kozuké.

Satomi Yoshizané (1417-1488)

Descendant of Yoshitoshi. He went from Kozuké to Awa, and built a castle at Shirahama.

Satomi Sanetaka (1483-1533)

2nd son of Shigeyoshi (1448-1505). He succeeded his elder brother Yoshimichi (1480-1518). He struggled to solidify his hold over the clan while expanding Satomi influence.

In 1526 Sanetaka led Uesugi forces at the Siege of Kamakura (Sagami) defended by a number of retainers of Hojo Ujitsuna (1487-1541), including members of the Ito and the Ogasawara, burning much of the city to the ground, including the Tsuru-ga-oka Hachiman-gu.

He suffered the defection of a number of his retainers, and committed suicide when under attack by his nephew Yoshitoyo.

Satomi Yoshitaka (1512-1574)

Eldest son of Sanetaka.

In 1533, Sanetaka's murder by his nephew Yoshitoyo, Yoshitaka immediately gathered loyal retainers to revenge his father, and sent a message to the Hojo of Odawara (Sagami) asking for their assistance. In 1534 his forces descended on Inamura Castle (Awa), and compelled Yoshitoyo to kill himself.

In 1538, defeated together with the Oyumi kubo "deputy Shogun" Ashikaga Yoshiaki (-1538) at the 1st Battle of Konodai (Shimosa) by Hojo Ujitsuna (1487-1541) and his son Ujiyasu (1515-1571), Yoshitaka saw a great number of his vassals abandon him.

In 1540 Yoshitaka recovered, and was able to turn back an Hojo incursion into Awa.

In 1553 Yoshitaka stormed the castle of Shiizu belonging to Takeda Nobumasa, forcing him to commit suicide.

In 1560 Yoshitaka's domain was attacked by the Hojo, and he called for the support of "the Dragon of Echigo" Uesugi Kenshin (1530-1578), who responded by leading an attack into the Kanto.

He built a castle at Kururi (Kazusa), and lived in it, leaving his son Yoshihiro the castle of Tateyama (Awa).

Satomi Yoshitoyo (1513-1534)

Eldest son of Yoshimichi.

In 1533 Yoshitoyo rebelled against his uncle Sanetaka, and forced him to commit suicide.

In 1534 Sanetaka's son Yoshitaka attacked Yoshitoyo at Inamura Castle (Awa) with overwhelming odds, and forced him to commit suicide.

Satomi Yoshihiro (1530-1578)

Eldest son of Yoshitaka.

In 1561 Yoshihiro participated in the Seige of Odawara (Sagami) by the Uesugi against the Hojo.

In 1564 Yoshihiro was defeated by Hojo Ujiyasu (1515-1571) and his son Ujimasa (1538-1590) at the 2nd Battle of Konodai (Shimosa), where his son Chokuro was killed by Matsuda Yasuyoshi, who later entered the clergy in remorse for killing such a young boy. Yoshihiro fled to Kazusa.

In 1567 Yoshihiro allied with Takeda Shingen (1521-1573), and fought against the Hojo and the Ota at the Battle of Mifuné-dai, where the enemy commander Ota Ujisuké was killed.

In 1570 Yoshihiro sent troops by sea to Izu to assist the Takeda's operations against the Hojo.

He died, evidently as the result of a stomach ulcer, without a son, and so his younger brother Yoshiyori succeeded him.

Satomi Yoshiyori (1542-1587)

3rd son of Yoshitaka. In 1578 he succeeded his elder brother Yoshihiro, who had died without an heir. He ruled from Tateyama Castle (Awa).

In 1580 Yoshiyori clashed with Masaki Noritoki, who had disputed his succession. In the following year Noritoki was assassinated.

Yoshiyori continued the war against the Hojo, who in 1581 had entered Kazusa and Awa.

Satomi Yoshiyasu (1573-1603)

Son of Yoshiyori.

Yoshiyasu submitted to Toyotomi Hideyoshi (1536-1598), and in 1590 took part in the Siege of Odawara (Sagami), thus being present for downfall of the Satomi's long-time enemy, the Hojo.

Afterwards Yoshiyasu was made to give up Kazusa and Shimosa, and his possessions were reduced to Awa (92,000 koku).

In 1600 Yoshiyasu sided with Tokugawa Ieyasu (1543-1616) in the Seki-ga-hara Campaign, and had his revenues raised to 120,000 koku.

Satomi Tadayoshi (1593-1622)

Son of Yoshiyasu. He was Awa no kami.

In 1614, being implicated in the Okubo plot against the Tokugawa Shogunate, Tadayoshi was dispossessed of his holdings, but at the petition of his samurai, he received Kurayoshi (Hoki - 40,000 koku).

He died without leaving an heir, and his family became extinct.

SUGIHARA

Revenues: 50,000 koku
Territory: Tajima
Castle: Toyo'oka (Tajima)

Ancient daimyo family descended from Taira Sadamori (10th century).

In 1601 the Sugihara obtained the fief of Toyo'oka (Tajima -- 35,000 koku).

The 2nd lord of the Sugihara clan Shigenaga died without a son, and his nephew Shigeharu became the head of the fief, but in 1653 he died at the age of 17 without an heir. Their domain then passed to the Tokugawa Shogunate.

Notable Ancestors

Sugihara Nagafusa (1574-1629)
Son of Ietsugu, uncle to the wife of Toyotomi Hideyoshi (1536-1598). Hoki no kami.

During the 1600 Seki-ga-hara Campaign, Nagafusa sided with Ishida Mitsunari (1560-1600), and defended at the Siege of Tanabé (Kii). Through the intercession of Asano Nagamasa (1546-1610), Nagafusa avoided losing his fief.

After serving the Tokugawa at the 1615 Osaka Summer Campaign, Nagafusa had his fief of Toyo'oka (Tajima) increased to 50,000 koku.

TERAZAWA

Revenues: 123,000 koku
Territories: Hizen, Higo
Castle: Karatsu (Hizen)

Daimyo family descended from Ki no Haseo.

Notable Ancestors

Terazawa Hirotaka (1563-1633)
Called also Masanari. He was Shima no kami, and Nagasaki bugyo "commissioner of Nagasaki."

In 1587 Hirotaka served Toyotomi Hideyoshi (1536-1598) in the Kyushu Campaign, and afterwards received in fief Karatsu (Hizen -- 83,000 koku).

Hirotaka took part in Toyotomi Hideyoshi's 1592-1598 Invasions of Korea.

In 1596 Hirotaka was baptised, but when the edicts of persecution were published, he apostatized, and became a persecutor.

In 1598 Hirotaka abandoned Nagoya Castle (Hizen), and used material from there to start work on the new Karatsu Castle. The Tokugawa Shogunate ordered neighboring tozama daimyo to contribute to its construction, which was completed in 1608.

In 1600 Hirotaka fought at the Battle of Seki-ga-hara (Mino) on the side of Tokugawa Ieyasu (1543-1616), and received the Amakusa islands (Higo) in reward, which brought his revenue total to 123,000 koku.

Hirotaka was partly responsible for the over-taxation and mismanagement of local government, which was continued by his son Katataka, and which instigated the Shimabara Rebellion (Hizen) a few years after his death.

Terazawa Katataka (1609-1647)
Son of Hirotaka. In 1633, upon his father's death, he inherited Karatsu (Hizen -- 123,000 koku).

In 1637 Katataka, through his exactions and tyranny, brought about the Shimabara Rebellion (Hizen). In 1638, after its suppression, he was dispossessed.

Katataka became insane, and committed suicide at the Senso-ji in Asakusa (Edo). He was the last scion of the family.

TANAKA

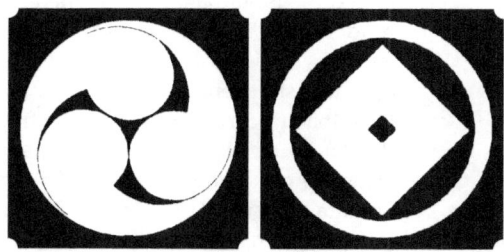

Revenues: 320,000 koku
Territories: Omi, Mikawa, Chikugo

Ancient daimyo family descended from the Tachibana, and installed at Tanaka (Omi).

NOTABLE ANCESTORS

Tanaka Yoshimasa (1548-1609)
Chikugo no kami, and hyobu daisuké "senior deputy minister of war." At first served Oda Nobunaga (1534-1582).

After Oda Nobunaga's death, Yoshimasa served Hashiba (later Toyotomi) Hideyoshi (1536-1598), who in 1583 gave him Yawata (Omi -- 30,000 koku).

In 1590 Yoshimasa was transferred to Okazaki (Mikawa -- 100,000 koku).

Named counselor of Toyotomi Hidetsugu (1568-1595), he revealed to the Taiko the ambitious designs of his adopted son.

In 1600 Yoshimasa sent his son Yoshimuné with an army of men to the Battle of Seki-ga-hara (Mino) to fight in the side of Tokugawa Ieyasu (1543-1616), who afterwards gave him the fief of Kurumé (Chikugo -- 320,000 koku).

Like Toyotomi Hideyoshi, Yoshimasa came from the humblest of roots, and gained high position due to his natural talents.

Tanaka Tadamasa/Yoshimuné (-1620)
Son of Yoshimasa.
In 1600 Yoshimuné fought at the Battle of Seki-ga-hara (Mino) for Tokugawa Ieyasu (1543-1616).
He died without an heir, and his domain reverted to the Shogun.

TOGAWA

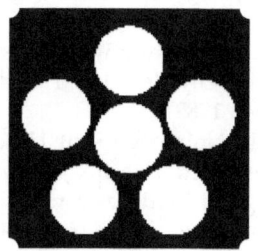

Revenues: 29,000 koku
Territory: Bitchu
Castle: Niwasé (Bitchu)

Daimyo family of Bingo.

In 1679 the clan became extinct when the 4th Togawa daimyo of Niwasé, Yasukazé, died without an heir.

SUCCESSION
1. Michiyasu (1569-1629)
2. Masayasu
3. Yasunobu
4. Yasukazé (-1679)

NOTABLE ANCESTORS

Togawa Hideyasu (-1598)
Higo no kami. He was a longtime vassal of Ukita Naoié (1530-1582) and his son Hideié (1572-1662) of Okayama (Bizen), with an income of 25,000 koku, fighting in many Ukita battles.

Togawa Satoyasu/Michiyasu (1569-1627)
Eldest son of Hideyasu. He was at first a retainer of Ukita Hideié (1572-1662).
In 1600 Michiyasu rebelled against his lord, and sided with the Tokugawa at the Battle of Seki-ga-hara (Mino). As reward he received Niwasé Castle (Bitchu -- 29,000 koku).

TOKUNAGA

Revenues: 60,000 koku
Territory: Mino

Ancient daimyo family coming from Omi, and descended from the Fujiwara.

During the late Azuchi-Momoyama Period (1573-1603) to the early Edo "Tokugawa" Period (1603-1868), one of its branches was the daimyo family which ruled Takasu (Mino -- 50,000 koku). It was dispossessed by the Shogunate, but later forgiven, and carried on as a high-ranking hatamoto family.

NOTABLE ANCESTORS

Tokunaga Toshimasa (1549-1612)
Served Toyotomi Hideyoshi (1536-1598), who in 1590 gave him the fief of Matsunaga (Mino -- 20,000 koku). In 1600 Tokugawa Ieyasu (1543-1616) transferred him to Takasu (Mino -- 60,000 koku).

Tokunaga Masashigé (1574-1642)
Son of Toshimasa. He was dispossessed in 1628 on account of his bad conduct, and exiled to Shinjo (Dewa) where he died.

Edo Period

TOYOTOMI

Castle: Osaka

Family from Owari, originally of the peasantry with no surname. Once its most influential figure Hideyoshi rose in rank in the service of Oda Nobunaga (1534-1582), he took the name Hashiba. In 1586 Hideyoshi received the name Toyotomi after he became Kanpaku "Regent to the Emperor," and by which he and his descendants are known in history.

For Hideyoshi's relatives who retained the name Hashiba, see the Azuchi-Momoyama Period (1573-1603) section under that name.

Notable Ancestors

Toyotomi Hideyoshi (1536-1598)

Son of a peasant-warrior named Yanosuké or Yaémon with no surname. Born in the village of Nakamura near Nagoya (Owari), the clan home of the Oda. His father dying soon after, his mother married into the Chikuami, by whom he was educated. In his childhood, he was called Hiyoshi.

His parents destined him to become a bonze, so they placed him in the Komyo-ji, a neighboring temple, but at the age of 15, he made his escape to search for adventure, and entered the service of the lord of Kuno Castle (Totomi) Matsushita Yukitsuna (1537-1598), who, having learned one day that Hiyoshi was from Owari, gave him 6 ryo to purchase for his master a coat of mail, like the one worn by Oda Nobunaga (1534-1582). The young man took the money, used it to procure clothes and weapons, but instead of returning to his master, he changed his name to that of Kinoshita Tokichiro, and went to Suruga to serve the Imagawa there.

Around 1557 he returned to Owari, and went to Oda Nobunaga, who admitted him into his service as a lowly servant, and nicknamed him Kozaru "Little Monkey" for his facial features and skinny form.

In 1560 he was one of Oda Nobunaga's sandal bearers at the Battle of Oké-ha-zama (Owari). He later acted as a foreman during the repair of Kiyosu Castle (Owari).

By 1564 he was known as Hideyoshi. That year he managed to bribe a number of Mino warlords to desert the Saito, including the clan's strategist Takenaka Shigeharu (1544-1579).

Hideyoshi carried out repairs on Sunomata Castle (Mino) with his younger half-brother Hidenaga (1540-1591) and the bandits Hachisuka Masakatsu (1526-1586) and Maeno Nagayasu (1528-1595). According to legend he constructed overnight a fort nearby, and discovered a secret route into the rear of Inaba-yama Castle. In 1567, when Oda Nobunaga came to attack the castle, he was able to take it with relative ease using this route. After this Hideyoshi became one of Nobunaga's most distinguished generals.

In 1570 Hideyoshi led troops in the Battle of Anegawa (Omi) against the Asai and the Asakura.

In 1573, after victorious campaigns against the Asai and the Asakura, Hideyoshi received in fief Nagahama Castle (Omi -- 220,000 koku), and the title of Chikuzen no kami. He later moved to the port of Imahama on Lake Biwa, and built a castle there. He took control of the nearby Kunitomo firearms factory that had been established previously by the Asai and the Asakura, and dramatically increased its firearms production.

That year Hideyoshi and Sakuma Nobumori (1528-1582) commanded troops at the 2nd Siege of Nagashima (Owari) against the Ikko-ikko, who defeated the Nobunaga forces when rain rendered 90% of his arquebuses useless.

Hideyoshi eventually took the name Hashiba by borrowing a character from the name of his two companions-in-arms, Niwa Nagahidé (1535-1585) and Shibata Katsuié (1522-1583). By this time, noticing his brilliant intellect, Oda Nobunaga had him marry Nené, a daughter of Sugihara Yoshifusa, who had been adopted by Asano Nagamasa (1546-1610). As Hideyoshi had no children, Nobunaga appointed his 4th son Hidekatsu (1568-1586) to be his heir.

In 1574 Hideyoshi fought at the 3rd Siege of Nagashima (Owari), where Oda Nobunaga and a fleet of ships led by Kuki Yoshitaka (1542-1600) finally defeated the Ikko-ikki, and completely destroyed the fortress.

In 1575 Hideyoshi fought at the Battle of Nagashino (Mikawa), where Oda Nobunaga and Tokugawa Ieyasu (1543-1616) soundly defeated Takeda Katsuyori (1546-1582).

In 1576 Oda Nobunaga sent Hideyoshi to Himeji Castle (Harima) to conquer the Chugoku "middle provinces" region. At that time, Mori Terumoto (1553-1625) had gradually joined ten provinces in the San'yodo and the San'indo to his domain, and now refused to submit to Nobunaga. Hideyoshi induced Ukita Naoié (1529-1582) of Okayama (Bizen) to join him, and with Akechi Mitsuhidé (1528-1582) successively besieged all the castles of the Mori.

In 1577 Hideyoshi fought at the Battle of Tedori-gawa (Kaga), where Oda Nobunaga suffered a devastating defeat to Uesugi Kenshin (1530-1578).

In 1578 Hideyoshi began the Siege of Miki (Harima) defended by Bessho Nagaharu (1558-1580), a retainer of the Mori. In 1580 the siege finally ended, and the castle fell to Hideyoshi. Afterwards, during an armistice, Hideyoshi went to Azuchi (Omi) to give an account of his exploits to Oda Nobunaga, by whom he was received with great honor. Soon after he moved from Nagahama to Himeji (Harima).

In 1582 Hideyoshi resumed the war by laying the Siege of Takamatsu (Bitchu). Mori's troops resisted with great energy, and Mori Terumoto himself came to their aid at the head of a great army. Hideyoshi asked Oda Nobunaga for support, and Akechi Mitsuhidé was sent to reinforce him. But Mitsuhidé, instead of leading his forces to the seat of war, killed Nobunaga in the Incident at the Honno-ji (Kyoto), and then at Azuchi Castle (Omi) attacked Nobunaga's eldest son and heir Nobutada (1557-1582), who committed suicide. Hideyoshi, on hearing this, hastened to conclude peace with the Mori, condemning the defender of Takamatsu, Shimizu Muneharu (1537-1582), to commit seppuku, and his soldiers to disperse. Going towards the capital, Hideyoshi met Nobunaga's 3rd son Nobutaka (1558-1583) at Amagasaki (Settsu), with whom he force-marched against the traitor. The vanguard of his army, commanded by Takayama Ukon (1552-1615), Nakagawa Kiyohidé (1556-1583), and Ikeda Tsuneoki (1536-1584), overtook Mitsuhidé, who was then defeated and killed at the Battle of Yamazaki (Yamashiro). Hideyoshi presented Mitsuhidé's head before Nobunaga's grave, and acted as the central figure at the funeral.

Hideyoshi then went to the castle of Kiyosu (Owari), and after having conferred with the great vassals of Oda, with the support of Niwa Nagahidé and Ikeda Tsuneoki, he nominated the son of Nobutada, and the grandson of Oda Nobunaga, Hidenobu (1580-1605), as heir, and appointed the child's two uncles, Nobukatsu (1558-1630) and Nobutaka (1558-1583), guardians till his majority.

Although Hideyoshi was *de facto* ruler of the Oda lands, and expected to obtain Oda Nobunaga's power in the government of the country, he was opposed by the Oda clan members who could not bear to see an upstart occupy that lofty position. Oda Nobutaka was the first to revolt, and calling Shibata Katsuié (1522-1583) to his help, he declared war against the usurper. Hideyoshi sent Nobukatsu to besiege his brother at Gifu Castle (Mino), and Nobutaka, being defeated, killed himself.

In 1583 Hideyoshi, with a large army, went to attack Shibata Katsuié. At the Battle of Shizu-ga-také (Omi), a number of Toyotomi warriors made a name for themselves, including Kato Kiyomasa (1562-1611) and Fukushima

Masanori (1561-1624). They defeated Sakuma Morimasa (1554-1583), and routed his army. Katsuié retreated to Kita-no-sho Castle (Echizen), and committed seppuku with his wife, Oda Nobunaga's sister O-ichi (1547-1583), whose three daughters from a previous marriage to Asai Nagamasa (1545-1573) were released to Hideyoshi, one of whom, Yodo-gimi (1569-1615), would become his chief consort, and the mother of his eventual heir, Hideyori (1593-1615).

In 1584 Oda Nobukatsu in his turn quarreled with Hideyoshi, and to be able to fight him, asked for the help of Tokugawa Ieyasu (1543-1616), who accepted, and engaged Hideyoshi's vanguard at Nagakuté (Owari), and routed it completely. The two armies then camped at Komaki-yama for a long time, facing each other, neither daring to bring battle, when finally Hideyoshi thought it prudent to negotiate. He first spoke to Nobukatsu, whom he easily brought to an agreement, and who then served as intermediary between him and Ieyasu. To cement the peace Hideyoshi gave his half-sister Asahi-no-kata (1543-1590) in marriage to Ieyasu, and the latter left his son Hideyasu as hostage.

In 1585, at the site of the Ishiyama Hongan-ji, which in 1580 Oda Nobunaga had burnt to the ground, Hideyoshi began the building of Osaka Castle, which was to be his residence, and which, in grandeur and richness, surpassed all that was ever seen in Japan. He then repressed the tumults occasioned by the warrior-monks of Negoro-dera and Saiga (Kii).

For the Invasion of Shikoku, Hideyoshi sent a large expedition commanded by Hashiba Hidenaga, Hashiba Hidetsugu (1568-1595), Ukita Hideié (1573-1655), Mori Terumoto, Kobayakawa Takakagé (1533-1597), and Kikkawa Motoharu (1530-1586) to reduce Chosokabé Motochika (1538-1599) to submission, and limited his domain only to Tosa. That year Hideyoshi also took control of Etchu.

After this, Hideyoshi's power was no more contested, and he wished his honor to be proportionate to his importance. He at first thought of the Shogunate, but this dignity could be given only to the descendants of the Minamoto. Instead he arranged to have himself adopted into the Fujiwara, and the udaijin "junior minister of state" Kikutei Harusué proposed to him the dignity of Kanpaku "Regent to the Emperor," and Hideyoshi having assented, Nijo Akizané (1556-1619) was induced to resign that office. Hideyoshi then created the go- bugyo "five magistrates" to help him in the administration of the government: Kyoto-shoshi-dai "governor of Kyoto" Maeda Gen'i (1539-1602) had charge of the police and the temples; Nagetsuka Masaié (1562-1600) of finance; Asano Nagamasa (1546-1610) of the laws; Ishida Mitsunari (1560-1600), of the public works; and Masuda Nagamori of justice. Hideyoshi was also made Dajo-daijin "Chancellor of the Realm." Then he issued an edict outlawing merchant guilds, and began a land survey of the whole country.

Late in 1585 Hidekatsu, the son Hideyoshi had adopted from Oda Nobunaga, suddenly died, with many believing he was killed on the orders of Hideyoshi.

In 1586 Hideyoshi was granted the family name of Toyotomi from the Emperor. His annual revenue at this time was 3,000,000 koku. Then leading an army towards the north, he had his authority recognized everywhere, almost without striking a blow: the Sassa in Etchu, the Uesugi in Echigo, the Anenokoji in Hida, the Sanada in Shinano, all made their submission, and consented to be his vassals.

In 1587 the Otomo, the Ryuzoji, etc., called on Hideyoshi to help suppress Shimazu Yoshihisa (1533-1611) of Satsuma, who had been waging war against his neighbors, and threatened to subjugate all of Kyushu. When Yoshihisa refused to recall his troops, Hideyoshi began his Kyushu Campaign, which in a few months pacified the island. Yoshihisa was ordered to retire, and was replaced by his younger brother Yoshihiro. The Shimazu were allowed to retain Satsuma, Osumi, and southern Hyuga; Konishi Yukinaga (1555-1600) received Higo; Kato Kiyomasa, Higo; Kuroda Yoshitaka (1546-1604), Bizen; and Kobayakawa Takakagé, Chikuzen. Hideyoshi then saw the Christians on the island as a dangerous destabilizing influence, and issued the 1st Christian Expulsion Edict and the Limitation on the Propagation of Christianity, forcing the missionaries to leave Japan, but allowed landholders to become Christian, although outlawing forced conversion.

Late that year Hideyoshi hosted the Grand Kitano Tea Ceremony near Kyoto, an extravagant event that saw the finest tea items on display.

In 1588 Hideyoshi held the opening his Juraku-dai Palace (Kyoto), and in the midst of splendid festivities received the visit of the Emperor Go-Yozei (1572-1617), the ex-Emperor Ogimachi (1517-1593), and the whole Imperial Court.

That same year Hideyoshi ordered the Great Sword Hunt, which forbade ordinary citizens from owning weapons, promising that the confiscate arms would be melted down to create a great statue of Buddha at the Hoko-ji (Kyoto).

In 1589 Hideyoshi distributedto the civil and military officials 365,000 ryo.

To complete the final act of the unification of Japan, in 1590 Hideyoshi invited all the daimyo to join in the Siege of Odawara (Sagami) against the Hojo, who after three months surrendered. Hojo Ujimasa (1538-1590) and his brother Ujiteru (1540-1590) were forced to commit seppuku, but Ujimasa's son Ujinao (1562-1591) was spared as he was the husband of Tokugawa Ieyasu's 2nd daughter Toku-himé (1565-1615), and thus his son-in-law. During the siege Ieyasu accepted Hideyoshi's offer to exchange the five provinces he controlled from Mikawa for the Hojo lands in Kanto, further from the capital. To the former Tokugawa lands Hideyoshi installed Asano Nagamasa in Kii, Kyogoku Takamoto in Shinano, Ikeda Terumasa (1565-1613) in Mikawa, and Yamauchi Kazutoyo (1545-1605) in Totomi.

In 1591 Hideyoshi ordered his tutor in cha-no-yu "way of tea," the great tea master Sen no Rikyu (1522-1591), to commit seppuku.

That year Hideyoshi issued his Edict on Changing Status, in which warriors were no longer allowed to become villagers, villagers were no longer allowed to become townspeople or to engage in trade, and the hiring of warriors who had deserted their previous lords were prohibited. Social mobility between the classes was essentially abolished, and the samurai were eventually ordered to live in the castle town of their lords.

Turning his attention to Korea, Hideyoshi sent So Yoshitoshi (1568-1615) of Tsushima to invite the king of that country Seonjo of Joseon (1567-1608) to become his vassal, and to allow his army to march unmolested into China. The king refused, and appealed to his sole lord, the Emperor of China Wanli (1563-1620). Hideyoshi then called upon all the daimyo, and ordered them to prepare for an expedition into Korea.

Also in 1591 Hideyoshi's only son Tsurumatsu died at the age of three, and shortly after his half-brother Hidenaga died also. In 1592 Hideyoshi then adopted his nephew Hidetsugu as heir, retired as the Kanpaku, and assumed that of Taiko "Retired Regent." He then began the construction of Fushimi Castle (Kyoto), wither he intended to retire in his old age.

Hideyoshi then launched his 1st Invasion of Korea from his new residence at Nagoya (Hizen). The fleet was commanded by Kuki Yoshitaka and Todo Takatora (1556-1630). The vanguard left under the command of Konishi Yukinaga and Kato Kiyomasa. The main army soon followed, and in a short time, all Korea was in the possession of the Japanese. The King Seonjo had fled to Ming China demanding help from the Emperor Wanli. On hearing of the intervention of the Chinese, Hideyoshi sent a reinforcement, but the Korean admiral Yi Sun-sin (1545-1598) successfully cut off his naval supply lines, forcing the invaders to retreat, and negotiate a ceasefire.

In 1593 Hideyoshi was informed that his consort Yodo-gimi had given birth to his 2nd son, Hideyori, whereupon he placed Maeda Toshiié (1539-1599) in charge, and hastily returned to Osaka. He began to quarrel with his adopted son Hidetsugu, who, though Kanpaku, thought only of pleasure. In 1595 Hideyoshi accused him of plotting against his life, and exiled him to Mount Koya (Kii), where he was ordered to commit seppuku.

In 1593 Hideyoshi sent Naito Joan (-1626) to present to the Chinese Emperor seven conditions, the principal being the marriage of a daughter of the Chinese Emperor to the Emperor of Japan, the continuation of former commercial relations between the two countries, the cession of the four southern provinces of Korea to Japan, etc.

In 1596 the Imperial Court of Beijing dispatched an embassy to Hideyoshi. Without mentioning any of the conditions conveyed through Naito, three conditions were proposed: the immediate recall of the Japanese troops yet in Fusan, the resumption of commercial relations, and peace with Korea. If these conditions proved acceptable, the Chinese envoy, in the name of his master, was to confer the title of King of Japan upon Hideyoshi, and to give him the golden seal and crown, emblems of his new dignity. At the reading of these propositions, Hideyoshi became furious, expelled the ambassador, and decided to resume the war.

In 1597, alarmed by the presence of the Spanish ship San Felipe in Japanese waters, and sure that the Jesuits were the forerunners of a military expedition, Hideyoshi publicly crucified Christians in Nagasaki (Hizen) as an example to those Japanese who contemplated converting to Christianity. Known as the "26 Martyrs of Japan," they included five European Franciscan missionaries, one Mexican Franciscan missionary, three Japanese Jesuits, and 17 Japanese laymen, including three young boys.

The 2nd Invasion of Korea commenced under the leadership of the Taiko's nephew Kobayakawa Hideaki (1577-1602). The army crossed the straits, but, fatigued by continued fighting, it was decimated by sickness and privation, had no success, and the expedition utterly failed. In 1598 Hideyoshi fell sick, and perceiving that his death was nigh, he ordered Tokugawa Ieyasu to call back the remnants of the army from Korea.

Fearing for his 5-year-old son's future, Hideyoshi then took great precautions to assure the succession to Hideyori. To that end, he appointed the Go-tairo "Five Elders," who were made to sign a loyalty pledge in blood to govern during the minority of Hideyori as co-Regents. These were the five greatest daimyo of Honshu: Tokugawa Ieyasu, Maeda Toshiié, Uesugi Kagekatsu (1556-1623), Mori Terumoto, and Ukita Hideié. Subject to the Go-tairo, the go-bugyo, created some ten years before, had charge of the administration. The san-churo "three adjudicators": Nakamura Kazuuji (-1600), Horio Yoshiharu (1543-1611), and Ikoma Chikamasa (1526-1603), were also chosen, and ranked between the Tairo and the bugyo; they were to settle any differences that might arise among the daimyo. Lastly, two most trustworthy men, Katagiri Katsumoto (1556-1615) and Koidé Masahidé, were charged to educate Hideyori. Hideyoshi made all these dignitaries swear fealty to their young master, and having thus arranged all things, he died in his palace of Fushimi.

One of the greatest figures of Japanese history, Hideyoshi came from low birth, but by his intelligence rose to the first rank to finally end the Sengoku "Warring States" Period (1467-1573). More a cunning politician than a skilful warrior, he was able to impose his authority upon the ambitious daimyo of these troubled times. He re-established order and prosperity in a country which had been ruined by civil wars during a century and a half. A dutiful servant of the Imperial Dynasty, he rebuilt the Kyoto Palace, and secured sufficient revenues for the Court to defray the necessary expenses, for which the Emperor Go-Yozei bestowed upon him the posthumous title of Toyokuni-Daimyo-jin. To his discredit, however, history records the disastrous expedition to Korea, inspired either by pride or the desire to check the too warlike military caste of Japan. Nor is it to be forgotten that Hideyoshi inaugurated religious persecution in Japan.

Few leaders have attracted as much adulation and hero-worship as Hideyoshi has from both the scholars and the general public in the pageantry of Japanese history.

Toyotomi Hidetsugu (1568-1595)

Son of Yoshifusa, who was Musashi no kami and lord of Oyama Castle (Owari). He successively bore the names of Kinoshita, Nagao, and Miyoshi. His mother Zuiryu-in was the elder half-sister of Toyotomi Hideyoshi.

In 1582, after the death of Oda Nobunaga (1534-1582), Hideyoshi gave Hidetsugu a 400,000 koku fiefdom in Omi as he was one his few relatives.

In 1583 Hidetsugu was ordered to fight Takigawa Kazumasu (1525-1586), and stormed the castle of Miné (Isé).

In 1584, at the Battle of Nagakuté (Owari), Hidetsugu sustained heavy losses against the forces of Tokugawa Ieyasu (1543-1616).

In 1585 Hidetsugu took part in the Siege of the Negoro-ji (Izumi), where the temple was set aflame, and the warrior-monks defeated. Also that year he proved himself in Hideyoshi's Invasion of Shikoku against the Chosokabé.

Hidetsugu built the Omi-Hachiman Castle near Lake Biwa, and developed a prosperous town there.

When Hideyoshi was named Kanpaku "Regent to the Emperor," Hidetsugu changed his name from Miyoshi to that of Hashiba, which Hideyoshi bore till then.

In 1590, during Hideyoshi's Odawara Campaign against the Hojo, Hidetsugu besieged and took Yamanaka Castle (Sagami). Afterwards he received five districts in Owari and Isé, and moved to Kiyosu Castle (Owari).

At the end of the same year, Hidetsugu, with Gamo Ujisato (1556-1595), conducted an expedition against Kunohé Masazané, who had caused trouble in Mutsu, and invaded the domains of Kimura Hidetoshi.

In 1592, after the death of both Hideyoshi's only son Tsurumatsu and his half-brother Hidenaga (1540-1591), he adopted his nephew Hidetsugu as heir, and retired. Hidetsugu succeeded as Kanpaku, and moved to the Juraku-dai (Kyoto), with the assumption that he would succeed Hideyoshi after his death.

Hidetsugu practiced shudo, a Japanese form of pederasty, as was common with men of stature, and had a number of wakashu "young lovers." Among the notable were Yamamoto Tonoma, Yamada Sanjuro, and his most beloved Fuwano Mansaku, who gained renown for his spirit and physical beauty.

Hideyoshi desired Hidetsugu to lead the expedition against Korea, but he refused, not daring to venture on such a distant and dangerous campaign. This irritated Hideyoshi, who soon found other reasons to complain of the conduct of his heir.

In 1593 the ex-Emperor Ogimachi (1517-1593) died, and before the official mourning was over, Hidetsugu had organized a hunting expedition. He also took the liberty to enter the monasteries of Mount Hiei (northeast of Kyoto) with his wife and daughters, an act altogether prohibited to women. Gamo Ujisato and Kuroda Yoshitaka (1546-1604) vainly tried to make him understand the impropriety of such acts, but he listened to nothing.

At this juncture, Hideyori (1593-1615) was born to Hideyoshi, who then thought of transmitting the succession from his nephew Hidetsugu to his new son. Henceforth the relation between Hideyoshi and Hidetsugu gradually became more strained. In 1595 Hidetsugu was accused of plotting against the Taiko by Ishida Mitsunari (1560-1600) and Masuda Nagamori, and perhaps Yodo-gimi (1569-1615), the mother of Hideyori, out of hatred to Hidetsugu. Upon hearing this, in a moment of fury, Hideyoshi confined Hidetsugu to the Seigan-ji on Mount Koya (Kii). Hidetsugu vainly tried to justify himself, but Fukushima Masanori (1561-1624) and Fukuhara Naotaka came to invest the place, and communicated to Hidetsugu the order to kill himself. With him died three wakashu, who committed seppuku with his assistance, along with a number of his vassals including Maeno Nagayasu and Watarasé Shigeaki.

At the request of Ishida Mitsunari, Hidetsugu's head was exposed in Kyoto. The following month his wife, daughters, and ladies-in-waiting, 34 in all, were decapitatated at the Sanjo-gawara. Only one was spared, his one-month-old daughter Okiku, who was adopted by her grandfather's nephew Goto Noriyoshi. Afterwards the Juraku-dai was dismantled, and many of its parts reassembled at Fushimi Castle (Kyoto).

Toyotomi Hideyori (1593-1615)

2nd natural son of Hideyoshi. His mother was Yodo-gimi, a niece of Oda Nobunaga (1534-1582). He was born at Fushimi Castle (Kyoto), and was first known as Hiroi.

In 1597, at the age of 3, Hideyoshi presented his son for the first time at the Imperial Palace, where he received the title of sakon-é-gon-shosho "senior deputy officer of the Imperial guard," and his new name Hideyori.

In 1598 Hideyori was given the title gon-chunagon "middle counselor." After the death of his father, he with his mother went to live at Osaka Castle, and the Go-tairo "Five Elders," appointed by Hideyoshi to rule on behalf of Hideyori during his minority, began jockeying for power.

In 1600, when the Toyotomi party was defeated at the Battle of Seki-ga-hara (Mino), Tokugawa Ieyasu (1543-1616) became *de facto* ruler of Japan, and Osaka Castle was greatly alarmed. Ieyasu however dared not lay hands on a child he had promised to protect, and allowed him to retain his castle and the three provinces of Settsu, Kawachi, and Izumi with a revenue of 650,000 koku.

In 1603 Hideyori was named naidaijin "minister of the center," and Tokugawa Ieyasu betrothed him to his granddaughter Sen-himé (1597-1666), then 6 years old. At this time the young boy practiced calligraphy with phrases wishing for peace in the world. Ieyasu however viewed him as a potential threat to the Tokugawa.

In 1611 Tokugawa Ieyasu came to Kyoto, and desired to see Hideyori at Nijo Castle. The trusted servants of the Toyotomi, fearing lest Ieyasu entertained some evil design, opposed the interview, but the widow of Hideyoshi, Kodai-in, was of a contrary opinion, and Kato Kiyomasa (1562-1611) and Asano Nagamasa (1546-1610) vouched that nothing unpleasant would happen to the young man. Thus Hideyori went to Kyoto, saw his dreaded protector, and returned without harm.

The same year Hideyori ordered the reconstruction of the Hoko-ji (Kyoto),

Toyotomi Hideyori

which his father had erected, but which was destroyed during the great earthquake of 1596. In 1614 the temple was finished, and a new bronze bell was cast successfully. Hideyori invited Tougawa Ieyasu to the opening ceremony. For some time already, Osaka had become the refuge of all those samurai who had been reduced to misery by the rising power of the Tokugawa. Ieyasu distrustfully looked upon this center of dissatisfaction and opposition, and longed for an occasion to destroy it. He thought he found it in the inscription on the bell. There happened to be two characters on the bell, which formed his name, but were separated by another character from each other. He affected to see an insult in this, and a curse upon his head. In an incident known as the Shomei Jiken, Ieyasu stopped the proceedings of the feast, asked an explanation, and even wanted to force the Emperor to suppress the ill-omened inscription, but Hideyori refused to submit to such unreasonableness. Vainly did Hideyori send Katagiri Katsumoto (1556-1615) to Sunpu to give explanations, but Ieyasu would listen to nothing, and war was resolved upon.

Hideyori then called on all his friends and protégés of his father. None of the daimyo in power answered his appeal, but some ancient daimyo and a great number of samurai came to increase his army in Osaka. It was commanded by Ono Harunaga (-1615), Sanada Yukimura (1567-1615), Goto Mototsugu (1565-1615), Chosokabé Morichika (1575-1615), Mori Katsunaga (-1615), Akashi Morishigé (-1618), etc.

In late 1614 Tokugawa Ieyasu, with his 3rd son Hidetada (1579-1632), and a great army appeared before Osaka, but after some fighting, known as the Winter Campaign of the Siege of Osaka, in early 1615 peace was concluded on condition that the walls of the castle be destroyed, and the moats filled in.

When Tokugawa Ieyasu, however, sent Honda Masazumi (1566-1637) to oversee the work done, Hideyori protested. The Summer Campaign of the Siege of Osaka then ensued. After a decisive Tokugawa victory at the Battle of Tenno-ji, where Toyotomi general Sanada Yukimura was killed, the castle was reduced to ashes. Although Sen-himé tried to persuade her grandfather to spare her husband's life, Hideyori, his mother Yodo-gimi, and most of the surviving samurai perished in the flames. Hideyori's 7-year-old son Kunimatsu-maro was taken as a prisoner to Kyoto and executed, and his -6-year-old daughter was sent to a Buddhist monastery. Sen-himé remarried, but later became a Buddhist nun. Thus ended the short lineage of the Toyotomi.

Such at least is the version of the Tokugawa. But legend says, after the destruction of Osaka, Hideyori and his family, with Tokugawa Ieyasu's consent, escaped on vessels put at their disposal by Hachisuka Iemasa, and retired to Satsuma, where under the name of Tanimura, they received rich presents from the great daimyo, ancient vassals of the Taiko, and their descendants lived to be one of the richest families of the province. Moreover the annals tell us that in 1645, a certain Tenshu-ni, a daughter of Hideyori, died at Kamakura, where she had been the abbess of the convent at the Tokei-ji.

TSUTSUI

Revenues: 120,000 koku
Territories:
 Yamato, Iga, Yamashiro, Isé
Castles: Tsutsui, Koriyama (Yamato), Ueno (Iga)

Ancient daimyo family descended from the Fujiwara. Vassal of the big temple of Kokoku-ji, it received the domain of Tsutsui (Yamato), and took its name.

NOTABLE ANCESTORS

Tsutsui Junsho (1523-1550)
Son of Junko. He became a minor daimyo in Yamato.

Tsutsui Junkei (1549-1584)
Son of Junsho. At first called Fujimasa or Fujikatsu. Etchu no kami.
When Junkei entered into possession of his father's estate, a large number of samurai were enlisting in the army of the then all-powerful daimyo Matsunaga Hisahidé (1510-1577), who in 1569 took Tsutsui Castle (Yamato) from him. To oppose such an adversary, Junkei placed himself under the protection of Oda Nobunaga (1534-1582).
When Oda Nobunaga laid the 1570-1580 Siege of the Ishiyama Hongan-ji (later Osaka), Junkei assisted.
In 1577, when Matsunaga Hisahidé revolted against Oda Nobunaga, Junkei was ordered to besiege him at Shigi-san (Yamato). He stormed the castle, and in reward received Yamato, and was allowed to build Koriyama Castle. In 1580 Nobunaga ordered him to supervise the destructions of castles in Yamato and Kawachi.

In 1581 Junkei participated in the Invasion of Iga, where he joined Gamo Ujisato (1557-1596) in laying the Siege of Hijiyama.
In 1582, after the murder of Oda Nobunaga, Junkei initially sided with his relative Akechi Mitsuhidé (1528-1582) and brought his troops to the Battle of Yamazaki (Yamashiro), but remarking the great strength of the army of Hashiba (later Toyotomi) Hideyoshi (1536-1598), he kept his army on the Hora-ga-také to watch the progress of the fight. When victory favored Hideyoshi, Junkei joined him, and contributed to the defeat of Mitsuhidé. Hence he received the nickname Hiyorimi Junkei "Heavenly-omen-watching Junkei." Hideyoshi however was not impressed, and reduced his revenue to 70,000 koku.

In 1584 Junkei supported Hashiba Hideyoshi in his campaign against the Tokugawa, and in a bloody fight took Matsu-ga-shima Castle (Isé) from Oda Nobukatsu (1558-1630).

Tsutsui Sadatsugu (1562-1615)
In 1571 he was adopted by his uncle Junkei of Yamato.
In 1584, at Junkei's death, Sadatsugu received Ueno Castle (Iga), with a revenue of 120,000 koku in Yamashiro and Isé.
In 1585 Sadatsugu joined Hori Hidemasa (1553-1590) when Hashiba (later Toyotomi) Hideyoshi (1536-1598) fought the bonzes at the Siege of the Negoro-ji (Izumi), killing them all, and setting their temple aflame.
In 1592 Sadatsugu received baptism, and became Christian.
In 1600 Sadatsugu sided with Tokugawa Ieyasu (1543-1616), accompanied him in the expedition against Uesugi Kagekatsu (1556-1623), and returned in time to assist at the Battle of Seki-ga-hara (Mino).
In 1608 Sadatsugu was accused by his kerai "vassals" of maladministration, was dispossessed, and banished to Matsuyama (Iyo). In 1615 he was invited to commit seppuku.

YURA

Revenues: 10,000 koku
Territories: Kozuké, Hitachi

Ancient family vassal of the Nitta. In the 16th century it was established at Kanayama (Kozuké), and afterwards transferred to Hitachi (10,000 koku). In 1621 it died out.

EDO PERIOD – TOMITA / YASHIRO

TOMITA

Revenues: 120,000 koku
Territory: Isé, Iyo
Castle: Anotsu (Isé)

Ancient daimyo family descended from the Minamoto.

NOTABLE ANCESTORS

Tomita Nobuhiro (late 16th century)
Served Toyotomi Hideyoshi (1536-1598), who in 1586 gave him Anotsu (Isé -- 100,000 koku).

Tomita Tomonobu (16th-17th century)
Son of Nobuhiro. He bravely defended his castle of Anotsu (Isé) against Mori Hidemoto (1579-1650), Kikkawa Hiroié (1561-1625), etc. His wife, a daughter of Ukita Tadaié, likewise distinguished herself and fought at his side.

In 1608, to reward Tomonobu for his services, Tokuwaga Ieyasu (1543-1616) transferred him to Uwajima (Iyo -- 120,000 koku).

In 1613 Tomonobu was dispossessed because he tried to save his father, Sakazaki Samon, guilty of murder, from the vengeance of justice.

He died at Iwakidaira (Mutsu), the place of his exile.

YASHIRO

Revenues: 10,000 koku
Territories: Shinano, Awa
Castle: Yashiro (Shinano)

Daimyo family descended from the Murakami-Genji Murakami Tamekuni.

NOTABLE ANCESTORS

Yashiro Yorikuni
Settled at Yashiro (Shinano), and took its name.

Yashiro Masakuni (-1575)
At first served Murakami Yoshikiyo, and held Yashiro Castle (Shinano). When the Takeda defeated the Murakami, he went to serve the victor.

In 1575 Masakuni was killed at the Battle of Nagashino (Mikawa) fighting for Takeda Katsuyori (1546-1582) against Oda Nobunaga (1534-1582) and Tokugawa Ieyasu (1543-1616).

Yashiro Hidemasa (-1623)
Younger brother to Masakuni. In 1600 he received the fief of Hojo (Awa -- 10,000 koku).

Yashiro Tadamasa (1594-1662)
In 1632 was dispossessed, and banished to Takata (Echigo), for not having kept stricter watch on the Suruga dainagon "major counselor" Tokugawa Tadanaga (1606-1633), who was his prisoner. Pardoned after 6 years, he regained his former domain.

Yashiro Tadanori (17th-18th century)
In 1712 was definitively dispossessed for bad administration.

Edo Period / Yuki

YUKI

Revenues: 670,000 koku

Territories: Shimosa, Mutsu, Iwaki, Echizen

Castles: Koga (Shimosa), Shirakawa (Mutsu)

Daimyo family descended from Fujiwara Hidesato (10th century).

The clan split into two branches during the Nanboku-cho Period (1336-1392) when one branch supported the Southern Imperial Court, and the other branch supported the Northern pretenders.

At the end of the 16th century the Shirakawa branch was destroyed by Toyotomi Hideyoshi (1536-1598). The Shimosa branch survived a short time longer as daimyo of Yuki domain (Shimosa), and through adoption they became absorbed into the Tokugawa as a branch family.

Notable Ancestors

Yuki Tomomitsu (1168-1254)

Son of Oyama Masamitsu, and descendant of Hidesato in the 10th generation. He received the fief of Yuki (Shimosa), and took the name of the place. His mother had been the nurse of Minamoto Yoritomo (1147-1199), and she advised her son to side with him against the Taira.

In 1189 Tomomitsu entered the Mutsu campaign against Fujiwara Yasuhira (1155-1189).

In 1200, when Kajiwara Kagetoki (1162-1200) revolted, Tomomitsu marched against him, and defeated him in Suruga. He later received the title of Kazusa no suké.

Yuki Tomohiro (13th century)

Son of Tomomitsu. He had two sons: the elder son Hirotsugu, kept the fief of Yuki and transmitted it to his descendants; in 1289 the younger son Sukehiro settled at Shirakawa (Mutsu), where his family resided for several centuries.

Yuki Munehiro (-1340)

Son of Sukehiro. Kozuké no suké and lord of Shirakawa Castle (Mutsu). At first served the Hojo. He shaved his head, and took the name Dochu.

In 1331 Munehiro joined the Hojo in the fight against the Emperor Go-Daigo (1288-1339) on Mount Kasagi (Yamashiro and Yamato). In 1333, when the Emperor escaped from Oki, and fled to Funanoé-sen (Hoki), he called all his faithful servants round. Munehiro then abandoned the Hojo party, joined Nitta Yoshisada (1301-1338), and with him entered Kamakura.

Munehiro went to Mutsu with Imperial Prince Yoshinaga, and fought against Ashikaga Takauji (1305-1358).

In 1338, defeated with Kitabaké Akiié (1318-1338) at Nara (Yamato), Munehiro took refuge at Yoshino (southern Yamato).

Returning to Mutsu, Munehiro levied another army, which he took to Anotsu (Isé) by sea, but had scarcely landed when he fell sick and died.

Yuki Chikatomo (-1347)

Eldest son of Munehiro. He sided with the Emperor Go-Daigo (1288-1339) against the Hojo, and then against the Ashikaga, but seeing his opponents successful everywhere, in 1340 he finally submitted to the Northern Dynasty.

Yuki Chikamitsu (-1336)

Son of Munehiro, and younger brother to Chikatomo.

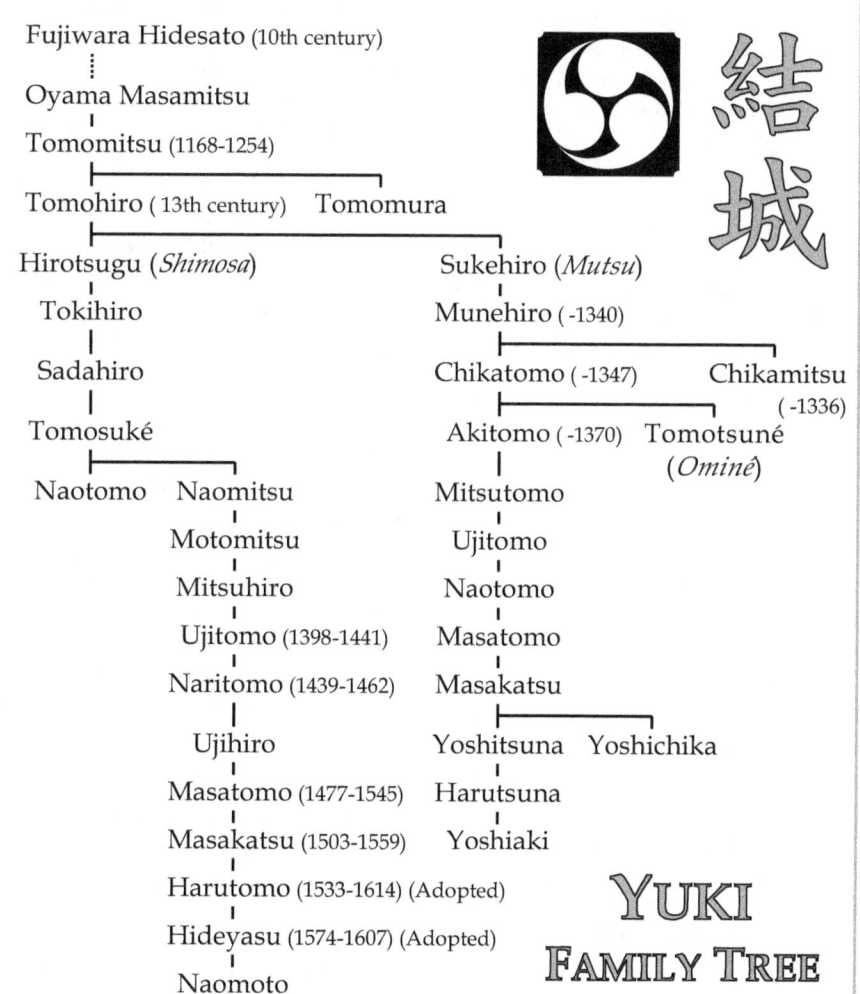

YUKI FAMILY TREE

SHOGUN & DAIMYO

In 1331, at the Siege of Akasaka (Kawachi) near Osaka, Chikamitsu sided with Daibutsu Sadanao and the Hojo against Kusunoki Masashigé (1294-1336), and helped take the fortress. Then in 1333 he was at the Rokuhara (Kyoto) in defense against the Imperial army. Later at Seta (Omi) he assisted in the defeat of Ashikaga Takauji (1305-1358).

When the Emperor Go-Daigo (1288-1339) fled to Mount Hiei (northeast of Kyoto), Chikamitsu remained at the capital, but being attacked by superior forces, he asked to surrender. Ashikaga Takauji mistrusting his intentions, sent Otomo Sadanori to negotiate with him. During the conference Chikamitsu attacked Sadanori, and killed him with one stroke. He then fell under the spears of the Ashikaga soldiers.

Yuki Akitomo (-1370)

Son of Chikatomo. He served the Ashikaga.

Together with Hatakeyama Takakuni, Akitomo fought Kitabataké Chikafusa (1293-1354), who was forced to escape to Yoshino (southern Yamato).

In 1350, when Ashikaga Tadayoshi (1306-1352) joined the Southern Dynasty, Akitomo intended to follow him, but Ashikaga Takauji (1305-1358) prevented him by threatening to confiscate his domain. He then joined him against Kitabataké Akinobu.

In 1369 Akitomo transferred his domain to his son Mitsutomo.

For two centuries, his descendants kept the fief of Shirakawa (Iwaki), until 1590, when Toyotomi Hideyoshi (1536-1598) dispossessed Yoshiaki.

Yuki Ujitomo (1398-1441)

Descendant of the senior branch. He inherited the fief of Yuki (Shimosa).

In 1440, after the failed rebellion of the 4th Kanto kubo "Kanto deputy Shogun" Ashikaga Mochiuji (1398-1439), Ujitomo led Mochiuji's sons Haruomaru and Yasuo-maru to his castle in Koga (Shimosa), but in 1441 Uesugi Kiyokata (-1442) came to besiege him, was defeated and killed, and his two wards were put to death.

Yuki Naritomo (1439-1462)

Son of Ujitomo. He succeeded when only 2 years old, whereupon he was taken by a faithful servant to Hitachi, where he was received as a guest by Sataké Yoshitoshi.

In 1454 the Ashikaga returned his domain in Shimosa. He was continually at war with the Uesugi.

Yuki Masatomo (1477-1545)

Grandson of Naritomo. He was obliged to fight his neighbors, the Utsunomiya, who sought to despoil him of his domain in Shimosa, but were repulsed.

Around 1525 Masatomo gave his domain to his son Masakatsu, and shaved his head, taking the name Kosho.

Yuki Masakatsu (1503-1559)

Son of Masatomo. Around 1525 he assumed family headship of their domain in Shimosa. He adopted his nephew Harutomo as son and heir.

Masakatsu was continually obliged to wage war against his vassals the Oda, the Tagaya, and others who attempted to become independent.

In 1556 Masakatsu completed the *Yuki-shi Shin Hatto* "Yuki-clan New Laws," 107 articles designed to regulate samurai conduct.

Yuki Harutomo (1533-1614)

Son of Oyama Takatomo. He was adopted by his uncle Masakatsu, and succeeded him in Shimosa. He continued the war against his neighbors. As he had no children, to retain the favor of Toyotomi Hideyoshi (1536-1598), he asked him to chose an heir. Hideyoshi selected Hideyasu, 2nd son of Tokugawa Ieyasu (1543-1616), who took the name of Yuki.

In 1590 Harutomo transferred the administration of his domain to Hideyasu.

When Hideyasu was transferred to Echizen, Harutomo accompanied him, retired to Katakatsu, and died there.

Yuki Hideyasu (1574-1607)

2nd son of Tokugawa Ieyasu (1543-1616). He was born Tokugawa Ogimaru, at Ofumi Village near Hamamatsu Castle (Totomi). His mother was Lady Oman, who was a servant of Lady Tsukiyama, Ieyasu's first wife. After Ieyasu impregnated Oman, he was fearful of Tsukiyama's wrath, so he sheltered her in the home of his retainer Honda Shigetsugu (1529-1596), where Ogimaru was born.

For some reason, the young Ogimaru was disliked by his father Tokugawa Ieyasu, and it was not until age 3 that he met his father, through a meeting arranged by his elder half-brother Matsu-

daira Nobuyasu (1559-1579). After the execution order from Oda Nobunaga (1534-1582) of Nobuyasu and his mother Lady Tsukiyama, Ogimaru was next in line to inherit the Tokugawa headship. He was instead sent to be adopted by Hashiba (later Toyotomi) Hideyoshi (1536-1598) as an hostage. Coming of age while with Hideyoshi, he took the name Hashiba Hideyasu, using a character from each of his fathers.

In 1587 Hideyasu took part in his 1st campaign in Toyotomi Hideyoshi's Kyushu Campaign, leading the assault on Buzen-Iwaishi Castle, and receiving honors for his distinction in the pacification of Hyuga.

In 1589 a son was born to Toyotomi Hideyoshi, and so in 1590 Hideyasu was given in adoption to Yuki Harutomo, whose niece he married, and succeeded to that clan's headship and the domain of Yuki (Shimosa -- 100,000 koku), and also became Mikawa no kami.

In 1590 Hideyasu took part in the Siege of Odawara (Sagami), and in the 1592 Invasion of Korea. His successes in these campaigns earned him the respect as an able field commander, despite his young age.

In 1601 Hideyasu was transferred from Shimosa to Fukui (Echizen -- 670,000 koku).

In 1604 Hideyasu took the surname Matsudaira. When he died, his eldest son Matsudaira Tadanao (1595-1650) succeeded him, and left the name Yuki to his 4th son Naomoto.

It is said that he had a twin brother who succeeded his mother's father as the priest of the Chiryu Shrine (Mikawa).

Samurai Cinema

Chanbara! "Sword Fighting"

Chanbara movies are excellent sources of ideas for samurai role-playing games. Also often spelled chambara, all films in this genré have samurai warriors and sword fighting, as well as an exotic, but usually historical, setting, much like the pseudo-European world of *Dungeons & Dragons*, albeit in feudal Japan. And most samurai films climax with a terrific sword fight at the end.

Chanbara is a subset of jidai-geki "Japanese period drama," which, like costume dramas, are often full of military regalia, fancy armor, and colorful kimono, and provide much insight into Japanese history and culture. Wikipedia claims, citing several sources, that *Star Wars* creator George Lucas devised the name Jedi from this term.

Chanbara movies are often compared to cowboy westerns, with similar themes of life & death, loyalty, honor, and duty; and where the line between good and evil are usually clear. Although samurai motion pictures have been around since the silent-movie era, the later films in the genré have been heavily influenced by Hollywood westerns, where the lone gunman is replaced by a wandering ronin with a sword for hire. The westerns in turn have likewise been inspired by samurai films such as *Seven Samurai* (1954) and *Yojimbo* (1961), which were remade respectively into *The Magnificent Seven* (1960) and *A Fistful of Dollars* (1964). Both samurai movies and Hollywood westerns feature one-on-one duels, skirmishes between a small band of armed men vs. an equal or larger foe, as well as large-scale battles between armies.

The scope of samurai cinema is actually wide enough that it can accommodate many other themes than just chanbara:

- Historical costume dramas (*Taira Clan Saga*)
- Psychological thrillers (*Gate of Hell*)
- Supernatural ghost stories (*Kuroneko, Aragami*)
- Mysteries (*Rashomon, Hanzo the Razor*)
- Science fiction (*G.I. Samurai*)
- Epic war stories (*Heaven and Earth, Samurai Banners*)
- Adventure (*The Hidden Fortress*)
- Shakespearean tragedy (*Ran, Throne of Blood*)
- Ninja spies (*Shinobi no mono, Samurai Spy*)
- Children stories (*Watari, Ninja Boy*)
- Comedy (*Samurai Saga*)
- Bloody teenage splatter movies (*Azumi*)
- Road pictures (*Bloody Spear on Mount Fuji, The Tale of Zatoichi*)
- Women fighters (*Crimson Bat*)
- Martial arts (*Festival of Swordsmen*)
- Social commentary (*Harakiri*)
- Male fantasy (*Hanzo the Razor*)
- Tearjerkers (*In Search of Mother*)
- Yakuza gangsters (*The Tale of Zatoichi*)
- Dark comedy (*Kill!*)
- Sex & violence exploitation films (*Quick-draw Okatsu, Hanzo the Razor*)
- Revenge (*Revenge, Chushingura*)
- Master swordsman (*Samurai Trilogy*)
- Romance (*The Samurai I Loved, Love and Honor*)
- Homosexuality (*Taboo*)
- Giant monsters (*Daimajin*)
- Fantasy (*The Great Bandit*)

Weapons of all types are portrayed: from the many varieties of swords and daggers, to bows and arrows, pole arms, spears, maces, trancheons, chain weapons, and even iron war fans. Unarmed combat is also depicted, along with deceptive ninja-style assassination techniques.

Samurai films are the among the most beautifully-photographed motion pictures in the world. Just about every shot is presented as a tightly-composed frame, and every scene is carefully choreographed and orchestrated. The quality of the background music however can run from being first-rate to deplorable, although the sound effects are usually just fine.

The caliber of subtitling can be spotty in the more obscure releases. When I first watched *Shinobi no mono* back in the 1960s, the word "ninja" never appeared in the subtitles although it was spoken in the dialog, and the word "occult" was substituted. This was presumably because the word "ninja" was not yet familiar to western audiences when the subtitles were originally written.

Characters in Chanbara

Samurai

The samurai are of course ubiquitous in chanbara. The warrior class included the Shogun, daimyo, roju "senior retainers," vassals, and ronin. The class also included their families, household attendants, and foot soldiers.

During the earlier part of the samurai era, class mobility was more fluid, and young men, usually of the peasant class, are depicted in cinema striving to become warriors. By the late 16th century however social classes were stratified and any movement between them was forbidden. Men of this period sometimes bemoaned that could not join a fight because they were mere peasants. Conversely, samurai occasionally complained that their responsibilities in society were onerous, or that it was "no fun" being a warrior during times of peace.

The way of the samurai is through death, and that is how they dealt with problems and obstacles on the silver screen. A daimyo coveting another's property would make war against him. A samurai who feels that he has been dishonored would challenge the offender to a swordfight. A corrupt official would be demanded that he commit seppuku. A vendetta would be settled by the killing of the perpetrator. To prevent dishonoring his family, a samurai would commit seppuku himself. Indeed, honorable death for a good cause is a prevalent theme in samurai films.

The Land of the Rising Sun was governed by the military class during the feudal era, and many samurai films are political in nature. They often involve corrupt government officials, bad policies, and poor ethics. In the movies, nefarious plots are often hatched by unscrupulous government officials. Samurai on film, and in literature, often had to choose between giri "duty" and ninjo "compassion." Bushido demanded absolute loyalty to one's lord, and many story plots revolved around whether to obey a superior's unjust command, or to defy the order, and perhaps commit seppuku in the end.

Ninja

The ninja were highly-trained spies and assassins, often hired by the samurai for clandestine activities that required the use of covert tactics.

Most ninja on film came from either Iga province or the nearby Koga region just to the north in Omi province. Whenever there was a conflict between two opposing sides, one side would hire one of the ninja groups and the other would hire the other group.

Magic is not often a component of samurai films, but ninjutsu is. Its magic-like skills include camouflage, explosives, smoke bombs, poison darts, etc. The ninja's legendary skills include flight (with or without the help of kites, birds, etc.), communicating with animals, control of weather, shapeshifting (especially into animals), teleportation, etc. How did they leap over the wall in a single bound? By pole-vaulting, of course.

Peasants

Peasants represent the oppressed class that celluloid samurai and ronin would come to rescue from their plight. In addition to farmers, they also included fishermen and hunters. The main agricultural crop was rice, but they also harvested commercial crops such as tea, indigo, tobacco, and cotton. Worms were also grown for silk.

Each farming village had a headman who was responsible for a variety of duties, including the collection of taxes, and was accountable to the local warlord.

When a daughter was sold into indentured servitude, often as prostitutes, it was usually by a poor farmer. Young peasant men would surreptitiously run off to towns to find a better life, although this was illegal from the end of the 16th century.

Yakuza

The yakuza represents the organized crime syndicate of Japan. They are known for their strict hierarchy and codes of conduct.

In Japanese cinema the yakuza are presented as organized gangs of delinquents and misfits involved in prostitution, gambling, loan sharking, protection, extortion, pornography, counterfeiting, drug trafficking, and other criminal activities.

Each yakuza group was headed by the oyabun "family boss," or "foster parent." The subordinates are called kobun "foster child" who owe allegiance to the oyabun to form a sworn brotherhood, and refer to each other as family members.

Lower-ranking members were often required to have permanent tattoos to show their loyalty, and to signify that membership is forever, and cannot be rescinded. Indeed many yakuza have full-body tattoos that takes year to complete to show their pride and dedication to the profession.

If a member commits a minor transgression, in the first instance, the tip of his little finger is severed as a form of penance or apology. Further infractions meant further severing of digits.

Although only the samurai were allowed to carry swords, on film yakuza members nominally carried one short sword.

WOMEN

Women appear in chanbara as mothers, wives, sisters, daughters, maids, attendants, concubines, geisha, prostitutes, nuns, etc. They usually play the part of a conspiring wife, a romantic interest, an innocent victim, or even a ghost. Those with martial arts skills are mostly samurai wives or ninja daughters.

In samurai flicks, women arguably have a bigger role in setting the course of the plot than they ever did in historical Japan. On the other hand, a lot more happen in the movies than they do in real life. This is likewise true in gaming, and female characters can add a lot of color to the plot; just keep in mind that historically women generally played a minor role in Japanese feudal society, and that you do not need to worry about giving them equal time just for the sake of political correctness.

TOWNSFOLK

- Craftsmen
  - Carpenters, sawyers, plasterers, masons, roofers
  - Tatami "straw mat" makers
  - Blacksmiths -- Swordmakers, armorers
  - Sword polishers
  - Bowyers and fletchers
  - Potters
  - Saké brewers
  - Weavers
  - Dyers
  - Umbrella makers
  - Sandle and clog makers
  - Candlemakers
  - Etc.
- Shopkeepers
  - Innkeepers -- Including cooks, maids, bath attendants
  - Sellers of rice, vegetables, fish, tofu, soy sauce, tea, saké, confectionary, kimono, ceramics, lacquerware, etc.
  - Eateries --Sushi restaurants, noodle shops, drinking establishments, etc.
  - Communal bathhouses
- Merchants -- They became ever richer and influential during the Edo Period (1603-1868).
  - Money lenders
  - Commodity brokers (rice, vegetables, fish, lumber, etc.)
  - Transporters, sailors, distributors
  - Porters, messengers
  - Etc.
- Intellectuals -- Confucianists, poets, calligraphers, tea masters, writers, artists, etc.
- Doctors, acupuncturists
- Police -- Non-samurai peacekeepers, guards, patrolmen
- Firemen -- Normally volunteers, they occasionally appear on film as gangs
- Geisha -- Personal entertainers highly-trained in the art of conversation. They were not considered prostitutes, but were often mistresses to rich patrons.
- Prostitutes -- Including courtesans at the licensed quarters, as well as streetwalkers at unlicensed areas
- Theater people -- Kabuki actors, puppeteers, playwrights, comics, dancers, singers, musicians, hucksters
- Sumo wrestlers
- Etc.

OTHERS

- Aristocrats -- Except for jidai-geki taking place during the per-samurai Heian Period (794-1185), nobles, including the Emperor, only appeared in the background as part of the scenery, and their involvement in movie plots was for the most part incidental, and rarely direct.
- Priests -- Monks and nuns. Buddhist temples and shinto shrines are often settings for festivals and samurai combat.
- Pilgrims
- Itinerant street performers -- Musicians, singers, dancers, animal trainers, acrobats, jugglers, clowns, storytellers, magicians
- Masseurs -- This was the only occupation normally available to blind people.
- Fortune tellers -- Diviners and mediums
- Foreigners -- They were important in the latter half of the 16th century when guns and other western technology were introduced and missionaries found some success. During the Edo Period (1603-1868) however foreigners and foreign trade was abolished, save for an occasional Dutch trader based in Nagasaki. In the Bakumatsu "Late Tokugawa" Period (1853-1867) foreign influence dominated Japanese politics when foreign powers demanded access to Japanese ports for trade and detente.
- Mendicants -- In addition to common street beggars, they include the komuso "mendicant Zen Buddhist monks" who wore straw baskets in their heads to manifest the absence of ego. They often played the shakuhachi "Japanese flute" for alms as a meditative practice to attain enlightenment. In film, samurai, ronin, ninja, and women would occasionally disguised themselves as komuso.
- Etc.

Recommendations for Gamers

Although there are many worthy samurai-themed movies that deserve viewing, including masterpieces of world cinema such as *Rashomon* and *Harakiri*, the following recommendations are for films that are of particular interest to gamers. The following list can be much longer, but only those movies that are commercially available in the West are included. As of this writing, all are available on DVD with English sub-titles, except *Heaven and Earth*, which is only procurable in VHS.

Gamers may dismiss the lone-ronin films as unsuitable for gaming, as they usually have only one protagonist-hero, and role-playing games invariably involve a party of several player-characters. You can however easily craft scenarios based on the plot of films of this type by simply giving the ronin an entourage of supporting characters to help him on his quest. In the *Samurai Trilogy*, when you have the master swordsman Musashi go on his musha-shugyo, a pilgrimage to hone his martial arts skills and to discover the true meaning of Bushido, you can have several disciples accompanying him in his travels. In *Sanjuro*, you can have the young samurai as the player-characters, and the ronin as a non-player character who comes to their aid.

For Role-Playing

The best period for role-playing a small party of samurai player-characters is without a doubt the Edo Period (1603-1868). The fact that most samurai films take place in this era is no accident. It was a time of peace and many unemployed samurai traveled the country as ronin looking for work and often causing troubles. The road network was complete, well-maintained, and serviced. Travel restrictions were liberalized for religious pilgrims and merchants, offering many opportunities for encountering people of all social classes and occupations. Bushido was codified in the 17th century and the conflict between giri "duty," or "social obligation," and ninjo "compassion" was obsessively debated.

Towards the end of the samurai era, after a long period of peace, questions arose as to the necessity of the class as a whole and how to deal with the ever-increasing incursions by foreign powers into the country they ruled. This is a great time for role-playing: After two-and-a-half centuries, the daimyo around the country began to challenge the rule of the Tokugawa Shogunate. A new era of samurai can be hypothesized without the country reverting to Imperial rule. Who will be the new Shogun? How will he deal with the foreigners?

- *The Hidden Fortress* (1958) Sengoku
- *Seven Samurai* (1954) Sengoku
- *Shinobi no mono* (1962) Sengoku
- *Hanzo the Razor: Sword of Justice* (1972) Edo
- *Samurai Trilogy* (1954-1956) Edo
- *Samurai Fiction* (1998) Edo
- *Sanjuro* (1962) Edo
- *13 Assassins* (2010) Edo
- *Chushingura* (1962) Genroku
- *Samurai Assassin* (1965) Bakumatsu
- *Daimajin* (1966) Non-specific

For Miniatures

For miniatures gaming, films taking place in the Sengoku "Warring States" Period (1467-1573), the Azuchi-Momoyama Period (1573-1603), and the Bakumatsu "Late Tokugawa" Period (1853-1867) offer the most examples of large armies in action.

Note that three of the movies on the recommended list below are not historical and have fictional, made-up armor, uniforms, and regalia: *Ran*, *Shogun*, and *The Last Samurai*.

- *Heaven and Earth* (1990) Sengoku
- *Ran* (1985) Sengoku
- *Samurai Banners* (1969) Sengoku
- *Kagemusha* (1980) Momoyama
- *Shogun* (1980) Edo
- *Chushingura* (1962) Genroku
- *The Last Samurai* (2003) Bakumatsu
- *Shinsengumi* (1969) Bakumatsu

Notes

The following list, for gaming purposes, is in chronological order based on the film's historical time period. Within each period, they are in alphabetical order by the title most often used for marketing in the U.S.

Movie ratings are as of this writing. They are subject to change as more people chime in with their appraisals.

All samurai-era names are in Japanese order with family name first. Names of modern Japanese are in Western order, as is customary in English text.

I should confess that I have not seen many of the following movies in decades, nor have I have personally watched every single movie listed. Some of the recommendations and plot descriptions are from other sources. Please see the bibliography.

There are literally thousands of samurai movies and TV shows. The following is just the tip of the iceberg. As the genré is seemingly gathering renewed interest, new chanbara will appear in the future, and hopefully more DVDs of older films will be made available to western audiences.

Heian "Aristocratic" Period (794-1185)

Gate of Hell (Jigokumon)

1953 Daiei, 86 minutes, color

- **Director:** Teinosuké Kinugasa
- **Cast:** Kazuo Hasegawa, Machiko Kyo, Isao Yamagata, et al
- **Recommendation:** Of historical background interest. A psychological thriller.
- **Ratings:** AllMovie 4/5, Amazon.com 4/5, IMDb 7.3/10, Rotten Tomatoes --/69%

In 1159, when samurai Endo Morito defends his lord from a coup attempt in the Imperial capital of Kyoto, he is to be rewarded with anything he desires. He asks to marry Lady Kesa, not realizing that she is already wed to Watanabé Wataru, one of the ruling family's lieges. Even after finding out, Morito clings to his wish, challenging the husband to release her, but Lady Kesa unshakably stays faithful, and Morito's stubborn obsession eventually leads to tragedy.

Awards: Cannes Film Festival (1954), Palme d'Or. New York Film Critics Circle Award, Best Foreign Language Film. 27th Academy Awards (1954), Best Costume Design, Best Foreign Language Film (honorary).

DVD: Region 1 (USA) version not commercially available

VHS: Home Vision Entertainment (2000)

Kuroneko "Black Cat" (Yabu no naka no kuroneko "Black Cat from the Grove")

1968 Toho, 99 minutes, b&w

- **Director:** Kaneto Shindo
- **Cast:** Nobuko Otowa, Kiwako Taichi, Kichiémon Nakamura, Kei Sato, et al
- **Recommendation:** Atmospheric and violent samurai ghost story, surprisingly erotic.
- **Ratings:** AllMovie 3/5, Amazon.com 4.7/5, IMDb 7.6/10, Netflix 4.1/5, Rotten Tomatoes 92%/87%

In the 10th century, Yoné and Shigé, mother and daughter, are raped and murdered by arrogant mercenaries at their farm just outside of Kyoto, south of the Rashomon "main city gate." Three years later their onryo "vengeful ghosts" begin to lure samurai to their haunted home and kill them. The Emperor himself orders general Minamoto Raiko (949-1021) to vanquish the menace. He sends the wild and fierce young warrior Gintoki, who discovers in an eerie, beautiful scene that the specters are his own mother and wife. After spiritual purification, he meets the demons in a thrilling fight.

DVD: Eureka Video (non-USA PAL region 2 version)

Rashomon

1950 Daiei, 88 minutes, b&w

- **Director:** Akira Kurosawa
- **Cast:** Toshiro Mifuné, Masayuki Mori, Machiko Mori, Takashi Shimura, et al
- **Recommendation:** Not of historical interest. No major samurai combat. Great plot. A masterpiece of world cinema, one of the finest films ever made.
- **Ratings:** AllMovie 5/5, Amazon.com 4.5/5, IMDb 8.5/10, Netflix 3.8/5, Rotten Tomatoes 100%/93%

A story of rape and murder told from wildly different, conflicting, and self-serving points of view.

The director said this of *Rashomon*: "Human beings are unable to be honest with themselves about themselves. They cannot talk about themselves without embellishing. This script portrays such human beings -- the kind who cannot survive without lies to make them feel they are better people than they really are." (Akira Kurosawa, *Something Like an Autobiography*)

Rashomon "main city gate" is the name of the southern gate built in ancient Nara and Kyoto.

Awards: National Board of Review (1951), Best Director, Best Foreign Film. Venice International Film Festival (1951), Lion of San Marco for Best Film. 24th Academy Awards (1952), Honorary Academy Award.

DVD: Criterion (2002), Essential Art House (2008)

Taira Clan Saga (Shin Heiké monogatari "New tales of the Taira Clan")

1955 Daiei, 108 minutes color

- **Director:** Kenji Mizoguchi
- **Cast:** Raizo Ichikawa, Ichijiro Oya, Michiyo Koguré, Tatsuya Ishiguro, et al

- **Recommendation:** Epic historical drama.
- **Ratings:** AllMovie 3/5, Amazon.com 3/5, IMDb 7.4/10, Rotten Tomatoes --/68%

In 1137 cloistered Emperor Toba (1103-1156) attempts to wrest control of the government from the Fujiwara Regents. He enlists the aid of Taira Tadamori (1096-1153) and his son Kiyomori (1118-1181), which leads to the beginning of samurai rule in Japan.

Based on the novel by Eiji Yoshikawa (1892-1962).

DVD: NYFA (2007)

SENGOKU "WARRING STATES" PERIOD (1467-1573)

G.I. Samurai (aka *Time Slip*) (*Sengoku jieitai*)

1979 Toho/Kadokawa/Toei, 139 minutes, color

- **Director:** Kosei Saito
- **Cast:** Sonny Chiba, Jun Eto, Toshitaka Ito, Haruki Kadokawa, et al
- **Recommendation:** Rousing action-adventure. Frenetic battle scenes. Appearances by many historical characters. Impressive costumes and samurai regalia. Cheesy special effects. Interesting theories about time travel.
- **Ratings:** AllMovie 2.5/5, Amazon.com 3.3/5, IMDb 6.8/10, Netflix 2.6/5, Rotten Tomatoes --/51%

Twenty-one members of modern-day Japanese Self-Defense Force suddenly find themselves centuries in the past, and under attack by samurai forces. Their leader Lieutenant Yoshiaki Iba befriends and allies with Nagao Kagetora (later Uesugi Kenshin, 1530-1578) to fight Takeda Shingen (1521-1573).

Despite their modern armament, including a tank, an APV, a jeep, a truck, and a helicopter, Yoshiaki and his men are eventually overwhelmed and outmaneuvered by Shingen's men.

DVD: Navarre (2008)

Heaven and Earth (*Ten to chi to*)

1990 Haruki Kadokawa Films, 104 minutes, rated PG-13, color

- **Director:** Haruki Kadokawa
- **Cast:** Takaaki Enoki, Masahiko Tsugawa, Tsunehiro Watasé, Atsuko Asano, et al
- **Recommendation:** Outstanding full-scale battle scenes. Beautifully photographed.
- **Ratings:** AllMovie 3/5, Amazon.com 4.6/5, IMDb 6.8/10, Rotten Tomatoes --/88%

Uesugi Kenshin (1530-1578) defends his province of Echigo against Takeda Shingen (1521-1573) of Kai, culminating in 1561 at the 4th Battle of Kawanaka-jima (Shinano).

DVD: Region 1 (USA) version not commercially available

VHS: Lion's Gate (1992)

The Hidden Fortress (*Kakushi toridé no san-akunin* "Three Villains of the Hidden Fortress")

1958 Toho, 139 minutes, b&w

- **Director:** Akira Kurosawa
- **Cast:** Toshiro Mifuné, Minoru Chiaki, Kamatari Fujiwara, Misa Uehara, et al
- **Recommendation:** Great plot! Very enjoyable adventure film.
- **Ratings:** AllMovie 4.5/5, Amazon.com 4.5/5, IMDb 8.0/10, Netflix 3.9/5, Rotten Tomatoes 100%/90%

In Kyushu, two peasants, Tahei and Matashichi, meet and travel with General Rokurota Makabé, who is secretly escorting Princess Yuki of Akizuki Castle to safety in neighboring Hayakawa territory to escape the enemy Yamana forces.

Peasant revolt, spear duel, fire festival, mounted samurai in sword combat, etc.

George Lucas has acknowledged the influence of *The Hidden Fortress* on his *Star Wars Episode IV: A New Hope* (1977).

Awards: 9th Berlin International Film Festival (1959), Silver Bear for Best Director

DVD: Criterion (2001), Essential Art House (2009)

Ran "Chaos"

1985 Toho, 162 minutes, rated R, color

- **Director:** Akira Kurosawa
- **Cast:** Tatsuya Nakadai, Akira Terao, Jinpachi Nezu, Daisuké Ryu, et al
- **Recommendation:** Ahistorical period piece. Beautifully filmed epic battles.
- **Ratings:** AllMovie 5/5, Amazon.com 4.3/5, IMDb 8.3/10, Netflix 3.9/5, Rotten Tomatoes 96%/94%

Lord Ichimonji Hidetora decides to retire and give control of his domain to his three sons. The eldest, Taro, is given leadership of the clan and receives the prestigious 1st Castle, while his brothers Jiro and Saburo receive the 2nd and 3rd Castles respectively. The sons battle each other for total control that leads to a tragic end.

Based partly on the life of legendary warlord Mori Motonari (1497-1571) and the tragic play *King Lear* by William Shakespeare (1564-1616).

Awards: 58th Academy Awards (1986), Best Costume Design (Emi Wada). 40th British Academy Film Awards (1986), Best Foreign Language Film, Best Makeup Artist (team of four recipients).

DVD: Criterion (2005)

Blu-ray: Lions Gate (2010)

Rise Against the Sword (*Abaré Goémon*)

1966 Toho, 101 minutes, b&w

- **Director:** Hiroshi Inagaki
- **Cast:** Toshiro Mifuné, Nobuko Otowa, Makoto Sato, Ryo Tamura, et al
- **Recommendation:** Ahistorical sieges, massacres, and full-scale battles. Farmers against the samurai.
- **Ratings:** AllMovie 2.5/5, IMDb 6.8/10

Abaré Goémon raises an army of militant farmers in Shinobu village to fight mercenary samurai. When he succeeds, local lord Asakura attempts to recruit him to fight in a conflict with the nearby Kaga clan of Enjo Castle.

DVD: Region 1 (USA) version not commercially available

Samurai Banners (Furin kazan "Wind, forest, fire, mountain")

1969 Toho, 165 minutes, color

- **Director:** Hiroshi Inagaki
- **Cast:** Toshiro Mifuné, Kinnosuké Nakamura, Yoshiko Sakuma, Kan'émon Nakamura, et al
- **Recommendation:** Spectacular battlefield regalia with immaculate costuming. A grand, larger-than-life, historical samurai epic with a cast of thousands. Must see!
- **Ratings:** AllMovie 3/5, Amazon.com 3.5/5, IMDb 6.9/10, Netflix 3.5/5, Rotten Tomatoes --/72%

Ruthless Yamamoto Kansuké (1501-1561) uses cunning and guile to become a general and strategist for Takeda Shingen (1521-1573). He arranges for the death of Suwa Yorishigé (1516-1542), lord of Kuwabara Castle (Shinano), whose daughter Yu becomes a reluctant concubine to Shingen. Later, in 1561 at the 4th Battle of Kawanaka-jima (Shinano), Shingen battles Uesugi Kenshin (1530-1578).

In 2007 NHK Taiga Drama aired a 50-episode version of the story based on *Furin kazan*, a novel by Yasushi Inoué (1907-1991).

DVD: AnimEigo (2005)

Seven Samurai (Shichinin no samurai)

1954 Toho, 207 minutes, b&w

- **Director:** Akira Kurosawa
- **Cast:** Takashi Shimura, Toshiro Mifuné, Yoshio Inaba, et al
- **Recommendation:** Great insight into the relationship between the samurai and the farmer classes. Excellent characterizations. Lots of action. An undisputed classic.
- **Ratings:** AllMovie 5/5, Amazon.com 4.7/5, IMDb 8.8/10, Netflix 4.1/5, Rotten Tomatoes 100%/96%

Village farmers recruit seven ronin to combat bandits who will return after the harvest to steal their crops.

Later remade into the Hollywood western *The Magnificent Seven* (1960).

Awards: Venice Film Festival (1954), Silver Lion.

DVD: Criterion (2006)
Blu-ray: Criterion Collection (2010)

Shinobi no mono "Covert agent" (Band of Assassins)

1962 Daiei, 104 minutes, b&w

- **Director:** Satsuo Yamamoto
- **Cast:** Raizo Ichikawa, Yunosuké Ito, Tomisaburo Wakayama, Shiho Fujimura, et al
- **Recommendation:** Exciting seminal ninja film based on real-life historical figures and events. Convoluted plot, but many displays of realistic ninja techniques. Highly recommended.
- **Ratings:** Amazon.com 3.8/5, IMDb 7/10, Netflix 3.4/5, Rotten Tomatoes --/79%

Ishikawa Goémon (1558-1594) is a clerk for the Iga ninja clan led by Momochi Sandayu, rival of Fujibayashi Nagato, leader of the other Iga ninja clan. He is tasked to go to Kyoto, and then to Azuchi Castle (Omi), to kill Oda Nobunaga (1534-1582), a notorious enemy of the ninja.

Seven sequels were released between 1962 and 1966.

DVD: AnimEigo (2007)

Throne of Blood (Kumonosu-jo "Cobweb Castle")

1957 Toho, 110 minutes, b&w

- **Director:** Akira Kurosawa
- **Cast:** Toshiro Mifuné, Isuzu Yamada, Minoru Chiaki, et al

- **Recommendation:** Features samurai armies, horsemen, forts, and lots of arrows. Tragic story of ambition.
- **Ratings:** AllMovie 4.5/5, Amazon.com 4.2/5, IMDb 8.1/10, Netflix 3.9/5, Rotten Tomatoes 97%/93%

General Washizu Taketori and his ruthless wife Lady Asaji plot their rise to power at their North Mansion on the slope of Mount Fuji. Taketori assassinates Lord Tsuzuki, whom he serves, and takes Kumonosu-jo "Cobweb Castle." Taketori's friend and fellow general Miki Yoshiaki arrives and is murdered, but the latter's son escapes and later returns to take the castle.

Based on the play *The Tragedy of Macbeth* by William Shakespeare (-1616), transposing the plot to feudal Japan.

DVD: Criterion (2003), Essential Art House (2009)

Watari, Ninja Boy (Daininjutsu eiga Watari)

1966 Toei, 86 minutes, color

- **Director:** Sadao Fuadoko
- **Cast:** Yoshinobu Kaneko, Ryutaro Otomo, Chiyoko Honma, Fuyukichi Maki, et al
- **Recommendation:** Complicated plot. Cartoonish non-stop ninja action with good old-school special effects and stunts. Contains many scenes of both villains and children being killed. Marketed to Japanese children, who culturally accept death as a part of life, but may not be appropriate for young non-Japanese audiences.
- **Ratings:** IMDb 7.8/10

In 16th-century Iga province, the Momochi and the Fujibayashi clans are training children in mountain camps to fill the ranks in their bitter feud. Features shuriken, smoke bombs, transfigurations, body separation, wicked ninja Dojun, multi-colored ninja monsters, the villain Joko, etc.

Adapted from a manga series by Sanpei Shirato (1932-). A Taiwanese sequel called *The Magic Sword of Watari* was later released.

DVD: Region 1 (USA) version not commercially available

Warring Clans (Sengoku yaro "Sengoku rascal")

1963 Toho, 98 minutes, b&w

- **Director:** Kihachi Okamoto
- **Cast:** Yuzo Kayama, Makoto Sato, Ichiro Nakaya, Jun Tazaki, et al
- **Recommendation:** Entertaining black comedy featuring ninja. Exciting swordfights.
- **Ratings:** AllMovie 2.5/5, IMDb 6.7/10

Ninja Oichi Kittan and Doko Harima meet the future Toyotomi Hideyoshi (1536-1598) who is transporting rifles for Oda Nobunaga (1534-1582).

DVD: Region 1 (USA) version not commercially available

AZUCHI-MOMOYAMA PERIOD (1573-1603)

Castle of Owls (Ninja hicho fukuro no shiro)

1963 Toei, 91 minutes, color

- **Director:** Eiichi Kudo
- **Cast:** Ryutaro Otomo, Minoru Oki, Chiyoko Honma, Choichiro Kawarazaki, et al
- **Recommendation:** Realistic ninja action.
- **Ratings:** IMDb 7.2/10

Toyotomi Hideyoshi (1536-1598) has conquered Japan and is the target of assassination by the Iga ninja Tsuzura Juzo.

Based on the 1959 award-winning ninja story by Ryotaro Shiba (1923-1996).

A remake, *Owl's Castle*, directed by Masahiro Shinoda, was released in 1999.

DVD: Region 1 (USA) version not commercially available

The Conspirator (Hangyakuji)

1961 Toei, 110 minutes, color

- **Director:** Daisuké Ito
- **Cast:** Kinnosuké Nakamura, Haruko Sugimura, Kaneko Iwasaki, Chiyonosuké Azuma, et al
- **Recommendation:** High production values. Good fictionalized retelling of a tragic historical event.

Story of Tokugawa Nobuyasu (1559-1579), 1st son of future Shogun Ieyasu (1543-1616) and Lady Tsukiyama, the niece of Imagawa Yoshimoto (1519-1560). Although he was married to the daughter of Oda Nobunaga (1534-1582), Tokuhimé (1559-1636), Nobunaga suspects Nobuyasu of conspiring with Takeda Katsuyori (1546-1582), and orders Ieyasu to have his son commit seppuku.

DVD: Region 1 (USA) version not commercially available

Kagemusha "Shadow Warrior"

1980 Toho/20th Century Fox, 179 minutes, rated PG, color

- **Director:** Akira Kurosawa
- **Cast:** Tatsuya Nakadai, Tsutomu Yamazaki, Daisuké Ryu, et al
- **Recommendation:** Fictionalized account of events following the death of Takeda Shingen. Sprawling epic. A classic.
- **Ratings:** AllMovie 4.5/5, Amazon.com 4.5/5, IMDb 7.9/10, Netflix 3.8/5, Rotten Tomatoes 84%/92%

When Takeda Shingen (1521-1573) is shot by a sniper, a body double, found by Shingen's brother Nobukado (1529-1582), is used to hide his death. Shingen's son Katsuyori (1546-1582) eventually takes over leadership of the clan, and is defeated by Oda Nobunaga (1534-1582) and Tokugawa Ieyasu (1543-1616) at the 1575 Battle of Nagashino (Mikawa).

Awards: Cannes Film Festival (1980), Palme d'Or.

DVD: Criterion (2005)

Blu-ray: Criterion (2009)

Rikyu

1989 Shochiku, 135 minutes, color

- **Director:** Hiroshi Teshigahara
- **Cast:** Rentaro Mikuni, Tsutomu Yamazaki, Yasosuké Bando, Hisashi Igawa, et al
- **Recommendation:** Story of the historical figure who made the preparation and serving of tea into a profoundly Japanese art. Insight into an important part of samurai culture beautifully presented.
- **Ratings:** AllMovie 4/5, Amazon.com 3.4/5, IMDb 6.9/10, Netflix 3/5, Rotten Tomatoes --/76%

Story of the real-life tea master Sen no Rikyu (1522-1591), who was a confidant of Toyotomi Hideyoshi (1536-1598). When Rikyu innocuously expresses misgiving about Hideyoshi's plans to conquer Korea and China, he is calumniated by the scheming Lord Mitsunari.

DVD: Sling Shot (2000)

Samurai Saga (aka Life of a Swordsman) (Aru kengo no shogai)

1959 Toho, 111 minutes, color

- **Director:** Hiroshi Inagaki
- **Cast:** Toshiro Mifuné, Yoko Tsukasa, Akira Takarada, Akihiko Hirata, et al
- **Recommendation:** Historical background. Swordfight at a Kabuki theater. Good adaptation of a tragic love story. Many memorable images.
- **Ratings:** AllMovie 2.5/5, IMDb 6.9/10, Rotten Tomatoes --/74%

In 1599 poet and swordsman Komaki Heihachi, a retainer of the Ishida clan with a hideously large nose, is in love with Lady Ochiyo, who has eyes for the

Samurai Movies – Tokugawa Period

handsome young samurai Karibé Jurota. Heihachi ends up writing sweet nothings for tongue-tied Jurota to help him woo Ochiyo for the sake of her own happiness.

At the 1600 Battle of Sekigahara (Omi) both fight on the losing side, but narrowly escape. Jurota commits suicide so Heihachi can make it back to Ochiyo, who then becomes a nun. Ten years later Heihachi is found and ambushed by Tokugawa forces, but before he dies, he visits Ochiyo one last time.

Based on the play *Cyrano de Bergerac* (1897) by Edmond Rostand (1868-1918).

DVD: Region 1 (USA) version not commercially available

Shogun's Ninja (Ninja bugeicho Momochi Sandayu)

1980 Toei, 115 minutes, rated R, color, dubbed in English (acceptable)

- **Director:** Norifumi Suzuki
- **Cast:** Hiroyuki Sanada, Sonny Chiba, Yuki Ninagawa, Isao Natsuyagi, et al
- **Recommendation:** Watch if you've run out of anything else to see; it's not half-bad.
- **Ratings:** AllMovie 1.5/5, Amazon.com 3.7/5, IMDb 6.1/10, Netflix 3/5, Rotten Tomatoes --/62%

In 1581 the legendary Iga ninja leader Momochi Sandayu falls victim to an evil scheme hatched by the Koga ninja leader Shiranui Shogen who is secretly working for Hashiba (later Toyotomi) Hideyoshi (1536-1598). Sandayu's young son Takamaru witnesses the murder of both his parents before being whisked off by an old family servant to China, where he is trained in the martial arts.

Takamaru returns to Japan all grown up, which is duly noted by Tokugawa master spy Hattori Hanzo (1541-1596).

Takamaru takes up with his old Iga clansmen who have been collectively thieving in the guise of the famous bandit Goémon Ishikawa (-1594), and declares the Momochi clan restored and vows revenge against Shogen and Hideyoshi.

Female seppuku. Town scenes. Castle scenes. Banners. Wanton slaughter of villagers, including women and children. Ninjutsu. Ninja action. Public execution by boiling alive. Martial arts.

Decent sound effects. Horrible music.

DVD: Vintage Home Entertainment (2003)

Taikoki: The Story of Hideyoshi

1987 TBS TV, 4 hours, color

- **Director:** Kihachi Okamoto
- **Cast:** Kyohei Shibata, Horoki Matsukata, Sonny Chiba, et al
- **Recommendation:** Sprawling historical TV drama.

TV story of Toyotomi Hideyoshi (1536-1598). Among the historical figures appearing are Oda Nobunaga (1534-1582), Akechi Mitsuhidé (1528-1582), Takeda Shingen (1521-1573), and Tokugawa Ieyasu (1543-1616). Historical events include the 1567 Battle of Inaba-yama (Mino), the 1570 Battle of Anegawa (Omi), the 1582 Battle of Yamazaki, and the two unsuccessful Invasions of Korea (1592-1598).

DVD: Region 1 (USA) version not commercially available

Torawakamaru, the Koga Ninja (Ninjutsu gozen-jiai)

1957 Toei, 63 minutes, b&w

- **Director:** Tadashi Sawashima
- **Cast:** Sentaro Fushima, Koinosuké Onoé, Chié Ueki, et al
- **Recommendation:** Arguably one of the greatest ninja films ever made.
- **Ratings:** IMDb 5.6

Tokugawa Ieyasu (1543-1616) orders Iga ninja Momochi Sandayu and his disciple Ishikawa Goémon (-1594) to assassinate Toyotomi Hideyoshi (1536-1598), and steal blueprints to a hidden fortress within Osaka Castle. Hideyoshi is protected by Koga ninja Tozawa Torawakamaru, and Ieyasu's plan is foiled. Frustrated, Ieyasu concocts a plot to pit the two ninja clans against each other.

DVD: Region 1 (USA) version not commercially available

Edo "Tokugawa" Period (1603-1868)

Agent Shiranui (aka Secrets of a Court Masseur) (Shiranui kengyo)

1960 Daiei, 91 minutes, b&w

- **Director:** Kazuo Mori
- **Cast:** Shintaro Katsu, Tamao Nakamura, Fujio Suga, Toru Abé, et al
- **Recommendation:** More yakuza than samurai. Edo underworld setting.
- **Ratings:** IMDb 7.6/10

Evil Shichinosuké was born blind, and eventually becomes a masseur named Suginoichi, who is sent on a errand to Kawasaki. Along the way he kills a man for his money, a deed witnessed by Edo thief Kurakichi, with whom Suginoichi splits the money to keep him quiet. The two end up working for Kurakichi's boss, Tobaya Tanji. Later, Suginoichi attains the coveted post of kengyo "temple administrator," the highest position a blind person in the Shiranui area can attain in feudal Japan.

Based on a kabuki play by Nobuo Uno (1904-1991).

DVD: Region 1 (USA) version not commercially available

Samurai Movies – Edo Period

Aragami

2003 Micott, 80 minutes, color

- **Director:** Ryuhei Kitamura
- **Cast:** Takao Osawa, Masaya Kato, Kanaé Uotani
- **Recommendation:** Supernatural samurai story. Suspenseful and creepy. Tight script. Good climatic swordfight.
- **Ratings:** AllMovie 3/5, Amazon.com 4.5/5, IMDb 6.7/10, Netflix 3.2/5, Rotten Tomatoes --/70%

Two seriously-wounded samurai take refuge from a storm at an isolated mountain temple, the home of a swordsman and a mysterious young woman. The next morning one of the samurai awakes to find not only his comrade dead, but that his own wounds have miraculously healed. He discovers that he was fed the liver of the dead samurai by the swordsman and is now nearly immortal. The swordsman reveals that he is in fact the legendary Miyamoto Musashi (1584-1645) and was never defeated in battle. Musashi is tired to living and wants to die in a duel.

DVD: Tokyo Shock (2004)

Azumi

2003 Toho, 128 minutes, rated R, color

- **Director:** Ryuhei Kitamura
- **Cast:** Aya Ueto, Shun Oguri, Hiroki Narimiya, Kenji Kohashi, et al
- **Recommendation:** Virtually non-stop, over-the-top action. Lots of gruesome bloody gore and exquisitely choreographed violence.
- **Ratings:** AllMovie 3.5/5, Amazon.com 4.3/5, IMDb 7/10, Netflix 3.7/5, Rotten Tomatoes 47%/81%

Orphan Azumi and nine other children are trained to become an assassin by Obata Gensai. When the group comes of age, they are told to pair up with whomever they feel the closest, and then are ordered to kill their partner in order to weed out those who are too weak to fulfill their life's mission. Azumi and the four other survivors are then sent out to assassinate all the warlords that oppose the new Shogun Tokugawa Ieyasu (1543-1616).

Based on the award-winning manga series by Yu Koyama (1948-). A sequel, *Azumi 2*, was released in 2005.

DVD: AsiaVision (2006)

Bandits vs. Samurai Squadron (*Kumokiri Nizaémon*)

1978 Shochiku, 163 minutes, color

- **Director:** Hideo Gosha
- **Cast:** Tatsuya Nakadai, Shima Iwashita, Somegoro Ichikawa, Tetsuro Tanba, et al
- **Recommendation:** Labyrinthine plot with numerous characters. A fusion of the yakuza and samurai genres. Considered a flawed masterpiece, a classic worth seeing.
- **Ratings:** Amazon.com 4.5/5, IMDb 6.8/10, Netflix 2.7/5, Rotten Tomatoes --/73%

In 1722 Fukagawa district of Edo, enigmatic master-thief Kumokiri Nakaémon tries to pull off an elaborate con while trying to outsmart the double-crossing hatamoto Abé Shikibu, the Shogunate's chief of arson and theft investigation, who realizes that in order to catch the thief, he will have to engage in some shady dealings of his own.

Based on a novel by Shotaro Ikenami (1923-1990).

DVD: Panorama Entertainment (2008)

The Betrayal (aka *Great Slaughter & the Serpent*) (*Daisatsujin orochi*)

1966 Daiei, 87 minutes, b&w

- **Director:** Tokuzo Tanaka
- **Cast:** Raizo Ichikawa, Kaoru Yachigusa, Shiho Fujimura, Ichiro Nakaya, et al
- **Recommendation:** Tragic tale of a samurai's fall from retainer to ronin to fugitive. Features probably the longest sword fighting sequence in chanbara history that lasts almost half the movie. Rivers of blood and mountains of corpses.
- **Ratings:** IMDb 7.2/10

An Iwashiro samurai challenges the Minazuki clan to a sword duel, but its swordmaster Issaka Yaichiro is currently away. On his way home, the samurai is killed by two members of the Minazuki, and the Iwashiro clan demands the perpetrator to be arrested and punished. Naive samurai Kobusé Takuma is pressured by his beautiful fiancé's father to take the blame and disappear for a year while he figures out a solution. He is betrayed, however, and is forced to battle single-handedly the police, the Iwashiro samurai, and his own clansmen.

DVD: Region 1 (USA) version not commercially available

A Bloody Spear on Mount Fuji (*Chiyari Fuji*)

1955 Toei, 94 minutes, b&w

- **Director:** Tomu Uchida
- **Cast:** Chiezo Kataoka, Teruo Shimada, Daisuké Kato, Motoharu Ueki, et al
- **Recommendation:** A samurai road film with many scenes inside town inns. Entertaining spear fighting. At first humorous, the second half turns serious and tragic in tone. Considered a minor classic.
- **Ratings:** IMDb 7.4/10, Rotten Tomatoes --/80%

Young samurai Sakawa Shojuro travels on the Tokaido to Edo with his two servants, Genta and spear-carrier Gonpachi, who were told by Shojuro's mother to prevent him from drinking. Along the way they meet street performer Osumi and her cherubic daughter Okin, precocious orphan-boy Jiro, highway cop Denji who is searching for the notorious thief Rokuémon, old Yomosaku who is selling his daughter Otané into prostitution, a blind masseur, among others.

DVD: Region 1 (USA) version not commercially available

Buraikan

1970 Toho, 104 minutes, color

- **Director:** Masahiro Shinoda
- **Cast:** Tatsuya Nakadai, Shima Iwashita, Shoichi Ozawa, Tetsuro Tanba, et al

- **Recommendation:** Sexy and suspenseful. Funny, complex, well-developed characters.
- **Ratings:** AllMovie 3/5, IMDb 6.7/10, Rotten Tomatoes --/100%

In 1842 chief roju "senior councilor" Mizuno Tadakuni (1794-1851), daimyo of Hamamatsu (Totomi -- 70,000 koku), instituted the Tenpo Reform which, among other things, banned most forms of entertainment and displays of wealth.

The story concerns several characters living in a red light district of Edo who become involved with a band of rebellious underground actors. They include the infamous fugitive Buraikan cleverly disguised as the monk Kochiyama Soshun, shiftless Kabuki performer and lazy fortune teller Kataoka Naojiro, and Ushimatsu who had just left his family.

DVD: Region 1 (USA) version not commercially available

The Ceiling at Utsunomiya Castle (aka *Ghost of Hanging in Utsunomiya*) (*Kaii Utsunomiya tsuri-tenjo*)

1956 Shin Toho, 80 minutes, b&w

- **Director:** Nobuo Nakagawa
- **Cast:** Ryuzaburo Ogasawara, Tetsuro Tanba, Masao Mishima, Akemi Tsukushi, et al
- **Recommendation:** Quaint historical film of political intrigue with supernatural elements.
- **Ratings:** IMDb 8/10

At Utsunomiya Castle (Shimotsuké) karo "chief vassal" Kawamura and his cohort, cruel merchant Kagiya, set up an elaborate trap to kill the 3rd Tokugawa Shogun Iemitsu (1604-1651) when he comes visiting on his way to the Toshogu Shrine in Nikko. Upon completion of the trap, the carpenters are poisoned, and one of them, Toémon, returns as a vengeful ghost. When ronin Ryutaro arrives, he starts asking asking a lot of questions and getting into a lot of sword fights.

Adapted from a novel by Tetsuji Godo.

DVD: Region 1 (USA) version not commercially available

Crimson Bat, the Blind Swordswoman (*Kurenai kawahori*)

1969 Shochiku, 88 minutes, color

- **Director:** Sadatsugu Matsuda
- **Cast:** Yoko Matsuyama, Isamu Nagato, Jun Tatara, Akitaké Kono, et al
- **Recommendation:** Not as good as the Zatoichi series. May be worth watching if you can find a copy from a good-quality print, which is reportedly virtually impossible to find.
- **Ratings:** IMDb 5.8/10

Abandoned young girl Oichi is struck blind by lightning, and is brought up by a caring elderly gentleman. When her guardian is later killed by a group of men, she learns that her mother is still alive and is a brothel owner in another town. On the way to find her, she is attacked by the same group of men, but the ronin Jubei comes to her rescue. He notices her keen instincts and reflexes and trains her to become a deadly swordswoman. She eventually becomes a bounty hunter, and travels the countryside to seek her mother and to avenge her adoptive father's death.

Three sequels were released, all within a year of this 1st film in the series.

Note: Crimson Bat is an appellation created outside Japan; the phrase never appears in the film.

DVD: Region 1 (USA) version not commercially available

Death Shadow (*Jittemai*)

1986 Shochiku, 115 minutes, color

- **Director:** Hideo Gosha
- **Cast:** Mariko Ishihara, Masanori Sera, Mari Natsuki, Tsunehiko Watasé, et al
- **Recommendation:** Yakuza story set in the samurai era. Off-the-wall theatrics, over-the-top action, eccentric direction.
- **Ratings:** IMDb 6.8/10

Three condemned criminals are spared from execution by the mysterious magistrate Utsumi on the condition that they become agents of the Shogun's Shadow Police. They are not to have personal lives and have their vocal cords cut to insure they never speak of their employer. One of them, Yasuké, however, has a relationship with a young woman named Osaki, and they have a daughter. Utsumi arrives, however, and separates Yasuké from his family.

Twenty years later, during a raid, Yasuké is attacked by masked woman who turns out to be his grown-up daughter Ocho. When Yasuké sacrifices himself to save his daughter, Ocho is recruited by the Shadow Police to collect evidence against corrupt official Genshiro.

This film served as an inspiration to Luc Besson's *La Femme Nikita* (1990).

DVD: Region 1 (USA) version not commercially available

Dora-heita "Alley cat"

2000 Nikkatsu, 111 minutes, color

- **Director:** Kon Ichikawa
- **Cast:** Koji Yakusho, Yuko Asano, Tsurutaro Kataoka, Ryudo Uzaki, et al
- **Recommendation:** Entertaining. Plot not historically significant. Anticipates the neo-samurai films of the new decade.
- **Ratings:** AllMovie 2.5/5, Amazon.com 4.5/5, IMDb 6.9/10, Netflix 3.4/5, Rotten Tomatoes --/70%

Mochizuki Koheita, a samurai with a reputation for debauchery, is appointed town commissioner by the daimyo of a small han "fief" to clean up the corrupt and lawless town of Horisoto. Koheita is aided by his cohorts Senba Gijuro and Yasukawa Hanzo to neutralize the town's three gangs, led by saké and prostitution boss Taju, gambling boss Saibei, and smuggling and money-laundering boss Nadahachi.

Based on the novel *Diary of a Town Magistrate* by Yamamoto Shugoro (1903-1967).

DVD: AnimEigo (2007)

Festival of Swordsmen (*Kengo tengu matsuri*)

1961 Toei, 90 minutes, color

- **Director:** Shigehiro Ozawa
- **Cast:** Ryutaro Otomo, Tomisaburo Wakayama, Shingo Yamashiro, Eiji Okada, et al
- **Recommendation:** Stylized acting and sword fighting. Numerous subplots. Appearances by many historical characters.
- **Ratings:** IMDb 6.7/10

In peaceful 1634 Okubo Hikozaémon, chief advisor to the 3rd Tokugawa Shogun Iemitsu (1604-1651), holds a public competition among martial artists from all over the country. Problems arise when some of the participants bring their personal grudges to the competition. Two of the strongest swordsmen are ronin Busshi Shirogoro and Iishino Shurinosuké. Shirogoro meets ninja princess Iso, 6th daughter of Sanada Yukimura (1567-1615), who introduces him

Samurai Movies – Edo Period

to legendary ninja Kakei Juzo. Iso joins the competition as a jujutsu master to avenge her father, who was killed at the Siege of Osaka Castle by Tokugawa forces.

DVD: Region 1 (USA) version not commercially available

Goyokin "Official gold"

1969 Toho, 124 minutes, color

- **Director:** Hideo Gosha
- **Cast:** Tatsuya Nakadai, Tetsuro Tanba, Yoro Tsukasa, Kinnosuké Nakamura, et al
- **Recommendation:** Some historical background. Beautifully filmed.
- **Ratings:** AllMovie 2/5, Amazon.com 4.1/5, IMDb 7.7/10, Netflix 3.5/5, Rotten Tomatoes --/84%

A ship laden with the Shogun's gold from the mines of Sado Island sinks and the fishermen of nearby Kurosaki village recover some of it intending to return it to the Tokugawa Shogunate. However Sabai clan karo "senior retainer" Rokugo Tatewaki appropriates the gold and massacres the peasants so they cannot report the stolen gold. A witness, Sabai retainer Wakizaka Magobei, loyally promises not to report the crime if Tatewaki promises not to do so again. Three years later, when assassins attempt to kill Magobei in Edo, he realizes Tatewaki intends to steal more gold and slaughter more innocents. He returns to Sado for a showdown.

DVD: Tokyo Shock (2006)

Hanzo the Razor: Sword of Justice (Goyokiba)

1972 Toho, 90 minutes, rated R, color

- **Director:** Kenji Misumi
- **Cast:** Shintaro Katsu, Ko Nishimura, Yukiji Asaoka, Daigo Kusano, et al
- **Recommendation:** Male fantasy. Lots of sex and violence.
- **Ratings:** Amazon.com 4.2/5, IMDb 6.8/10, Netflix 3.2/5, Rotten Tomatoes --/73%

Itami Hanzo is an incorruptible Edo constable who uses his well-endowed phallus to interrogate women, pleasuring them to give up information. When Hanzo finds out that a mistress of his chief, Onishi Magobei, is the ex-girlfriend of an escaped convict, the trail leads him to the Shogun's Inner Castle.

Based on the manga "Japanese comic book" series by Kazuo Koiké, two sequels were later released, *The Snare* (1973) and *Who's Got the Gold?* (1974).

DVD: Bonzai. Home Vision Entertainment (boxed set of all three films in the series, 2005)

Harakiri (Seppuku)

1962 Shochiku, 135 minutes, b&w

- **Director:** Masaki Kobayashi
- **Cast:** Tatsuya Nakadai, Rentaro Mikuni, Shima Iwashita, Akira Ishihama, et al
- **Recommendation:** Disturbing insight into the hypocrisy between the Bushido ideals of giri "duty" and ninjo "compassion." Uncompromising tragic tale, Shakespearean in emotional scope. A scathing denouncement of military rule.
- **Ratings:** AllMovie 4.5/5, Amazon.com 4.9/5, IMDb 8.3/10, Netflix 4.1/5, Rotten Tomatoes -- /96%

In 1630 Tsugumo Hanshiro, who became ronin after his clan was abolished some ten years earlier, appears at the compound of the Ii clan, and tells the karo "clan elder" Saito Kageyu that he can no longer go on living in poverty, and wishes to die honorably by seppuku in their courtyard. Before granting his wish, Kageyu recounts a story of another ronin, Chijiwa Motomé, who had made the same request earlier that year. It was apparent that he had made the request assuming that it would be denied, and offered money to leave and not sully the clan household. In order to stop this extortion scam from getting out of hand, Motomé was forced to go ahead with the suicide even though he had already sold his sword to feed his family, and only carried a bamboo substitute, making the disembowelment excruciatingly painful. Hanshiro confesses that Motomé was his son-in-law, and after the latter's death his daughter Miho and his grandson Kingo died of illness. Hanshiro blames Ii retainers Omodaka Hikokuro, Yazaki Hayato, and Kawabé Umenosuké for Motomé's death.

A remake was released in 2011, directed by Takashi Miiké, the 1st samurai movie ever in 3D.

Awards: Cannes Film Festival (1963), Special Jury Prize

DVD: Criterion (2007)

Blu-ray: Criterion (2010)

Hunter in the Dark (Yami no karyudo)

1979 Shochiku, 137 minutes, color

- **Director:** Hideo Gosha
- **Cast:** Tatsuya Nakadai, Yoshio Harada, Sonny Chiba, Ayumi Ishida, et al
- **Recommendation:** Lots of blood, flying limbs, and deaths. Great film noir acting. Labyrinthine plot with many twists and turns.
- **Ratings:** AllMovie 2.5/5, Amazon.com 5/5, IMDb 7/10, Rotten Tomatoes --/67%

In 1784, Edo yakuza boss Gomyo Kiyoémon hires Tanigawa Yataro, a one-eyed ronin, as yojimbo "bodyguard." Corrupt roju "senior counselor" Tanuma Okitsugu (1719-1788) conspires with Shimoguni Samon to seize control of Japan's northern island of Ezo.

DVD: Panorama (2008)

Incident at Blood Pass (Machibusé "Ambush")

1970 Toho, 117 minutes, color

- **Director:** Hiroshi Inagaki
- **Cast:** Toshiro Mifuné, Yujiro Ishihara, Ruriko Asaoka, Shintaro Katsu, Kinnosuké Nakamura, et al
- **Recommendation:** Nice photography. Complex plot. Claustrophobic in feel. Slow pacing. Not much action until the end.
- **Ratings:** Amazon.com 4.2/5, IMDb 7/10, Netflix 3.5/5, Rotten Tomatoes --/53%

A nameless ronin accepts a mysterious assignment to go to a remote mountain pass and await orders at an isolated teahouse where he is served by the woman he had recently saved from an abusive husband. There he becomes aware of an elaborate plot involving a Shogunate officer, a gang of bandits, a disgraced doctor, and a convoy of Shogunate gold.

DVD: AnimEigo (2005)

Inn of Evil (Inochi bo ni furo "We give our lives for nothing")

1971 Toho, 121 minutes, b&w

- **Director:** Masaki Kobayashi
- **Cast:** Tatsuya Nakadai, Shintaro Katsu, Shin Kishida, Yosuké Kondo, et al
- **Recommendation:** Slow pacing leads to a fantastic finale.
- **Ratings:** IMDb 6.9/10

At the Easy Tavern on an island in Fukagawa (Edo), river smuggler Sadashichi the Aloof spends his days with a criminal gang of misfits comprised of the inn keeper Ikuzo, bisexual ex-monk Yohei the Living Buddha, consumptive Genzo, irascible Maaji, stuttering Bunta, youngster Senkichi, and joker Yoshiko. Despite being protected by government officials, the bribe-hungry police continue to torment them. When the group decides to help a young man who is trying to save his girlfriend from prostitution, things begin to unraval.

Based on the novel *Fukagawa anrakutei* by Shugoro Yamamoto (1903-1967).

DVD: Region 1 (USA) version not commercially available

In Search of Mother (Mabuta no haha)

1962 Toei, 140 minutes, color

- **Director:** Tai Kato
- **Cast:** Kinnosuké Nakamura, Hiroki Matsukata, Michiyo Koguré, Kensaku Hara, et al
- **Recommendation:** More yakuza than samurai. Great tearjerker. Very emotional.
- **Ratings:** IMDb 6.4/10

Young yakuza Banba Chutaro is going to Edo to search for his mother who had abandoned him at age 5, but before he does, he helps his pal Kanamachi Hanjiro who is out to avenge the death of his boss Shigezo by the Iioka gang. When Chutaro finds his mother, he finds that his mother has married into wealth and social position, and has no intention of uniting with her outcast yakuza son.

Based on the modern kabuki play *Mabuta no haha* (1931) by Shin Hasegawa (1884-1963).

DVD: Region 1 (USA) version not commercially available

Kill! (Kiru)

1968 Toho, 115 minutes, b&w

- **Director:** Kihachi Okamoto
- **Cast:** Tatsuya Nakadai, Etsushi Takahashi, Atsuo Nakamura, Shigeru Koyama, et al
- **Recommendation:** Dark comedy with exaggerated exploration into the meaning of being a samurai. Interesting plot and highly entertaining.
- **Ratings:** AllMovie 2.5/5, Amazon.com 3.9/5, IMDb 7.4/10, Netflix 3.6/5, Rotten Tomatoes --/89%

In 1833 disillusioned ex-samurai Hyodo Yagenta (Genta) meets Tabata Hanjiro (Hanji), a farmer aspiring to become samurai. In Joshu (Kozuké) Genta tries to save a band of seven samurai, led by Oikawa Tetsutaro, who have been sent by villainous chamberlain Ayuzawa Tamiya to kill his rival, karo "chief vassal" Mizoguchi Sachu. Meanwhile Tamiya hires Hanji to kill Genta, and sends swordmaster Arao Jurota to kill the seven samurai, as well as his brother Kinzaburo to kill both Jurota and Tetsutaro's group.

Based on the same short story as *Sanjuro, Nichi-nichi heian "Peaceful Days"* by Shugoro Yamamoto (1903-1967).

DVD: Criterion (2005)

Lone Wolf and Cub: Sword of Vengeance (Kozuré Okami: Kowokashi udekashi tsukamatsuru "Wolf with Child in Tow: Child and Expertise for Rent")

1972 Toho, 83 minutes, color

- **Director:** Kenji Misumi
- **Cast:** Tomisaburo Wakayama, Akihiro Tomikawa, Yunosuké Ito, Saburo Daté, et al
- **Recommendation:** Among the goriest samurai films of all time. Plenty of dismemberment; not for the squeamish. Cult favorite and guilty pleasure to many.
- **Ratings:** Amazon.com 4.3/5, IMDb 8/10, Netflix 3.9/5, Rotten Tomatoes 71%/91%

Ogami Itto, a disgraced former executioner to the Shogun, with his 3-year-old son Daigoro in a makeshift baby cart, wanders the countryside as an assassin for hire. He is pursued by Yagyu clan leader Retsudo.

Itto is hired by Oyamada clan karo "senior retainer" Gyobu Ichigé to kill his rival Sugito and his gang of henchmen who pose a threat to his lord.

Based on a 28-volume manga "Japanese comic book" series by Kazuo Koiké (1936-) published from 1970 to 1976, this is the 1st of a six-film series that was released from 1972 to 1974. From 1973 to 1976, three 26-episode seasons were aired on TV starring Kinnosuké Nakamura. From 2002 to 2004 another TV series aired with Kinya Kitaoji as Ogami Itto.

DVD: AnimEigo (2003), boxed set of all six films in the series (2005)

Momotaro zamurai

1957 Daiei

- **Director:** Kenji Misumi
- **Cast:** Raizo Ichikawa, Yoko Uraji, Saizaburo Kawazu, Michiyo Koguré, et al
- **Recommendation:** Virtually impossible to find, I have not seen this film, nor have I seen any reviews of it. I have seen the first two seasons of the TV series, and it features a light-hearted look at Edo culture.

Wakagi Shinnosuké is living in the tenements of Edo as the ronin Momotaro to protect his daimyo brother, who is his older twin brother.

Based on the novel by Kiichiro Yamaté (1899-1978).

This film was the 2nd featuring the ronin. The 1st was in 1952, the 3rd was in 1960 starring Kotaro Satomi, and the 4th in 1963 starring Kojiro Hongo. A popular TV series of 258 episodes aired from 1976 to 1981 starring Hideki Takahashi, with specials in 1992 and 1993. In 2006 eight episodes of a new TV series called *Shin Momotaro zamurai* aired, starring Masahiro Takashima.

DVD: Region 1 (USA) version not commercially available

Mushuku mono (Homeless Drifter, aka Lone Wanderer)

1964 Daiei, 89 minutes, color

- **Director:** Kenji Misumi

Samurai Movies – Edo Period

- **Cast:** Raizo Ichikawa, Eiko Taki, Jun Fujimaki, Kenjiro Ishiyama, et al
- **Recommendation:** Beautifully photographed, excellently directed. A tragic samurai tale.
- **Ratings:** IMDb 6.2/10

Wandering yakuza gambler Ipponmatsu "Lone Pine" meets young ronin Kuroki and they begin traveling together. Ipponmatsu is seeking the murderer of his father who five years earlier was slain at Sasago Pass while transporting 4,000 ryo with his guards. The main suspect is the missing guard Yaichiro, who had survived the ambush. Ipponmatsu learns that Kuroki is the son of Yaichiro and is out to clear his father's name.

When they come to a small coastal village, they learn that the local yakuza boss had suddenly become very wealthy at the time of the ambush. As they investigate this tale, they discover that there is a power behind the scenes, and an even shadowier figure behind him.

DVD: Region 1 (USA) version not commercially available

Quick-draw Okatsu (Hitokiri Okatsu)

1969 Toei, 89 minutes, color

- **Director:** Nobuo Nakagawa
- **Cast:** Junko Miyazono, Reiko Onobuta, Ko Nishimura, Kenji Imai, et al
- **Recommendation:** Disturbing sex and violence exploitation film set in the feudal era. Bloody spectacle with extremely violent scenes of merciless cruelty, torture, and gore. Not for the faint of heart.
- **Ratings:** Amazon.com 3.8/5, IMDb 6.9/10, Netflix 2.9/5, Rotten Tomatoes --/71%

Okatsu is raped, and her adoptive father, Kogen sword school sensei Makabé Yahei, is tortured to death by corrupt official Shiozaki. Later her brother Rintaro is murdered and his pregnant girlfriend Saki is sold into prostitution by the devious Okiwa and her dim-witted husband Jinkuro. When Okatsu sets out on revenge she is aided by her sexy sidekick Rui.

Marketed in the U.S. as the middle film in the "Legends of the Poisonous Seductress" trilogy of films starring Junko Miyazono, but although the names and plot are the same or similar, each film is independent, with characters that are different, and with storylines that do not follow each other.

DVD: Synapse (2007)

Revenge (Adauchi)

1964 Toei, 87 minutes, b&w

- **Director:** Tadashi Imai
- **Cast:** Kinnosuké Nakamura, Tetsuro Tanba, Yoshiko Mita, Eitaro Shindo, et al
- **Recommendation:** Good premise. Tense, violent, and tragic. A political allegory.
- **Ratings:** IMDb 6.5/10

At Wakisaka clan's Tatsuno Castle (Harima), when low-ranking samurai Ezaki Shinpachi kills government inspector Okuno Magadayu in a forbidden private duel, he is banished to the mountains. When he is pursued there by Magadayu's brother Shumé, he kills him too. Then the youngest brother, Tatsunosuké, backed by the Wakisaka clan, comes to take revenge, and Shinpachi's fate is sealed.

DVD: Region 1 (USA) version not commercially available

Ronin Gai

1990 Shochiku, 121 minutes, color

- **Director:** Kazuo Kuroki
- **Cast:** Yoshio Harada, Kanako Higuchi, Shintaro Katsu, Renji Ishibashi, et al
- **Recommendation:** Exploration into the depravity of the era.
- **Ratings:** Amazon.com 4/5, IMDb 6.5/10, Netflix 3.2/5, Rotten Tomatoes --/55%

In 1836, hedonistic ronin Aramaki Gennai and Tanomo Gonbei are staying at a brothel in the outskirts of Edo. A band of Shogun's retainers start to righteously kill prostitutes. The drunken ronin sober up, and, along with the bouncer Goémon and another ronin Magohachiro, retaliate for a chance to redeem themselves.

Remake of a 3-part silent film series released from 1928.

DVD: Home Vision Entertainment (2005)

Samurai Trilogy

Samurai I: Miyamoto Musashi

1954 Toho, 93 minutes, color

Samurai II: Duel at Ichijoji Temple (Zoku Miyamoto Musashi: Ichijo-ji no ketto)

1955 Toho, 103 minutes

Samurai III: Duel at Ganryu Island (Miyamoto Musashi kanketsuhen: ketto Ganryu-jima)

1956 Toho, 105 minutes

- **Director:** Hiroshi Inagaki
- **Cast:** Toshiro Mifuné, Koji Tsuruta, Kaoru Yachigusa, Mariko Okada, et al
- **Recommendation:** Must see. Epic storytelling. Good example of a samurai going on a musha shugyo. Plenty of warrior philosophies. Many well-choreographed swordfights.
- **Ratings:** AllMovie I 4, II 3, III 3/5; Amazon.com 4.2/5; IMDb I 7.7 , II 7.4, III 7.9/10, Netflix I 3.8, II 3.8, III 3.7/5, Rotten Tomatoes I --/84%, II --/85%, III --/94%

Based on the historical novel *Musashi* (1935) by Eiji Yoshikawa (1892-1962). The trilogy is a fictionalized account of the life of legendary swordsman Miyamoto Musashi (1584-1645), a powerful young samurai who learns the error of his wild ways.

The 1st movie begins right after the 1600 Battle of Sekigahara (Mino), and the 3rd ends after his climatic duel with Sasaki Kojiro (1585-1612) at Ganryu-jima (between Honshu and Kyushu), featuring one of the greatest duels in samurai cinema.

There are dozens of Japanese films based on the life of Musashi going back to the silent era. This version is the most famous outside Japan. There is an in-depth NHK Taiga Drama series titled *Musashi* (2004), which ran 49 episodes, of 45 minutes each, weekly for a year, also based on Yoshikawa's novel. It was broadcast in the U.S. with English subtitles on stations that aired Japanese programming, but this sub-titled version is presently not available commercially on DVD.

Historical cameos: Takuan Soho (1573-1645), Ikeda Terumasa (1565-1613), Shishido Baiken (-1607), Hon'ami Koetsu (1558-1637).

Awards: Academy Award (1955) Best Foreign Language Film (honorary)

DVD: Criterion (2004)

Ultimate Samurai Miyamoto Musashi

Zen and Sword (Miyamoto Musashi)

1961 Toei, color

Samurai Movies – Edo Period

Miyamoto Musashi: Showdown at Hannyazaka Heights (Miyamoto Musashi: Hannya-zaka no ketto)

1962 Toei, 110 minutes, color

Two-Sword Fencing Is Born (Miyamoto Musashi: Nito-ryu kaigen)

1963 Toei, 104 minutes, color

Miyamoto Musashi: The Duel at Ichijoji (Miyamoto Musashi: Ichijo-ji no ketto)

1964 Toei, 128 minutes, color

Miyamoto Musashi: Ganryu-jima no ketto

1965 Toei, 121 minutes, color

- **Director:** Tomu Uchida
- **Cast:** Kinnosuké Nakamura, Wakaba Irié, Ken Takakura, et al
- **Rating:** Amazon.com 5/5, IMDb (in above order) 6.9, 6.4, 7.0, 6.7, 6.7/10, Rotten Tomatoes 100%

Another epic Miyamoto Musashi movie series, also based on the historical novel *Musashi* (1935) by Eiji Yoshikawa (1892-1962). This five-part version is actually more popular and better known in Japan than the Inagaki version.

DVD: AnimEigo (2010)

Samurai Fiction (SF: Episode One)

1998 Pony Canyon, 111 minutes, b&w (with spot coloring)

- **Director:** Hiroyuki Nakano
- **Cast:** Morio Kazama, Mitsuru Fukikoshi, Tomoyasu Hotei, Tamaki Ogawa, et al
- **Recommendation:** Funny and entertaining with good performances. Both a parody and homage to chanbara. Well shot. Scenes feature contemporary music to evoke appropriate mood.
- **Ratings:** AllMovie 3/5, Amazon.com 4.3/5, IMDb 7.2/10, Netflix 3.5/5, Rotten Tomatoes --/81%

In 1696 Nagashima clan's precious ceremonial sword, bestowed some eighty years earlier by Tokugawa Ieyasu (1543-1616) himself, is stolen by the ronin Kazamatsuri Rannosuké. Heishiro insists on retrieving the sword against the advice of his father, clan karo "senior retainer" Inukai Kanzen. Heishiro is accompanied by two fellow samurai, Kurosawa Tadasuké and Suzuki Shintaro, and two ninja, Hayabusa and Akakagé. Rannosuké dispatches the companions and wounds Heishiro, who is nursed back to health by Mizoguchi Hanbei and his lovely daughter Koharu. When Heishiro hears that Rannosuké is acting as a bodyguard for female yakuza boss Okatsu, he confronts Rannosuké for a final battle to retrieve the clan sword.

Director Quentin Tarantino spoofed a few scenes from this film in his *Kill Bill Vol. 1* (2003).

DVD: Tokyo Shock (2003)

The Samurai I Loved (Semishiguré "Autumn Rain of the Cicadas")

2005 Toho, 131 minutes, color

- **Director:** Mitsuo Kurotsuchi
- **Cast:** Somegoro Ichikawa, Yoshino Kimura, Koji Imada, Ryo Fukawa, et al
- **Recommendation:** Beautifully shot and superbly crafted. Realistic swordfights. Subtle and profoundly emotional. A bittersweet romantic neo-samurai film. As close to a chick-flick the samurai genre can get.
- **Ratings:** Amazon.com 4/5, IMDb 7.2/10, Netflix 3/5, Rotten Tomatoes --/61%

When Maki Sukezaémon is ordered to commit seppuku when he is wrongfully accused of plotting against the clan, his wife and son Bunshiro are forced to live in squalor. But Bunshiro is a talented and loyal swordsman, and after a time he becomes a crop inspector for the fief. He discovers that the political maneuvering which led to his father's death is still widespread, and that his childhood sweetheart Fuku, now one of the lord's concubines, has given birth to the lord's son, and a rival faction has decided to kill the boy and blame Bunshiro.

Based on a novel by Shuhei Fujisawa (1927-1997).

DVD: AnimEigo (2009)

Samurai Rebellion (Joi-uchi: Hairyo tsuma shimatsu "Rebellion: Result of the Wife Bestowed")

1967 Toho, 128 minutes, b&w

- **Director:** Masaki Kobayashi
- **Cast:** Toshiro Mifuné, Tatsuya Nakadai, Takeshi Kato, Shigeru Koyama, et al
- **Recommendation:** Preparation of a house for combat. Highly entertaining.
- **Ratings:** AllMovie 4/5, Amazon.com 4.9/5, IMDb 8.2/10, Netflix 4/5, Rotten Tomatoes 100%/91%

In 1725, Sasahara Isaburo's son Yogoro is ordered by the clan karo "senior retainer" Takahashi Geki to marry Ichi, a cast-off concubine of Lord Matsudaira Masakata (1681-1731) of Aizu (Mutsu -- 280,000 koku). When she is later ordered to return to the castle, Isaburo and Yogoro decide to defend their family honor.

Awards: Venice Film Festival (1967), FIPRESCI Prize (Masaki Kobayashi)

DVD: Criterion (2005)

Samurai Reincarnation (Makai tensho)

1981 Toei, 122 minutes, color

- **Director:** Kinji Fukasaku
- **Cast:** Sonny Chiba, Kenji Sawada, Akiko Kana, Ken Ogata, Hiroyuki Sanada, et al
- **Recommendation:** Campy. Flawed. Historical background but totally fictional tale.
- **Ratings:** AllMovie 1.5/5, Amazon.com 3.4/5, IMDb 6.5/10, Netflix 2.9/5, Rotten Tomatoes --/71%

Amakusa Shiro (1621-1638), the teenage leader of the Shimabara Rebellion (Hizen) who was beheaded along with 27,000 other Christian rebels by the Shogunate forces, supernaturally comes back to life, renounces Christianity, and vows to take revenge against the Shogun.

Many historical figures appear in the film, including Hosokawa Gracia (1563-1600), Miyamoto Musashi (1584-1645), Yagyu Jubei (1607-1650), Hozo Inshun (1589-1648), Yagyu Munenori (1571-1646), Tokugawa Ietsuna (1641-1680), and Muramasa Sengo.

Remade in 2003 as *Samurai Resurrection* starring Yosuké Kubozuka.

DVD: Tokyo Shock (2004)

Samurai Spy (Ibun Sarutobi Sasuké)

1965 Shochiku, 102 minutes, b&w

- **Director:** Masahiro Shinoda
- **Cast:** Koji Takahashi, Rokuhiro Toura, Testuro Tanba, Eiji Okada, et al

Samurai Movies – Edo Period

- **Recommendation:** Historical background. Cryptic tale of intrigue and secrecy. Samurai film noir.
- **Ratings:** AllMovie 2.5/5, Amazon.com 4.2/5, IMDb 7.1/10, Netflix 3.4/5, Rotten Tomatoes --/72%

In 1614, ninja samurai Sarutobi Sasuké of the Sanada clan is caught between rival groups of spies, those working for the Tokugawa and those supporting the Toyotomi. The Tokugawa spies are led by Yagyu clan members Takatani Sakon and Koriyama Tatewaki, and the Toyotomi by Koremura Shigeyuki and his sadistic lieutenant Nojiri Takanosuké. Sasuké, who believes another war is brewing, is approached by another Toyotomi spy, Inamura Mitsuaki, to help him from the cruel local magistrate Kuni Genba.

Loosely adapted from the novel *Ibun Sarutobi Sasuké* by Koji Nakada.

DVD: Criterion (2005)

Samurai Wolf (*Kiba Okaminosuké*)

1966 Toei, 75 minutes, b&w

- **Director:** Hideo Gosha
- **Cast:** Isao Natsuyagi, Junko Miyazono, Ryohei Uchida, Tatsuo Endo, et al
- **Recommendation:** Solid action-packed samurai entertainment with exceptionally well-choreographed sword fighting. Many interesting characters. Good camera work and editing. A minor classic.
- **Ratings:** IMDb 7.2/10, Rotten Tomatoes --/63%

At a mountain relay post, ronin Kiba Okaminosuké aids express messengers who are under attack by a gang out to take over the lucrative delivery service. Leader of the gang Nizaémon hires another ronin Akizuki Sanai to deal with Okaminosuké.

A sequel, *Samurai Wolf II* (*Kiba Okaminosuke jigoku giri*), appeared in 1967.

DVD: Region 1 (USA) version not commercially available

Sanjuro (*Tsubaki Sanjuro*)

1962 Toho, 96 minutes, rated PG-13, b&w

- **Director:** Akira Kurosawa
- **Cast:** Toshiro Mifuné, Tatsuya Nakadai, Keiju Kobayashi, Yuzo Kayama, et al
- **Recommendation:** Highly entertaining and often humorous. Unforgettable iai "quick draw" duel at end.
- **Ratings:** AllMovie 3.5/5, Amazon.com 4.4/5, IMDb 8.1/10, Netflix 4/5, Rotten Tomatoes 100%/94%

In the mid-19th century a ronin who calls himself Tsubaki Sanjuro "Camellia tree, 30-year-old," essentially the same character as that in the previous film *Yojimbo* (1961), helps nine young samurai who are determined to clean up the corruption in the leadership of their clan. The idealistic group doubt the cynical ronin's nobility, but Sanjuro has a deep commitment to justice and honor underneath his dirty, abrasive exterior.

Loosely based on the short story *Nichi-nichi heian "Peaceful Days"* by Shugoro Yamamoto (1903-1967).

DVD: Criterion (2007)
Blu-ray: Criterion (2010)

The Secret of the Urn (*Tangé Sazen: Hien iai giri*)

1966 Toei, 91 minutes, color

- **Director:** Hideo Gosha
- **Cast:** Kinnosuké Nakamura, Tetsuro Tanba, Isao Kimura, Keiko Awaji, et al
- **Recommendation:** Above-average samurai action. Well-beloved character in Japan.
- **Ratings:** IMDb 6.9/10

This is the definitive version of the story of loyal samurai Tangé Samanosuké, who is betrayed, attacked, and loses one eye and one arm. A year later he appears as the ronin Tangé Sazen searching for a valuable old jar that holds the key to a fortune.

Tangé Sazen originally appeared as a supporting character in a serial novel featuring the exploits of Ooka Tadasuké (1677-1752).

The story originally appeared in the 1935 film *The Million Ryo Pot* (*Tangé Sazen yowa: Hyakuman-ryo no tsubo*) starring Denjiro Okochi. Four films starring Ryutaro Otomo as Tangé Sazen appeared from 1958 to 1961. A shot-by-shot remake of the 1935 film was released in 2004 directed by Toshio Tsuda.

DVD: Region 1 (USA) version not commercially available

Shogun (aka *James Clavell's Shogun*)

1980 NBC, 549 minutes, rated PG-13, color

- **Director:** Jerry London
- **Cast:** Richard Chamberlain, Toshiro Mifuné, Yoko Shimada, Frankie Sakai, et al
- **Recommendation:** Hugely-popular TV miniseries. Epic big-budget production. Ahistorical story of a foreigner slowly assimilating into Japanese culture.
- **Ratings:** AllMovie 4/5, Amazon.com 4.5/5, IMDb 8.3/10, Netflix 3.9/5

Ship-wrecked English pilot John Blackthorne helps warlord Toranaga Yoshi compete with others for the position of Shogun, while fending off European missionaries and traders seeking influence over Japan.

Based on the 1975 novel by James Clavell (1924-1994). The story is loosely based on the exploits of navigator William Adams (1564-1620), the 1st Englishman to set foot on Japan.

Awards: Peabody Award (1981). Golden Globe (1981). Emmy (1981).

DVD: Paramount (2003)

Shogun's Samurai (*Yagyu ichizoku no inbo* "Yagyu clan conspiracy")

1978 Toei, 130 minutes, color

- **Director:** Kinji Fukasaku
- **Cast:** Kinnosuké Nakamura, Sonny Chiba, Hiroki Matsukata, Tetsuro Tanba, Toshiro Mifuné, et al
- **Recommendation:** Fictionalized account of historical events. Big production with an all-star cast. Violent scenes of dismemberments, beheadings, massacres, etc.
- **Ratings:** Amazon.com 3.9/5, IMDb 7.1/10, Netflix 3.4/5, Rotten Tomatoes --/74%

The 2nd Tokugawa Shogun Hidetada (1579-1632) has died under suspicious circumstances, and a succession dispute develops between his two sons Iemitsu (1604-1651) and Tadanaga (1606-1633). Ruthless Yagyu Munenori (1571-1646), the instructor of swordsmanship to the Shogun, supports Iemitsu. Munenori's son Jubei (1607-1650) enlists the help of the Negoro clan of mountain ninja.

DVD: Adness (2004)

The Shogun's Vault (*Gokinzo yaburi*)

1964 Toei, 93 minutes, color

- **Director:** Teruo Ishii

Samurai Movies – Edo Period

- **Cast:** Hashizo Okawa, Shiezo Kataoka, Tetsuro Tanba, Toru Abé, et al
- **Recommendation:** Exciting, suspenseful, lots of action. A classic heist film.

Disillusioned ex-samurai "Red Peony" Hanji, named for his flower tattoo, is thrown into Tenma-cho Prison where he gets involved with "Smoke" Tomizo in a plot to steal the Shogun's gold in Edo Castle with the help of Lady Oko. Tomizo is trailed by nosy cop Kanbei who is out to catch the old thief in the act. Yakuza boss Yatagoro and his henchman Kasuké plan to poach the loot once the pair steal the gold.

DVD: Region 1 (USA) version not commercially available

Sleepy Eyes of Death 1: The Chinese Jade (*Nemuri Kyoshiro 1: Sappocho*)

1963 Daiei, 82 minutes, color

- **Director:** Tokuzo Tanaka
- **Cast:** Raizo Ichikawa, Tamao Nakamura, Tomisaburo Wakayama, Sonosuké Sawamura, Saburo Daté, Shinobu Araki, et al
- **Recommendation:** Unrealistic ninja action. Unbelievable display of swordfighting and martial arts skills.
- **Ratings:** Amazon.com 4.7/5 (for the boxed set of 1st four films in the series), IMDb 6.9/10, Netflix 3/5, Rotten Tomatoes --/60%

Nemuri Kyoshiro, a stereotypically cynical super-swordsman ronin, is attacked in Edo by ninja sent by Lord Maeda Nariyasu (1811-1884) of Kanazawa (Kaga -- 1,025,000 koku) to test his skills. Nariyasu is trying to get back a jade statuette from the merchant Zeniya Gohei. He send his daughter Chisa to hire Kyoshiro as her yojimbo "bodyguard."

Kyoshiro is summoned by the monk Chen Sun, the 13th descendant of a Chinese master of Shorinji-style boxing, to Tsukuda-shima (off Edo), where he meets Gohei, who also tries to hire him, and tells him about the secret of the Chinese Jade.

Based on a series of novels by Renzaburo Shibata, this is the 1st in a series of 12 films starring Raizo Ichikawa in the title role, the last released in 1969. This series was preceded by three films that were released from 1956 to 1958 and starred Koji Tsuruta. After Ichikawa's death in 1969, two more Sleepy Eyes of Death films appeared that year starring Hiroki Matsukata. Four made-for-TV movie specials appeared from 1989 to 1998 starring Masakazu Tamura.

DVD: AnimEigo (2009, boxed set of 1st four films in the series)

The Tale of Zatoichi (*Zatoichi monogatari*)

1962 Daiei, 96 minutes, b&w

- **Director:** Kenji Misumi
- **Cast:** Shintaro Katsu, Shigeru Amachi, Masayo Banri, Ryuzo Shimada, et al
- **Recommendation:** More yakuza than samurai. Good background scenes of towns and countryside. Standard plot. Highly entertaining with good performances.
- **Ratings:** AllMovie 2.5/5, Amazon.com 4.7/5, IMDb 7.6/10, Netflix 3.7/5, Rotten Tomatoes 100%/84%

In Iioka (Shimosa), the blind masseur Zatoichi is hired by yakuza boss Sukejoro to fight his rival, Shigezo of nearby Sasagawa, who has hired the skilled ronin Hiraté Miki. Zatoichi and Miki develop a strong friendship based on mutual respect, but in the end fate forces them to duel.

This is the 1st film of an immensely-popular series featuring the blind masseur, gambler, and deadly swordsman created by the novelist Kan Shimozawa. A total of 25 films were made from 1962 to 1973, and the 26th was made in 1989. The 1st two were in b&w and the rest in color. From 1974 to 1979, 100 episodes were made for a TV series featuring Zatoichi. All these starred Shintaro Katsu in the title role.

In 2003 Takeshi Kitano wrote, directed, and starred in a new high-budget film titled simply *Zatoichi*. It premiered at the Venice Film Festival where it received the Silver Lion award.

DVD: Home Vision Entertainment (2002)

Whirlwind (*Shikonmado -- Dai tatsumaki*)

1964 Toho, 108 minutes, color

- **Director:** Hiroshi Inagaki
- **Cast:** Somegoro Ichikawa, Yosuké Natsuki, Toshiro Mifuné, Makoto Sato, et al
- **Recommendation:** Samurai spectacle with recreation of the siege and burning of Osaka Castle. Adventure, romance, and action!
- **Ratings:** AllMovie 2.5/5, IMDb 6.5/10

In 1615, during the Summer Campaign of the Siege of Osaka Castle, three samurai within the compound know the end is near. Fierce warrior Kusanagi Shuri plans to fight to the death, young Fukami Jubei opts for seppuku, and Kyunosuké just wants to run away.

Based on the novel *Shikonmado* by Norio Danjo.

DVD: Region 1 (USA) version not commercially available

Yojimbo "Bodyguard"

1961 Toho, 110 minutes, b&w

- **Director:** Akira Kurosawa
- **Cast:** Toshiro Mifuné, Tatsuya Nakadai, Yoko Tsukasa, Isuzu Yamada, et al
- **Recommendation:** Great iconic ronin story. Violent with plenty of action. A must-see classic.
- **Ratings:** AllMovie 5/5, Amazon.com 4.7/5, IMDb 8.3/10, Netflix 4/5, Rotten Tomatoes 97%/96%

It is the 1860s and many out-of-work samurai wander the country. A ronin who calls himself Kuwabataké Sanjuro "Mulberry field, 30-year-old" arrives at a small town where competing crime lords make their money from gambling. On the one side is Seibei, his wife Orin, and their son Yoichiro, who are allied with the silk merchant Tazaémon. On the other is Ushitora and his brothers Inokichi and Unosuké, who are allied with the saké brewer Tokuémon. After

the tavern keeper Gonji apprises the ronin of the war between the two yakuza gangs, Sanjuro tells him, "I'll cause some trouble and pay you. In this town I'll get paid for killing, and this town is full of men who are better off dead."

Later remade into Sergio Leone's 1st spaghetti western *A Fistful of Dollars* (1964) starring Clint Eastwood, the Prohibition-era gangster thriller *Last Man Standing* (1996) directed by Walter Hill and starring Bruce Willis, among others.

DVD: Criterion (2007)

Blu-ray: Criterion (2010)

GENROKU "GOLDEN AGE OF EDO" PERIOD (1688-1704)

Chushingura (*Chushingura: Hana no maki, yuki no maki*)

1962 Toho, 207 minutes, color

- **Director:** Hiroshi Inagaki
- **Cast:** Hakuo Matsumoto, Yuzo Kayama, Chusha Ichikawa, Toshiro Mifuné, et al
- **Recommendation:** Must see! Classic bushido story of unwavering loyalty and dedication of the ideal samurai. One of the most beautiful films of Japanese cinema. Big-budget production. Magnificently-choreographed battle scene at end.
- **Ratings:** AllMovie 3/5, Amazon.com 4.3/5, IMDb 7.7/10, Netflix 3.7/5, Rotten Tomatoes --/66%

Based on actual events known as the Revenge of the 47 Ronin.

On the 14th day of the 3rd month, 1701, Lord Asano Naganori of Ako (Harima -- 53,000 koku) attacks master-of-ceremonies Kira Yoshinaka in Edo Castle for insults Yoshinaka directed at Naganori when he would not sufficiently bribe him. Yoshinaka survives with a minor wound. As any sort of violence in the Shogun's residence is completely forbidden, Lord Asano is unjustly ordered to commit seppuku that very evening. His clan is abolished, his domain confiscated, and his retainers become ronin.

Although the Shogunate prohibited revenge in this case, the Asano clan karo "senior retainer" Oishi Yoshio blames Yoshinaka for the tragic events, and seeks vengeance.

On the 14th day of the 12th month, 1702, on a snowy night, after secretly planning their attack for over a year and a half, 47 of the ex-men of Ako storm Yoshinaka's residence in Edo. After beheading the object of their vendetta, they take the head to the Sengaku-ji, and present it before Lord Asano's grave.

Countless versions of the venerable 47 Ronin story have appeared on film and TV -- over 80 feature films alone. This rousing epic classic is the most well known in the West. In 1999 NHK Taiga Drama presented a year-long, 49-episode, detailed version called *Genroku Ryoran*.

DVD: Image Entertainment (2001)

47 Ronin (*Shiju-shichi-nin no shikaku*)

1994, 132 minutes, color

- **Director:** Kon Ichikawa
- **Cast:** Ken Takakura, Ko Nishimura, Koji Ishizaka, Hisaya Morishigé, et al
- **Recommendation:** A solid entry to the Chushingura canon. A more thoughtful retelling than the rousing Inagaki version.
- **Ratings:** AllMovie 2.5/5, Amazon.com 4/5, IMDb 6.9/10, Netflix 3.3/5, Rotten Tomatoes --/57%

See *Chushingura* above.

DVD: AnimEigo (2007)

Hana: The Tale of a Reluctant Samurai (*Hana yori mo naho*)

2006 Shochiku, 127 minutes, color

- **Director:** Hirokazu Koré'eda
- **Cast:** Jun'ichi Okada, Rié Miyazawa, Arata Furuta, Katsuo Nakamura, et al
- **Recommendation:** Unorthodox samurai story. Low-key and humanistic. A thoughtful neo-samurai film.
- **Ratings:** Amazon.com 3.6/5, IMDb 6.9/10, Netflix 3/5, Rotten Tomatoes --/52%

In 1702, when the ronin of the dispossessed Asano clan of Ako are planning their revenge, another samurai, gentle Aoki Sozaémon from Matsumoto, must avenge the death of his father and secure his family's honor. It's been two years, however, and he is content to teach reading and writing to kids in the Edo tenement area, where he now lives. When he stumbles on the killer, Kanazawa Jubei, he finds a way to reconcile his fate.

DVD: Funimation (2008)

The Loyal 47 Ronin (*Chushingura*)

1958 Daiei, 166 minutes, color

- **Director:** Kunio Watanabé
- **Cast:** Kazuo Hasegawa, Shintaro Katsu, Koji Tsuruta, Raizo Ichikawa, et al
- **Recommendation:** Great all-star cast, big-budget production.
- **Ratings:** Amazon.com 4.7/5, IMDb 7.7/10, Netflix 3.6/5, Rotten Tomatoes --/100%

See *Chushingura* above. Many Japanese consider this the best film version.

DVD: AnimEigo (2009)

Samurai Vedetta (*Hakuoki "Chronicle of Pale Cherry Blossoms"*)

Samurai Movies – Bakumatsu Period

1959 Daiei, 109 minutes, color
- **Director:** Kazuo Mori
- **Cast:** Shintaro Katsu, Raizo Ichikawa, Miki Chitosé, Gen Shimizu, et al
- **Recommendation:** Classic samurai story of love and revenge.
- **Ratings:** Amazon.com 4/5, IMDb 6.7/10, Netflix 3.6/5

In 1694, at Takada-no-baba (Edo), Nakayama (later Horibé) Yasubei (1670-1703) aids his uncle and members of his Horiguchi Itto school in a sword battle against the Murakami brothers of the Chishu Shinden school. Through fate, government official Tangé Tenzen, a member of the latter school, and Yasubei end up aiding each other, forming a friendship of sorts, although often at opposing sides. After Tenzen's wife Chiharu is raped, her infuriated brother cuts off Tenzen's right arm. After healing, Tenzen goes after the five men who had raped his wife. Meanwhile, Yasubei joins the Asano clan in Ako, and participates as one of the 47 ronin who attacked and killed Kira Yoshinaka (1641-1703) to avenge the death of their late Lord Asano Naganori (1667-1701).

DVD: AnimEigo (2010)

Shura

1971 Matsumoto Productions, 135 minutes, color
- **Director:** Toshio Matsumoto
- **Cast:** Katsuo Nakamura, Yasuko Sanjo, Juro Kara, Masao Imafuku, et al
- **Recommendation:** Shockingly burtal violence, disturbingly gruesome carnage. Expressionistic and *avant garde*.
- **Ratings:** AllMovie 2/5, IMDb 7.4/10

Bankrupt ronin Gengobei suddenly receives 100 ryo "gold pieces" from loyal old servant Hachiémon. The money is badly needed for the vendetta of the 47 ronin. Gengobei however is in love with Koman, and uses the money to redeem her instead. He later realizes she and her cohort Sangoro are scam artists, and it was all a con. Gengobei pursues them to take bloody revenge.

Based on the kabuki play *Kamikaketé sango taisetsu* (1825). Back story is from an early kabuki version of *Chushingura* with the names changed.

DVD: Region 1 (USA) version not commercially available

Bakumatsu "Late Tokugawa" Period (1853-1867)

The Ambitious (*Bakumatsu*)

1970 Toei, 120 minutes, color
- **Director:** Daisuké Ito
- **Cast:** Kinnosuké Nakamura, Toshiro Mifuné, Tatsuya Nakadai, Keiju Kobayashi, et al
- **Recommendation:** Unusually slow and plodding for a samurai film. Mostly dialog.
- **Ratings:** IMDb 6.6/10

Story of rebel samurai Sakamoto Ryoma (1836-1867) of Tosa province, a leader in the movement to overthrow the Tokugawa Shogunate.

DVD: Region 1 (USA) version not commercially available

Assassination (*Ansatsu*)

1964 Shochiku, 104 minutes, b&w
- **Director:** Masahiro Shinoda
- **Cast:** Tetsuro Tanba, Shima Iwashita, Eiji Okada, Isao Kimura, et al
- **Recommendation:** Historical setting. Complex story about a complex man.
- **Ratings:** AllMovie 4/5, IMDb 7.3/10, Rotten Tomatoes --/55%

Low-ranking samurai Sasaki Tadasaburo is tasked to kill Kiyokawa Hachiro (1830-1863), who had formed the Roshigumi, a group of ronin recruited to protect the Shogun during his visits to Kyoto. After initially failing in his mission, Tadasaburo is given another chance to redeem himself. To better understand the man he is going to kill, he looks into Hachiro's past life.

Based on a story by Ryotaro Shiba (1923-1996).

DVD: Region 1 (USA) version not commercially available

Blood End (*Tengu-to*)

1969 Daiei, 102 minutes, color
- **Director:** Satsuo Yamamoto
- **Cast:** Tatsuya Nakadai, Go Kato, Shigeru Koyama, Ayako Wakao, et al
- **Recommendation:** Based on historical events. Good sword fighting with bloody violence.
- **Ratings:** IMDb 6.5/10

In 1864 infamous gambler Sentaro is in Edo, and reluctantly joins Kada Gentaro and his anti-Shogunate group, the Tengu-to from Mito. He is quickly repulsed by the group's reckless tactics.

DVD: Region 1 (USA) version not commercially available

Destiny's Son (*Kiru* "Kill")

1962 Daiei, 71 minutes, color
- **Director:** Kenji Misumi
- **Cast:** Raizo Ichikawa, Eijiro Yanagi, Yoshio Inaba, Masayo Banri, et al
- **Recommendation:** See it if you get the chance. A minor classic.
- **Ratings:** IMDb 7.1/10, Rotten Tomatoes --/100%

The lord of the Iida clan had a mistress that held power over him. This worried the clan karo "senior retainer" enough that he directed Fujiko, a lady-in-waiting, to kill her. The upset Lord Iida sentences her to death. As no Iida clansman is willing to do the beheading, Fujiko's lover Tada Soji, a Nagaoka samurai, volunteers. Afterwards Soji becomes a monk and goes to live in the forest. The couple's infant son is adopted by Takakura Shuémon and is named Shingo.

At the age of 20, not knowing his true past, Shingo sets out on a three-year musha shugyo, and returns a master swordsman. He gains notoriety for his skills, but spurs jealousy within the clan, and Shingo's father and sister are murdered. He takes bloody revenge on the assassins, fellow clansmen Ikebé and his son. Before his foster father's death, Shingo is told about his birth. The swordsman then sets off to find his biological father Soji.

When Shingo finds his father, Soji shows his son the grave of his mother Fujiko.

Shingo then sets off on his path as ronin. Along the way the he helps Tadokoro Mondo and his beautiful sister, who are on the run from the government for murdering some corrupt officials.

Eventually Shingo is hired as a yojimbo "bodyguard" for the Shogunate minister Matsudaira during the Mito Rebellion (1864-1865).

Note: This film should not be confused with the 1968 film *Kill!* (*Kiru*) directed by Kihachi Okamoto.

DVD: Region 1 (USA) version not commercially available

Samurai Movies – Bakumatsu Period

The Hidden Blade (*Kakushi ken: Oni no tsumé*)

2004 Shochiku, 132 minutes, rated R, color

- **Director:** Yoji Yamada
- **Cast:** Masatoshi Nagasé, Takako Matsu, Hidetaka Yoshioka, Yukiyoshi Ozawa, et al
- **Recommendation:** Comical scenes of samurai in Western military training. Romantic and low-key with compelling characters. Solid neo-samurai film.
- **Ratings:** Amazon.com 4.3/5, IMDb 7.7/10, Netflix 3.7/5, Rotten Tomatoes 87%/50%

After being caught in a failed political intrigue in Edo, Hazama Yaichiro is sent home in disgrace to his Unasaka clan in northwest Japan and imprisoned. When he escapes, honest and noble low-ranking samurai Katagiri Munezo is ordered by the clan karo "senior retainer" Hori to prove his innocence from complicity by killing his old friend.

Based on a short story by Shuhei Fujisawa (1927-1997).

DVD: Tartan Video (2006)

The Last Samurai (*Okami yo rakujitsu o kiré*)

1974 Shochiku, 159 minutes, color

- **Director:** Kenji Misumi
- **Cast:** Hideki Takahashi, Ken Ogata, Kiwako Taichi, Keiko Matsuzaka, et al
- **Recommendation:** Complex story of historical events seriously and sincerely told. Unsparing gore. Elaborate battle sequences.
- **Ratings:** IMDb 7/10

Ronin Suji Toranosuké returns to his home town of Edo after many years. He meets and befriends Shinsengumi swordsman Okita Soji (1842-1868), Satsuma samurai Nakamura Hanjiro (1838-1877), and Mimawarigumi member Iba Hachiro (1843-1869). They take part in the 1864 Ikeda-ya Incident, the 1868 Battle of Toba-Fushimi, the 1868 Battle of Ueno (Edo), and the 1877 Satsuma Rebellion.

Note: This film should not be confused with the 2003 film with the same title starring Tom Cruise.

DVD: Region 1 (USA) version not commercially available

The Last Samurai

2003 Warner Bros., 154 minutes, rated R, color

- **Director:** Edward Zwick
- **Cast:** Tom Cruise, Ken Watanabé, Hiroyuki Sanada, Masato Harada, et al
- **Recommendation:** A historical story loosely based on the last stand of samurai Saigo Takamori (1828-1877) against Japan's transformation into a Western-style nation. Includes obligatory scenes of cultural differences. Although ultimately unbelievable, the film is tasteful and better than expected. Beautifully shot with noteworthy performances.
- **Ratings:** AllMovie 3/5, Amazon.com 4.1/5, IMDb 7.8/10, Netflix 3.8/5, Rotten Tomatoes 65%/82%

In 1876 alcoholic U.S. Army captain Nathan Algren is hired by the Meiji government to train Japan's new Western-style army. After the initial training of conscripts, in his first battle, Nathan is wounded and captured by traditionalist samurai, led by the resourceful Lord Katsumoto Moritsugu, conducting an armed insurrection against the modernization campaign.

The film's plot was inspired by the 1876 Satsuma Rebellion led by Saigo Takamori, and also on the story of Jules Brunet, a French army captain who fought alongside Enomoto Takéaki in the 1868-69 Boshin War.

DVD: Warner Home Video (full-screen 2004, HD 2006, widescreen 2009)

Blu-ray: Warner Home Video (2006)

Love and Honor (*Bushi no ichibun*)

2006 Shochiku, 121 minutes, rated PG-13, color

- **Director:** Yoji Yamada
- **Cast:** Takuya Kimura, Rei Dan, Takashi Sasano, Mitsugoro Bando, et al
- **Recommendation:** Realistic atmosphere and convincing performances. Comparatively simple plot. Perhaps the best of the recent crop of neo-samurai films.
- **Ratings:** Amazon.com 4.7/5, IMDb 7.6/10, Netflix 3.7/5, Rotten Tomatoes 79%/83%

An official food taster for the clan lord, low-ranking samurai Mimura Shinnojo becomes blind when he samples a toxic shellfish. As Shinnojo's stipend of rice is clearly at risk, his loyal wife Kayo goes to Shimada Toya, a high-ranking samurai officer, for his assistance. Toya forces himself on her and blackmails Kayo into giving him sexual favors. A message arrives from the castle that the stipend will remain the same, but when Shinnojo finds out about the tryst, he angrily divorces his wife. When Shinnojo later finds out that the continuing stipend was due to the gratitude of the lord, and that Toya had nothing to do with it, he sets up a duel with him, despite his blindness.

Based on a novel by Shuhei Fujisawa (1927-1997).

DVD: Funimation (2008)

Mask of the Moon (*Tsukigata Hanpeita*)

1961 Toei, color

- **Director:** Masahiro Makino
- **Cast:** Hashizo Okawa, Isao Yamagata, Satomi Oka, Sonosuké Sawamura, et al
- **Recommendation:** Fictionalized version of historical events with plenty of great swordplay. Good cast.

Tsukigata Hanpeita is a member of an anti-Shogunate clan from Choshu (aka Nagato). He befriends Hayasé, a members of the pro-Shogunate Mimawarigumi, which is assigned primarily to protect the Imperial Palace in Kyoto, and is headquartered in Nijo Castle. The 200-member group is made up entirely of sons of Tokugawa hatamoto.

Ever since the silent era, many film versions of this story have appeared.

DVD: Region 1 (USA) version not commercially available

SAMURAI MOVIES

Red Lion (Akagé "Red hair")

1969 Toho, 115 minutes, color

- **Director:** Kihachi Okamoto
- **Cast:** Toshiro Mifuné, Etsushi Takahashi, Shigeru Koyama, Minori Terada, et al
- **Recommendation:** Historical background, but the plot is of the typical "save the village from corrupt officials" theme. Entertaining blend of humor and tragedy.
- **Ratings:** AllMovie 2.5/5, Amazon.com 4.7/5, IMDb 7/10, Netflix 3.2/5, Rotten Tomatoes --/67%

In 1869, a year into the Imperial Restoration, the transition of power is not complete. When an advance troop of peasant recruits approach one of the villages on their way to Edo, one of its members, Gonzo, announces that he is from that village, and begs to ride ahead to notify the villagers of the coming of the Imperial Army. So he can have some authority when delivering the message, Gonzo is allowed to don the large red wig of an officer.

When Gonzo arrives at the village of Sawado, which he has not been to in ten years, he learns that corrupt Shogunate officials have been heavily overtaxing the villagers over the years, causing much suffering.

DVD: AnimEigo (2005)

Samurai Assassin (Samurai)

1965 Toho, 122 minutes, b&w

- **Director:** Kihachi Okamoto
- **Cast:** Toshiro Mifuné, Keiju Kobayashi, Michiyo Aratama, Yunosuké Ito, et al
- **Recommendation:** Detailed account of an important historical incident. Ironic, suspenseful, violent, and tragic.
- **Ratings:** AllMovie 2.5/5, Amazon.com 4.4/5, IMDb 7.1/10, Netflix 3.6/5, Rotten Tomatoes --/73%

Based on actual events leading to the Sakurada-mon Incident. In 1860, on a bleak snowy day, outside the Sakurada Gate of Edo Castle, a group of ronin from Mito (Hitachi), led by Hoshino Kenmotsu, assassinates the Shogun's tairo "chief minister" Ii Naosuké (1815-1860).

The story is told from the point of view of the ronin Niiro Tsurichiyo, an illegitimate son of a high-ranking official, who is befriended by the aristocratic samurai Kurihara Einosuké.

DVD: AnimEigo (2005)

Satan's Sword (Daibosatsu togé "Boddhisattva Pass")

1960 Daiei, 106 minutes, color

- **Director:** Kenji Misumi
- **Cast:** Raizo Ichikawa, Tamao Nakamura, Kojiro Hongo, Fujiko Yamamoto, et al
- **Recommendation:** Historical background. Good cast.
- **Ratings:** IMDb 7.1/10

Psychopathic master swordsman Tsukué Ryunosuké kills Utsuki Bunnojo in a big sword tournament, rapes his wife, and is pursued by his brother Hyoma.

Based on an unfinished historical novel by Kaizan Nakazato (1885-1944) of over 41 volumes published from 1913 to 1941. The lead characters is based on real-life Fuda Ryuzaburo Takafumi, a swordsman of the Kogen Itto-ryu.

1st film in a series, two sequels were made. The stand-alone film, *Sword of Doom* (1966), based on the same novel, essentially tells the same story as this film.

DVD: Region 1 (USA) version not commercially available

Shinsengumi (aka Band of Assassins, Assassins of Honor)

1969 Toho, 122 minutes, color

- **Director:** Tadashi Awashima
- **Cast:** Toshiro Mifuné, Rentaro Mikuni, Kinya Kitaoji, Keiju Kobayashi, et al
- **Recommendation:** Detailed historical drama. Big-budget production.
- **Ratings:** AllMovie 2/5, Amazon.com 4.1/5, IMDb 7.1/10, Netflix 3.5/5, Rotten Tomatoes --/67%

In 1863 Serizawa Kamo (1826-1863) and Kondo Isami (1834-1868) form the Shinsengumi, a special police force funded by the Tokugawa Shogunate to keep peace in Kyoto. Isami later murders Kamo, and takes over the leadership of the group. In 1864 the Shinsengumi discovers a plot to set Kyoto aflame, which leads to the Ikeda-ya Incident.

The film features many historical figures.

In 2004 NHK Taiga Drama aired a 50-episode version of the story, titled *Shinsengumi!*, written by Koki Mitani (1961-).

DVD: AnimEigo (2007)

Shinsengumi Chronicles: I Want to Die a Samurai (Shinsengumi shimatsu-ki)

1963 Daiei, 93 minutes, color

- **Director:** Kenji Mitsumi
- **Cast:** Raizo Ichikawa, Tomisaburo Wakayama, Shiho Fujimura, Shigeru Amachi, et al
- **Recommendation:** Thoroughly-detailed depiction of historical events. Starts slow, ends with a bang.
- **Ratings:** IMDb 8.1/10, Netflix 2.9/5

In 1863 ronin Yamazaki Susumu (1833-1868) joins the pro-Shogunate Shinsengumi in Kyoto out of admiration for its leader Kondo Isami (1834-1868). After Isami's lieutenant Hijikata Toshizo (1835-1869) assassinates rival faction leader Serizawa Kamo (1826-1863), in 1864 the group famously prevents the torching of Kyoto by pro-Imperialist ronin from Choshu (aka Nagato) and Tosa provinces in the raid known as the Ikeda-ya Incident.

Adapted from a book by Shimazawa Kan (1892-1968).

DVD: AnimEigo (2010)

The Sword of Doom (Dai-bosatsu togé "Boddhisattva Pass")

1966 Toho, 119 minutes, b&w

- **Director:** Kihachi Okamoto
- **Cast:** Tatsuya Nakadai, Yuzo Kayama, Michiyo Aratama, Ko Nishimura, et al
- **Recommendation:** Impressive swordplay. Lots of killing.
- **Ratings:** AllMovie 4/5, Amazon.com 4.1/5, IMDb 8/10, Netflix 3.7/5, Rotten Tomatoes 71%/90%

The sociopathic ronin Tsukué Ryunosuké is a swordsman of pure evil. He is hired by Serizawa Kamo (1826-1863) to join the violent Shinchogumi, the Edo counterpart of Kyoto's Shinsengumi. Ryunosuké is eventually driven mad by visions of people he has killed.

Based on a 41-volume historical novel by Kaizan Nakazato (1885-1944). The story has been filmed many times, and this is the most well-known version. A more complete version was released earlier as the *Satan's Sword Trilogy* (1960-1961) starring Raizo Ichikawa.

DVD: Criterion (2005)

Samurai Movies – Bakumatsu Period

Sword of the Beast (*Kedamono no ken*)

1965 Shochiku, 85 minutes, b&w

- **Director:** Hideo Gosha
- **Cast:** Mikijiro Hira, Go Kato, Shima Iwashita, Kunié Tanaka, et al
- **Recommendation:** Melodramatic story of loyalty, greed, and betrayal. Excellent swordplay.
- **Ratings:** Amazon.com 3.6/5, IMDb 7.6/10, Netflix 3.6/5, Rotten Tomatoes --/83%

In 1857 lowly samurai Yuki Gennosuké of the Ota clan of Kakegawa domain (Totomi -- 50,000 koku) is tricked into assassinating his clan's karo "senior retainer" Yamaoka Kenmotsu. He is pursued by the karo's daughter Misa, her fiancé Torio Daizaburo, the clan's master swordsman Katori Gundayu, and other clan members. He comes upon the theif Tanji who enlists him into poaching gold from the Shogun's Mount Shirané (Kozuké). There Gennosuké encounters another samurai, Yamané Jurota, and his wife Taka, who are on a mission to steal gold for their clan.

DVD: Criterion (2005)

Taboo (*Gohatto*)

1999 Shochiku, 100 minutes, color

- **Director:** Nagisa Oshima
- **Cast:** Takeshi Kitano, Ryuhei Matsuda, Tadanobu Asano, Masa Tommies, et al
- **Recommendation:** A view into the homosexuality of the samurai. Realistic historical background. Moody. A neo-samurai film.
- **Ratings:** AllMovie 4/5, Amazon.com 4/5, IMDb 6.8/10, Netflix 3/5, Rotten Tomatoes 67%/69%

In 1865 androgynous Kano Sozaburo is admitted to the Shinsengumi in Kyoto by commander Kondo Isami (1834-1868) and captain Hijikata Toshizo (1835-1869). Fellow recruit Hyozo Tashiro is suspected of being his lover, stirring up jealousy and gossip among the other men, which includes Inoué Genzaburo (1829-1868) and Okita Soji (1842-1868).

DVD: New Yorker Video (2002)

Tenchu (*Hitokiri "Killer"*)

1969 Shochiku, 140 minutes, color

- **Director:** Hideo Gosha
- **Cast:** Shintaro Katsu, Tatsuya Nakadai, Yukio Mishima, Yujiro Ishihara, et al
- **Recommendation:** Astonishing sword fights amidst an historical background.
- **Ratings:** AllMovie 2/5, IMDb 7.6/10

In 1862 Okada Izo (1832-1865) is hired by Takechi Hanpeita (1829-1865) as an assassin for the Loyalist faction from Tosa dedicated to restoring Imperial rule.

Also appearing are historical figures Sakamoto Ryoma (1836-1867), a leader of the movement to overthrow the Tokugawa Shogunate, and Tanaka Shinbei (1832-1863), another assassin working for Hanpeita, who was involved in the assassination of the Shogun's tairo "chief minister" Ii Naosuké (1815-1860).

DVD: Region 1 (USA) version not commercially available

The Thirteen Assassins (*Jusan-nin no shikaku*)

1963 Toho, 125 minutes, b&w

- **Director:** Eiichi Kudo
- **Cast:** Chiezo Kataoka, Ko Nishimura, Ryohei Uchida, Isao Natsuyagi, et al
- **Recommendation:** Superbly choreographed epic final battle.
- **Ratings:** IMDb 7.3/10, Rotten Tomatoes --/85%

Shimada Shinzaémon is recruited to assassinate the younger brother to the 12th Tokugawa Shogun Ieyoshi (1793-1853), the cruel and evil lord Matsudaira Naritsugu, whose scandalous rapes and reckless killings threaten the Shogunate. Shinzaémon gathers twelve others to help him set up a death trap against a force of bodyguards four times greater.

Remade as *13 Assassins* (2010) directed by Takashi Miiké, and starring Koji Yakuso.

DVD: Region 1 (USA) version not commercially available

Twilight Samurai (*Tasogaré Seibei*)

2003 Shochiku, 129 minutes, color

- **Director:** Yoji Yamada
- **Cast:** Hiroyuki Sanada, Ren Osugi, Tetsuro Tamba, Rié Miyazawa, et al
- **Recommendation:** Life of a rural samurai. One of the more romantic samurai tales. A solid neo-samurai film and an instant classic.
- **Ratings:** Amazon.com 4.6/5, IMDb 8.1/10, Netflix 4/5, Rotten Tomatoes 99%/93%

Widower Iguchi Seibei is a supply clerk for the rural Unasaka clan. He has two young daughters and a senile mother to support, and is deeply in debt. He has become disheveled and unkempt, and is scolded by the lord of the clan for not keeping clean. His uncle Tozaémon suggests remarrying, but Seibei declines. His childhood sweetheart Tomoé returns to town, recently divorced from her abusive husband Kodo Toyotaro. When Toyotaro drunkenly comes to fetch Tomoé, Seibei incapacitates him with a wooden stick. Seibei is soon ordered to kill renegade samurai Yogo Zenémon, whose circumstances are very similar to his own.

Based on a novel by Shuhei Fujisawa (1927-1997).

DVD: First Run Features (2004)

When the Last Sword is Drawn (*Mibu gishi den*)

2003 Shochiku, 143 minutes, color

- **Director:** Yojiro Takita
- **Cast:** Kichi Nakai, Koichi Sato, Miki Nakatani, Yui Natsukawa, et al
- **Recommendation:** Loosely based on historical events. Gorgeous cinematography. Detailed sets and costumes. First-rate production. A neo-samurai film.
- **Ratings:** AllMovie 3/5, Amazon.com 4.7/5, IMDb 7.5/10, Netflix 3.8/5, Rotten Tomatoes --/87%

In flashbacks, ex-Shinsengumi member Saito Hajimé (1844-1915) recounts the life of Yoshimura Kan'ichiro (1840-1868), a Nanbu clan samurai from Morioka (Mutsu -- 100,000 koku). In 1864 the two participates in the Ikeda-ya Incident in Kyoto. In 1867, when Ito Kashitaro (1835-1867) defects to form the Goryo Eji, an anti-Shogunate group, the two are part of the Shinsengumi assault team that ambushes them at the Incident at Aburano Koji. In 1868 they are decisively defeated at the Battle of Toba-Fushimi (between Kyoto and Osaka) by Imperial forces while defending Fushimi Castle.

Based on the novel by Jiro Asada (1951-).

DVD: Fox Lorber (2005)

Non-Specific

Daimajin "Great Evil Spirit"

1966 Daiei, 86 minutes, color

- **Director:** Kimiyoshi Yasuda

Samurai Movies – Bakumatsu Period

- **Cast:** Miwa Takada, Jun Fujimaki, Yoshihiko Aoyama, Ryutaro Gomi, et al
- **Recommendation:** Monster movie set in the samurai era.
- **Ratings:** AllMovie 3/5, Amazon.com 4.3/5, IMDb 5.9/10, Netflix 3.1/5 (for the complete series), Rotten Tomatoes --/77%

In the mountains is a Daimajin "Great Evil Spirit" which is kept at bay by a giant stone village god. At Yamanaka Castle (Izu), the local Lord Hanabusa Kozasa is overthrown by his karo "senior retainer" Odaté Samanosuké and his henchman Gunjuro. Loyal clan retainers Chuma and Kogenta take the lord's young son Tadafumi and young daughter Kozasa to safety.

Ten years later, Lord Odaté sends Gunjuro and some men to destroy the stone statue, but the monster appears before the deed is done, and wreaks havoc and mayhem.

This film was followed by two sequels: *Wrath of Daimajin* (1966) and *Return of Daimajin* (1966).

DVD: ADV Films (2005)

The Great Bandit (aka *Samurai Pirate* and *The Lost World of Sinbad*) (*Dai tozoku*)

1963 Toho, 96 minutes, color

- **Director:** Senkichi Taniguchi
- **Cast:** Toshiro Mifuné, Tadao Nakamaru, Mié Hama, Kumi Mizuno, et al
- **Recommendation:** Low-budget special effects. Goofy costumes. More fantasy than samurai, kids will enjoy this swashbuckler film.
- **Ratings:** AllMovie 2/5, IMDb 6.1/10

Sukezaémon, a wealthy shipping merchant of Sakai (Izumi), is falsely accused of being a pirate and is sentenced to death. He escapes with a bribe and sets sail with his men. A storm immediately wrecks his ship and he washes ashore on a Pacific island.

There Sukezaémon meets the island's beautiful princess, whose father is dying, and is awaiting her prince from Ming China. He must stop the dastardly chancellor from usurping the throne, as well as help rid an old witch who turns people to stone.

DVD: Region 1 (USA) version not commercially available

Kwaidan "Ghost Stories" (*Kaidan*)

1964 Toho, 183 minutes, color

- **Director:** Masaki Kobayashi
- **Cast:** Rentaro Mikuni, Keiko Kishi, Michiyo Aratama, Misako Watanabé, Tatsuya Nakadai, et al
- **Recommendation:** Atypical ghost stories, even for the Japanese. Although a classic, this is perhaps the least interesting film on this list for samurai fans. Stunning cinematography.
- **Ratings:** AllMovie 4/5, Amazon.com 4.4/5, IMDb 8.0/10, Netflix 3.6/5, Rotten Tomatoes 81%/89%

Kwaidan means "ghost story" and this film consists of four separate and unrelated episodes based on stories from Japanese folk tales collected by Lafcadio Hearn (1850-1904).

In "The Black Hair," a poor samurai in Kyoto divorces his wife to marry a wealthy wife, but he is unhappy with his marriage and returns to his wife. After spending the night with her in their now-dilapidated house, he wakes up to a horrifying discovery which drives him insane.

In "The Woman of the Snow," a woodcutter is saved from a snow storm by a spirit of a snow woman on the condition that he never tell anyone about her. Years later he marries a beautiful woman and eventually breaks his promise and tells her about his encounter to grave consequences.

In "Hochi the Earless," the scene begins with a re-enactment of the Battle of Dan-no-ura, and then cuts to a blind biwa "Japanese lute" player performing the tale at the Amada-ji in Akama-ga-hara. He is invited by a samurai to perform the epic ballad for his lord. After going out several nights to do so, Hochi begins to look like life is draining away from him. The monks find out he has been playing to ghosts at the cemetery where the Heiké in his song are buried. They cover him by writing a holy mantra all over his body to make him invisible, except they forget his ears. Hochi returns safe, but with his ears cut off.

"A Cup of Tea" takes place in 1680 at a temple in Hongo (Edo). The samurai Kannai sees a samurai's face on the surface of the water in his cup. He is later haunted by his spirit, leading to a shocking ending.

Awards: Cannes Film Festival (1965), Special Jury Prize

DVD: Criterion (2000)

100 Monsters (*Yokai hyaku monogatari* "100 ghosts story")

1968 Daiei, 90 minutes, color

- **Director:** Kimiyoshi Yasuda
- **Cast:** Miwa Takada, Jun Fujimaki, Ryutaro Gomi, Takashi Kanda, et al
- **Recommendation:** Many traditional ghosts from Japanese folklore. Considered suitable for children in Japan, despite all the killing. Kids will certainly enjoy it.
- **Ratings:** Amazon.com 4/5, IMDb 6.7/10, Netflix 2.8/5

Ghosts get involved when yakuza boss Tajimaya Reimon, supported by the shrine magistrate Hotta, threatens to tear down a tenement building and put up a brothel. Living in the tenement is the kindly landlord's daughter Okiku, and the mysterious ronin Yasutaro.

1st of a trilogy, followed by *Yokai Monsters: Spook Warfare* (1968) and *Yokai Monsters: Along With Ghosts* (1969). In 2005 a new film called *The Great Yokai War*, directed by Takashi Miiké, was released.

DVD: ADV Films (2003)

Three Outlaw Samurai (*Sanbiki no samurai*)

1964 Shochiku, 95 minutes, b&w

- **Director:** Hideo Gosha
- **Cast:** Tetsuro Tanba, Isamu Nagato, Mikijiro Hira, Miyuki Kawano, et al
- **Recommendation:** Exciting and entertaining story. Solid chanbara action. See it if you can find it.
- **Ratings:** IMDb 7.5/10, Rotten Tomatoes --/86%

Wandering ronin Shiba Sakon encounters three peasants, led by Junbei, who have kidnapped Aya, the local magistrate's daughter. The local farmers are starving, and are desperate to have their petition to reduce taxes heard. Sakon is eventually joined by two other ronin, Sakura Kyojuro and Kikyo Einosuké.

Sakon makes a deal with the magistrate: he will accept punishment for the peasant's crimes on the condition that there are no other retributions. After 100 lashes, the magistrate reneges and has the peasants killed. Aya, who has fallen in love with Sakon, helps him escape, but when he goes after the magistrate, she pleads for her father's life.

DVD: Platinum Classics (Hong Kong)

Kanji Primer

Chinese Characters 漢字

The Japanese were first introduced to Chinese characters in the early part of the 1st millenium A.D. Japanese legend has it that around the 4th century A.D., Wani, a Korean-Baekje scholar, brought to the Japanese islands the *Senji-mon* "*The Scroll of a Thousand Characters*" and ten volumes of Analects by Confucius. The scroll was used as a primer for learning Chinese writing. Previously, the Japanese language did not have a written form.

The first written documents of the Imperial Court of Japan were probably written by Chinese immigrants in the Chinese language. Over time, the Chinese characters were adapted to conform to the rules of Japanese grammar. The Japanese used their pronunciations for the Chinese characters, and added hiranaga and katakana for the additional sounds that are needed for the Japanese language. Kanji is the modified Japanese version of the Chinese character set. The Chinese readings, however, are still used regularly in Japan and are part of its language, much like how French words exist in English.

The kanji in this primer are provided for those interested in rudimentary knowledge of the Japanese written language.

The first line of each entry lists the Japanese pronunciations. If the verbalization is preceded by a hyphen, it is an alternate enunciation that is sometimes used when the kanji is employed as a suffix. *Italicized* entries are Chinese pronunciations that are commonly used by the Japanese.

Topographical

川	kawa, -gawa, *sen* "river"
山	yama, *san, zan* "mountain"
原	hara, -bara, -wara, *gen* "field"
平	sawa, -zawa, *hei* "plain"
島	shima, -jima, *to* "island"
坂	saka, -zaka, *han* "hill"
峠	togé "mountain pass"
湖	mizu'umi, *ko* "lake"
湾	*wan* "bay" "gulf"
海	umi, *kai* "ocean" "sea"

Arboreal

木	ki, *boku* "tree" "wood"
森	mori, *shin* "forest" "grove"
松	matsu, *sho* "pine tree"

Man-Made Constructs

田	ta, -da, *den* "rice paddy"
井	i, *sei* "well"
道	michi, *do* "road" "way" "path"
寺	tera, -dera, *ji* "temple"
宮	miya, *gu* "shrine"
橋	hashi, -bashi, *kyo* "bridge"
城	shiro, *jo* "castle" "citadel"
門	kado, *mon* "gate" "door"
村	mura, *son* "village" "hamlet"
町	machi, *cho* "town" "city"
国	kuni, *koku* "country" "province"

Size

大	ō, *dai, tai* "big" "great" "grand"
小	ko, o, *shu* "small" "minor

Kanji Primer

Compass Directions

北	kita, *hoku* "north"	京	higashi, *to* "east"
南	minami, *nan* "south"	西	nishi, *sai* "west"

Seasons

冬	fuyu, *to* "winter"	夏	natsu, *gé* "summer"
春	haru, *shun* "spring"	秋	aki, *shu* "autumn"

Heavenly

日	hi, *nichi* "sun" "day"
月	tsuki, *getsu* "moon" "month"
天	*ten* "heaven" "sky"
空	sora, *ku* "sky" "air"
雨	amé, *u* "rain" "rainfall"
雪	yuki, *setsu* "snow" "snowfall"

Positional

上	ué, *jo* "top" "up" "upper" "over"
下	shita, *ka, gé* "bottom" "down" "lower" "under"
中	naka, *chu* "middle" "inner"

Things

本	moto, *hon* "source" "book"
石	ishi, *seki* "stone"
口	kuchi, -guchi, *ko, ku* "mouth" "opening"
水	mizu, *sui* "water (cold)"
火	hi, *ka* "fire" "flames"
金	kané, *kin* "money" "gold"
土	tsuchi, *do* "earth" "soil" "ground"
米	komé, *mai* "rice"
酒	saké, *shu* "rice wine"
馬	uma, *ba* "horse"

Human

人	hito, *jin, nin* "person"
男	otoko, *dan, nan* "man" "male"
女	onna, *jo* "woman" "female"
子	ko, *shi, su* "child"

Martial

武	*bu, mu* "martial"
士	samurai, *shi*
刀	katana, *to* "sword"
弓	yumi, *kyu* "bow"
矢	ya, *shi* "arrow"

Numerical

一	hito, *ichi* "one" "single"	二	futa, *ni* "two"	五	itsu, *go* "five"	八	ya, *hachi* "eight"
		三	mi, *san* "three"	六	mu, *roku* "six"	九	kokono, *ku* "nine"
		四	yo, *shi* "four"	七	nana, *shichi* "seven"	十	to, *ju* "ten"
		百	*hyaku* "hundred"	千	chi, *sen* "thousand"	万	*man* "ten thousand"

Campaign Setting

Samurai Role-Playing

The following is a suggestion for an ahistorial samurai campaign setting. Modify as necessary to suit your particular scenario.

Ahistorical Campaign

An ahistorical setting allows for the use of any historical or fictional character, or interaction in any historical event, without regard to the actual timeline of history. The full panorama of Japanese history can be used in this type of setting.

Keep geography accurate, however. Castles and temples should at their historical locations. Unless magic or science fiction is introduced, travel from one place to the next should be along plausible routes, e.g. characters will have to travel by sea to get from island to island.

The Tabi "Pilgrimage"

A clan has a tradition of sending the heirs of its daimyo on a series of pilgrimages soon after his genbuku "coming-of-age ceremony." During the pilgrimage, he will visit his clan domain, practice the martial arts, learn about the country, and experience its people, places, and things.

The sankin-kotai "alternate attendance" system is in effect, and so the family resides in Edo. Allowing the heir to leave the capital and go off on a pilgrimage requires the permission of the Shogun himself, and the daimyo must make the request personally.

The tabi will start a week or two after the daimyo returns in the early spring from a year in his domain to remain in the capital for the following year. The initial pilgrimage is for six months so the young heir is expected to return to the capital sometime in the fall.

The Pilgrim Party

The daimyo's son will be accompanied by a group of supporting characters:

- **Waka-tono "young lord"** -- The heir is around 15-years-old, trained at least in the martial arts of swordsmanship, archery, and horsemanship. He leaves behind his father, mother, and at least one brother and one sister from the same mother, and several half-siblings from different mothers.
- **Senior bodyguard** -- An experienced samurai in his 30s or 40s, perhaps an uncle, who has traveled between the capital and the clan domain

UENO (IGA)

DAI-JINGU, KASHIMA (HITACHI)

ISHIYAMA-DERA, LAKE BIWA (OMI)

– From the woodcut print series Famous Places in the Sixty-odd Provinces *by Utagawa Hiroshigé (1797-1858).*

several times, accompanying the daimyo in his sankin-kotai trips.

- **Junior bodyguard** -- A young samurai in his early 20s, who is the young lord's cousin, or perhaps a son of the clan karo "senior retainer" in Edo. In addition to his bodyguard duties, he will serve as an older brother and companion to the young lord. He has been to the clan domain at least once before.
- **Female attendant** -- Young, but with some experience, she is in her mid-20s. She was selected by the boy's mother from among the attendants in the clan mansion in Edo, and will serve as an older sister to the young lord. Her primary responsibility, other than that of the safety of the boy, is to make sure the party's domestic needs are met. She will also keep a daily log of the party's activities, which she will present to the clan at the end of the trip.
- **Senior ninja** -- In his late 20s or early 30s, he will travel ahead of the party in plain traveler's garb to gather intelligence from other ninja cohorts along the way to find out whether there is anything that may jeopardize the young lord's safety.
- **Junior ninja** -- In his early 20s, he will travel behind the party to look out for any suspicious characters that may be acting to harm the group. He will both walk in plain traveling clothes on the road, and in camouflage off the road.

Both ninja are masters of disguise, and will regularly make costume changes.

Party Protocol

The first stop, after setting off from his home, will be to the temple, where the family worships while in Edo, to offer prayers for a safe journey.

When on the road, the young lord, the two samurai, and the attendant will generally start walking in the early morning together to their next destination. Sometime during the afternoon, the older bodyguard will go ahead to make arrangements for that that night's lodging; sometimes it will be the younger bodyguard; and occasionally, if permitted and considered safe enough, the attendant will go. When crossing checkpoints, the party will usually do so together.

The party is allowed to stay in honjin "official lodgings" reserved for daimyo and Shogunate officials, but will generally board overnight at superior inns at post towns.

The young lord will receive martial arts training from the two samurai when opportunities arise. The older samurai will supervise sword practice while the young lord spars with the younger samurai.

The young lord will know about the senior ninja, but not necessarily the junior ninja following the group, at least initially. Occasionally, the young lord will receive ninjutsu training from the older ninja.

Once the party settles into their respective lodgings, both samurai and one or both of the ninja will meet in secret to exchange any pertinent information, and to make plans for the next day and, if required, for the rest of the trip. The young lord will take part in these meetings only when necessary. The attendant will keep the young lord company while the meeting is held.

The young lord will send a messenger every few days with a report on the party's progress to his father, and occasionally to his mother and siblings. He will frequently send small souvenirs of local craft items, dried foods, charms, and art prints along with his message. Any messages from the clan to the heir will be routed to a rendezvous point based on the latest itinerary.

The Route

The first leg of the journey depends on the location of the clan's domain. If it is to the south of Edo, the southern route will be taken first. If it is to the north, the party will initially travel the northern route.

The Southern Circuit

This route takes the pilgrims on the famous Tokaido "Eastern Sea Road" from the Shogun's capital to the Emperor's capital in Kyoto, with a side trip along the way to the Isé Jingu "Grand Shrine" (Isé). The Tokaido minimally takes 12 or 13 days to travel, and the Isé side trip will add 4 or 5 days.

From Kyoto, the party will travel the Osaka Kaido to Osaka. From there they will cross the Inland Sea to the island province of Awaji, then to Awa at the eastern end of Shikoku. The travelers will cross the island to the west side along the Nankaido, and travel to Bungo on the eastern end to Kyushu. They will then go clockwise around the island to Buzen along the Saikaido, cross the Shimo-no-seki Straits to Hagi (Nagato). From there the pilgrims will take the San'yodo along the coast of the Inland Sea back to Kyoto. From Kyoto they will head back to Edo via the Nakasendo.

This southern circuit will require seven to eight weeks of constant travel, so at least three months will be allocated for this leg of the pilgrimage.

The Northern Circuit

This route starts at Edo and heads north on the Oshu Kaido to its terminus at Shirakawa (Mutsu). From there the young lord and his group will take the Sendaido to its terminus at Sendai (Mutsu), and then on the Matsumaedo to its Tappisaki (Mutsu) terminus at the northern tip of Honshu. They will pass through more than 100 post stations in this leg of the trip, and will require over three weeks of constant travel by foot.

From there the travelers will take a trip across the Tsugaru Strait to visit Hakodaté (Ezo) before heading south along the Japan Sea side of Honshu to Nikko (Shimotsuké), and then on the Nikko Kaido back to Edo.

The whole northern circuit will take about seven weeks of constant travel, so two-and-a-half to three months is normally allocated for this route.

Notes

- A young lord on this type of pilgrimage will normally stay 4 or 5 days at his clan's domain, to inspect the estate lands and meeting with as many of his subjects possible. Along with any messages from his clan in Edo, he will bring his relatives and the clan's hittogaro "head chamberlain" small gifts of dried food, craft items, and artwork.
- The side trip to Isé takes one-and-a-half days to get there from the Tokaido. Pilgrims spend at least two whole days there, so the round trip visit will require a minimum of five days.
- The party will stay at least four days in Kyoto, and a few days in Osaka.
- Sickness and injury will add to the travel time, as will poor weather and flooded rivers.
- It will not be unusual for the pilgrimage to take more than the allotted six months. Changes to the itinerary will be mentioned in the young lord's regular messages back to his clan in Edo.

For Adults Only

It was important for a daimyo to have male heirs, whether with his official wife or with concubines. If there is no heir, the Shogunate can dispossess the daimyo and officially disband the clan. Their domain would be either confiscated by the Shogun or assigned to another clan. The clan can petition to adopt an heir, but this required substantial influence as well as the support of the Shogunate.

To this end the clan will initiate the young lord's sexual education in his early teens, as soon as he reaches puberty. When he starts showing interest in the opposite sex, the waka-tono will be taken to a private room for his first sexual intercourse. The event will be somewhat ritualized. The boy will be escorted to the room by his uncle or an older cousin. Upon entering the room, the sexual partner will prostrate and introduce herself with an assumed name for the night. The room will have futon "bedding" already laid out, and with the lights dimmed. There will be two or three female attendants present, along with his escort, to provide any necessary assistance and support, and to make sure no problems arise.

The female partner would be young, but sexually experienced, perhaps a widow. The boy would have been advised to not fall in love with the woman, and this will be the only time he will ever see her. Different partners will be provided for him every night, so long as he is able and willing, but he will never see any of them ever again, unless the young lord is especially insistent. After a few successful engagements, only the female attendants will be present, and depending on the heir's desires, they may be requested to wait behind a curtain or a room divider.

During the pilgrimage, both the senior bodyguard and the female attendant will arrange suitable partners for the young lord, based on his disposition. The attendant will be present during the encounters, but may be behind a room divider, or even in a separate connecting room, if security is less of a concern.

Both samurai and the attendant will answer any questions the boy may have, and will counsel him on sexual techniques. The attendant will go as far as showing the boy exactly what to do by using her own body. As it is important that he enjoys the act of procreation, she will use various methods to pleasure the young man. She will inform the arranged partners regarding his preferences, as well as encourage them to use their personal expertise to consummate a satisfactory encounter.

It is quite possible that the boy will develop fondness for the female attendant. She will try to discourage this by acting like a motherly older sister. If all else fails, and the infatuation continues, she may end up being a concubine to the young lord later on, if there are no objection from the family.

If the boy shows interest in members of his own sex, this will not at all be discouraged as many Japanese men during the feudal era were bisexual. He will, of course, be counseled on the importance of producing male heirs.

Please note that customs differed from clan to clan. This is just a suggestion for this particular family in a fictional role-playing setting.

ROADS

GOKAIDO

In 1601 Tokugawa Ieyasu (1543-1616) started construction of five major roads, called the Gokaido "Five Routes," from Edo to facilitate his control over the country politically, economically, and militarily.

Each of the Five Routes all commenced at Nihonbashi in Edo. They were:

- **Tokaido** -- Connected to Kyoto via a Pacific coast route.
- **Nakasendo** -- Connected to Kyoto to via a central mountain road.
- **Koshu Kaido** -- Connected to Kai province.
- **Oshu Kaido** -- Led north to Mutsu province.
- **Nikko Kaido** -- Connected with Nikko (Shimotsuké).

Official post stations were set up along these routes that provided rest stops, local food, and beverages. Most also offered lodgings, tourist spots, and sightseeing opportunities. There were also many tea houses between stations. Overnight lodging for non-local travelers were only allowed at designated post towns with hatago "inns."

A typical hatago was two-storied, with four guestrooms on the upper floor. Each room typically was eight tatami "straw mats" in size, about 12x12 feet/ 3.6x3.6 meters, and accommodated up to four travelers. Cost was around 200 to 300 mon, about US$40 to $60 per person in a shared room. Names of guests were optionally posted on wooden boards outside the inns so messengers and other parties looking for them can find the travelers.

Every inn had a hot bath for their guests. The better ones provided freshly-cleaned yukata "cotton robes" for lounging and sleeping in; a set dinner, with saké costing extra; next morning's breakfast; and a bento lunch to take with them. Meals were usually served in the guestroom on a small low table, laden with food, for each person. A maid usually stayed in the room during meals to act as a server, and occasionally told local stories, sang songs, or provided other forms of light entertainment for tips.

The cheapest lodgings for the poorest of travelers charged around 50 mon, about $10, and only provided firewood for self-cooking.

Many post stations also had one or more honjin "official lodgings," reserved for daimyo, Shogunal officials, and aristocrats, where common travelers were not allowed, regardless of their wealth and status. These honjin were usually the personal residences of village and town leaders. They had walls and guarded gates, and several buildings, the largest of which typically had twenty or more rooms.

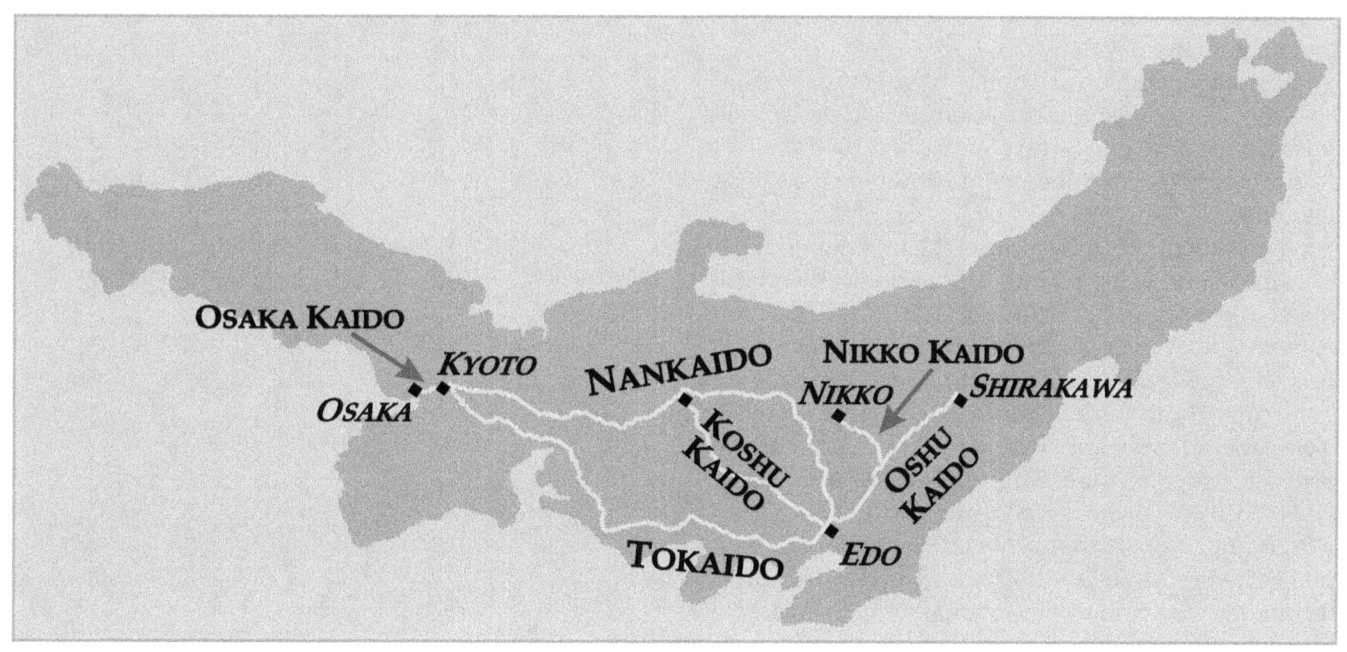

Roads

In addition, there were waki-honjin "sub-honjin" which were similar, but smaller, than honjin. When two official parties stayed at a post town with one honjin and one waki-honjin, the less powerful stayed in the sub-honjin. The waki-honjin, however, were allowed to accept common travelers, if they were not otherwise occupied, and the guests had enough money or sufficient status.

Although prostitution was officially illegal, it was common practice for inns to have maids who would provide sexual services. In 1718 the Tokugawa Shogunate issued a law restricting the maid-prostitutes to two per hatago, which effectively acknowledged the practice.

For special entertainment, geisha "female entertainers" were available at most major post towns. In many cases arrangements should be made as early as possible with the innkeeper. Depending on their skills, they can dance, sing, recite poetry, play music, and provide engaging conversation. Although they flirted and engaged in playful innuendo, traditional geisha are not necessarily prostitutes, and the highest members of the occupation were not available to common travelers; they were available only to their patron and his guests, and at honjin. The higher the class of the geisha, the less they will be inclined to participate in paid sex. Arrangements for sex should made prior to engaging the geisha with the innkeeper. If this is not possible, customers would just hire a prostitute at the hatago, if available, or simply go elsewhere where it was available.

The roads were proactively maintained and sometimes paved with small stones. It was often lined with rows of closely-planted trees to provide shade from the sun, and cover from rain and snow. Rivers had bridges, ferries, or other crossing services, and were occasionally flooded, when they become impassable, but rarely for longer than a day or two.

Palanquins, porters, and horses were generally available for hire between post stations. Handlers usually traveled for only one or two towns, and then the load was transferred to another set of carriers in a tag-team manner.

Wheeled vehicles were rare as the mountainous terrain, the many river crossings, and periodically muddy roads were not conducive to their use. Indeed, the paranoid Shogunate purposefully kept the roads narrow to restrict large-scale rebellions and armed attacks from occurring. The Imperial Court used carriages drawn by oxen, but normally only within the environs of Kyoto. Wheeled wagons were used only necessary, such as when transporting heavy stones for castle walls.

Although more than seventy official sekisho "checkpoints" were strategically-placed by the Shogunate throughout the country, individual domains were not allowed to have gates or barriers of any kind on the main roads, nor were they allowed to charge tolls or fees of any kind for passage.

Due to the heavy traffic, and with all the daimyo traveling to fulfill their sankin-kotai obligations, the Tokaido and all the major roads generally provided safe passage during the Edo Period. This was not however necessarily the case in previous times, especially in the more remote areas where bandits roamed.

Other Routes

In addition to the Five Routes, there were many other minor routes that crisscrossed the entire country. Depending on the traffic level, these roads did not necessarily provide all the amenities available at the major routes. Although they may not have been as rigorously controlled and maintained as the Gokaido, many were important trade routes that had been in use for centuries.

Notes on Gazetteers

- Station names are normally followed by the suffix -shuku or -juku "station," e.g., Tokaido station 1 is Shinagawa-juku.
- The following gazetteers are in the present tense, as though written during the Edo Period, so not all of the following information applies today.
- Major post stations where travelers would most likely lodge overnight are listed in SMALL CAPS.
- Random shops mentioned in the gazetteers can be considered business advertising.

Roads

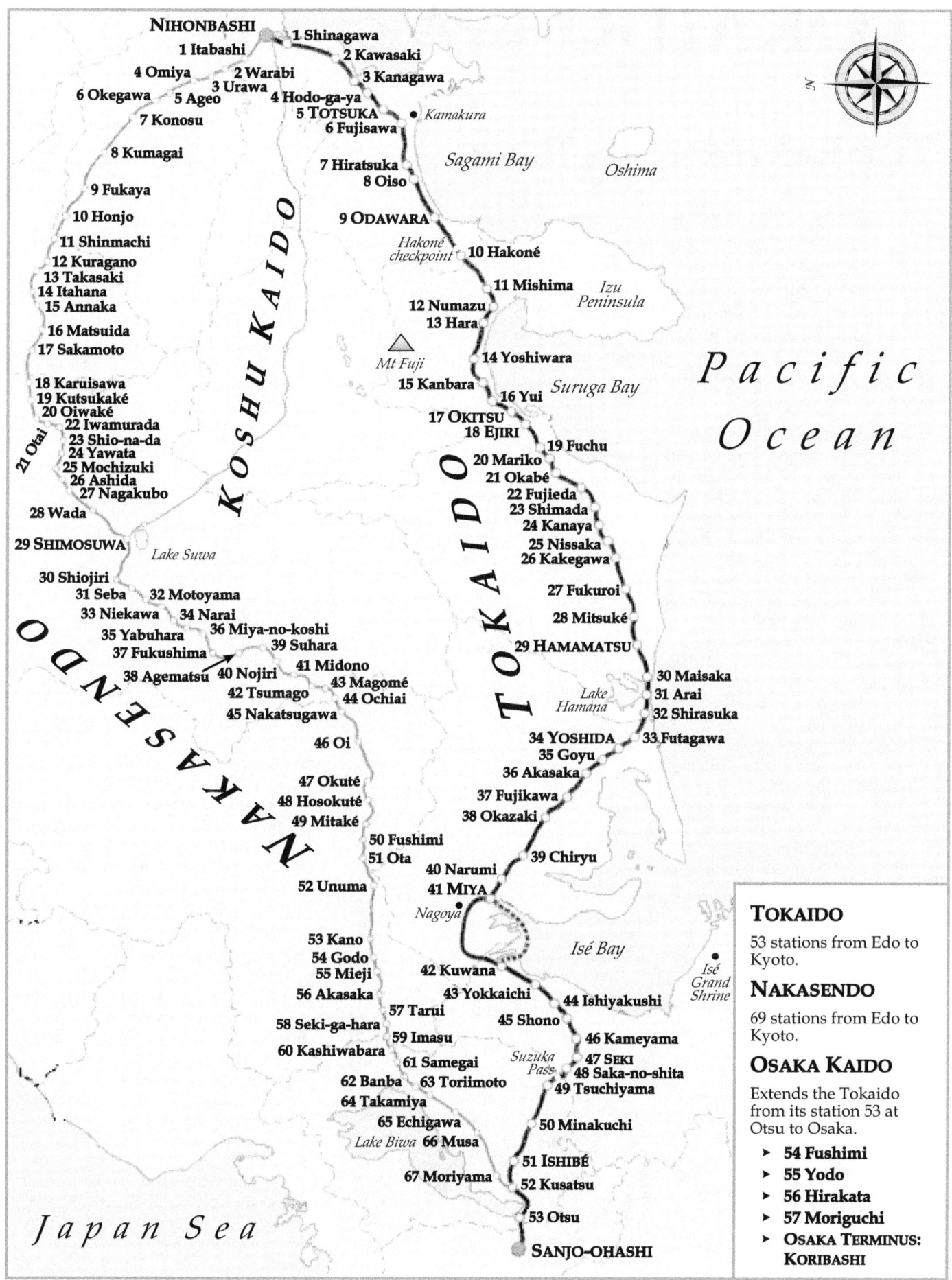

TOKAIDO
53 stations from Edo to Kyoto.

NAKASENDO
69 stations from Edo to Kyoto.

OSAKA KAIDO
Extends the Tokaido from its station 53 at Otsu to Osaka.

- 54 Fushimi
- 55 Yodo
- 56 Hirakata
- 57 Moriguchi
- OSAKA TERMINUS: KORIBASHI

GAMERS GUIDE TO FEUDAL JAPAN — SHOGUN & DAIMYO

TOKAIDO GAZETTEER

THE EASTERN SEA ROAD 東海道

The Tokaido runs from Edo to Kyoto along the southern coast of Honshu. At this time, the Tokaido is believed to be the most heavily traveled road in the world. The distance is 127 ri, or about 310 miles/500 km, and took about 12 or 13 days on foot. There are 53 shukuba "post stations" in between, averaging about 5.75 miles/9.25 km apart from each other, and travel distances are commonly gauged based on the number of stations to get to a destination. Pedestrians generally cover four or five stations per day, depending on actual distance, travel conditions, and walking speed.

EDO TERMINUS: NIHON-BASHI

Initially known as Edo-bashi, the official starting point of the Tokaido is a wooden bridge built in 1603 that spans the Nihon-bashi River. The center of the bridge is the point from which all distances from Edo are measured. It is also the terminus for the Nakasendo.

The area is a bustling mercantile center with many major businesses.

- **Echigo-ya** -- A dry goods department store, with a branch in Kyoto, that began in 1673 by Mitsui Takatoshi (1622-1694), who had a major wholesaling business in the area. In 1683 the Shogunate granted Takatoshi permission to act as a money changer; he then developed a new system for inter-city money lending. In 1691 the Mitsui family was officially chartered as a merchant to the Tokugawa Shogunate. By the end of the Edo Period, the family was the richest and most eminent family in Japan.
- **Uogashi "Fish Quay"** -- A nearby wholesale fish market (predecessor of present-day Tsukiji Fish Market). When Tokugawa Ieyasu (1542-1616) invited fishermen to provide food for Edo Castle, fish not bought by the castle were sold at this market.

1 Shinagawa (Musashi)

Near the Meguro River, as the first rest stop from Edo, it is one of the busiest along the Tokaido. Many daimyo processions rest here on their return journey to Edo before entering the city.

Many Edoites frequent here as the town is famous for its unofficial pleasure quarter where hundreds of entertainment options are available.

The area is famous for its cherry blossoms.

- **Tokai-ji** -- Temple constructed especially for the Tokugawa family, for which the 3rd Tokugawa Shogun Iemitsu (1604-51) invited the Rinzai Zen Buddhist priest Takuan Soho (1573-1645) to be its first abbot.
- **Shinagawa-jinja** -- Built in 1187, the shrine features a torii "traditional Japanese gate" made of stone with images of dragons carved on its pillars. An annual festival is held here to celebrate the victory of Tokugawa Ieyasu (1543-1616) at the 1600 Battle of Seki-ga-hara (Mino).
- **Yoshida-ya** -- Soba "buckwheat noodles" shop, in business since 1856.

2 Kawasaki (Musashi)

Post station established in 1623 by the local magistrate Hasegawa Nagatsuna. It was the last station to be built along the Tokaido.

On the western side of the Rokugo River (aka Tama-gawa) ferry-boat crossing, for people from Edo, crossing the river meant they were leaving the city and entering the countryside. For most people coming from Kyoto, it signified the end of their journey.

- **Heiken-ji** (aka Daishi Temple) -- A famous Buddhist temple founded in 1128, it is the headquarters of the Chizan Shingon Buddhism. Many locals pray here, especially as their hatsumodé, the first place of worshipping in the new year.

3 Kanagawa (Musashi)

This post station parallels the Kanagawa Port, and also serves as part of the route that goods traveled on the way to Sagami. The views of the seashore from the inns along the road are superb.

It was here in 1854 that the Nichibei Washin-joyaku "Japan-U.S. Treaty of Amity and Friendship" was concluded between Commodore Matthew C. Perry (1794-1858) of the U.S. Navy and the Tokugawa Shogunate. This treaty began the opening of Japan to foreign trade after centuries of virtual, self-imposed isolation from the rest of the world.

NIHONBASHI, EDO

4 Hodo-ga-ya (Musashi)

The western-most post station in Musashi. It is a crossroads of many other roads, including those that lead to Kamakura, Kanazawa, and the Komeiji. It has a honjin and several inns.

There is a stone Buddhist statue that people often pray for safety while traveling along the Tokaido.

▶ **Ni-hachi** -- Soba-ya "buckwheat noodle shop" near the Shinmachi Bridge.

5 TOTSUKA (Sagami)

The eastern-most post station in Sagami, it is the 2nd largest post town on the Tokaido after Odawara. As it is approximately 23 miles/37 km from Nihon-bashi, many people who leave Edo at dawn stop here to spend the night at one of its two honjin, owned by the Sawabé and the Uchida families, and numerous inns.

Totsuka is also at the intersection of the Kamakura Kaido and the Atsugi Kaido.

▶ **Tsurugaoka Hachiman-gu** -- Most important Shinto shrine in Kamakura, about 5 miles/8 km from Totsuka, dedicated to the guardian god of warriors. Originally built in another part of the city in 1063 by Minamoto Yoriyoshi (988-1075), it was moved to its present location by Minamoto Yoritomo (1147-1199). Next to the main stairway is a 1000-year-old ginkgo tree. It is said that this is the tree where in 1219 Kugyo (1200-1219), son of the 2nd

Minamoto Shogun Yoriié (1182-1204), hid behind when he murdered the 3rd Minamoto Shogun Sanetomo (1192-1219).

6 Fujisawa (Sagami)

Known as a temple town, this station has one honjin and many inns. Prior to 1745, the Horiuchi residence was used as the honjin, but since then the honjin has been at the Maita residence.

Also located on a fork along the Odawara Kaido, the station served as a the commercial center for the surrounding fishing villages.

The locality is the subject of a number of poems.

▶ **Yugyo-ji** (officially Shojoko-ji) -- Founded in 1325 by Kagehira Matano, its founding priest was Donkai (1265-1327). This is the head temple of the Ji sect of Jodo "Pure Land" Buddhism, which has hundreds of seminaries and training centers throughout Japan. It features a nice garden. The Tokaido branches at this temple for the nearby Enoshima-jinja.

▶ **Enoshima-jinja** -- Founded in 853 by the Buddhist priest Ennin (794-864), the shrine features a rather unusual naked statue of Benzaiten (the Japanese name for the Hindu goddess Saraswati), the goddess of music and entertainment, who is said to have raised the island from the bottom of sea in the 6th century. At low tide people can walk to the island, otherwise coolies are available for carrying pilgrims on their shoulders; fares vary depending on the depth of the water. The island is known for its beauty, abundant nature, and seafood. Hundreds of ukiyo-é prints have been drawn of the island, almost all with Mount Fuji in the background. It will require at least one whole day of travel and sightseeing for this side trip.

▶ **Eisho-ji** -- Convent with many graves of meshimori onna "servant maids" who worked at the local inns, often as prostitutes.

7 Hiratsuka (Sagami)

In 1655 this post station was renamed Shin-hiratsuka-juku. It has one honjin, one sub-honjin, and 54 inns. The Banyu River crossing is located here. The station is at the foot of Korai-zan, a hill with maple trees.

8 Oiso (Sagami)

Around this post station, in 1604 Tokugawa Ieyasu (1543-1616) planted a 2.4-mile/3.9-km colonnade of pine and hackberry trees, to provide shade for the travelers. The station faces Sagami Bay to the south and Mount Korai to the north.

Famous in poetry and legend, in the warrior tale *Soga Monogatari* "*Revenge of the Soga Brothers*" it was here that the beautiful courtesan Tora-gozen lived, and on the 28th day of the 5th month, 1193, she had to part with her lover, one of the Soga brothers. Her copious and bitter tears turned to rain, and it is said that it always rains in Oiso on the 28th day of the 5th month of each year.

Tokaido Gazetteer

9 Odawara (Sagami)

Facing Sagami Bay and located near the banks of the Sakawa River, Odawara-juku is the first post station on the Tokaido from Edo that is a castle town. In 1850 it had a population of 12,700 and some 2,500 travelers passed through it daily, with another 1,000 staying overnight at one of its 121 inns. It is the largest post town on the Tokaido.

Odawara is the gateway to Hakoné, and is famous for its plum and cherry trees, and kamaboko "fish cakes."

▸ **Odawara Castle** -- Built in 1447 by Omori Yoriharu (-1469), in 1495 Hojo Soun (1432-1519, aka Isé Shinkuro) took over the castle soon after he gained control of Izu Peninsula. The castle successfully blocked invasions by Uesugi Kenshin (1530-1578) in 1561, and by Takeda Shingen (1521-1573) in 1569, before Toyotomi Hideyoshi (1536-1598) captured it in 1590 on his way to Odawara after a 100-day siege, when Hojo Ujinao (1562-1591) finally surrendered. During the subsequent Edo Period, as the castle ruled over a strategically-important post town, it was held by a succession of fudai daimyo clans: from 1590 the Okubo, from 1620 the Abé, from 1632 the Inaba, and finally from 1686 the castle reverted back to the Okubo.

Hakoné Sekisho "Checkpoint" (Sagami)

Established in 1619 by the Tokugawa Shogunate at the extremely difficult Hakoné Pass, all travelers passing through this part of the Tokaido must stop at this official checkpoint and present their travel papers and baggage for inspection. As 130 daimyo of western domains pass through this checkpoint for sankin-kotai, this is a daily occurrence during spring. Unlucky travelers will face a long wait.

During the Warring States Period (1467-1573), there was an often quoted saying: "Those who control Hakoné, control Japan."

▸ **Ama-zaké Cha-ya** "Sweet Saké Tea House" -- One of the many rest stops between Odawara and Hakoné, it serves hot sweet saké, tea, and snacks.

10 Hakoné (Sagami)

At an elevation of 2,380 feet/725 m, it is the highest post station on the Tokaido. Rows of tall cedar trees line this part of the road. The area is noted for its cherry blossoms in the spring.

Many popular onsen "hot springs" with indoor and outdoor mineral baths are nearby. The seven most famous are Yumoto, Tonosawa, Miya-no-shita, Dogashima, Sokokura, Kiga, and Ashi-no-yu.

▸ **Owaku-dani** "Great Boiling Valley" -- Lying in the ancient crater of Kamiyama "God Mountain," it is a volcanic hot spot full of sulfurous springs and geysers, where eggs are cooked directly in the boiling water. Known as black eggs, as the sulfurous water turns the shells black, according legend, every one you eat will add seven years to your life.

▸ **Ashi-no-ko** "Lake Ashi" -- Offers beautiful views of Mount Fuji, but only on clear days.

▸ **Hakoné-jinja** -- Located on the eastern shore of Lake Ashi, the shrine was founded in 757 by the Buddhist priest Mangan, and represents an amalgam of Buddhist and Shinto elements. In 1180, when Minamoto Yoritomo (1147-1199) was defeated by the Taira at the Battle of Ishibashi-yama in his first major battle, he took refuge here. Since then it has attracted many Kanto samurai, but Toyotomi Hideyoshi (1536-1598) burned down the shrine when he attacked the area. It was rebuilt by Tokugawa Ieyasu (1543-1616) before he became Shogun. Many travelers pray here for a safe journey.

11 Mishima (Izu)

The only post station located within Izu Peninsula, it has two honjin and 74 inns.

Izu is under direct control of the Shogun, with Mishima as its capital, and is the seat of government for the hatamoto that rules over the province.

As the town is located at the foot of Mount Fuji, clear mountain water flows here, and Mishima is referred to as the "Capital of Water."

▸ **Mishima-jinja** -- The ichi-no-miya "first shrine" of Izu, its foundation is lost in history. A popular pilgrimage stop, the shrine is dedicated to the Mishima Daimyojin, an amalgamation of Ohoyamatsumi, the elder brother to Amaterasu the Sun Goddess and an important god of mountain, sea, and war, and his consort. In his boyhood, Miyamoto Yoritomo (1147-1199) was exiled to Nirayama in Izu about 6 miles/ 10 km south of the shrine. Before setting off to battle the Taira, it is said he worshipped here daily for 100 days to ask for good luck and divine assistance. After his success, he rebuilt the shrine on a large scale.

ODAWARA-JO 小田原城

Worship of the Mishima Daimyojin has become popular with the samurai as it came to be associated with victory in battle, and the shrine was patronized by the Odawara Hojo, the Imagawa, and the Tokugawa. Among the Cryptomeria trees, a fragrant olive tree planted around 800 A.D. still stands in the temple grounds.

12 Numazu (Suruga)

The eastern-most post station of the province, facing Suruga Bay, it is a castle town with three honjin, one sub-honjin, and 55 inns. A part of the road to this town follows the Kisé River.

In 1601 Tokugawa Ieyasu promoted Okubo Tadasuké (1537-1613) to daimyohood of Numazu for his efforts at the Battle of Seki-ga-hara (Mino), but when he passed without an heir, the domain reverted back to the Shogunate.

- **Numazu Castle** -- In 1777 Mizuno Tadatomo (1731-1801) was transferred here from Mikawa, and in 1780 built Numazu Castle on the site of the ruins of Sanmaibashi Castle.

13 Hara (Suruga)

This post station is considered one of the best view points for seeing Mount Fuji. The road is lined with pine tress in the western part of town.

14 Yoshiwara (Suruga)

This post station was moved further inland twice after destructive tsunami in 1639 and in 1680. Because of a bend in the road, travelers from Edo would see Mount Fuji on their left.

15 Kanbara (Suruga)

Minor post station located on the eastern bank of the rapidly-flowing Fuji River near its mouth at Suruga Bay.

- **Kanbara Castle** -- In 1569 the castle was taken in a siege by Takeda Katsuyori (1546-1582), son of Takeda Shingen (1521-1573), from Hojo Tsunashigé (1515-1587), nephew of Hojo Soun (1432-1519).

16 Yui (Suruga)

Located at the base of the Satta Mountain and the mouth of the Yui River, the area is known for its sakura ebi, a type of small shrimp. The spectacular view from Satta Pass of Suruga Bay, dotted with the white sails of boats, with Mount Fuji in the background, is considered priceless.

17 Okitsu (Suruga)

Established in 1601, this post station has two honjin, two sub-honjin, and 34 inns. The Tokaido crosses the Okitsu River here.

- **Seiken-ji** -- Temple where Tokugawa Ieyasu (1543-1616) studied while he was a hostage to the Imagawa. He frequently visited Seiken-ji throughout his life, and the plum trees he planted still bloom here. Originally a Tendai Buddhist temple, in 1261 it became associated with the Rinzai Zen sect. It is considered one of the most magnificent temples in Japan. Travelers passing this temple along the Tokaido are required to pay a tributary tax for its maintenance and public safety. The temple supports 49 monks and a staff of 13 others.

18 Ejiri (Suruga)

This castle and port town, located on the lower reaches of the Tomoé River, has two honjin, three sub-honjin, and 50 inns. It is famous for its view of Mount Ashitaka.

PINE GROVE OF MIHO EJIRI

- **Miho-no-matsubara** "Pine grove of Miho" -- Located on Miho Peninsula, one of the pine trees is said to be the one featured in the legend Hagoromo in which a fisherman finds hanging on a branch a beautiful feather robe that belonged to a celestial maiden who needed it to go back home to heaven. There are many versions of the story, including a famous noh play, but most often the fisherman hides the robe and the maiden is compelled to become his wife. The Miho Shrine nearby preserves a piece of her plumage.

19 Fuchu (Suruga)

Castle town with a view of Mount Shizuhata. The famous Abé River crosses here. Fuchu is the birthplace of Jippensha Ikku (1765-1831) who wrote the book *Hizakurigé "Shank's Mare*,*"* a comic novel about the misadventures of two travelers on the Tokaido.

- **Sunpu Castle** -- Known as the "Castle of the Floating Isle," it was built in 1585 by Tokugawa Ieyasu (1543-1616), who retired there in 1605. In 1607 it was rebuilt with a triple moat system, keep, and palace. Subsequently, the castle burned down several times, and rebuilt to certain extents. It is the seat of government for the Sunpu domain, which is owned by the Tokugawa Shogunate, and governed by the Sunpu jodai "castle lord."

SUNPU-JO 駿府城

Tokaido Gazetteer

- **Mirokuja-ya** -- Teahouse selling the popular Abé-kawa mochi, a type of sweet rice dumpling.

20 Mariko (Suruga)

One of the smallest post stations on the Tokaido, it has close association with the Minamoto, the Imagawa, and the Tokugawa.

Located on the western bank of the Abé River, the region is famous for its views, bountiful mandarin orange groves, and yam porridge.

21 Okabé (Suruga)

A small post town built in 1602. Although the town has only a few inns, one of the more prosperous hatago is the Kashiba-ya.

Near Mount Utsu, the Tokaido merges with the Tsuta-no-hosomichi "Narrow Road of Ivy" here. The area is known for its moon viewing, and the ivy and maples in autumn.

The tea houses down in the valley are famous for their rice dumplings strung together in groups of ten for easy carrying and eating on the road.

22 Fujieda (Suruga)

Castle town of the Tanaka domain with 37 inns. Near the Fujié River, it is also a commercial town on the Unuma Kaido which leads to the salt-producing area of Sagara (Totomi).

- **Tanaka Castle** -- Began as a fortification built by the Isshiki around 1537 under the orders of the Imagawa. The castle, the only circular one in Japan, and moat was built after Takeda Shingen (1521-1573) conquered the area in 1570. After his fall, the castle fell under the control of Tokugawa Ieyasu (1543-1616), who came here for hawking whenever he was at Sunpu Castle. It is well known as the place where Ieyasu ate too much fish tempura, which supposedly contributed to his death. The Tanaka domain has been ruled by a succession of fudai daimyo.

23 Shimada (Suruga)

Located on the Edo side of the Oi River. For security reasons, the Tokugawa Shogunate has expressly forbidden the construction of any bridge or ferry service over the river, so travelers must wade across its shallows. When it floods due to strong rains, it is impossible to pass, so travelers may have to wait a day or more at this post town.

24 Kanaya (Totomi)

Eastern-most post station of Totomi, located on the Kyoto side of the Oi River. There are three honjin, one sub-honjin, and 51 inns.

25 Nissaka (Totomi)

At the western end of Sayo no Nakayama, one of the three most difficult mountain passes along the Tokaido.

The area is famous for its warabi-mochi "kudzu root rice cakes."

- **Koto-no-mama Hachiman-gu** -- Shrine at the western entrance of the post station. Although records say it was founded some time during the reign of the Emperor Seimu (84-190), its exact foundation is unknown. Enshrined here are the Empress Jingu (169-269), the Emperor Ojin (late 3rd century), and Tamayori-himé no Mikoto, the mother of the 1st Emperor of Japan Jimmu (7th century B.C.). In 1062 Minamoto Yoritomo (1047-1099) invited the deities of Iwashimizu Hachiman-gu here, and since then it has been referred to as a shrine for Hachiman, the god of warriors. Many huge old trees grow in the spacious shrine grounds, including a pair which are about 1,000 years old.

- **Yonaka-ishi** "Midnight Stone" -- A large rock that marks a place of murder of a pregnant woman by bandits. Later a passing priest heard the stone cry out, found the dead woman, and delivered the unborn baby. The rock continued to cry every night until Kukai (774-835), when passing the village, heard the crying stone, prayed to Amida Buddha, carved a part of a sutra on the rock, and the stone stopped crying. Another version of the story has the goddess Kannon saving the child, who was brought up on sweets, and later avenged his mother's death.

26 Kakegawa (Totomi)

Wealthy castle town that also serves as a post station along a salt road that runs between Sagara (Totomi) and Hamamatsu (Totomi). There is an earth-covered bridge for crossing the Shioi River. From the town, a distant view of Mount Akiba can be seen.

- **Kakegawa Castle** -- Seat of Kakegawa domain, it was built by Asahina Yasuhiro in the latter half of the 15th century on the orders of Imagawa Yoshitada (1436-1476) to consolidate his holdings in Totomi. The Asahina retained the castle until the defeat of the Imagawa at the 1560 Battle of Okehazama (Owari), when in 1568 Asahina Yasutomo (1538-) surrendered the castle to Tokugawa forces without resistance. In 1590, when Tokugawa Ieyasu (1543-1616) traded his domains and moved to the Kanto region, it was assigned to Toyotomi retainer Yamauchi Kazutoyo (1545-1605), who completely rebuilt the castle. After the establishment of the Tokugawa Bakufu, the domain was successively assigned to over a dozen fudai daimyo clans.

TOKAIDO STATION 22
FUJIEDA

- **Akiba Shrine** -- Located at the summit of Mount Akiba, it is one of the oldest in Japan, and attracts many worshippers from all over the country who come to pray to Hifusé, the god of fire prevention and protection against fire.

27 Fukuroi (Totomi)

Established in 1616, the post station has three honjin and 50 inns, and is approximately the half-way point on the Tokaido between Edo and Kyoto. The area is famous for its green tea.

- **Hattasan Sonei-ji** -- Under the edict of Emperor Shomu (701-756), the temple was founded in 725 by the Buddhist priest Gyoki (668-749). Famous for its cherry trees, many people come here to pray and eat the bad-luck-removing dango "dumplings" sold here. Talismans for good luck in the battlefield, peace in the realm, and abundant harvest of crops are also available.
- **Kasuisai** -- Soto Zen temple founded in 1394 by the monk Jochu Tengin (1363-1437). In 1572 Tokugawa Ieyasu (1543-1616) took refuge at a cave in the temple precincts after his loss to the Takeda at the Battle of Mikata-ga-hara (Totomi). The temple is splendidly ornamented with many artworks. Its beautiful garden is filled with many cherry and maple trees, orchids, peonies, and azaleas.
- **Yusan-ji** -- Shingon Buddhist temple best known for its three-storied pagoda built in 1611. It is said the temple can cure eye problems and strengthen feet.

28 Mitsuké (Totomi)

The name of this post station means "View Point" as it is the first place where travelers can get a nice look at Mount Fuji when coming from Kyoto.

Located on the Edo-side of the Tenryu River, which is so swift-flowing that it can only be crossed by boats. When the river overflows, travel through the town is impossible.

- **Mitsuké Tenjin Shrine** -- Ancient shrine where stands a bronze statue of Shippei-taro, a legendary dog that helped to kill a mountain spirit and end the sacrificing of maidens.

29 Hamamatsu (Totomi)

A castle town with six honjin and 94 inns, situated next to Lake Hamana, and on the Kyoto-side of the Tenryu River, it is the largest post station in Totomi and Suruga.

- **Hamamatsu Castle** -- Originally called Hikuma Castle, Tokugawa Ieyasu (1543-1616) renovated and greatly expanded the castle, although a keep was never built. He renamed it Hamamatsu Castle in 1577. After Ieyasu, many fudai daimyo clans have occupied the castle, and is considered a stepping stone to higher offices within the Tokugawa Shogunate, such as roju "senior counselor" or waka-doshiyori "junior counselor."
- **Mikata-ga-hara** -- In the distance is the famous battlefield where in 1573 Takeda Shingen (1521-1573) defeated Tokugawa Ieyasu (1543-1616), forcing him to retreat to Hamamatsu Castle.

30 Maisaka (Totomi)

Located in the eastern shores of Lake Hamana, it has the first view of the open sea since Suruga Bay. Originally there was a land bridge to the next post station, but it was washed away in the great tidal wave of 1499, and now travelers must cross the lake on ferry boats, called the Imagiri Crossing, to reach Arai-juku.

Popular with fishermen and clam diggers, good seafood, especially eel, is available here.

31 Arai (Totomi)

Located on the western shores of Lake Hamana. Right at the ferry landing is the Arai Checkpoint where women have to show documents, but the men only have to give their name and address.

- **Kii-no-kuni-ya** -- A rest stop for official travelers coming from Kii.

32 Shirasuka (Totomi)

Western-most post station of Totomi, it is mid-sized with 27 inns, and noted for its picturesque views of the hills of Shiomi-zaka.

33 Futagawa (Mikawa)

Eastern-most post station of Mikawa, it has one honjin, one sub-honjin, and 30 inns. Beyond the station lies the broad desolate plain called Sarugababa, where the soil is poor and trees stunted. The road here is barren and monotonous to walk through.

34 Yoshida (Mikawa)

Bustling castle and port town, Yoshida is known for its maids that serve at inns. It has two honjin, one sub-honjin, and 65 inns. West of the castle, a bridge has been built for crossing the Toyo River, one of the few in Japan that never dries, even in the winter. Mount Hiraiji, a holy place for pilgrims, can be seen in the far distance.

- **Yoshida Castle** -- Built by Makino Naritoki at the end of the 15th century. During the Edo Period, it has been held by a succession of fudai daimyo clans.

35 Goyu (Mikawa)

A thriving post town with four honjin and many inns, known for their maids.

The road from here to the next station at Akasaka is lined with beautiful pine trees.

The Motosaka Road branches from here toward Motosaka Pass.

- **Toyokawa Inari** -- Founded in 1441 by Tokai Gieki, this is a Soto Buddhist temple, but it is also popularly known as a shrine dedicated to the Shinto god of fertility, rice, agriculture, foxes, industry, and worldly success.

HAMAMATSU-JO

- **Zaika-ji** -- Ancient Buddhist temple established around the 9th century. There is a pair of statues from the 11th or 12th century depicting guardian deities.

36 Akasaka (Mikawa)

A popular post station with three honjin, one sub-honjin, and 62 inns, it is well known as having the friendliest maids along the Tokaido.

- **Ohashi-ya** -- Inn which opened in 1649.

37 Fujikawa (Mikawa)

This post station has one honjin, one sub-honjin, and 36 inns. This area is known for its murasaki mugi "purple wheat."

38 Okazaki (Mikawa)

A flourishing castle town, it is also the terminus for Shio-no-michi's Sanshu Kaido which led to Nakasendo station 30 at Shiojiri (Shinano).

There is a bridge for crossing the Yahagi River, the longest on the Tokaido. From here, Mount Moto can be seen in the distance.

The area is famous for its high-quality hatcho miso "soy bean paste," which takes three years to ferment, and was a favorite of the Tokugawa army.

- **Okazaki Castle** -- Birthplace of Tokugawa Ieyasu (1543-1616), it was built back in 1455 by Saigo Tsugiyori, and taken in 1524 by Ieyasu's grandfather Matsudaira Kiyoyasu (1511-1536). During the Edo Period, it has been successively occupied by the fudai daimyo clans of the Honda, the Mizuno, the Matsudaira (Matsui), and again by the Honda.

39 Chiryu (Mikawa)

Western-most post station in Mikawa, it is a distribution center for cotton cloth. A horse fair is held here every summer.

- **Chiryu-jinja** -- Shinto shrine built by Yamato Takeru (4th century) during the reign of Emperor Keiko. Formerly called the Chiryu Dai-Myojin, it is the namesake of the post town. It is popular among religious pilgrims as it enshrines the god for repelling vipers, bringing rain, and safe journey.
- **Muryoju-ji** -- The original temple was called Ryoun-ji, and was founded in 704 by an unknown founder. In 822 the Shingon Buddhist priest Mitsuen moved the temple to its present location. In 1670 it was converted by Genten to the Rinzai Zen sect. It is renowned for its iris garden.
- **Henjo-in** -- Shingon Buddhist temple founded in 822 by Kukai (774-835), whose self-portrait statue is worshiped here. The statue is only displayed once a year, on the 21st day of the 3rd month, the anniversary of the founder's death.

40 Narumi (Owari)

Post town with one honjin, two sub-honjin, and 68 inns. It is famous for its fine light-weight silks for summer kimono, decorated with shibori, a complex form of tie-dye cotton fabric, produced in nearby Arimatsu.

- **Cho'o-ji** -- Founded in 1582, the temple is famous for its statue of Yakushi, the Mahayana Buddha of healing and medicine.
- **Seigan-ji** -- Temple famous for being the first to honor the master poet Matsuo Basho (1644-1694), with a statue carved by Takashima Ka'émon, one of the six Narumi students of Basho.
- **Dengaku-hazama** -- Nearby is the location of the 1560 Battle of Okéhazama, a decisive victory for the Owari warlord Oda Nobunaga (1534-1582) over the powerful daimyo Imagawa Yoshimoto (1519-1560) of Suruga.

41 MIYA (Owari)

As this temple town is the terminus for two other roads, the Saya Kaido and the Minoji, it has the most inns of any post station along the Tokaido, some 250, in addition to its two honjin.

Travelers can use the Saya Kaido overland route to the next station at Kuwana, or enjoy a boat trip that takes about four hours to cross the 17 miles/27 km.

The next post station along the Minoji is the castle town of Nagoya. The road eventually leads to Nakasendo station 57 at Tarui (Mino).

- **Atsuta-jingu** -- Ancient Shinto shrine on Isé Bay believed to have been established during the reign of Emperor Keiko around the 2nd century to house the legendary sword Kusanagi "Grass-cutting Sword," one of the three Imperial Regalia of Japan. The shrine is considered the 2nd most revered shrine after the Isé Grand Shrine. One of the shrine's festivals is the Uma-oi "Horsechase" that is held at night and lit by bonfires.

42 Kuwana (Isé)

Situated at a point where three rivers, the Ibi, the Nagara, and the Kiso, flow into Isé Bay, Kuwana is a castle and major port town that serves as the gateway to the Isé Grand Shrine for those coming from Edo.

The area is known for its fresh seafood, especially clams.

- **Kuwana Castle** -- Founded in 1601 by Honda Tadakatsu (1548-1610), the strategically-placed castle has been occupied by the shinpan Matsudaira clan, relatives of the Tokugawa.

TOKAIDO STATION 38 OKAZAKI

- **Tado-taisha** -- Shinto shrine famous for its annual festival featuring a horse race up a muddy slope.

43 Yokkaichi (Isé)

Busy port town that intersects the Isé Sangu Kaido, which travelers use to go to the Isé Grand Shine. A major market is held here on the 4th, 14th, and 24th day of every month. Near the Mié River, it is known for its seed oil, ceramics, somen noodles, and tea.

44 Ishiyakushi (Isé)

Established in 1616, it is named after the nearby temple. There is one honjin, managed by the Ozawa family, and several inns.

- **Ishiyakushi-ji** -- Buddhist temple built during the Nara Period (710-794) with a stone image of Yakushi, the Mahayana Buddha of healing and medicine.

45 Shono (Isé)

One of the last post stations to be designed on the Tokaido, it has one honjin, one sub-honjin and several inns. Part of the road around Shono follows the Suzuka River. The area is mainly agricultural with a small population.

46 Kameyama (Isé)

Castle town situated on the banks of the Suzuka River. The area is famous for its candles.

- **Kameyama Castle** -- Originally built in 1254 by Seki Sanetada, the present castle was built by Okamoto Munenori in 1590.

47 Seki (Isé)

This temple town also intersects the Isebetsu Kaido and the Yamato Kaido. As the station name implies, there are three checkpoints here that close whenever there is an incident in the Yamato region. Since prosperous travelers often stop here, the town with its two honjin and many inns is famous for its large number of prostitutes.

48 Saka-no-shita (Isé)

A flourishing post town at the eastern entrance of the Suzuka Pass, one of the most hardest to cross on the Tokaido, with a view of Mount Fudesuté. The story goes that when master painter Kano Motonobu (1476-1559) came here to paint the mountain, he realized it was beyond his powers and in his despair threw away his brush. The honjin here is considered the most luxurious on the Tokaido.

TOKAIDO STATION 47
SEKI

49 Tsuchiyama (Omi)

A flourishing post town at the western entrance of the Suzuka Pass. The Tamura River runs through this town. The area is known for its Koga ninja history, the many tea plantations, and plentiful rainfalls.

50 Minakuchi (Omi)

Castle town known for its quality ceramics. The area is known for its Koga ninja history, loach soup, and dried gourd shavings used as a relish in Japanese cooking. Part of the road around this station follows the Yokota River.

- **Minakuchi Castle** -- Constructed in 1634 by the 3rd Tokugawa Shogun Iemitsu (1604-1651) as a rest stop where he could stay during his travels between Edo and Kyoto, it was modeled after Nijo Castle in Kyoto. It has been assigned to the Kato clan since 1682.

51 Ishibé (Omi)

A desolate post station with two honjin and 32 inns. As it was approximately a one-day journey from Kyoto, many travelers stay overnight here. The town boasts many historical points of interst.

- **Joraku-ji, Choju-ji, Zensui-ji** -- A trio of ancient Tendai Buddhist temples.
- **Isé-ya** -- Inn in the nearby village of Mekawa where many travelers stop to eat and drink saké.

52 Kusatsu (Omi)

On the eastern banks of the Kusatsu River, this major post town has two honjin, two sub-honjin, and 72 inns. The Nakasendo joins the Tokaido here as its station 68.

53 Otsu (Omi)

Also Nakasendo station 69, this prosperous and thriving village, located on the southwestern shore of Lake Biwa, the largest in Japan, is the last post station before Kyoto. It has two honjin, one sub-honjin, and 71 inns. Famous for its scenery, there are many popular shrines and temples nearby. Shops here sell Otsu-é, the famous folk paintings of Otsu.

Travelers going to Osaka can leave the Tokaido here for Osaka Kaido station 54 at Fushimi.

KYOTO TERMINUS: SANJO OHASHI

The terminus of the Takaido and the Nakasendo is a bridge in Kyoto that spans the Kamo River as part of the Sanjo-dori "Third Avenue." There is a panoramic view of the Imperial capital from this bridge.

OSAKA KAIDO GAZETTEER

THE OSAKA MAIN ROAD   大阪街道

This road to Osaka is an extension of the Tokaido starting at its station 53 at Otsu. The numbering continues from there with four more post stations before terminating at Osaka. Travel from Kyoto, or between the termini, can be made in one day, albeit a long one if made on foot. The road generally follows the Yodo River, which flowed from Lake Biwa at Otsu, and ferry service is available all the way to Osaka, which can be quicker and more pleasant in good weather.

54 Fushimi (Yamashiro)
Successful castle and port town on the Yodo River founded in 1619.

- **Fushimi Castle** -- The original castle was completed in 1594 as a place of retirement by Toyotomi Hideyoshi (1536-1598). It was demolished by an earthquake two years later and rebuilt soon afterwards. In 1600 the castle fell to Ishida Mitsunari (1560-1600) after being defended famously by Torii Mototada (1539-1600). In 1602 the castle was rebuilt, but in 1623 it was dismantled as part of the one-castle-per-domain law and abandoned. Many of its rooms and buildings were incorporated into castles and temples across Japan.

55 Yodo (Yamashiro)
Castle town founded in 1619 and situated between the Yodo and Katsura Rivers.

- **Yodo Castle** -- Constructed in 1623. It has been held by a succession of fudai daimyo.

56 Hirakata (Kawachi)
Flourishing port station along the Yodo River, approximately midpoint between Kyoto and Osaka, it was also a major travel intersection. It has one honjin, two sub-honjin, and numerous inns.

57 Moriguichi (Kawachi)
Long an important travel center, it was officially established as a post station in 1616. It has one honjin and 27 inns.

OSAKA TERMINUS: KORIBASHI
The terminus of Osaka Kaido is a bridge spanning the Higashi Yokobori River. The area is a major financial center as well as Osaka's principal shopping and tourist district.

- **Dotonbori** -- In 1621 the Tokugawa Shogunate designated the urban street as the entertainment district of Osaka. By 1662 the avenue boasted six kabuki and five bunraku "puppet" theaters.
- **Shinsaibashi** -- Major shopping district of Osaka, just north of Dotonbori.
- **Ebisu Shrine** -- Dedicated to the god of fishermen, good luck, workingmen, and the health of small children. Ebisu is one of the Seven Gods of Fortune, and the only one to originate from Japan.
- **Osaka Castle** -- Completed in 1597 by Toyotomi Hideyoshi (1536-1598) on the site of the Ikko-ikki fortress temple of Ishiyama Hongan-ji. The castle fell in the 1615 Summer Siege of Osaka Castle when Tokugawa Ieyasu (1543-1616) took it from Hideyoshi's son Toyotomi Hideyori (1593-1615), marking the end of the Toyotomi clan. In 1620 the 2nd Tokugawa Shogun Hidetada (1579-1632) began reconstruction of the castle.

OSAKA-JO   大坂城

NAKASENDO GAZETTEER

INNER MOUNTAIN ROAD 中山道

Also called the Kisokaido, the Nakasendo connects Edo with Kyoto via an inland route. It is 332 miles/534 km long, with 69 stations between the termini. The road is well-developed, and many people prefer the Nakasendo over the Tokaido, as it does not require the fording of any rivers, and is less crowded.

EDO TERMINUS: NIHON-BASHI
See Tokaido Gazetteer.

1 Itabashi
A flourishing post station named after the bridge spanning the Shakuji River. It has one honjin and many inns. Many warehouses of wholesalers are located here.
▶ **Itabashi keijo** "execution grounds" -- One of three sites in the vicinity of Edo that the Tokugawa Bakufu executes criminals.

2 Warabi (Musashi)
Castle town with two honjin, one sub-honjin, and 23 inns. There is a ferry service over the nearby Toda River.
▶ **Warabi Castle** -- Built in 1457 by Shibukawa Yoshikané. In 1525 the castle was taken by the Hojo of Odawara.

3 Urawa (Musashi)
A flourishing medium-sized post town with a view of Mount Asama.

4 Omiya (Musashi)
Post station with the largest number of sub-honjin on the Nakasendo, of which there were nine. Mount Fuji can be seen from here.
▶ **Hikawa-jinja** -- Shrine established in 473 B.C., during the reign of the Emperor Kosho, in honor of Susano'o, the Shinto god of the sea and storms.

5 Ageo (Musashi)
A rest stop that became a Nakasendo post station in 1603. Although relatively a small town, it has the 2nd largest honjin after the one in Nakasendo station 30 at Shiojiri. There are also three sub-honjin and several inns. The area is famous for its flower trade.

6 Okegawa (Musashi)
Prospering post town with one honjin and 36 inns. The area is a center of safflower production.

7 Konosu (Musashi)
Large post station with one honjin, two sub-honjin, and 58 inns. Its roads connect to Matsuyama (Musashi), Nin (Musashi), and Kisaichi (Musashi).

Fukiagé (Musashi)
A rest stop and post station 10 on Nikko Wakiokan, an alternate sub-route to the Nikko Kaido. The area is known for its production of Japanese-style socks.
▶ **Oshi Castle** -- Completed around 1479 by Narita Akiyasu. It was taken by the army of Toyotomi Hideyoshi (1536-1598) in his assault on the Kanto. After the Tokugawa moved to Edo, the castle was placed in charge of the Matsudaira.

8 Kumagai (Musashi)
A large post town, but with two honjin and only 19 inns.
▶ **Yukoku-ji** -- Pure Land Buddhist temple built in 1192 by the famous Genji soldier Kumagai Naozané (1141-1208), who was born in the area. Favored by Tokugawa Ieyasu (1543-1616), the temple is particularly attractive when the hydrangeas are in full bloom.

9 Fukaya (Musashi)
Large post town with one honjin and 80 inns, known for its wild entertainment quarters. The area is a big producer of leeks, and silkworms for silk thread production.
▶ **Fukaya Castle** -- Castle held by a branch of the Uesugi.
▶ **Takinomiya-jinja** -- Large Shinto shrine.

10 Honjo (Musashi)
A center for the silk trade and a major market town. In 1781, to encourage travel along the Nakasendo, a local businessman started construction on a bridge to span the Kamo River, but he ran out of funds, and the bridge was built only part way. Ferry boats are available for crossing the remaining distance.

NAKASENDO STATION 9
FUKAYA

Nakasendo Gazetteer

The Nakasendo becomes gradually hilly from here.

11 Shinmachi (Kozuké)

Last station to be developed on the Nakasendo, it is fairly large with 43 inns.

12 Kuragano (Kozuké)

Port town for trader ships on the Karasu River with one honjin, two sub-honjin, and 32 inns. When the water is high enough, passenger boat service down to Edo is available.

The post station also serves as the starting point of the Nikko Reiheishi Kaido, which people from Kyoto use to travel to Nikko (Shimotsuké).

13 Takasaki (Kozuké)

Castle town overlooking Lake Haruna. Although one of the largest post stations on the Nakasendo, it has no honjin or sub-honjin, and just 15 inns for travelers.

The town also serves as the starting point of the Mikuni Kaido, which leads to the castle town of Nagaoka (Echigo).

- **Daruma-ji** -- Temple that popularized the use of papier-maché Daruma dolls as good luck charms. The dolls are modeled after Bodhidharma (5th or 6th century), the founder of Zen Buddhism. The roly-poly dolls are made so that they always return to an upright position after being tipped over, symbolizing the ability to achieve success after overcoming adversity and recovering from misfortune.
- **Haruna-jinja** -- Shinto shrine located on nearby Mount Haruna. It was founded in 586, the first year of the reign of the Emperor Yomei (518-587). In the 14th century, it became affiliated with Tendai Buddhism.
- **Minowa Castle** -- One of the largest castles in the province, it was built in 1526 by the Uesugi retainer Nagano Narimasa (1491-1561). In the 1566 Siege of Minowa, the castle fell to Takeda Shingen (1521-1573). After the siege it was held by the Takeda, the Oda, and then the Hojo. In 1590 Ii Naomasa (1561-1602) became lord of the castle, until 1598 when he moved to Takasaki Castle, and Minowa Castle was decommissioned. It has been abandoned since then.
- **Takasaki Castle** -- Ii Naomasa began construction of the castle in 1597 under the orders of Tokugawa Ieyasu (1543-1616). It has since been held by the Sakai, the Ando, and the Okochi.

14 Itahana (Kozuké)

Post town with one honjin and 54 inns. As the two post station on either side are castle towns with watchful daimyo, this town had an active nightlife with over 80 professional entertainers, and over 100 lesser servers.

15 Annaka (Kozuké)

Lining the roads around this castle town are many steles of Bato Kannon, the horse-headed Buddhist protector of animals. The town has 17 inns for travelers.

- **Annaka Castle** -- Castle which was the residence of a succession of daimyo.

16 Matsuida (Kozuké)

Post station located at the foot of Mount Myogi. Travelers wishing to avoid the checkpoint before the next post station can take a detour that will take them over the mountains to station 20 at Oiwaké.

- **Matsuida Castle** -- Ancient castle deserted since 1590.

Usui Checkpoint (Kozuké)

A major checkpoint on the western edge of the province, the barrier is located on a group of mountains that separate Kozuké from Shinano. During the 16th century the area was the scene of several battles between the Takeda and the Uesugi.

17 Sakamoto (Kozuké)

Located at the eastern entrance to the treacherous Usui Pass. A comparatively large station, there are two honjin, two sub-honjin, and 40 inns.

At the top of the pass is a cluster of rest stops with spectacular panoramas of Mount Asama to the northwest and Mount Miyogi to the south.

18 Karuisawa (Shinano)

On the slopes of Mount Asama and located at the western entrance to the Usui Pass, it is a flourishing post town with two honjin, three sub-honjin, and over 100 inns that are famous for their maids.

The area abounds with its famous blueberries and strawberries.

To the east of the post town, a bridge is available for crossing the Yakazaki River.

19 Kutsukaké (Shinano)

Post station with one honjin and several inns.

20 Oiwaké (Shinano)

As it is also the terminus to the Hokkoku Kaido, which leads to Takada (Echigo) on the Japan Sea, this busy post town can hold over 200 guests. Oiwaké is also the highest post station on the Nakasendo.

Travelers wishing to avoid the Usui Checkpoint after the Nakasendo station 17 at Sakamoto can take a detour that will take them over the mountains to station 16 at Matsuida.

Nakasendo Station 17 Sakamoto

21 Otai (Shinano)

Originating in the late 5th century, there are one honjin, one sub-honjin, and only five inns in this small post town. Its location is through a desolate field at the foot of Mount Asama.

22 Iwamurada (Shinano)

Castle town with several inns, but no honjin or sub-honjin. The Saku-Koshu Kaido intersects here.

▶ **Iwamurada Castle** -- From 1693 the residence of the Naito daimyo.

23 Shionada (Shinano)

Located on the east bank of the Shinano River, Japan's longest, which can be forded or crossed via a ferry service. It has two honjin, one sub-honjin, and about ten inns.

▶ **Fudo Falls** -- Scenic spot good for resting.

24 Yawata (Shinano)

Located on the west bank of the Shinano River, this post town, perhaps the smallest on the Nakasendo, is also a distribution center for rice. It has one honjin, four sub-honjin, and just three inns.

Travelers from Kyoto get their first close view of Mount Asama on the road leading to this town. The fact that the mountain is active, and a benign plume of smoke emanates from its crest, deters travelers from staying in this town, hence the small number of inns.

25 Mochizuki (Shinano)

Located at the base of Mount Tateshina, this small town has one sub-honjin and only nine inns serving travelers. The area is known for its horses.

▶ **Mimaki-ga-hara** -- An Imperial pasture northeast of the post town.

Motai (Shinano)

Unofficial post station. Overnight lodging is not available to non-local travelers.

▶ **Ozawa Saké Brewery** -- Small factory which welcomes visitors to sample its locally brewed saké.

26 Ashida (Shinano)

Located near the eastern entrance to the Kasadori Pass, this small post station has one honjin, which claims to be the oldest on the Nakasendo, and just six inns. The area is well-known for its silk production and a magnificent view of Mount Asama.

NAKASENDO STATION 29 SHIMO-SUWA

27. Nagakubo (Shinano)

Bustling post town between the Wada Pass and the Kasadori Pass. There are 43 inns available to travelers with a full complement of maids and entertainers. The area is known for its production of ginseng. There is a bridge for crossing the Yoda River.

28 Wada (Shinano)

At the entrance to the difficult Wada Pass, highest on the Nakasendo. Although a quiet mountain town, because the post station at Shimo-Suwa is over 12 miles/20 km away, it flourishes with one honjin and many inns. The area is known for its vast resources of obsidian.

29 SHIMO-SUWA (Shinano)

Also the terminus of the Koshu Kaido which leads to Nihon-bashi at Edo along a road between the Nakasendo and the Tokaido. A flourishing post town overlooking Lake Suwa, due to its location between the Wada Pass and the Shiojiri Pass, it has one honjin, one sub-honjin, and 40 inns. It is popular for its numerous onsen "hot springs."

▶ **Suwa Taisha** "Suwa Grand Shrine" -- Built around the 8th century, it is one of the oldest shrines in Japan. It is famous for its Onbashira, a festival held only every six years, on the years of the monkey and the tiger. It lasts several months starting in April, and involves the cutting down of huge trees to be placed as the new supports for the foundation of the shrine buildings.

30 Shiojiri (Shinano)

Located west of Shiojiri Pass, the area was originally developed by Tokugawa retainer Okubo Nagayasu (1545-1613). A large post town with panoramic views of Mount Fuji and the Yatsu-ga-také Mountains, it has one honjin, one sub-honjin, and 75 inns. The area is noted for its fine lacquer ware.

The post station also serves as the terminus for the Sanshu Kaido, a trade route that leads to Tokaido station 38 at Okazaki (Mikawa), and brought salt to Japan's interior.

31 Seba (Shinano)

Established in 1614, the name of this post station means "washing horse," and it originates from when Minamoto Yoshinaka (1154-1184) had his horse washed in the Ota River nearby.

At the center of town is an official weigh station that checks baggage carried by porters, which is not supposed to exceed 85 pounds/40 kg according to the regulations of the Tokugawa Shogunate.

32 Motoyama (Shinano)

Established in 1614, this post town is known as the birthplace of soba "buckwheat noodles."

33 Niékawa (Shinano)

This peaceful post town was the terminus of the Kisoji, an old trade route that stretched to Nakasendo station 43 at Magomé (Shinano). The eleven post stations became part of the Nakasendo when it was established.

Nakasendo Gazetteer

The town has 25 inns for travelers. There is a checkpoint at one of town. The area is noted for its onsen "hot springs" that warm the local river.

34 Narai (Shinano)

This post town boasts the highest elevation along the Kisoji. The town flourishes due to the Torii Pass, which is the most difficult part of the Nakasendo, and many travelers stop and rest here before continuing. The area is famous for its lacquer ware.

- **Taiho-ji** -- Temple built in the 16th century by Narai Yoshitaka. There is a garden where visitors can enjoy beautiful views of azaleas in June and maple tress in autumn.
- **Kiso-no-hashi** -- Famous bridge spanning the Kiso River.

35 Yabuhara (Shinano)

Located on the western side of the Torii Pass, from where travelers from Edo can first view the sacred Mount Ontaké.

The area is famous throughout Japan for its Oroku combs made of local wood that many passersby purchase here as souvenirs. Using the comb every morning and evening reputedly cures headaches and other sicknesses of the head.

- **Yabuhara Castle** -- Built in 1555 by Takeda Shingen (1521-1573).

36 Miya-no-koshi (Shinano)

Post town established in 1605, it was the childhood home of Minamoto Yoshinaka (1154-1184).

- **Hataagé Hachiman-gu** -- Shrine from where in 1180 Minamoto Yoshinaka rose in arms to march against the Taira.

37 Fukushima (Shinano)

Approximately the midpoint between Edo and Kyoto on the Nakasendo, this bustling post town with 14 inns hosts people going on a religious pilgrimage to climb Mount Ontaké, considered one of the holiest mountains in Japan..

A large checkpoint is located at the northern end of this town.

- **Kozen-ji** -- Tendai Buddhist temple and training center founded in 860 by the priest Honjyo, during the reign of the Emperor Seiwa (850-880). The beautiful grounds are surrounded by many huge and ancient trees.

38 Agematsu (Shinano)

Flourishing logging town where loggers and travelers congregate to bring a lively atmosphere. It has 35 inns, the most of any town in the Kiso Valley. The neighborhood around this post station is known for its many scenic spots.

The famous Kiso cypress from this area is used as the sacred tree of the Isé Grand Shrine.

- **Kiso Bridge** -- A dangerous bridge made of woven wisteria vine that spans several hundred meters over the cliffs of the Kiso River.
- **Nezamé-no-toko** -- Gorge along the Kiso River known for its fascinating white granite rock formations and the beautiful green color of the river. It is especially beautiful in autumn when the fall colors of the leaves reflect on the water. Upon seeing the gorge, many writers and poets have recorded their experiences in their writings and verses.

39 Suhara (Shinano)

Oldest post station on the Kisoji with 24 inns.

- **Josho-ji** -- Oldest temple of Myoshin Rinzai Zen Buddhism, famous for its dry rock garden.

40 Nojiri (Shinano)

This post town is characterized by its winding streets, originally built to inhibit the invasion of enemies. It has 19 inns for travelers.

41 Midono (Shinano)

Prosperous post town with 32 inns. Apricots are grown in the area.

42 Tsumago (Shinano)

Prosperous but relatively small post town located on the east side of Magomé Pass, it has one honjin, one sub-honjin, and 31 inns. From here Mount Ena can be seen in the distance to the south.

- **Kabuto Kannon-jinja** -- Ancient shrine built around 1180, and dedicated to Minamoto Yoshinaka (1154-1184).
- **Tsumago Castle** -- Built by Kiso Yoshimasa (1540-1595), who in 1584 sided with Toyotomi Hideyoshi (1536-1598), and was unsuccessfully besieged in the castle by Suganuma Sadatoshi acting under orders from Tokugawa Ieyasu (1543-1616). It was dismantled in 1615 under orders of the Tokugawa Shogunate. From its abandoned grounds, there is a wonderful view of both Midono and Tsumago stations.
- **Rurisan Kotoku-ji** -- Temple founded in 1500, and famous for its cherry trees and nightingale "chirping" floors.

43 Magomé (Shinano)

A remote, but relatively prosperous, post town, it is located on the west side of Magomé Pass, with one honjin, one sub-honjin, and 18 inns. It also marks the western terminus of the old Kisoji. The town also offers a fine view of Mount Ena. Popular regional cuisine includes gohei mochi "rice cakes on sticks," soba "buckwheat noodles,"

Nakasendo Gazetteer

and kuri-kinton "sweet mashed-chestnut confectionary."

44 Ochiai (Mino)

The Jikkoku Pass on the east side of the post station marks the border between Shinano and Mino. The post town has one honjin, one sub-honjin, and 14 inns.

- **Ino-ji** -- Located in the outskirts of Ochiai, it is famous for its valuable tanuki "raccoon dog" ointment.

45 Nakatsugawa (Mino)

Largest post town on the Nakasendo, many people, including those from afar, come to visit its popular market held on the 3rd and 8th of each month. This station has over 30 inns to serve its many visitors. There is a bridge for crossing the nearby Yotsumé River.

46 Oi (Mino)

A medium-sized post town located on the banks of the Agi River, and on the east side of Jusan Pass, where there are three illegal gambling houses. Lining the roads in the area are many statues of Jizo, the bodhisattva guardian of children and travelers.

47 Okuté (Mino)

Established in 1604, it was built on the east side of Biwa Pass and the west side of Jusan Pass. From here you can see Mount Ibuki, Mount Hakusan, and Isé Bay far in the distance.

- **Shinmei-jinja** -- Shrine with an old cedar tree planted around the 7th century.

48 Hosokuté (Mino)

Mountaintop post town established in 1610 due to the long distance between Okuté and Mitaké. Located on the west side of Biwa Pass, a view of Mount Ontaké can be had here.

- **Benten-iké** -- An ancient lily pond.
- **Daikoku-ya** -- An inn for travelers.

49 Mitaké (Mino)

Temple town, one of the original Nakasendo post stations.

- **Ganko-ji** -- Temple dedicated to Yakushi, founded in 998 by the nun Gyochini, daughter of Emperor Ichijo (980-1011).

50 Fushimi (Mino)

The last post town to be established on the Nakasendo, it was founded in 1694. It has a port named Niimura on the Kiso River, where rice is loaded onto barges destined for Inuyama (Owari) or Kuwana (Isé).

51 Ota (Mino)

Prosperous post town and economic center, the Hida River convergences with the Kiso River here. The Kiso river at this point is too wide for a bridge, so it is served by ferry boats, which is considered a major bottleneck of the Nakasendo.

The Hida Road and the Gujo Road also branches off from here.

The post station has one honjin, one sub-honjin, and 20 inns.

- **Yusen-ji** -- Temple constructed in 1474.
- **Komatsu-ya** -- Family-run store with supplies for travelers.

52 Unuma (Mino)

One of the oldest post station on the Nakasendo, it is located at the west side of the Uto Pass, and is served by only eight inns. The road along here is paved with stones and beautiful hydrangeas. The area is known for its Hachiya persimmons and spectacular views of Kiso River.

It also serves as the terminus of the Inagi Kaido.

- **Unuma Castle** -- Castle taken from Osawa Jiroémon by Oda Nobunaga (1534-1582).
- **Inuyama Castle** -- Overlooking the Kiso River, it was built in 1440, and augmented in 1537 by Oda Nobuyasu. Since 1617, it has been held by the Narusé clan.

Shinkano (Mino)

Unofficial post station. Overnight lodging is not available to non-local travelers.

53 Kano (Mino)

Largest post town in Mino.

- **Kano Tenman-gu** -- Shrine founded in 1445 by Saito Toshinaga (-1490) dedicated to Tenjin, the Shinto god of scholarship.
- **Kano Castle** -- Saito Toshinaga began the castle's construction in 1445. In 1603 Okudaira Nobumasa (1555-1615) moved into the castle, and after his retirement, began the development of the town around the castle. After his lineage died out, the castle has been occupied by a succession of fudai daimyo.

54 Godo (Mino)

Flourishing post town next to the Nagara River served by ferries. There are only eight inns for guests.

Since the 9th century, the river's fishermen has used cormorants to catch the local ayu "sweetfish." Master poet Matsuo Basho (1644-1694) has written two haiku about the famous activity.

55 Mié-ji (Mino)

Post town next to the Goroku River which floods frequently, and is considered the station with the worst conditions on the Nakasendo. It has eleven inns served by maid-prostitutes, that are frequented by wandering thieves, gamblers, and other down-and-outs. Many travelers do not lodge in this notoriously lawless town by choice.

Nakasendo Station 34 Narai

Nakasendo Gazetteer

Yoro Falls (Mino)

- **Mié-ji** -- Tendai Buddhist temple said to have been built to offers prayers to protect against the flooding of the three major rivers in the area, the Kiso, the Nagara, and the Ibi.

56 Akasaka (Mino)

Located in a fertile valley next to a river, this bustling post town has one honjin, one sub-honjin, and 17 inns. There is a bridge for crossing the Kuisé River.

A popular rainy-season activity at this post town is firefly watching in the evening from boats along the river.

57 Tarui (Mino)

One of the oldest post towns on the Nakasendo, it has served travelers since at least the 12th century. Sitting on the banks of the Ai River, this rather large town has one honjin, one sub-honjin, and 45 inns. It is also the terminus of the Minoji, which leads south to Tokaido station 41 at Miya (Owari).

- **Nangu Taisha** -- Ancient shrine first built during the reign of Japan's 1st Emperor Jimmu (7th century B.C.), it was completely burnt to the ground in 1600, and rebuilt in 1642 by the 3rd Tokugawa Shogun Iemitsu (1604-1651).

58 Seki-ga-hara (Mino)

Large post station that is also connected to the Hokkoku Kaido and the Isé Kaido. Site of the 1600 Battle of Seki-ga-hara, the town has one honjin, one sub-honjin, and 33 inns.

- **Kurochi-gawa** "Black Blood River" -- Place where the Tokugawa army washed the cut-off heads of those fallen in the Battle of Seki-ga-hara.
- **Lake Mishima** -- Famous spot with a profusion of fireflies.

Fuwa-no-seki (Mino)

Barrier station raised in 673 by the Emperor Temmu (631-686).

59 Imasu (Mino)

Flourishing post town that is also connected with the Kurihan Kaido. It has one honjin, two sub-honjin, and 13 inns, and is the western-most post station in Mino.

60 Kashiwabara (Omi)

Large post station established in 646 with hundreds of inns. Nestled against Mount Ibuki, it is the eastern-most post in Omi. The area is known for its wormwood, an herb used for moxa healing.

61 Samegai (Omi)

Old rest stop popular for its scenic sights and refreshing water from nearby springs. The post station serves travelers with its eleven inns.

- **Kamo-ji** -- Temple famous for its Isamé Spring, the water of which has been praised since ancient times for its healing and soothing properties.

62 Banba (Omi)

Post station located on the east side of Surihari Pass with one honjin, one sub-honjin, and ten inns.

63 Toriimoto (Omi)

Flourishing post town on the west side of Surihari Pass with one honjin, two sub-honjin, and many inns. It is part of other pathways, including the Chosenji Kaido, which leads to Nakasendo station 66 at Musa (Omi) via a route closer to Lake Biwa.

- **Taga Taisha** -- Important Shinto shrine dedicated to the god of longevity.
- **Hikoné Castle** -- Built in 1606 by the fudai daimyo Ii Naokatsu (1590-1662), and has been held since then by the clan's successors.

64 Takamiya (Omi)

Post town originally founded during the Sengoku "Warring States" Period (1467-1573), it is located on the banks of the Inukami River. Although the largest post town in Omi, it only has 33 inns to serve travelers. The area is known for its production of persimmons and hemp cloth.

65 Echigawa (Omi)

Thriving post town and commercial center with one honjin, two sub-honjin, and 28 inns. For most travelers from Kyoto going to Edo, this is the traditional place for the first overnight stay.

It is recorded that Court noble Kitabataké Akiié (1318-1338) stayed here in 1336.

66 Musa (Omi)

Post station with one honjin, one sub-honjin, and 23 inns. It is also part of the Chosenji Kaido, which connects to the Nakasendo station 63 at Toriimoto (Omi) via a route closer to Lake Biwa. The area is known for its cotton and flax production.

67 Moriyama (Omi)

Comparatively large post station with two honjin, one sub-honjin, and 30 inns.

- **Moriyama Castle** -- Built around 1525 by the Oda clan.
- **Enryaku-ji** -- Tendai Mahayana Buddhist monastery on Mount Hiei, overlooking Kyoto, established by Saicho (767-822). When the temple became militant and powerful, and started to hire mercenaries to march on the capital to make monastic demands, Oda Nobunaga (1534-1582) leveled the temple and slaughtered its warrior monks. Many of its buildings were reconstructed when the Tokugawa Shogunate began its rule.

68 Kusatsu (Omi)

See Tokaido Gazetteer.

69 Otsu (Omi)

See Tokaido Gazetteer.

Kyoto Terminus: Sanjo Ohashi

See Tokaido Gazetteer.

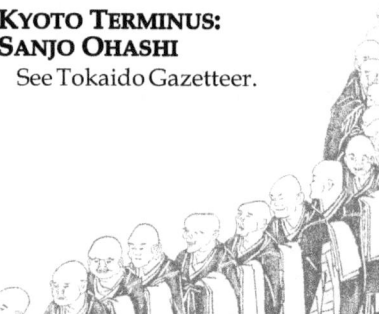

MINOJI GAZETTEER

THE MINO WAY

美濃路

A short secondary road that connects Tokaido station 41 at Miya (Owari), near Nagoya, with Nakasendo station 57 at Tarui (Mino), near Seki-ga-hara. It is only 37 miles / 60 km long.

Unlike the Tokaido and the Nakasendo, the termini of the Minoji are often included in the numbering of the post stations as follows:

1 Miya (Owari)
See Tokaido Gazetteer.

2 Nagoya (Owari)
Castle town with no honjin, no sub-honjin, and several inns.
- **Nagoya Castle** -- Built in 1525 by Shiba Yoshimuné (1513-1554) for his son-in-law Imagawa Ujitoyo (1521-), from whom in 1532 Oda Nobuhidé (1510-1551) seized the castle. Although abandoned around 1582, Tokugawa Ieyasu (1543-1616) began rebuiling the castle in 1610. Since then, it has been the residence of the Owari branch of the Tokugawa clan, and headquarters of the Owari Domain.

3 Kiyosu (Owari)
Formerly the castle town for Kiyosu Castle.
- **Kiyosu Castle** -- Built between 1394 and 1427, it first belonging to Shiba Yoshishigé (1371-1418). Upon completion, it was held by Oda Toshisada. In 1555 Oda Nobunaga (1534-1582) captured it from his uncle Oda Nobutomo (1516-1555). After Nobunaga's death, his 2nd son Oda Nobukatsu (1558-1630) came into control of the castle, and began large-scale renovations in 1586. When Tokugawa Ieyasu (1543-1616) decided to rebuild Nagoya Castle in 1609, Kiyosu Castle was demolished, and parts of it were used for the new construction.

4 Inaba (Owari)
Post town originally built in 1584 by Oda Nobukatsu (1558-1630).
- **Gifu Castle** -- Originally built in 1203 and called Inaba Castle, Oda Nobunaga (1536-1582) took it in 1564, and changed its name to Gifu Castle.

5 Hagiwara (Owari)
Located on the banks of the Nikko River, it is the smallest post station on the Minoji.

6 Okoshi (Owari/Mino)
Post station established on the edge of the Kiso River, and on the border of Owari and Mino.

7 Sunomata (Mino)
Active castle town between the Nagara River and the Ibi River.

It is also a stop on the Kamakura Kaido, which connected Kyoto with Kamakura (Sagami).
- **Sunomata Castle** -- Constructed in 1566 by Toyotomi Hideyoshi (1536-1598) during the siege on Inabayama Castle by Oda Nobunaga (1534-1582). Although considered a legend, there are records detailing how Hideyoshi actually built the castle in just one day.
- **Hokoku-jinja** -- Shrine dedicated to the god of success.

8 Ogaki (Mino)
Castle town. The area is very pretty during cherry blossom season.
- **Ogaki Castle** -- Built in 1535 by Miyagawa Yasusada by the orders of the 12th Ashikaga Shogun Yoshiharu (1510-1550). In 1546 it was captured by Oda Nobuhidé (1510-1551). After the defeat of Oda Nobutaka (1558-1583) in 1583, Toyotomi Hideyoshi (1536-1598) gave it to Ikeda Tsuneoki (1536-1584). When Hideyoshi realized the castle's strategic importance, in 1595 he had Ito Sukemori build a donjon "main keep." In 1600 it served as the base for the forces of Ishida Mitsunari (1560-1600) during the Battle of Seki-ga-hara (Mino). In 1635 Toda Ujikané (1576-1655) took over the castle, and his descendants have rule it ever since.

9 Tarui (Mino)
See Nakasendo Gazetteer.

NAGOYA-JO

Family Crests

Mon

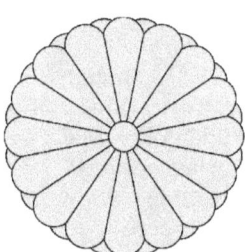

Imperial Mon

Tokugawa Mon

Mitsubishi Group Corporate Logo

Mon "family crests" are Japanese emblems used to identify a family, similar to the coats of arms of European heraldry. The origin of Japanese family crests goes back to the 11th century when high-ranking aristocrats started using specific textile designs on their formal costumes that they wore at the Imperial Court. After the warrior class took over the government at the end of the 12th century, the bushi began adopting the practice, and by the Muromachi Period (1336-1573) the use of mon by samurai clans was universal.

Except for a few designs, such as the chrysanthemum mon reserved for the Imperial Family and the three hollyhock leaves inside a circle motif reserved for the Tokugawa, family crests were not officially regulated in Japan, nor were they legally formalized. There were no set rules as to their design and usage; the basic design was monochrome, and can be drawn in any color. Strict social controls however were quite effective in informally governing their use.

Customs and traditions varied over time regarding the adoption of mon by a family. The following rules may be adopted for gaming purposes:

- Flags and banners displayed the mon of the daimyo to identify their armies.
- Retainer wore their respective family crests on their armor for individual identification.
- It was considered improper to unilaterally adopt a crest that was already in use by another family. When conflicts occurred, the lower-ranking clan would change their mon to avoid offending the superior-ranking clan.
- It was however a great honor for a retainer to be allowed the use his lord's mon as a reward.
- New cadet branches of a family may continue to use the clan mon, or adopt a slight variant, or adopt an entirely new mon.

Depending on clan tradition, as part of an official dress code, there may have been rules regarding the display of mon on the retainers' formal and informal clothing. Most often they are seen on the center of the back and both sleeves of a samurai's kimono.

Eventually all Japanese had a family crest. Families used their mon to identify their stores and shops, and were eventually adopted by the business as a sort of company logo. One of the most famous corporate logos in Japan using a mon style is the three water chestnuts design of the Mitsubishi Group conglomerate.

Like corporate logos, over time, mon were imprinted ubiquitously, wherever the placement of a family emblem would be appropriate for identification purposes.

For many of the warlords in this survey, I was unable to find their mon design. The following table is provided for the assigning of a random crest to a particular family with the roll of a D100.

Random Mon Generator

 **01** Icho "Gingko"

 **02** Igeta "Well crib"

 **03** Ishi "Stones"

 **04** Ikari "Anchor"

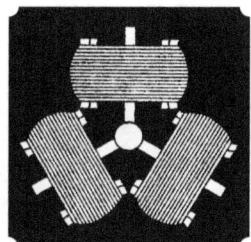 **05** Ito-maki "Spools"

 **06** Roku no ji The character "six"

 **07** Hagoita "Battledore"

 **08** Hamaguri "Clams"

 **09** Robuchi "Hearth rim"

 **10** Hato "Pigeon"

 **11** Basho "Plantain"

 **12** Hagi "Clover"

 **13** Hasami "Scissors"

 **14** Hasu "Lotus"

 **15** Botan "Peony"

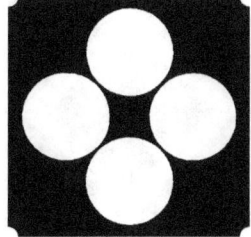 **16** Hoshi "Stars"

 **17** Koma "Tops"

 **18** Honaga "Ferns"

 **19** Ho "Sail"

 **20** Hei-shi "Saké bottle"

 **21** Hei "Sacred staff with cut paper"

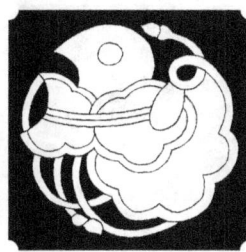 **22** Tori-kabuto "Monk's hood"

 **23** Tomoé "Commas"

 **24** Torii "Shinto gate"

 **25** Ito-maki "Spools"

Family Crests – Random Mon Generator

 **26** Choji "Cloves"
 **27** Choban "Gong board"
 **28** Rindo "Bellflowers"
 **29** Ryo "Dragon"
 **30** Ryugo "Juggling objects"

 **31** Wachigai "Joined rings"
 **32** Omodaka "Water plantains"
 **33** Warabi "Fernbrake"
 **34** Katabami "Wood sorrel"
 **35** Kaku-ji "Chinese character"

 **36** Kasa "Umbrellas"
 **37** Kanawa "Iron rings"
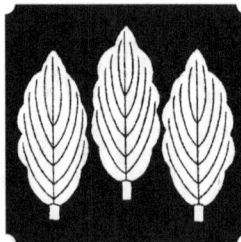 **38** Kashiwa "Oak leaves"
 **39** Kabura "Turnip"
 **40** Kakitsubata "Iris"

 **41** Kaji "Paper mulberry"
 **42** Karahana "Chinese flower"
 **43** Kari "Wild geese"
 **44** Kama-shiki "Trivet"
 **45** Kaku "Shape"

 **46** Kaku "Shapes"
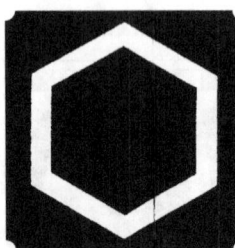 **47** Kaku "Shape"
 **48** Kama "Sickles"
 **49** Kani "Crab"
 **50** Kaki "Fence"

Family Crests – Random Mon Generator

 **51** Yo-tsumé "Four-eye pattern"
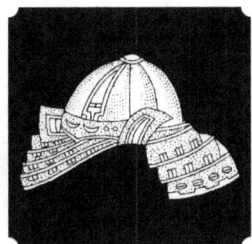 **52** Kabuto "Helmet"
 **53** Tachibana "Mandarin orange blossons"
 **54** Takaha "Hawk feathers"
 **55** Tsuru "Crane"

 **56** Tsuru "Cranes"
 **57** Soroban "Abacus beads"
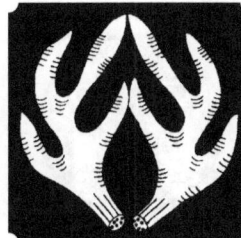 **58** Tsuno "Antlers"
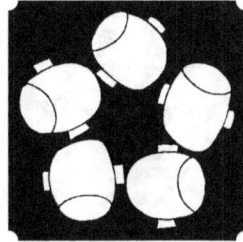 **59** Tsuchi "Mallets"
 **60** Tsuki "Moon"

 **61** Zukin "Hoods"
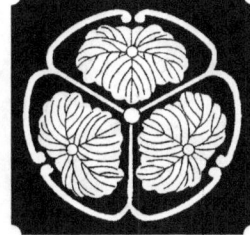 **62** Tsuta "Ivies"
 **63** Nami "Waves"
 **64** Nadeshiko "Wild pink"
 **65** Nashi "Pear blossoms"

 **66** Mukadé "Centipedes"
 **67** Umé-bachi "Plum blossoms"
 **68** Kara-uchiwa "Chinese fans"
 **69** Hané-uchiwa "Plume fan"
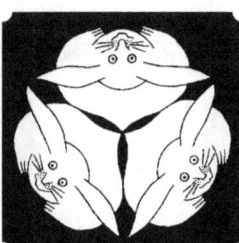 **70** Usagi "Rabbits"

 **71** Uma "Horse"
 **72** Uroko "Fish scales"
 **73** Noshi "Dried abalone strips"
 **74** Kutsuwa "Horse bits"
 **75** Kugi-nuki "Nail extractor"

Family Crests – Random Mon Generator

 **76** Kan-nuki "Bolt"

 **77** Yama-buki "Yellow rose"

 **78** Ya "Arrows"

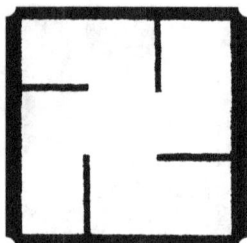 **79** Man-ji "Buddhist cross"

 **80** Ken "Sword"

 **81** Mamori "Talisman"

 **82** Fuji "Wisteria"

 **83** Fukuro "Pouch"

 **84** Budo "Grapes"

 **85** Funé "Ship"

 **86** Fusen-ryo "Dragon balloon"

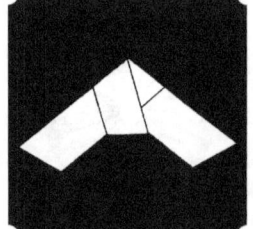 **87** Fumi "Folded letter"

 **88** Fundo "Balance weights"

 **89** Kohoné "Candocks"

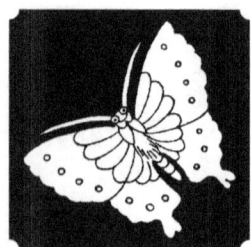 **90** Cho "Butterfly"

 **91** Tessen "Clematis"

 **92** Awa "Millet"

 **93** Asa "Flax leaf"

 **94** Sasa "Bamboo leaves"

 **95** Kikyo "Balloon flower"

 **96** Myoga "Ginger"

 **97** Shichi-ho "Seven-treasures shape"

 **98** Mokko "Papaya"

 **99** Momiji "Maple leaves"

 **00** Sugi "Cedar trees"

Prefectures

In July 1871, the Meiji government abolished the han "fief" system of provinces and established the haihan-chiken "prefecture system." At first the prefectures for the most part reflected the individual fiefs, but by 1885 they were quickly consolidated into 45 prefectures. Adding Hokkaido and Okinawa produced the current total of 47 prefectures.

Many sources today locate places in terms of the new prefectures. To find the corresponding traditional provincial locations, consult the list below. Next to the prefecture name in parenthesis is the name of the Japanese region in which the prefecture is located (see map below).

Note that some provinces were split to occupy parts of two or more prefectures, and many new prefectures consolidated two or more provinces.

Prefecture to Province Conversion

- **Aichi** (Tokaido) -- Mikawa (Nagashino, Okazaki), Owari (Inuyama, Kiyosu, Nagoya)
- **Akita** (Tosando) -- Dewa (Akita), Mutsu
- **Aomori** (Tosando) -- Mutsu
- **Chiba** (Tokaido) -- Awa, Kazusa, Shimosa
- **Ehimé** (Nankaido) -- Iyo
- **Fukui** (Hokurikudo) -- Echizen, Wakasa
- **Fukuoka** (Saikaido) -- Buzen, Chikugo, Chikuzen (Hakata)
- **Fukushima** (Tosando) -- Mutsu (Aizu-Wakamatsu)
- **Fukuyama** (Hokurikudo) -- Etchu
- **Gifu** (Tosando) -- Hida, Mino (Gifu, Seki-ga-hara)
- **Gunma** (Tosando) -- Kozuké
- **Hiroshima** (San'yodo) -- Aki (Hiroshima), Bingo
- **Hokkaido** -- Ezo (Hakodaté)
- **Hyogo** (San'indo/San'yodo/Nankaido) -- Awaji, Harima (Himeji), Settsu (Ichi-no-tani, Kobé), Tajima
- **Ibaraki** (Tokaido) -- Hitachi, Shimosa
- **Ishikawa** (Hokurikudo) -- Kaga (Kanazawa), Noto
- **Iwaté** (Tosando) -- Mutsu
- **Kagawa** (Nankaido) -- Sanuki (Yashima)
- **Kagoshima** (Saikaido) -- Osumi, Satsuma (Kagoshima)
- **Kanagawa** (Tokaido) -- Musashi (Kawasaki, Yokohama), Sagami (Hakoné, Kamakura, Odawara)
- **Kochi** (Nankaido) -- Tosa
- **Kumamoto** (Saikaido) -- Higo
- **Kyoto** (Kinai/San'indo) -- Tanba, Tango, Yamashiro (Fushimi)
- **Mié** (Tokaido) -- Iga, Isé, Shima
- **Miyagi** (Tosando) -- Mutsu (Sendai)
- **Miyazaki** (Saikaido) -- Hyuga
- **Nagano** (Tosando) -- Shinano (Kawanaka-jima)
- **Nagasaki** (Saikaido) -- Hizen (Nagasaki), Tsushima
- **Nara** (Kinai) -- Yamato (Nara)
- **Niigata** (Hokurikudo) -- Echigo, Sado
- **Oita** (Saikaido) -- Bungo (Funai)
- **Okayama** (San'yodo) -- Bitchu, Bizen (Okayama), Mimasaka
- **Osaka** (Kinai) -- Izumi (Sakai), Kawachi, Settsu
- **Saga** (Saikaido) -- Hizen, Iki
- **Saitama** (Tokaido) -- Musashi
- **Shiga** (Tosando) -- Omi
- **Shimané** (San'indo) -- Iwami, Izumo, Oki

Goshichido
Traditional Regions of Japan

Family Crests – Random Mon Generator

- **Shizuoka** (Tokaido) -- Izu, Suruga (Sunpu), Totomi
- **Tochigi** (Tosando) -- Shimotsuké (Nikko)
- **Tokushima** (Nankaido) -- Awa
- **Tokyo** (Tokaido) -- Musashi (Fuchu)
- **Tottori** (San'indo) -- Hoki, Inaba
- **Toyama** (Hokurikudo) -- Etchu
- **Wakayama** (Nankaido) -- Kii
- **Yamagata** (Tosando) -- Dewa
- **Yamaguchi** (San'yodo) -- Nagato (Dan-no-ura), Suo
- **Yamanashi** (Tokaido) -- Kai (Kofu)

Other Regional Names

- **Chinzei** "Western Defense" -- Kyushu
- **Chubu** "Central Region" -- Aichi, Fukui, Gifu, Ishikawa, Nagano, Niigata, Shizuoka, Toyama, Yamanashi, Mié
  Its sub-regions are:
  - **Hokuriku** -- Toyama, Ishikawa, Fukui, Niigata
  - **Koshin'etsu** -- Yamanashi, Nagano, Niigata
  - **Tokai** -- Shizuoka, Aichi, Gifu, Mié
- **Chugoku** "Middle Provinces" -- Horoshima, Yamaguchi, Shimané, Tottori, Okayama
- **Dazaifu** (northern Kyushu) -- From the Nara Period (710-794) through the Heian "Aristocratic" Period (794-1185) and to the Kamakura Period (1185-1333), it was one of the military and administrative centers of Japan. During the 8th and 9th centuries it was known as the "distant capital." With the Mongol Invasions (1274, 1281) and the decline of the Imperial authority, it became less politically significant. In the Muromachi "Ashikaga" Period (1336-1573) the political center of Kyushu was moved to Hakata (Chikuzen).
- **Hokurikudo** "Northern Region"
- **Home Provinces** -- See Kansai
- **Hondo** -- Another name for the island of Honshu
- **Kansai** -- Nara, Wakayama, Kyoto, Osaka, Hyogo, Shiga (sometimes also Mié, Fukui, Tokushima, Tottori)
- **Kanto** "Eastern Provinces" -- Gunma, Tochigi, Ibaraki, Saitama, Tokyo, Chiba, Kanagawa
- **Kibi** -- Bizen, Mimasaka, Bitchu, Bingo
- **Kinai** -- See Kansai
- **Kinki** -- See Kansai
- **Kishu** -- Another name for Kii province
- **Koshu** -- Another name for Kai province
- **Oshu** "Northern Provinces" -- Mutsu and Dewa
- **Saikoku** "Western Provinces" -- Kyushu and the neighboring islands
- **Soshu** -- Another name for Shimosa province
- **Tohoku** "Northeast" -- Akita, Aomori, Fukushima, Iwaté, Miyagi, Yamagata
- **Tsukushi** -- Ancient name for Chikuzen and Chikugo provinces, and also for the whole of Kyushu
- **Ugo** -- In 1869 Dewa was split into two: Ugo and Uzen. It is presently part of Akita prefecture.
- **Uzen** -- In 1869 Dewa was split into two: Ugo and Uzen. It is presently part of Yamagata prefecture.
- **Yoshino** -- A wild and sparsely populated mountainous region of southern Yamato province. It was separated from the province around 716, but abolished sometime after 738, and absorbed back into Yamato. The area continues to be referred to as Yoshino.

Hot Springs near Shuzen-ji (Izu)

Salt-making, Takatsu (Iwami)

Bonito Fishermen (Tosa)

- From the woodcut print series Famous Places in the Sixty-odd Provinces *by Utagawa Hiroshigé (1797-1858).*

Glossary

Titles & Offices

ama -- A Buddhist nun. The ama, also called bikuni, were bound to celibacy, and lived together in nunneries called ama-dera.

azechi, ansatsu-shi "inspector general" -- Title of an inspector created by the Empress Gencho (683-748) in 719 to superintend the administration of provincial governors. Later the office was intrusted to the Chinjufu shogun.

Bakufu (Lit.: government of the tent) "military government" -- Synonymous with Shogunate. Name first given to the Shogunal government organized in Kamakura by Minamoto Yoritomo (1147-1199) in 1190. It was thus denominated because the former Shogun, in their expeditions, had no fixed residence and administered from their camp.

betto "superintendent" "director" "chief" -- Senior bureaucratic head of a department

bozu, bonze -- A Buddhist monk or friar. Bonzes were formerly bound to celibacy and to abstain from fleshmeat. Shinran-shonin (1173-1263), the founder of the Buddhist Jodo Shinshu sect, was the first to dispense his disciples from this obligation in 1124.

bugyo "chief administrator" "commissioner" -- The name formerly given to the chief of an administration. Thus, the machi-bugyo had charge of the city affairs; the kanjo-bugyo, of the finances; the jisha-bugyo, of the temples, etc.

buké -- The military class, the samurai

bushi -- Samurai, warrior, soldier; military class

Chinjufu shogun "commander-in-chief of the Northern Defenses" "defender of the north" -- At the beginning, when the army was sent against the Ebisu, it was commanded by a Chinto shogun, or a Sei-Ezo shogun, or a Chin-teki shogun. These shogun however bore their title only for the time of the expedition and had no fixed residence. In 725 Ono Azumabito (-757) was created Azechi-ken Chinju shogun and took up his residence at Taga Castle (Mutsu). Otomo Otomaro (731-809) and Sakanoué Tamuramaro (758-811) were invested with the same title under Kammu-tenno (737-806). But it was only in 812 that Izawa Castle (Mutsu) was selected as the seat of the Chinjufu, which was composed of a shogun "commander-in-chief," a gunkan "inspector," and several inferior officers. When Minamoto Yoritomo (1147-1199) had obtained the title of Sei-i-tai-shogun, that of Chinjufu shogun was suppressed. In 1326 the Emperor Go-Daigo (1288-1339) re-established it in favor of Kitabataké Akiié (1318-1338), but under the Ashikaga Shogunate (1336-1573), it was definitively abolished.

Chinzei shogun "commander-in-chief of the Western Defenses"

Chinzei tandai "military governor of Kyushu" -- See Kyushu tandai.

chunagon "middle counselor" -- Counselors at the Court, ranking after the dainagon. Their number was not always the same: at the end of the 12th century there were as many as ten.

daijin -- Honorific implying important person

Daijo-daijin "Chancellor of the Realm" "Grand Minister of State" "Prime Minister" -- Head of the Daijo-kan "Grand Council of State"

Daijo-kan "Grand Council of State" -- Supreme Council of the Emperor, established in 702. It was composed of the Daijo-daijin "Chancellor of the Realm," the sadaijin "minister of the left," the udaijin "minister of the right," the naidaijin "minister of the center," the four dainagon "grand counselors," and the three shonagon "minor counselors." Afterwards the chunagon "middle counselors" were created and the number of dainagon and shonagaon increased.

daikan -- Official who, under the Hojo (1203-1333) and the Ashikaga (1338-1573), governed the great fiefs in the absence of the titulars (koku-shi, shugo), then mostly at the capital.

Under the Tokugawa (1603-1868), the title was given to the administrators of the domains of the Shogun.

daimyo (Lit: great name) -- A noble, a lord in feudal times. The possessors of great domains were first called myoden; then by and by the term daimyo prevailed. Daimyo were classified into koku-shu, governors of one or several provinces; ryo-shu, governors of a smaller territory; and jo-shu, commanders of a castle. Before Tokugawa Ieyasu (1543-1616), there were 18 koku-shu, 32 ryo-shu, and 212 jo-shu. From the time of Ieyasu, all those whose revenues were above 10,000 koku of rice were daimyo. He divided them into two classes: the fudai-daimyo, numbering 176, who had sided with him before the Sekigahara Campaign (1600), and the tozama-daimyo, numbering 86, who had submitted to his authority only after been defeated.

dainagon "grand counselor" "major counselor" -- Counselors of the Imperial Court. The Taiho Code (702) created four dainagon. Towards the end of the 12th century the number of dainagon was raised to eight. At the beginning, they were called oimono-mosu-tsukasa.

daizen-shiki "office of the Imperial Household" -- Had charge of the collection and employment of taxes in kind destined for the Imperial Court.

daizen-tayu "minister of the Imperial Household" -- From the time of the Tokugawa Shogunate (1603-1868) the office was hereditary to the Mori of Choshu.

Dazai daini "governor of Kyushu"

Dazai shoni "vice-governor of Kyushu" -- The title of one of the principal officials of the Dazai-fu "military government of Kyushu." In 1196 Muto Sukeyori received this title from Minamoto Yoritomo (1147-1199), and his descendants made it their family name, Shoni.

Glossary – Titles & Offices

emon-fu "Imperial guard" -- A guard of the Imperial Palace. At the beginning, this function was performed by two families, the Otomo and the Kumebé. In 643 the Empress Kogyoku (594-661) created the emon-fu, which comprised the the Kadobé, the Mononobé, the Eji, the Hayato, etc.

eta -- An inferior class of ancient society, a sort of pariah to whom those trades were reserved which were considered impure, such as those of flayers, tanners, curriers, etc.

It is said that the eta were descendants of ancient Korean prisoners or shipwrecked people that settled in Japan.

The eta in Edo had Danzaémon for their chief, who gradually became very rich.

fudai -- A hereditary vassal or retainer. Tokugawa Ieyasu (1543-1616) gave the title of fudai-daimyo to those who had embraced his party before the Seki-ga-hara Campaign (1600); they numbered 176. All important functions were reserved for them.

fushin-bugyo -- An office created in 1652 and entrusted to two officials whose functions were to superintend the reparations of the walls, moats, etc., of the Edo castle as well as other undertakings of the Bakufu in the town.

hatamoto (Lit.: at the foot of the standard) -- Formerly the camp of a Shogun, next the samurai that guarded it. Under the Tokugawa Shogunate (1603-1868), the direct vassals of the Shogun, ranking below the daimyo and above the go-kenin. The class of the hatamoto comprised three degrees: the kodai-yoriai, the yoriai and the kofushin.

go-kenin "Shogunal vassal" -- A name given to the samurai in the service of the Shogun. In the beginning this term applied to high officials such as the shugo and the jito. Under the Tokugawa Shogunate (1603-1868) it was only given to samurai inferior in rank to the hatamoto.

gon-dainagon "acting grand counselor" -- In 828 Jun'a-tenno (786-840) added some gon-dainagon to the Imperial Court.

Go-Tairo -- The five members of the council of state created by Toyotomi Hideyoshi (1536-1598) and who were to assist his son Hideyori (1593-1615) in the government: Tokugawa Ieyasu (1543-1616), Maeda Toshiié (1539-1599), Mori Terumoto (1553-1625), Uesugi Kagekatsu (1556-1623), and Ukita Hideié (1573-1655). They were above the five bugyo and were to form the council of the regency during the minority of Hideyori.

gyobu-sho "ministry of justice" -- Duties encompassed the administration and conduct of trials, determination of punishment, and regulation of fines, imprisonments, and penal servitude.

heimin -- Commoners. A class of people comprising farmers, artisans, and merchants. Above them were the samurai, and below the eta and hinin.

hyobu-kyo "minister of war" -- Usually a son or a close relative of the Emperor. Responsible for directing all military matters. Beginning in the late-12th century, empowered to work with the Shogunate on the Emperor's behalf. In the Edo "Tokugawa" Period (1603-1868) titles associated with the ministry became merely ceremonial.

hyobu-sho "ministry of the military" "ministry of war" -- Formerly the war department. In ancient times, military affairs were superintended by the Otomo and the Mononobé. In 683 the Emperor Temmu (631-686) created the hyosei-kan which in 702 was changed into the hyobu-sho or tsuwamono-no-tsukasa. The minister was also called hyobu-no-kami, later hyobu-kyo.

Hyojo-bugyo "Chief of the Council of State" -- Title created in 1249 under the Kamakura Shogunate (1185-1333). Adachi Yoshikagé (-1255) was the first to bear this title. The same office was created at Kyoto under the Ashikaga Shogunate (1336-1573).

Hyojo-shu "Council of State" "Board of Counselors" -- The highest decision-making body in the Kamakura Shogunate (1185-1333), it was composed of the high officials, who, with the Shikken, assembled at the Mandokoro in order to deliberate on government affairs. Established in 1225 by the 3rd Hojo Shikken Yasutoki (1183-1242). Initially there were 11 members, and the number steadily increased to 28. They were formerly chosen among the families of literati: the Oé, the Kiyohara, the Nakahara, the Miyoshi, the Nikaido, the Saito, etc., among whom this office became hereditary; later they were chosen among the principal daimyo: the Miura, the Chiba, the Adachi, the Yuki, the Sasaki, the Utsunomiya, etc., but without hereditary privileges.

Under the Ashikaga Shogunate (1336-1573) the Hyojo-shu, who had been re-established in 1354, were chosen from the families of the Settsu, the Ota, the Machino, the Iio, the Fusé, etc., all descended from the Nakahara or the Miyoshi.

insei "cloister government" -- The administration of a retired Emperor. The first was that of Shirakawa-tenno (1053-1129) when he abdicated in 1087 in favor of his son Horikawa-tenno (1079-1107).

jibu-sho "ministry of ceremonies" "ministry of the interior" -- One of the eight executive departments creaetd by the Taika Reform (649). The administrator of his department had charge of the genealogies, successions, marriage and funeral rites, and public mourning, of theaters and music, of the Imperial tombs, the reception of foreigners, etc.

Jiro "Little Brother"

jisha-bugyo "commissioner of religious affairs" "commissioner of temples and shrines" -- The official who, under the Kamakura Shogunate (1185-1333), had charge of things concerning the Buddhist and Shintoist priests, the temples and their properties, the ceremonies, etc. This title was created in 1293, and Hojo Tokitsura was the first who received it.

The function was reestablished by the Tokugawa Shogunate (1603-1868) in 1613. In 1635 three jisha-bugyo were nominated: they performed their office alternately, each during one month.

jito "land steward" "deputy administrator" -- Formerly the administrators of the domains of high court officials. This title existed before the Kamakura Shogunate (1185-1333), and those invested with it had charge of collecting the taxes. In 1186, Minamoto Yoritomo (1147-1199) placed the shugo at the head of provinces and the jito at the head of the shoen (domains taken from the jurisdiction of the shugo). After the Jokyu War (1221) bonzes and even women received this title, which became hereditary.

GLOSSARY – TITLES & OFFICES

Under the Ashikaga Shogunate (1336-1573), the domains bestowed on nobles were called ryochi, and their possessors, ryoshu. During the long civil wars of the 15th and 16th centuries, many ryoshu lost their possession, which passed over to samurai vassals of the shugo, and jito were replaced by simple hatamoto; this was continued under the Tokugawa Shogunate (1603-1868).

jodai -- Anciently the military governor of a castle in the absence of the lord. Under the Tokugawa Shogunate (1603-1868), the castles of Osaka, Fushimi, etc., belonging to the Bakufu were guarded by a jodai.

kami "governor" -- A title corresponding to that of governor of a province: Settsu no kami, Iga no kami, etc. From the time of the Ashikaga, the title, in most cases, became merely honorific: there were, for instance, several Shinano no kami at the same time, and having no jurisdiction over that province. The Shimazu, daimyo of Kagoshima, however bore the hereditary title of Satsuma no kami; the So, that of Tsushima no kami, etc.

kamon -- A title given to daimyo families related to the Tokugawa. They were: the different branches of the Sanké (Owari, Kii, Mito), of the Sankyo (Shimizu, Tayasu, Hitotsubashi), and of the Matsudaira of Echizen, all descended from the Shogun.

kanjo-bugyo "finance minister" -- Superintendent of the treasury under the Tokugawa Shogunate (1603-1868). In 1603 Okubo Nagayasu (1545-1613) was the first to discharge this function. In 1682 their number was increased to four, two of whom had the title of kuji-gata, and two others that of katté-gata. They had a great number of employees under their direction.

Kanpaku "Regent to the Emperor" -- From 882 to 1868 the highest dignity at the Imperial Court. First called Azukari-mosu, the Kanpaku was all powerful at the Imperial Court. He represented the Emperor, and at times even took his place in all important questions. He served as intermediary between the Emperor and the officials.

kanrei, kanryo "deputy Shogun" -- A title of two high officials during the Ashikaga Period (1336-1573): one, Kyoto kanrei, the Shogunal deputy in Kyoto, was always taken from the Shiba, the Hosokawa, or the Hatakeyama families, which were for that reason called the san-kan; the other, Kanto kanrei, governor of Kanto, was first taken from the younger branch of the Ashikaga, then from the Uesugi, etc.

Kanto bugyo -- During the Kamakura Shogunate (1185-1333) an official serving as intermediary between the daimyo, officers of the Bakufu, etc., and the Imperial Court of Kyoto, for demanding and granting titles, offices, etc. That charge was maintained by the Ashikaga Shogunate (1336-1573) and from 1370 it became hereditary in the family of Settsu Mitsuchika.

Kanto kanrei "Kanto governor-general" "eastern deputy Shogun" -- Post created by Ashikaga Takauji (1305-1358) following the fall of the Kamakura Shogunate (1185-1333), and the abolition of the Rokuhara tandai position. When Ashikaga Motouji (1340-1367) assumed the title Kanto kubo, he transferred the Kanto kanrei position to the Uesugi, who had previously held the hereditary title of shitsuji, and who dominated the position until it was abolished in 1552.

Kanto kubo, Kanto gosho "Kanto deputy Shogun" -- Kamakura-based representative of the Kyoto Ashikaga regime. The five recorded by history are Ashikaga Motouji (1340-1367) and his bloodline, Ujimitsu (1359-1398), Mitsukané (1378-1409), Mochiuji (1398-1439), and Shigeuji (1438-1497).

karo, garo "senior retainer" -- Formerly the intendant of a daimyo. Also called o-karo or go-karo depending on clan tradition or local idiom. During sankin-kotai, a daimyo had two karo, one in his home han and one in Edo. A karo in charge of a castle was called jodai-karo, and the one in Edo was called Edo karo.

kebiishi "chief of police" -- Established in 839, the office was charged with the policing and the punishment of crimes. In 857 the Emperor Montoku (827-858) placed an office in each province. The influence of the office began to wane when the 1st Kamakura Shogun Minamoto Yoritomo (1147-1199) assigned to the daimyo the right of justice in their estates.

kerai "vassal" -- Vassal of a daimyo, or servant attached to a house.

kiroku-sho "record office" -- A council created in 1069 by the Emperor Go-Sanjo (1032-1073) to deal with administrative and judicial matters. It was presided over by the Emperor in person and took cognizance of all the matters reserved until then to the kurodo-dokoro, with the aim of opposing the all-powerful influence of the Fujiwara. It cut down the number of shoen, and endeavored to put the Imperial finances on a surer footing. It ceased to exist at the close of the 14th century, in the reign of Go-Komatsu (1377-1433).

koké (Lit.: the high families) -- A title given during the Tokugawa Shogunate (1603-1868) to some great dispossessed daimyo: the Takeda, the Yokosé, the Hatakéyama, the Yura, the Imagawa, the Oda, the Otomo, the Osawa, the Kira, etc. They had neither castle nor domains and received from the Bakufu a pension of less than 1,000 koku. But certain privileged missions were reserved to them: they carried the Shogun's messages to the Imperial Palace; they treated the Imperial envoys at Edo; they represented the Shogun at certain ceremonies of Nikko, etc. They also regulated the ceremonies to be observed in the Shogun's palace. They were instituted in 1608, and in 1845 their number was 26.

Below the koké, about ten families bore the title of omoté-koké.

koku-shi "provincial governor" "provincial administrator" "Imperial governor" -- Official sent from the central Imperial government to oversee a province. There were four levels: kami, suké, jo, and sakan.

kon'efu "Imperial Guard" -- A corp of the Imperial Guard. It was divided into sakon'é and ukon'é. The officers bore the title of taisho, chujo, shosho, shogen, shoso, fusei, bancho, toneri, etc.

Kotaishi "Crown Prince" -- The heir apparent to the Chrysanthemum Throne. He was also called Taishi, Haru-no-

GLOSSARY – TITLES & OFFICES

miya, Togu, Shoyo, Chokun, Choni, Hitsugi-no-miya, Hitsugi-no-miko, etc. The Emperor Keitai was the first to appoint his successor by an Imperial decree in 531: this custom was generally followed afterwards. Neglected during the civil wars, in 1683 it was re-established by Reigen-tenno (1653-1732). At the rittaishi "crowning ceremony," in which the title of Kotaishi was conferred, a sword called Tsubokiri-no-tsurugi was presented to the Prince. Orders issued by the Prince Imperial were called reishi; his travels, gyokei; petitions addressed to him, jokei. He had the right to the title of denka. His palace Togu-no-miya was administered by a taifu. His wives were called Nyogo or Miyasu-dokoro.

kugé -- Nobles of the Imperial Court. Most of them belonged to the Fujiwara, the Sugawara, the Taira, the Minamoto, the Kiyohara, the Abé, the Urabé, etc. This nobility was distinct from the military nobility (daimyo), over which it had precedence at the Imperial Court.

Kumonjo "Archives Bureau" "Office of Documents" -- Established by Minamoto Yoritomo (1147-1199) at Kamakura in 1184. The kugé Oé Hiromoto (1148-1225) was its first titulary. It was absorbed into the Mandokoro in 1192.

kunai-sho "ministry of the Imperial Household" -- Established in 645 by the Taika Reforms, its minister had the title of Kunai-kyo and was empowered to collect the revenues of the provinces and domains of the Crown, etc. It came to be responsible for everything to do with supporting the Emperor and the Imperial Family.

kurodo, kurando "administrative official" -- Officials of the kurodo-dokoro

kurodo-dokoro -- Office created in 810 by the Emperor Saga (785-842) to manage administrative matters and the wording of Imperial decrees. Fujiwara Fuyutsugu (775-826) and Kosé Notari were its first titularies. In 897 its minister received the title of betto, which was assigned to Fujiwara Tokihira (871-909). Its members were at first kugé of high rank. Later on three members of the 5th rank and four of the 6th rank were added to their number. They were called higero and managed the daily routine work, the repasts of the Courts, etc. Moreover, young men of high families were intrusted with the commissions, the messages etc., They were the hi-kurodo. Besides them, there were eight zoshiki, 20 tokoroshu, 20 takiguchi-bushi, three suito, six kotoneri, etc.

Kyoto daikan -- During the Tokugawa Shogunate (1603-1868), an official commissioned to administer the five provinces of Kinai. The charge was first filled by the machi-bugyo; in 1680 it became a special office under the authority of the Kyoto shoshidai. From the close of the 18th century, it became hereditary in the Kobori family. It was also called Kyoto-gundai.

Kyoto kanrei "Kyoto deputy Shogun" -- During the Muromachi "Ashikaga" Period (1336-1573), assisted the Shogun in administering the Bakufu. One important responsibility was to oversee the shugo "military governors." Three warrior families, the Shiba, the Hosokawa, and the Hatakeyama, shared this position on a rotating basis.

Kyoto machi-bugyo "Kyoto city magistrate" -- During the Tokugawa Shogunate (1603-1868), an official residing at Kyoto and entrusted with the collection of taxes in the five provinces of Kinai and of Omi, Tanba, and Harima. This office was established in 1600 and was filled by an official first called Kyoto-gundai. In 1665 two officials were appointed who received the title of machi-bugyo, and were moreover empowered to judge lawsuits and superintend the temples.

Kyoto shoshidai "Kyoto governor-general" "Shogunal representative to the Imperial Court" -- In the Ashikaga Period (1336-1573), the chief of the samurai-dokoro bore the title of shoshi. He had himself sometimes replaced by a shoshidai. The office of Kyoto shoshidai was created by Oda Nobunaga (1534-1582). In 1600 Tokugawa Ieyasu (1543-1616) granted the title to Okudaira Nobumasa (1555-1615), then to Itakura Katsushigé (1545-1624). The duty of the shoshidai, official representative of the Shogun at Kyoto, was to inspect the Imperial Court, the kugé; to judge lawsuits, etc. He had authority over the bugyo of Kyoto, Fushimi and Nara, over the Kyoto daikan, over the officials of the Nijo (Shogun's palace at Kyoto), etc. Every five years he had to repair to Edo to render an account of his administration to the Shogun. A former Osaka jodai or a waka-doshiyori was generally selected for the office of shoshidai. He received annually 10,000 koku and had under him 50 yoriki and 100 doshin.

Kyushu tandai "military governor of Kyushu" -- Created in 1275, the title was first conferred on Hojo Sanemasa, commissioned to organize the national defence against the Mongols, and until the end of the Kamakura Shogunate (1185-1333), this office was always filled by a Hojo. The last, Hidetoki, was defeated and slain in 1333 by the Otomo.

During the Ashikaga Period (1336-1573), the title was maintained: Imagawa Ryoshun (1326-1420) bore it from 1371-1396.

machi-bugyo "city magistrate" -- Under the Tokugawa Shogunate (1603-1868), mayors or governors of the cities of Edo, Kyoto, Osaka, and Sunpu. From the year 1719 there were in the city of Edo two such governors who exercised their power by turns. They received 3,000 koku, and had under their command 25 yoriki and 128 doshin.

Mandokoro "Administrative Board" -- Established in 1191 by Minamoto Yoritomo (1147-1199). It took over the functions of the Kumonjo as the main executive and general administrative office of the Kamakura Shogunate (1185-1333). After the Hojo Regency assumed control of the Bakufu, the Mandokoro's sole responsibility was to oversee the government's finances. During the Muromachi "Ashikaga" Period (1336-1573) it was retained by the Bakufu.

metsuké "inspector" -- Under the Tokugawa Shogunate (1603-1868), officials whose duty it was to watch over the keeping of the rules. The metsuké were created in 1617, and numbered 16 members, but at any given time there were as many 24. They were under the authority of a waka-doshiyori. The overseeing of the daimyo was made by the ometsuké, and that of the hatamoto by the metsuké. Every year, one of them was sent to Nagasaki to inspect. In the pal-

Glossary – Titles & Offices

ace of the Shogun, there were always two of them on watch, in the hall called Kikyo-no-ma.

minbu-kyo "minister of taxation"

minbu-sho "ministry of taxation" -- One of the eight ministries created at the time of the Taika Reforms (646). Initially established for the controlling of agriculture, it came to be concerned with census records, land surveys, collection of taxes, infrastructure maintenance, etc.

mokudai "acting provincial governor" -- From the beginning of the 12th century it became customary for the koku-shi "provincial governors" to remain in Kyoto, whilst an official named mokudai or rusu-shoku replaced them in their provinces.

Monchujo -- High Court of Justice established at Kamakura in 1184 by Minamoto Yoritomo (1147-1199): Miyoshi Yasunobu was its 1st minister. Installed first in the palace of the future Shogun, it was in 1199 transferred outside the city. It was the supreme court for all legal matters, especially lawsuits and appeals.

It continued in existence under the Ashikaga Shogunate (1336-1573), the charge of shitsuji "minister" being controlled in turn by the members of the Ota and Machino families. Many of its responsibilities were eventually reassigned to the Mandokoro, and the office was reduced to record keeping.

musha -- See bushi

musha-dokoro -- From the 10th century, the apartments of the samurai who attend an Emperor after his abdication

myoden -- In the Middle Ages, when a person had cleared some wasteland in order to change it into rice fields, he became the proprietor thereof, and to distinguish these lands from koden "government rice-fields," they received a special name and were designated by the general term of of myoden. Their possessor was called myoju: if his domains were considerable, he was a daimyo; if not, he was only shomyo. At the time of the feudal system, these terms daimyo and shomyo were reserved to the families of the military class according to the extent of their fiefs.

naidaijin "inner minister" "minister of the center" -- Formerly minster, who, under the udaijin and the sadaijin took part in the administration of the state. In 662 Fujiwara (Nakatomi) Kamatari (614-669) was the first raised from the title of naijin to that naidaijin; after him, in 771 Fujiwara Yoshitsugu (716-777) and in 779 Fujiwara Uona (721-783) bore the same title; but, as it was not embodied in the Taika and Taiho codes, it had no permanent possessor. It was first called uchi-no-o'omi or uchi-no-otodo.

nairan "Imperial inspector of documents" -- Official created by Minamoto Yoritomo (1147-1199) and charged with inspecting the Imperial Court, to inform the Shogun of all that occurred there. This title corresponds to the Kyoto shoshidai of the Tokugawa Shogunate (1603-1868).

nakatsukasa-sho "ministry of the center" -- One of the eight offices created at the Taika Reforms (649). Placed as a liaison between the Emperor and the Daijo-kan "Council of State," he transmitted the Imperial orders and the petitions of the functionaries, drew up the laws, decrees, and historical annals, kept the registers of the employments, dignities, taxes, etc. The minister had the title of nakatsukasa-kyo. He had under him: one tayu, one shoyu, one taijo, two shojo, two sakan, etc. Eight jiju "chamberlains" attended the Emperor; 90 toneri formed the bodyguard; two dai-naiki, two chu-naiki, and two sho-naiki were charged with drawing up the Imperial messages; two dai-kenmotsu, four chu-kenmotsu, and four sho-kenmotsu kept the keys of the kura "storeroom" and supervised the entrance and exit of all the necessary objects.

nyudo "religious person" -- Monk or nun

Ogosho "Retired Shogun" -- When Tokugawa Ieyasu (1543-1616) retired in 1605, he held this title, and was called Ogosho Ieyasu until his death.

okura-sho "ministry of the treasury" -- From remote times storehouses were built to receive the objects sent to the Imperial Court as presents or taxes; they were first called iwaifura and were intrusted to the Imubé clan. In the reign of Richu-tenno (early 5th century) uchi-kura were built, which were called okura in the reign of Yuryaku-tenno (mid 5th century). At the time of the Taika Reforms (645), a ministry was established with an okura-kyo at its head. It was intrusted with the collection of taxes, the distrubtion of pensions, the verification of measures, the fixing of the prices of the most necessary staples, coinage, etc. The minister had under his control five secondary offices: Tenju, Kmon, Urushibé, Nuibé, Oribé.

ometsuké "chief inspector" "inspector general" -- Officials under the Edo Shogunate (1603-1868) commissioned to look to the strict observance of the laws, to revised lawsuits, to control the proceedings of the daimyo and functionaries, to secure the execution of edicts against the Christians, to superintend the escort of the Shogun when he traveled, to control the adoptions made by the daimyo families, etc. These officials, four in number, were first appointed in 1633, and bore the title of sometsuké; later on their number was increased to five and their name was changed to ometsuké. They reported to the roju.

onsho-gata "office of awards" -- Established by the Emperor Go-Daigo (1288-1339)

oryoshi "provincial governor" -- Ancient title created in 878, at the time of a revolt of the Ebisu in Dewa, and given to Minabuchi Akisato, commissioned to put down brigands, to render justice, etc. In 940 the title and functions of oryoshi were assigned to the governors of Shimosa, Shomotsuké, Iumo, Awaji, Mutsu, and Dewa. This position disappeared during the Kamakura Period (1185-1333) when it was replaced by that of shugo.

Osaka jodai "keeper of Osaka Castle" -- Representative of the Shogun in Osaka Castle. The first who filled this charge was Naito Masanobu (1619). He was commissioned to maintain the fortifications in good condition, to settle lawsuits among the inhabitants of the city and the neighboring villages, to control the acts of the machi-bugyo, etc. It was one of the highest functions of the Shogunate and was generally assigned to the soshaban or jisha-bugyo and at the end of his term, the jodai became Kyoto shoshidai or roju. For some years (1652-1662) there existed at the same time

GLOSSARY – TITLES & OFFICES

six titulars who served in turns, but after 1662 the custom prevailed of appointing a single titular. The Osaka jodai, besides the revenues of his territory, received every year 10,000 koku.

Osaka machi-bugyo "Osaka city magistrate" -- A title created in 1617 and assigned to two officials commissioned to administer, in the name of the Shogun, the city of Osaka and its environs. One was posted in the east of the city, the other in the west.

rensho "associate Regent" -- In the Kamakura Period (1185-1333) the highest official after the Shikken. Also called ren-pan, gohan, kaban. As he shared with the Shikken the right to seal the official documents of the Bakufu, they were called ryo-shikken, ryo-shitsuji, ryo-koken. The rensho was always taken from the Hojo family, and Tokifusa (1175-1240) was the first to receive the title in 1224.

roju, rochu "elder" "senior counselor" -- During the Tokugawa Period (1603-1868), members of the Shogun's council.

This title, corresponding to the rensho of Kamakura or the Kyoto kanrei, was assigned to five officials chosen among daimyo having a revenue of at least 25,000 koku. The Osaki jodai and the Kyoto shoshidai generally became roju at the end of their term; others were taken from among the soba-yonin, the waka-doshiyori, the soshaban, etc. The roju performed their duties in turn, each one serving a month. The hall assigned to the roju in the Shogunal palace was called Go-yo-geya, and was at first near that of the Shogun; but from the time when the Tairo Hotta Masatoshi (1634-1684) was killed there by Inaba Masayasu (1640-1684), it was transferred elsewhere and the roju and the waka-doshiyori had rarely access to the Shogun.

Rokuhara tandai "military governor of Kyoto" -- After the Jokyu Incident (1221), Hojo Yoshitoki (1163-1224) sent his son Yasutoki (1183-1242) and his brother Tokifusa (1175-1250) to take over the administration of the capital and its environs; the former took a north position, the latter, south of Rokuhara; such was the beginning of what was called ryo-Rokuhara "two Rokuhara." Henceforth the two chiefs were the higher-ranking kita-kata "northern governor," and the lower-ranking minami-kata "southern governor." In imitation of what had been done at Kamakura, they were assisted by some hyojoshu (1263), generally taken from among the Goto and Kamedani families, by some hikitsukeshu, etc. Gradually they came to rule over all the departments of administration. The two tandai were always taken from among the Hojo family. The agency was destroyed in 1333 with the fall of the Kamakura Shogunate.

ronin -- A samurai who, freely or on compulsion, left the service of his lord and gained his living by pledging himself to any that needed bold men to make some daring attempt. The famous 47 samurai of Ako became ronin after the death of their lord Asano Naganori (1667-1701); but the Japanese called them gishi "faithful samurai."

sadaiben "senior controller" -- Official having charge of the revision of the affairs of the nakatsukasa-sho, the shikibu-sho, the jibu-sho, the minbu-sho, the Daijo-kan, etc. When there was no uben-kan, he performed the latter's functions.

sadaijin "senior minister of state" "minister of the left" -- The 2nd of the three principal ministers, inferior to the Daijo-daijin, and superior to the udaijin: shared the administration with them, revised the judgments of the Daijo-kan "Council of State," but his special duty was to superintend the affairs pertaining to the Imperial Palace. He was also called ichi-no-kami and safu.

sakon'é "senior officer of the Imperial Guard"

sakon'é-taisho "senior commander of the Imperial Guard"

samurai -- Military man, warrior, man of arms. This word comes from the verb samurau, or better saburau, which signifies: to be on one's guard, to guard; it applied especially to the soldiers who were on guard at the Imperial Palace. The samurai received a pension from their daimyo, and had the privilege of wearing two swords. They intermarried in their own caste and the privilege of samurai was transmitted to all the children, although the heir alone received a pension.

samurai-dokoro "board of retainers" -- Under the Kamakura Shogunate (1185-1333), a bureau that attended to all affairs concerning the military class: guard of the Shogun's Palace, nomination of officials, military tribunals, etc.

sangi "Imperial advisor" -- Counselors of the Daijo-kan "Council of State." They took part in the deliberations but could not vote.

Sanké -- The three branches of the Tokugawa family descended from the three last sons of Ieyasu (1543-1616): Yoshinao (1601-1650), who became daimyo of Nagoya (Owari); Yorinobu (1602-1671), daimyo of Wakayama (Kii), and Yorifusa (1603-1661), daimyo of Mito (Hitachi). They were usually called the families of Owari, Kii, and Mito. When a Shogun died without an heir, his successor could be chosen from these families only. Thrice the Kii branch and once the Mito branch benefitted by this privilege.

Sankyo -- The three branches of the Tokugawa family: Tayasu, Hitotsubashi, and Shimizu. The 1st was established by Munetaké (-1769), son of the 8th Tokugawa Shogun Yoshimuné (1684-1751); the 2nd, by Munetada (1721-1764), brother of the above; the 3rd, by Shigeyoshi (1745-1795), son of the 9th Tokugawa Shogun Ieshigé (1712-1761).

They did not possess castles, but resided at Edo and had their domains superintended by a daikan.

Sei-i-tai-shogun -- See Shogun

Seiwa-Genji -- Patronymic of the families descended from Sadazumi-shinno (874-916), son of Emperor Seiwa, and which received the name of Minamoto.

sensei "teacher" "master"

Sessho "Regent to the Child Emperor" -- At the death of Chuai-tenno (late 2nd century), Empress-consort Jingu (169-269) for 69 years acted as regent instead of her son Ojin-tenno (late 3rd century): it was the first time that this happened in Japan. Later on, Prince Shotoku (574-622) was regent during the reign of the Empress Suiko (554-628). At the death of Montoku-tenno (827-858), his successor Seiwa-tenno (850-880) was only 9 years old, and his grandfather

GLOSSARY – TITLES & OFFICES

Fujiwara Yoshifusa (804-872) was named Sessho during the minority of the Emperor, a custom that was followed afterwards.

shikibu-kyo "chief of protocol" -- Minister of the shikibu-sho. Subject to him were one tayu, one shoyu, two taijo, two shojo, etc.

shikibu-sho "ministry of civil services" "ministry of ceremonies" -- Created in 649, its functions were to examine into the merits of the officials in reference to their advancement, to fix the rewards, to superintend the University, etc.

Shikken "Regent to the Shogun" -- First minister of the Shogun of Kamakura. This title had its equivalent in the Sessho and the Kanpaku of Kyoto. In 1203, Minamoto Yoriié (1182-1204), having handed over the shogunate to his brother Sanetomo (1192-1219), then only 11 years old, their maternal grandfather Hojo Tokimasa (1138-1215) took upon himself the direction of affairs and received the title of Shikken, which he transmitted two years later to his son Yoshitoki (1163-1224). In 1213, after the defeat of Wada Yoshimori (1147-1213), Yoshitoki assumed the title of samurai-dokoro-betto, and, as he was already mandokoro-betto, he then held both the bun "civil" and bu "military" authority, which his descendants inherited and exercised till 1333.

-shinno "Imperial Prince" "Crown Prince"

shitsuji "deputy Shogun" "minister" -- Under the Kamakura Shogunate (1185-1333), minister of the Mandokoro. Its chief had the title of betto, reserved to the Shikken Hojo. The shitsuji acted as first minister of the Shikken. After the fall of Kamakura, it replaced the Rokuhara tandai.

Under the Ashikaga Shogunate (1336-1573), Ashikaga Takauji (1305-1358) named two shitsuji at Kyoto, Ko Moronao (-1351) and Uesugi Tomosada. In 1362 the title of shitsuji, then borne by Shiba Yoshimasa (1350-1410) was changed to kanrei. At Kamakura, Takauji's son Ashikaga Yoshiakira (1330-1367), having assumed the title of Kanto kanrei, Uesugi Noriaki received that of shitsuji, but when Ashikaga Motouji (1340-1367) assumed the title Kanto kubo, the Uesugi were promoted to the Kanto kanrei position.

The vice minister of the Monchujo also had the title of shitsuji, which, under the Kamakura and the Kyoto Shogun, was hereditary in the Ota and the Machino families.

shobanshu "Shogun's private guard" -- Officials of high rank who, during the Ashikaga Shogunate (1336-1573), accompanied the Shogun in his travels. In 1421 Ashikaga Yoshimochi (1386-1428), being invited to visit Isé Sadatsuné, for the first time gave this title to Hatakeyama Mitsuié (1372-1433). The members of the Shiba, the Hosokawa, and the Hatakeyama families, before being named kanrei, and also the daimyo skilful in military exercises, were chosen as shobanshu.

Shogun "Military Dictator," **Sei-i-tai-shogun** "Commander-in-Chief against the Barbarians" -- Such was the title under which the Minamoto (1192-1219), the Fujiwara (1220-1244), some Imperial Princes (1245-1334), the Ashikaga (1336-1573), and lastly the Tokugawa (1603-1868), exercised unlimited power to which the Emperors themselves were obliged to yield. This state of affairs caused Europeans for a long time to believe that Japan was governed by two Emperors, one retired in his palace of Kyoto, the descendant of the gods, busied only with religious matters; the other, the acting sovereign, governing and administering as he pleased. This notion though false was a correct estimate of the situation. The investiture of the Shogun was at all times received from the Emperor, who seems never to have had either the desire or the power to refuse it. From the time of Minamoto Yoritomo (1147-1199), the title of Shogun was reserved for the descendants of the Minamoto (Seiwa-Genji), and for this reason, Oda Nobunaga (1534-1582), descendant of the Taira, and Toyotomi Hideyoshi (1536-1598), who was of low extraction, never bore that title.

Shogunate -- See Bakufu

shoji -- Formerly a title given to the possessors of the shoen

shomyo -- Formerly, especially under the Ashikaga Shogunate (1336-1573), lord of a small domain, as opposed to daimyo.

shonagon "minor counselor" -- Officials of the Daijo-kan, equivalent to a 2nd-class secretary, who transacted business of small importance. There were at first three, but later increased.

shoshidai -- See Kyoto shoshidai

shugo, shugo-shoku "constable" "military governor" -- In 1185, on the advice of Oé Hiromoto (1148-1225), Minamoto Yoritomo (1147-1199) created an official in the provinces formerly belonging to the Taira, and not depending directly on him, to assist the koku-shi "governor": he named him shugo or shugo-shoku. In the shoen, they were called jito. At the head of the Kanto provinces, which depended directly upon him, he placed kuni-bugyo.

The shoku, who at first were called sotsui-bushi, had to secure the payment of the taxes, render justice, levy troops in case of war, etc. Gradually they extended their power over the shoen, and the jito were reduced to a secondary position. Under the Ashikaga Shogunate (1336-1573), the shugo became still more powerful, some governing several provinces, for in 1440, the Yamana lorded it over 11 provinces. After the Onin War (1469), they began to replace the koku-shi and formed the class of daimyo, whilst the jito and the gokenin were called shomyo.

shugo-dai, shugo-daikan "deputy constable" -- Official who replaced the shugo when absent from his fief. As the case occurred frequently, the shugo-dai increased in importance and at times even overthrew the shugo.

shuri-tayu, shuri-dayu -- Court title

soba-shu -- Under the Tokugawa Shogunate (1603-1868), samurai on duty at the Palace of Edo. Among them, some had to read the reports of the roju to the Shogun, and to write down the observations he made. They settled in advance the days of audience of the daimyo and the hatamoto. After a period judged sufficiently long, the soba-shu were usually raised to the rank of waka-doshiyori. The custom for each Shogun to raise one soba-shu to the rank of a daimyo began at the commencement of the 18th century.

soshaban -- Under the Tokugawa Shogunate (1603-1868), an official whose duty it was to introduce the samurai to audience with the Shogun at New Year and certain festivals, to read the list of presents given by the Shogun, to regulate the details of the ceremony, etc. Created in 1632, this office was discharged by two soshaban, but their number was subsequently raised to 24, who performed their duties by turn. In 1658 the jisha-bugyo exercised it in connection with his own office.

sotsui-bushi "constable-general" "chief constable" -- In 1185 Minamoto Yoritomo (1147-1199) sent to all the provinces, high officials who replaced the governors. These officials wre called sotsui-bushi (later on they were called shugo), and Yoritomo himself was known by the title of Nihon sotsui-bushi or 66-koku-no-sotsui-bushi.

Taiko "Retired Regent to the Emperor" -- Title taken by a Kanpaku, when he was succeeded in office by his son: if he transmitted it to another, he had no claim that title. If, when being succeeded by his son, he shaved his head, and became bonze, he was called Zenko. Although this title occurs several times in history, it is especially given to Toyotomi Hideyoshi (1536-1598), who in 1592 took it when the office of Kanpaku passed to his adopted son Hidetsugu (1568-1595).

tairo "great elder" "chief minister" -- Under the Tokugawa Bakufu (1603-1868), the first minister of the Shogun. He was also called genro or o-toshiyori. In 1638 the first to receive this title were Doi Toshikatsu (1573-1644) and Sakai Tadakatsu (1587-1662). Later on the office was given to one official usually chosen from the Sakai, the Ii, and the Hotta families. A tozama-daimyo was never raised to the dignity of tairo. From 1709, the time of the 6th Tokugawa Shogun Ienobu (1662-1712), till 1760, that of the 9th Tokugawa Shogun Ieshigé (1712-1761), this office was vacant. One of the best known tairo is the famous Ii Naosuké (1815-1860), signer of the first treaty with the foreign powers, who was assassinated in 1860.

Taro "Big Brother"

-tenno "Emperor"

tozama-daimyo -- Formerly this term was applied to the daimyo who were not vassals of the Shogun. Ieyasu gave that name to the 86 daimyo who submitted to him only after the Battle of Seki-ga-hara (1600), whilst he called those who had sided with him from the beginning of the campaign, fudai-daimyo: these numbered 176.

The most powerful among the tozama-daimyo were: Maeda (Kaga), Daté (Sendai), Shimazu (Satsuma), Mori (Choshu). They took rank immediately after the Sanké; were the guests of the Shogun when they came to Edo for their annual visit, and were received by a special joshi "envoy" sent as far as Shinagawa or Senju.

udaiben "junior controller" -- 1st secretary in the hyobu "ministry of war," gyobu "ministry of justice," okura "ministry of finance," and kunai "ministry of the Imperial Palace." He was superior to the uchuben and the ushoben.

udaijin "junior minister of state" "minister of the right" -- From 645, the 3rd of the three principal ministers, inferior to the sadaijin.

ukon'é "junior officer of the Imperial Guard"

ukon'é-taisho "junior commander of the Imperial Guard"

waka-doshiyori -- Under the Tokugawa Bakufu (1603-1868), members of the Council of the Shogun, below the roju. Their functions were to supervise officials and the hatamoto. In 1633 the 3rd Tokugawa Shogun Iemitsu (1604-1651) created the following six: Matsudaira Nobutsuna (1596-1662), Miura Masatsugu, Abé Tadaoki, Ota Sukemuné (1600-1680), Hotta Masamori (1606-1651), and Abé Shigetsugu. This number was always retained.

yoriki-doshin -- Under the Tokugawa Shogunate (1603-1868), minor officials subject to a bugyo. These offices were hereditary. The yoriki were divided into two classes: go-fudai-gumi and o-kakaé-gumi. The doshin belonged to the kakaé-gumi.

Zenko -- Title given to a Kanpaku who transmitted his office to his son, shaved his head and became a bonze. When he remained in public life after his resignation, he took the title of Taiko.

OTHER

Aino, Ainu -- The Aino, who call themselves Ainu "men" are the last remnants of the aboriginal race of Japan. Japanese history calls them Ebisu "barbarians." Gradually driven back by the invaders from the southwest, they were not brought under complete subjection before the 18th century. Nearly all reside in the northern island of Ezo.

Buké-shohatto "Points of Law for Warrior Houses" -- A code promulgated by Tokugawa Ieyasu (1543-1616), containing in 13 chapters the laws to be observed by the daimyo and the samurai.

Bun'ei no Eki -- This is the name given to the war resulting from the first expedition of the Mongols to Japan (1274). The invaders, after having ravaged Tsushima and Iki, were repulsed from Kyushu, their general was killed, and a tempest dispersed their fleet.

Bunroku-no-kenchi -- Toyotomi Hideyoshi (1536-1598) had a register made of all the provinces from 1589-1595. New measures were used for that survey (1 tan = 300 tsubo, 1 cho = 10 tan). From that time the revenues were no more appraised in money but koku of rice. This reform was called Bunroku-no-kenchi, or Tensho-no-koku-naoshi.

Bushido (Lit. the way of the samurai) -- This term is applied to the principles of loyalty and honor which were always to be followed by the samurai. Bushido borrowed stoic endurance, scorn of danger and death from Buddhism; religious worship of country and sovereign from Shintoism; a certain literary and artistic culture, as well as the social moral of the go-rin "five relations," from Confucianism. This amalgam was to form the code of the perfect knight. It may be summed up in three words: the samurai is a man of few words; he does not serve two masters; for duty he sheds his blood, "like the cherry-tree drops its flowers." Such was to be the ideal samurai.

Dan-no-ura (Nagato) -- A bay near Shimonoseki, where in 1185 the celebrated naval battle was fought that consummated the ruin of the Taira and the triumph of the Minamoto. The latter's victory was principally due to the bravery of Minamoto Yoshitsuné (1159-1189), who, among other feats, in one bound, leapt over eight (?) hasso-tobi

Glossary – Other

"boats" to reach an enemy. The ex-Emperor Antoku (1178-1185), 7 years old, and his grandmother Nii-no-ama (1126-1185), the widow of Taira Kiyomori (1118-1181), perished in the sea with a great number of their partisans.

Ebisu "barbarians" -- A name given to the aborigines in the east and north of Japan. Those that lived in the most remote provinces were called Ara-Ebisu, Tsugaru-Ebisu. The Aino are their descendants.

eboshi-na -- At the time of the genbuku, a kinsman or a friend was chosen as eboshi-oya "sponsor" who putting the eboshi (a kind of hat) on the head of the young man, gave him a name: it was the eboshi-na, or kammei.

Edo Jidai -- The period of the Tokugawa Shogunate in Edo, from 1603 till 1867; it is also called Tokugawa Jidai.

Eikyo no Ran -- A civil war which arose in Kanto when the kanrei Ashikaga Mochiuji (1398-1439), irritated at not having been made Shogun, refused obedience to the elected 6th Ashikaga Shogun Yoshinori (1394-1441), commenced war against Uesugi Norizané (1410-1466), and was finally condemned to commit harakiri.

genbuku, genpuku -- A ceremony during which a minor is declared to be of age. For the Emperor, since the reign of Seiwa-tenno (850-880), it consisted in the receiving of a collar. The sons of kugé had their headdress arranged according to the Court fashion and received the kanmuri (the black hat seen on portraits). Among the officials, the young man changed the name he bore in childhood and received the eboshi from a relation or a patron, called eboshi-oya or kanmuri-oya. During the Tokugawa Period (1603-1868), the genbuku for boys consisted in having the top of the head shaved; and for girls, in having the eyebrows shaved and the teeth blackened.

Genko no Ran -- The civil war during the Genko Era. In 1326, the Kotaishi Kuninaga-shinno having died, the Emperor Go-Daigo (1288-1339) wished to replace him by his son Morinaga-shinno (1308-1335), but was prevented by Hojo Takatoki (1303-1333) who had Kazuhito-shinno (1313-1364) a son of Go-Fushimi-tenno (1288-1336), nominated. Go-Daigo appointed Morinaga chief of the Enryaku-ji of the Tendai sect, and with the help of the bonzes, prepared to get rid of the Hojo. It was then that Takatoki marched against Kyoto with a numerous army: the Emperor fled to Mount Kasagi, but being taken prisoner, he was confined to the Rokuhara and afterwards exiled to Chiburi Island (Oki).

Go-san-nen no Eki -- The Earlier Three Years War (1086-1089). During the Nine Years' War (1053-1062), Kiyohara Takenori had helped Minamoto Yoriyoshi (988-1075) to defeat Abé Yoritoki (-1057) and his sons, and in return for his services, had been nominated Chinjufu shogun. His son Kiyohara Sadahira governed six districts of the province of Mutsu, when Kiyohara Iehira (-1087), the latter's brother, aided by his uncle Kiyohara Takehira, revolted against him; soon the war extended over the whole province. Minamoto Yoshiié (1039-1106) was sent to support Sadahira. In 1089 he besieged Iehira and Takehira in the castle of Kanazawa (Dewa). The rebels set fire to the castle and escaped, but were killed in their flight.

han (Lit.: hedge, palisade) -- A fief or territory governed by a daimyo. The han were established by degrees during the 12th century and regularly organized by Minamoto Yoritomo (1147-1199). Under the Ashikaga Bakufu (1336-1573) it was not by the will of the Emperor or of the Shogun that the titulars were designated, but by force of arms. Tokugawa Ieyasu (1543-1616) renewed the regulation of the ancient Bakufu and raised the number of the han to over 300. They were divided into three classes, according to the importance of their revenue: the dai-han, above 400,000 koku of rice; the chu-han, from 100,000 to 400,000 koku; the sho-han, below 100,000 koku.

harakiri (Chinese: seppuku) -- A manner of suicide peculiar to Japan. It was of two kinds, one obligatory and the other voluntary. The first took place after condemnation to death: daimyo and samurai then had the privilege of opening the abdomen, instead of being beheaded by the executioner. Such is the meaning of the words harakiri or seppuku. This was the case in 1702 with the 47 ronin of Ako, in 1867 with the murders of the French sailors at Sakai, etc. The principal motives in committing voluntary harakiri were: the desire of not falling alive into the hands of the enemy after a defeat; to give proof of fidelity by committing suicide on the tomb of a deceased master; to protest against the conduct of a superior, etc. Formerly harakiri was performed in a most brutal manner and at times death came only after hours of suffering. Subsequently the patient made only a slight incision, and at the same time a faithful friend cut off his head with a sword. Obligatory harakiri has been completely expunged from the present legislation, but the voluntary harakiri occurs yet from time to time.

Heiji no Ran -- The civil war of the Heiji Period (1159), Fujiwara Nobuyori (1133-1160) and Minamoto Yoshitomo (1123-1160) revolted against the Taira, but they were vanquished and killed.

Hogen no Ran -- The civil war of the Hogen Era (1156). At the death of Emperor Konoé (1139-1155), the ex-Emperor Sutoku (1119-1164) expected to see his son Shigehito-shinno raised to the throne, but despite his efforts the previous Emperor Toba (1103-1156) had another of his sons, Go-Shirakawa (1127-1192) nominated. Sutoku was supported by the Minamoto and Go-Shirakawa by the Taira who ultimately conquered. Sutoku was exiled to Sanuki, Shigehito was obliged to become bonze and the others were put to death or banished, but the most striking result was the strengthening of the ever increasing authority of Taira Kiyomori (1118-1181).

Ikko-to no Ran (Lit.: the civil war of the adherents of the Ikko sect) -- The 8th successor of Shinran (1173-1263), Rennyo-shonin (1415-1499), forced to flee from Kyoto, spread the doctrines of the sect in the provinces of Echizen, Kaga, and Noto, where it became prosperous. The bonzes, not content with the domains they received from their adherents, made themselves masters of a great number of others and declared war against the daimyo. The 16th century to the times of Oda Nobunaga (1534-1582) was full of these wars, which were felt especially in Echizen, Isé, Settsu, and Mikawa.

Glossary – Other

Jinshin no Ran -- The civil war that occupied the short reign of the Emperor Kobun (648-672) and was brought to a close by the triumph of his uncle, the Emperor Temmu (631-686). It took its name from the year of the sexagesimal cycle during which it happened (672).

Jokyu no Ran -- The civil war of the Jokyu Era. After the death of the 3rd and last Minamoto Shogun Sanetomo (1192-1219), Kujo (Fujiwara) Yoritsuné (1218-1256), then 2 years old, was chosen by the Hojo to succeed him, and the 2nd Hojo Shikken Yoshitoki (1163-1224) continued to govern. A little later in 1221, Emperor Juntoku (1197-1242) abdicated in favor of his son. There then were three ex-Emperors: Go-Toba (Ichi-in), Tsuchimikado (Chu-in), and Juntoku (Shin-in). Go-Toba and Juntoku resolved to get rid of the Hojo, and an order was sent to all the provinces to levy troops and march against them. On hearing this, Yoshitoki, after taking the advice of his sister Minamoto (née Hojo) Masako (1156-1225) and Oé Hiromoto (1148-1225), sent a large army against Kyoto under the command of his sons Hojo Yasutoki (1183-1242) and Hojo Tomotoki and his brother Hojo Tokufusa. The several thousands of samurai who had answered the call of the Emperor were defeated at Uji and at Seta: the victorious Kamakura army entered Kanto, and Yoshitoki took his revenge. The young Emperor Chukyo (1218-1234) was deposed, his father Juntoku exiled to Sado, and Go-Toba to Oki. Although Tsuchimikado had kept himself secluded, he was notwithstanding exiled to Shikoku. Thus ended the Jokyu War. The Hojo were thus to remain all powerful during one more century.

junshi -- Formerly, at the death of a great personage, his servants were buried with him: it was the junshi. In 2 B.C., the Emperor Suinin, on the advice of Nomi no Sukuné, interdicted that practice, but the custom to commit suicide at the loss of one's master was introduced as a sign of fidelity. In the 16th century, when a general or daimyo died, many vassals put an end to their lives by seppuku. At the death of the 3rd Tokugawa Shogun Iemitsu (1604-1651) five great daimyo committed suicide in order not to survive him. It was only in 1668, that by very severe ordinances, the 4th Tokugawa Shogun Ietsuna (1641-1680) succeeded in suppressing that abuse.

Kakitsu no Hen (Lit.: the advent of the Kakitsu Era) -- An expression to designate the assassination of the 6th Ashikaga Shogun Yoshinori (1394-1441) by Akamatsu Mitsusuké (1381-1441). Yoshinori hated Mitsusuké and proved it to him in many ways; finally, he wished to despoil him of his domains in order to bestow them on Akamatsu Sadamasa. Mitsusuké, concealing his anger, invited the Shogun to a feast during which he assassinated him; next he put fire to his own house and fled to Harima. There he proclaimed Giun, a bonze and grandson of Ashikaga Tadafuyu, heir of Yoshinori. Meanwhile, the Hosokawa, the Takeda, the Yamana, etc., recognized Yoshinori's son Ashikaga Yoshikatsu (1434-1443), and marched against Mitsusuké, who, being besieged in his castle at Shirahata (Harima) and defeated after a short resistance, killed himself by harakiri.

kami -- The gods and goddesses of Shintoism

Kanto (Lit.: east of the barrier) -- A name given first to the region which extended east from the Osaka barrier (Omi), near lake Biwa, and later on to the provinces situated east from the old Hakoné barrier (Sagami).

Kawanaka-jima (Shinano) -- A district comprised between the two rivers Sai-gawa and Chikuma-gawa, to the northeast of the province. Was from 1553 to 1563 the scene of many engagements between Uesugi Kenshin (1530-1578) and Takeda Shingen (1521-1573). In the Tokugawa Period (1603-1868) it was the domain of the Matsudaira daimyo (1603-1619), and the Fukushima (1619-1624).

koden -- Formerly rice-fields leased as a reward for services rendered to the country. There were four kinds: taiko, permanent lease; joko, leased for three generations; chuko, for two generations; geko, which passed over to the son, and after his death, reverted to the public domain.

koku -- Measure of capacity, equal to 180.4 liters, or 5.1 bushels, the amount of rice needed to feed one person for one year. It was in koku of rice that from the 16th century onwards the revenues of daimyo and salaries of officials were estimated. During the Tokugawa Period (1603-1868), a revenue of 10,000 koku at least, was necessary to entitle one to the rank of daimyo. The value of the koku has naturally undergone variations. In 1787, for instance, it was 5.5 ryo, so that the revenue of a domain of 30,000 koku was 165,000 ryo.

koku-daka (Lit.: the amount of koku) -- Until the close of the 16th century, the revenues of the daimyo, and the salaries of officials were valued in kan (kan-daka), a coin equal to 1/10 of a ryo. Hideyoshi substituted the valuation in koku of rice. From 1589 to 1596, a new survey was made of the whole Empire (see Bunroku-no-kenchi). Until then, 360 bu made 1 tan, 10 tan made 1 cho; thenceforth, 30 bu made 1 sé, 300 bu or tsubo made 1 tan, 3,000 bu made 1 cho. Thus the old tan was equaled to 1 tan and 2 sé of the new system, and 1 cho made 1 cho 2 tan. It was with these new measures that the area of the domains and their revenues were estimated. This modification was termed Bunroku-no-kenchi or Tensho-no-koku-naoshi.

Muromachi Jidai -- The period of the Shogunate of the Ashikaga, beginning in 1392, date of the fusion of the two dynasties of the North and of the South, and lasting till 1490, accession of the 10th Ashikaga Shogun Yoshitané (1466-1523).

musha-shugyo -- At the time of the prosperity of the Bushido, a great number of fencing schools were established, whose graduates spread over the provinces to place their learning at the service of the daimyo: they were called musha-shugyo.

nengo -- Era, period of years. During the first 10 centuries of their history, the Japanese reckoned their years either from the enthronement of Jimmu-tenno (660 B.C.), or after the sexagesimal cycle, or again from the commencement of each reign. Kotoku-tenno (596-654) borrowed from China the custom of giving a name to the years, and decided that the 1st year of his reign should be the 1st of the Taika Era (645). Six years after, the Emperor, having received the present of a white pheasant from the province of Nagato, concluded that this event merited to be handed down to history and changed the name of the era to that of Hakuchi

Glossary – Other

"White Pheasant": this was the 1st kaigan "change of era." Kotoku-tenno died in the 5th year of Hakuchi (654), and his two immediate successors, Empress Saimei (594-661) and Emperor Tenji (626-671), suppressed the nengo. Temmu-tenno (631-686) re-established them in 672, and since then the custom was followed without interruption: the accession of an Emperor to the throne, an important event, happy or unhappy, brought about a change in the era. In the reign of Murakami-tenno (947-967) the astronomer Abé Seimei (921-1005) introduced the Chinese custom of changing the name of the era in the 1st (ki-no-é no né) and the 57th (ka-no-to no tori) year of the cycle. The reigns which counted the greatest number of nengo are those of the Emperors Go-Daigo (1319-1338) and Go-Hanazono (1429-1465), which each had eight. From the Taika Era (645) to the Imperial Restoration (1868) there have been 229 nengo.

Onin no Ran -- Civil war that broke out in the Onin Era. The 8th Ashikaga Shogun Yoshimasa (1436-1490), having no children, adopted his brother Ashikaga Yoshimi (1438-1491), and in 1464 gave him as hosa "tutor" Hosokawa Katsumoto (1430-1473). But the following year, a son, Ashikaga Yoshihisa (1465-1489), was born to him, upon which he intended to deprive his brother of his rights to the succession. Meanwhile, Hatakeyama Mochikuni, after having adopted his nephew Hatakeyama Masanaga (1442-1493), also had a son and, and dismissed his adopted son. Similar difficulties arose in the Shiba family, where two rivals, Shiba Yoshitoshi (1430-1490) and Shiba Yoshikado (-1480) disputed the inheritance of Shiba Yoshitaké (-1452). The malcontents appealed to the great daimyo and two parties were formed, headed by Hosokawa Katsumoto and Yamana Mochitoyo (1404-1473). It was not long before war broke out, which continued without decisive advantage for either side, during 11 years (1467-1477). Kyoto and its environs were laid waste and the struggle was ended only by the exhaustion of both parties.

ryo -- Gold coin. Value and weight fluctuated widely over time.

Sankan Seibatsu -- The expedition in 200 led by Empress-consort Jingu (169-269) for the purpose of subjugating Korea. The Korean annals do not mention the fact.

sankin-kotai -- Law enacted in 1634 by the 3rd Tokugawa Shogun Iemitsu (1604-1651) which obliged all the daimyo to reside alternately in their domains and in Edo, and to leave their wife and children as hostages in that city. The time of residence was no strictly determined but most of the daimyo remained one year at Edo and one year in their domains. Those of the Kanto province changed their residence every 6 months. This law was abrogated in 1862.

Seki-ga-hara (Mino) -- Village thus called because it was situated in the plain near the ancient seki "gate" of Fuwa. It was also called Fuwa-no, Ao-no-hara. At that place, Oct 21, 1600, Tokugawa Ieyasu (1543-1616) gained a decisive victory over the army of Toyotomi Hideyori (1593-1615), commanded by Ishida Katsushigé (1557-1600). This battle, which raised the Tokugawa to supreme power, is the most important event of Japanese history. Ieyasu was at the head of 80,000 men; his opponents had 130,000 and left 30,000 dead on the battlefield.

Sengoku Jidai -- Period from 1490 to 1600, during which Japan was completely involved in civil war.

seppuku -- See harakiri.

shoen -- Formerly, domains with which the Emperor rewarded Princes or high officials. The possessors of shoen, called shoji, at first had only the product of these lands, the land itself remaining Imperial property; but they were exempt from taxes and not subject to provincial government. Their number gradually increased; some lords, on their own authority, gave the name of shoen to their domains, dispensed justice, levied heavy taxes, etc. In the 11th century, half of the country was thus converted into shoen domains. Vainly did some Emperors enact laws against this state of affairs. Minamoto Yoritomo (1147-1199), however, succeeded in notably diminishing their number and imposed on all an annual taxation of 5 sho (9 litres) of rice per tan (10 acres).

The shoji were often absent from their domains and had them administered by a jito.

Shokyu no Ran -- See Jokyu no Ran

Tenkei no Ran -- The civil war brought about by the rebellion of Taira Masakado (-940) during the Tenkei Era.

BIBLIOGRAPHY

For a more complete listing of peripheral references, please see *Daimyo of 1867*.

MAIN SOURCES

Deal, William E. -- *Handbook to Life in Medieval and Early Modern Japan* (Oxford University Press, New York 2006)
Frédéric, Louis -- *Japan Encyclopedia* (The Belknap Press of Harvard University Press, Cambridge, Massachusetts 2002)
Papinot, E. -- *Historical and Geographical Dictionary of Japan* (Charles E. Tuttle Company, Rutland, Vermont 1972)
Reischauer, Edwin O. -- *Japan: The Story of a Nation* (Alfred A. Knopf, New York 1970)
The Samurai Archives (www.samurai-archives.com)
Wikipedia (www.wikipedia.org)

HISTORY

Ehara, Tadashi -- *Daimyo of 1867: Samurai Warlords of Shogun Japan* (Different Worlds Publications, San Francisco 2010)
Grossberg, Kenneth Alan -- *Japan's Renaissance: The Politics of the Muromachi Bakufu* (East Asia Program, Cornell University, Ithaca, New York 2001)
Hall, Whitney; Nagahara, Keiji; and Yamamura, Kozo (eds.) -- *Japan Before Tokugawa: Political Consolidation and Economic Growth, 1500 to 1650* (Princeton University Press, Princeton, New Jersey 1981)
Statler, Oliver -- *Shimoda Story* (Random House, New York 1969)
Totman, Conrad D. -- *Politics in the Tokugawa Bakufu, 1600-1843* (University of California Press, Berkeley 1988)

BUSHIDO

Cleary, Thomas -- *Code of the Samurai: A Modern Translation of the Bushido Shoshinshu of Taira Shigesuke* (Tuttle Publishing, Rutland, Vermont 1999)
Clements, Jonathan -- *A Brief History of the Samurai: The Way of Japan's Elite Warriors* (Running Press, Philadelphia 2010)
de Lange, William -- *Famous Japanese Swordsmen of The Period of Unification* (Floating World Editions, Warren, Connecticut 2008)
Miyamori, Asataro -- *Katsuno's Revenge and Other Tales of the Samurai* (Dover Publications, Mineola, New York 2006)
Sato, Hiroaki -- *The Sword & the Mind* (The Overlook Press, Woodstock, New York 1985)
Varley, Paul -- *Warriors of Japan: As Portrayed in the War Tales* (University of Hawai'i Press, Honolulu 1994)
Wilson, William Scott -- *Ideals of the Samurai: Writings of Japanese Warriors* (Ohara Publications, Santa Clarita, California 1982)
Yagyu Munenori -- *The Life-Giving Sword: Secret Teachings from the House of the Shogun* (Kodansha International, Tokyo 2003)

CULTURE

Dalby, Liza -- *Geisha* (Vintage Books, New York 1985)
Dunn, Charles J. -- *Everyday Life in Traditional Japan* (Charles E. Tuttle Company, Rutland, Vermont 1972)
Statler, Oliver -- *Japanese Inn* (University of Hawai'i Press, Honolulu 1982)

MON "JAPANESE CRESTS"

Harimaya -- "Sengoku Daimyo Clan List" (http://www2.harimaya.com/sengoku/bk_1ran.html)
The Matsuya Company -- *Japanese Crest Design: CD-ROM and Book* (Dover Publications, Mineola, New York 2006)
Matsuya Piece-Goods Store -- *Japanese Design Motifs* (Dover Publications, New York 1972)
Wikimedia Commons -- "Family crest of Japan" (commons.wikimedia.org/wiki/Category:Family_crest_of_Japan)

SAMURAI CINEMA

All Movie Guide (www.allmovie.com)
Amazon.com (www.amazon.com)
Galloway, Patrick -- *Stray Dogs & Lone Wolves: The Samurai Film Handbook* (Stone Bridge Press, Berkeley, California 2005)
Galloway, Patrick -- *Warring Clans, Flashing Blades: A Samurai Film Companion* (Stone Bridge Press, Berkeley, California 2009)
The Internet Movie Database (www.imdb.com)
Rotten Tomatoes (www.rottentomatoes.com)
Silver, Alain -- *The Samurai Film* (The Overlook Press, New York 2005)
Thorne, Roland -- *Samurai Films* (Kamera Books, Herts, UK 2008)

TRANSLATIONS

Babylon -- "Japanese Translation" (translation.babylon.com/Japanese)
Saiga -- "Japanese Kanji Dictionary" (www.saiga-jp.com/kanji_dictionary.html)
WorldLingo -- "Free Online Language Translator" (www.worldlingo.com/en/products_services/worldlingo_translator.html)

ILLUSTRATIONS

Bing, Siegfried (ed.) -- *Artistic Japan: 300 Traditional Spot Illustrations* (Dover Publications, Mineola, New York 2009)

Bibliography

Cotton Town -- "Japanese Prints" (www.cottontown.org/page.cfm?pageid=513&language=eng)

Grafton, Carol Belanger (ed.) -- *Traditional Japanese Vector Motifs* (Dover Publications, Mineola, New York 2009)

A Mirror of Japanese Ornament: 600 Traditional Designs (Dover Publications, Mineola, New York 2010)

Museum of Fine Arts, Boston -- "Educators Online: Bring art from the MFA into your classroom" (educators.mfa.org)

Nakamura, Shigeki -- *Pattern Sourcebook: Japanese Style* (Rockport Publishers, Beverly, Massachusetts 2008)

Nakamura, Shigeki -- *Pattern Sourcebook: Japanese Style 2* (Rockport Publishers, Beverly, Massachusetts 2009)

Narazaki, Muneshige -- *Hiroshige: The 53 Stations of the Tokaido* (Kodansha International, Tokyo 1969)

National Diet Library -- "Meiji and Taisho Eras in Photographs" (www.ndl.go.jp/scenery/e/index.html)

Orban-Szontagh -- *Japanese Floral Patterns and Motifs* (Dover Publications, Mineola, New York 1990)

Wikimedia Commons (commons.wikimedia.org/wiki/Main_Page)

The Woodblock Prints of Ando Hiroshige (www.hiroshige.org.uk)

Unless otherwise noted, all photos and historical illustrations used in this survey are from Wikipedia or Wikimedia Commons. For licensing info, please go to Wikimedia Commons and find the photo by searching the appropriate keywords.

According to articles 51 and 57 of the copyright laws of Japan, under the jurisdiction of the Government of Japan all non-photographic works enter the public domain 50 years after the death of the creator (there being multiple creators, the creator who dies last) or 50 years after publication for anonymous or pseudonymous authors or for works whose copyright holder is an organization.

Photographic images published before December 31st 1956, or photographed before 1946 and not published for 10 years thereafter, under jurisdiction of the Government of Japan, are considered to be public domain according to article 23 of old copyright law of Japan and article 2 of supplemental provision of copyright law of Japan.

The official position taken by the Wikimedia Foundation is that "faithful reproductions of two-dimensional public domain works of art are public domain, and that claims to the contrary represent an assault on the very concept of a public domain."

Special Thanks

- Randy Schadel of the Samurai Archives for information on the Hojo mon and Takeda Shingen's death
- Google (google.com)
- Dictionary.com (dictionary.reference.com)
- Thesaurus.com (thesaurus.reference.com)

Indices

Index of Clans

Abé (Heian) 53
Adachi (Kamakura) 90
Akamatsu (Muromachi) 120
Akaza (Momoyama) 164
Akechi (Momoyama) 163
Amako (Momoyama) 165
Anegakoji (Momoyama) 172
Asai (Momoyama) 168
Asakura (Momoyama) 170
Ashikaga (Muromachi Shogun) 32
Ashikaga (Muromachi) 114
Ashina (Momoyama) 173
Aso (Momoyama) 174
Bessho (Edo) 221
Chiba (Momoyama) 175
Chikusa (Momoyama) 176
Chosokabé (Edo) 219
Daibutsu (Kamakura) 91
Daidoji (Momoyama) 176
Fujiwara (Heian) 54
Fukushima (Edo) 222
Furuta (Edo) 223
Gamo (Edo) 224
Hasebé (Momoyama) 177
Hashiba (Momoyama) 178
Hatakeyama (Momoyama) 179
Hatano (Momoyama) 183
Hiki (Kamakura) 91
Hineno (Edo) 223
Hiraiwa (Edo) 225
Hiratsuka (Momoyama) 176
Hojo (Kamakura Shikken) 26
Hojo (Kamakura) 92
Horio (Edo) 229
Hosokawa (Muromachi) 122
Imagawa (Muromachi) 127
Ina (Edo) 226
Isé (Muromachi) 126
Ishibashi (Muromachi) 130
Ishida (Momoyama) 184
Ishido (Muromachi) 130
Ishikawa (Momoyama) 177
Isshiki (Momoyama) 185
Itagaki (Muromachi) 131
Itami (Muromachi) 131
Itami (Edo) 226
Izumi (Kamakura) 91
Jinbo (Muromachi) 132
Jo (Kamakura) 94
Kagaé (Momoyama) 178
Kagami (Kamakura) 91
Kakimi (Momoyama) 182
Kanamori (Edo) 227
Kasai (Momoyama) 183
Kasuya (Momoyama) 185
Katata (Momoyama) 186
Kato (Edo) 228
Kikuchi (Muromachi) 133
Kimura (Momoyama) 186

Kimura (Edo) 227
Kira (Muromachi) 137
Kitabataké (Momoyama) 187
Kiyohara (Heian) 77
Ko (Muromachi) 138
Kobayakawa (Momoyama) 190
Kobori (Edo) 226
Kodera (Momoyama) 186
Konishi (Momoyama) 189
Kono (Momoyama) 192
Koriki (Edo) 230
Kudo (Kamakura) 94
Kumagai (Kamakura) 95
Kusunoki (Muromachi) 139
Kuwayama (Edo) 230
Maeda (Edo) 231
Maita (Edo) 231
Maki (Momoyama) 191
Marumo (Momoyama) 193
Masuda (Edo) 232
Matsukura (Edo) 233
Matsunaga (Momoyama) 194
Matsushita (Edo) 232
Minagawa (Edo) 234
Minamoto (Kamakura Shogun) 22
Minamoto (Kamakura) 96
Miura (Kamakura) 109
Miyabé (Momoyama) 193
Miyoshi (Muromachi) 142
Mizunoya (Edo) 232
Mogami (Edo) 235
Momonoi (Muromachi) 136
Mori (Edo) 234
Munakata (Momoyama) 195
Murakami (Edo) 236
Nagao (Muromachi) 147
Naito (Edo) 237
Nakamura (Edo) 234
Nanjo (Momoyama) 195
Nasu (Edo) 238
Nawa (Kamakura) 95
Nigao (Edo) 237
Nikaido (Kamakura) 111
Nikki (Muromachi) 141
Nishina (Momoyama) 196
Nitta (Muromachi) 145
Oba (Heian) 78
Oda (Muromachi) 141
Oé (Kamakura) 111
Ogawa (Momoyama) 195
Ogigayatsu (Muromachi) 148
Oimi (Muromachi) 136
Okamoto (Momoyama) 196
Okubo (Edo) 238
Ono (Heian) 78, 79
Onodera (Momoyama) 197
Onoki (Momoyama) 196
Otani (Momoyama) 197

Otaté (Muromachi) 144
Otomo (Edo) 239
Ouchi (Muromachi) 149
Oyama (Muromachi) 151
Rokkaku (Muromachi) 152
Ryuzoji (Momoyama) 198
Saigo (Edo) 242
Saito (Muromachi) 154
Sakanoué (Heian) 80
Sakazaki (Momoyama) 199
Sakuma (Edo) 243
Sano (Edo) 242
Sasaki (Muromachi) 156
Sassa (Momoyama) 200
Sato (Heian) 80
Satomi (Edo) 245
Shiba (Muromachi) 158
Shibata (Echigo) (Momoyama) 202
Shibata (Owari) (Momoyama) 201
Shibukawa (Muromachi) 153
Shimokabé (Kamakura) 112
Shoni (Muromachi) 155
Suganuma (Edo) 242
Sugihara (Edo) 246
Suzuki (Muromachi) 157
Tagaya (Momoyama) 203
Taira (Heian) 81
Takahashi (Momoyama) 203
Takayama (Momoyama) 204
Takeda (Momoyama) 206
Takeda (Aki) (Muromachi) 160
Takenaka (Edo) 244
Takigawa (Momoyama) 205
Tanaka (Edo) 247
Tawara (Muromachi) 159
Terazawa (Edo) 246
Togashi (Muromachi) 161
Togawa (Edo) 247
Tokugawa (Edo Shogun) 39
Tokunaga (Edo) 247
Tomita (Edo) 254
Toyotomi (Edo) 248
Tsukushi (Momoyama) 212
Tsutsui (Edo) 253
Ueno (Muromachi) 157
Ujiié (Momoyama) 213
Ukita (Momoyama) 214
Urakami (Muromachi) 162
Utsunomiya (Momoyama) 218
Wada (Kamakura) 113
Wada (Muromachi) 161
Wada (Momoyama) 215
Wakiya (Muromachi) 162
Yamagata (Momoyama) 213
Yamana (Momoyama) 216
Yashiro (Edo) 254
Yuki (Edo) 255
Yura (Edo) 253

INDEX OF NOTABLE ANCESTORS

To provide a comprehensive listing of all the warlords in both this book and *Daimyo of 1867*, they are listed together in alphabetical order below. Entries for *Daimyo of 1867* are in italics. Some of the daimyo in that book have only their illustration; these are noted by an asterisk next to the page number.

Abé Hirafu (575-664) 53 (Heian)
Abé Masahiro (1819-1857) 232* (Bingo)
Abé Masakatsu (1541-1600) 104 (Mutsu), 173 (Kazusa), 232 (Bingo)
Abé Masato (11th century) 54 (Heian)
Abé Masatsugu (1569-1647) 173 (Kazusa), 232 (Bingo)
Abé Muneto (1032-1108) 54 (Heian)
Abé Norito (11th century) 54 (Heian)
Abé Sadato (1019-1062) 53 (Heian)
Abé Yoritoki (-1057) 53 (Heian)
Adachi Kagemori (-1248) 90 (Kamakura)
Adachi Morinaga (1135-1200) 90 (Kamakura)
Adachi Tokiaki (-1333) 90 (Kamakura)
Adachi Yasumori (1231-1285) 90 (Kamakura)
Adachi Yoshikagé (-1255) 90 (Kamakura)
Akamatsu Enshin (1277-1350) 120 (Muromachi)
Akamatsu Masanori (-1577) 121 (Muromachi)
Akamatsu Mitsusuké (1381-1441) 121 (Muromachi)
Akamatsu Norifusa (1559-1598) 121 (Muromachi)
Akamatsu Norimura (1277-1350) 120 (Muromachi)
Akamatsu Norisuké (1312-1371) 121 (Muromachi)
Akamatsu Sadamura (15th century) 121 (Muromachi)
Akamatsu Suéfusa (12th century) 120 (Muromachi)
Akamatsu Yoshinori (1358-1427) 121 (Muromachi)
Akamatsu Yoshisuké (-1576) 121 (Muromachi)
Akaza Naoyasu (-1606) 164 (Momoyama)
Akaza Shichiroémon (-1582) 164 (Momoyama)
Akechi Mitsuharu (1537-1582) 164 (Momoyama)
Akechi Mitsuhidé (1528-1582) 163 (Momoyama)
Akechi Mitsukuni (-1538) 163 (Momoyama)
Akechi Mitsutada (1540-1582) 164 (Momoyama)
Akechi Mitsutsuna (-1538) 163 (Momoyama)
Akechi Mitsuyasu (-1552) 163 (Momoyama)
Akechi Mitsuyoshi (1569-1582) 164 (Momoyama)
Akita Sanesué (1576-1659) 105 (Mutsu)
Akita Toshisué (1598-1649) 105 (Mutsu)
Akizuki Tanemichi 271 (Hyuga)
Akizuki Tanenaga 271 (Hyuga)
Akizuki Taneo 271 (Hyuga)
Akizuki Tanezané 271 (Hyuga)
Amako Akihisa (1514-1561) 166 (Momoyama)
Amako Haruhisa (1514-1561) 166 (Momoyama)
Amako Hisayuki (-1541) 166 (Momoyama)
Amako Katsuhisa (1553-1578) 167 (Momoyama)
Amako Kunihisa (1492-1554) 166 (Momoyama)
Amako Masahisa (1488-1518) 166 (Momoyama)
Amako Masahisa (-1554) 166 (Momoyama)
Amako Okihisa (1497-1534) 166 (Momoyama)
Amako Takahisa (14th century) 165 (Momoyama)
Amako Tsunehisa (1458-1541) 165 (Momoyama)
Amako Yoshihisa (1536-1610) 167 (Momoyama)
Ando Nobumasa (1819-1871) 100 (Mutsu)
Ando Naotsugu (1564-1635) 242 (Kii)
Ando Shigenaga (1600-1657) 100 (Mutsu)
Ando Shigenobu (1558-1622) 100 (Mutsu)
Akimoto Nagatomo (-1628) 94 (Kozuké)
Akimoto Takatomo (1647-1714) 94 (Kozuké)
Akimoto Yasutomo (1580-1642) 94 (Kozuké)
Anegakoji Koretsuna (1540-1587) 172 (Momoyama)
Anegakoji Tadatsuna (-1411) 172 (Momoyama)
Anegakoji Yoshiyori (1520-1571) 172 (Momoyama)
Arima Harunobu (1567-1612) 126 (Echizen)
Arima Haruzumi 126 (Echizen)
Arima Kiyozumi 126 (Echizen)
Arima Naozumi 126 (Echizen)
Arima Noriyori (-1602) 254 (Chikugo)
Arima Toyouji (1570-1642) 254 (Chikugo)
Arima Tsunezumi 126 (Echizen)
Arima Yoshisada (-1577) 126 (Echizen)
Arima Yoshisuké 254 (Chikugo)
Asahina Saburo Yoshihidé (1175-) 113 (Kamakura)
Asai Hisamasa (1524-1573) 168 (Momoyama)
Asai Inori (-1573) 169 (Momoyama)
Asai Manpuku-maru (1563-1573) 169 (Momoyama)
Asai Sukemasa (1495-1546) 168 (Momoyama)
Asakura Hirokagé (1255-1352) 170 (Momoyama)
Asakura Kagé'akira (1529-1574) 171 (Momoyama)
Asakura Kagetaka (1495-1543) 171 (Momoyama)
Asakura Kagetaka (108-1570) 171 (Momoyama)
Asakura Kagetaké (1529-1574) 172 (Momoyama)
Asakura Kagetoshi (1505-1572) 171 (Momoyama)
Asakura Kagetsura (-1570) 171 (Momoyama)
Asakura Nobumasa (1583-1637) 172 (Momoyama)
Asakura Norikagé (1477-1555) 170 (Momoyama)
Asakura Sadakagé (1473-1512) 171 (Momoyama)
Asakura Takakagé (1493-1546) 171 (Momoyama)
Asakura Toshikagé (1428-1481) 170 (Momoyama)
Asakura Ujikagé (1449-1486) 170 (Momoyama)
Asakura Yoshikagé (1533-1573) 171 (Momoyama)
Asano Nagaakira (1586-1632) 234 (Aki)
Asano Nagamasa (1546-1610) 158 (Kai), 233 (Aki)
Asano Naganori (1667-1701) 234 (Aki)
Asano Yoshinaga (1576-1613) 159 (Kai), 234 (Aki)
Asano Yukinaga (1576-1613) 159 (Kai)
Ashikaga Haruuji (1503-1560) 119 (Muromachi)
Ashikaga Ietoki (13th century) 115 (Muromachi)
Ashikaga Masatomo (1436-1491) 116 (Muromachi)
Ashikaga Masauji (-1531) 119 (Muromachi)
Ashikaga Mitsukané (1378-1409) 118 (Muromachi)
Ashikaga Mochiuji (1398-1439) 118 (Muromachi)
Ashikaga Motouji (1340-1367) 117 (Muromachi)
Ashikaga Shigeuji (1434-1497) 119 (Muromachi)
Ashikaga Tadafuyu (ca. 1327-1400) 116 (Muromachi)
Ashikaga Tadayoshi (1306-1352) 115 (Muromachi)
Ashikaga Takauji (1305-1358) 32 (Muromachi Shogun)
Ashikaga Ujimitsu (1359-1398) 117 (Muromachi)
Ashikaga Yoshiaki (-1538) 119 (Muromachi)
Ashikaga Yoshiaki (1537-1597) 38 (Muromachi Shogun)
Ashikaga Yoshiakira (1330-1367) 33 (Muromachi Shogun)
Ashikaga Yoshiharu (1510-1550) 37 (Muromachi Shogun)
Ashikaga Yoshihidé (1564-1568) 37 (Muromachi Shogun)
Ashikaga Yoshihisa (1465-1489) 36 (Muromachi Shogun)
Ashikaga Yoshikané (1147-1196) 115 (Muromachi)
Ashikaga Yoshikatsu (1434-1443) 35 (Muromachi Shogun)
Ashikaga Yoshikazu (1407-1425) 34 (Muromachi Shogun)
Ashikaga Yoshimasa (1435-1490) 35 (Muromachi Shogun)
Ashikaga Yoshimi (1439-1491) 117 (Muromachi)
Ashikaga Yoshimitsu (1358-1408) 33 (Muromachi Shogun)
Ashikaga Yoshimochi (1386-1428) 34 (Muromachi Shogun)

INDICES

Ashikaga Yoshinori (1394-1441) 34 (Muromachi Shogun)
Ashikaga Yoshitané (1465-1522) 36 (Muromachi Shogun)
Ashikaga Yoshiteru (1536-1565) 37 (Muromachi Shogun)
Ashikaga Yoshiuji 97 (Shimotsuké)
Ashikaga Yoshiuji (1189-1254) 115 (Muromachi)
Ashikaga Yoshiuji (16th century) 119 (Muromachi)
Ashikaga Yoshiyasu (1126-1157) 115 (Muromachi)
Ashikaga Yoshizumi (1478-1510) 36 (Muromachi Shogun)
Ashina Morihisa (-1444) 173 (Momoyama)
Ashina Morikiyo (1490-1553) 173 (Momoyama)
Ashina Morimasa (1386-1432) 173 (Momoyama)
Ashina Morinori (1431-1466) 173 (Momoyama)
Ashina Morishigé (1575-1631) 173 (Momoyama)
Ashina Moritaka (1448-1517) 173 (Momoyama)
Ashina Moritaka (1560-1583) 173 (Momoyama)
Ashina Moriuji (1521-1580) 173 (Momoyama)
Ashina Yoshihiro (1575-1631) 173 (Momoyama)
Aso Koremitsu (1582-1593) 174 (Momoyama)
Aso Korenao (-1336) 174 (Momoyama)
Aso Koretoyo (1543-1584) 174 (Momoyama)
Aso Korezumi (14th century) 174 (Momoyama)
Atagi Fuyuyasu (1528-1564) 143 (Muromachi)
Bessho Harusada (1561-1579) 221 (Edo)
Bessho Nagaharu (1558-1580) 221 (Edo)
Bessho Toyoharu (1578-) 221 (Edo)
Chbia Kanetané (early 15th century) 175 (Momoyama)
Chiba Sadatané (1291-1351) 175 (Momoyama)
Chiba Sanetané (15th century) 175 (Momoyama)
Chiba Shigetané (16th century) 175 (Momoyama)
Chiba Takatané (15th century) 175 (Momoyama)
Chiba Tanenao (-1455) 175 (Momoyama)
Chiba Toshitané (1528-1559) 175 (Momoyama)
Chiba Tsunetané (1118-1201) 175 (Momoyama)
Chikusa Tadaharu (16th century) 176 (Momoyama)
Chikusa Tadamoto (16th century) 176 (Momoyama)
Chikusa Takamichi (14th century) 176 (Momoyama)
Chosokabé Chikakazu (1567-1587) 220 (Edo)
Chosokabé Chikatada (1572-1600) 221 (Edo)
Chosokabé Chikataké (-1589) 220 (Edo)
Chosokabé Kunichika (1504-1560) 219 (Edo)
Chosokabé Morichika (1575-1615) 221 (Edo)
Chosokabé Nobuchika (1565-1587) 220 (Edo)
Chosokabé Motochika (1539-1599) 219 (Edo)
Daibutsu Sadafusa (-1306) 91 (Kamakura)
Daibutsu Yorimori (13th century) 91 (Kamakura)
Daidoji Kanekatsu (15th or 16th century) 176 (Momoyama)
Daidoji Masashigé (1533-1590) 176 (Momoyama)
Daidoji Naoshigé (1573-1628) 176 (Momoyama)
Daidoji Shigehisa (17th century) 176 (Momoyama)
Daidoji Shigé'oki (15th or 16th century) 176 (Momoyama)
Daidoji Shigesuké (1639-1730) 176 (Momoyama)
Daidoji Shigetoki (15th century) 176 (Momoyama)
Daté Masamuné (1566-1636) 107 (Mutsu)
Daté Tadamuné (1600-1658) 107 (Mutsu)
Daté Tsunamuné (1650-1711) 107 (Mutsu)
Doi Toshikatsu (1573-1644) 128 (Echizen), 148 (Mikawa), 179 (Shimosa)
Fujiwara Akiko (829-899) 76 (Heian)
Fujiwara Akiko (988-1074) 76 (Heian)
Fujiwara Akimitsu (944-1021) 64 (Heian)
Fujiwara Akira-keiko (829-899) 76 (Heian)
Fujiwara Akisué (1055-1123) 74 (Heian)
Fujiwara Akisuké (1090-1155) 74 (Heian)
Fujiwara Akitada (898-965) 62 (Heian)
Fujiwara Arihira (892-970) 61 (Heian)
Fujiwara Asakari (8th century) 59 (Heian)
Fujiwara Atsutada (906-943) 62 (Heian)
Fujiwara Fuhito (659-720) 56 (Heian)
Fujiwara Fujifusa (1295-1380) 73 (Heian)
Fujiwara Fusasaki (681-737) 57 (Heian)
Fujiwara Fuyutsugu (775-826) 59 (Heian)
Fujiwara Hamanari (724-790) 59 (Heian)
Fujiwara Hidehira (1096-1187) 71 (Heian)
Fujiwara Hidesato (10th century) 62 (Heian)
Fujiwara Hirotsugu (715-741) 58 (Heian)
Fujiwara Ietaka (1158-1237) 75 (Heian)
Fujiwara (Konoé) Iezané (1180-1243) 72 (Heian)
Fujiwara Ishi (999-1036) 76 (Heian)
Fujiwara Itsuko (1351-1406) 77 (Heian)
Fujiwara Kamatari (614-669) 54 (Heian)
Fujiwara (Takatsukasa) Kanehira (1228-1294) 73 (Heian)
Fujiwara Kaneié (929-999) 63 (Heian)
Fujiwara Kanemichi (925-977) 63 (Heian)
Fujiwara Kanesué (14th century) 73 (Heian)
Fujiwara Kanezané (1149-1207) 70 (Heian)
Fujiwara Kenshi (994-1027) 76 (Heian)
Fujiwara Kimiko (1232-1304) 76 (Heian)
Fujiwara Kinsué (957-1029) 63 (Heian)
Fujiwara Kinto (966-1041) 64 (Heian)
Fujiwara Kintsugu (1175-1227) 72 (Heian)
Fujiwara Kinzané (1053-1107) 67 (Heian)
Fujiwara Kiyohira (1056-1128) 70 (Heian)
Fujiwara Kiyokawa (706-778) 57 (Heian)
Fujiwara Korechika (974-1010) 66 (Heian)
Fujiwara Korekata (-1125) 69 (Heian)
Fujiwara Koremichi (1093-1165) 67 (Heian)
Fujiwara Korenari (953-989) 64 (Heian)
Fujiwara Koretada (924-972) 63 (Heian)
Fujiwara Kuraji-maro (734-775) 59 (Heian)
Fujiwara Kusuko (-810) 76 (Heian)
Fujiwara Maro (695-737) 57 (Heian)
Fujiwara Masako (1122-1182) 76 (Heian)
Fujiwara Masuko (1140-1201) 76 (Heian)
Fujiwara Mataté (716-767) 58 (Heian)
Fujiwara Michiié (1193-1252) 72 (Heian)
Fujiwara Michikané (955-995) 65 (Heian)
Fujiwara Michinaga (966-1028) 65 (Heian)
Fujiwara Michinori (-1159) 69 (Heian)
Fujiwara Michitaka (953-995) 64 (Heian)
Fujiwara Miyako no Iratsuné (-754) 76 (Heian)
Fujiwara Momokawa (732-779) 58 (Heian)
Fujiwara Morokata (1300-1332) 73 (Heian)
Fujiwara Moromichi (102-1099) 67 (Heian)
Fujiwara Moromitsu (-1177) 69 (Heian)
Fujiwara Moronaga (1137-1192) 70 (Heian)
Fujiwara Morosuké (908-960) 62 (Heian)
Fujiwara Morozane (1042-1101) 67 (Heian)
Fujiwara Motofusa (1144-1230) 70 (Heian)
Fujiwara Motohira (-1157) 71 (Heian)
Fujiwara Motomichi (1160-1233) 72 (Heian)
Fujiwara Mototoshi (1055-1138) 67 (Heian)
Fujiwara Mototsuné (836-891) 60 (Heian)
Fujiwara Motozané (1143-1166) 69 (Heian)
Fujiwara Muchimaro (680-737) 56 (Heian)
Fujiwara Nagaté (714-771) 58 (Heian)
Fujiwara Nakahira (875-945) 61 (Heian)
Fujiwara Nakamaro (706-764) 57 (Heian)
Fujiwara Nakanari (774-810) 59 (Heian)
Fujiwara Narichika (1138-1178) 69 (Heian)
Fujiwara Nariko (1117-1160) 76 (Heian)
Fujiwara Naritsuné (-1202) 69 (Heian)
Fujiwara Nobuyori (1133-1159) 68 (Heian)
Fujiwara Norimichi (996-1075) 66 (Heian)
Fujiwara Oguro-maro (733-794) 59 (Heian)
Fujiwara Omiya (1140-1201) 76 (Heian)
Fujiwara Onshi I (872-907) 76 (Heian)

INDICES

Fujiwara Onshi II (885-954) 76 (Heian)
Fujiwara Otsugu (773-843) 59 (Heian)
Fujiwara Renshi (1301-1359) 77 (Heian)
Fujiwara Sadaié (1162-1241) 75 (Heian)
Fujiwara Sadako (977-1001) 76 (Heian)
Fujiwara Sadayori (995-1045) 66 (Heian)
Fujiwara Sanesuké (957-1046) 63 (Heian)
Fujiwara Saneuji (1194-1269) 73 (Heian)
Fujiwara Saneyori (900-970) 62 (Heian)
Fujiwara Seika (1561-1619) 75 (Heian)
Fujiwara Seishi (1122-1182) 76 (Heian)
Fujiwara Senshi (962-1002) 76 (Heian)
Fujiwara Shoko (1101-1145) 76 (Heian)
Fujiwara Shoshi (988-1074) 76 (Heian)
Fujiwara Shunzei (1114-1204) 74 (Heian)
Fujiwara Son'ondo (756-818) 59 (Heian)
Fujiwara Sugané (856-908) 60 (Heian)
Fujiwara Sukemasa (944-998) 64 (Heian)
Fujiwara Sumitomo (-941) 64 (Heian)
Fujiwara Tadabumi (873-947) 61 (Heian)
Fujiwara Tadahira (880-949) 61 (Heian)
Fujiwara Tadahira (-1189) 72 (Heian)
Fujiwara Tadamichi (1097-1164) 68 (Heian)
Fujiwara Tadanobu (967-1035) 66 (Heian)
Fujiwara Tadazané (1078-1162) 67 (Heian)
Fujiwara Takaié (979-1044) 66 (Heian)
Fujiwara Takanobu (1142-1205) 75 (Heian)
Fujiwara Tamako (1101-1145) 76 (Heian)
Fujiwara Tameaki (-1364) 73 (Heian)
Fujiwara Tameié (1198-1275) 75 (Heian)
Fujiwara Tametaka (1070-1130) 67 (Heian)
Fujiwara Tanetsugu (737-785) 59 (Heian)
Fujiwara Teika (1162-1241) 75 (Heian)
Fujiwara Teishi (977-1001) 76 (Heian)
Fujiwara Tokihira (871-909) 61 (Heian)
Fujiwara Tokuko (1117-1160) 76 (Heian)
Fujiwara Tokushi (1117-1160) 76 (Heian)
Fujiwara Toshimoto (-1331) 73 (Heian)
Fujiwara Toshinari (1114-1204) 74 (Heian)
Fujiwara Toyonari (704-765) 57 (Heian)
Fujiwara Tsuginawa (727-796) 59 (Heian)
Fujiwara Tsunetsugu (796-840) 59 (Heian)
Fujiwara Uchimaro (756-812) 59 (Heian)
Fujiwara Umakai (694-737) 57 (Heian)
Fujiwara Uona (721-783) 58 (Heian)
Fujiwara Yamakagé (824-888) 60 (Heian)
Fujiwara Yasuhira (-1189) 72 (Heian)
Fujiwara Yasuko (1292-1357) (Heian)
Fujiwara Yasumasa (958-1036) 74 (Heian)
Fujiwara Yasunori (825-895) 60 (Heian)
Fujiwara Yorimichi (992-1074) 66 (Heian)
Fujiwara Yorinaga (1120-1156) 68 (Heian)
Fujiwara Yoritada (924-989) 63 (Heian)
Fujiwara (Kujo) Yoritsugu (1239-1256) 24 (Kamakura Shogun)
Fujiwara (Kujo) Yoritsuné (1218-1256) 23 (Kamakura Shogun)
Fujiwara Yoshifusa (804-872) 59 (Heian)
Fujiwara Yoshikado (9th century) 60 (Heian)
Fujiwara Yoshikané (957-1008) 64 (Heian)
Fujiwara Yoshiko (1225-1292) 76 (Heian)
Fujiwara Yoshisuké (813-867) 60 (Heian)
Fujiwara Yoshitsugu (716-777) 58 (Heian)
Fujiwara (Kujo) Yoshitsuné (1169-1206) 72 (Heian)
Fukushima Masanori (1561-1624) 222 (Edo)
Fukushima Masayori (16th-17th century) 222 (Edo)
Furuta Oribé (1545-1615) 223 (Edo)
Furuta Shigeharu (early 17th century) 223 (Edo)
Furuta Shigekatsu (1561-1600) 223 (Edo)
Furuta Shigenari (1545-1615) 223 (Edo)
Furuta Shigetsuné (1598-1648) 223 (Edo)
Gamo Hideyuki (1583-1612) 225 (Edo)
Gamo Katahidé (1534-1584) 224 (Edo)
Gamo Tadasato (1603-1627) 225 (Edo)
Gamo Tadatomo (1605-1634) 225 (Edo)
Gamo Ujisato (1557-1596) 224 (Edo)
Hachisuka Iemasa (1558-1638) 243 (Awa-Tokushima)
Hachisuka Masakatsu (1525-1585) 243 (Awa-Tokushima)
Hachisuka Mochiaki (1846-1918) 243* (Awa-Tokushima)
Hachisuka Yoshishigé (1586-1620) 243 (Awa-Tokushima)
Hangaku-gozen (12-th-13th century) 94 (Kamakura)
Hasebé Nobutsura (-1217) 177 (Momoyama)
Hasebé Tsunatsura (-1576) 177 (Momoyama)
Hashiba Hidekatsu (1567-1594) 178 (Momoyama)
Hashiba Hidenaga (1540-1591) 178 (Momoyama)
Hashiba Hidetoshi (1577-1594) 178 (Momoyama)
Hatakeyama Dosei (-1364) 180 (Momoyama)
Hatakeyama Kunikiyo (-1364) 180 (Momoyama)
Hatakeyama Masanaga (1442-1493) 181 (Momoyama)
Hatakeyama Mitsuié (1372-1433) 180 (Momoyama)
Hatakeyama Mochikuni (1397-1455) 180 (Momoyama)
Hatakeyama Motokuni (1352-1406) 180 (Momoyama)
Hatakeyama Naonobu (-1534) 181 (Momoyama)
Hatakeyama Sadamasa (-1584) 181 (Momoyama)
Hatakeyama Shigetada (1164-1205) 179 (Momoyama)
Hatakeyama Shigeyasu (-1205) 180 (Momoyama)
Hatakeyama Takamasa (1527-1576) 181 (Momoyama)
Hatakeyama Yoshifusa (1495-1545) 182 (Momoyama)
Hatakeyama Yoshihidé (-1532) 181 (Momoyama)
Hatakeyama Yoshikuni (1521-1580) 182 (Momoyama)
Hatakeyama Yoshimuné (-1480) 182 (Momoyama)
Hatakeyama Yoshinari (1454-1493) 181 (Momoyama)
Hatakeyama Yoshitaka (1557-1577) 182 (Momoyama)
Hatakeyama Yoshito (1331-1379) 180 (Momoyama)
Hatakeyama Yoshitoyo (-1499) 181 (Momoyama)
Hatakeyama Yoshitsugu (1552-1586) 182 (Momoyama)
Hatakeyama Yoshitsuna (1536-1594) 182 (Momoyama)
Hatakeyama Yoshizumi (early 13th century) 180 (Momoyama)
Hatakeyama Yukishigé (late 16th century) 181 (Momoyama)
Hatano Hideharu (1541-1579) 183 (Momoyama)
Hiki Yoshikazu (-1203) 91 (Kamakura)
Hineno Hironari (1518-1602) 223 (Edo)
Hineno Takayoshi (1539-1600) 223 (Edo)
Hineno Yoshitomo (1588-1658) 223 (Edo)
Hiraiwa Chikayoshi (1542-1611) 225 (Edo)
Hiratsuka Tamehiro (late 16th century) 176 (Momoyama)
Hisa'aki-shinno (1276-1328) 24 (Kamakura Shogun)
Hisamatsu Toshikatsu 247 (Iyo)
Hojo Hirotoki (1279-1315) 30 (Kamakura Shikken)
Hojo (Minamoto) Masako (1157-1225) 92 (Kamakura)
Hojo Masamura (1205-1273) 28 (Kamakura Shikken)
Hojo Moritoki (1295-1333) 31 (Kamakura Shikken)
Hojo Morotoki (1275-1311) 30 (Kamakura Shikken)
Hojo Mototoki (1286-1333) 30 (Kamakura Shikken)
Hojo Munenobu (1259-1312) 30 (Kamakura Shikken)
Hojo Nagatoki (1230-1264) 28 (Kamakura Shikken)
Hojo Nagauji (1432-1519) 195 (Kawachi)
Hojo Sada'aki (1278-1333) 31 (Kamakura Shikken)
Hojo Sadatoki (1271-1311) 29 (Kamakura Shikken)
Hojo Shigetoki (1198-1261) 93 (Kamakura)
Hojo Soun (1432-1519) 195 (Kawachi)
Hojo Takatoki (1303-1333) 30 (Kamakura Shikken)
Hojo Tokifusa (1175-1240) 93 (Kamakura)
Hojo Tokimasa (1138-1215) 26 (Kamakura Shikken)
Hojo Tokimuné (1251-1284) 28 (Kamakura Shikken)
Hojo Tokiuji (1203-1230) 93 (Kamakura)
Hojo Tokiyori (1227-1263) 28 (Kamakura Shikken)

INDICES

Hojo Tokiyuki (1322-1353) 93 (Kamakura)
Hojo Tomotoki (1193-1245) 93 (Kamakura)
Hojo Tsunetoki (1224-1246) 27 (Kamakura Shikken)
Hojo Ujinori (1545-1600) 196 (Kawachi)
Hojo Ujitsuna (1487-1541) 195 (Kawachi)
Hojo Ujiyasu (1515-1570) 195 (Kawachi)
Hojo Yasutoki (1183-1242) 26 (Kamakura Shikken)
Hojo Yoshitoki (1163-1224) 26 (Kamakura Shikken)
Honda Masakatsu (1614-1671) 147 (Mikawa), 221 (Harima)
Honda Masanaga 147 (Mikawa), 221 (Harima)
Honda Tadakatsu (1548-1610) 104 (Mutsu), 147 (Mikawa), 221 (Harima)
Honda Tadataka 147 (Mikawa)
Honda Tadatsugu (1549-1613) 75 (Omi), 140 (Isé)
Honda Yasushigé (1554-1611) 87 (Shinano)
Honda Yasutoshi (1570-1622) 75 (Omi), 140 (Isé)
Hori Chikayoshi (1580-1637) 89 (Shinano)
Hori Naomasa (-1608) 89 (Shinano), 132 (Echigo)
Hori Naoyori (1577-1639) 132 (Echigo)
Horio Tadaharu (1596-1633) 229 (Edo)
Horio Tadauji (1575-1604) 229 (Edo)
Horio Yoshiharu (1543-1611) 229 (Edo)
Hoshina Masamitsu (1561-1631) 101 (Mutsu)
Hoshina Masanao (1542-1601) 101 (Mutsu), 174 (Kazusa)
Hosokawa Akiuji (-1352) 123 (Muromachi)
Hosokawa Fujitaka (1534-1610) 186 (Hitachi), 268 (Higo)
Hosokawa Harumoto (1519-1563) 125 (Muromachi)
Hosokawa Jozen (14th century) 124 (Muromachi)
Hosokawa Katsumoto (1430-1473) 124 (Muromachi)
Hosokawa Kiyo'uji (-1362) 123 (Muromachi)
Hosokawa Masamoto (1466-1507) 124 (Muromachi)
Hosokawa Mitsumoto (1378-1426) 124 (Muromachi)
Hosokawa Mochiyuki (1400-1442) 124 (Muromachi)
Hosokawa Nobuyoshi (-1615) 126 (Muromachi)
Hosokawa Okimoto (-1618) 186 (Hitachi)
Hosokawa Shigekata (1718-1785) 269 (Higo)
Hosokawa Sumimoto (1489-1520) 125 (Muromachi)
Hosokawa Sumiyuki (1489-1507) 125 (Muromachi)
Hosokawa Tadaoki (1564-1645) 269 (Higo)
Hosokawa Tadatoshi (1586-1641) 269 (Higo)
Hosokawa Takakuni (1484-1531) 125 (Muromachi)
Hosokawa Tatsutaka 269 (Higo)
Hosokawa Ujiharu (-1387) 123 (Muromachi)
Hosokawa Yoriharu (1299-1352) 186 (Hitachi), 268 (Higo)
Hosokawa Yoriharu (1299-1352) 123 (Muromachi)
Hosokawa Yorimoto (1343-1397) 123 (Muromachi)
Hosokawa Yoriyuki (1329-1392) 123 (Muromachi)
Hotta Masaharu 178 (Shimosa)
Hotta Masamori (1606-1651) 78 (Omi), 96 (Shimotsuké), 178 (Shimosa)
Hotta Masanaka (1660-1694) 178 (Shimosa)
Hotta Masanobu (1629-1677) 78 (Omi)
Hotta Masatora (1662-1729) 178 (Shimosa)
Hotta Masatoshi (1631-1684) 96 (Shimotsuké), 178 (Shimosa)
Hotta Masayasu 78 (Omi)
Hotta Masayoshi 178 (Shimosa)
Ichibashi Nagakatsu 77 (Omi)
Ii Naokatsu 135 (Echigo)
Ii Naomasa (1561-1602) 76 (Omi), 134 (Echigo)
Ii Naosuké (1815-1860) 76 (Omi)
Ii Naotaka (1590-1659) 76 (Omi)
Ikeda Akimasa 227 (Bizen)*
Ikeda Harumasa 227 (Bizen)*
Ikeda Harumichi 210 (Inaba)*
Ikeda Mitsumasa (1609-1682) 226 (Bizen)
Ikeda Mitsunaka 210 (Inaba)*
Ikeda Mochimasa 227 (Bizen)*
Ikeda Munemasa 227 (Bizen)*
Ikeda Muneyasu 210 (Inaba)*
Ikeda Narikuni 210 (Inaba)*

Ikeda Narimasa 227 (Bizen)*
Ikeda Narimichi 210 (Inaba)*
Ikeda Naritoshi 210 (Inaba), 227* (Bizen)*
Ikeda Nobuteru (1536-1584) 209 (Inaba), 226 (Bizen)
Ikeda Shigenobu 210 (Inaba)*
Ikeda Tadakatsu (1602-1632) 210 (Inaba)
Ikeda Tadatsugu (1599-1615) 209 (Inaba)
Ikeda Terumasa (1564-1613) 209 (Inaba), 226 (Bizen)
Ikeda Toshitaka (1584-1616) 226 (Bizen)
Ikeda Tsugumasa 227 (Bizen)*
Ikeda Tsunakiyo 210 (Inaba)*
Ikeda Tsunamasa (1638-1714) 227 (Bizen)*
Ikeda Yoshimasa 227 (Bizen)*
Ikeda Yoshinori 210 (Inaba)*
Ikeda Yoshitaka 210 (Inaba)*
Ikeda Yoshiyasu 210 (Inaba)*
Ikeda Yoshiyuki 210 (Inaba)*
Imagawa Kuniuji (1243-1282) 127 (Muromachi)
Imagawa Norikuni (1295-1384) 127 (Muromachi)
Imagawa Norimasa (1364-1433) 128 (Muromachi)
Imagawa Norinobu (1829-1887) 130 (Muromachi)
Imagawa Noritada (1408-1461) 128 (Muromachi)
Imagawa Noriuji (1316-1365) 127 (Muromachi)
Imagawa Ryoshun (1326-1420) 127 (Muromachi)
Imagawa Sadayo (1326-1420) 127 (Muromachi)
Imagawa Ujichika (1473-1526) 128 (Muromachi)
Imagawa Ujizané (1538-1615) 129 (Muromachi)
Imagawa Yasunori (1334-1409) 128 (Muromachi)
Imagawa Yoshimoto (1519-1560) 129 (Muromachi)
Imagawa Yoshitada (1436-1476) 128 (Muromachi)
Ina Tadamasa (16th-17th century) 226 (Edo)
Ina Tadatsugu (1551-1607) 226 (Edo)
Inaba Masanari (1571-1628) 171 (Awa-Chiba), 189 (Yamashiro)
Inaba Sadamichi (1551-1606) 259 (Bungo)
Isé Sadchika (1417-1473) 126 (Muromachi)
Isé Sadayuki (14th-15th century) 126 (Muromachi)
Ishibashi Kazuyoshi (14th century) 130 (Muromachi)
Ishida Kazushigé (1560-1600) 184 (Momoyama)
Ishida Masatsugu (-1600) 184 (Momoyama)
Ishida Mitsunari (1560-1600) 184 (Momoyama)
Ishida Shigenari (1589-1641) 184 (Momoyama)
Ishido Yorifusa (14th century) 130 (Muromachi)
Ishido Yorishigé 130 (Muromachi)
Ishido Yoshifusa (14th century) 130 (Muromachi)
Ishikawa Ienari (1534-1600) 140 (Isé), 187 (Hitachi)
Ishikawa Sadakiyo (-1625) 177 (Momoyama)
Ishikawa Tadafusa (1572-1650) 140 (Isé), 187 (Hitachi)
Ishikawa Yasumichi (1554-1607) 140 (Isé), 187 (Hitachi)
Isshiki Akinori (-1406) 185 (Momoyama)
Isshiki Kimifuka (late 13th century) 185 (Momoyama)
Isshiki Yoshiharu (late 15th century) 185 (Momoyama)
Isshiki Yoshikiyo (-1582) 185 (Momoyama)
Isshiki Yoshimichi (-1579) 185 (Momoyama)
Isshiki Yoshinao (-1483) 185 (Momoyama)
Isshiki Yoshisada (-1582) 185 (Momoyama)
Isshiki Yoshitsura (1400-1440) 185 (Momoyama)
Itagaki Nobukata (1489-1548) 131 (Muromachi)
Itami Katsumori (-1698) 226 (Edo)
Itami Katsunaga (1601-1662) 226 (Edo)
Itami Yasukatsu (1571-1649) 226 (Edo)
Itakura Katsukiyo (1823-1889) 229 (Bitchu)*
Itakura Katsushigé (1542-1624) 94 (Kozuké), 105 (Mutsu), 229 (Bitchu)
Itakura Shigehiro 105 (Mutsu)
Itakura Shigemasa (1588-1638) 105 (Mutsu), 230 (Bitchu)
Itakura Shigemuné (1587-1656) 94 (Kozuké), 229 (Bitchu)
Itakura Shigenori (1617-1673) 105 (Mutsu), 230 (Bitchu)
Itakura Shigesato (1620-1660) 229 (Bitchu)
Itakura Shigetané (1640-1705) 105 (Mutsu)

INDICES

Itami Chikaoki (16th century) 131 (Muromachi)
Ito Suketaka (1541-1600) 231 (Bitchu), 273 (Hyuga)
Ito Sukeyoshi (1588-1636) 231 (Bitchu), 273 (Hyuga)
Ito Yoshimasu (-1569) 272 (Hyuga)
Ito Yoshisuké (1512-1584) 231 (Bitchu), 272 (Hyuga)
Iwaki Sadataka (1584-1621) 116 (Dewa)
Iwaki Tsunetaka (1566-1590) 116 (Dewa)
Izumi Chikahira (-1213) 91 (Kamakura)
Jinbo Kiyoshigé (-1554) 132 (Muromachi)
Jinbo Nagakiyo (-1511) 132 (Muromachi)
Jinbo Nagamoto (-1572) 132 (Muromachi)
Jinbo Nagatsuna (-1511) 132 (Muromachi)
Jinbo Ujiharu (1528-1592) 132 (Muromachi)
Jinbo Yoshikata (-1581) 132 (Muromachi)
Jinbo Yoshimuné (-1520) 132 (Muromachi)
Jo Nagamochi (-1201) 94 (Kamakura)
Jo Sukemori (-1202) 94 (Kamakura)
Jo Sukenaga (-1182) 94 (Kamakura)
Kagaé Shigemochi (-1600) 178 (Momoyama)
Kagaé Shigemuné (-1584) 178 (Momoyama)
Kagami Hisatsuna (-1221) 91 (Kamakura)
Kakimi Iezumi (-1600) 182 (Momoyama)
Kakizaki Nobuhiro 74 (Ezo)
Kakizaki Suehiro 74 (Ezo)
Kamei Korenori (1567-1617) 215 (Iwami)
Kamei Masanori (1590-1619) 215 (Iwami)
Kanamori Nagachika (1524-1607) 227 (Edo)
Kanamori Yoshishigé (1559-1616) 227 (Edo)
Kasai Kiyoshigé (12th-13th century) 183 (Momoyama)
Kasuya Takenori (1562-1607) 185 (Momoyama)
Katata Horozumi (-1600) 186 (Momoyama)
Kato Akinari 75 (Omi)
Kato Akitomo 75 (Omi)
Kato Kiyomasa (1562-1611) 228 (Edo)
Kato Mitsuyasu (1537-1595) 158 (Kai), 250 (Iyo)
Kato Sadayasu (1581-1624) 250 (Iyo)
Kato Tadahiro (1597-1653) 229 (Edo)
Kato Yoshiaki (1563-1631) 75 (Omi)
Kensho-in (-1622) 212 (Momoyama)
Kikkawa Hiroié (1561-1625) 235 (Suwo)
Kikkawa Motoharu (1530-1586) 235 (Suwo)
Kikuchi Jiro Takanao (-1185) 133 (Muromachi)
Kikuchi Jiro Takefusa (1245-1285) 133 (Muromachi)
Kikuchi Jiro Takemasa (1342-1374) 135 (Muromachi)
Kikuchi Jiro Tokitaka (1287-1304) 134 (Muromachi)
Kikuchi Mochitomo (1409-1446) 135 (Muromachi)
Kikuchi Noritaka (11th century) 133 (Muromachi)
Kikuchi Takehito (1321-1401) 135 (Muromachi)
Kikuchi Takekané (-1532) 136 (Muromachi)
Kikuchi Takemitsu (1319-1373) 135 (Muromachi)
Kikuchi Taketomo (1363-1407) 135 (Muromachi)
Kikuchi Takeshigé (1307-1338) 135 (Muromachi)
Kikuchi Taketoki (1293-1334) 134 (Muromachi)
Kikuchi Taketoshi (-1341) 135 (Muromachi)
Kikuchi Yoshitaka (13th century) 133 (Muromachi)
Kikuchi Toshitaké (1505-1554) 136 (Muromachi)
Kikuchi Yoshiyuki (1482-1504) 136 (Muromachi)
Kimura Hidetoshi (late 16th century) 186 (Momoyama)
Kimura Shigekoré (-1595) 227 (Edo)
Kimura Shigenari (1594-1615) 227 (Edo)
Kinoshita Iesada (1543-1608) 230 (Bitchu), 259 (Bungo)
Kinoshita Nobutoshi (1577-1642) 259 (Bungo)
Kinoshita Toshifusa (1573-1637) 230 (Bitchu)
Kinoshita Toshimasa (1602-1661) 230 (Bitchu)
Kira Mitsusada (14th century) 137 (Muromachi)
Kira Yoshinaka (1641-1703) 137 (Muromachi)
Kiso (Minamoto) Yoshinaka (1154-1184) 106 (Kamakura)
Kitabataké Akiié (1317-1338) 188 (Momoyama)

Kitabataké Akinobu (early 14th century) 188 (Momoyama)
Kitabataké Akiyasu (1360-1402) 188 (Momoyama)
Kitabataké Akiyoshi (-1383) 188 (Momoyama)
Kitabataké Chikafusa (1293-1354) 187 (Momoyama)
Kitabataké Harutomo (1496-1563) 188 (Momoyama)
Kitabataké Masasato (1449-1508) 188 (Momoyama)
Kitabataké Mitsumasa (1377-1440) 188 (Momoyama)
Kitabataké Nobuoki (late 16th century) 189 (Momoyama)
Kitabataké Noritomo (1423-1471) 188 (Momoyama)
Kitabataké Tomonori (1528-1576) 189 (Momoyama)
Kiyohara Fusanori (9th century) 77 (Heian)
Kiyohara Iehira (-1087) 78 (Heian)
Kiyohara Motosuké (908-990) 77 (Heian)
Kiyohara Natsuno (782-837) 77 (Heian)
Kiyohara Takenori (11th century) 78 (Heian)
Ko Morofuyu (-1351) 138 (Muromachi)
Ko Moronao (-1351) 138 (Muromachi)
Ko Moroyasu (-1351) 138 (Muromachi)
Kobayakawa Hidéaki (1577-1602) 191 (Momoyama)
Kobayakawa Hidekané (1566-1601) 190 (Momoyama)
Kobayakawa Takakagé (1532-1597) 190 (Momoyama)
Kobori Enshu (1579-1647) 226 (Edo)
Kobori Masakata (18th century) 226 (Edo)
Kobori Masakazu (1579-1647) 226 (Edo)
Kodera Norimoto (mid 16th century) 186 (Momoyama)
Koidé Masahidé (1539-1604) 202 (Tanba)
Koidé Yoshimasa (1565-1613) 202 (Tanba)
Konishi Yukinaga (1555-1600) 189 (Momoyama)
Kono Michiari (late 13th century) 192 (Momoyama)
Kono Michimori (-1362) 192 (Momoyama)
Kono Michinao (-1572) 192 (Momoyama)
Kono Michinao (-1587) 192 (Momoyama)
Kono Michinobu (1156-1223) 192 (Momoyama)
Kono Michinobu (-1581) 192 (Momoyama)
Kono Michitaka (-1374) 192 (Momoyama)
Konoé (Fujiwara) Iezané (1180-1243) 72 (Heian)
Koreyasu-shinno (1264-1326) 24 (Kamakura Shogun)
Koriki Kiyonaga (1530-1608) 230 (Edo)
Koriki Masanaga (1558-1599) 230 (Edo)
Koriki Tadafusa (1583-1655) 230 (Edo)
Koriki Takanaga (1604-1676) 230 (Edo)
Kudo Shigemitsu (-1181) 94 (Kamakura)
Kudo Suketsuné (-1193) 231 (Bitchu), 272 (Hyuga)
Kudo Suketsuné (-1193) 94 (Kamakura)
Kujo (Fujiwara) Michiié (1193-1252) 72 (Heian)
Kujo (Fujiwara) Yoritsugu (1239-1256) 24 (Kamakura Shogun)
Kujo (Fujiwara) Yoritsuné (1218-1256) 23 (Kamakura Shogun)
Kujo (Fujiwara) Yoshitsuné (1169-1206) 72 (Heian)
Kuki Moritaka 200 (Settsu), 205 (Tanba)
Kuki Yoshitaka (1542-1600) 200 (Settsu), 205 (Tanba)
Kumagai Naosada (12th century) 95 (Kamakura)
Kumagai Naozané (1141-1208) 95 (Kamakura)
Kuroda Mototaka (1524-1585) 252 (Chikuzen)
Kuroda Nagamasa (1568-1623) 252 (Chikuzen)
Kuroda Yoshitaka (1546-1604) 252 (Chikuzen)
Kurushima Michichika (1580-1611) 257 (Bungo)
Kurushima Michifusa (1562-1597) 257 (Bungo)
Kusunoki Masaié (-1348) 140 (Muromachi)
Kusunoki Masakatsu (late 14th century) 141 (Muromachi)
Kusunoki Masamoto (-1402) 141 (Muromachi)
Kusunoki Masanori (-1390) 140 (Muromachi)
Kusunoki Masashigé (1294-1336) 139 (Muromachi)
Kusunoki Masatora (16th century) 141 (Muromachi)
Kusunoki Masatsura (1326-1348) 140 (Muromachi)
Kusunoki Mitsumasa (-1429) 141 (Muromachi)
Kutsuki Mototsuna (1549-1632) 203 (Tanba)
Kutsuki Nobutsuna 203 (Tanba)
Kutsuki Tanetsuna (-1550) 203 (Tanba)

Kutsuki Tanetsuna 203 (Tanba)
Kutsuki Yoshitsuna 203 (Tanba)
Kuwayama Shigeharu (1524-1606) 230 (Edo)
Kuzé Hironobu (1561-1626) 180 (Shimosa)
Kuzé Hiroyuki (1609-1679) 180 (Shimosa)
Kyogoku Tadataka (1593-1637) 246 (Sanuki)
Kyogoku Takamichi (1603-1665) 207 (Tango)
Kyogoku Takatomo (1571-1621) 207 (Tango)
Kyogoku Takatsugu (1560-1609) 246 (Sanuki)
Maeda Gen'i (1539-1602) 231 (Edo)
Maeda Hidenori Sakon (1577-1602) 231 (Edo)
Maeda Munehisa (1539-1602) 231 (Edo)
Maeda Munetoshi (16th-17th century) 231 (Edo)
Maeda Toshiié (1538-1599) 95 (Kozuké), 129 (Kaga), 130 (Etchu)
Maeda Toshinaga (1562-1614) 129 (Kaga), 131 (Etchu)
Maeda Toshitsuné (1593-1658) 130 (Kaga), 131 (Etchu)
Maki Shumé (late 16th century) 191 (Momoyama)
Manabé Akifusa 125 (Echizen)
Manabé Akikatsu 125 (Echizen)
Marumo Chikayoshi (16th-17th century) 193 (Momoyama)
Masuda Moritsugu (17th century) 232 (Edo)
Masuda Nagamori (1645-1615) 232 (Edo)
Matsudaira Akitsuna 146 (Mikawa)
Matsudaira Harusato (1751-1818) 212* (Izumo)
Matsudaira Hideyasu (1574-1607) 92 (Kozuké), 124 (Echizen), 133 (Echigo), 212 (Izumo), 219 (Harima), 225 (Mimasaka)
Matsudaira Ienobu (1569-1638) 202 (Tanba)
Matsudaira Ienori (1561-1600) 81 (Mino), 149 (Mikawa)
Matsudaira Ietada (1547-1582) 202 (Tanba)
Matsudaira Ietada (1555-1600) 267 (Hizen)
Matsudaira Katamori (1836-1893) 101 (Mutsu)
Matsudaira Katsutoshi (1556-1586) 181 (Shimosa)
Matsudaira Koretada (1537-1575) 267 (Hizen)
Matsudaira Masamitsu (1561-1631) 101 (Mutsu)
Matsudaira Masatsuna (1576-1648) 91 (Kozuké), 146 (Owari), 175 (Kazusa)
Matsudaira Masayuki (1609-1672) 101 (Mutsu)
Matsudaira Mitsunaga (1615-1707) 225 (Mimasaka)
Matsudaira Munesuké (1629-1699) 206 (Tango)
Matsudaira Nobuhira (1564-1657) 93 (Kozuké)
Matsudaira Nobukazu (1548-1632) 88 (Shinano), 109 (Dewa)
Matsudaira Nobukiyo 93 (Kozuké)
Matsudaira Nobutomi 225 (Mimasaka)
Matsudaira Nobutsuna (1596-1662) 91 (Kozuké), 146 (Mikawa)
Matsudaira Nobuyoshi (1576-1621) 109 (Dewa)
Matsudaira Norimasa (1480-1541) 81 (Mino), 149 (Mikawa), 258 (Bungo)
Matsudaira Sadaaki (1847-1908) 142 (Isé)
Matsudaira Sadafusa 248 (Iyo)
Matsudaira Sadakatsu (1560-1624) 141 (Isé), 247 (Iyo)
Matsudaira Sadanobu (1758-1829) 142 (Isé)
Matsudaira Sadatsuna (1592-1651) 141 (Isé)
Matsudaira Sadayasu (1835-1882) 212 (Izumo)
Matsudaira Sanenori (1553-1582) 81 (Mino), 149 (Mikawa)
Matsudaira Sanetsugu (1577-1646) 149 (Mikawa)
Matsudaira Shigekatsu (1548-1620) 260 (Bungo)
Matsudaira Shigeyoshi (1493-1580) 260 (Bungo)
Matsudaira Tadaaki/Tadaakira (1583-1644) 91 (Kozuké), 170 (Musashi)
Matsudaira Tadahiro (1628-1700) 91 (Kozuké), 170 (Musashi)
Matsudaira Tadamasa (1597-1645) 124 (Echizen)
Matsudaira Tadanao (1595-1650) 225 (Mimasaka)
Matsudaira Tadatoshi (1582-1632) 267 (Hizen)
Matsudaira Toshikatsu 141 (Isé), 181 (Shimosa)
Matsudaira Yasunaga (1562-1632) 84 (Shinano)
Matsudaira Yasunobu (1600-1682) 202 (Tanba)
Matsudaira Yoshikagé (1511-1556) 267 (Hizen)
Matsui Yasuchika (1521-1583) 169 (Musashi)
Matsu Yasushigé (1568-1640) 169 (Musashi)
Matsukura Katsuié (-1638)

Matsukura Nobushigé (1522-1586) 233 (Edo)
Matsukura Shigeharu (-1638) 233 (Edo)
Matsukura Shigemasa (1574-1630) 233 (Edo)
Matsukura Shigetoshi (17th century) 233 (Edo)
Matsumaé Akihiro (1775-1833) 74 (Ezo)
Matsumaé Sadahiro 74 (Ezo)
Matsumaé Takahiro (1829-1866) 74* (Ezo)
Matsumaé Yoshihiro 74 (Ezo)
Matsunaga Hisahidé (1510-1577) 194 (Momoyama)
Matsunaga Hisamichi (-1577) 194 (Momoyama)
Matsushita Nagatsuna (17th century) 232 (Edo)
Matsushita Shigetsuna (1580-1628) 232 (Edo)
Matsushita Yoshitsuna (16th-17th century) 232 (Edo)
Matsushita Yukitsuna (1538-1598) 232 (Edo)
Matsuura Atsunobu 264 (Hizen)
Matsuura Shigenobu 264 (Hizen)
Matsuura Takanobu 264 (Hizen)
Matsuura Yoshi 264 (Hizen)
Minagawa Hiroteru (-1625) 234 (Edo)
Minagawa Takatsuné (-1645) 234 (Edo)
Minamoto Akira (814-853) 97 (Kamakura)
Minamoto Hidéakira (-940) 99 (Kamakura)
Minamoto Hikaru (845-913) 97 (Kamakura)
Minamoto Hiromasa (918-980) 98 (Kamakura)
Minamoto Ichiman (1198-1203) 108 (Kamakura)
Minamoto Kugyo (1200-1219) 108 (Kamakura)
Minamoto Makoto (810-868) 97 (Kamakura)
Minamoto (Hojo) Masako (1157-1225) 92 (Kamakura)
Minamoto Masanobu (920-993) 99 (Kamakura)
Minamoto Masazané (1059-1127) 99 (Kamakura)
Minamoto Michichika (1149-1202) 99 (Kamakura)
Minamoto Mitsunaka (912-997) 100 (Kamakura)
Minamoto Morofusa (1009-1077) 99 (Kamakura)
Minamoto Moroyori (1070-1139) 99 (Kamakura)
Minamoto Nakatsuna (-1180) 104 (Kamakura)
Minamoto Noriyori (1156-1193) 106 (Kamakura)
Minamoto Sadamu (815-863) 97 (Kamakura)
Minamoto Sanetomo (1192-1219) 23 (Kamakura Shogun)
Minamoto Senju-maru (1201-1214) 108 (Kamakura)
Minamoto Shitago (911-983) 97 (Kamakura)
Minamoto Taka'aki (914-982) 98 (Kamakura)
Minamoto Takakuni (1004-1077) 98 (Kamakura)
Minamoto Tametomo (1139-1170) 105 (Kamakura)
Minamoto Tameyoshi (1096-1156) 103 (Kamakura)
Minamoto Tomonaga (1144-1160) 106 (Kamakura)
Minamoto Toru (822-895) 97 (Kamakura)
Minamoto Toshiaki (1044-1114) 98 (Kamakura)
Minamoto Toshifusa (1035-1131) 99 (Kamakura)
Minamoto Toshikata (959-1027) 98 (Kamakura)
Minamoto Tsuné (812-854) 97 (Kamakura)
Minamoto Tsunemoto (894-961) 99 (Kamakura)
Minamoto Yoriié (1182-1204) 22 (Kamakura Shogun)
Minamoto Yorimasa (1106-1180) 103 (Kamakura)
Minamoto Yorimitsu (944-1021) 101 (Kamakura)
Minamoto Yorinobu (968-1048) 101 (Kamakura)
Minamoto Yoritomo (1147-1199) 22 (Kamakura Shogun)
Minamoto Yoriyoshi (998-1082) 102 (Kamakura)
Minamoto Yoshichika (-1117) 103 (Kamakura)
Minamoto Yoshihira (1140-1160) 105 (Kamakura)
Minamoto Yoshiié (1041-1108) 102 (Kamakura)
Minamoto Yoshikata (-1155) 105 (Kamakura)
Minamoto Yoshikiyo (1075-1149) 206 (Momoyama)
Minamoto Yoshikuni (1082-1155) 103 (Kamakura)
Minamoto Yoshimitsu (1045-1127) 103 (Kamakura)
Minamoto (Kiso) Yoshinaka (1154-1184) 106 (Kamakura)
Minamoto Yoshinari (1200-1219) 108 (Kamakura)
Minamoto Yoshishigé (-1202) 145 (Muromachi)
Minamoto Yoshitomo (1123-1160) 104 (Kamakura)

INDICES

Minamoto Yoshitsuna (1042-1134) 103 (Kamakura)
Minamoto Yoshitsuné (1159-1189) 107 (Kamakura)
Minamoto Yoshiyasu (1126-1157) 115 (Muromachi)
Minamoto Yukiié (-1186) 105 (Kamakura)
Miura Mitsumura (-1247) 110 (Kamakura)
Miura Tamemichi (11th century) 109 (Kamakura)
Miura Taneyoshi (-1221) 110 (Kamakura)
Miura Yasumura (1204-1247) 110 (Kamakura)
Miura Yoshiaki (1093-1181) 109 (Kamakura)
Miura Yoshiatsu (-1516) 110 (Kamakura)
Miura Yoshimoto (-1516) 110 (Kamakura)
Miura Yoshimura (-1239) 110 (Kamakura)
Miura Yoshitsura (12th century) 110 (Kamakura)
Miura Yoshizumi (1127-1200) 110 (Kamakura)
Miyabé Keijun (1528-1599) 193 (Momoyama)
Miyabé Nagafusa (1581-1634) 193 (Momoyama)
Miyabé Nagahiro (1581-1634) 193 (Momoyama)
Miyabé Tsugimasu (1528-1599) 193 (Momoyama)
Miyoshi Chokei (1523-1564) 143 (Muromachi)
Miyoshi Fuyuyasu (1528-1564) 143 (Muromachi)
Miyoshi Jikkyu (1527-1562) 143 (Muromachi)
Miyoshi Masanaga (1508-1549) 142 (Muromachi)
Miyoshi Motonaga (-1532) 142 (Muromachi)
Miyoshi Nagamoto (-1532) 142 (Muromachi)
Miyoshi Nagateru (-1520) 142 (Muromachi)
Miyoshi Nagayoshi (1523-1564) 143 (Muromachi)
Miyoshi Yoshikata (1527-1562) 143 (Muromachi)
Miyoshi Yoshitsugu (1551-1573) 144 (Muromachi)
Miyoshi Yukinaga (-1520) 142 (Muromachi)
Miyoshi Yukitora (1527-1562) 143 (Muromachi)
Miyoshi Yukiyasu (1527-1562) 143 (Muromachi)
Mizuno Katsunari (1564-1651) 177 (Shimosa)
Mizuno Nobumoto (-1576) 155 (Suruga), 176 (Kazusa), 177 (Shimosa)
Mizuno Tadamasa (1493-1543) 117 (Dewa), 155 (Suruga), 176 (Kazusa), 177 (Shimosa), 242 (Kii)
Mizuno Tadashigé (1541-1600) 155 (Suruga), 176 (Kazusa), 177 (Shimosa)
Mogami Yoshiaki (1546-1614) 235 (Edo)
Mogami Yoshimori (1521-1590) 235 (Edo)
Mogami Yoshitoshi (-1631) 235 (Edo)
Momonoi Naotsuné (14th century) 136 (Muromachi)
Momonoi Yoshitané (13th century) 136 (Muromachi)
Mori Hidemoto (1579-1650) 238 (Nagato)
Mori Hidenari (1595-1651) 237 (Nagato)
Mori Katsunaga (-1615) 234 (Edo)
Mori Katsunobu (-1601) 234 (Edo)
Mori Motokiyo 238 (Nagato)
Mori Motonari (1497-1571) 237 (Nagato)
Mori Motonori (1839-1896) 238 (Nagato)
Mori Nagakazu (1558-1584) 223 (Harima)
Mori Nagayoshi (1558-1584) 223 (Harima)
Mori Narihiro 238 (Nagato)
Mori Suemitsu (-1221) 237 (Nagato)
Mori Tadamasa (1570-1634) 224 (Harima)
Mori Takamasa (1556-1628) 258 (Bungo)
Mori Takamoto (1523-1563) 237 (Nagato)
Mori Terumoto (1553-1625) 237 (Nagato)
Mori Tokichika 237 (Nagato)
Mori Yoshinari (1523-1570) 223 (Harima)
Morikawa Shigetoshi (1584-1632) 181 (Shimosa)
Morikuni-shinno (1301-1333) 24 (Kamakura Shogun)
Moriyoshi-shinno (1308-1335) 24 (Kamakura Shogun)
Munakata Kiyo'uji (early 10th century) 195 (Momoyama)
Munakata Okiuji (early 16th century) 195 (Momoyama)
Munakata Ujihiro (mid 15th century) 195 (Momoyama)
Munakata Ujikuni (late 12th century) 195 (Momoyama)
Munakata Ujio (-1551) 195 (Momoyama)
Munakata Ujisada (-1586) 195 (Momoyama)

Munetaka-shinno (1242-1274) 24 (Kamakura Shogun)
Murakami Yorikiyo (11th century) 236 (Edo)
Murakami Yoshiakira (-1624) 236 (Edo)
Murakami Yoshikiyo (1501-1573) 236 (Edo)
Murakami Yoshiteru (-1333) 236 (Edo)
Nabeshima Katsushigé (1580-1657) 262 (Hizen)
Nabeshima Naohiro (1846-1921) 261 (Hizen)
Nabeshima Naomasa (1815-1871) 261 (Hizen)
Nabeshima Naoshigé (1537-1619) 261 (Hizen)
Nabeshima Shigenao 261 (Hizen)
Nagai Naokatsu (1563-1629) 83 (Mino), 194 (Yamato), 199 (Settsu)
Nagai Naomasa (1587-1668) 83 (Mino), 194 (Yamato)
Nagai Naomitsu 194 (Yamato)
Nagai Naonaga 194 (Yamato)
Nagai Naoyuki 194 (Yamato)
Nagao Fujikagé (16th century) 147 (Muromachi)
Nagao Harukagé (-1553) 147 (Muromachi)
Nagao Kageharu (15th century) 147 (Muromachi)
Nagao Kagenao (16th century) 147 (Muromachi)
Nagao Kageyasu (-1545) 147 (Muromachi)
Nagao Masakagé (-1564) 147 (Muromachi)
Nagao Tamekagé (-1542) 147 (Muromachi)
Naito Genzaémon (16th century) 237 (Edo)
Naito Ienaga (1546-1600) 108 (Mutsu), 150 (Mikawa), 272 (Hyuga)
Naito Joan (1549-1626) 237 (Edo)
Naito Masanaga (1568-1634) 108 (Mutsu), 150 (Mikawa), 272 (Hyuga)
Naito Nobunari (1545-1612) 133 (Echigo)
Naito Yukiyasu (1549-1626) 237 (Edo)
Nakagawa Hidemasa 257 (Bungo)
Nakagawa Hidenari (1570-1612) 257 (Bungo)
Nakagawa Kiyohidé (1542-1583) 257 (Bungo)
Nakamura Kazuuji (-1600) 234 (Edo)
Nakamura Tadakazu (1590-1609) 234 (Edo)
Nakayama Nobuyoshi (1576-1642) 183 (Hitachi)
Nanbu Mitsuyuki 102 (Mutsu)
Nanbu Nobunao (1546-1599) 102 (Mutsu)
Nanbu Toshinao (1576-1632) 102 (Mutsu)
Narinaga-shinno (1325-1338) 25 (Kamakura Shogun)
Narusé Masakazu (1538-1620) 145 (Owari)
Nasu Sukefusa (17th century) 238 (Edo)
Nasu Sukeharu (1546-1609) 238 (Edo)
Nasu Sukeié (12th century) 238 (Edo)
Nasu Suketané (-1583) 238 (Edo)
Nasu Takasuké (-1551) 238 (Edo)
Nawa Nagatoshi (-1336) 95 (Kamakura)
Nawa Tadafusa (12th century) 95 (Kamakura)
Nigao Takanobu (1560-1623) 237 (Edo)
Nishina Morinobu (1557-1582) 196 (Momoyama)
Nishina Morito (-1221) 196 (Momoyama)
Nishio Yoshitsugu (1530-1606) 154 (Totomi)
Nikaido Sadafuji (14th century) 111 (Kamakura)
Nikaido Yukifuji (1246-1302) 111 (Kamakura)
Nikaido Yukimasa (12th century) 111 (Kamakura)
Nikaido Yukimori (1182-1254) 111 (Kamakura)
Nikki Sanekuni (13th century) 141 (Muromachi)
Nikki Yoriaki (1299-1359) 141 (Muromachi)
Nikki Yoshinaga (-1367) 141 (Muromachi)
Nitta Sadakata (-1410) 146 (Muromachi)
Nitta Taro (-1202) 145 (Muromachi)
Nitta Yoshiaki (-1337) 146 (Muromachi)
Nitta Yoshimuné (1335-1368) 146 (Muromachi)
Nitta Yoshioki (-1358) 146 (Muromachi)
Nitta Yoshisada (1301-1338) 145 (Muromachi)
Nitta Yoshisuké (-1340) 146 (Muromachi)
Niwa Mitsushigé 106 (Mutsu)
Niwa Nagahidé (1535-1585) 106 (Mutsu)
Niwa Nagahiro (1859-1886) 106* (Mutsu)
Niwa Nagakuni (1834-1904) 106* (Mutsu)

Niwa Nagashigé (1571-1637) 106 (Mutsu)
Niwa Nagtomi (1803-1866) 106* (Mutsu)
Oba Kagechika (-1180) 78 (Heian)
Oba Kageyoshi (-1210) 78 (Heian)
Oda Chikazané 119 (Dewa)
Oda Nagamasu (1548-1622) 193 (Yamato)
Oda Nobuhidé (1510-1551) 119 (Dewa), 193 (Yamato)
Oda Nobukatsu (1558-1630) 119 (Dewa)
Oda Nobunaga (1534-1582) 120 (Dewa)
Oda Haruhisa (-1352) 141 (Muromachi)
Oda Tomoshigé (12th century) 141 (Muromachi)
Oé Asatsuna (886-957) 111 (Kamakura)
Oé Chisato (9th century) 111 (Kamakura)
Oé Hiromoto (1148-1225) 112 (Kamakura)
Oé Koretoki (888-963) 111 (Kamakura)
Oé Masafusa (1041-1111) 112 (Kamakura)
Oé Otondo (811-877) 111 (Kamakura)
Oé Tadahira (952-1012) 111 (Kamakura)
Ogasawara Hidemasa (1569-1615) 222 (Harima), 255 (Buzen), 266 (Hizen)
Ogasawara Nagahidé 127 (Echizen), 222 (Harima), 255 (Buzen), 266 (Hizen)
Ogasawara Nagakiyo (1162-1242) 127 (Echizen), 222 (Harima), 255 (Buzen), 266 (Hizen)
Ogasawara Nagatoki (1519-1583) 127 (Echizen), 222 (Harima), 255 (Buzen), 266 (Hizen)
Ogasawara Sadamuné (1294-1350) 127 (Echizen), 222 (Harima), 255 (Buzen), 266 (Hizen)
Ogawa Suketada (1549-1601) 195 (Momoyama)
Ogigayatsu Akisada (14th century) 148 (Muromachi)
Ogigayatsu Mochitomo (1416-1467) 148 (Muromachi)
Ogigayatsu Sadamasa (1443-1494) 148 (Muromachi)
Ogigayatsu Tomo'oki (1488-1537) 148 (Muromachi)
Ogigayatsu Tomosada (1525-1546) 148 (Muromachi)
Ogigayatsu Tomoyoshi (-1518) 148 (Muromachi)
Okabé Nagamori (1568-1632) 196 (Izumi)
Okamoto Shigemasa (1542-1600) 196 (Momoyama)
Okochi Akitsuna 91 (Kozuké)
Okubo Nagayasu (1545-1613) 238 (Edo)
Okubo Tadachika (1553-1628) 160 (Sagami)
Okubo Tadakazu (1510-1582) 99 (Shimotsuké), 160 (Sagami)
Okubo Tadamoto (1604-1670) 161 (Sagami)
Okubo Tadatsuné (1580-1611) 161 (Sagami)
Okubo Tadayo (1531-1593) 160 (Sagami)
Okubo Tadazané (1778-1837) 161 (Sagami)
Okudaira Nobumasa (1555-1615) 256 (Buzen)
Omura Sumitada (1532-1587) 263 (Hizen)
Omura Sumiyori (-1619) 263 (Hizen)
Omura Tadazumi 263 (Hizen)
Omura Yoshisaki (1568-1615) 263 (Hizen)
Ono Harukazé (-899) 78 (Heian)
Ono Michikazé (894-966) 79 (Heian)
Ono Takamura (802-853) 79 (Heian)
Ono Yoshifuru (888-968) 79 (Heian)
Onodera Terumichi (-1598) 197 (Momoyama)
Onodera Yoshimichi (1566-1645) 197 (Momoyama)
Onoki Shigekatsu (-1600) 196 (Momoyama)
Ōoka Tadasuké (1677-1751) 150 (Mikawa)
Ota Sukekiyo (1411-1493) 153 (Totomi)
Ota Sukekuni 153 (Totomi)
Ota Sukemuné 153 (Totomi)
Ota Sukenaga (1432-1486) 153 (Totomi)
Ota Suketaka 153 (Totomi)
Ota Yasusuké 153 (Totomi)
Otani Yoshitaka (1559-1600) 197 (Momoyama)
Otani Yoshitsugu (1559-1600) 197 (Momoyama)
Otaté Ieuji (13th century) 144 (Muromachi)
Otaté Muneuji (14th century) 144 (Muromachi)
Otaté Ujiaki (-1341) 144 (Muromachi)
Otaté Ujikiyo (1337-1412) (Muromachi)
Otawara Harukiyo (1567-1631) 97 (Shimotsuké)
Otomo Chikaié (1561-1641) 241 (Edo)
Otomo Chikamori (1567-1643) 241 (Edo)
Otomo Chikasada (-1570) 241 (Edo)
Otomo Chikayo (14th century) 240 (Edo)
Otomo Sadamuné (early 14th century) 239 (Edo)
Otomo Sadanori (-1336) 240 (Edo)
Otomo Sorin (1530-1587) 240 (Edo)
Otomo Yoshiaki (1502-1550) 239 (Edo)
Otomo Yoshimuné (1558-1605) 241 (Edo)
Otomo Yoshinao (late 12th century) 239 (Edo)
Otomo Yoshinobu (-1639) 241 (Edo)
Otomo Yoshinori (1502-1550) 239 (Edo)
Otomo Yoshishigé (1530-1587) 240 (Edo)
Otomo Yoshitaka (16th-17th century) 241 (Edo)
Ouchi Hiroyo (14th century) 149 (Muromachi)
Ouchi Masahiro (1446-1495) 150 (Muromachi)
Ouchi Mochiyo (1395-1442) 149 (Muromachi)
Ouchi Morifusa (12th century) 149 (Muromachi)
Ouchi Teruhiro (-1569) 151 (Muromachi)
Ouchi Yoshihiro (1356-1399) 149 (Muromachi)
Ouchi Yoshinaga (1532-1557) 151 (Muromachi)
Ouchi Yoshioki (1477-1528) 150 (Muromachi)
Ouchi Yoshitaka (1507-1551) 150 (Muromachi)
Oyama Hidetomo (-1335) 151 (Muromachi)
Oyama Masamitsu (12th century) 151 (Muromachi)
Oyama Tomomasa (1155-1238) 151 (Muromachi)
Oyama Yoshimasa (-1382) 151 (Muromachi)
Rokkaku Mitsutaka (-1413) 152 (Muromachi)
Rokkaku Sadayori (1495-1552) 152 (Muromachi)
Rokkaku Takayori (-1520) 152 (Muromachi)
Rokkaku Ujiyori (1326-1370) 152 (Muromachi)
Rokkaku Yasutsuna (13th century) 152 (Muromachi)
Rokkaku Yoshiharu (1545-1612) 153 (Muromachi)
Rokkaku Yoshikata (1521-1598) 152 (Muromachi)
Rokkaku Yoshisuké (1545-1612) 153 (Muromachi)
Rokugo Masanori (1567-1634) 111 (Dewa)
Ryuzoji Iekané (1454-1546) 198 (Momoyama)
Ryuzoji Ienobu (1563-1622) 199 (Momoyama)
Ryuzoji Ietané (-1593) 199 (Momoyama)
Ryuzoji Masaié (1556-1607) 199 (Momoyama)
Ryuzoji Naganobu (-1603) 199 (Momoyama)
Ryuzoji Nobuchika (-1608) 199 (Momoyama)
Ryuzoji Takanobu (1530-1584) 198 (Momoyama)
Ryuzoji Tanehidé (1524-1548) 198 (Momoyama)
Saganuma Sadamitsu (1542-1604) 242 (Edo)
Saganuma Sadayoshi (16th-17th century) 242 (Edo)
Saigo Iezané (-1597) 242 (Edo)
Saigo Masakatsu (-1561) 242 (Edo)
Saigo Masakazu (1593-1638) 242 (Edo)
Saigo Nobukazu (1614-1697) 242 (Edo)
Saigyo Hoshi (1118-1190) 80 (Heian)
Saito Dosan (1494-1556) 154 (Muromachi)
Saito Nagatatsu (-1582) 155 (Muromachi)
Saito Sanemori (1111-1183) 154 (Muromachi)
Saito Tatsuoki (1548-1573) 155 (Muromachi)
Saito Toshimasa (1494-1556) 154 (Muromachi)
Saito Yoshitatsu (1527-1561) 154 (Muromachi)
Sakai Ietsugu (1564-1619) 118 (Dewa), 172 (Awa-Chiba)
Sakai Masachika (-1576) 93 (Kozuké), 123 (Wakasa), 125 (Echizen), 172 (Awa-Chiba), 217 (Harima)
Sakai Shigetada 93 (Kozuké), 217 (Harima)
Sakai Tadakatsu (1587-1662) 123 (Wakasa), 125 (Echizen), 172 (Awa-Chiba)
Sakai Tadakiyo (1624-1681) 93 (Kozuké), 218 (Harima)
Sakai Tadatoshi (1562-1627) 123 (Wakasa), 125 (Echizen), 172 (Awa-Chiba)

INDICES

Sakai Tadatsugu (1527-1596) 118 (Dewa)
Sakakibara Toshinaga 137 (Echigo)
Sakakibara Yasumasa (1548-1606) 137 (Echigo)
Sakanoué Karita-maro (728-786) 80 (Heian)
Sakanoué Tamura-maro (758-811) 80 (Heian)
Sakazaki Naomori (1563-1616) 199 (Momoyama)
Sakazaki Narimasa (1563-1616) 199 (Momoyama)
Sakazaki Tadaié (-1609) 199 (Momoyama)
Sakuma Genba Morimasa (1554-1583) 243 (Edo)
Sakuma Masakatsu (late 16th century) 243 (Edo)
Sakuma Nobumori (1528-1582) 243 (Edo)
Sakuma Yasumasa (1555-1627) 243 (Edo)
Sakuma Yasutsugu (1556-1638) 244 (Edo)
Sakurai Tadayori 198 (Settsu)
Sanada Masayuki (1544-1608) 86 (Shinano)
Sanada Nobuyuki (1566-1658) 86 (Shinano)
Sanada Yukimura (1570-1615) 86 (Shinano)
Sanada Yukitaka (1512-1574) 86 (Shinano)
Sano Masatsuna (16th-17th century) 242 (Edo)
Sasaki Doyo (1306-1373) 157 (Muromachi)
Sasaki Hideyoshi (1112-1184) 156 (Muromachi)
Sasaki Nariyori (11th century) 156 (Muromachi)
Sasaki Nobutsuna (-1242) 157 (Muromachi)
Sasaki Saburo Moritsuna (12th century) 156 (Muromachi)
Sasaki Sadatsuna (12th century) 156 (Muromachi)
Sasaki Takatsuna (1160-1214) 157 (Muromachi)
Sasaki Takauji (1306-1373) 157 (Muromachi)
Sassa Magosuké (-1556) 200 (Momoyama)
Sassa Narimasa (1539-1588) 200 (Momoyama)
Satake Hideyoshi (1151-1228) 110 (Dewa)
Satake Yoshiaki 110 (Dewa)
Satake Yoshinari 110 (Dewa)
Satake Yoshinobu (1570-1633) 110 (Dewa)
Satake Yoshinori (1395-1462) 110 (Dewa)
Satake Yoshishigé (1547-1612) 110 (Dewa)
Sato Norikiyo (1118-1190) 80 (Heian)
Sato Tadanobu (1160-1185) 80 (Heian)
Sato Tsuginobu (1158-1185) 81 (Heian)
Satomi Sanetaka (1483-1533) 245 (Edo)
Satomi Tadayoshi (1593-1622) 245 (Edo)
Satomi Yoshihiro (1530-1578) 245 (Edo)
Satomi Yoshitaka (1512-1574) 245 (Edo)
Satomi Yoshitoshi (12th-13th century) 245 (Edo)
Satomi Yoshitoyo (1513-1534) 245 (Edo)
Satomi Yoshiyasu (1573-1603) 245 (Edo)
Satomi Yoshiyori (1542-1587) 245 (Edo)
Satomi Yoshizané (1417-1488) 245 (Edo)
Sengoku Hidehisa (1551-1614) 208 (Tajima)
Sengoku Tadamasa 208 (Tajima)
Shiba Ieuji (13th century) 158 (Muromachi)
Shiba Takatsuné (-1367) 158 (Muromachi)
Shiba Yoshikado (-ca. 1480) 158 (Muromachi)
Shiba Yoshikané (1540-1580) 159 (Muromachi)
Shiba Yoshimasa (1350-1410) 158 (Muromachi)
Shiba Yoshimuné (1513-1554) 159 (Muromachi)
Shiba Yoshisato (-1521) 159 (Muromachi)
Shiba Yoshitaké (-1452) 158 (Muromachi)
Shiba Yoshitoshi (1430-1490) 158 (Muromachi)
Shibata Katsuhisa (1568-1583) 202 (Momoyama)
Shibata Katsuié (1530-1583) 201 (Momoyama)
Shibata Katsumasa (1557-1583) 202 (Momoyama)
Shibata Katsutoyo (-1583) 202 (Momoyama)
Shibata (Echigo) Nagaatsu (-1580) 202 (Momoyama)
Shibata (Echigo) Naganori (-1580) 202 (Momoyama)
Shibata (Echigo) Shigeié (-1587) 202 (Momoyama)
Shibukawa Mitsuyori (-1446) 153 (Muromachi)
Shibukawa Yoshiaki (13th century) 153 (Muromachi)
Shibukawa Yoshikané (15th century) 153 (Muromachi)
Shibukawa Yoshiyuki (14th-15th century) 153 (Muromachi)
Shimazu Hisamitsu (1820-1887) 275 (Satsuma)
Shimazu Iehisa (-1587) 274 (Satsuma)
Shimazu Nariakira (1809-1858) 275 (Satsuma)
Shimazu Tadahisa (-1227) 271 (Hyuga), 274 (Satsuma)
Shimazu Tadatsuné (1576-1638) 275 (Satsuma)
Shimazu Tadayoshi (1840-1897) 275 (Satsuma)
Shimazu Takahisa (1514-1571) 274 (Satsuma)
Shimazu Yoshihiro (1535-1619) 274 (Satsuma)
Shimazu Yoshihisa (1533-1611) 274 (Satsuma)
Shimokobé Yukihira (12th century) 112 (Kamakura)
Shimokobé Yukiyoshi (12th century) 112 (Kamakura)
Shinagawa Takahisa (1576-1639) 130 (Muromachi)
Shinjo Naoyori (1538-1613) 187 (Hitachi)
Shoni Fuyusuké (-1375) 155 (Muromachi)
Shoni Kagesuké (-1285) 155 (Muromachi)
Shoni Masasuké (-1506) 155 (Muromachi)
Shoni Sadatsuné (-1336) 155 (Muromachi)
Shoni Sukemoto (1497-1532) 155 (Muromachi)
Shoni Sukeyori (12th century) 155 (Muromachi)
Shoni Tokinao (-1556) 155 (Muromachi)
Shoni Yorihisa (14th century) 155 (Muromachi)
Shoni Yorizumi (14th century) 155 (Muromachi)
So Sadamori (1385-1452) 273 (Tsushima)
So Sukekuni (-1274) 273 (Tsushima)
So Tomomuné 273 (Tsushima)
So Yoshitomo (1568-1615) 273 (Tsushima)
Sugihara Nagafusa (1574-1629) 246 (Edo)
Suwa Morishigé 85 (Shinano)
Suwa Yorishigé (1516-1542) 85 (Shinano)
Suwa Yoritada (1536-1606) 85 (Shinano)
Tachibana Muneshigé (1567-1642) 253 (Chikugo)
Taira Atsumori (118-1184) 88 (Heian)
Taira Hirotsuné (12th century) 86 (Heian)
Taira Iesada (12th century) 83 (Heian)
Taira Kagekiyo (-1185)
Taira Kiyomori (1118-1181) 84 (Heian)
Taira Korehira (10th century) 83 (Heian)
Taira Koremochi (10th century) 83 (Heian)
Taira Koremori (1160-) 89 (Heian)
Taira Kunika (-935) 81 (Heian)
Taira Masakado (-940) 83 (Heian)
Taira Moritoshi (-1184) 85 (Heian)
Taira Munekiyo (12th century) 86 (Heian)
Taira Munemori (1147-1185) 86 (Heian)
Taira Norimori (1129-1185) 85 (Heian)
Taira Noritsuné (1160-1185) 89 (Heian)
Taira Sadamori (10th century) 81 (Heian)
Taira Sadayoshi (12th century) 83 (Heian)
Taira Shigehira (1158-1185) 88 (Heian)
Taira Shigemori (1138-1179) 86 (Heian)
Taira Tadamori (1096-1153) 84 (Heian)
Taira Tadanori (1144-1184) 85 (Heian)
Taira Tadatsuné (967-1031) 83 (Heian)
Taira Takamochi (9th century) 81 (Heian)
Taira Takamuné (804-867) 81 (Heian)
Taira Tokitada (1130-1189) 86 (Heian)
Taira Tokuko (1155-1213) 88 (Heian)
Taira Tomomori (1152-1185) 87 (Heian)
Taira Tomoyasu (12th century) 86 (Heian)
Taira Yasuyori (12th century) 85 (Heian)
Taira Yorimori (1132-1186) 85 (Heian)
Takahashi Mototané (late 16th century) 203 (Momoyama)
Takahashi Shigetané (1544-1586) 203 (Momoyama)
Takahashi Shoun (1544-1586) 203 (Momoyama)
Takatsukasa (Fujiwara) Kanehira (1228-1294) 73 (Heian)
Takayama Shigetomo (1552-1615) 204 (Momoyama)
Takayama Tomoteru (1531-1596) 204 (Momoyama)

Indices

Takayama Ukon (1552-1615) 204 (Momoyama)
Takeda Harukiyo (1557-1582) 212 (Momoyama)
Takeda Harunobu (1521-1573) 208 (Momoyama)
Takeda Katsuyori (1546-1582) 211 (Momoyama)
Takeda (Aki) Motoshigé (-1517) 160 (Muromachi)
Takeda Nobuchika (1541-1582) 211 (Momoyama)
Takeda Nobukado (1529-1582) 210 (Momoyama)
Takeda Nobumasa (1447-1505) 206 (Momoyama)
Takeda Nobumitsu (1162-1248) 206 (Momoyama)
Takeda Nobumitsu (-1417) 206 (Momoyama)
Takeda Nobushigé (1386-1450) 206 (Momoyama)
Takeda Nobushigé (1525-1561) 210 (Momoyama)
Takeda Nobutora (1493-1574) 207 (Momoyama)
Takeda Nobutoyo (-1582) 212 (Momoyama)
Takeda Nobuyoshi (1128-1186) 206 (Momoyama)
Takeda Nobuyoshi (1583-1603) 212 (Momoyama)
Takeda Nobuzané (-1575) 211 (Momoyama)
Takeda Shingen (1521-1573) 208 (Momoyama)
Takeda Yoshikiyo (1075-1149) 206 (Momoyama)
Takeda Yoshinobu (1538-1567) 211 (Momoyama)
Takenaka Hanbei (1544-1579) 244 (Edo)
Takenaka Shigeharu (1544-1579) 244 (Edo)
Takenaka Shigekado (1573-1631) 244 (Edo)
Takenaka Shigemoto (1498-1560) 244 (Edo)
Takenaka Shigetsuku (-1634) 244 (Edo)
Takigawa Kazumasu (1525-1586) 205 (Momoyama)
Tamura Muneyoshi (1637-1678) 108 (Mutsu)
Tanaka Tadamasa (-1620) 247 (Edo)
Tanaka Yoshimasa (1548-1609) 247 (Edo)
Tanaka Yoshimuné (-1620) 247 (Edo)
Tanuma Okikazu 151 (Totomi)
Tanuma Okitomo (-1784) 151 (Totomi)
Tanuma Okitsugu (1719-1788) 151 (Totomi)
Tanuma Okiyuki 151 (Totomi)
Tawara Chikataka (16th century) 159 (Muromachi)
Terazawa Hirotaka (1563-1633) 246 (Edo)
Terazawa Katataka (1609-1647) 246 (Edo)
Toda Kazuaki (1542-1604) 82 (Mino), 148 (Mikawa)
Toda Munemitsu 82 (Mino), 84 (Shinano), 98, 99 (Shimotsuké)
Toda Tadamasa (1632-1699) 98 (Shimotsuké)
Toda Tadatsugu (1532-1598) 98, 99 (Shimotsuké)
Toda Tadazané (1651-1729) 98 (Shimotsuké)
Toda Takatsugu (1565-1615) 98, 99 (Shimotsuké)
Todo Takatora (1556-1630) 139 (Isé)
Togashi Iekuni (11th century) 161 (Muromachi)
Togashi Ienao (late 12th century) 161 (Muromachi)
Togashi Masachika (-1488) 161 (Muromachi)
Togashi Tadayori (11th century) 161 (Muromachi)
Togashi Takaié (early 14th century) 161 (Muromachi)
Togashi Yasutaka (-1504) 161 (Muromachi)
Togawa Hideyasu (-1598) 247 (Edo)
Togawa Michiyasu (1569-1627) 247 (Edo)
Togawa Satoyasu (1569-1627) 247 (Edo)
Toki Mitsunobu 90 (Kozuké)
Toki Sadamasa (1551-1597) 90 (Kozuké)
Toki Sadayoshi (1579-1618) 90 (Kozuké)
Tokiwa Gozen (1123-1180) 104 (Kamakura)
Tokugawa Akitaké (1853-1910) 182 (Hitachi)
Tokugawa Chikatada (1418-1480) 163 (Edo)
Tokugawa Chikauji 163 (Edo)
Tokugawa Hidetada (1579-1632) 163* (Edo)
Tokugawa Hidetada (1579-1632) 43 (Edo Shogun)
Tokugawa Hirotada (1526-1549) 163 (Edo)
Tokugawa Ieharu (1737-1786) 47 (Edo Shogun)
Tokugawa Iemitsu (1604-1651) 163* (Edo)
Tokugawa Iemitsu (1604-1651) 44 (Edo Shogun)
Tokugawa Iemochi (1846-1866) 49 (Edo Shogun)
Tokugawa Ienari (1773-1841) 47 (Edo Shogun)

Tokugawa Ienobu (1662-1712) 159 (Kai)
Tokugawa Ienobu (1662-1712) 45 (Edo Shogun)
Tokugawa Iesada (1824-1858) 48 (Edo Shogun)
Tokugawa Ieshigé (1712-1761) (Edo Shogun)
Tokugawa Ietsugu (1709-1716) 46 (Edo Shogun)
Tokugawa Ietsuna (1641-1680) 44 (Edo Shogun)
Tokugawa Ieyasu (1543-1616) 164 (Edo)
Tokugawa Ieyasu (1543-1616) 39 (Edo Shogun)
Tokugawa Ieyoshi (1793-1853) 48 (Edo Shogun)
Tokugawa Kiyoyasu (1511-1536) 163 (Edo)
Tokugawa Mitsukuni (1628-1700) 182 (Hitachi)
Tokugawa Mochinaga (1831-1884) 145* (Owari)
Tokugawa Nagachika (1442-1510) 163 (Edo)
Tokugawa Nariaki (1800-1860) 182 (Hitachi)
Tokugawa Nobumitsu (1390-1465) 163 (Edo)
Tokugawa Nobutada (1489-1531) 163 (Edo)
Tokugawa Tadanaga (1606-1634) 157 (Suruga)
Tokugawa Tsunashigé (1644-1678) 159 (Kai)
Tokugawa Tsunayoshi (1646-1709) 45 (Edo Shogun)
Tokugawa Yasuchika (1369-1412) 163 (Edo)
Tokugawa Yorifusa (1603-1661) 182 (Hitachi)
Tokugawa Yorinobu (1602-1671) 241 (Kii)
Tokugawa Yoshikatsu (1824-1883) 145* (Owari)
Tokugawa Yoshimuné (1684-1751) 241* (Kii)
Tokugawa Yoshimuné (1684-1751) 46 (Edo Shogun)
Tokugawa Yoshinao (1601-1650) 145 (Owari), 159 (Kai)
Tokugawa Yoshinobu (1837-1913) 50 (Edo Shogun)
Tokugawa Yoshisué 163 (Edo)
Tokugawa Yoshitomi (1846-1866) 241* (Kii)
Tokunaga Masashigé (1547-1642) 247 (Edo)
Tokunaga Toshimasa (1549-1612) 247 (Edo)
Tomita Nobuhiro (late 16th century) 254 (Edo)
Tomita Tomonobu (16th-17th century) 254 (Edo)
Torii Mototada (1539-1600) 96 (Shimotsuké)
Torii Tadaharu (1608-1651) 96 (Shimotsuké)
Torii Tadamasa (1567-1628) 96 (Shimotsuké)
Torii Tadatsuné (-1636) 96 (Shimotsuké)
Toyotomi Hidetsugu (1568-1595) 251 (Edo)
Toyotomi Hideyori (1593-1615) 252 (Edo)
Toyotomi Hideyoshi (1536-1598) 248 (Edo)
Tozawa Masamori (1585-1648) 121 (Dewa)
Tozawa Moriyasu (1566-1590) 121 (Dewa)
Tsugaru Nobuhira (1586-1631) 103 (Mutsu)
Tsugaru Nobuyuki (1800-1862) 103 (Mutsu)
Tsugaru Tamenobu (1550-1608) 103 (Mutsu)
Tsugaru Yasuchika (1765-1833) 103 (Mutsu)
Tsukushi Hirokado (1548-1615) 212 (Momoyama)
Tsukushi Korekado (1531-1567) 212 (Momoyama)
Tsutsui Junkei (1549-1584) 253 (Edo)
Tsutsui Junsho (1523-1550) 253 (Edo)
Tsutsui Sadatsugu (1562-1615) 253 (Edo)
Uesugi Akisada (1454-1510) 113 (Dewa)
Uesugi Fusaaki (1432-1466) 113 (Dewa)
Uesugi Harunori (1751-1822) 115 (Dewa)
Uesugi Kagekatsu (1555-1623) 115 (Dewa)
Uesugi Kagetora (1552-1579) 115 (Dewa)
Uesugi Kenshin (1530-1578) 114 (Dewa)
Uesugi Kiyokata (-1442) 113 (Dewa)
Uesugi Mochinori (1844-1919) 115* (Dewa)
Uesugi Noriaki (1306-1368) 112 (Dewa)
Uesugi Norifusa (-1355) 112 (Dewa)
Uesugi Norifusa (1466-1524) 115 (Dewa)
Uesugi Noriharu (-1379) 113 (Dewa)
Uesugi Norikata (1335-1394) 113 (Dewa)
Uesugi Norimasa (1522-1579) 115 (Dewa)
Uesugi Norimoto (1383-1418) 113 (Dewa)
Uesugi Noritada (1433-1454) 113 (Dewa)
Uesugi Norizané (1410-1466) 113 (Dewa)
Uesugi Sadakatsu (1603-1645) 115 (Dewa)

INDICES

Uesugi Shigefusa 112 *(Dewa)*
Uesugi Tsunakatsu (-1664) 115 *(Dewa)*
Uesugi Yoshinori (-1378) 113 *(Dewa)*
Ujiié Bokuzen (-1571) 213 (Momoyama)
Ujiié Kinyori (12th-13th century) 213 (Momoyama)
Ujiié Naomoto (-1571) 213 (Momoyama)
Ujiié Yukihiro (1546-1615) 213 (Momoyama)
Ujiié Yukitsugu (16th-17th century) 213 (Momoyama)
Ukita Hideié (1572-1662) 215 (Momoyama)
Ukita Naoié (1530-1582) 214 (Momoyama)
Ukita Okiié (-1536) 214 (Momoyama)
Ukita Tadaié (-1609) 215 (Momoyama)
Ukita Yoshiié (-1534) 214 (Momoyama)
Urakami Munekagé (mid-16th century) 162 (Muromachi)
Urakami Muramuné (-1524) 162 (Muromachi)
Urakami Norimuné (-1502) 162 (Muromachi)
Utsunomiya Hirotsuna (1543-1590) 218 (Momoyama)
Utsunomiya Hisatsuna (1519-1546) 218 (Momoyama)
Utsunomiya Kintsuna (1302-1356) 218 (Momoyama)
Utsunomiya Kunitsuna (1568-1607) 218 (Momoyama)
Utsunomiya Tadatsuna (15th-16th century) 218 (Momoyama)
Utsunomiya Toshitsuna (1437-1477) 218 (Momoyama)
Utsunomiya Ujitsuna (-1370) 218 (Momoyama)
Wada Kenshu (14th century) 161 (Muromachi)
Wada Korenaga (-1573) 215 (Momoyama)
Wada Koremasa (1536-1571) 215 (Momoyama)
Wada Masatada (14th century) 161 (Muromachi)
Wada Masataké (14th century) 161 (Muromachi)
Wada Masatomo (-1352) 161 (Muromachi)
Wada Masauji (-1336) 161 (Muromachi)
Wada Sukehidé (14th century) 161 (Muromachi)
Wada Yoshimori (1147-1213) 113 (Kamakura)
Wakebé Mitsuyoshi 77 *(Omi)*
Wakisaka Yasuharu (1554-1626) 220 *(Harima)*
Wakisaka Yasumoto (1581-1654) 220 *(Harima)*
Wakiya Yoshiharu (mid-14th century) 162 (Muromachi)
Wakiya Yoshisuké (-1340) 146 (Muromachi)
Yagyu Jubei Mitsuyoshi (1607-1650) 191 *(Yamato)*
Yagyu Munefuyu (1613-1675) 191 *(Yamato)*
Yagyu Munenori (1571-1646) 191 *(Yamato)*
Yagyu Munetoshi (1529-1606) 191 *(Yamato)*
Yagyu Toshiyoshi (1579-1650) 191 *(Yamato)*
Yamagata Masakagé (1524-1575) 213 (Momoyama)
Yamana Koretoyo (15th century) 217 (Momoyama)
Yamana Masatoyo (15th century) 217 (Momoyama)
Yamana Mitsuyuki (-1395) 217 (Momoyama)
Yamana Mochitoyo (1404-1473) 217 (Momoyama)
Yamana Sozen (1404-1473) 217 (Momoyama)
Yamana Tokihiro (-1435) 217 (Momoyama)
Yamana Tokiuji (-1372) 216 (Momoyama)
Yamana Toyokuni (1548-1626) 217 (Momoyama)
Yamana Ujikiyo (1345-1392) 217 (Momoyama)
Yamana Ujiyuki (late 14th century) 217 (Momoyama)
Yamana Yoshimasa (late 14th century) 217 (Momoyama)
Yamana Yoshinori (12th-13th century) 216 (Momoyama)
Yamanouchi Kazutoyo (1546-1605) 244 *(Tosa)*
Yamanouchi Moritoyo 244 *(Tosa)*
Yamanouchi Toshimichi 244 *(Tosa)*
Yanagisawa Yoshiyasu (1658-1714) 136 *(Echigo),* 159 *(Kai),* 190 *(Yamato)*
Yashiro Hidemasa (-1623) 254 (Edo)
Yashiro Masakuni (-1575) 254 (Edo)
Yashiro Tadamasa (1594-1662) 254 (Edo)
Yashiro Tadanori (17th-18th century) 254 (Edo)
Yashiro Yorikuni 254 (Edo)
Yuki Akitomo (-1370) 256 (Edo)
Yuki Chikamitsu (-1336) 255 (Edo)
Yuki Chikatomo (-1347) 255 (Edo)

Yuki Harutomo (1533-1614) 256 (Edo)
Yuki Hideyasu (1574-1607) 92 *(Kozuké),* 124 *(Echizen),* 133 *(Echigo),* 212 *(Izumo),* 219 *(Harima),* 225 *(Mimasaka)*
Yuki Hideyasu (1574-1607) 256 (Edo)
Yuki Masakatsu (1503-1559) 256 (Edo)
Yuki Masatomo (1477-1545) 256 (Edo)
Yuki Munehiro (-1340) 255 (Edo)
Yuki Naritomo (1439-1462) 256 (Edo)
Yuki Tomohiro (13th century) 255 (Edo)
Yuki Tomomitsu (1168-1254) 255 (Edo)
Yuki Ujitomo (1398-1441) 256 (Edo)

About the Author

Born in Sapporo, Japan, Tadashi Ehara came to the U.S. when he was 6 years old. He has played games and watched samurai movies and TV shows from when he was very young. Later he began reading many historical novels and history books about Japan. He was a publisher at Chaosium, Inc., an editor of *Different Worlds* magazine, and is presently the publisher of Different Worlds Publications. His day job is as a marketing manager for a high-tech company in Silicon Valley.

The author lives in San Francisco with his family.